BUILDING
CO-OPERATION

BUILDING CO-OPERATION

*A Business History of
The Co-operative Group, 1863–2013*

JOHN F. WILSON
ANTHONY WEBSTER
and
RACHAEL VORBERG-RUGH

OXFORD
UNIVERSITY PRESS

OXFORD

UNIVERSITY PRESS

Great Clarendon Street, Oxford, OX2 6DP,
United Kingdom

Oxford University Press is a department of the University of Oxford.
It furthers the University's objective of excellence in research, scholarship,
and education by publishing worldwide. Oxford is a registered trade mark of
Oxford University Press in the UK and in certain other countries

First Edition published in 2013

Impression: 1

Published in the United States of America by Oxford University Press
198 Madison Avenue, New York, NY 10016, Unites States of America

British Library Cataloguing in Publication Data

Data available

ISBN 978-0-19-965511-3

Printed in Italy by
L.E.G.O. S.p.A. Lavis (TN)

ACKNOWLEDGEMENTS

The origins of this book can be traced to a meeting in July 2009 between two of the authors, Russell Gill (Head of Membership, The Co-operative Group), Mervyn Wilson (Chief Executive and Principal, the Co-operative College), and Gillian Lonergan (Head of Heritage Resources, the Co-operative College). While mulling over various possible projects that the two authors might undertake on behalf of The Co-operative Group, it was the latter who noted that as 2013 would mark the 150th anniversary of the creation of the Co-operative Wholesale Society, this would provide a worthwhile exercise. This prompted not only the recruitment of the third author, but also three years of intense archival research. As a team, we are enormously grateful to Gillian for her suggestion, because it has provided a marvellous opportunity to delve into a rich archive replete with written and pictorial records. Gillian and the National Co-operative Archive's team, Sophie Stewart, Adam Shaw, and Heather Roberts, have also responded energetically and patiently to our multiple requests for advice, material, and their extensive knowledge of co-operative history. Similarly, Mervyn Wilson and his enthusiastic colleague, Vice-Principal for Research and International, Dr Linda Shaw, have been extremely helpful over the course of the last three years, providing sound guidance on the complexities of co-operative history. A word must be offered on the Co-operative College, which remains one of the best and most distinctive educational organizations in the world. Few places of learning enjoy the dynamism, enthusiasm, and commitment to education and humanity which pervades those offices on the second floor of Holyoake House. It is a beacon of enlightenment, goodwill, and ideas, and should be recognized for the national (and international) treasure that it is.

We are also grateful to the many co-operative leaders who shared their time and their insight into the more recent decades of co-operative experience, in particular present and former chief executives Peter Marks, Martin Beaumont, Sir Graham Melmoth, and Sir Dennis Landau. It has also been a pleasure to interview several members of the co-operative movement, including: John Bowes, Bob Burlton, Martin Hulme, Roger Jones, Moira Lees, John Sandford, Bill Shannon, Paul Smedley, Christine Tacon, and Simon Williams. As part of the project, we were invited to present our provisional findings to assemblies of co-operative members and officials all over the country—including London, Newcastle, Beamish, Newport, Bath, Taunton, Belfast, Manchester, Birmingham, the Isle of Man, and elsewhere (as we write, invitations are still arriving), as well as at Co-operatives 2009 in Windsor and Co-operatives 2010 in Plymouth. We were also lucky enough to have the advice of scholars and active co-operators from all over the world at two major conferences held at The Co-operative Group's headquarters in Manchester in 2009 and 2012. The Co-operative Group was also gracious enough to invite us to help develop and present some learning materials and a module for their elected member training scheme. Special thanks go to Rachael Vorberg-Rugh for her exemplary work on these. The point about all these events is that the authors learned at least as much from their audiences as they did from us—such is the vitality, outspokenness, openness, and good fellowship which prevails in the movement. Their views have shaped this book, and we found it an enjoyable, fascinating, humbling, and very moving experience.

Over the course of the last three years, a large number of individuals have also helped the team. A key person has been Angela Whitecross, who has contributed on several fronts, from compiling a substantial database to drawing up the bibliography. Christine Nuttall and Kathryn Heatley have also provided invaluable research assistance, photographing significant numbers of documents for the team. From the academic world, Professor Leigh Sparks (Stirling University) has been an especially good friend, offering his highly authoritative knowledge of British retailing most generously. Dr Jim Quinn (University College, Dublin) was also generous with his time and data. Finally, conversations with many people at various conferences and workshops have improved our analysis, in particular Stephen Yeo, Mary Hilson, Peter Wardley, John K. Walton, Martin Purvis, David Stewart, Alyson Brown, Nicole Robertson, Martin Purvis, Steve Toms, Anna Tilba, Peter Gurney, and Katarina Friberg. The authors are also indebted to their partners and families, without whose support this volume would not have been possible.

Finally, we would like to express our sincere thanks to Russell Gill, because not only has he funded the research from his departmental budget, but also through managing the project from start to finish he has opened our eyes to what co-operation truly means. Ably supported by his PA, Anneke Schoemaker, Russell has arranged meetings, read chapters, and ensured that the final manuscript is accurate and balanced. Business historians the world over will appreciate the value of having such a supporter.

John Wilson, Anthony Webster, and Rachael Vorberg-Rugh, January 2013

CONTENTS

PART II. RETREAT AND RENAISSANCE

LIST OF FIGURES

List of Tables

LIST OF PLATES

CHAPTER 1

....

INTRODUCTION

....

In the spring of 1864 the following notice appeared under the heading 'The North of England Co-operative Wholesale Industrial and Provident Society':

This society commenced business on the 14th of March, and is now in a position to supply stores with any or all of the following articles:—Tea and coffee, chicory, cocoa, sugar, syrups, treacle, dried fruits, rice, sago, spices, pot barleys, soap, soda, starch, mustard, butter, cheese, grocers' papers, & c.& c.[1]

If its products were modest, so too were its offices, consisting of two small rooms in 3 Cooper Street, Manchester. Despite the unremarkable premises, however, those involved in the fledgling Co-operative Wholesale Society (CWS) were convinced that they were part of a business revolution—and they were right. Their enterprise would grow to become one of Britain's most successful and long-lasting businesses, and become a model for co-operative enterprises across the globe. Although they were confident they would succeed, the CWS's founders would be astonished at the scope of their organization 150 years on. Now known as The Co-operative Group, it employs more than 100,000 people in a family of businesses including food retailing, banking, insurance, pharmacy, funerals, and legal services, with an annual turnover of more than £13 billion. Yet what many contemporaries find most surprising about The Co-operative Group today—its status as a consumer-owned business governed on the principle of 'one member, one vote', which distributes a portion of its profits to members on the basis of use—would be refreshingly familiar to the co-operators of the 1860s.

There is more than one way of doing business. Although the investor-owned model that developed out of Britain's Industrial Revolution has become the dominant form of enterprise in the twenty-first century, it is not the only business type. *Building Co-operation* is the history of a different kind of business, also born from the experience of industrialization but developed according to a very different set of principles from those of the firms with which it competes. By definition, a co-operative is 'an autonomous association of persons united voluntarily to meet their common economic, social, and cultural needs and aspirations through a jointly-owned and democratically-controlled

---

[1] *The Co-operator* [Manchester] (May 1864), 180.

enterprise'.[2] Co-operative businesses operate in the competitive marketplace but join individual enterprise to collective goals through practices rooted in a defined set of values: self-help; self-responsibility; democracy; equality; equity; and solidarity. In Britain, co-operative enterprises have existed since at least the mid-eighteenth century. For 150 years, The Co-operative Group has stood at the centre of co-operative business. Born from the efforts of the Rochdale Pioneers and others who established successful co-operatives across Britain in the 1840s and 1850s, by the 1860s the proponents of the CWS were ready to pioneer a new effort: a federation of co-operative societies, democratically run and collectively owned, that would enable co-operatives to become their own suppliers. From humble origins the CWS grew into one of Britain's largest businesses within a generation, pioneering modern retailing and distribution on a national scale and expanding into production and financial services. Since the inauguration of the CWS in 1863 the commercial landscape has changed nearly beyond recognition, and the co-operative business model has had to evolve to meet new conditions. Yet there is also continuity in the principles that are central to co-operative enterprise, which have remained relevant to succeeding generations.

This book represents the first effort in many decades to address the development of Britain's largest co-operative enterprise from its inception to the present day. Through the lens of The Co-operative Group, *Building Co-operation* explores the co-operative business model as it developed in Britain over the course of 150 years. It will attempt to explain the trajectory of co-operative business experience, including its speedy rise to dominance from the mid-nineteenth century, its steady but conflicted growth through the first half of the twentieth century, the protracted period of decline, and the extraordinary 'renaissance' in co-operative enterprise since the 1990s. It is a story with many twists and turns, as the CWS moved into new areas of business, absorbed other co-operatives, and evolved from a co-operative federation into a hybrid structure that now includes more than 7 million individual members. The authors hope this study will appeal to business historians and interested scholars, but also to co-operative members and a wider public interested in the genesis and development of an alternative business model.

1.1 WHY THIS BOOK, AND WHY NOW?

The milestone of 150 years of continuous business seems an opportune time for reflection, and this project was designed with The Co-operative Group's sesquicentennial in mind. Although the authors have tried to avoid the pitfalls of a Whiggish homage to the co-operative past, there is nonetheless a tradition of anniversary histories in the

---

[2] International Co-operative Alliance (hereafter ICA), 'Statement of Co-operative Identity, Values and Principles'; see: <http://2012.coop/en/what-co-op/co-operative-identity-values-principles> (accessed 1 December 2012).

co-operative movement, which has long been prone to what Wrigley has termed 'the commemorative urge'.[3] Nonetheless it has been more than thirty-five years since a book-length study of Britain's largest co-operative business appeared in print, whilst those who wish to learn more about the origins and developments of the CWS before the Second World War continue to rely on histories prepared in celebration of the Wholesale's fiftieth and seventy-fifth anniversaries, in 1913 and 1938.[4] Since these publications, business history as an academic discipline has evolved considerably, moving away from straightforward institutional studies to a more multifaceted approach that includes organizational dynamics, multiple stakeholder perspectives, and the interrelationship between individual enterprises and the wider social, economic, and political context in which they operate.[5] This methodology is particularly well suited to the study of co-operative business, which includes amongst its fundamental values a refusal to divorce economic activity from its societal consequences. In short, the time is ripe to bring the story of The Co-operative Group up to date.

The paucity of business histories or studies of The Co-operative Group is surprising for many reasons, not the least of which is the richness of the subject matter. Leaving aside its importance in developing an innovative and successful model of co-operative business, the organization can claim a number of 'firsts' which have since become standard procedures in consumer-facing enterprises of all kinds. In the nineteenth century alone, the CWS created Britain's first national distribution network, devised some of the earliest 'own brand' products in retailing, and expanded its international supply chain through direct buying operations in Europe, North America, and Australasia. In the twentieth century, its innovations included the introduction of self-service shopping, in-store banking facilities, and the mainstreaming of 'green' and Fairtrade products. Despite such fertile material it remains true that co-operatives rarely feature in course syllabi or textbooks—a situation which contributes to the relative invisibility of an important and influential business type. As will be discussed, specialist academic interest in co-operatives has grown in recent decades but, in the main, British undergraduate and postgraduate programmes in business show 'a startling lack of awareness of and curiosity about co-operation and co-operatives'.[6] Amazingly, even in studies of business attitudes to environmental and social practice, 'the role of co-operatives in the evolution of corporate social responsibility often goes unacknowledged.'[7] Given that schools and universities are only just beginning to pay attention to different forms of enterprise, it is unsurprising to find that the co-operative business model is poorly understood by the British public. With the exception of a small proportion of active co-operative members, it is unlikely that more than a few shoppers on the high street today would be able to explain the difference between 'the Co-op' and food retailing rivals such as Tesco, Sainsbury's, ASDA, and Morrison's. Some older consumers have fond memories of 'the Co-op' of their childhood, and can recite their families' 'divi numbers'. Others view The Co-operative Group as a more ethical, community-minded business—yet few would

[3] C. Wrigley (2009).   [4] Richardson (1977); Redfern (1913) and (1938).
[5] Wilson (1995), 'Introduction', 1–20.   [6] Webster et al. (2011), 4.   [7] Hingley (2010), 113.

identify co-operatives as a different business type. There is a certain irony to this, for although Britain did much to inspire today's international movement, it is likely that co-operatives are better understood outside the UK than within it.

This study's arrival on the heels of the United Nations' International Year of Co-operatives (IYC) in 2012 is particularly opportune. Under the strapline 'Co-operative Enterprises Build a Better World', during the year national co-operative apex organizations and the International Co-operative Alliance (ICA) engaged in a widespread campaign to increase public awareness about co-operatives and their contributions to socio-economic development. The IYC represented the growing confidence of co-operative businesses in championing their distinctive identity at the national and international level, even as the movement recognized the need to demonstrate co-operatives' considerable contributions to the world economy.[8] In Britain and elsewhere, there is a pressing need for co-operative business models to be better understood in theory and in practice. The longstanding presence of co-operatives in many different national contexts and economic sectors suggests that we have much to learn about how, and why, these businesses survive and thrive. Recent research has highlighted key attributes of co-operatives that may contribute to their greater resilience during periods of crisis, arguing that co-operative ownership models tend to privilege long-term sustainability over short-term gain, generate greater legitimacy and trust through more accountable and transparent governance, and distribute resources more equitably amongst stakeholders than investor-owned corporations.[9] Particularly in the aftermath of the global financial crisis of 2007–8, these are topics of considerable relevance.

Historical studies of co-operative organizations and their evolution in different economic and social contexts have an important contribution to make. *Building Co-operation* analyses the co-operative movement's first successful federal model, analysing the conditions under which it developed and the ways in which it evolved across 150 years of enormous social, economic, and political change. Other countries would develop their own distinctive movements and models, for just as Rochdale was not the first or only type of co-operative enterprise, the CWS's federal structure was not the only framework in existence. However, the CWS provided an influential prototype and by the early twentieth century federal models were in place across Europe.[10] In addition to addressing the absence of co-operatives from histories of British business, *Building Co-operation* is a significant contribution to the burgeoning literature into co-operatives and mutuals, both in the UK and internationally. The authors have been fortunate in their access to a wealth of primary documents, dating from the inception of the CWS in the nineteenth century to its evolution into The Co-operative Group of the twenty-first. Many of these materials have been unavailable to scholars before now, and some are quite recent discoveries. As well, the authors have interviewed many CWS and The Co-operative Group leaders, who offered their insights into the developments of the last half-century. Readers

---

[8] See Mills and Davies (2012); and ICA et al. (2012).
[9] See Birchall and Kettison (2009); and Sanchez Bajo and Roelants (2011).
[10] Ekberg (2012b), 222–4.

will find much in these pages to generate new questions and debates about the history and future of co-operative business. We hope that *Building Co-operation* will inspire continued research into this vital and vibrant arena of scholarship.

1.2 *BUILDING CO-OPERATION*—SOME CAVEATS

In any historical study, particularly one covering such an extensive period of time, it is necessary to establish clear parameters for the scope of the project. In 2009, when research for this book began, it became apparent that strict limits would be necessary to bring the project to fruition, as the mountains of available material would keep a team of historians happily employed for decades. Thus, although this study covers 150 years of co-operative history, it is by no means exhaustive. Because it focuses on the co-operative business model in the specific context of the CWS and The Co-operative Group, there are many aspects of co-operation which receive limited attention. For example, despite the presence of many types of co-operatives in Britain, it was the consumer model which dominated and retail societies made up the bulk of co-operative membership and trade. Although worker co-operatives have been and remain important to the story of co-operative business, in this study they appear only in terms of their relations with the CWS/Group. The same is true of the agricultural sector.[11] The authors have taken a similar approach to the movement's other national organizations, including Co-operatives UK (formerly the Co-operative Union), the Co-operative Party, and the Women's Co-operative Guild.[12] As will be discussed, much of the extant literature on co-operatives is focused on its political, social, and educational aspects, which were predominantly (though not exclusively) the province of these organizations. Whilst these activities and organizations were significant in their own right, they appear in our analysis through their impact on, and relationship to, co-operative enterprise. In one area the authors faced a particularly vexing challenge: how to treat the Scottish Co-operative Wholesale Society (SCWS), which was established as a separate institution in 1868 but amalgamated with the CWS in 1973. The two Wholesales had close working relationships with one another from the very beginning. Before the SCWS was established a few Scottish societies were members of the Manchester-based business, and the CWS provided assistance to Scottish leaders in framing their rules in the late 1860s. The organizations

---

[11] On producer and worker co-operatives, see Jones (1894); more recent studies include Pérotin (2012) and Toms (2012). The National Co-operative Archive (hereafter NCA) also holds several journals focused on producer co-operation, including *The Co-operators' Yearbook* (1897–1960). There is little published material on agricultural co-operation in Britain, excepting the chapter 'Britain and Eire' in Digby (1951), 8–25. However NCA holds an extensive run of the *Plunkett Foundation Yearbook*, a journal with an agricultural focus established in 1926.

[12] The Co-operative Union (hereafter CU) is covered in most general co-operative histories; there is also Flanagan (1969). On the Co-operative Party, see Carbery (1969); Manton (2009); Stewart (2011); and Whitecross (forthcoming). On the Women's Co-operative Guild (hereafter WCG) see Scott (1998); Blaszak (2000); and Vorberg-Rugh (forthcoming).

worked together both formally and informally from the 1870s, and eventually institutionalized their joint arrangements through the establishment of the English & Scottish Joint Co-operative Wholesale Society (E&SCWS) in 1924. Despite these ties, there were also notable differences in scale and scope, strategy and organization, and the overall commercial context in which they operated. The SCWS has its own voluminous set of records and a long and vibrant history worthy of further research; however, an earlier business history, produced by Kinloch and Butt, offers a solid analysis of the organization across its lifespan.[13] Therefore, prior to 1973 the SCWS is treated as a separate business and is included in our analysis through its relationship to the CWS and in the Wholesales' joint actions. Following the merger, Scotland is included in our study alongside the other regions of the CWS and The Co-operative Group.

If *Building Co-operation* is not a comprehensive history of British co-operation, nor can it claim coverage of the entirety of The Co-operative Group and its component organizations. An all-encompassing chronicle of the CWS and The Co-operative Group across such a vast span a time would run to several volumes and test the patience of even the staunchest co-operative enthusiast! Our focus on the development of the overarching business model has meant that much material of value remains outside the scope of this study. For instance, each of the existing 'family of businesses' has a long and important history of its own, and all deserve greater attention than they receive here. The diversity of interests is extraordinary, and there is much to be learned from detailed examination of The Co-operative Group's involvement in farming, funeral provision, travel, and in its other specialist operations. The movement's provision of banking, insurance, and financial services is worthy of particular attention, and our analysis highlights the vital importance of these functions from the CWS's earliest days.[14] Whilst food retailing remains the dominant component of co-operative enterprise in Britain, the authors are keenly aware that The Co-operative Group's diverse business interests are important to the evolution of its distinctive model. Where possible we have provided examples of these contributions, but the authors remain conscious that there is scope for much further research.

The landscape of British co-operation becomes even more crowded when one considers the large numbers of retail societies that existed across this period. The number of UK consumer societies peaked at just over 1,400 in the early twentieth century and continued to be measured in the hundreds until the 1990s. Local and, after the Second World War, regional societies retained their distinctiveness. Local societies in England and Wales were the basic unit of CWS membership for most of its history, whilst regional identities coalesced around CWS branches in Newcastle, London, and (later) Bristol, Cardiff, and Northampton. In modern times, The Co-operative Group's local and regional area committees and the presence of independent co-operative societies as 'corporate members' illustrate the vital importance of understanding the British co-operative model in a geographical context. The authors have drawn upon archival materials and published histories of retail societies and, when extant, minutes of CWS branch

---

[13] Kinloch and Butt (1981).   [14] Garnett (1968).

committees, to set the context. However, given the large volume of co-operative society records, and their widely dispersed locations, our coverage of the range of member societies remains somewhat impressionistic. Local and regional studies have great value, and more are needed to provide a more nuanced view of co-operative business. In particular, much fruitful work could be done through regional comparative studies, testing the impact of national events on local experience, and vice versa. However, in *Building Co-operation* the focus is on the national business model, and by necessity our analysis tends more to the centre than the periphery.

A further under-explored area is that of the CWS's international operations, which are worthy of greater attention than they can receive in a single-volume study. The CWS developed its international supply chains with remarkable speed, establishing buying operations in Scandinavia, Western Europe, and North America from the 1870s. In the early twentieth century it looked to Australasia, West Africa, and South America for sources of food and raw materials. International supplies were a vital component of the early CWS business model and remained a significant feature throughout the twentieth century. However, the need for additional, more detailed research into CWS enterprises abroad is acute and there remain vast gaps to be filled. The opportunity exists to explore the interrelationships between the CWS's international outposts and domestic co-operative movements in both colonial and post-colonial contexts.[15] This would be an enormous contribution to the co-operative research agenda, particularly as a great deal of new source material has recently come to light.

In fact, the wealth of primary sources available on British co-operatives presents both opportunity and constraint. The sheer volume of extant material, and the level of detailed information it provides, is an extraordinary feature of British co-operative business over the course of 150 years. The co-operative commitment to openness, transparency, and education included the printing and distribution of balance sheets and accounts, verbatim coverage of CWS quarterly meetings in the *Co-operative News*, and numerous publications whose goal was to ensure its members and customers were well informed about the enterprise in which they were part-owners. These considerable resources are available in Manchester through the National Co-operative Archive, of which we have made extensive use. The co-operative tradition of openness clearly extends to the present, for The Co-operative Group, in addition to facilitating interviews with past and present members, Board leaders, and senior executives, allowed the authors access to the entirety of the extant Board minutes of the past 150 years. During the lifetime of this project, even more co-operative records have surfaced. As The Co-operative Group prepared to move into its new headquarters at 1 Angel Square, it spearheaded a project in conjunction with the Archive to recover records stored in the many buildings of Manchester's 'co-operative quarter'. By the end of 2012, the project had recovered more than

[15] In this context, the ambitious project of Mary Hilson and Silke Neusinger, who gathered international co-operative scholars in Stockholm in May 2012 to discuss 'A Global History of Consumer Co-operatives', is particularly noteworthy. See <http://www.arbark.se/forskning/projekt/co-op/> (accessed 1 December 2012).

750 linear metres (2,400 feet) of archival materials, many of outstanding historical value. The 'finds' range from the original minutes of the Jumbo Farm meeting in 1860 to photographs and minutes related to the CWS depots in West Africa in the years before and after the First World War, and the reports of Fred Lambert in the 1960s, whose insights were invaluable to our analysis of the Co-operative Independent Commission of the 1950s in Chapter 6. At times it seemed that every week brought a new discovery, and whilst we have endeavoured to make use of the materials we are conscious that much more is available for a new generation of co-operative research.

1.3 TOWARDS A CO-OPERATIVE BUSINESS HISTORY

The development of British retailing and consumer-oriented business has an extensive literature; so too does the co-operative movement. However, until quite recently there was little cross-fertilization between the two in contemporary scholarship. Indeed, as Kalmi demonstrates, whereas in the nineteenth and early twentieth century the co-operative model was a feature of mainstream business and economics texts, after 1945 it virtually disappeared.[16] In subsequent decades, awareness of co-operative business models was limited to the 'silos of the converted and committed', whilst the dominance of a neo-liberal economic orthodoxy did little to promote their further study.[17] In fact, co-operation seemed to fare extremely badly in the later twentieth century, as co-operation across Europe either declined markedly (as in Britain) or virtually collapsed, as in France, Germany, and Austria. This seemed to confirm the neo-liberal prejudice that co-operatives were a socialistic and anachronistic relic of a former time. In the decades following Jefferys's landmark 1954 work *Retail Trading in Britain*, which included extensive coverage of co-operatives, it was a rare study indeed which subjected co-operatives to any substantial degree of analysis.[18] Inside the movement itself the tradition of self-produced textbooks on the movement's history and practices remained, as evidenced by Bonner's *British Co-operation*,[19] but such texts were intended for an internal co-operative audiences and did little either to set the movement's experiences in the context of the overall business environment or to expose co-operative methods to a wider public. As co-operatives began to lose market share, movement-produced studies waned and a narrative of decline became apparent in the national business press. Meanwhile, although in the 1930s and 1940s studies by Carr-Saunders and G. D. H. Cole[20] had bridged the gap between the academy and the movement, in the post-war decades this gulf widened. What academic attention there was tended to focus on the nineteenth-

---

[16] Kalmi (2007).   [17] Webster and Walton (2012), 'Introduction', 825–6.
[18] Jefferys (1954). The only notable study of retail history that included co-operatives in its analysis prior to the 1990s was Winstanley (1983).
[19] Bonner (1961).   [20] Carr-Saunders et al. (1938); Cole (1944).

century movement. More recent co-operative experience received little attention. By the mid-1990s, Lancaster and Maguire commented that much of the academic literature seemed 'as detached from the movement as historical studies of Chartism or Puritanism, consigning a still active movement very firmly into the past tense'.[21]

In the second half of the twentieth century, most academic studies of co-operatives came from scholars interested in working-class social and political movements. Co-operatives were generally categorized with trade unions and socialist parties, and the predominant focus was the dynamics of class consciousness rather than with co-operatives as a distinct organizational type. In this framework co-operatives' business activities received less attention than their educational, social, and political endeavours. Amongst the post-war generation of labour historians, even sympathetic observers tended to view the movement's commercial growth as a capitulation to capitalism. Writing in the 1960s Pollard argued that, whilst there was some continuity between the movement's early experiments and its 'shopkeeping period', the Rochdale model's dividend on purchases represented a significant breach with the idealism of the Owenite era.[22] Many commentators before and since have equated co-operatives' mid-nineteenth-century success with the philosophical 'failure' of the Co-operative Commonwealth to supplant capitalist enterprise. For these scholars, co-operatives came to represent 'the very epitome of Engel's black-coated workers', and helped to incorporate the working classes into the capitalist project.[23] Thus, the literature tended to overemphasize a line of demarcation between co-operative enterprise and co-operative ideals, which were more often dealt with in the context of co-operative social, educational, and political efforts. Such a 'business versus ideals' dualism neglects the interchange between the movement's economic and socio-political goals. Even at their most pragmatic, co-operative business practices were part of a larger effort to reconstruct socio-economic relations around concepts of mutuality, fairness, and participation. In his 1996 book, Gurney put forth an important corrective, commenting that 'the dividend itself was an "ideal" despite the fact that it put food in bellies and clothes on backs'.[24] Since Gurney's important work, social and political historians interested in the development of consumer society have brought new attention to co-operatives.[25] In Robertson's recent comparative study of eight British retail societies, she demonstrates the variety of co-operatives' local experience, as societies emphasized different elements of co-operative ideology and varied their economic, social, and educational services to suit the needs of members in specific environments.[26] Robertson's work is particularly valuable in examining the multi-layered nature of co-operative institutions, bringing new attention to the intersections and disjunctions between national co-operative policies and grass roots practices.

---

[21] Lancaster and Maguire (1996), 5.   [22] Pollard (1960), 95.
[23] Lancaster and Maguire (1996), 6. For an example of the 'incorporation' argument, see Kirk (1985).
[24] Gurney (1996), 9–10.
[25] Hilton (2003); Trentmann (2008). See also the edited collection of essays on co-operation and consumerism, Black and Robertson (2009).
[26] Robertson (2010).

Since the 1990s, co-operatives have begun to re-emerge as a topic of interest for business scholars. In a lengthy 1993 article, Sparks developed the first substantive critique of British co-operative performance after 1945, highlighting the movement's difficulties in adapting to massive shifts in the consumer environment and its failure to arrest its falling market share in food retailing.[27] Sparks in particular is scathing about what he sees as a general failure in the leadership of the movement. Other social scientists, notably Birchall and Spears, contributed historical and contemporary studies which helped revive interest in co-operatives in the context of social enterprise and the social economy.[28] A turning point came in 1998, when a special issue of the journal *Business History* on the history of retailing appeared which included articles by Bamfield and Purvis. The issue highlighted co-operatives' contributions to British retail development and encouraged new scholarship, notably into the movement's twentieth-century experience. Purvis in particular offered important new insights into the commercial strategies of co-operative retail societies in the period from the 1850s to the 1870s, and their relations with the emergent CWS.[29] In this, he built upon earlier work on the geographical spread of co-operation in England and Wales in the later nineteenth century, which considered the factors which assisted the rise of co-operative business in some areas, and those which impeded it in others.[30] Since that time, co-operatives have continued to feature in the journal, notably in Shaw and Alexander's work on the introduction of self-service retailing in Britain in the 1950s.[31] The revival of the British co-operative movement in the first decade of the twenty-first century, and the major crisis in mainstream international capitalism precipitated by the financial crash of 2008, have helped create a new impetus for the study of co-operative economic models. A series of edited volumes, one focusing on the British example, but others seeking to draw international comparisons, have evaluated co-operatives' performance in a range of differing historical and contemporary contexts. Of particular importance is Black and Robertson's edited volume *Consumerism and the Co-operative Movement in Modern British History*.[32] The essays in this volume explore a range of different facets of the British movement, including the reasons for its decline in membership from the 1950s, an evaluation of the Co-operative Independent Commission's work between 1956 and 1958, and two essays comparing the British movement with those of Norway and Sweden. The volume explores a number of different aspects of the British movement, including political and cultural as well as business developments. The two edited volumes on international co-operation were the products of two major international conferences convened in honour of the then impending International Year of Co-operation of 2012. The first of these, *The Hidden Alternative*, offers essays which explore a wide range of the ideological, business, and cultural

[27] Sparks (1994) and (2002).
[28] See Birchall (1994) and (1997). Roger Spear, long-time chair of the Open University's Co-operative Research Unit, has published widely on British and international co-operatives since the 1980s, when he co-edited the volume Cornforth et al. (1988).
[29] Purvis (1998).   [30] Purvis (1990).
[31] Shaw and Alexander (2008) and Alexander (2008).   [32] Black and Robertson (2009).

manifestations of co-operation in a variety of historical and contemporary contexts. There are chapters on the development of co-operation in China, India, South Africa, Italy, and Spain, and amongst these were a number of contributions on the variety of business models which co-operative movements have developed.[33] The other volume was Schröter and Battilani's *The Co-operative Business Movement, 1950 to the Present*, the essays in which have a sharper focus on the post-1950 period, and on co-operative business models.[34] In 2012, this work was joined by a new special issue of *Business History*, this time focused entirely on co-operative business history.[35] Featuring articles on a range of British and international co-operative topics, the volume is further evidence of co-operatives' rising profile amongst business scholars. Of particular importance for the development of the British movement in that volume were the contributions of Whyman, Toms, Robertson, Ekberg, and Gurney. Toms's work is a direct challenge to the notion that workers' or producers' co-operatives are inherently less efficient than traditional capitalist enterprises. Focusing upon some of the experiments in producer co-operation in the British textile industry in the later nineteenth century, Toms shows that these organizations stood up well in comparison with their competitors.[36] Gurney's article sets the inter-war British co-operative movement within the context of an emergent consumer society, building on themes in earlier work on consumerism and co-operation, which focused on the post-war period.[37] Robertson illuminates a much neglected aspect of co-operative retail society development in the nineteenth and twentieth centuries—how these organizations supported their members through the provision of financial advice and services, especially during periods of economic difficulty.[38] Robertson's work is strongly complemented by Samy's study of the role of the Co-operative Permanent Building Society in promoting home-ownership among co-operative society members.[39] Ekberg's piece outlines the parallels and differences between co-operative movements across Europe in the post-war period, a comparative theme which appears in much of his other work.[40] Whyman provides a rare attempt to place thinking about co-operatives within the wider context of economic theory; which is of itself a vitally important task, given the gradual fading of co-operation from much of the literature about economics and business.[41]

Despite the recent surge in studies of co-operative businesses, detailed accounts of the CWS and The Co-operative Group are comparatively rare. The best known of these are the 1913 and 1938 histories written by Percy Redfern, who worked for the Wholesale's press agency and served for many years as the editor of the monthly *Wheatsheaf* magazine. Exhaustively researched, the lengthy volumes chronicle the origins and rise of the CWS in great detail and remain an exceptional resource. Yet for all the wealth of material the Redfern studies are very much 'official histories', valuable in articulating the view of the Wholesale's leaders but more than a little one-sided in their analysis of CWS

---

[33] Webster et al. (2011).   [34] Battilani and Schröter (2012).
[35] Webster and Walton (2012).   [36] Toms (2012).
[37] Gurney (2012); see also Gurney (2005).   [38] Robertson (2012).
[39] Samy (2012).   [40] Ekberg (2012a).   [41] Whyman (2012).

relations with retail societies and the movement's other national bodies.[42] This was certainly felt to be the case at the time, and readers may sympathize with the 1938 reviewer who criticized the 'picture of a CWS which is always triumphantly right'.[43] The same year, Carr-Saunders and his team published a more objective critique of co-operative business as it had developed up to the 1930s.[44] An invaluable resource for understanding the co-operative model as it had developed by the inter-war period, the Carr-Saunders study went so far as to opine that: 'The future historian of the movement will date the modern phase of Co-operation, not from 1844, but from the foundation of the Co-operative Wholesale Society'.[45] However, while Carr-Saunders and his colleagues saw in the CWS the natural centre for co-operative business, they also noted the need for better operational planning and more strategic management if the Wholesale was to help unify the movement in the face of increasingly fierce competition. The only subsequent book to focus on the CWS is by Sir William Richardson, who covers developments during the troubled times between 1938 and 1976. Given the period covered, its tone is substantially less triumphalist than that of the Redfern volumes, but Richardson does little to assess the movement in relationship to the wider commercial and socio-economic environment. However, his work highlights the key role of the CWS's accumulated resources in sustaining the movement during trying times.

In the 2000s, two studies appeared which have made important contributions to understanding the CWS up to the time of its transformation into The Co-operative Group. The first of these, by Yeo, was originally intended as the opening chapter of a larger project and outlines the period of the greatest transformation in the history of the British movement, 1973–2001.[46] Yeo, whose edited volume was instrumental in reviving social historians' attention to co-operatives in the 1980s,[47] brings to his work decades of active engagement with co-operatives through the Co-operative College. His insight into the redevelopment of the business model and the importance of the specialist businesses in this process is a significant contribution to the present volume. A second study, Ekberg's Ph.D. thesis comparing the experiences of the CWS and the Norwegian co-operative wholesale NKF between 1950 and 2002, provides retail historians with an incisive and detailed account.[48] Like Sparks, Ekberg concentrates on the period of the British movement's decline, but his more detailed study offers an incisive analysis of the complex interplay between the movement's internal organizational structures and culture with the wider socio-economic business environment. By comparing the CWS with its more successful Norwegian counterpart, Ekberg challenges the inevitability of the narrative of decline surrounding co-operative movements after 1950, and instead examines the combination of internal and external factors which impacted the two movements' ability to confront the competitive challenges of the post-war period.

---

[42] See for example Redfern's treatment of the acquisition of CIS in the 1913 volume and, in 1938, his brief dismissals of both the General Co-operative Survey and the National Co-operative Authority.

[43] E. Topham in *The Co-operative Review* (November 1938), 329.

[44] Carr-Saunders (1938).   [45] Carr-Saunders (1938), 36.

[46] Yeo (2002).   [47] Yeo (1988).   [48] Ekberg (2008).

In terms of the British movement, Ekberg and others have argued that only crises precipitated real change; unless economic necessity intervened efforts to rationalize and reform the sprawling retail and distribution empire proved ineffectual, largely because the internal political obstacles to coordinated reform became more intractable.[49] There is more than a grain of truth in this assessment, and crises have certainly been an important catalyst for change. However, this perspective provides few insights into the 'renaissance' of the contemporary movement. Ekberg's study ends in 2002, at a time when Britain's co-operative revival was still in its infancy and co-operative's food retail market share was at its nadir; the present study offers the opportunity to take the story forward in time. Moreover, Ekberg's work on the CWS is focused entirely on its food retailing and distribution operations to the exclusion of the broader family of co-operative businesses, a common feature of most of the extant literature. While it would be folly to ignore the primacy of the food business to The Co-operative Group, past and present, Yeo's work and the authors' own research suggest that the specialist businesses were integral to the revitalization of the business model. In particular The Co-operative Bank's growing profitability and its spearheading of the 'ethical business' approach was a key feature of the co-operative revival in the latter years of the twentieth century.

During the latter half of the twentieth century the British co-operative movement 'fell between different spheres' of scholarship,[50] resulting in a fragmented picture of co-operative experience that has hindered the development of a holistic understanding of co-operative enterprises in mainstream business scholarship and among the general public. Business historians lagged behind their counterparts interested in the political and social history of the movement. While these topics are valuable in their own right, in the final analysis the culture of co-operation was equally about economic enterprise. In the early twenty-first century, co-operative models are beginning to reassert themselves, and business scholars are rediscovering the co-operative and mutual sector's contributions as 'people-centred businesses'.[51] As an influential, innovative British enterprise and one of the oldest, most resilient co-operative businesses, The Co-operative Group offers historians an unparalleled opportunity for empirical analysis of the co-operative business model.

1.4 THE CO-OPERATIVE BUSINESS MODEL AND THE CO-OPERATIVE GROUP

In 1993, Davis and Worthington summarized the challenge at the heart of the co-operative business model: the objective 'to alter radically the basis by which business is undertaken whilst competing on equal terms in the very marketplace it seeks to reform'.[52]

[49] Ekberg (2008), 300.   [50] Robertson (2010), 5.
[51] Birchall (2011).   [52] Davis and Worthington (1993), 849.

This was true at the time of the formation of the CWS in 1863 and remains central to understanding The Co-operative Group 150 years on. The early CWS leaders shared a desire to supplant the capitalist economy with a co-operative one, and their successful business was proof to some that a Co-operative Commonwealth could be practically achieved within, and then overtake, existing market practice. However, co-operative ideals and practices are not static, nor do they exist in isolation from their cultural, political, and economic contexts. Over time the business model has had to adapt to the changing needs of co-operative societies and their members, with varying degrees of success, amidst the numerous shifts and shocks of the nineteenth, twentieth, and early twenty-first centuries. Whilst few co-operative leaders today would express an ambition to replace capitalism, co-operative enterprises have nonetheless shaped, and continue to influence, wider business practice. Thus it is essential to understand co-operative enterprises in *both* their co-operative and wider commercial contexts, in order to understand the structures they develop, the strategies they employ, and how these have changed over time.

The CWS's federal structure was rooted in the Rochdale model of the 1840s, and reflected the needs of co-operative retail societies in the mid-nineteenth century. It was designed to incorporate co-operative principles into a democratic organization that would help societies compete against their business rivals. It is unsurprising that the CWS founders, who included amongst them three of the original Pioneers, would seek a joint solution to the needs of numerous, distinct co-operative businesses. However, the creation of a viable 'co-operative of co-operatives' was no easy task, requiring a balance between the collective needs of member societies and their interests as autonomous organizations rooted in particular communities. Like the Rochdale Pioneers, the new CWS was both an expression of ideological purpose and a pragmatic solution. Societies purchasing shares in the CWS were able to pool their risks, reduce costs through greater economies of scale, and collectively raise capital to support expansion, without losing their separate, local identities or limiting their independent action. The federal model enabled the nineteenth-century movement to grow on a national scale and become a significant manufacturer of goods, but over time this organizational framework shaped CWS development in a very different manner from that of private businesses operating in the same field. In comparison with other large firms developing in the same period, the CWS's ownership structure was inverted. Rather than 'parent companies' controlling individual enterprises, in the co-operative federation the local co-operative societies governed from the bottom up.[53] Member societies elected the CWS Board, and could both propose new policies and practices at quarterly meetings as well as vote for or against Board decisions. As the number of individual societies grew, tensions arose between the local aims of co-operative societies and the goals of the CWS's national leadership. For societies, the primary motivation was to sustain their community position, using local market knowledge to provide the appropriate goods and services and

[53] Ekberg (2012b), 224–5.

achieve levels of dividend which could attract and retain members. Societies' members were far more concerned with local trade than with wider co-operative business trends, and their management committees were responsible to a local membership, not the CWS Board. However, as the CWS developed into an increasingly powerful, national enterprise, local societies' tendency to pull in different directions was a significant brake on the CWS's ability to take full advantage of its purchasing power.

The ties and tensions between national and local incentives run throughout the history of the British co-operative movement and its central institutions. From its inception, the rules of the CWS prevented it from selling to non-co-operative enterprises. Local societies were under no similar obligation to buy exclusively from the CWS, and many chose to purchase at least some goods from local suppliers, on the basis of price but also to spread risks and assure continued community support. Under some circumstances, the need to compete for societies' business served as a hothouse environment that promoted innovation at the CWS, pushing the Wholesale to create its national supply network and expand its buying operations overseas very early on in its development. Member societies' interests were also influential in directing CWS into new business arenas, such as banking in the 1870s, as societies lacked access to essential financial services.[54] Over time, however, the increasing concentration of resources in CWS created its own centrifugal force, and gave CWS directors significant leverage in their dealings with local societies. Particularly during times when retail societies' businesses were under pressure, the influence of the CWS's financial arm could be considerable. Nonetheless, the voluntary nature of the co-operative model meant that the CWS authority was based on its power to persuade. The relationship between the CWS Board and local co-operative societies thus bore little resemblance to the more centralized, 'command and control' structures of the multiple retail firms developing from the late nineteenth century.

As the number of local societies declined, slowly in the early twentieth century and then with increasing speed after 1960, the federal dynamic changed considerably. It evolved from being a federal system made up entirely of society members to The Co-operative Group's current hybrid structure in which individual membership predominates. Changes to the CWS's organizational structure took place in reaction to shifting business conditions, but also within a co-operative context, as co-operative societies and their members balanced pragmatic needs with the desire to maintain co-operative values and principles and prove their relevance in new circumstances. There were also issues of path dependency, as past decisions influenced the range of choices available in present circumstances. Thus, alongside its business activities co-operative democratic structures have evolved, adapting to address the commercial and organizational needs of different eras. The British co-operative model remains a complicated one, with many overlapping structures that defy easy categorization. In tracing the CWS/The Co-operative Group model over time, the authors address several key questions. How did co-operative businesses adapt to the changing needs of members over time? How did issues of centre

[54] Webster (2012), 883–904.

and periphery impact CWS business development, and that of retail societies? What are the challenges and opportunities of a federal structure that combines both 'top down' and 'bottom up' elements? And, perhaps most crucially, how can we assess the co-operative model's strengths and weaknesses in comparison to that of PLCs, in different times and environments?

The co-operative business model raises particular questions related to management and leadership. Co-operative democratic structures create a different environment from PLC models, allowing for active participation in governance by members at several organizational levels. Co-operatives' multi-layered structures and scepticism of central authority suggest that different leadership qualities were required of co-operative business leaders than their private counterparts. The need for an informed membership helped spur co-operative businesses' commitment to transparent governance, as member-owners (whether individuals or societies) had to be persuaded of the wisdom of management policies and practices. However, there are questions to be raised regarding the speed with which co-operatives were able to adapt, given their complex structures and the time-consuming nature of achieving consensus. This is particularly important in regard to the movement's efforts to reform itself in the twentieth century through its various surveys and commissions, which identified problems but found great difficulty in implementing solutions. Access to positions of leadership were also different in co-operatives, as its personnel were drawn largely from the working classes at least until the mid-twentieth century, and the movement offered different paths to authority, through elected office or direct employment. The movement's ideological commitment to education paralleled the pragmatic need to provide training and information to largely self-educated nineteenth-century co-operative leaders, spurring the development of co-operative management training programmes at a very early stage in comparison to private firms. However, CWS and other co-operative leaders debated the balance between the need for technical training and more specifically ideological co-operative education. Over time, the professionalization of management also had an influence on the CWS, which had to balance the need to attract and retain talented managers with an internal movement culture that valued 'promotion from within'. A number of related questions remain, which will be addressed throughout our analysis. Is there a relationship between the size of co-operative societies and the effectiveness of their democratic structures? What role do leaders, 'active members', and customers play in relationship to each other and in the development of the model over time?

All co-operative businesses—local and national, large and small—respond not only to their own internal dynamics but also to shifts in the overall commercial environment. As comparative studies illustrate, the CWS's development was marked by its arrival in an already complex, mature retail environment. In contrast, in Scandinavian countries co-operative wholesalers faced little competition for societies' trade, and retail societies developed under less competitive pressure from private shopkeepers.[55] The presence of

---

[55] See Chapter 8.

formidable rivals and the early pressure to compete had a dramatic influence on the CWS's development in the nineteenth century, even as co-operative innovations in distribution and retailing spurred change in the wider marketplace. As co-operative business leaders have learned many times throughout the past 150 years, there is no rule that prohibits competitors from adopting one's innovations, and practices that were once market leaders can quickly become the norm. In Britain, the pace of change accelerated throughout the twentieth century. Consumers had more options and co-operative businesses had to do more to draw their custom. As both Gurney and Schwartzkopf demonstrate, co-operative notions of consumption contrasted with those of many of their competitors, leading to differences in the movement's approach to advertising, marketing, and branding.[56] However, as incomes rose and living standards increased the incentive power of co-operative dividends as a competitive advantage diminished and the co-operative brand had to adapt to changing consumer interests. This raises the question of the degree to which competitive pressures have influenced co-operative efforts to innovate and reform, and the extent to which co-operative practices have permeated the marketplace. Throughout the chapters to come, the authors will assess the impact of the CWS and The Co-operative Group on their competitors, and vice versa.

Co-operatives have not only responded to internal and commercial changes, but also to the remarkable social, political, and cultural upheavals that have occurred since the mid-nineteenth century. These range from the global watershed events of war and economic depression to more gradual shifts, as the British economy transitioned from one based on manufacturing to one centred around services, and standards of living rose to create a culture of affluence with very different perceptions of needs and wants. Political developments too influenced co-operative business and culture, from the rise of universal suffrage to the growing role of the state in providing education, health care, and unemployment benefits. The social and cultural changes of the period are staggering, changing the interaction between individuals of different classes, genders, and ethnicities and the interaction between individuals, organizations, and the natural environment. Throughout our analysis, we will address the role of broader societal changes on co-operative developments, focusing on two key questions: how has the co-operative business model adapted to, and helped shape, these key transformations in British society? And, how have the CWS and The Co-operative Group impacted the role of business in relationship to societal change?

1.5 ORGANIZATION

In Part I: Rise and Reign, the authors explore the development of the co-operative business model from its nineteenth-century origins to the start of the Second World War—a period of near-continuous growth. Chapter 2 traces the origins of co-operative

---

[56] See Chapter 9.

ideology and the development of the consumer co-operative model, providing the essential context for the CWS's establishment in 1863. Chapter 3 charts the founding and early development of the CWS as it expanded its distribution network at home and abroad and made its first moves into manufacturing and banking. This chapter demonstrates the strengths and weaknesses of the federal model as the movement grew, highlighting the influence of the pre-existing commercial environment and the Wholesale's need to compete for societies' custom in driving CWS innovations in developing international supply chains. By 1890 the essential features of the CWS business model were in place. As Chapter 4 details, the CWS and the movement continued to expand at a remarkable pace in the years before the First World War. The CWS further increased its productive capacity, vertically integrated its supply chains, and developed overseas sources for raw materials such as tea, palm oil, and cocoa. Co-operatives began to extend their reach beyond the 'heartland' regions of the industrial North, and swelled the range of goods and services on offer. However, expansion came with challenges of its own. The mushrooming number of retail societies added to the complexity of co-operative business and reduced the potential for economies of scale, while more efficient multiple retailers grew more competitive. Tensions in the federal model became more apparent, as the CWS and other national bodies sought greater authority to enforce co-operative policy and local societies resisted efforts that might limit their autonomy.

Although internecine co-operative conflicts did not disappear, as Chapter 5 demonstrates, in the period between 1914 and 1938 external battles of various kinds would have the greatest impact on the co-operative business model. The First World War was as much a watershed event for the co-operative movement as it was for Britain as a whole, reshaping co-operatives' relationship with their members, their competitors, and with the state. The creation of the Co-operative Party in 1917 brought the movement into the political arena, and throughout the inter-war years the CWS would struggle to defend its interests on both the political left and right. Britain's changing position in the global economy, a series of crises in international financial markets, and the shifting geography of decline and growth in British industry were external challenges to which the CWS had to adapt. This was the period in which the CWS Retail Society (later CRS) came into being as a means of support for failing co-operative societies, whilst other initiatives sought to unify societies in the face of increasing multiple competition and a largely hostile political environment. Still, for the CWS the inter-war years were predominantly ones of phenomenal growth, and as the Second World War approached co-operatives were at the height of their economic power.

In the book's second part, 'Retreat and Renaissance', the authors analyse the co-operative business model throughout a period of ever-intensifying competition and enormous socio-political change. Chapter 6, covering the period from the Second World War to the early 1970s, shows the movement's efforts to adapt its business methods and practices as the 'consumer revolution' entered a new phase. Although co-operatives enjoyed strong market share in the immediate post-war period, by the 1960s it was apparent that co-operatives were beginning to lose ground to the growing multiple firms. Changes in living standards, consumer behaviour, and social structure all contributed to new patterns of retail trade, to which co-operatives found it difficult to adapt. Although the movement sought to reform itself, instigating the Co-operative Independent Commission of the 1950s and developing plans to reduce the number of societies and rationalize its operations, coordinated efforts were difficult to achieve. From the centre, the CWS instituted reforms to its own structure and used its resources to push for more streamlined buying and modernized operations. However, co-operative societies continued to pull in different directions, and multiple competitors continued to increase their market share at co-operatives' expense.

In the decades following the merger of the two Wholesales in 1973, the situation remained bleak. Chapter 7 traces the continued decline in market share up to 1990, as co-operative societies merged at a rapid pace but failed to build a consensus around strategic reform. Paradoxically, the larger regional societies that formed in this era tended to seek greater independence from the CWS, as did the CRS, further weakening efforts to unify the movement. The absorption of SCWS required the CWS to adapt its governance model to include individual members and its business model to include Scottish retail operations, which later expanded to include those of other societies who merged into the CWS. However, despite the decline in food retailing this period saw new developments that played a role in the movement's revival, notably the growing importance of The Co-operative Bank and other specialist businesses. In Chapter 8, the authors focus on the watershed decade of 1990–2000, as the movement responded to crises in governance and the attempted hostile takeover of the CWS, moved away from manufacturing, and grew into the largest co-operative retailer, in the process redeveloping its business strategies based on a modernized conception of the movement's values and principles. The CWS and retail societies found new ways to work together through joint buying operations, whilst the longstanding rivalry with CRS finally came to a conclusion through the formation of The Co-operative Group. Chapter 9, the last in this section, brings the story up to date, through the important mergers with United Co-operatives and Britannia Building Society, continued developments in ethical retailing and Fairtrade initiatives, and the evolution of new democratic structures that incorporated local and regional identities into a national framework. An extensive rebranding initiative brought the specialist concerns into closer connection across the family of businesses, whilst The Co-operative Group expanded market share through improved operations and by acquiring retail competitors such as Alldays and Somerfield.

In the concluding chapter, the authors offer their analysis of the business model as it stands today. The Co-operative Group continues to evolve, and events still coming to fruition as this book is published will take the business model in new directions. Inevitably, it is difficult as historians to predict how all this might take shape. The Co-operative Group's significant investment in the legal services sector, the strong performance of its specialist businesses despite difficult economic conditions, and the recent introduction of a new, more all-embracing marketing strapline—'Here for you for life'—are indications to consumers and stakeholders of an enhanced interest in services other than food retailing and banking. Although we have no crystal ball, we can confidently claim that the last fifteen years have demonstrated the organization's ability to adapt to both internal and external challenges, developing a structural dynamic that can effectively respond, even in the teeth of one of deepest economic recessions of the last century. What lies ahead will be the subject of a future research team's project.

PART I

RISE AND REIGN

CHAPTER 2

··

THE ROOTS AND RISE OF BRITISH CO-OPERATION, C.1780–1863

··

In Britain, the emergence of the co-operative movement tends to be associated with the name of a place in east Lancashire—Rochdale. The Rochdale Pioneers, who established their famous consumer co-operative in 1844, have become international icons, celebrated in popular culture, especially within the international labour movement. In addition to the voluminous literature on the Pioneers, from Holyoake onwards, their lives have even been the subject of co-operative movement sponsored films, in 1944 ('Men of Rochdale') and 2012 ('The Rochdale Pioneers'). The first store they established in the town at Toad Lane has been a museum for decades, and has recently been refurbished with the benefit of Heritage Lottery Funding. In Kobe, Japan, there is even a replica of Toad Lane—several times the size of the original!

There is no doubt that the success of Rochdale was an important milestone, arguably a turning point, in the fortunes of British co-operation. But as this chapter will demonstrate, the roots of co-operation ran deeper than Rochdale, which was, in many respects, the cumulative result of developments which preceded it by several decades. This chapter will address several key questions. First, what were the social and economic conditions which gave rise to the organization, by ordinary working people, of consumer or producer co-operatives? While the hardship of life in the early stages of the industrial revolution was certainly a factor, it will be seen that the successful establishment of co-operatives required much more than just widespread poverty. The presence of other factors was equally essential for the establishment of co-operatives, including the existence of common interests and social bonds amongst those who established the early societies, as well as equally less tangible attributes such as education and prevailing cultural and value systems. As will be seen, this made for very uneven geographical patterns of co-operative development across the country. Secondly, what were the intellectual foundations of what became much more than a pragmatic response to immediate difficulty? Which of the currents of contemporary philosophical thought fed into the emergence of co-operation not only as a practical commercial strategy, but as a championed alternative social, political, and economic order to capitalism? Thirdly, why did most of the attempts up to the 1840s to establish sustainable local co-operatives fail, while Rochdale and those which followed its model achieved not only more members and greater commercial success, but also lasted much longer? This pattern of abortive initiatives suddenly being transformed into lasting and sustained success was to be repeated in the quest to try to establish a national system for supplying the local societies through some kind of co-operative wholesaling system. Attempts to create a national wholesale system for co-operatives in England were made in the early 1830s and in the 1850s, by co-operators in Liverpool, London, and Rochdale, but all of these failed. It was not until 1863 that the movement established the English Co-operative Wholesale Society, with its Scottish counterpart being established a few years later.

This chapter will first examine the earliest efforts to establish co-operative societies of various kinds, highlighting both the sociological factors and ideas behind these initiatives. The reasons for the instability and unsustainability of these first experiments will be explored. Secondly, it will outline the emergence of the Rochdale Pioneers and their model in the mid-1840s, and will consider the reasons for the durability and startling popularity of this model; whilst also considering why it spread rapidly in some parts of the country and social environments whilst it struggled elsewhere. Finally, the chapter will examine the efforts to establish a wholesale organization capable of supplying co-operative societies across the country, and why these only came to fruition in the 1860s.

2.1   Co-operative initiatives before the 1840s

It is widely accepted that the effects of the economic changes of the eighteenth and nineteenth centuries were pivotal in stimulating a wave of self-help and co-operative initiatives in Britain. Land enclosures and industrialization prompted unprecedented social change, as new agricultural methods reduced demand for labour in the countryside, and the rise of factory production drew large numbers of people into the fast growing towns and cities. While there is much historical debate about the pace of urbanization, it is clear that economic change was accompanied by major shifts in social relations. In his famous essay on the origin of food riots in the late eighteenth century, E. P. Thompson described the breakdown of what he termed the 'Moral Economy' of life in towns and agricultural districts.[1] Thompson argued that much of British life in the eighteenth century was governed by notions of traditional obligations between levels of what was regarded by contemporaries as quite a fixed social hierarchy. The lower orders subjected themselves to the authority of the landed elite and their allies, in return for paternalistic

[1] Thompson (1971), 76–136.

regard for their welfare. One manifestation of this was an accepted notion of what constituted a fair and socially acceptable price for bread, especially in circumstances of economic hardship. Thompson described how the increasing monetization of the economy and growing prevalence of market pressures led to growing number of millers, bakers, and grocers departing from pricing strategies based on social norms to ones more in tune with a rapidly marketizing economy. The result was a sense of betrayal, isolation, fear, and rage among many of those most affected by rising food prices. Without political representation they sought redress for their grievances through violent disorder: rioting. Other historians have traced such acts of resistance against the attack on traditional and customary economic and social relations unleashed by industrialization and the emergence of the market economy. Randall traces the often violent and clandestine activities of working people, both in the countryside and the developing industrial towns, from the riots of the eighteenth century, through the Luddite uprisings in the textile industries of Yorkshire and Nottinghamshire in 1811–12, to the widespread attacks on landowners across the south of England by the rural poor during the 'Swing Riots' of the late 1820s.[2] Navickas shows how the nature of this resistance, no matter how widespread it appeared to be, was profoundly shaped by local circumstances and local grievances, and the ability of the aggrieved to respond through collective action, which frequently depended upon the extent to which local populations perceived their common interests.[3]

While the formation of co-operatives in the early nineteenth century perhaps lacked the dramatic and direct impact of collective violence against property, it was no less part of this collective response by the poor and dispossessed to the frightening and seemingly amoral world being created by agricultural and industrial change, urbanization, and the emerging hegemony of the market. Bamfield's work has thrown important new light on responses by the lower classes to the challenges of marketization and industrialization.[4] First, he shows that the growth of mutual self-help organizations was more strongly established before the early nineteenth century than suggested in the work of historians such as G. D. H. Cole and Birchall.[5] While both the latter trace the roots of working-class co-operative organization back to the mid-eighteenth century, Bamfield shows that these were by no means isolated experiments, and that the longevity of some of these earlier organizations, like the Hull Anti-Mill society in Figure 2.1, was much more impressive than the experiments in co-operation of the early nineteenth century which followed the ideological principles of Robert Owen and William King.[6] Bamfield also shows the very strong correlation between food rioting and the emergence of the variety of mutual societies in his study, which were variously engaged in purchasing corn and milling flour, baking and retailing bread at as close to cost price as possible, and in some instances vertically integrating the whole process

[2] Randall (1991 and 2006).   [3] Navickas (2011), 59–73.
[4] Bamfield (1998), 16–36.   [5] Cole (1944), 13–16; Birchall (1994), 4–5; Bamfield (1998), 17.
[6] Bamfield (1998), 31; Bamfield calculates that the average lifespan of the bread and flour societies in his sample was over forty-eight years.

FIGURE 2.1. **Hull Anti-mill co-operative corn mill.** Established in 1795 as a response to the high prices of local millers and shopkeepers, the Hull Anti-mill society continued into the 1890s.

from purchasing corn to selling bread. Thirty-eight of the forty-six such societies identified in Bamfield's study were established in areas of the country notorious for food riots in the later eighteenth century.[7]

Bamfield and other historians have recently offered some important new insights into why these mutual organizations came into existence at this time, and why they flourished in some areas but not in others. Some of the reasons offered are of course not new. The correlation between close-knit employment groups and the emergence of mutual organizations is well known. Birchall identifies those occupations which experienced the most extreme effects of industrialization as ones which were in the forefront of co-operative formation, notably mining and handloom weaving.[8] Such trades were characterized by strong recognition of common interests among workers, expressed in a variety of guises, including militancy, strikes, trade union formation, as well as the establishment of co-operatives, Friendly Societies, or other forms of mutual organization. Thus

---

[7] Bamfield (1998), 20–1.   [8] Birchall (1994), 4–5.

Bamfield and Cole single out the role of Chatham shipwrights and Portsmouth dock workers as examples of the importance of occupational solidarity in the formation of the flour and bread societies.[9] Similarly, other historians have identified the importance of key occupational groups in co-operative formation throughout the nineteenth century; notably coal miners and railway workers.[10] More recent research on the nature of emergent industrial communities and the social dynamics within them, however, points to perhaps a less obvious socio-psychological factor which made mutual self-help organization especially attractive. Snell's recent work on notions of home, community, and friendship among the English poor during this period points to how migration from the countryside into towns and cities had a massive psychological impact upon the young people, many with families, who broke—often decisively and permanently—with their rural communities.[11] Many felt a powerful sense of loss and anxiety, with the severing of social ties which were at the heart of their sense of identity and security. This supports the notion that a vital aspect of the formation of mutual organizations in the later eighteenth century was a yearning for the establishment of new ties of loyalty and friendship to replace what had been lost as a result of departure from village life.[12] Such a perspective also helps to explain the attraction of the 'communitarian' ideas of co-operation preferred by leaders such as Owen and King, who saw co-operative forms of business not as an end in themselves, but as a means of creating new, self-sufficient communities run on principles of co-operation and equality.[13] It is perhaps significant that for these early co-operative thinkers, communities were to involve the acquisition and working of the land, an aspiration which must have appealed to those who had recently cut their ties with village homes. Perhaps this explains the appeal of co-operation as an idealistic or utopian answer to the predicament of life in an increasingly market dominated and industrializing environment.

Of course there were also practical concerns which promoted the spread of mutuals and co-operative societies. Scola's work on the developing food supply for Manchester in the eighteenth and nineteenth centuries shows just how haphazard and uncertain the systems for victualling a major industrial conurbation could be.[14] Scola shows that while market-driven provisioning, on the whole, did meet the needs of Manchester, there were areas of weakness, especially in serving the needs of the very poor, and in ensuring quality at a time when official safeguards were virtually non-existent. Furthermore, it is clear that rapid urban growth was sometimes accompanied by a 'time lag' in provisioning keeping pace with the influx of population. This meant that established grocers (either in shops or markets) were well placed to charge exploitative prices.[15] This in itself was a factor which prompted co-operative or other mutual responses to problems of food supply. Blackman also shows that the physical infrastructure needed to house market facilities in a city like Sheffield was only expanded after the growth of demand and political pressure for an official response; suggesting that there were periods when urban needs were not adequately

[9] Cole (1944), 14; Bamfield (1998), 17.   [10] Purvis (1990), 314–31; Walton (1996), 17–28.
[11] Snell (2012), 1–25.   [12] Gorsky (1998), 507.   [13] Birchall (1994), 18–24.
[14] Scola (1992).   [15] Blackman (1967), 111.

met by existing market-driven food supply chains.[16] Then there were the infamous episodes of unscrupulous employers insisting that their employees purchase their supplies
from stores owned and run by the employer, sometimes the employer even insisting on
paying his workers in tickets exchangeable only at the local shop. This practice, known as
the 'Truck System', usually involved high prices and poor quality, and became one of the
most hated aspects of life in some of the more isolated industrial towns and villages. Birchall makes the point that even though truck was outlawed in 1831, its practice continued
for some time in a few of the more isolated and intimidated industrial communities.[17]
Indebtedness was another serious problem for many poorer families in their dealings with
those grocers or other shopkeepers who enjoyed near monopoly advantages in locations
with a scarcity of retail outlets. High prices led to a reliance on credit, which in turn led to
the accrual of such debts by some households that they were obliged to purchase from
their creditor shops, regardless of price and possible alternatives. Of course, food prices
were artificially supported by the Corn Law of 1815, which was designed to bolster the price
of bread and landed incomes by restricting food imports. In addition, food adulteration
was a health-threatening—sometimes life-threatening—hazard which all faced in the
early nineteenth century, but one which perhaps posed the biggest danger to underfed
poorer households. Milk was frequently watered; bread whitened by the addition of alum,
and virtually every processed food was bulked out with additional material, some of it poi-
sonous. All of these obstacles to health and nourishment were compounded by a deliberate state policy of increasing the misery and terror of the poor, exemplified by the Poor
Law Amendment Act of 1834, which introduced a punitive regime for the destitute in the
form of the workhouse. Such problems were powerful spurs for working people to take
matters into their own hands to resolve shortages and problems of food quality.

Of course, co-operation also appealed as an ideal to those who sought to lead, but
were not of, the impoverished masses. Industrialization and the rapid social and economic changes associated with it alienated those who believed these forces threatened
notions of an ordered and morally based society. Much is made of the prevalence of the
new philosophy of the dominance of the market in the late eighteenth and nineteenth
centuries, especially the ideas of Adam Smith, as expressed in his *The Wealth of Nations*
published in 1776. It is certainly true that a new generation of thinkers postulated theo-
ries which did not augur well for the poor. Thomas Malthus contended that an inevitable
consequence of the population growth which came with economic modernization
would be mass poverty and starvation, and that to seek to ameliorate this with state or
other assistance for the poor was ultimately self-defeating and a waste of resources.
David Ricardo argued that a world economic system was emerging, based on national
specialization in different lines of production (comparative advantage) which would be
dominated by the market, and to the needs of which labour would have to conform. But
even amongst the advocates of the new order, there were acknowledgements that markets were open to distortion and rigging. Adam Smith's famous comment that collectively the tendency among capitalists was to 'fix' the market against the public interest

---

[16] Blackman (1963), 94.   [17] Birchall (1994), 11–13.

was just one example of the market system being problematic even for those who supported it. By the 1840s and 1850s there was a strong Christian movement whose dismay at the social consequences of unfettered capitalism was so strong that they became powerful advocates of co-operation, developing a critique of capitalism, which they saw as essentially amoral, and proposing in its place a new social order built around co-operatives. Christian Socialism, as it became known, emerged as a powerful intellectual leadership championing co-operation in the early 1850s, led by such voices as J. M. Ludlow the barrister, Reverend F. D. Maurice, Professor of Theology at King's College London, the poet and novelist the Reverend Charles Kingsley, Thomas Hughes, author of *Tom Brown's Schooldays*, and Edward Vansittart Neale, who was to become possibly the co-operative movement's leading intellectual by the 1860s and 1870s, as well as a highly capable problem-solver and legal adviser.[18]

But this movement owed much to two earlier famous advocates of co-operation, whose pioneering of the concept influenced many of the later ideas of the Christian Socialists, even though one of these earlier advocates was an avowed atheist. Robert Owen and Dr William King were unique in their attempts to combine development of co-operation as an idea with engagements in practical experiments in the philosophy. Robert Owen (see Figures 2.2 and 2.3) is perhaps the better known of the two. His statue may be found in what has become known as the 'co-operative quarter' of Manchester. Born in Newtown, Wales, in 1771, Owen rose from a modest background, with little or no formal education, to become, by the age of 21, manager of the Chorlton Twist Mills in Manchester. By then, Owen was already known for his concern about the social conditions wrought by industrialization, and was a member of the Manchester Board of Health. But he came to wider attention following his marriage to the daughter of David Dale, joint owner of a cotton mill at New Lanark in Scotland in 1799. By 1800 Owen was manager at New Lanark, and he set about establishing a 'model factory' and community, which provided not only better working conditions for its employees, but also decent housing and education for the workers and their families. New Lanark became a focus for much interest among those concerned by the effects of industrialization. Owen went on first to champion reform through Parliament, and then to support the idea of establishing co-operatives to help fund the creation of separate communities of the poor, that would enable them to free themselves from the tyranny of capitalism. Owen adopted the term socialism to describe his idea that capitalism would gradually be displaced by the spread of co-operative land-based communities, in which wealth would be created and shared on a communal basis. His efforts to turn these ideas into practice met with limited success. He established short-lived communities in the 1820s in Orbiston in Scotland and famously 'New Harmony' in Indiana, USA, both of which failed after a brief period.[19] The experiments dented his personal wealth, and by the 1830s he had become more of a propagandist for co-operation and socialism than an entrepreneur. In the early 1830s he experimented

[18] Bonner (1961), 60–1.   [19] Clayton (1908).

FIGURE 2.2. **Robert Owen (1771–1858).** Often called the 'Father of Co-operation', Owen's writings inspired many co-operative societies and communitarian experiments in the 1820s and 1830s.

with new systems of exchange through the short-lived National Equitable Labour Exchange, and became involved with the equally unsuccessful Grand National Consolidated Trade Union, which sought to unify the nation's workers into one organization, only to collapse in 1834.[20] In addition to other initiatives he sustained an involvement with the co-operative movement, becoming briefly Governor of the Queenwood community in Hampshire, before it failed in 1839. An atheist, Owen believed that human nature is profoundly shaped by the environment in which it is nurtured, and in that respect made a seminal contribution to socialist and co-operative thought. In light of these failures, Owen's prominence in the history of co-operation and socialist ideology is slightly curious. A difficult man to work with, he was notoriously authoritarian in temperament, insisting that his communities follow his commands. At times he was quite scathing about those who saw co-operation solely as a practical strategy for survival or betterment within the prevailing social and economic order, rather than the foundation of a new moral and social order. Ultimately his projects were not successful; but he was a successful propagandist, and in that capacity played an important role in the popularization of co-operation. The eminent co-operative historian R. G. Garnett perhaps captures the significance of Owen's career best:

Robert Owen's unique contribution was not his grand co-operative solution to combat the evils of the new industrialism, rather it was to be found in his optimism, in his raising of hopes of

---

[20] Claeys (2002), 194–9.

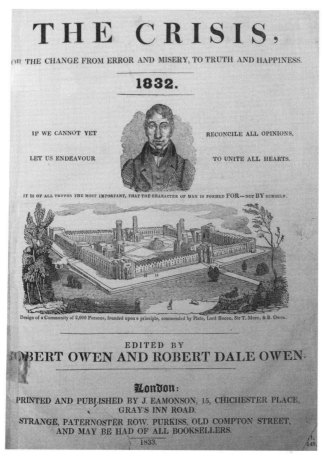

FIGURE 2.3. *The Crisis*, 1832. Robert Owen edited *The Crisis* between 1832 and 1834, following his return from America. The cover features a design for a model co-operative community.

betterment—that low wages, squalor and misery could be eradicated without bloody revolution or the destruction of Britain's industrial leadership.[21]

Arguably more significant in the development of co-operative ideas was Dr William King, who also emerged in this period as powerful propagandist for co-operation. King, shown in Figure 2.4, was born in Ipswich in 1786. The son of a vicar, he studied history and philosophy at Cambridge, becoming subsequently a medical doctor and a Fellow of the Royal College of Physicians. As a doctor with a strong sense of religious obligation and social conscience he provided medical treatment for the poor. He became heavily involved in charity work, helped to establish a friendly society and also a Mechanics Institute, at which he gave lectures on issues of public importance. In the late 1820s he became involved with William Allen and a group of other working men who established the Brighton Co-operative Society. The experience was life-changing. In 1828 he

---

[21] Garnett (1972), 235.

FIGURE 2.4. Dr William King (1786–1865). Having helped establish co-operative societies in Brighton in the 1820s, King edited a monthly journal, *The Co-operator*, from 1828 to 1830. A copy owned by James Smithies, one of the Rochdale Pioneers, was later donated to the Pioneers' library, and is now held by the National Co-operative Archive.

launched *The Co-operator*, an influential journal which supported co-operation.[22] Though it only lasted two years, it proved so inspirational that another journal was set up by Henry Pitman in its honour in the late 1850s with the same name, and with the same fundamental values. Many watched King's experience in building *The Co-operator* and decided to follow his example, resulting in a temporary flourishing of the co-operative press during the early 1830s.[23] Unlike Owen, King's motivation was partly religious, and he inspired those who were later to build the Christian Socialist movement. Like Owen, King saw co-operatives as the means to accumulate capital for the establishment of co-operative communities based on the land which would be able to separate themselves from and renounce capitalist society.

King's work of course coincided with one of the most radical and turbulent periods of British history. The clamour for widening the franchise, which had been building since the 1790s, reached its crescendo in the period between 1828 and the mid-1830s, resulting in the Great Reform Act of 1832 which gave the vote to the emergent middle classes. Working-class organizations which had supported the popular agitation for change felt cheated by its result, and the exclusion of working people from parliamentary representation fuelled

[22] Cole (1944), 23.   [23] Cole (1944), 23.

the Chartist agitation of the 1840s. The spread of co-operation was part of this phenomenon, and by the middle of 1830, King could boast that as many as 300 co-operative societies had come into existence across the country during the previous five years. Such was the confidence of the movement at this time that a series of national co-operative congresses were held between 1831 and 1835.[24] There was even an attempt to establish a national wholesale supply system for the co-operatives in 1831, in the form of the North West of England United Co-operative Company, set up in Liverpool in 1831.[25] Generally, as with the Owenite experiments, this blossoming of co-operative initiatives proved short-lived, with many societies dissolving and disappearing from the historical record as quickly as they had appeared. By the later 1830s, as with much of the radical impetus of the early 1830s, co-operation seemed to have stalled, with many of the societies of the earlier 1830s having been disbanded.

The reasons for the short life of these early co-operatives and co-operative communities, and indeed for the general instability and unsustainability of the flourishing of the labour movement during this period, were several fold. First, like many capitalist commercial organizations, both co-operative societies, and the communities which many of them founded, faced one of the most turbulent periods in British economic history. The severe fluctuations in the economy hit both societies and communities hard, and made it difficult for them to sustain themselves, since they could not completely insulate themselves from the wider world. Secondly, the legal status of co-operative societies was always highly suspect, since legislation to empower such organizations as co-operatives to conduct their own affairs as corporate bodies, and without relying on the vesting of financial rights and responsibilities in individuals, was not introduced until the 1850s. This meant that the early co-operatives and communities were always vulnerable to financial maladministration and fraud. This undoubtedly contributed to the demise of many of them, though it should be noted that by the 1840s a newer generation of consumer co-operatives, notably the Rochdale Pioneers and their imitators, seemed to manage the difficulties more effectively. Perhaps the failure of the earlier co-operatives reflected a third and more severe flaw; weakness in both the co-operative education of the working people who joined them and the absence of sufficiently strong incentives for people to remain as members. Ultimately, the notion of joining self-sufficient communities to escape wider industrial British society was not as appealing as their advocates believed. This is perhaps not hard to understand. After all, industrial society, for all its difficulties, did at times offer higher wages and living standards, at least when the economy was booming. Ultimately, separate communities did not always seem to offer the prospect of a better life to working people with a practical eye on income and material well-being, regardless of the claims of the well-meaning socialist elite. As will be seen, these were problems which the next generation of co-operatives from the mid-1840s would address.

---

[24] Bonner (1961), 28–9.   [25] Bonner (1961), 31–2.

2.2 THE ROCHDALE PIONEERS AND THE ROCHDALE MODEL

In August 1844, a group of weavers, cloggers, and men from other associated trades established a co-operative society in the east Lancashire mill town of Rochdale. Their society, the 'Rochdale Equitable Pioneers Society', won the reputation as being the parent of the modern British co-operative movement. The Pioneers proved not only to be an extremely durable society which inspired the establishment of similar societies across the North of England and the rest of the country, in due course, they also established a series of organizational principles which came to be seen as the very basis of modern co-operation. Many of these remained in essence the same throughout the movement's history, but their precise meaning was adapted to meet changing contexts, and through evolving practice, these principles were added to and developed.[26] This process has involved the conscious updating of the principles from time to time, most recently in 1995. But the Rochdale Pioneers have become internationally renowned within the co-operative movement, and its original store in Toad Lane, a kind of shrine to the origins of modern consumer co-operation (see Figure 2.5 and Plate 20).

But the iconic status of the Pioneers within co-operative folklore has been a source of historical debate. To what extent were the Rochdale Pioneers actually a break with the past? How original were they in developing the key principles behind the 'Rochdale model'? Why did this model of co-operation prove so successful in Rochdale and its surrounding villages? Who were the Pioneers? How have different generations of historians seen them? And finally: what were the principles and why did they inspire a new wave of co-operative formation, moreover co-operatives which proved more successful and durable than their predecessors?

The story of the establishment of the Rochdale Pioneers is well known. The early 1840s was a period of considerable hardship and political turbulence, especially in the industrial North of England. Economic depression had resulted in large scale unemployment and hunger, compounding the difficulties of poor housing and public squalor which beset most of the country's growing industrial towns. In response, working-class resistance took various forms; trade union formation and strikes, support for further parliamentary reform and the enfranchisement of working men (Chartism), the creation of separatist Owenite communities, and the formation of consumer co-operatives. The situation in Rochdale seemed to encapsulate all of these factors. A cotton town, not only was Rochdale suffering from the effects of a short-run downturn in economic activity, but also, as a major centre for handloom weaving, many of its inhabitants had experienced a long-term decline in living standards, as the industrial firms who provided them with work drove down wages and prices in an effort to remain competitive. The social and political environment of the town was

---

[26] Fairbairn (1994).

FIGURE 2.5. **Rochdale Pioneers Museum (interior).** The Pioneers opened for business on 21 December 1844, in the front room of a former wool sorting warehouse. The co-operative movement has operated a museum on the site since 1931; this photo was taken in the 1960s.

also distinctive. As Walton shows, not only was Rochdale the scene of varied religious affiliations and debates, worshippers also seem to have enjoyed a high degree of engagement with theology and philosophy generally, even some of those with little formal education. This undoubtedly contributed to the intellectual engagement with such ideas as co-operation, as did the presence in the town of strong Owenites. Walton shows that at least four of the Pioneers had invested funds in the earlier Owenite community at Harmony Hall in 1843, while Charles Howarth, one of the leading founder members, had been active in the Owenite movement since an earlier and short-lived attempt to establish a co-operative society in Rochdale in the early 1830s.[27] The fact that Rochdale was a close-knit community, in which there were powerful bonds of friendship, trust, and familiarity, also helped provide the foundations upon which lasting organizations of all kinds could flourish. As mentioned, trade unionism was strong in the town, but it has been suggested that it was the defeat of a strike by the Weavers' Union which convinced many that an alternative to industrial militancy was

[27] Walton (2012).

needed to improve the lot of Rochdale's workers.[28] Walton also shows that in some cases the close-knit ties which held the town together cut across boundaries of social class, equipping some of the Pioneers with wealthy middle-class allies prepared to lend support to the new venture. Thus, the Pioneers were the product of a quite distinctive industrial and social environment, and a particular confluence of factors.

But some historians have questioned whether the Pioneers were the first or in any way unique in the development of consumer co-operatives in Britain. The famous co-operator and writer G. J. Holyoake, shown in Figure 2.6, undoubtedly led in thrusting the Pioneers forward as the unique 'taproot' of modern consumer co-operation. His highly readable and widely read 1859 study established the case for the Pioneers as the first and leaders in the movement, and for a very long time constituted the final authority on the question.[29] But more recent historians have contended that the Pioneers and their model were not unique, and that other organizations have a claim to be 'the first'. Certainly there is evidence that Rochdale was by no means alone in experimenting with and developing co-operative societies.[30] Nonetheless, whether or not it was the first modern consumer co-operative, and whether or not it represented a decisive new direction compared to earlier experiments, it is clear that Rochdale did seem to capture the imagination of the movement, and certainly inspired many imitators. Inevitably, the background and character of the men who established the Pioneers have also come under scrutiny, and there has been a tendency for historians to interpret them in light of wider perceptions of the nature of the movement. Walton shows that there has been a tendency to see the Pioneers as part of a new emergent and 'respectable' labour aristocracy in Britain, which was essentially non-revolutionary and with little solidarity with the poorer and lower sections of the working class.[31] 'Rochdale Man' as one historian dubbed the 'ideal' Pioneer and the type of working-class person he represented, was thrifty, self-educated, God-fearing, and determined to command a respectable position in society.[32] He eschewed notions of revolution, confrontation, and violence. The implication is that the Pioneers were not typical of the very poor of Rochdale; rather they were relatively well off, with reasonable resources, and enjoyed some measure of education and some influential and affluent connections. This is an interpretation which historians have challenged on a number of counts. First, Walton, from an analysis of several sources on the Pioneers, shows that while there were relatively prosperous individuals in their number, with many being skilled workers, particularly handloom weavers, several were on very modest incomes with young families to support.[33] Secondly, Kirk makes the point that co-operation in Lancashire was not confined to an 'aristocracy' of better-off labourers, but reached down to the far less well off.[34] What is interesting here is how the Pioneers have been 'reinvented' to serve particular versions of the role of consumer co-operation in British history. It is a point which also applies to efforts to interpret the

---

[28] Cole (1944), 43–4.   [29] Holyoake (1893a).
[30] Hibberd (1968), 531–7; P. Davis, in Lancaster and Maguire (1996), 198–215.
[31] Foster (1974).   [32] Rose (1977).   [33] Walton (2012).   [34] Kirk (1998), 46–8.

FIGURE 2.6. George Jacob Holyoake (1817–1906). Involved in the Owenite movement from the 1830s, Holyoake became a leading propagandist for co-operation and wrote the first history of the Rochdale Pioneers, in 1858.

Pioneers in other media, notably the famous 1944 film *Men of Rochdale* and its recent remake, *The Rochdale Pioneers*, to commemorate the UN Year of Co-operation in 2012.

Whatever the truth of contrasting depictions and interpretations of the Pioneers, there is no doubt that they became associated with a particular model of consumer co-operation which was especially well adapted to the challenges of the time, and which was adopted by the large number of societies which sprang into existence from the 1840s onwards. The principles of this model both spread across the world and survived to the present as the 'ideal'. The 'Rochdale Principles' encapsulated a whole philosophy and strategy of business organization, and it is important to explore these principles, and how they contributed to the success of the movement from the mid-nineteenth century. At the heart of the model was the basic concept of democracy, of one member one vote and a structure of accountability for the management and leadership of the society. The rules of the society, from the outset, established regular general meetings and the election of officers and directors on the basis of one member one vote. The quantity of shares held by a member was in no way allowed to interfere with the one member one vote principle. Birchall shows that there is plenty of evidence to suggest that in the early years, lively debate and disagreement was a healthy feature of this developing democratic culture.[35] In the context of working-class Rochdale, this democratic principle had

---

[35] Birchall (1994), 54–6.

particularly important political symbolism. At a time when the Chartists were trying to challenge elite perceptions that the working class were intellectually and educationally unfit to be enfranchised, a business being run by working-class people on democratic lines was of powerful significance. It demonstrated that such people were not only capable of exercising responsible judgement in a democratic context, but that they were able to understand and operate within a disciplined constitutional structure. The message was clear: if working-class people could exercise judgement and democratic power to run a business, they were also surely fit to vote. Moreover, the principle was an important check on the danger of the slightly wealthier or better educated coming to dominate the organization.

A second principle called for open membership, for the admittance of all who could pay the membership subscription, regardless of creed or gender. This was not just an egalitarian principle to overcome the social and religious differences which existed in Rochdale as they did elsewhere. It was also a highly practical recognition that a co-operative society consisting of relatively poor people needed a large critical mass of members if it was to overcome problems of limited capital resources. Initially the Pioneers did limit membership to about 250 on the basis that any more than this would make it difficult to operate an effective and flourishing democracy. But it soon found that by establishing branches around the town a much larger active membership could be drawn in. It was extremely successful. By 1855 the Pioneers had 1,400 members, and by 1870, 5,560.[36] What underpinned this principle was the notion of tolerance of differences of political and religious opinion among members, and to support it another principle, that of religious and political neutrality, was adopted. Religious neutrality was especially important, as both Owenite secularists and Unitarian worshippers were amongst the members, and the potential for internal disagreements were substantial. Birchall makes the point that in its early years there were tensions between Methodists and other members, the former wanting to close the meeting room and library on Sundays. The move was defeated, but resulted in a temporary suspension for six months of the admission of new members.[37] It is clear that the neutrality of the organization was not intended to stifle inevitable debates among members over the important issues of the day, but rather to ensure that differences would not lead to the exclusion of potential members and thereby limit the scope for growth.

A fourth principle was that only fixed and limited interest should be paid on share and loan capital. This principle was designed to balance two counteracting considerations: first the need to attract investment into the society by rewarding members' shares with interest; whilst at the same time ensuring that interest payments did not swallow up essential resources needed for reinvestment in the business. Capital had to be rewarded, but it should not be, as in a capitalist enterprise, at the head of the queue when it came to commanding surplus and resources of the society. This was reinforced by a decision in 1845 to limit the size of shareholdings to just £4, a move designed to prevent the effective domination of the society by wealthy individuals with large shareholdings. This provi-

[36] Cole (1944), 81.   [37] Birchall (1994), 62.

sion was relaxed as a result of the 1852 Industrial and Provident Societies Act, which gave the societies limited liability and better protection for their assets in law. The Act allowed for shareholdings of up £100, and loans to societies of £400. Once again, an important idea at work here was the desire to prevent domination of the society by powerful and wealthy individuals.[38]

Perhaps the most famous of all the principles, however, was the idea of distributing the surplus (profit) of the society on the basis of dividend on purchase. In simple terms, if you were a member of the society, the more you bought from the co-operative store, the more you received in dividend. This marked an important break with the intended purpose of accumulated society surpluses as envisaged by the earlier generation of co-operative idealists; namely to use it to purchase land on which to establish 'co-operative communities'. It was of course crucial in both attracting new members and retaining them by offering substantial material rewards for membership. It rewarded customer loyalty, and ensured that surplus would benefit a wide body of people rather than a few wealthy shareholders as was often the case in capitalist organizations. Such an egalitarian idea was in harmony with the whole moral purpose of co-operation in helping poorer people obtain a greater share of the wealth generated by economic activity. Practically it also bound members to the society store and incentivized their trade with it, strengthening the commercial position of the society. The 'divi', of course, has become an unmistakable symbol of co-operation in Britain. Many older people, who were not even members, are able to recall their parents' 'divi' numbers from errands to the local 'co-op'. The dividend proved to be hugely beneficial for many poorer members, not simply because it augmented incomes, but because members frequently found it beneficial to allow their dividends to accumulate in the society, building up effectively a hedge of savings against unemployment or sickness. At a time when banks could be notoriously unreliable and unwelcoming to working-class savers, the society was able to allow its members to accumulate savings safely, learning in the process how to manage their finances in a more sophisticated and remunerative way. The failure of the Rochdale Savings Bank in 1849 underlined the problems faced by many working-class people trying to save through institutions which were not stable or trustworthy.[39] The Pioneers benefited directly from the failure. This emphasis on the dividend as an appeal to working-class material self-interest has led to a tendency by some to see it as the main if not the sole driver of co-operative membership and involvement, implying that the other functions of societies (educational, ideological, or social) were peripheral.[40] This has led to a tendency to see co-operation as a rather materialistic and conservative working-class movement which essentially reconciled co-operative members and their families to the prevailing capitalist order by allowing successful adaptation to it, rather than posing an alternative.[41] This interpretation of co-operation has been fiercely challenged by Gurney and Robertson, who argue that the impact of the social connections and activi-

---

[38] Birchall (1994), 57.   [39] Holyoake (1893b), 16.
[40] See for example Johnson (1985), 143.   [41] Stedman-Jones (1984), 179–238; Kirk (1985), 25.

ties of co-operation have been hugely underestimated by these earlier historians, as has the role co-operation played in strengthening working-class identity and solidarity.[42] It will become clear that the work of Gurney and Robertson has important implications for not just the political and social impact of co-operation, but also how societies and the movement at large developed as a business entity.

On the question of the role of co-operation in enhancing working-class life, two other important principles played a central role. The Pioneers, and following their example the movement at large, were committed to selling pure and adulterated goods. At a time when food was rarely of reliable quality or freshness, and there was little enforcement of the few legal restraints governing quality, this was a hugely important commitment. Good, reliable food could be a matter of life or death, not merely of health. As such, it was a commitment which had great significance for working-class well-being. It also helped to build and consolidate the relations of trust which were so crucial for the growth of movement. Thus shopping at the co-operative store became not just a habit for personal or household material gain, but also based on a strong belief that to do so was inherently safer. The other important principle which underpinned this strong social dimension was the commitment of the Pioneers to providing educational facilities for members, particularly a library and reading room. It was an example followed by societies across the country. There were numerous benefits connected with this. First, at a time when there was no state provision of education, co-operatives began to fulfil an essential function in helping working-class advancement, if only by introducing members to classes which helped them to read, write, and use basic arithmetic. It also provided members with the knowledge and skills to engage fully in the business of the society, and to keep its conduct under proper scrutiny. Education also provided an opportunity for more gifted and committed members to rise within the society by becoming store managers or buyers, assisting upward social mobility whilst simultaneously creating a supply of personnel who could fill important roles in the business. Education facilities also served an important political function. At a time when the clamour for universal manhood suffrage gathered momentum between the 1840s and 1860s, it strengthened the case that working-class people were 'fit' to be given the vote and capable of being equipped to use it properly. Finally, as Gurney and Robertson both show, educational activities and spaces such as reading rooms provided opportunities to build collective social activities and events (festivals, study groups, etc.) which strengthened understanding of and support for co-operative ideology, and strongly embedded societies within their localities.

The final key principle was one which, though strictly adhered to by the Pioneers (see Figure 2.7), and most of the societies which emerged during the 1850s and 1860s, began to be departed from as the century went on. The Pioneers committed themselves to cash-only trading, refusing to offer credit to members on any terms. At first sight this might appear to present a disincentive to join the society, especially for those working families in especially straitened circumstances. Undoubtedly it was, and contributed a tendency in the nineteenth century, noted by many historians, for societies to be mainly successful

[42] Gurney (1996); Robertson (2010).

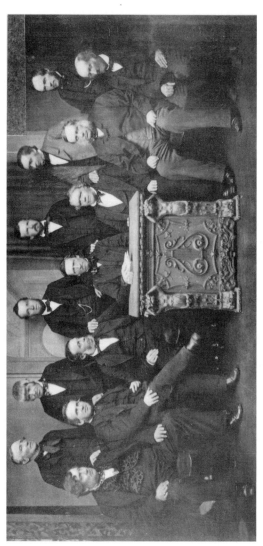

FIGURE 2.7. **Thirteen of the original Rochdale Pioneers, 1865.** The most famous image in the co-operative movement was taken twenty-one years after the Pioneers founded their society. Back row (left to right): James Manock, John Collier, Samuel Ashworth, William Cooper, James Tweedale, and Joseph Smith. Front row: James Standring, John Bent, James Smithies, Charles Howarth, David Brooks, Benjamin Rudman, and John Scowcroft.

in attracting better-off sections of the working class. But the calculation was that credit trading posed numerous potentially fatal dangers to co-operatives, principally through the accumulation of large quantities of bad debt. It was also recognized that the propensity towards indebtedness to private traders had been one of the banes of working-class life, exposing debtors to undue pressure from their creditors to continue trading at the creditor's store, often on increasingly unfavourable terms. An important function of cash-only trading was therefore educational. The aim was to help instil in members the importance of thrift, of staying within a weekly budget without having recourse to credit. Admirable though the principle was, by the latter decades of the century many societies departed from it, partly in response to demands from members, and partly to meet competition from private traders who continued to attract customers by the provision of credit.

The significance of the 'Rochdale Principles' is that they provided a blueprint which other societies could imitate. These principles accomplished two objectives. First, they provided the basis for building a sustainable co-operative business which would prove attractive for working-class people to join, offering material rewards as well as important social and educational facilities. Secondly, they also enshrined key co-operative objectives of raising the status of working-class people by providing the means for their own self-elevation through education, wider wealth sharing, and an opportunity to run wealth-making enterprises rather than just being employed by them. It was a model which was to prove attractive and successful in Britain from the mid-nineteenth century onwards and in turn across the globe. What were the first steps in this process?

2.3 The spread of co-operation in England and experiments in wholesaling, 1844–63

One reason why the Pioneers have become so central to the history of co-operation in Britain was that they were formed on the eve of a wave of unprecedented growth in co-operative societies, especially across northern industrial England. The reasons for this were complex, and some were related to substantial changes in the economic climate. The first half of the nineteenth century had been characterized by rapid economic growth, but also volatility, with spurts of rapid growth being curbed by devastating downturns characterized by widespread bankruptcies, sudden increases in unemployment and poverty, and occasionally social unrest. But even historians who are sceptical about claims that Britain then moved into a period of uninterrupted growth and prosperity which lasted from 1850s to 1873 concede that there was a real and largely sustained rise in working-class living standards.[43] This undoubtedly helped the advancement of

---

[43] Crouzet (1982), 54–8.

co-operation during this period, and indeed Jeffreys argues that it, together with the advent of modern rail transport, helped create the circumstances for a 'retail revolution', which saw over the ensuing decades the rise of fixed shops which took great care to present their wares attractively, the advent of modern advertising, branding, manufacturer-led pricing and commodity promotion, and eventually by the end of the nineteenth century the emergence of multiple chains of shops.[44] While this interpretation has been criticized for its oversimplification of the chronological pattern of change, it is clear that greater prosperity in the latter half of the century undoubtedly helped the spread of consumer co-operation. How this process occurred is still a subject which would benefit from further research; but it is clear that deliberate efforts to 'spread the word' by the Rochdale Pioneers and their sympathizers played a very important role, as did coverage by the popular press.

By December 1860, the co-operative journal *The Co-operator* reported that there were almost 200 consumer co-operatives in existence across the country, from the cluster of towns which surrounded Rochdale to Sunderland in the north-east, London in the south-east, and Plymouth in the south-west.[45] Of course, this was merely a snap shot of a process which had involved many society commencements and many failures; but it is clear that the trend was towards the proliferation of societies across the country. Purvis shows that the trend was stronger in some areas than in others, reflecting a variety of factors. These included the presence of large, homogeneous communities of people in the same occupations, for example among miners in the north-east of England or strong religious ties which held the community together such as in South Wales. In both of these contexts, a strong sense of communal identity was clearly important in generating sustainable co-operatives.[46] But Purvis shows that other influences determined the distribution of co-operatives across England and Wales, including the degree of hostility and resistance encountered from private shopkeepers and employers, and the extent to which limited local economic growth negated the need for additional or improved retail provision.[47] The upshot was that while the number of co-operative societies grew rapidly in the later nineteenth century, reaching almost 1,400 by 1900, the wider geographical distribution was uneven, with a marked preponderance of co-operatives in the industrial areas of the North and the Midlands. This by the end of the nineteenth century would be the source of much concern, with the perception that large swathes of the south, and particularly London, were effectively 'co-operative deserts'.[48] It is worth considering the position of these new co-operative societies carefully. Most sprang up in urban environments, typically where there was a strong sense of identification with community frequently engendered by occupational commonalities. Often the new societies' stores faced tough and resentful competition from private shopkeepers who viewed them as unwelcome interlopers trading on the unfair basis of the dividend. In such circumstances, as Gurney shows, it was essential that commercial advantages such as the dividend be supplemented with the fostering of strong social and cultural loyalties among

[44] Jefferys (1954), 1–39.   [45] *The Co-operator* (December 1860), 96.
[46] Purvis (1990).   [47] Purvis (1990), 328–9.   [48] Purvis (1999), 225–43.

members. The upshot was a movement of fiercely independent local consumer co-operative societies, which were deeply embedded in their local urban environments. They
had developed finely tuned commercial strategies for competing effectively with the
non-co-operative sector, by securing member and customer loyalty through a battery of
social and commercial measures, the latter including competitive prices as well as the
'divi'. This meant that co-operative society store managers had to be sophisticated local
operators, procuring supplies carefully to ensure low prices and high quality, and working hard to keep key local interests such as wholesalers firmly on-side, in the face of
potential pressure from private traders not to supply the societies.[49] While such powerful localism and pragmatic adaptation to prevailing market conditions were instrumental in the rise and proliferation of co-operative societies, it would, in due course, present
barriers to the construction of a coherent national business strategy.

But it was not only consumer co-operation which seemed to be making giant strides
during this period. The late 1840s saw the flourishing of a different kind of co-operative:
the producer co-operative, a producer/industrial organization owned at least partly by
the workforce, which shared the profits of the organization after meeting essential commitments like interest on loans, wages, and other costs. As with consumer co-operatives,
the roots of this branch of the movement can be traced back much earlier. Producer co-
operatives had been set up in the late eighteenth and early nineteenth centuries, notably
the Hull Anti-Mill and a tailors' society in Birmingham. This branch of co-operation
became closely associated with the Christian Socialist movement which emerged in the
late 1840s, and took a keen interest in co-operation until the mid-1850s. But its antecedents were much earlier, and can be traced back to some of the early Owenite experiments
in the 1830s. In the late 1840s, there was a strong, Owenite-influenced producer movement around Leeds, known as the 'Redemption of Labour' movement.[50] True to its
Owenite roots, the Redemptionists aspired to acquire land to create separatist co-operative
communities, but their aspirations also included the establishment of industrial productive workshops as well as farming. They acquired an estate in South Wales for their
communitarian experiment, which ran until the mid-1850s. The Leeds Redemption
Society established branches as far afield as London, Bury, Stockport, and Norwich, and
though the movement (including the Leeds Redemption Society itself) was wound up
in the mid-1850s, it still had a surplus which was redistributed to sympathetic causes.[51]

At the same time, though apparently without links to or knowledge of the Redemptionists, the Christian Socialist movement was established by John M. F. Ludlow, Frederick D. Maurice, and Charles Kingsley, three committed Christian intellectuals who
were deeply disturbed by the impact of industrialization on the lives of the very poor.
They were joined by the writer Thomas Hughes (shown in Figure 2.8), and Edward Vansittart Neale (Figure 2.9), who developed a lasting connection with the co-operative
movement. Eventually, from the mid-1850s they became predominantly concerned with
education as a vehicle for social improvement, but between 1850 and 1855 they were
focused upon producer co-operation as a way of helping the poor out of their predica-

[49] Purvis (1998), 55–78.   [50] Cole (1944), 100–1.   [51] Cole (1944), 101.

ment. Their strategy was to set up what became known as the Working Men's Associations. The associations were assiduously promoted by the Society for Promoting Working Men's Associations, an organization, controlled by a Christian Socialist dominated board, which advanced capital to new working men's societies. After some early mistakes, the Society became much more rigorous in its evaluations of the credibility of requests for funding, and effectively came to exercise considerable powers of patronage over the working men's associations it sponsored. These were mainly located in London and the south-east of England, and included such bodies as the Working Tailors Association, the London Builders Association, and several boot and shoe making co-operatives.[52] But ultimately few of these organizations survived for long. This partly reflected the peculiarly hazardous environment which producer co-operatives faced during the later nineteenth century: a still unpredictable and occasionally volatile market, cut-throat competition from wealthier private entrepreneurs, and all too frequently a deficit in the expertise needed to make the enterprise work. Bonner argues that the working men's associations were also excessively dependent on capital from the Society, with too little commitment and investment from the members themselves.[53] This might have been so,

FIGURE 2.8. Thomas Hughes (1822–96). Better known to many as the author of *Tom Brown's School Days*, Hughes was a Christian Socialist and a proponent of producer co-operatives. With E. V. Neale, he helped craft the Industrial & Provident Societies legislation of the 1850s and 1860s; the two co-wrote *A Manual for Co-operators* in 1881.

[52] Cole (1944), 102.   [53] Bonner (1961), 64–5.

FIGURE 2.9. **Edward Vansittart Neale** (1810–92). Another of the Christian Socialists, Neale established an early co-operative wholesale in London, the Central Co-operative Agency. He helped organize the 1869 Co-operative Congress and eventually the Co-operative Union, of which he was General Secretary from 1873 to 1891.

but the high mortality rate seems to have been characteristic of all producer co-operative initiatives in this period. The trade union movement also made several efforts to promote producer co-operation in the late 1840s and early 1850s, especially the Amalgamated Society of Engineers, but these came to little, as the trade unions found themselves bogged down in a series of expensive strikes and lock-outs.[54]

The main achievement associated with the Christian Socialists in respect of co-operation was the role they played in securing a major change in the legal status of co-operatives of all kinds. Up until the early 1850s, the legal position of co-operatives was extremely precarious. Under the Friendly Societies Act of 1846 a society had to be certified as legal by the Registrar of Friendly Societies, and property could only be held through trustees, upon whose honesty the security of the co-operative's assets consequently depended. One problem that especially inhibited the retail consumer societies was the so-called 'Frugal Investment' clause of the 1846 Act, which constrained a society's trading activities to its own members, thereby capping the potential for the growth of its trade. The effect on producer pocieties was even more severe, since it effectively meant that they had no legal protection at all, since all of their commerce was, by definition, with customers external to themselves. It effectively meant

[54] Cole (1944), 99–100.

that many societies had little or no recourse to law in the event of their members steal-ing from them. Furthermore, if a society had less than twenty-five members, those members were deemed to be partners in the concern, each with the power to pledge the resources and credit of the society without any control or restraint. Societies with more than twenty-five members would have no legal protection at all, unless they reg-istered as joint stock companies, which would be inappropriate for a co-operative organization. Leading Christian Socialists such as Ludlow, Neale, Hughes, and Lloyd Jones, together with the Shrewsbury MP R. A. Slaney, managed to accomplish a major change in the law, through a determined parliamentary campaign. Slaney's involve-ment was quite significant. Slaney was not only a champion of working-class enter-prise; he was also heavily involved in campaigns for major legislative reform of business, especially in clarification of the implications of limited liability. Slaney led the call for a Royal Commission to review the whole legal apparatus governing pri-vate business, what became known as the Mercantile Laws Commission of 1854.[55] The catastrophic financial crisis of the late 1840s had raised many concerns about the legislative framework governing business governance and investment, and led to major attempts at reform in the 1850s. The impetus for greater legal protection for co-operatives should be seen in this wider reforming context, and was very much part of an attempt to create an environment of more trustworthy and stable busi-nesses. The Industrial and Provident Societies' Act of 1852 transformed the position of co-operatives, giving for the first time tailor-made legal protection for co-operative societies. There were limitations. Banking and mining outside the UK were prohib-ited, the rate of interest payable could not exceed 5 per cent, and members were still liable for the society's debts (the Act did not allow for limited liability). Sharehold-ings by individuals could not exceed £100 in value, but an important defence of co-operative status was embodied in restrictions on how members could dispose of their shares in the society. Members could only sell their shares to the society itself, or to another person approved by the society's committee.[56] Crucially, though, the law did not provide for the formation of a co-operative whose membership consisted of other co-operatives, thus the possibility of a federation of co-operatives would require further changes of legislation in the Industrial and Provident Societies' Act of 1862.

2.4 MORE CONCRETE MOVES TOWARDS A WHOLESALE SOCIETY

But perhaps the most important development during the 1850s was a growing realiza-tion that if co-operation was to continue to flourish, it needed to secure its sources of raw materials and essential supplies. Dependence on private wholesalers and capitalist

---

[55] Bryer (1997), 40–1.   [56] Bonner (1961), 66–7.

suppliers was always recognized as a potentially serious weakness. The profit motive and the amorality of capitalism (as co-operators believed) inevitably led to a danger of exploitation by unscrupulous suppliers, brokers, and wholesalers. Ultimately, it was an axiom of co-operation that the closer procurement could get to the source of supply, the less danger there was of poor quality and inflated prices. Then, as local societies began to encounter a measure of local opposition, the potential danger of private traders taking collective action to cut off supplies to the societies began to be seen as a real danger. Little wonder that the idea of the movement establishing its own wholesaling system had emerged in the earliest years of its development. In 1831 the first Congress of the Co-operative Movement had established the North West of England United Co-operative Company, based in Liverpool. Its remit was to supply local co-operative societies with imported produce.[57] It seems to have folded in a very short period of time. Almost at the same time, in London a new initiative was launched which was designed to provide 'Equitable Labour Exchanges' at which co-operative societies could exchange goods on the basis of the amount of labour invested in the production of commodities (based on the Labour Theory of Value). The main exchange was established at Grays Inn Road in London.[58] But this movement also failed in 1833.[59] The next major initiative was led by the Christian Socialists in the early 1850s, and was again focused on London. The Central Co-operative Agency, managed by Lloyd Jones, opened in May 1851 on Charlotte Street, with the aim of supplying co-operative societies and providing a means through which the working men's associations could sell their produce. But this was undermined by the establishment of a rival organization; the Universal Provider in 1852. After a brief period of prosperity, both disappeared, the Central Co-operative Agency being wound up in 1857.[60] As early as 1850, the Rochdale Pioneers had committed themselves to developing a wholesale wing to support local societies, and by 1851 it was up and running. Throughout the 1850s at a national level co-operative congresses debated the need for a separate and truly national wholesale organization, and during this time Rochdale seemed to fulfil an important function. But running it placed a financial strain on the Pioneers, and in 1856 the wholesale function became the source of major disagreements within the society.[61] Though the pro-wholesale lobby, led by pro-wholesalers like J. T. W Mitchell and Abraham Greenwood, won the day, eventually the losses incurred led to the closure of the wholesale department in 1858.

The failure of these initiatives, however, did not remove the perceived need of a major joint co-operative venture into co-operative wholesaling. As a result, many of those who had been involved in these efforts at wholesaling, including leading members of the Pioneers like Mitchell, and Christian Socialists like Neale and Lloyd Jones, adopted a new strategy, which would change the law and pave the way for a new approach to establishing a national wholesale system through the creation of a federation of co-operatives to run that service: in effect a co-operative of co-operatives. The closure of the Rochdale wholesale department in 1858 was the catalyst for the launch of a new initiative in this direction.

---

[57] Bonner (1961), 31.   [58] Bonner (1961), 33.
[59] Cole (1944), 128.   [60] Bonner (1961), 65.   [61] Bonner (1961), 71.

The momentum for change came from three main sources. First, that stalwart of Rochdale co-operation, Abraham Greenwood, seems to have been instrumental in rallying a group of co-operators in the Manchester area to focus on the question of winning an Act which would legalize a co-operative of co-operatives to become a new national wholesaling organization. In this he was helped by two rising co-operators in the region, J. C. Edwards and Edward Hooson. In 1859, it was this group which drew in Neale, Ludlow, and others to begin the campaign for a change in the law.[62] Secondly, 1860 saw the establishment of a new national voice for co-operation, the monthly newspaper *The Co-operator*. The first edition of the paper, edited first by Edward Longfield and then Henry Pitman, appeared in June 1860. So popular did it prove to be that Longfield was able to boast in the second issue of a rapid growth of orders for the journal. Five hundred copies were ordered by J. D. Stiles of London for societies there, the Queenshead Industrial Society of Huddersfield also asked for 500 copies, while a range of other societies put in orders for more modest quantities.[63] The result was that the journal rapidly became a rallying point and promoter of the idea of a national wholesale society. In October 1860 it offered enthusiastic support for a national conference of co-operative societies at which, it believed, 'the subject of wholesale agents and stores in central districts, from which stores at a distance might be supplied with every description of commodities, could be considered'.[64] Throughout the following years, the journal became an assiduous supporter of a national wholesale society.[65] Thirdly, a group of co-operators in the Manchester district addressed the question of what such an organization might be like and how it would function. The rise of co-operative societies here, in Rochdale, Oldham, Manchester, and in the cluster of mill and other industrial towns in this part of Lancashire, created a network of activists who were quick to perceive the necessity and advantages of greater collaboration between co-operative societies in a range of fields, from the promotion of producer co-operative ventures to the question of a co-operative wholesale organization. On the latter question, the presence of well-developed retail competitors, who were increasingly resentful of co-operative success, undoubtedly focused their attention. The failure of the Rochdale wholesale experiment seems to have spurred them into action.

In March 1859, William Cooper, one of the original Rochdale Pioneers, read a paper advocating a wholesale organization run collaboratively by Rochdale and other societies in the district. Though the proposal was rejected, the basic idea had been floated, and crucially had won the interest of the network of co-operative activists in east Lancashire.[66] The next development has become part of popular co-operative mythology. In mid-August 1860, a group of co-operative activists met at Lowbands farm near Middleton, right at the heart of the network of east Lancashire co-operative societies. The farm, depicted in Figure 2.10, was run by a co-operative society, and the 'Jumbo Farm' as it was known, had long been a meeting place for co-operators.[67] The meeting

[62] Bonner (1961), 485–6; Cole (1944), 139.
[63] E. Longfield, 'Our Journal', *The Co-operator* (July 1860), 23.
[64] Editorial, *The Co-operator* (October 1860), 65.   [65] Cole (1944), 139–40.
[66] Redfern (1913), 18–19.   [67] Cole (1944), 140.

FIGURE 2.10. 'Jumbo Farm', Middleton. The 'Lowbands Farm' in Jumbo was established as a co-operative farm in 1851, along the lines of Feargus O'Connor's Chartist Land Scheme. Conveniently located to Rochdale, Manchester, and Oldham, the farm was host to early meetings that led to the formation of the CWS.

addressed a number of common issues, including the establishment of a cotton mill by co-operators in Oldham, as well as the question of a new wholesale agency.[68] Co-operative luminaries attending included William Marcroft, William Nuttall, and Edward Ingham of Oldham, William Cooper of Rochdale, and George Booth of the Jumbo Farm co-operative.[69] The legal impediments to the establishment of a 'co-operative of co-operatives' appear to have been discussed, and the need to change the law. The result was a further meeting in Oldham a few weeks later, followed by a conference in Rochdale in October, at which a committee was set up to lead the campaign for legal reform which would make a co-operative wholesale society of co-operatives achievable. Dyson chaired the first meeting of this body, and William Cooper was made secretary (see Plate 1).[70] Other members of this body included a strong Rochdale contingent of Abraham Greenwood, James Smithies, Samuel Stott, Thomas Cheetham, William Marcroft of Oldham, Charles Howarth (formerly of Rochdale, now of Heywood), John Hilton (Middleton), Edward Hooson, and J. C. Edwards (Manchester).[71] The committee organized a major conference in Manchester on 25 December 1860, attended by about

[68] *The Co-operator* (October 1860), 63.   [69] Redfern (1913), 19–21.
[70] Jumbo Minute Book (4 November 1860), 4, NCA.
[71] Cole (1944), 141.

sixty delegates from societies mainly in the north-west of England.[72] This set up a smaller committee, consisting of Greenwood, Stott, and Cooper, which was tasked with liaising with Neale to coordinate a campaign to change the law in Parliament.[73] Meanwhile, the larger committee established in Rochdale focused on developing the idea and practicalities of a co-operative wholesale society.

Over the next two years, these bodies set about their tasks with great energy and determination. While a change to the law had to wait until 1862, the support of Slaney and Richard Cobden in the house made it a certainty. The Industrial and Provident Society Act of 1862 allowed the principle of limited liability for co-operatives, and crucially permitted co-operatives to invest in each other, making a federation of co-operatives possible. Interestingly, the idea of co-operative federation was not a Lancashire monopoly. Exploratory discussions were undertaken among societies in the north-east around Newcastle upon Tyne, and a federal society of fourteen local societies was established at Northampton, which survived until 1870.[74] This seems to have spurred the Lancashire men on and a battery of meetings and conferences throughout 1861 and 1862 ensued, as the detailed workings of the new wholesale organization were debated and hammered out. Interestingly, Greenwood and the committee argued at a conference held in December 1862 for a minimalist wholesale agency, which would buy at cost price and sell on commission. But this proved unacceptable for the movement and at a special conference of 200 delegates in Ancoats in April 1863 they insisted upon the establishment of both an agency and a physical depot, and this view won the day.[75] The name of the new organization was to be the North of England Co-operative Wholesale Agency & Depot Society Ltd (NECWADS), and it was to be registered under the new 1862 Industrial and Provident Societies Act.[76] Because of limits in the Act which restricted society subscriptions to £200, it was decided that the new organization would have some individual as well as society members. This reflected some concern that the new body would initially be short of funds if it was unable to attract as many societies to join as was hoped. The individual members could also subscribe up to £200 each, and it was envisaged that the individuals concerned would be furnished with funds for their individual membership by the societies which they represented. Thus Smithies, Greenwood, Cheetham, Cooper, and Stott of Rochdale, Hewkins and Marcroft of Oldham, Howarth of Heywood, Hooson, Dyson, and Edwards from Manchester, and Hilton of Middleton all became individual members.[77] From this point matters moved swiftly. By August 1863 the rules of the organization had been agreed upon, and it had been legally enrolled.[78] By late October, forty-eight co-operative societies had agreed to join NECWADS. A provisional general committee was elected at the first general meeting in November, and perhaps unsurprisingly it was dominated by the men who had been working towards the creation of the organization over the previous years. Greenwood was the first president, Cheetham was

---

[72] Cole (1944), 141.   [73] Jumbo Minute Book, Conference (25 December 1860), 11–12.
[74] Cole (1944), 142.   [75] Jumbo Minute Book (25 December 1862), 38–41; Cole (1944), 143.
[76] Jumbo Minute Book, conference in Ancoats (3 April 1863), 49.
[77] Cole (1944), 143.   [78] Redfern (1913), 424.

made treasurer, and Edwards became secretary. Initially the plan had been to register the organization in Liverpool, but this was eventually dropped in favour of Manchester, which was quickly becoming the natural geographical centre of a body which was initially dominated by societies in the towns near that city. Trading finally began at the small warehouse at 3 Cooper Street, Manchester, on 14 March 1864. Initially trading could only be on a small scale. But as will be seen—the growth of the new organization was so impressive that it rapidly exceeded all expectations.

CHAPTER 3

THE RISE OF THE CWS, 1863 TO 1890

The Birth and Leadership of a Corporate Giant?

THE foundation of the Co-operative Wholesale Society (CWS) in 1863 ushered in a new phase in the development of the co-operative movement. As shown, the movement had emerged in response to the problems and insecurity caused by the turbulence of early British industrialization and urbanization, and the long list of co-operative failures as well as successes reflected the extraordinary difficult circumstances in which British co-operation first flourished. But in the wake of the great crises of the 1840s, the British economy entered calmer waters of greater stability and growth, which began to bring benefits to a larger portion of the country's population. As a result, the numbers of co-operatives established in Britain grew in the 1850s, and many proved to be much more durable than their predecessors. Living standards rose, and as the incomes of co-operative members became more reliable, their ability to buy from the local store grew. As shown, this flourishing of co-operation in the 1850s had already prompted several attempts to address a nagging problem faced by consumer co-operatives: how to ensure a reliable supply of food and other commodities of the right quality and price to sell in the co-operative stores. Supplying shops and stores of all kinds was of course problem-atic in Britain in the 1850s. While the rail network was fast developing, difficulties in transporting goods over large distances at affordable freight rates was, as yet, a chal-lenge. But the situation for co-operatives was compounded by the suspicions and resentment towards them harboured by non-co-operative competitors, many of whom saw co-operative practices such as the dividend as inherently unfair, since they seemed to offer additional rewards to entice customers away from 'ordinary' private capitalist traders. There was always the possibility that such opponents might organize and pressure wholesale suppliers to discriminate against or even boycott their co-operative customers. Then of course there was the problem of ensuring the quality of goods supplied on the free market, at a time when legislative guarantees were few and largely unenforced.

Taking control of the supply chain thus came to be seen by co-operative leaders as the best strategy to ensure both the security of their trading activities and the promise of higher-quality produce. From very modest beginnings in Manchester's Cooper Street (shown in Figure 3.1), the CWS rose to become a major international commercial organization within a quarter of a century. In 1864, in its first year of trading, the CWS's sales amounted to £51,875, based on a capital (drawn from co-operative society shareholdings) of £2,445, to a monumental £7,429,073 of sales in 1890, with a capital of £434,017.[1] The total number of individual members of those societies which were affiliated to the CWS rose from just 18,337 in 1864 to 721,316 in 1890. During the intervening years the CWS established a national network of wholesaling facilities across England and Wales, with major branches in Newcastle and London, and the headquarters in Manchester. There were depots in Leeds, Blackburn, Bristol, Nottingham, and Huddersfield. The CWS had also become a major manufacturer, with a factory making biscuits and confectionery in Crumpsall, Manchester, a soap works in Durham, shoe works in Leicester and Heckmondwike, as well as textile mills in Batley, Yorkshire. The rapid growth of the CWS as a producer was matched by the organization's international reach. A branch was established in New York in the mid-1870s, which began to purchase agricultural produce (wheat, cheese, and meat) from the eastern states and in due course from the mid west, especially Chicago, where the CWS undertook extensive operations. By the mid-1880s it had branches in Copenhagen and Hamburg, buying Danish and northern German foodstuffs, including butter, wheat, and bacon. It maintained a steady trade with France through its branch in Rouen and its agents in Calais and Paris. Its international expansion continued into the twentieth century, and by the outbreak of the First World War it had a branch in Sydney, Australia, and tea plantations in India and Ceylon (now Sri Lanka).

This chapter will address a number of key questions related to this meteoric rise in the later nineteenth century. How did co-operation adapt to the context of continuing British socio-economic development, as the country matured as a modern urban and industrial society? To what extent was the success of co-operation assisted by the wider phenomenon of British industrialization, and how far did co-operatives and the CWS have to adjust and adapt their principles to meet the challenges of industrial maturation? How did the emerging urban environments of Britain's industrializing towns and cities shape the relationship between retail co-operative societies, their local competitors and suppliers, and the newly established CWS and other national co-operative bodies? What strategies were adopted by the CWS to develop their business with retail societies during the period? How successful were they?

---

[1] *People's Year Book* (1950), 131–2.

FIGURE 3.1. First CWS offices, Manchester. Located at 3 Cooper Street in Manchester, the CWS's first offices were in two rooms on the first floor (the man standing in the doorway shows the entry). By November 1864 offices moved to 28 Cannon Street, and in summer 1865 new premises were taken at 53 Dantzic Street—not far from today's 'co-operative quarter'.

3.1 THE CONTEXT OF CO-OPERATIVE DEVELOPMENT: BRITISH ECONOMIC AND SOCIAL DEVELOPMENT, 1860–90, AND THE 'RETAIL REVOLUTION'

As shown, a common feature in the establishment of co-operatives of all kinds in the early and mid-nineteenth century was the need to adapt to difficulties caused by the early stages of industrialization. These included problems of access to safe and reasonably priced food, chronic insecurity in employment caused by violent economic fluctuations, and the paltry level of state support for those in dire need, as exemplified by the punitive regime of the 1834 Poor Law. It also reflected the absence of any reliable provision of education at a time when the poorest in society were unrepresented in the political system and many working-class activists were striving to prove the fitness of ordinary people for the vote. The 'Rochdale model' proved to be the most durable of a variety of forms of co-operative organization which had been attempted earlier in the nineteenth century.

But from the 1850s, economic and social conditions began to change in Britain. The severity of the economic fluctuations which beset Britain's early industrial economy tended to lessen later in the century, as the economic benefits of industrialization for the lower ranks of society became more apparent, and as the spread of new technologies across a range of industries helped to open more global markets and provide more employment.[2] Working-class living standards rose, even as the country's towns and cities entered into a period of unprecedented growth. The urban population spiralled. The population of Manchester rose from 252,000 in 1841 to 645,000 in 1902; Liverpool from 299,000 to 704,000, and Birmingham from 202,000 to 781,000 in the same period.[3] London, always the giant among British cities, rose from about 2.2 million to 6.5 million, if one includes the outer suburbs of the city.[4] A similar trend was identifiable in the towns—especially in highly industrialized regions such as the north-west of England. Urban spaces expanded into the local countryside as the population of the towns swelled, and the more affluent middle classes sought to distance themselves from the poorer and more polluted districts, taking advantage of improvements in local transport.

The effect of these changes on patterns of consumption and the structure of retailing has received considerable attention from historians, perhaps the most influential study being one by Jefferys in 1954.[5] He contended that rising living standards after 1850, cheaper and better rail transport, combined with less economic volatility laid the foundations for a major transformation in the way people obtained the day-to-day necessities of life. Beginning in the 1850s, these changes gathered momentum in the last quarter of the nineteenth century. They included the emergence of 'proactive' selling through advertising, carefully designed window displays and the emergence of fixed and steady prices, a growing presence for manufacturers in retailing through branding, resale price maintenance, and advertising by the manufacturers themselves; and the emergence by the end of the century of multiple chains of shops and large department stores.[6] Significantly, Jefferys saw the spread of co-operative retail societies and the establishment of a national supply network, partly through the CWS, as integral to this revolution in retailing, citing the movement as a leading innovator in developing international as well as national supply chains. Significantly, Jefferys himself played an important role on the Co-operative Independent Commission established in 1956 to modernize the movement in the face of growing competition from the non-co-operative sector. Sitting alongside such political

[2] Mathias (1983), 224–6.   [3] Crouzet (1982), 97.   [4] Crouzet (1982), 96.
[5] Jefferys (1954).   [6] Jefferys (1954), 1–39.

giants as Hugh Gaitskell and Tony Crosland, Jefferys's appointment was a clear recognition of the ground-breaking nature of his work on British retail development, and its potential to inform future policy.[7] For modern academic historians seeking to meet new demands that their work should have contemporary relevance, especially in the commercial sphere, Jefferys's study was an early model of academic 'impact'.

Inevitably, of course, later historians have both challenged and refined Jefferys's conclusions. Some of this later work has important implications for the path of development of the co-operative movement in Britain. Two main qualifications of Jefferys's analysis have emerged from this body of work. First, the change in retailing practice, culture, and organization is now widely acknowledged to have been much more gradual than Jefferys suggests. At one extreme, Blackman suggests that the emergence of modern retailing techniques began much earlier in the mid-nineteenth century.[8] This is reinforced by Stobart and Hann, who show that some of the 'modern' techniques of retailing identified with the later nineteenth century can actually be traced back to the eighteenth century.[9] At the other end of the spectrum, Blackman and others also cite the surprising durability of some 'older' retailing practices well into the twentieth century. Wide disparities in household incomes meant that in many places there was space for smaller players, operating on tighter margins, to function alongside the new multiples and other sophisticated retailers. Thus Rubin shows that very small retailers like tallymen and packmen were important in serving poor communities long after 1900.[10] Hodson shows that in many parts of Lancashire the local market trader was successful in holding off the fierce competition of the new shops, principally because of their ability to meet the needs of the poorer sections of local communities.[11] Scola's seminal work on food supplies in Manchester to 1870 also reinforces this picture of complexity; of older retail systems surviving, such as the activities of street and door-to-door hawkers, well into the supposed new era of multiples, marketing, and branding.[12] The alleged novelty of some of the new methods of retailing, such as branding, shop displays, and basic advertising, has also been challenged, as Stobart and Hann's work shows.[13] Nor has the importance of local conditions in shaping the variety and configuration of retail types been missed by historians. Mutch's study of the development of a chain of public houses in Liverpool by Peter Walker showed that the business model proved difficult to export to other cities and towns.[14] Porter's work on department store development in the late nineteenth and early twentieth centuries demonstrates that the organization of these innovative retail operations was much more responsive to local circumstances than was once assumed.[15] But it is perhaps Michael Winstanley's rich survey of the development

---

[7] See section 6.4.   [8] Blackman (1963), 96–7; and (1967), 116–17.
[9] Stobart and Hann (2004), 189–90.   [10] Rubin (1986), 221.   [11] Hodson (1998), 109–10.
[12] Scola (1975), 153–67 and (1992).   [13] Stobart and Hann (2004).   [14] Mutch (2006), 12–16.
[15] Porter (1971), 71.

of the British shopkeeper in the pre-First World War period which best captures this complex, heavily localized, and gradually evolving landscape of new multiple and co-operative operations and enduring 'traditional' retail forms.[16]

In essence this meant that the environment in which co-operative retail societies and the CWS developed from the 1860s was highly complex, locally varied, and subject to accelerating change as the century progressed. Purvis has analysed the expansion of

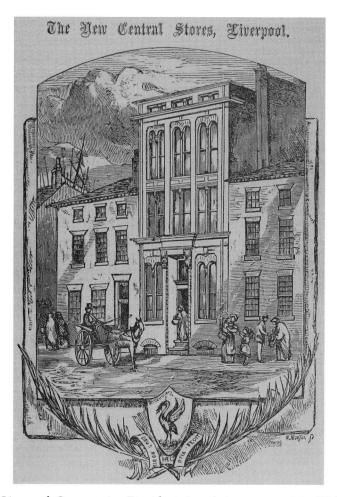

FIGURE 3.2. Liverpool Co-operative Provident Association stores, 1863. With over 3,000 members, 'the Provident' was one of the largest societies in England in spring 1863 when it opened its new Camden Street premises, announced in *The Co-operator*. However, the society declined precipitously in the later 1860s and the society let the building to tenants. Today it is home to the Merseyside Dance & Drama Centre.

[16] Winstanley (1983), 3 and 8–16.

co-operatives across Britain during the late nineteenth century, and highlights an uneven pattern of development in which the most fertile places for co-operative formation and survival tended to be the industrial and urban environments of north and north-west England (see Figure 3.2).[17] In contrast, as late as the 1890s, London was identified as a co-operative desert. The reasons for the greater success of the movement in some areas are inevitably complex and varied, but certain factors do seem to be common. Shared experiences in working and social life certainly seem to have been important, thus the success of co-operatives in areas where particular industries were the main source of employment, such as the coal mines of county Durham or the textile industry in Lancashire.[18] Conversely, heterogeneity of employment, particularly where there was a prevalence of unstable and casual jobs, was a much tougher environment for co-operation to master. Indeed, Purvis shows that such difficulties contributed very significantly to a high rate of co-operative failure nationally, with many of them succumbing to fierce local competition from private retailers, or sudden collapse of custom and membership among poor working-class people hit hard by the effects of economic downturns. As a result, the pattern of co-operative development was highly varied and contingent upon local conditions—as were the strategies adopted by co-operative retail societies to ensure survival and growth.

3.2 THE CO-OPERATIVE MOVEMENT AND THE 'DOMINANCE OF LOCALISM'

An important point about the acceleration of co-operative growth in the mid-nineteenth century is that the movement was taking off in what was already quite a well-developed urban and industrial society. By 1850 Britain's towns and cities had already experienced rapid growth and by then many accommodated sophisticated business and retail communities. Wilson, Popp, and Carnevali have shown that by this period, a lot of northern industrial cities hosted substantial numbers of small businesses, many of which served and supported each other through complex networks of business relationships.[19] They show that these 'clusters' of businesses were mutually supportive by keeping transactions costs to a minimum, and by enabling each of them to outsource key activities and supplies which helped keep running costs down. Fostering trust and co-operation between firms and their owners was the key. The point for the rise of co-operatives in Britain during this period was that local retail societies were very much part of this local business landscape, and found it very much in their interest to cultivate local relationships with wholesalers and the wider business community. At a time when local supply chains were still very important, particularly in food, and long-term transport costs were still

[17] Purvis (1990).   [18] Purvis (1990), 327.
[19] Wilson and Popp (2003), Introduction, 1–18; Carnevali (2004).

relatively high notwithstanding the developing railway network, co-operative societies depended heavily upon good relations with local wholesalers, farmers, and the local community generally. Moreover, the need to compete with local rival retailers meant that co-operative retail societies had to prioritize low prices and high quality of the produce they sold, in order to stay in business, and to generate surplus to pay attractive dividends.

Local co-operators had to be especially sensitive to local opinions and interests. Retail societies faced considerable and growing hostility from private retailers, many of whom regarded the co-operative dividend on purchases as unfair trading. Some retailers tried to take matters into their own hands. In April 1886, the *Co-operative News* published an editorial condemning efforts by private traders in Scotland to organize boycotts of co-operatives among wholesalers, a campaign which rapidly turned into a newspaper campaign against co-operation in general.[20] Winstanley shows that by the end of the nineteenth century, such journals as *The Tradesmen and Shopkeeper* were leading campaigns of vilification against co-operative societies and the 'divi', occasionally resorting to slightly bizarre tactics, such as the publication of a song in what purported to be a northern dialect, 'Co-ops and Divi'.[21] Some anti-co-operative initiatives even targeted the employers of leading co-operators. In 1886, grocers in Maryport, Cumberland, lobbied the Maryport and Carlisle Railway Company to pressurize a number of their employees who were prominent in the local co-operative society to desist from their co-operative activities; and also to instruct their other employees to buy from local traders rather than the society. The grocers threatened to use a rival railway line if the Maryport and Carlisle Railway Company did not comply. Ultimately that company decided not to give in to these threats, chiefly because it earned substantial revenues from freighting co-operative goods! But the episode showed just how potentially vulnerable co-operative societies might be to organized attempts to undermine their trade.[22] In May 1886, a CWS buyer reported that committee members of the Birmingham Industrial Society were being intimidated by their employer, the Midland Railway Company, with threats of dismissal unless they stood down from their co-operative activities.[23] Other opponents were cruder and more direct. A meeting called to establish a co-operative society in Salisbury in Wiltshire in January 1887 was broken up by a rowdy gang of youths and shopkeepers who noisily objected that the working class of Salisbury had no need of co-operation.[24]

In this context, maintaining good relations with at least some of the local commercial community, especially wholesalers and other suppliers, was most prudent. There is a substantial body of evidence from a range of co-operative society records that care was taken to ensure that local wholesalers would enjoy reliable custom with them. Purvis's

[20]   *Co-operative News* (17 April 1886), 372.
[21]   Winstanley (1983), 85–7.
[22]   Editorial, 'The Grocers' New Weapon', *Co-operative News* (8 May 1886), 444–5.
[23]   Minutes of the Grocery and Provisions Committee (13 May 1886), 78–9.
[24]   *Co-operative News* (5 February 1887), 137.

study of societies in the north-east of England in the 1860s and 1870s shows that they were careful to spread their purchases across a range of favoured suppliers, to ensure best price and highest quality whilst promoting the acceptance by these suppliers of co-operatives as a legitimate section of the local business community.[25] Such policies were sustained over extended periods of time. Between 1882 and 1886, the Great Grimsby society consistently purchased from prominent local wholesalers such as W. Marshall & Son, Jarman & Flint, and R. Pringle.[26] In the early 1880s, the Bridge End Equitable Progressionists of Todmorden operated a policy of consistently purchasing butter from several well-established suppliers, of which the CWS was just one. For example, on 21 July 1881 25 firkins of butter were purchased from John Binns, and 25 from the CWS. On 18 August 25 firkins were ordered from the CWS, and 25 from J. Clanchy. Similarly, on 21 September, 25 firkins were purchased from the CWS and 25 from John Flynn. This pattern of transactions continued throughout the periods from 7 April 1881 to 30 March 1882, and 7 January to 29 July 1886. A similar strategy of 'spread purchasing' was evident in the procurement of tea, soap, and biscuits.[27]

Other studies of the co-operative movement have shown that the development of social and cultural activities by local co-operatives was driven by practical as well as ideological considerations. Local festivals, the establishment of reading rooms, and the emergence of vibrant social communities in which members participated not only ensured consumer loyalty to the local store, it also helped build a core of local activists who could campaign to defend the society in the face of political challenges. Walton in particular stresses the importance of cultural and social initiatives in promoting involvement in co-operatives in the towns of Lancashire, particularly in the cotton manufacturing centres.[28] Peter Gurney's important book on co-operative politics and cultural life shows that the success of the movement rested upon much more than just the 'divi'. It involved the mobilization of local communities of members through social activities as well as commercial transactions. This was a crucial weapon in the defence of local societies.[29] There was an important political dimension here. By the 1890s mobilization against anti-co-operative campaigns strengthened the local identities of many retail societies.[30] While most societies eschewed overt party political affiliations, many active co-operators held Liberal views and were drawn into the groundswell of working-class political activism following the Reform Acts of 1867 and 1884, and the rise of New Unionism in the late 1880s.[31] Thus many co-operators emerged as important players in the flourishing local working-class political cultures of the late nineteenth century. This reinforced the preoccupation of co-operators with local issues.

---

[25] Purvis (1998), 55–78.

[26] Minutes of the Great Grimsby Co-operative Company Ltd, 1882 and 1886, 1–50 (1882); 448–502 (1886), NCR/2/17/5/1/2, NCA.

[27] Minutes of Bridge End Equitable Progressionists, 1881 and 1886, NCRS/2/4/1/1/4–10, NCA.

[28] Walton (1996), 27.   [29] Gurney (1996), 199–201.   [30] Gurney (1996), 199–200.

[31] Cole (1944), 194–5; see also Creighton (1996), 35–8.

In terms of developing loyalty and trust between co-operatives and their members, this socio-cultural aspect of local society life yielded real commercial and social benefits. Samy's work on the success of the Co-operative Permanent Building Society (CPBS—now of course the Nationwide Building Society) in promoting working-class home-ownership in the late nineteenth century places particular emphasis upon the close relationship which frequently existed between store managers and local society members. Samy shows that the CPBS operated through local co-operative store managers, who also acted as de facto mortgage managers, using their knowledge of the local membership to advise which members were and were not good risks. Samy makes the point that the repayment record of the CPBS's debtors was especially impressive during this period, since the need to maintain a good reputation with the local society persuaded many member mortgagees to prioritize repaying their mortgage debts.[32] Thus the intense social and personal links which existed between society and member played a very important role in the commercial operations of the former. In February 1875, the *Co-operative News* vividly captured the importance of these relationships in societies in the north-east of England:

Each of these stores is a little centre of power in its district, and the public spirit of the leading men has contributed in no small degree to consolidate the co-operative idea in the mind of the masses of the people. Though no organized system of propaganda has been established, still at annual tea parties and by private effort much has been done to spread knowledge of the advantages their societies confer on those who have the wisdom to join them.[33]

This fierce sense of local independence was further entrenched by societies developing a wide range of productive activities and other services, either on their own or with other societies, though rarely with the CWS.[34] Thus the 1893 *Co-operative Directory* listed a very wide range of business functions commonly carried on by societies, including ironmongery, drapery, tailoring and shoe repairs, baking, corn milling, and jewellery.[35]

But such localism was to prove quite problematic for the developing relationship between the CWS and its member societies. From the start, the Wholesale's principal function was to supply co-operative societies with produce. As a 'co-operative of co-operatives', the CWS's members were the hundreds of co-operative societies across England and Wales who joined the CWS. A separate Scottish Co-operative Wholesale Society (SCWS) was established on a similar basis in 1868. Thus the local retail societies were masters of the CWS. They elected the General Committee, eventually referred to as the Board of Directors, and ratified, amended, or rejected proposals from it at regular delegate meetings. These were held every six months at first, and latterly every three months. One might expect that this control and sense of ownership would have engendered a powerful sense of loyalty to the Wholesale—after all, dividends generated by business with the CWS would be a welcome addition to local society resources. But in

---

[32] Samy (2012), 184–8.

[33] 'Northern Letter', J. McKendrick, *Co-operative News* (6 February 1875), 67.

[34] Friberg (2005), part 1.   [35] *Co-operative Directory* (1893), 9.

fact, many societies proved to be extremely lukewarm in their commercial relations with the Wholesale. One reason for this was that it took the CWS a number of years before its operations were substantial enough to furnish societies with more than a fraction of their supplies; yet the 1860s and 1870s saw a rapid proliferation of local co-operative societies. These societies had to develop their own local and national supplies of produce with relatively little support from the CWS. This further entrenched the strong spirit of local independence which characterized the movement.

Society localism and independence led to a fundamental difference between the perceptions of the CWS's role held by the committees and buyers of a large number of local societies, and those of the people who led and worked for the Wholesale. For many local retail societies, especially their managers and buyers, CWS was certainly an important supplier, useful not only for sourcing products but also demonstrating to wholesalers and suppliers generally that the local co-operative society had alternative sources, should their private suppliers not meet society expectations in terms of price or quality. But few of them welcomed the idea of the CWS becoming the sole or even the main supplier of commodities. Rather they saw the Wholesale as a strategic player in the wholesale market, ensuring that other suppliers were forced to supply local retail societies with high-quality goods at competitive prices, and that they would be reluctant to succumb to calls from private competitors for boycotts of supplies to co-operative societies. Most local society committees and buyers were more than happy to purchase from the Wholesale, and certainly believed that this was both a moral obligation and an act of self-interest (especially given the dividend). But there were limits to how far many retail society managers were prepared to take such considerations. Ultimately, there was a very commonly held view that the CWS could expect the loyal custom of societies only if they competed effectively, and provided goods which were as cheap and as good as those procurable on the open market. Some society managers were quite open about such views, even at CWS meetings when there was considerable pressure from the Board and officials to buy more from the CWS. For example, in March 1882, at a meeting of society buyers at CWS headquarters in Balloon Street, chaired by J. T. W. Mitchell (CWS Chair), buyers of local societies were treated to a long and assertive paper by one Noah Briggs of the Prestwich Society, stressing the duty of all co-operative society buyers to prioritize the CWS as their main supplier. The *Co-operative News* reported that one Mr Hague of Barnsley was quite blunt in his response, saying that:

While he agreed with the writer of the paper that the Wholesale was a centre to which all the buyers ought to look up, he thought that a little competition was a good thing even to the buyers of the Wholesale.

He concluded by saying that 'competition does no harm, even in the co-operative movement'.[36] Such views were not new. In March 1876, Mr Tell, an official of the Gloucester Society, wrote to the *Co-operative News*, asserting:

---

[36] Report on conference of co-operative society buyers and managers at Balloon St on 14 March 1882, *Co-operative News* (18 March 1882), 172.

Now I think it is the duty of all committees to study the interest of their own society, and if they can purchase better from the Wholesale it is their duty to do so. If, on the other hand, they can purchase from the merchants as good a quality and at a cheaper rate, the opportunity should not be thrown away.[37]

Five years later, T. Gisley of the Plymouth Society made exactly the same point, telling a conference in Exeter that the ferocity of competition from private shopkeepers in the town forced the society to buy as cheaply as possible, and that loyalty to the CWS came a very poor second in the face of such stark practical considerations.[38] An additional problem was that many co-operative societies were deeply critical of the quality of some CWS goods. In March 1882 the Langley Mill and Aldercar Co-operative Society ranked CWS coffee as inferior to at least two other suppliers, who got the society's orders.[39] In 1886 the same society even voted against the proposal that the CWS move into cocoa and woollen goods production, so unimpressed was it with Wholesale goods.[40] In the late 1870s, certain societies, notably Bury and Leeds, were cited by leading CWS buyers as being openly hostile to the CWS.[41] The antipathy of some local buyers was noted in 1878 by a Mr Scott of the Newbottle Society, who commented that the average co-operative society buyer had as much warm feeling for the CWS as 'a cat has for a mouse, or a Muscovite has for an Ottoman'.[42] In the south, some societies seemed completely adrift from the CWS. In 1885 one society correspondent calculated that across 176 societies in the south of England, only just over a quarter of goods purchased came from the CWS.[43] In 1893, *The Co-operative News* lamented the stubborn indifference of the Stratford Society in London and for clinging

more or less lovingly, and lastingly, to its old habit of buying in the so-called open market. The occasions upon which the Wholesale has been able to 'charm' this very shy collective co-operative entity have been fitful and few. The 't'other dear charmer' was there first, in the shape of the private firm, and the first love manages, in some way, in the main to hold the field. The Stratford Committee seem to be quite willing to be 'happy with either'; nevertheless the old love gets the cake and the Wholesale the crumbs.[44]

Some even claimed that leading officials of the CWS itself acknowledged that they were not necessarily the first port of call. In 1877, William Barnett of the Equitable Provident Society of Macclesfield claimed that some CWS officials had told him that they regarded any society which sourced only a third of its goods from the CWS as loyal.[45]

---

[37] Letter: 'Dealing with the Wholesale Society', *Co-operative News* (11 March 1876), 123.

[38] Co-operative Conference at Exeter, 2 April 1887, *Co-operative News* (16 April 1887), 370.

[39] Minutes of Langley Mill and Aldercar Co-operative Society (23 March 1882), MID/1/2/3/1/1/3, NCA.

[40] Minutes of Langley Mill and Aldercar Co-operative Society (11 November 1886).

[41] CWS Grocery and Provisions Committee minutes (8 May and 11 September 1878), NCA.

[42] Letter from G. Scott, 18 June 1878, *Co-operative News* (29 June 1878), 429.

[43] Letter, 'The Southern Societies and their Loyalty to the Wholesale', 1 August 1885, *Co-operative News* (22 August 1885), 779.

[44] *Co-operative News* (22 July 1893), 795.

[45] Letter, 'The Trade of the Wholesale', *Co-operative News* (30 June 1877), 349.

But notwithstanding such claims there were strong aspirations, both moral and commercial, within CWS leadership that it should become, in time, the principal supplier of goods and services to local co-operative societies. For some CWS leaders this was essential if co-operation was to improve the lot of the British people. Some believed that in due course the CWS would prove unsurpassable in ensuring steady supplies of cheap and wholesome food and the other necessities of life, if only societies would become loyal customers. The CWS would prove unbeatable by moving into production on its own account, and by developing robust and complex supply chains which would take the organization as close to the point of production as possible. In 1877, R. Whittle, a CWS director, articulated this aim in a debate about the CWS tea trade:

The very principle of the Wholesale, as far as I have understood it, is to do away with all middlemen and dealers—and of course save their profits—and to get as near as possible to the grower, the producer and the manufacturer, and, as the principle gets more developed, even to manufacture ourselves articles of general consumption. This, so far, has been the policy of the Wholesale.[46]

In the late 1880s, so convinced was the Board of its rightful position as the principal supplier for the movement that it launched a series of major conferences around the country, which focused upon the question of loyalty to the Wholesale. None other than Mitchell himself presided over several of these conferences, and he was forthright about the obligation of societies to support the CWS. In October 1890 he harangued a meeting of co-operative society representatives at Long Eaton, Nottinghamshire, for taking some £200,000 of trade outside the CWS during the course of the previous year.[47] At a conference in Yorkshire in July of the following year he even 'named and shamed' two societies for their especially poor record of trading with the CWS.[48] The desire on the part of CWS leaders that it should become the hub and engine of British co-operation was thus openly stated, and it enjoyed considerable support in some of the key organs of the movement. The Co-operative News consistently championed the notion that co-operative societies had a duty to purchase as much as possible from the CWS. It regularly published lists of how much societies purchased from the CWS per member, with the aim of shaming those societies with especially poor records.[49] Much to their embarrassment, even the Rochdale Pioneers appeared among the names of the censured![50] The CWS Annual of 1892 went a step further and produced a national survey of retail societies in England and Wales which showed the percentage of their total purchases by value which came from the CWS. The picture was damning. In 1890, societies across the country sourced only 37 per cent by value of their produce from the Wholesale.[51]

[46] Paper by R. Whittle (undated), CWS General Committee minutes, Special Meeting of CWS Directors (11 August 1877), Vol. 5, 188.

[47] Co-operative News (1 November 1890), 1102.

[48] Co-operative News (18 July 1891), 728.

[49] 'The Trade of the Wholesale', Co-operative News (6 April 1876), 175.

[50] 'The Wholesale and the Retail Societies', Co-operative News (15 March 1879), 171. The article showed that Rochdale's purchases from CWS were only 16 per cent by value of Rochdale Pioneers' sales.

[51] 'Co-operative Societies and the Wholesale', Co-operative Wholesale Society Ltd Annual (1892), 489–521, 518.

The situation in Lancashire, that citadel of co-operation and the home of the CWS, mirrored almost exactly the national position. Societies there only obtained 36.9 per cent of their total supplies from the CWS.[52] Results elsewhere were even worse. The 10 societies in Devon procured just 17.7 per cent of goods by value from the Wholesale. The 19 societies in Glamorgan obtained just 19.7 per cent. There were some pockets of relative loyalty such as Middlesex (59.7 per cent for 24 societies), Kent (45.2 per cent for 25 societies), Buckinghamshire (57.4 per cent for 9 societies), Cambridgeshire (61.6 per cent for 5 societies), and Bedfordshire (50.2 per cent for 8 societies). Notwithstanding some considerable variations, though, the national picture was disappointing.

Right from the start, the CWS encountered a fundamental clash with its member retail co-operative societies over the nature of the Wholesale's purpose. The CWS's leaders were clear in their own minds that their long-term aim was to become the main if not the sole supplier of goods for the retail societies, a substantial proportion of which would be produced by the CWS itself. This, in its view, was how the co-operative movement would ultimately displace the privately owned market system. Implicit in this was an aspiration for the CWS to effectively lead the movement, as it would become the central hub for supplying the retail societies which would enable them to beat the private competition. The problem was that the retail societies never accepted this version of the role of the CWS. For them, the CWS was important as one, reliable supplier among many, which could be used to keep private wholesalers on their mettle by offering to societies high-quality produce at competitive prices. It was also a strategic source of goods and support in the event of boycotts or other anti-co-operative campaigns from private traders. Loyalty was owed to the CWS, but only if it could genuinely offer supplies on terms which were competitive with private sources. Thus, from the beginning, there was a fundamental difference over what the CWS was for. It was a difference which persisted throughout the next 130 or so years of the movement's existence. At heart the movement was a federation, but given this conflict over the role of the Wholesale, a quite dysfunctional one. Moreover, it presented the CWS with a major problem which took up most of its effort and ingenuity in the years which followed: how best to secure the custom of its member societies in the face of fierce competition?

3.3   Building the CWS: The competitive 'hothouse' and the rise of a commercial giant

From the outset therefore the Wholesale had to strive to make itself a strong competitor under what were unequal circumstances. The ordinary private wholesalers faced no restrictions. They could sell to private and co-operative retailers alike, while the CWS

---

[52] 'Co-operative Societies and the Wholesale', 490.

could only sell, by the terms of its remit, to co-operative societies. It had to strive even harder than private wholesalers to win and sustain the loyalty of this more restricted clientele, for it had no alternative market to turn to. It was effectively 'hothoused': placed in a context of artificially heightened competition which made survival and success more difficult to achieve, and innovation absolutely essential. The Wholesale proved remarkably resourceful in meeting this challenge. Between 1863 and 1890 it grew into a highly sophisticated multinational organization which engaged in a wide range of activities, including wholesaling to co-operative societies, banking, shipping, a global import business with branches across the world and the production of a wide range of commodities, including shoes, boots, biscuits, textiles, pottery, and soap. It became a major employer, with a sophisticated hierarchy of workers, from highly skilled accountants, buyers, engineers, and experts in specified commodities, to warehouse and factory workers. All this was driven by the need to win as much of the commerce of co-operative societies as possible; how this spectacular growth emerged out of strategies designed to beat off the competition will now be explored.

The success of the Wholesale is captured by the statistical evidence of spectacular growth in Table 3.1. The total individual membership of societies affiliated to the CWS rose from 18,337 in 1864 to 721,316 in 1890. Net sales grew from £51,875 in 1864 to £7,429,073 in 1890. By 1900, net sales exceeded £16 million. Net surplus (profits) rose from £306 in 1864, to £126,979 in 1890 and almost £290,000 by the end of the century. CWS leaders were constantly bullish about the organization's progress, notwithstanding concern about the CWS's share of retail societies' business. Expansion of CWS production between 1863 and 1890 was funded partly by profits and partly through capital accumulated by retail society share purchases in the CWS, which grew rapidly as new societies joined the CWS. Another source was deposits in the CWS Bank by retail societies, together with accumulating reserves. The capital resources of the CWS grew from £40,658 in 1870, to £1,474, 466 in 1890, and made possible rapid expansion of the Wholesale's international trade and its development of production.[53]

How did the CWS effect such a rapid growth in its business? What role did its leaders play in this successful expansion? How were the management structures of the CWS developed to enable it to run what was an increasingly diverse and international organization? Moreover, how did the CWS's phenomenal growth impact upon its wider relations with other emergent national co-operative bodies such as the SCWS and the Co-operative Union? In terms of leadership, it is clear that the CWS enjoyed the advantage of several of the most energetic and resourceful business minds of the late nineteenth century. An element of caution is required here. The great strength of the CWS in this early phase of its development lay in the fact that most of its leaders had enjoyed considerable business experience in their own societies before joining the CWS, and that its decision-making was collective and subject to the regular scrutiny of the membership. As such, leadership within the CWS was a different role from that which applied in many capitalist businesses, in which individual owners or entrepreneurs 'ruled the

[53] Redfern (1913), 418–19.

Table 3.1. CWS share capital, sales and profits 1864–90

Year	No. of weeks	No. of individual members in all member societies	Share capital (£)	Net sales (£)	Net surplus (profits, £)
1864	30	18,337	2,455	51,875	306
1865		24,005	7,182	120,754	1,850
1866		31,030	10,968	175,489	2,235
1868	65	59,349	11,276	331,744	4,411
1869		74,737	14,888	412,240	4,862
1870		79,245	16,556	507,217	4,248
1871	65	89,880	19,015	677,734	7,626
1872		114,588	24,104	758,764	7,867
1873		134,276	31,352	1,153,132	11,116
1874		168,985	48,126	1,636,950	14,233
1875		198,608	60,930	1,964,829	20,684
1876		249,516	78,249	2,247,395	26,750
1877	53	276,522	94,590	2,697,366	36,979
1878		274,649	103,091	2,827,052	29,189
1879		305,161	117,657	2,705,625	34,859
1879	50	331,625	130,615	2,645,331	42,746
1880		361,523	146,061	3,339,681	42,090
1881		367,973	156,052	3,574,095	46,850
1882		404,006	171,940	4,038,238	49,658
1883		433,151	186,692	4,546,889	47,885
1884	53	459,734	207,080	4,675,371	54,491
1885		507,772	234,112	4,793,151	77,630
1886		558,104	270,679	5,223,179	83,328
1887		604,800	300,953	5,713,235	65,141
1888		634,196	318,583	6,200,074	82,490
1889	53	679,336	342,218	7,028,944	101,984
1890		721,316	434,017	7,429,073	126,979

Source: People's Year Book (1950), 131–2.

roost'. CWS leaders had to be effective communicators, able to persuade member societies and their delegates of the wisdom of CWS decisions. The democratic traditions of
the movement also demanded a spirit of egalitarianism in the day-to-day functioning
of the organization, and especially in the workings of the General Committee (or Board
of Directors as it became known). This was different from the organizational culture
which existed in many of the family-dominated and -owned businesses of the period.
Notwithstanding this caveat, two figures especially stand out in the period of rapid
growth in the later nineteenth century. Abraham Greenwood, the first President/

THE RISE OF THE CWS, 1863 TO 1890 69

Chairman of the CWS until 1870, was pivotal in the fragile early years, when building supply chains for the CWS, and also developing business with co-operative societies, were at a premium. The son of a small blanket manufacturer, Greenwood (pictured in Figure 3.3) brought a wealth of business experience and co-operative contacts to the role of Chair. He had been a member of the Rochdale Pioneers since 1846, rising quickly to its management committee. He had been instrumental in the establishment of the Rochdale Corn Mill Society, acting as its first chairman. He had also been at the heart of the Rochdale experiment in wholesaling in the 1850s.[54] This breadth of business experience equipped him with the versatility needed to turn his hand to a range of activities. As Chair of the CWS, he was prepared to become directly involved in the development of the business, and regularly acted as 'visitor' for the Board, a job which involved inspecting the CWS premises and operations in Manchester.[55] He was also prepared to take member societies to task personally if they did not pay their bills to the CWS. In December 1868 he resolved to visit the Wolverhampton society in person to ensure that they settled their account.[56] His reputation was also invaluable. In September 1865, he and another former Rochdale man, Smithies, approached the Rochdale Corn Mill Society for a loan to the CWS of £2,000.[57] Greenwood also seems to have been instrumental in securing the services of Henry Pitman of *The Co-operator* as a travelling advocate of the CWS who would visit societies all over the country.[58] In return, the CWS bought 500 copies of *The Co-operator* and distributed them among co-operative societies.[59] It was Greenwood's combination of commercial acumen and versatility and his impeccable reputation within the movement which made him an ideal first Chair. He possessed the breadth of commercial knowledge to oversee the CWS's first steps into sourcing a range of commodities, including the appointment of a butter buyer in Ireland.[60] He also commanded the respect and loyalty of co-operators across the country, helping the CWS to win new member societies. Perhaps the lasting testament to his importance was the decision in 1874 to appoint Greenwood as manager of the CWS Bank from 1874 to 1898, a period in which it became central to the cementing of relations between the CWS and many member societies, who turned to the bank for loans to develop their businesses. Greenwood was also a founder and Director of the Co-operative Insurance Company, as well as a member of the Central Board of the Co-operative Union.

The other major figure during this period was of course John Thomas Whitehead Mitchell, who was elected to the Board of the CWS in 1869, and was its Chair from 1874 until his death in 1895. As shown, this period was a remarkable one for the CWS, which

---

[54] Bonner (1961), 485–6.
[55] Minute Book 1863–8: The North of England Co-operative & Wholesale Industrial Society Ltd (27 August 1864), 24, NCA.
[56] Minute Book 1863–8 (31 December 1868), 203–5.
[57] Minute Book 1863–8 (16 September 1866), 50.
[58] Minute Book 1863–8 (3 June 1865), 44–5.
[59] Minute Book 1863–8 (7 June 1865), 45–6.
[60] Minute Book 1863–8 (12 May 1866), 66.

FIGURE 3.3. **Abraham Greenwood (1824–1911).** Born in Rochdale, Greenwood was an early member of the Rochdale Pioneers' society, helping to develop its educational activities and its wholesaling efforts. He chaired the committee that established the CWS, and became its first president. Greenwood left the Board to become the CWS's first bank manager in 1874, retiring in 1898.

saw it develop into a banker, shipper, producer, employer, and international commercial presence. Inevitably, Mitchell (pictured in Figure 3.4) was the focus of much contemporary interest, as well as subsequently from historians. The son of a domestic servant, Mitchell worked in a cotton mill at the age of 10. He grew up to be devoutly Christian and a supporter of the Temperance movement, which underpinned his lifelong commitment to co-operation. A bachelor, Mitchell's life was consumed by his involvement in co-operation. He joined the Rochdale Pioneers in 1853, rising to the management committee in 1856. He was elected onto the CWS Board in 1869, and onto the Central Board in 1872, becoming a major force in the deliberations of the Co-operative Union. One of the difficulties which all national co-operative leaders were to face from the late 1860s onwards was how to rally and unite a movement with numerous separate national bodies, some of which claimed leadership of the movement in their own right. The 1860s saw the foundation of the Co-operative Insurance Company (1867), the Scottish Co-operative Wholesale Society (SCWS—1868), and, following a series of national congresses late in the decade, the Central Board in 1870—a body which gradually became known as the Co-operative Union over the next two decades, culminating in its official registration as such in 1889 under the Industrial and Provident Societies Act.[61] The Co-operative Union evolved into the political voice and debating forum of the movement, and societies joined and held a democratic voice in it, much in the same way as

[61] Bonner (1961), 81–3.

FIGURE 3.4. J. T. W. Mitchell (1828–95). Another Rochdale man, Mitchell was connected with the Rochdale Pioneers' society from 1853, was elected to the CWS Board in 1869, and replaced Greenwood as its president in 1874. He was pivotal to many CWS developments, notably its entry into manufacturing, the growth of its overseas supply operations, and its strong support for the Manchester Ship Canal, which opened the year before Mitchell's death (see Figure 4.11).

they did in the CWS. As such it became a rival centre of potential national leadership in the 1870s and 1880s. Its annual Congresses became especially important for providing a platform for debates, while the Co-operative Union, with its own regional representative structures and permanent officials, became crucial in promoting the spread of co-operation and in providing national support for educational initiatives. In the long run, as the CWS became larger and wealthier, this would lead to friction between the two bodies, as each developed their own ideas about the best way forward for the movement. But for much of the period from the 1870s to the 1890s, relations between the two bodies were reasonably amicable and collaborative, with close joint work in the field of promoting the spread of co-operation through the joint propaganda committee. This was helped greatly by the presence on both bodies of Mitchell and other senior CWS figures. However, it could not prevent, in the long run, a growing tension and even struggle for dominance between the two bodies, as will be clear in subsequent chapters.[62] There was also successful collaboration between the CWS and SCWS, which increasingly worked together in the tea trade through a special joint committee, and in relations with the CWS's overseas branches.

---

[62] See sections 4.5 and 5.3.

Mitchell gained a reputation as the leading advocate of consumer co-operation as the principal form to be pursued in Britain, with the CWS, as well as the Co-operative Union, being a prominent force shaping the development of the movement. In this capacity he became a critic of those, like Neale and Thomas Hughes, who argued for a more traditional version of co-operation, which laid particular emphasis upon independent producer co-operatives, and in the creation of some kind of partnership between CWS and its employees.[63] He was branded by some, such as Beatrice Webb, the eminent Fabian Socialist, as the dominant figure on the Board, with a concern principally for the commercial success of the CWS rather than the development of co-operation as a coherent ideology or alternative to the capitalist system.[64] Webb's rather patronizing account of Mitchell's simple working-class personal style, and her description of him and his board as 'neither more nor less than simple tradesman', has been fiercely contested by Stephen Yeo, who demonstrates convincingly that Mitchell had a real grasp of how British society and economy might be transformed by consumer co-operation, and how such a system could reconcile divisions between people as consumers and producers. For Yeo, Mitchell was an idealist with a real sense of the moral purpose of co-operation, but one with a hard-headed grasp of the realities of survival in the face of hostile capitalist competitors. This was certainly evident in Mitchell's active promotion of the CWS's growing involvement in production and in his support of the internationalization of its activities; and in his support for the professionalization of the CWS's growing body of specialist managers. It was also the case that Mitchell was a powerful personality who was unafraid of confrontation with his opponents. His exhaustive involvement in the day-to-day work of the various subcommittees of the General Committee which supervised the work of the CWS strongly suggests that he was a powerful and active influence in the organization's development. But such a conclusion should be tempered by recognition that as the CWS got bigger, and as more societies joined, its management became even more of a collective enterprise. Elected members in Manchester, Newcastle, and London were joined by a growing army of professional managers employed by the CWS in shaping the organization's policy and business strategy, and all of course, were answerable to frequently boisterous and challenging quarterly meetings in Manchester and the main branches. In this respect, the CWS was never subject to the type of central, personal leadership evident in so many mainstream capitalist organizations.

Indeed the managerial structure of the CWS had to evolve rapidly to meet the demands of its burgeoning commercial empire. Throughout the period to 1890, the central executive body was the General Committee, increasingly referred to as the Board of Directors, consisting of twelve directors, elected annually by the quarterly general meeting of delegates from member societies. With the creation of the Newcastle and London branches, there were effectively three separate quarterly meetings, one in Manchester, and one each in London and Newcastle which took place the week before the Manchester event, and

---

[63] Cole (1944), 168.   [64] Yeo (1995), 26–7.

which were attended by delegates from the societies within the branch's region (see Figure 3.5). Quarterly meetings were frequently lively events, at which the judgement of the Board was challenged, and issues of the day debated at great length. The *Co-operative News* covered many of the heated arguments about a range of issues, from directors' travel expenses to more fundamental questions such as how to spread co-operation success-fully to the increasingly fraught question of the relationship between producer and con-sumer co-operation. It meant that the Board had to constantly keep an eye on political developments in the movement, and the quarterly meetings became the focus of some major personal rivalries, most notably between James Crabtree and J. T. W. Mitchell in the 1870s.[65] But within this constraint, the Board proved a remarkably efficient tool for overseeing the development of a growing, national organization. It accomplished this through two main devices. First, the Board delegated much of its detailed work to a series of subcommittees tasked with direction of specific areas of CWS activity. By 1880, there were committees for Finance, Grocery and Provisions, Shipping, and Drapery.[66] The Finance Committee became central to overseeing not only the general financial affairs of the CWS, but more specifically the work of the CWS Bank. The rather innocuously named Grocery and Provisions Committee was central to the whole organization's operations. It not only took charge of procuring supplies and liaising with the fast-developing produc-tive centres of the CWS, it also supervised most of the CWS's relations with its overseas branches. The Drapery Committee grew in importance as the CWS became more heavily involved in textile manufacturing and the supply of cloth and similar products to local societies; while the Shipping Committee rose with the development of the CWS fleet. Other subcommittees were established to deal with specific issues from time to time. As most subcommittees consisted of three or four directors, each of the directors gained very thorough experience and understanding of major aspects of CWS business. The Chair in particular was very active on a day-to-day basis in several of the more important commit-tees (especially Finance), which accounts in part for Mitchell's reputation as an especially effective leader. When the Newcastle and London branches (see Figure 3.6) were estab-lished, 'mirror' versions of these subcommittees were set up there—but these (as with the General Committees in the branches) remained subordinate to the Manchester Head Office Board and subcommittees, even if, from time to time, they tried to challenge deci-sions from there which they did not like. Secondly, as will be seen, the CWS proved adept not only at appointing and developing some highly capable managers as employees, they were also integrated very successfully into the working of the General and Subcommittees, frequently attending meetings of these bodies to offer expert advice. Full-time employees (such as London branch manager Ben Jones, shown in Figure 3.7) and elected Board members became accustomed to working side by side, and frequently visited local co-operative societies together as part of their duties, ensuring that both possessed a good working knowledge of the CWS's market. It was, in many ways, an ideal blend of political/elected leadership and employed professional expertise. Some of the more important

---

[65] Yeo (1995), 16–17.

[66] CWS General Committee minutes (18 September 1880), Vol. 6, 1–5.

managers were also supported by substantial departments, with additional clerical and other staff to support them. There was, for example, a substantial Tea and Coffee Department based in London which ran this part of the business under the direction of Charles Fielding, the highly remunerated professional manager. Thus, over time, the CWS managed to build a quite efficient democratic structure, which was nonetheless able to respond effectively to the market and the demands of business efficiency. It proved responsive to the demands of member societies both at quarterly meetings and, insofar as this was possible in light of the fierce commercial independence of retail co-operative societies, in terms of supplies of CWS produce.

The key to much of the CWS's success was in its recruitment and development of employees at the cutting edge of the business: in dealing directly with the retail societies. From the start it was clear that the CWS would need skilled personnel if it was to succeed in winning the custom of co-operative societies. In particular it was vital to secure the services of a skilled buyer who could not only identify good quality produce and negotiate good prices, but who also understood the needs and wants of co-operative society managers and buyers to whom he would have to sell. Within a fortnight of being formed the North of England Co-operative & Wholesale Industrial Society Ltd (as the CWS was first called) tried to head hunt the Rochdale Pioneers' senior buyer, a move

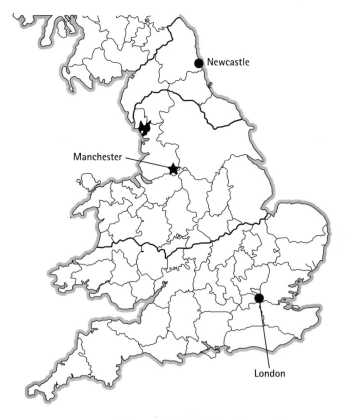

FIGURE 3.5. Map of CWS districts, 1874–1936.

FIGURE 3.6. **CWS London branch, 1881.** Although its first London premises were at 118 Minories East, in 1879 CWS purchased land near Leman Street, fronting Hooper Square and Rupert Street in East London. Mitchell and Hughes laid the foundation stone for the building, above, which was completed in early 1881.

beaten off by the latter increasing the man's salary to top the Wholesale's offer.[67] After working with a stop-gap, a recruitment drive in early 1864 resulted in the appointment of Mr Simpson on an annual salary of £200. Over 200 people were interviewed in the process.[68] There was a high turnover of buyers in the 1860s, in what was a very competitive retail management environment.[69] However, by the early 1870s a strong team of buyers had been assembled by the names of Kay, Cockshaw, Pearson, and Heyes. They played a vital role in the early expansion of the business.[70] The emerging role of buyer was both complex and pivotal for the whole organization. They were essential intermediaries

[67] Minute Book 1863–8 (7 and 21 November 1863), 3–4.
[68] Minute Book 1863–8 (16 and 28 January 1864), 10–12.
[69] Redfern (1913), 35.
[70] CWS Grocery and Provisions Committee minutes (1 April 1874), 3–6.

FIGURE 3.7. **Benjamin Jones (1847–1942).** First employed by CWS in Manchester as an assistant bookkeeper in 1866, Jones rose through the ranks to head the London branch from 1874 to 1902. During his tenure he helped promote co-operative development in London and oversaw the expansion of the CWS in southern England and Wales. He was present for the opening of the original Rochdale Pioneers' store as a museum in 1931.

between the processes of ascertaining society demands in terms of price and quality of produce, and ensuring that procurement met these requirements. They bought for the CWS, travelled around societies to promote CWS goods, and dealt with complaints. They reported directly to the Grocery and Provisions Committee, a subcommittee of the Board manned by elected Board members, and in this capacity came to shape many aspects of CWS strategy both in managing relations with societies and in developing systems of procurement.

Of crucial importance was personal contact with retail society committees and managers, a fact acknowledged by the Grocery Committee in July 1876 when it appointed a Mr John Andrews as travelling salesman for the department. Andrews's remit was to spend his days travelling around retail societies in Lancashire, Yorkshire, and the Midlands.[71] Travellers and buyers were also appointed for the subsidiary CWS branches established in Newcastle and London in the 1870s, and for some of the larger depots established across the country in the following decades. These men were the eyes and ears of the Wholesale. They experienced at first hand the attitudes to the CWS of retail society managers and activists, and as such were the single most important source of commercial intelligence for the organization. They reported to the Grocery Committee

[71] CWS Grocery and Provisions Committee minutes 2/0/1 (1 July 1876), 53.

about complaints, attitudes to CWS produce, and information about the activities of rival wholesalers. Andrews was to prove a tireless champion of CWS interests in the North during the late 1870s. For example, in just one month between 7 November and 7 December 1877 Andrews visited societies in Hyde, Ashton, Todmorden, Bradford, Great Horton, Bingley, Keighley, Windhill, Rochdale, Lancaster, Ulverston, Dalton, Preston, Batley, and Wakefield, securing many orders as he went. At Preston he persuaded the manager to shift his orders for tea from a Manchester firm to the CWS.[72] Occasionally he encountered resistance bordering on hostility. On a tour of east Lancashire societies in May 1878 he found the Bury Society utterly obdurate in matters concerning the CWS:

At Bury no impression can be made on them to purchase from the Wholesale. Only now and then an order is given by the manager for Burys blacking. At nearly all the other societies he got an order but only for small lots.[73]

But his fortunes picked up later in the month as he progressed into Yorkshire and Derbyshire, visiting societies in Huddersfield, Bradford, and Glossop, picking up orders for the CWS from some societies for the very first time.[74] At times, one suspects that Andrews must have felt like a missionary for the Wholesale. He certainly had to listen to complaints about the price or alleged shortcomings of CWS produce. In February 1879, at Lane Dyehouse Society in Huddersfield he was harangued with complaints stretching back two or three years.[75] Andrews and other CWS travellers were barometers of opinion and economic welfare in retail societies, and important in alerting the CWS to the activities of competitors. Thus in December 1878 he reported that societies in east Lancashire were struggling desperately because of the economic downturn and that private merchants were giving sugar away free to societies which ordered substantial amounts of tea and coffee from them.[76] Three months later, he reported that members of societies in east Lancashire were withdrawing their money because of continuing economic hardship.[77] Andrews's successors continued these vital functions of salesmen and intelligence gatherers. In August 1886 Mr Turner, a CWS traveller, reported that a number of societies in the West Midlands were so desperate for money that there was a real danger that they would turn to 'some pushing wholesale grocer' who would undercut the CWS and win their trade.[78] Some reports from buyers revealed worrying trends in society behaviour. Thus in October 1887 it was reported that many societies were being compelled by competition from private shopkeepers to increase their sales and purchases of butterine.[79] Little wonder then that the position of CWS traveller was well

[72] CWS Grocery and Provisions Committee minutes 2/0/1 (7 November 1877), 215; (14 November 1877), 216; (7 December 1877), 226.
[73] CWS Grocery and Provisions Committee minutes 2/0/1 (8 May 1878), 290.
[74] CWS Grocery and Provisions Committee minutes 2/0/1 (15 May 1879), 293; (12 June 1878), 304.
[75] CWS Grocery and Provisions Committee minutes 2/0/2 (26 February 1879), 41.
[76] CWS Grocery and Provisions Committee minutes 2/0/2 (27 December 1878), 12.
[77] CWS Grocery and Provisions Committee minutes 2/0/2 (27 March 1879), 54.
[78] CWS Grocery and Provisions Committee minutes 2/0/6 (26 August 1886), 180–2.
[79] CWS Grocery and Provisions Committee minutes 2/0/7 (5 October 1887), 98.

remunerated and widely coveted. In January 1884 there were no fewer than 78 applications for one position as traveller, including ten from within the CWS itself. The lucky candidate, a Mr Turner, was offered an initial salary of £120 per annum.[80] In fact this role of intelligence gatherer hardly changed in almost a hundred years. The CWS statement to the Independent Co-operative Commission in 1956 still stressed the importance of travellers' visits to societies in ensuring that relations with the Wholesale were as harmonious as possible.[81]

Another method of promoting the CWS in the eyes of retail societies was the physical development of CWS premises in Manchester, Newcastle, and London. These were more than mere places of business; they were statements of the organization's wealth, sophistication, and unique commercial values. The headquarters in Manchester (see Figure 3.8) in particular became a showcase for the Wholesale, impressing representatives from societies to quarterly meetings with the opulence and grandeur of the CWS. Societies across the country organized tours to visit the CWS premises in Manchester[82] From the late 1870s, retail society buyers were wined and dined for free in the CWS's Manchester headquarters.[83] By 1880 the 'co-operative quarter' in Manchester was emerging, trumpeting the success of the CWS through architecture. CWS branches in Newcastle, London, and elsewhere followed suit, imposing a physical presence for the CWS on the nation's urban landscape.

Inevitably, the CWS tried to win the loyalty of retail societies by appealing to them ideologically. Only by remaining loyal to the CWS, it was argued, could the co-operative movement develop into a viable alternative system to free market capitalism. CWS leaders repeatedly claimed loyalty to the Wholesale was central to the creation of the 'Co-operative Commonwealth'; a society and economy organized on co-operative principles. This was stressed by CWS Board members, employees, and supporters, at co-operative events, meetings, conferences, talks to societies, and through the pages of *Co-operative News* and other publications. The creation of the 'Co-operative Commonwealth', it was argued, was contingent upon the CWS becoming the central commercial organization of the movement. Societies were condemned as 'anti-co-operative' if they sourced their supplies on the open market, and disloyalty to CWS was frequently depicted as disloyalty to co-operation in general.[84] On the other hand, buying from CWS was seen as the best way of 'weakening the resistance to a greater extension of our principles'.[85] But as seen, many local societies rejected this

---

[80] CWS Grocery and Provisions Committee minutes 2/o/4 (21 January 1884), 360–1; (29 January 1884), 366–7.

[81] Statement of the CWS to the Independent Co-operative Commission, 6. See also section 6.4.

[82] For example, 50 members of the Oxford Society were entertained to a 'knife and fork tea' at the CWS on 13 August 1887, only one of many such visits by societies from around the country. CWS General Committee minutes (5 August 1887), Vol. 11, 294.

[83] CWS Grocery and Provisions Committee minutes 2/o/1, Special Meeting of the Grocery and Provisions Committee (23 July 1878), 247.

[84] Editorial, 'The Trade of the Wholesale', *Co-operative News* (8 April 1876), 175.

[85] Editorial, 'The Trade of the Wholesale', *Co-operative News* (3 July 1875), 354.

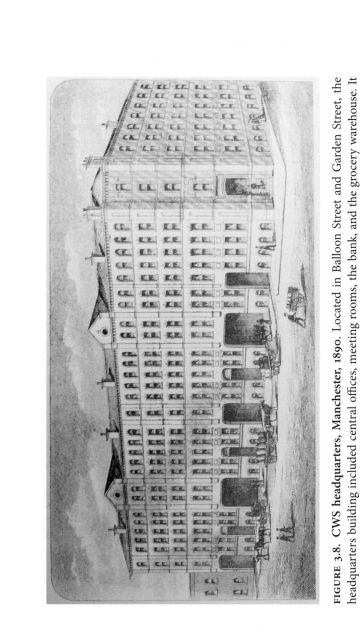

FIGURE 3.8. CWS headquarters, Manchester, 1890. Located in Balloon Street and Garden Street, the headquarters building included central offices, meeting rooms, the bank, and the grocery warehouse. It was replaced by new headquarters in the early twentieth century (see Figure 4.19).

argument. They asserted that co-operation was best served by obtaining produce as cheaply as possible on the open market, in which the CWS would have to compete. In the end, CWS demands for society loyalty cut little ice, because there was little agreement about what exactly the role of the CWS should be.

Such differences about the role of the CWS extended into other areas. One particular source of friction was the relationship of the CWS and consumer co-operation with the numerous producer co-operatives beginning to spring up at this time. The Wholesale saw itself as a commercial intermediary between producer and consumer co-operatives, purchasing goods from the former to sell to the latter. It also tried to help producer co-operatives by providing loans and credit through the CWS Bank. In the 1870s, there were a number of experimental co-operatives in coal mines and engineering, possibly the most famous of which was the Ouseburn Engineering Works on Tyneside.[86] But during the 1870s and early 1880s CWS relationships with producer co-operatives proved problematic. The difficult economic climate of the 1870s wreaked havoc among a number of producer societies, and major flagship enterprises such as Ouseburn failed disastrously. As a major creditor for some of these societies, the CWS found itself drawn into taking some of these organizations over, when it became clear that they were unable to settle their debts to the Wholesale. The CWS lost large amounts in defaulted loans, and some were compounded by further losses following CWS takeover. The Wholesale was hit hard in this way in a number of coal mines.[87] Then in June 1881 the CWS was forced to write off £32,000 of debts. Many member retail societies were infuriated by what they saw as financial imprudence on the part of the CWS and the fundamentally unsound basis of producer co-operative organization. There was even a brief attempt by some retail societies to prohibit CWS loans to producer societies, and though this was defeated, the legacy of the spat was a longstanding division and tension between producer and consumer co-operatives which lasted to the second half of the twentieth century.[88] Thus the CWS could not lead by ideological persuasion alone.

Problems in supporting producer co-operatives were related to another emerging strategy for winning the custom of retail societies: the growth of the CWS as a major manufacturer in its own right. An increasingly important principle which underpinned CWS thinking was the notion of vertically integrating the Wholesale's operations to take it as close as possible to the point of production. The logical implication of this was the CWS's move in the early 1870s into making goods themselves. This was seen not only as a way of minimizing costs, but also as a way of maximizing quality. The CWS opened its first factory in Crumpsall, Manchester, in January 1873, producing sweets and biscuits

---

[86] Bonner (1961), 106–7.

[87] In 1878 CWS lost £7,351 0s. 3d. on loans and investments in the Eccleshill Coal Company. Minutes of General & Branch quarterly Meetings, December 1878, Committee's report (printed), CWS General Committee minutes, Vol. 5, 69–74.

[88] Minutes of General Quarterly Meeting, Manchester (18 June 1881), CWS General Committee minutes, Vol. 6, 143–4; also motion to quarterly general meeting of CWS (18 June 1881) adopted by the Newcastle branch, 'That in future no loans or overdrafts be allowed to other than distributive co-operative societies or to societies whose shares are held by such societies'.

FIGURE 3.9. **CWS biscuit works, Crumpsall, 1890.** One of the first factories established by the CWS in 1873, in 1890 the Crumpsall works produced biscuits, sweets, jams, and marmalade, as well as dry and soft soap for the Manchester district.

(see Figure 3.9). Also in 1873 it commenced shoe and boot production in Leicester. So promising did the latter prove that in 1880 the CWS opened a second footwear factory in Yorkshire, in Heckmondwike. Soap production began at the CWS Durham Soap Works in 1874 (see Figure 3.10). After over a decade of steadily increasing production, and many battles to secure the custom of retail societies for CWS produce, a second wave of productive innovation followed in 1887–8. A woollen mill was opened at Batley in Yorkshire and the CWS built upon its solid trade in coffee and tea by moving into cocoa production.[89] In the 1890s, the CWS implemented a programme of expansion to build upon and develop this earlier foray into manufacturing. It custom-built a large flour mill at Dunston, Newcastle on Tyne, and opened a new soap works at Irlam in Manchester, with access to the Manchester Ship Canal.[90] By the end of the century the Wholesale had opened a factory to process tobacco (Manchester). It was only a beginning. The twentieth century saw a massive expansion of CWS activity into agriculture, as well as the further expansion of industrial production.[91]

The CWS travellers enthusiastically promoted Wholesale products, seeking to improve quality whenever possible. CWS industrial managers and buyers often visited private manufacturers in search of the latest and most efficient production methods and

---

[89] Jones (1894), i. 218–19.   [90] Redfern (1913), 427–8.   [91] See sections 4.3 and 4.4.

FIGURE 3.10. CWS soap works, Durham, 1890. In 1874, the CWS purchased a former candle factory and converted it into its first soap works. By 1890, it produced more than twenty varieties of soap, including 'Wheatsheaf' and 'Congress' soap tablets.

technologies.[92] But progress was not without difficulty, although there was an overall increase in sales between the 1870s and 1890. Leicester boot and shoe sales rose from £91,985 (368,964 pairs) in 1883 to £172,266 (747,563 pairs) in 1889.[93] In 1890 this success led to the relocation of the Leicester works to a larger site.[94] Sales of Crumpsall produce grew from *c.* £20,000–25,000 in 1883 to *c.* £41,000 in 1889. Durham soap sales rose from £14,751 for 1883 to £24,643 by 1889.[95] CWS officials were extremely concerned about quality, and this was particularly evident in the tea and coffee department. In its first years the CWS acquired tea and coffee through a London tea merchant, Joseph Woodin, who had a reputation for pro-co-operative sympathies. But a growing conviction that the CWS would serve societies best by entering specialist trades in its own capacity prompted in November 1882 the foundation of the CWS tea department.[96] The Wholesale took scrupulous care in efforts to find the best possible leadership for the department. In

---

[92] For example, in June 1876 Pearson went with the manager of the CWS Durham soap works to the soap factories of Crossfields and Goodwins, and was able to report back that much had been learnt to improve quality. CWS Grocery and Provisions Committee minutes 2/0/1 (1 July 1876), 53.

[93] Figures from quarterly reports of the CWS for this period, held in CWS General Committee minutes.

[94] Printed report of CWS presented to the quarterly meetings (November and December 1889), in CWS General Committee minutes, Vol. 15, 41.

[95] Figures from quarterly reports of the CWS for this period, held in CWS General Committee minutes.

[96] Report on CWS meeting with Woodin and his sons, 16 October 1880, in CWS General Committee minutes, Vol. 6, 25; Redfern (1913), 426.

July 1882 a special committee, chaired by J. T. W. Mitchell himself, interviewed eight men of wide and impressive experience for the post.[97] The successful candidate, Charles Fielding, was highly experienced and commanded impressive remuneration. By 1890 he was the highest-paid CWS employee in Britain, at £1,000 per annum, matched only by the CWS manager in New York, John Gledhill.[98] Fielding faced a tough challenge to satisfy the diverse range of co-operative society tastes in tea. In response, by 1890 the CWS employed 300 people to supply 350 different blends of tea.[99] Tea sales grew from 3,199,111 lbs (£287,344) in 1884, to 5,785,406 lbs (£476,109) in 1889. Coffee sales rose from 759,490 lbs (£39,541) in 1884 to 1,113,234 lbs (£61,539) in 1889.[100] Fielding was quite prepared to accompany CWS travellers to meet retail society committees and buyers in an effort to promote CWS tea and to gather information about how to blend tea to meet local tastes. Thus in September 1885 he visited societies in Haslingden, Warrington, Runcorn, and Ramsbottom to promote CWS tea. In Haslingden he had a long debate with the committee about the respective qualities of Hornimans and CWS tea.[101] The general pattern was that most CWS productive branches were profitable, albeit with occasional quarterly losses. One exception in the period was textile production at Batley Mill, which returned several years of unacceptable losses. In response, the CWS showed that it was no more prepared to tolerate failure than were most private commercial enterprises. In August 1889 it forced Mr Hall, the Batley Mill manager, to resign.[102] There are many other examples of such ruthlessness in the CWS records. The CWS was also aware that it was in charge of distinctive brands to rival those of private producers. In November 1886 Irwen Brothers of Liverpool asked the CWS for permission to use the Wheatsheaf trademark on their hams, and were briskly rejected by the CWS.[103] Then in June 1890 it was approached by the private firm Krienger & Co. who wanted to use a logo closely similar to the CWS Wheatsheaf trademark. Again the CWS refused.[104] The Wholesale was no less jealous of brand in its dealings with co-operative societies. They even stopped the Oxford Co-operative Society using it on their bags of pastry flour.[105]

A major problem for what was essentially Britain's first major national wholesaling organization was the relatively high cost of long-distance land transport by rail, in a period before the emergence of modern road transport. Rail freight charges added substantially to the price of CWS goods. This was compounded by the costs of transporting

---

[97] CWS Grocery & Provisions Committee minutes 2/0/4, Special Sub Committee appointed to appoint a tea buyer (29 July 1882), 5–8.

[98] List of salary rises from 18 February 1889, Minutes of Joint Committee of CWS branches and SCWS (5 March 1889), in CWS General Committee minutes, Vol. 13, 415.

[99] *CWS Annual* (1892), 460–7.

[100] Figures from quarterly reports of the CWS for this period, held in CWS General Committee minutes.

[101] CWS Grocery & Provisions Committee minutes 2/0/5, Special Committee Meeting (28 September 1885), 332.

[102] CWS General Committee minutes (23 August 1889), Vol. 14, 289.

[103] CWS Grocery & Provisions Committee minutes 2/0/5 (4 November 1885), 363.

[104] CWS General Committee minutes (13 June 1890), Vol. 15, 400.

[105] CWS General Committee minutes (18 January 1889), Vol. 13, 317.

goods from rail head to store. For more remote locations, this could be a serious problem. Cumberland and the Lake District was one such area. In response to complaints about rail carriage costs in May 1886, Tweedale and Lobb, senior buyers for CWS, visited societies in Westmorland, Cumberland, and Furness.[106] Their solution initially proved to be controversial. They decided to route flour from Germany to these districts by private shipping line from Hamburg to Liverpool, and then by private coasting vessel from Liverpool to Whitehaven, Maryport, Barrow, and Ulverston. The CWS Grocery Committee initially objected to this arrangement, as CWS ran its own shipping line between Goole and Hamburg, and would have expected flour to be routed from Goole by rail to the north-west. But it was forced to concede that Tweedale and Lobb had an unshakable justification for their strategy. It cost 9s. 2d. to transport a ton of flour from Hamburg to Liverpool by non-CWS vessel, well in excess of the 5s. 2d. per ton charged on the CWS Goole–Hamburg Line. But costs of rail carriage wiped out the CWS's advantage completely. It cost 14s. 2d. per ton to transport flour by rail from Goole to the Lake District, compared to just 4s. 6d. per ton by private vessel from Liverpool to the north-western ports. The example showed just how severe the problem of carriage costs could be.[107] Even at a local level, the CWS found it difficult at times to secure transport at the right price. In 1877, after several years of using the firm of Carvers in Liverpool, the CWS decided to put carting of their goods out to tender.[108] But they struggled to find an alternative, and Carvers ended up with the contract until 1888, when it was put out to tender and was won by Binnie & Co.[109] Binnie and Sons were then dismissed in 1890 for trying to increase the freight rate to 1s. per ton.[110] A further effort to contract out carting in Liverpool ended with a Messrs Hall & Co. agreeing to cart at 11s. 5d. per ton.[111] CWS Liverpool was also deeply dissatisfied with the high warehousing charges imposed by the Lancashire & Yorkshire Railway at North Dock in the city, and they negotiated fiercely to drive these down, though with only limited success. High carriage costs were frequently cited by retail societies for buying elsewhere than the Wholesale. Some argued that the CWS should follow the example of some private traders and deliver goods carriage paid, as did the South East London Co-operative Baking Society in June 1890.[112] As always, the CWS refused on the grounds that the cost of doing so would be ruinous. In 1889, the London branch acquired stables to do its own carting around the city.[113] In the same year, the Long Eaton Society in Nottinghamshire spoke for many when it grumbled about the unreliability of CWS deliveries.[114] The cost of carriage

---

[106] CWS Grocery & Provisions Committee minutes 2/0/6 (26 May 1886), 90.

[107] CWS Grocery & Provisions Committee minutes 2/0/6 (9 June 1886), 111.

[108] CWS Grocery & Provisions Committee minutes 2/0/1 (15 December 1877), 231.

[109] CWS Grocery & Provisions Committee minutes 2/0/7 (23 April 1888), 308–9.

[110] CWS General Committee minutes (24 January and 7 February 1890), Vol. 15, 137 and 162.

[111] CWS General Committee minutes (7 March 1890), Vol. 15, 225.

[112] Letter from the Committee of the SE London Co-operative Baking Society, *Co-operative News* (25 June 1890), 687.

[113] Printed report presented to the quarterly meetings of Manchester and the London and Newcastle branches (August/September 1889), in CWS General Committee minutes, Vol. 14, 320.

[114] Conference at Long Eaton, 25 October 1890, in *Co-operative News* (1 November 1890), 1102.

problem was never entirely overcome in this period. An important initiative to improve transport nationally was the decision by the CWS to become major shareholders in the Manchester Ship Canal.[115] It also haggled with the railway companies over terms of carriage. When in 1889 the railway companies tried to get parliamentary approval for their freight rate increases and the reclassification of goods, the CWS objected in the strongest terms.[116]

Probably the most effective of the CWS's responses to this was to open major subsidiary branches in Newcastle (1871, see Figure 3.11) and London (1874), and later a series of depots across the country, thereby reducing the problem of distance.[117] These soon came to emulate the splendour and architectural presence of the 'co-operative quarter' in Manchester. By the end of the 1870s it was clear that many more local depots or salesrooms would be needed. In June 1881, a meeting of CWS shareholders in Wakefield clamoured for a Yorkshire branch. It was shown, using the CWS's own sales figures, that the further a society was from Manchester, the lower its volume of trade with the Wholesale. This was especially evident among the Yorkshire societies.[118] The CWS responded to the argument.[119] It opened a salesroom in Leeds in October 1882; some way short of the original request for a full-scale branch, but enough to dramatically improve supplies to the Yorkshire societies.[120] The CWS followed this with the establishment of depots at Bristol in September 1884, Huddersfield in August 1885 (see Figure 3.12), Nottingham in April 1886, and Blackburn in May 1890.[121] By 1893 there were also depots in Cardiff and Birmingham. In October 1885 the Western Section of the Co-operative Union in Pontypridd spoke for many Welsh societies in hoping that the Bristol depot would dramatically improve the lamentably weak trade between CWS and societies there. The situation was especially worrying. Of £179,839 of business done by 16 societies in Glamorganshire in 1883, only £1,508 was with the CWS. A similar pattern was evident across Wales and in Cornwall, Devon, Somerset, and Herefordshire, a problem which the Bristol depot was intended to rectify.[122] In time, though, the Wholesale did establish a network of outlets which could more readily respond to the needs of local societies and supply them more cheaply. Interestingly, this strategy pre-dated the branch location policies of private multiple retail chains which helped them win so much of the national market in the twentieth century.[123] Significantly, the 'command and control' management structures of the private multiple chains made it much easier for them to implement

[115] Redfern (1913), 117.
[116] Paper by T. Brodrick, 'Some objections to the proposed maximum rates and charges' to meeting of co-operative societies, Special Meeting of the General Committee, in CWS General Committee minutes (4 May 1889), Vol. 14, 88–91.
[117] Redfern (1913), 58 and 88.
[118] Report on meeting in Wakefield in June, in CWS General Committee minutes (29 July 1881), Vol. 6, 163–4.
[119] Report on meeting in Wakefield in June, 159.
[120] CWS General Committee minutes (20 October 1881), Vol. 7, 69.
[121] Redfern (1913), 426–7.
[122] Western Section Conference (15 October 1885), in Co-operative News (24 October 1885), 968.
[123] Shaw et al. (1998).

FIGURE 3.11. **CWS Newcastle branch, 1890.** Established in rented premises in 1872, in 1874 the CWS purchased land in Waterloo Street. By 1890 the premises had expanded, and there were separate drapery and furnishing warehouses nearby. Still further expansion came in 1899, with the erection of new premises in West Blandford Street, which now house Newcastle's Discovery Museum.

this policy. In contrast, the CWS had to sensitively pick its way through the competing demands of societies which controlled CWS through the organization's democratic structure. Nonetheless its efforts were usually the result of diligent research and planning. Thus in April 1886 the Nottingham salesroom's new manager designed a colour-coded map, identifying the societies close to Nottingham which would be served by his team of travelling salesmen.[124]

Perhaps the most striking effect of the enormous pressure to win custom was the expansion overseas of the CWS's procurement activities. This began with the establishment of butter buying agents in Ireland in the early 1870s, and the opening of branches/depots in Ireland (Limerick 1868, Armagh and Waterford 1873, Tralee 1874, and Cork 1877). Overseas branches were intended to reduce dependence on middlemen in importing produce. High brokers' commission charges forced CWS buyers to buy larger quantities of produce than immediately demanded by retail societies, in order to

---

[124] CWS General Committee minutes (16 April 1886), Vol. 10, 64.

FIGURE 3.12. CWS saleroom, Huddersfield, 1909. Established in 1885, the Huddersfield sale-room was part of the CWS's expanding domestic distribution network. It operated from rented premises until 1904, when the saleroom took over the former CWS brush works buildings (shown here) at Upperhead Row and Spring Street.

get favourable terms. This resulted in the build up of excessive stocks in ports such as Liverpool, which then had to be sold at a loss to non-co-operative buyers.[125] The CWS became so dissatisfied with the arrangements with Liverpool brokers that they prohib-ited the use of brokers entirely, and sacked two buyers when they disobeyed this instruction.[126] As a result of such problems, the CWS's overseas activities quickly expanded into a global operation.[127] In the early 1870s, it began dealings with the USA and Canada through local agents.[128] So promising were these that as early as April 1874 the CWS was already considering the appointment of a permanent buyer across the Atlantic.[129] In September 1875 it decided to establish a full branch in New York.[130] In November, John Gledhill, a fast rising young buyer was appointed to lead it, on a lucra-tive salary of £550 per annum, a sum which signalled the Wholesale's seriousness about its American enterprise.[131] New York quickly began to supply cheese, bacon, lard, ham,

[125] CWS Grocery and Provisions Committee minutes 2/0/1 (30 May 1877), 155.
[126] Special meeting of the Grocery and Provisions Committee (13 September 1880), and meeting (December 1880), in CWS Grocery and Provisions Committee minutes 2/0/3, 13 and 68.
[127] CWS Grocery & Provisions Committee minutes (unnumbered) 1874–5, 3–6.
[128] CWS Grocery & Provisions Committee minutes (1 April 1874), 11.
[129] CWS Grocery & Provisions Committee minutes.
[130] CWS Grocery & Provisions Committee minutes (16 September 1875), 170.
[131] CWS Grocery & Provisions Committee minutes (3 November 1875), 175–6.

tinned meats, flour, and other foodstuffs to societies in Scotland as well as England and Wales. In September 1876 Gledhill made an ominous observation to the Board in Manchester: to get the best prices on American produce in many cases he would have to purchase quantities in excess of CWS demand for them, implying that it might be pragmatic for the Wholesale to make exceptions to the general rule that it should only sell to co-operative organizations. The Board gave him permission to proceed.[132] Thus within a few years, the CWS branch in New York came to supply and deal with numerous non-co-operative organizations in Britain. By 1882, the lard firm, Kilverts, were using the CWS to import hog fats from the USA, which were sourced in Chicago.[133] In July 1885 the CWS agreed to supply the Liverpool firm of Fowlers and a Mr Marples with American cheese.[134] At the end of that month they established a similar relationship with Dixon & Co. of Manchester.[135] Gledhill commended not just the commissions this work generated, but also the market knowledge gained through working on this basis. It also enabled him to buy larger quantities of commodities, thereby facilitating the negotiation of better prices.[136] By December 1886, the New York branch was supplying several British companies with sugar purchased in New York, including the major firm of McFie's in Liverpool.[137] The branch also shipped resin for the firm of Goodwin Bros in 1888.[138]

Under Gledhill's leadership the CWS became an important international player among New York's merchants and brokers. In March 1882, Abraham Hodgson & Sons and D. H. Lewis of New York were asking him to arrange for quotations of cheese prices in Liverpool to be cabled daily to the Butter, Cheese & Egg Exchange in New York. He agreed to do this for a fee.[139] On 21 June of that year, Gledhill was elected as a manager on the New York Produce Exchange (see Figure 3.13), sweeping the board with 1,328 votes out of a possible 1,612.[140] In the following January Gledhill even moved the headquarters of the New York CWS branch into the Produce Exchange Building.[141] In June 1888, Gledhill's deputy, Percival, was also elected as a manager on the Produce Exchange.[142] CWS New York strove hard to negotiate the best deals, using the basic co-operative principle of dealing with those as close to the point of production as possible, thereby reducing intermediary costs. Thus in June 1883, with the agreement of the Board, Gledhill sought to buy tinned meat from packing firms rather than the brokers in New York with whom he normally dealt.[143] He was not successful, but clearly the New York branch was

---

[132] CWS Grocery & Provisions Committee 2/0/1 (27 September 1876), 78.
[133] CWS Grocery & Provisions Committee 2/0/1 (5 April 1882), 311.
[134] CWS Grocery & Provisions Committee 2/0/5 (1 July 1885), 264–5.
[135] CWS Grocery & Provisions Committee 2/0/5 (30 July 1885), 287–8.
[136] CWS Grocery & Provisions Committee 2/0/5 (30 July 1885), 285.
[137] CWS Grocery & Provisions Committee minutes 2/0/6 (2 December 1886), 280.
[138] CWS General Committee minutes (31 August 1888), Vol. 13, 55.
[139] CWS Grocery & Provisions Committee minutes 2/0/1 (29 March 1882), 303, and (5 April 1882), 308.
[140] CWS Grocery & Provisions Committee minutes 2/0/1 (21 June 1882), 353.
[141] CWS Grocery & Provisions Committee minutes 2/0/4 (17 January 1884), 356.
[142] CWS Grocery & Provisions Committee minutes 2/0/7 (20 June 1888), 361.
[143] CWS Grocery & Provisions Committee minutes 2/0/4 (13 June 1883), 207, and (21 June 1883), 218.

FIGURE 3.13. New York Produce Exchange, 1890. The CWS's New York City buying offices were located in the Exchange building, which was completed in 1884 and stood at 2 Broadway. Designed by noted architect George B. Post, the building was famed as his 'commercial masterpiece', but was demolished in 1957.

striving hard to secure the best deals for the CWS.[144] Interestingly, even in the USA there was evidence of efforts by British private traders to stifle the co-operative movement. The American firm Washbourne Crosby supplied CWS New York with flour, but in November 1884 they asked Gledhill to advise Manchester to remain silent about the relationship 'on the other side', lest it lead to Washbourne's other British customers forcing them to cease supplying the CWS through threats of boycotts.[145] Other firms were happy to supply the CWS with their goods with CWS labels, as the tinned meat firm Armour did in December 1884.[146] Indeed, co-operative society buyers in Britain pressed strongly in January 1887 for the New York branch to extend the practice wherever

[144] CWS Grocery & Provisions Committee minutes 2/0/4 (8 August 1883), 246.
[145] CWS Grocery & Provisions Committee minutes 2/0/5 (19 November 1884), 102.
[146] CWS Grocery & Provisions Committee minutes 2/0/5 (10 December 1884), 124.

agreement could be reached with the suppliers concerned.[147] By 1890, the New York branch had become a major presence in the American market, purchasing flour and meat as far west as Chicago and Minneapolis, and already planning to expand its activities into Canada.

But of course New York was not the only major scene of international activity by CWS. Branches in Rouen (1879), Copenhagen (1881), and Hamburg (1884) supplied large amounts of foodstuffs of competitive price and quality. The professionalism, strategic acumen, and quite revolutionary nature of these operations were especially evident in the case of the Copenhagen branch (see Plate 10). It became not only very successful at supplying butter, bacon, and a range of commodities for British co-operative societies, it also came to exemplify the possibilities of international collaboration between quite different co-operative movements. Denmark had undergone a major agricultural revolution since the 1870s, which had been led by farmer co-operatives. The rise of grain imports from the USA during this period hit European farmers hard, and like others, Danish farmers adapted to survive. They did so principally by moving into dairying and butter production, employing the latest methods and technologies based on 'winter feeding' which not only produced high-quality milk and butter, but ensured continued production and sales even during the winter months, which was traditionally a season of low production in dairying in Europe.[148] Central to this transformation was the formation by Danish farmers of co-operative creameries, which played a major role in providing centralized facilities for processing milk, and for disseminating crucial knowledge of the new techniques.[149] In due course, Danish butter acquired a reputation for reliable quality which was second to none, a reputation which was jealously guarded after 1888 by the Danish state through its Agricultural Commissioner in London, who proactively pursued and prosecuted all those suspected of passing off as Danish, sub-standard butter from other sources.[150] Britain became a major market for Danish butter in the late nineteenth century. Average annual butter exports grew from 11,760 tons in the period 1870 to 1879, to 53,810 thousand tons between 1890 and 1899.[151] Both ideological conviction and practical considerations made the CWS a most welcome actor in the Danish market when it opened its Copenhagen branch in 1881. The CWS's own commitment to high-quality produce, and the fastidiousness of its co-operative society customers, dovetailed with the Danish industry's and state's concern to protect the reputation for quality. Significantly, John Andrews, the first head of the new branch, soon made important friends in the Danish co-operative movement, and the agricultural establishment. On 12 April 1882, just ten months after setting up operations in the Danish capital, Andrews met the President of the Royal Agricultural Society of Denmark, holding discussions

[147] The brand they wanted was the 'Pioneer' brand, a concept which neatly encompassed images of Rochdale and the American frontier. CWS Grocery & Provisions Committee minutes 2/0/6 (13 January 1887), 325.
[148] Henriksen and O'Rourke (2005).   [149] Henriksen and O'Rourke (2005), 547–8.
[150] Higgins and Mordhorst (2008), 195.   [151] Higgins and Mordhorst (2008), 185.

with him and a deputation of farmers for nearly three hours.[152] In the following December, Andrews even accepted an invitation from Tesdorf, the President of the Society, for the CWS to join the organization, and to supply it with general information about the butter trade in Britain.[153] Andrews also wrote for the *Farmers Journal* in Denmark about the trade on occasion.[154] In February 1885 he was made a Burgher of Copenhagen, and was then able to trade on exactly the same terms as any Dane.[155] Then in March 1885 Andrews won the custom of Herr Donnersgaard, a very prominent farmer, who was an MP and President of the Danish Co-operative Wholesale Society. Donnersgaard instantly wanted to explore the possibility of closer relations with the English CWS.[156] At the end of the month Andrews spoke to the annual meeting of the Danish Wholesale Society, beginning a close relationship between the two organizations.[157] As a consequence, in December 1885 the English CWS shipped a large consignment of rice to their Danish counterparts.[158]

Andrews proved to be a very adept operator on the Copenhagen market. Formerly a highly experienced traveller for the CWS, who knew the tastes and demands of retail societies, Andrews brought that knowledge to bear in his purchasing operations. His strategy was informed by the co-operative principle of sourcing goods where possible at the point of production. Within two months of his arrival in Copenhagen in June 1881, Andrews made clear his intention to establish supply chains with Danish farmers, rather than just rely on Copenhagen merchants and brokers. He immediately met resistance from those merchants who had initially welcomed the arrival of the CWS in the capital.[159] By October, a group of the Copenhagen merchants were even threatening to boycott business with the CWS, unless Andrews agreed not to build relationships with farmers.[160] But Andrews called their bluff, and boasted in January 1882 that of 270 casks of butter he had shipped in the first week of the new year, 46 had been sourced directly from the farm.[161] The arrangement gave Andrews leverage in his dealings with the Copenhagen merchants, enabling him to negotiate the best prices and highest quality. Thus in October 1882 Andrews quite happily offended a number of them by rejecting their butter because of its poor quality.[162] Andrews even advanced money to dairy farmers, to encourage supplies.[163] From November 1883, the CWS Copenhagen branch was advertised in a leading Danish farmers' journal.[164] Andrews even put on lavish enter-

---

[152] CWS Grocery & Provisions Committee minutes 2/o/3 (12 April 1882), 312–13.
[153] CWS Grocery & Provisions Committee minutes 2/o/4 (28 December 1882), 87.
[154] CWS Grocery & Provisions Committee minutes 2/o/4 (27 June 1883), 223.
[155] CWS Grocery & Provisions Committee minutes 2/o/5 (26 February 1885), 176.
[156] CWS Grocery & Provisions Committee minutes 2/o/5 (4 March 1885), 182.
[157] CWS Grocery & Provisions Committee minutes 2/o/5 (31 March 1885), 203.
[158] CWS Grocery & Provisions Committee minutes 2/o/5 (16 December 1885), 404.
[159] CWS Grocery & Provisions Committee minutes 2/o/3 (24 August 1881), 205.
[160] CWS Grocery & Provisions Committee minutes 2/o/3 (19 October 1881), 230.
[161] CWS Grocery & Provisions Committee minutes 2/o/3 (11 January 1882), 269.
[162] CWS Grocery & Provisions Committee minutes 2/o/4 (18 October 1882), 52.
[163] CWS Grocery & Provisions Committee minutes 2/o/4 (4 October 1883), 288.
[164] CWS Grocery & Provisions Committee minutes 2/o/4 (22 November 1883), 316.

tainments at his home for farmers visiting Copenhagen.[165] By August 1885, CWS Copenhagen was receiving butter from 101 farmers across Scandinavia.[166] As early as 1883, operations were very substantial. In the year ended 23 June 1883, CWS Copenhagen's shipments had been worth £261,073, exceeding the New York branch, which supplied goods worth £211,976.[167] Copenhagen's operations were also beginning to extend across Scandinavia. In October 1883 Andrews reported agreeing orders from a major landowner in Sweden.[168] By March 1885, Andrews boasted that he was shipping butter and flour worth £9,000–10,000 per week:

He [Andrews] says this exceeds by far anything like it done by any other firm in Scandinavia, in Germany, in France, in Italy, in the United States or even by any one firm anywhere under the British empire in butter alone.[169]

In September 1887, the Grocery & Provisions Committee reflected on the meteoric rise of the Danish trade, which by then dealt with merchants and farmers across Scandinavia (see Tables 3.2 and 3.3). When the Hamburg branch was opened in 1884, again with a strong remit to purchase butter, Dilworth, an experienced traveller for the CWS, was

Table 3.2. Statement of shipments of Swedish and Danish butter by CWS to England and Scotland, June 1886 to June 1887

	Casks (#)	Value (£-s.-d.)
Denmark	59,948	343,720-0-8
Sweden	37,759	205,265-12-5
Total	97,527	548,955-13-1

Source: CWS Grocery & Provisions Committee minutes 2/0/6 (7 September 1887), 69.

Table 3.3. Statement of shipments of Swedish and Danish butter purchased directly by CWS from producers, June 1886 to June 1887

	Casks (#)	Value (£-s.-d.)
Denmark	7,477	41,642-7-0
Sweden	8,907	49,357-6-6
Total	16,384	90,999-13-6

Source: CWS Grocery & Provisions Committee minutes 2/0/6 (7 September 1887), 69.

---

[165] CWS Grocery & Provisions Committee minutes 2/0/4 (31 January 1884), 369.
[166] CWS Grocery & Provisions Committee minutes 2/0/5 (19 August 1885), 303.
[167] CWS Grocery & Provisions Committee minutes 2/0/4 (4 October 1883), 289.
[168] CWS Grocery & Provisions Committee minutes 2/0/4 (15 November 1883), 312.
[169] CWS Grocery & Provisions Committee minutes 2/0/5 (11 March 1885), 186.

Table 3.4. CWS Hamburg branch butter purchases, September 1886 to June 1887

Quarter ended	Spot purchases		Direct purchases	
	Casks (#)	Value (£-s.-d.)	Casks (#)	Value (£-s.-d.)
September 1886	4,117	17,012-0-10	533	2,216-9-11
December 1886	2,079	11,264-6-11	422	2,129-13-10
March 1887	7,776	37,415-5-3	1,963	9,117-7-7
June 1887	11,709	45,184-11-0	2,571	9,736-12-1
Total	25,681	111,476-3-8	5,489	23,200-4-3

Source: CWS Grocery & Provisions Committee minutes 2/0/7 (12 October 1887), 101.

placed in charge. Andrews was instructed to advise him on how to build and conduct trade with local merchants and farmers.[170] Like Andrews, Dilworth also faced resistance and hostility from merchants when they discovered that he was dealing directly with local farmers.[171] But like Andrews, Dilworth resisted this pressure, and by 1887 he was able to report a thriving business purchasing from both merchants and local farmers (see Table 3.4).

The CWS's overseas commerce was also assisted by the acquisition of its own shipping lines (see Figure 3.14), running from Goole to Calais (and later Hamburg) and Garston to Rouen. These were run down in the early twentieth century, as the CWS found it cheaper to contract out to regular shipping lines; but in the initial phase of development of the CWS, they played an important role.[172] The CWS sourced goods from all over Europe. Thus, in November 1878 the buyer Kay was sent to purchase French butter in response to shortages in Britain.[173] By the end of the 1880s, the CWS commanded a network of suppliers across the continent. Deputations to Greece and Turkey to secure supplies of dried fruit travelled overland, making deals en route for apples, potatoes, flour, and other commodities in Belgium, France, Germany, Austria, and the Balkans.[174] Just as it did in New York, to finance its European operations, the CWS relaxed its restrictions on doing business with non-co-operative organizations. Its shipping lines exported coal for private mining firms, notably Pope & Pearson.[175] Ultimately, the intense competitive pressures it faced in England and Wales forced the CWS to become a sophisticated international enterprise.

[170] CWS Grocery & Provisions Committee minutes 2/0/4 (24 April 1884), 428; CWS Grocery & Provisions Committee minutes 2/0/5 (25 March 1885), 195.

[171] CWS Grocery & Provisions Committee minutes 2/0/5 (19 November 1885), 104.

[172] Redfern (1913), 135.

[173] CWS Grocery & Provisions Committee minutes 2/0/1 (6 November 1878), 365.

[174] Tweedale's Report (printed) to CWS General Committee on his visit to Greece 30 July–27 September 1886 (dated October 1886), 3–9, NCA.

[175] For example, CWS General Committee minutes (10 November 1882), Vol. 7, 82.

FIGURE 3.14. *SS Pioneer*, 1904. Launched in 1879, the *Pioneer* was the CWS's first new-built steamship; it had purchased the *SS Plover* in 1874. The *Pioneer* was the first vessel to enter the Manchester Ship Canal in 1894 (see Figure 4.11).

Another vitally important branch of activity was the financial services offered to societies through the CWS Bank, established in 1872. The bank strengthened relations between the CWS and societies, through the provision of loans and overdrafts. Business grew rapidly, with bank turnover rising from £15–16 million in 1884, to £22–23 million in 1889. The number of current accounts increased from 156 in the quarter ended December 1883 to 256 by the end of June 1890.[176] Of crucial importance were the loans and overdrafts granted to societies, which funded local expansion. In the period June 1878 to 12 September 1890, the bank gave loans or overdrafts amounting to £438,000 to 158 different societies.[177] Loans varied in size and terms. In May 1879, the large society at Blaydon in the north-east, was awarded £6,000 at 5 per cent. By contrast, in May 1881 the much smaller society at Wigan received just £50.[178] Loans and overdrafts encouraged loyalty to the CWS. They also generated annual profits for the CWS of about £3,000 to £4,000 by the end of the 1880s.[179] Buildings and equipment were funded by CWS loans. In 1886, the Penge Society borrowed £1,000 to build stables and a bakery.[180] In 1902, the

[176] Figures from quarterly reports of the CWS for this period, held in CWS General Committee minutes.

[177] These figures are calculated from entries in CWS General Committee minutes, Vols. 5 to 16.

[178] Blaydon loan: CWS General Committee minutes Vol. 134; Wigan loan: General Committee minutes Vol. 6, 125.

[179] According to CWS quarterly reports for this period, in CWS General Committee minutes.

[180] CWS General Committee minutes (26 November 1886), Vol. 10, 377.

Hull Society was awarded an overdraft of £6,000 to purchase property, while the Brandon and Byshottle Co-operative Society received £5,000 for building its central stores, and the Berkhamsted Society got £4,500 to buy 2 acres of land.[181] In this way, the CWS Bank encouraged greater loyalty among societies and promoted the CWS's position at the centre of the movement.

3.4 THE CWS BY 1890: A SUCCESSFUL LEADER OF THE CO-OPERATIVE MOVEMENT?

By the beginning of the 1890s, the position of the CWS showed reasons for both satisfaction and concern. Sales had grown spectacularly and rapidly. The CWS had grown into a major producer, shipper, and international trader. But the aspiration to become the movement's unquestioned leader had not been achieved. In particular, the CWS had yet to command the degree of loyal custom from societies to which it felt entitled. This has led some historians to view the organization rather critically. The celebrated American business historian Alfred Chandler compared the CWS's managerial structure unfavourably with that of the leading US distributor Sears Roebuck. Chandler's depiction of the CWS and the co-operative movement follows his general view of British business in the late nineteenth century. Chandler argued that the cheapness of British labour and the relative smallness of the British market served to entrench traditional business methods and retard the development of modern 'scientific' management. In contrast, shortages of labour and the presence of a substantial domestic market in the USA encouraged the adoption there of sophisticated management, production, and marketing systems run by complex managerial hierarchies. Chandler argues that even though the large scale of CWS activities and production created some competitive advantages, the relatively small range of commodities it produced and the democratic decision-making structures of the movement stifled the development of modern systems of managerial control. Sears Roebuck, on the other hand, had to satisfy diverse demands from consumers spread across a wide geographical area. Consequently it had to develop highly sophisticated management systems.[182] The implication is that the CWS's limited success in winning the custom of member societies arose at least partly from its limited and uncoordinated system of business management.

But this analysis is fundamentally wrong. Chandler seemed to assume that co-operative societies were customers upon whom the CWS could rely. He even described the CWS's trade with retail societies as 'assured sales'.[183] Tellingly, Chandler refers to the retail societies as the CWS's 'hundreds of retail shops'.[184] The federal nature of CWS

---

[181] CWS Financial Committee minutes (1 July 1902), Vol. 37, 1–2, NCA.
[182] Chandler (1990), 259–61.   [183] Chandler (1990), 257.   [184] Chandler (1990), 260.

relations with local societies was simply overlooked. For Chandler, the CWS moved into production because the retail societies were reliable CWS customers. But in reality the CWS did this to compete against private manufacturers whose produce societies generally preferred. Backward integration by the CWS into production was a product of competition—not the presence of a reliable internal market within the movement. Chandler is also wrong in his low estimation of the leadership and management systems of the CWS. He described the CWS as a loose federation, in which decision-making power was largely devolved to its branches and depots, and buyers operated independently with little control.[185] CWS management was described by Chandler as 'non-hierarchical', with the grocery and drapery committees, run by elected officials, running the organization.[186] But this description does not bear scrutiny. The General Committee (or Board of Directors) in Manchester carefully supervised the activities of the branches, and most major decisions were taken by a regular joint committee of the branches, which also co-opted members from the SCWS.[187] It set the salaries of production managers, buyers (drapery, grocery, and others), branch officials, and overseas employees. Regular conferences of CWS buyers, usually including SCWS buyers, imposed common methods of operation. Appointments at all of the branches, and at all levels, had to be approved by the General Committee in Manchester. All branch decisions were carefully scrutinized by that body.[188] In reality, the CWS was a highly centralized organization, over which the General Committee asserted a consistent body of policies and strategies. It was also served by a highly professional staff of managers, buyers, and salespeople, many with long experience. The latter were highly rewarded, and constituted a quite clearly defined managerial hierarchy. In this period the CWS was much more like Sears Roebuck than Chandler realized. Chandler also ignored certain key CWS activities such as banking. He also seemed unaware of the rapid internationalization of the CWS's commercial activities. The CWS was a sophisticated corporate body with a well-developed managerial structure—a rarity in Britain according to the 'Chandler thesis'.

In fact, in the late nineteenth century the CWS was a national leader in methods of management, leadership, and recruitment. It could boast some outstanding senior figures of real inspiration. As shown, J. T. W. Mitchell, Chair of the CWS Board from 1878 to 1895, was a leader of extraordinary talent.[189] Mitchell offered a vision of the future of the CWS and the co-operative movement in general. He led the way in the development of the CWS as a major producer, and as a shipper, banker, and international

---

[185] Chandler (1990), 260.   [186] Chandler (1990), 261.

[187] See for example the minutes of the Joint Committee (18 February 1884), in CWS General Committee minutes, Vol. 8, 68.

[188] For example, the General Committee meeting of 29 February 1884 made several decisions which demonstrated its final authority in all appointments. It overturned the appointment of a Mr Bottomley as boot and shoe traveller because it was unhappy with his references. It confirmed the appointment of Mr A. Hill in the tea department in London at 7s. per week, and approved the prosecution of two workers in the same department for theft. CWS General Committee minutes, Vol. 8, 74–7.

[189] Yeo (1995).

operator. As a result, he experienced much criticism from within the ranks of the move-ment.[190] Thus individual leadership was vital in the early, formative years of CWS devel-opment. But the temptation to sanctify any individual co-operative leader should be resisted. Mitchell proved a divisive leader on occasion.[191] He was partly responsible for the bitter divisions between producer and consumer co-operation, and, as seen, his bluntness at the conferences to win society loyalty to the CWS alienated as many as they won over. Probably more central to CWS success was the cultivation of a cadre of managers who ran through the CWS hierarchy like the veins of a rich cheese. They were the product of sophisticated and modern methods of managerial recruitment, and of serious attention to their professional development. When it appointed a senior tea buyer in July 1882, the Grocery & Provisions Committee interviewed eight candidates, most with tea selling experience outside the movement, especially in Yorkshire and Lancashire. Charles Fielding was appointed head of the CWS tea and coffee depart-ment.[192] Similar competition was evident for more lowly positions. In 1884, when a vacancy appeared for a CWS traveller, seventy-eight applications were received.[193] The key to advancement was knowledge of what retail societies wanted to buy. This was why figures such as John Andrews, W. Dilworth, and John Gledhill rose so quickly—because of their strong understanding of the fundamental relationship with retail soci-eties which was at the heart of CWS activities.[194] Bad managers were not tolerated. Thus in August 1889 the CWS pushed out its Batley Mill textile factory manager because of continuously poor performance.[195] In this way, the CWS became probably the most advanced business organization of the period.

Why did the CWS grow into a large and complex organization at a time when such firms were rare in Britain? A key reason was the fierce competitive pressures imposed by member societies who were not prepared to pledge total loyalty to the CWS. Such pref-erence for the open market reflected an important characteristic of nineteenth-century British economic development in the industrial heartlands. The work of Wilson and Popp shows how the location of British industrial firms in close proximity with each other in highly developed localities promoted the outsourcing of key services by those firms. This diminished the need for the complex managerial structures generated by US firms to cope with labour shortages, and geographically dispersed resources and mar-kets.[196] A similar logic drove the decision-making of retail societies in respect of sourc-ing goods. It was frequently cheaper to buy locally rather than rely on the CWS. The CWS had to be able to sell the best at the lowest prices to compete with local suppliers. Thus the CWS's moves into production, banking, and international trade were attempts

---

[190] Yeo (1995), 58–62.   [191] Yeo (1995), 10–16.

[192] CWS Grocery and Provisions Committee minutes 2/0/4 (29 July 1882), 5–8.

[193] CWS Grocery and Provisions Committee minutes 2/0/4 (21 January 1884), 366–7.

[194] CWS Grocery and Provisions Committee minutes (unnumbered) (16 September 1875), 170; Grocery & Provisions Committee minutes 2/0/4 (24 April 1884), 428.

[195] General Committee minutes (23 August 1889), Vol. 14, 289.

[196] Wilson and Popp (2003), 1–18.

to beat off local competitors through vertical integration. The CWS was propelled towards managerial innovation by the 'hothouse' of competition with local suppliers. All this challenges assumptions (many still current) that co-operatives are inherently less efficient than the private sector. By 1890 the CWS was a national leader in the development of British business organization. But as will be seen, some major challenges were already looming on the horizon.

CHAPTER 4

THE AGE OF EXPANSION, 1890–1914

By the 1890s, co-operators had become accustomed to national membership and sales figures rising annually, and it certainly continued between 1890 and 1914. Already well established in the industrial centres of northern England and Scotland, after 1900 co-operatives spread to other regions—even to such 'co-operative deserts' as London. Existing societies also expanded their businesses, opening new branches in adjoining neighbourhoods and launching new departments to supply their members with a greater variety of goods. By 1914 co-operatives supplied between 7 and 9 per cent of the nation's total retail trade, and from 17 to 19 per cent of the trade in groceries and provisions.[1] In serving co-operative societies, the CWS became one of Britain's largest businesses and its own operations expanded in scale and scope. Although the British economy experienced fluctuations in the 1890s and the rising cost of living worried many in the early 1900s, co-operatives continued to enjoy growing success until 1914.

But success exacerbated old difficulties and caused new ones. National leaders in the Wholesales and the Co-operative Union recognized that the establishment of new consumer societies across the UK—the total number of which was about 1,400 in the early 1900s, aggravated difficulties in the coordination of strategy, policy, and practice. Conversely, local co-operative society leaders, protective of their independence, viewed the expansion of the CWS with suspicion. Meanwhile, as the range and complexity of co-operative activities increased, the movement's national bodies struggled to adapt their organizations to meet changing needs, and sparred with one another over their proper sphere of action. Yet the decentralized nature of co-operative governance and the lack of alignment between the movement's local and national aims meant that effective structural reform was difficult to achieve. Moreover, co-operatives were not the only businesses whose sales and profits were rising. From the 1890s private multiple retailers captured greater market share and manufacturers produced an increasing variety of low-cost, heavily advertised commodities—particularly the foodstuffs and household items that made up the bulk of co-operative goods. Independent shopkeepers were also

---

[1] Jefferys (1954), 29 and 163.

responding to co-operative competition by forming local and national associations which launched intensive anti-co-operative campaigns.

As co-operative institutions matured, their personnel changed. Many of those who had established the Wholesales and the Co-operative Union retired or died in the 1890s. E. V. Neale died in 1892, followed in 1895 by J. T. W. Mitchell, while Abraham Greenwood retired in 1898. Whilst earlier co-operators battled over the merits of producer and consumer models, the rising generation interpreted co-operative ideals almost exclusively through the experience of the retail co-operative society. It was in this era that co-operative federalism, exemplified by the CWS, was elevated 'almost to a co-operative principle in its own right'.[2] But notwithstanding the stress on the importance of co-operation as a consumer movement, there were new champions of the movement's role in addressing major social, political, and economic issues. Between 1890 and 1914 working-class activism increased, as the New Unionism swelled trade union membership to four million by 1914 and socialist and labour organizations developed into a significant political force. In this environment, new interest groups and auxiliary organizations developed that sought to influence the direction of co-operative policy and practice. The co-operative response to these situations reflected its dual nature as both business and social movement, as it struggled to reconcile its role as a major employer of labour, participated in debate about the role of the state in regulating business and providing for its citizens' welfare, and reconsidered the movement's abstinence from party politics. The CWS participated in all of these debates.

4.1 THE CO-OPERATIVE MOVEMENT AND RETAILING, 1890–1914

The transformation of British retailing begun in the mid-nineteenth century accelerated between 1890 and 1914. Rising living standards, falling food prices, better transportation, and improved manufacturing technologies all contributed to dynamic growth in the distributive trades. Businesses developed new methods of producing, processing, and selling household goods and foodstuffs, and targeted them at working-class consumers. While such developments varied regionally, a 'retailing revolution' was under way.[3]

In this environment consumer co-operatives expanded—in trade and membership, in numbers of societies, the range of their departments and branches, and in their locations. Individual members of British societies grew from 1 million in 1890 to 1.7 million in 1900, and over 3 million in 1914. Such growth is even more impressive in light of the policy of many societies to limit membership on a one per family basis. Also, many societies undertook significant trade with non-members, suggesting that the number of

---

[2] Fairbairn (1994), 14.   [3] Winstanley (1983), 8–9.

people interacting with co-operatives was much greater than these figures suggest.[4] Members' investments also rose, and societies' total share capital reached £38 million in 1914. Sales figures climbed, with the combined turnover reaching nearly £88 million. This expanding co-operative market benefited the Wholesale societies, both of which significantly extended their operations before the First World War.

While the movement grew all over Britain, there were national and regional variations (see Table 4.1). On the basis of co-operative members as a percentage of the total population, it is possible to estimate the degree of co-operative penetration in different localities. As Figure 4.1 demonstrates, by 1900 Scotland and the industrial regions of the English north-east, north-west, and parts of the Midlands all had percentages over 5 per cent, with Durham at the top with over 12 per cent. In these regions co-operative societies were a powerful presence in working-class neighbourhoods. In addition to new societies being formed, membership grew significantly in existing societies. By 1910, while these heartland areas continued to lead on this measure, parts of the Midlands

Table 4.1. British co-operative membership as per cent of population, 1901 and 1911

	Members 1901	Members 1911	As % of population 1901	As % of population 1911
England	1,454,829	2,166,560	4.7	6.4
Scotland	301,626	406,411	6.7	8.5
Wales	24,462	53,982	1.4	2.7

Source: General Co-operative Survey (hereafter GCS), Third Interim and Fourth (Final) Report, 95–96.

were catching up, and there were areas of south-west England reaching over 5 per cent. In these areas of more recent growth, formation of new societies was prominent in the rise in membership.

Although co-operators were fewer outside the northern heartlands, the pace of expansion was accelerating all over. Between 1901 and 1916, the number of co-operators in Wales increased by over 260 per cent, doubled in England, and rose by 70 per cent in Scotland. As Figure 4.2 illustrates, in England the fastest growth took place in the south-west and the south-east, with significant expansion in London and its surrounding counties. Between 1900 and 1914, the former co-operative deserts were becoming the major new areas of growth. This trend, even more pronounced in the inter-war period, was evident before 1914.

---

[4] One-per-family restrictions on membership were changing over this period, both in response to reduced concerns over 'surplus capital' and to a widespread campaign for 'open membership' by the Women's Co-operative Guild; see Vorberg-Rugh (forthcoming).

Table 4.2. CWS domestic sales, England and Wales, 1890–1915

	Manchester (£)	% of total	Newcastle branch (£)	% of total	London branch (£)	% of total	Total (£)
1890	4,294,048	61.8	1,615,610	23.3	1,034,607	14.9	6,944,265
1895	5,671,536	60.1	2,215,596	23.5	1,557,498	16.5	9,444,630
1900	8,373,348	56.9	3,751,971	25.5	2,601,173	17.7	14,726,492
1905	11,159,849	57.4	4,193,160	21.6	4,080,541	21.0	19,433,550
1910	14,570,574	58.0	4,872,912	19.4	5,660,194	22.5	25,103,680
1915	23,004,846	55.5	7,419,278	17.9	11,032,401	26.6	41,456,525

Source: CWS balance sheets, 1890–1915, NCA.

As retail societies grew, so did the CWS, together with its travelling sales staff and its system of depots and salesrooms to attract co-operative buyers. In 1890 the Blackburn saleroom completed the Wholesale's northern network. Building on its success with the Bristol depot (1884), in 1891 it opened a saleroom in Cardiff to better access the growing societies of South Wales. By 1905 the expansion of the Cardiff business necessitated the acquisition of the former Town Hall building to accommodate trade (see Figure 4.3). New salerooms in the Midlands included Northampton (1890) and Birmingham (1892). This expanded distribution network facilitated trade growth in southern England and Wales. Although the bulk of CWS sales still flowed through the Manchester headquarters, by 1914 the London branch accounted for about a quarter of its trade (see Table 4.2).

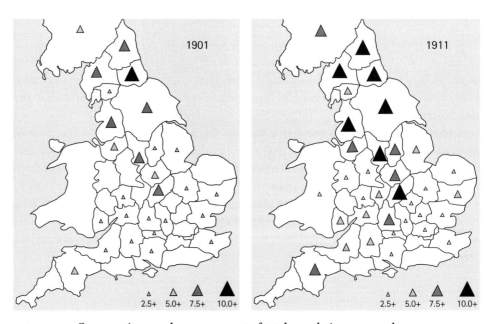

FIGURE 4.1. Co-operative members as per cent of total population, 1901 and 1911.

FIGURE 4.2. Per cent increase in co-operative membership, 1901 to 1916.

Although the timing and extent of societies' growth varied, a common pattern of expansion is discernible. Starting with single stores in small rented premises, societies began by selling groceries and basic household provisions. As membership and sales grew, they opened additional grocery branches in neighbouring districts. They also expanded the types of goods on offer. As they grew larger, societies generally purchased land and built new central premises with several departments, usually including drapery, footwear, clothing, furnishing, and hardware. If branches were geographically distant from the centre then drapery, boot, or other departments might be added, or societies might start delivery services. Local variations in demands and needs dictated the types of services on offer, which could be quite diverse (see Table 4.3). Nonetheless, staple household needs dominated, and by 1910 over 90 per cent of the societies which responded to a Co-operative Union survey had grocery, drapery, and footwear departments, while a considerable number also dedicated departments to hardware, furnishings, housewares, flour, and coal. Growing numbers of societies opened butchers' shops and chemists, or operated milk delivery rounds, trends that would accelerate in the inter-war period. In addition to retailing, many societies also produced their own goods for sale, including bakeries, shoe making and repairing shops, and tailoring and dress-

FIGURE 4.3. CWS depot, Cardiff, 1909. The first Cardiff depot opened in 1891, and by 1901 trade had expanded to require its own building (shown here), located on Bute Terrace. In 1913 even greater expansion was needed, and the CWS purchased the former town hall site at St Mary's Street, demolishing the building and erecting a new eight storey facility during the First World War. Located near the Millenium Stadium, the building is now known as Hodge House.

making departments. Again, there was a considerable degree of local diversity in this field. Overall the proportion of societies engaged in production was considerably less than in distribution (see Table 4.4). Moreover, as co-operative reports tended to divide departments into only two categories, many activities that figured under the 'productive' heading would be more accurately defined as services, such as laundries and building and decorating departments. In the inter-war era, services, including both travel and funeral departments, would be a significant area of growth for retail societies. Over time, the production of co-operative goods would become almost the sole province of the Wholesales. Ultimately, although it sold clothing, furnishings, and other goods, it was food and provisions that made up the bulk of CWS sales and remained its core business. In 1914 more than 80 per cent of its sales were groceries (see Table 4.5). There were regional variations, with the Newcastle district buying more shoes, drapery, furniture, and other items than the other districts, but even here between 70 and 75 per cent of its purchases were food and provisions. Given the large number of societies, the volume of their records, and the diversity of record-keeping standards, it is impossible to estimate with any accuracy the average amount of supplies co-operative societies purchased from the CWS in this period. Some societies did publish

Table 4.3. British retail societies' distributive departments, 1910 and 1916

	1910		1916	
	UK	% of Total*	UK	% of Total*
Grocery	1,253	99.7	1,264	99.8
Drapery	1,147	91.2	1,180	93.1
Boots & Shoes	1,140	90.7	1,166	92.0
Hardware	992	78.9	1,073	84.7
Furnishing	870	69.2	890	70.2
Earthenware	811	64.5	810	63.9
Flour	778	61.9	718	56.7
Coal	725	57.7	749	59.1
Butchering	620	49.3	614	48.5
Ironmongery	619	49.2	712	56.2
Tailoring	584	46.5	556	43.9
Millinery	379	30.2	380	30.0
Jewellery	207	16.5	186	14.7
Milk	141	11.2	123	9.7
Restaurant	86	6.8	83	6.6
Chemists	34	2.7	49	3.9
Greengrocery	29	2.3	38	3.0
Fish, Game &c	24	1.9	36	2.8
Beer, Wines, & Spirits	22	1.8	22	1.7
Oil	8	0.6	8	0.6
Baking	6	0.5	100	7.9
Outfitting	6	0.5	30	2.4
Clogging	5	0.4	64	5.1
Hairdressing	4	0.3	6	0.5

* 1,257 UK retail societies responded to the survey in 1910, and 1,267 in 1916.

Other departments (4 or less respondents)

Undertaking; Laundry; Mantles; Tobacco; Carriers; Colours; Dentistry; Dyeing and Cleaning; Fire Insurance; Fishing Tackle; Hosiery; Insurance Agency; Manure; Meals and Feeding Stuffs; Lime; Musical Instruments; Opticians; Paper Hanging; Picture Framing; Post Office; Poultry; Provender; Ready-made Clothing; Stationery; Vegetarian Food Specialties; Grain & Corn; Fruit; Agricultural Implements; Egg Merchants; Seeds; Colonial Meat; Florists; Excursion Agency; Botanic Drinks; Building Materials; Cinematograph Theatre; Dentistry Agents; Furniture Removing; Light Refreshments; Photography Agents; Saddlery

Source: GCS (1919), 105–8.

Table 4.4. British retail societies' productive departments, 1910 and 1916

	1910		1916	
	UK	% of Total*	UK	% of Total**
Baking	646	51.4	719	56.7
Boot Making & Repair	406	32.3	500	39.5
Tailoring	254	20.2	300	23.7
Dressmaking	201	16.0	201	15.9
Millinery	184	14.6	232	18.3
Clogging	95	7.6	135	10.7
Farming	44	3.5	73	5.8
Butchering**	−	0.0	94	7.4
Painting & Decorating	30	2.4	37	2.9
Joinery	20	1.	25	2.0
Corn Milling	17	1.4	26	2.1
Building	15	1.2	18	1.4
Knitting/Hosiery	14	1.1	18	1.4
Confectionery	13	1.0	−	0.0
Cabinetmaking	12	1.0	12	0.9
Plumbers	10	0.8	13	1.0
Bacon Curing	9	0.7	10	0.8
Sausage Making	7	0.6	35	2.8
Jewellery	5	0.4	9	0.7
Laundry	5	0.4	15	1.2
Mantlemaking	5	0.4	3	0.2
Blacksmiths	4	0.3	8	0.6
Upholstery	3	0.2	7	0.6
Wheelwrights	3	0.2	6	0.5

* 1,257 UK retail societies responded to survey in 1910, and 1,267 in 1916.
** not classified as productive dept, 1910

Other departments (4 or less respondents)

Shirtmaking; Undertaking; Gardening; Mineral Water Manufacture; Tinsmiths; Tobacco Manufacture; Butter Making; Glazing; Baking Powder Manufacture; Brushmaking; Chemists; Clothing Manufacture; Cycle Repairing; Dairy; Electricians; Firewood Factory; Paper Bag Making; Picture Framing; Pork Butchering; Printing; Saddlery; Self-Raising Flour; Spice Boiling; Tea Packing; Tripe Dressing; Works Dept; Furniture Manufacture; Cooked Meats; Meat Preparation; Sundries Packing; Underclothing; Baking Powder Packing; Bone; Blood Manure; Brewery; Clog Sole Making; Contractors; Dyeing & Cleaning; Engineering; Estate Development; Furniture Polishing; Grocery Sundries; Jam Making; Ladies Outfitting; Livestock; Mattress & Bed Making; Nurserymen; Plain Sewing; Salt Packing; Small Goods; Small Meats; Tallow; Window Cleaning

Source: GCS (1919), 105–8.

Table 4.5. Per cent of CWS domestic sales in grocery category, 1890–1915

	Manchester	Newcastle branch	London branch	Total*
1890	84.4	72.7	86.3	82.0
1895	82.2	74.7	85.3	81.0
1900	83.3	70.5	84.0	80.2
1905	84.6	73.7	86.5	82.6
1910	85.4	75.1	85.9	83.5
1915	85.0	76.9	85.4	83.7

* Domestic trade does not include trade with SCWS or the E&SCWS

Source: CWS balance sheets, 1890–1915

the amounts of goods that they purchased 'from co-operative sources' in their balance sheets, and the Co-operative Union attempted to record these figures in its statistical returns between 1895 and 1901. However many societies did not make such returns and the totals did not disaggregate items purchased from the Wholesales from other co-operative sources. Nevertheless at least one society, in Leicester, did publish both the amount of supplies it bought from the CWS and from other sources, as well as the types of goods it purchased, for the best part of four decades. No single society's experience can be taken as typical, as there were many variables influencing the procurement strategies societies used to choose their suppliers—local consumer preferences, prices and carriage costs, reputation, and even ideology could play a role. Thus the choices of the Leicester Co-operative Society (LCS) vis-à-vis the CWS should be examined within its local context. Nonetheless, the LCS records offer an example of how one society made use of the CWS.

Thirty years old in 1890, the Leicester society had grown large, with around 7,000 members and a turnover of £200,000. In addition to groceries, LCS had departments for drapery, boot & shoe, coal, butchery and furniture. In 1888 it took over the local co-operative corn mill, which it had helped establish in 1875, and by the 1890s had started to cure its own bacon. By 1900 its operations included a dairy and a café. Ten years later, there was a central hub and thirty grocery branches, about half as many butchers' shops, and two branches selling drapery and boots. In common with many societies, LCS grew rapidly between 1890 and 1914, tripling its membership to more than 21,000 and growing turnover above £530,000, while offering a 2 shilling dividend.[5] As Tables 4.6 and 4.7 demonstrate, before 1914 the Leicester society purchased between one-third and one-half of its supplies from the CWS—and at least three-quarters of these goods were

[5] For membership figures, see CU Congress Report (1891), 119, and (1915), 604–5. On LCS history, see Thomson (1911).

FIGURE 4.4. **Dalton in Furness Co-operative Society, *c*.1900.** This Cumbrian society's window advertised CWS Pelaw products alongside Cadbury's cocoa. Most co-operative societies stocked both private brands and co-operative productions.

groceries or other food items. Supplies from the LCS's own mill reached 11 per cent by the 1910s. Other local co-operatives (many of them producer societies) accounted for 2 per cent of LCS purchases in most years. But worrying for the CWS was the growth of LCS purchases after 1904 from private suppliers. This trend (see, for example, Figure 4.4) became a growing concern for the CWS in subsequent decades.

Of course, private multiple retail firms also grew rapidly between 1890 and 1914, and competed fiercely for a share of growing working-class consumer demand. By 1890, firms such as Home and Colonial (tea) and Eastman's (butchers) were among the first to operate more than 100 branches each. Others followed. By 1914, big retail operations were far more common and had become even larger. By 1914 Eastman's had more than 1,000 branches while Home & Colonial, Maypole (dairy), and Lipton (tea) had around 500. Moreover, where once chain retailers had been confined largely to the provisions and footwear sectors, multiples were appearing in an increasing number of categories, including chemists such as Boots and 'penny bazaars' like those of Marks & Spencer.[6] Like the CWS these firms bought in bulk, but unlike co-operatives they specialized in a

---

[6] According to Jefferys (1954), 27, around 1914 about 72 per cent of retail sales of multiples was in foodstuffs (83 per cent for Co-ops), 15 per cent in clothing, 8 per cent other, and 5 per cent confectionery, reading and writing material, tobacco. Unlike co-operatives, there was no regional bias in where they appeared.

Table 4.6. Leicester Co-operative Society purchases by source, 1898–1914

	CWS (%)	Other co-ops	LCS Corn Mill	Other sources*
1898	40.7	3.2	14.5	41.8
1899	46.1	2.5	9.7	41.8
1900	47.2	2.6	8.4	41.8
1901	49.8	3.5	8.6	38.0
1902	52.1	2.3	6.7	38.9
1903	50.2	1.7	9.8	38.3
1904	50.8	1.8	10.7	36.7
1905	50.6	2.0	10.5	36.9
1906	50.8	1.9	9.4	37.9
1907	49.9	2.0	10.1	38.0
1908	48.5	2.2	11.1	38.2
1909	48.0	2.0	11.0	39.0
1910	45.9	2.1	11.0	41.0
1911	39.0	2.2	11.4	47.4
1912	36.4	2.1	11.7	49.8
1913	33.8	2.2	11.0	53.1
1914	32.7	2.4	11.0	53.9

* Other sources were predominantly private suppliers, but the overall total may also include a small number of internal transfers from LCS departments (not tallied separately in this period).

Source: LCS balance sheets, NCA.

limited range of goods, and standardized their stores and methods of selling. Shops were usually located in working-class neighbourhoods and operated with few amenities and on a cash-only basis.[7] As Jefferys noted, 'every effort was made to advertise in spectacular and noisy ways the goods for sale and the low prices at which they were being offered'.[8] The success of multiple stores worried co-operative leaders. As early as 1887 Edinburgh's Thomas Ritchie feared that multiple shops had become 'the most formidable rival to the store', commenting: 'The people flock to them, as the moth to the candle, attracted by the low price of the goods. As long as members of stores insist upon getting a dividend of from 3s. to 4s. per £, there is no hope of competing with these traders'.[9] Co-operatives' focus on maintaining dividends rather than reducing prices troubled many in the movement throughout this period. Moreover, chain stores were not their only concern, as independent shopkeepers were also becoming increasingly active, joining together in trade associations and launched anti-co-operative campaigns.

---

[7] Jefferys (1954), 21–8.   [8] Jefferys (1954), 27.   [9] Ritchie (1887), 10–11.

Table 4.7. Leicester Co-operative Society purchases from CWS, 1898–1914

(%)	Grocery	Drapery	Clothing	Boot & shoe	Furnishing	Butchery	Bakery
1898	76.7	6.9	1.9	6.2	8.3	–	–
1899	78.0	5.8	2.1	5.0	9.1	–	–
1900	78.7	7.0	2.2	4.4	7.6	–	–
1901	80.2	6.6	3.1	4.0	7.4	–	–
1902	78.8	7.1	2.9	3.4	6.3	–	–
1903	79.8	7.8	3.0	3.1	5.6	0.6	–
1904	79.1	9.1	2.9	3.3	5.0	0.6	–
1905	81.6	7.4	3.0	3.0	4.2	0.8	–
1906	81.9	6.8	2.9	3.0	4.3	1.0	–
1907	81.4	7.6	2.5	3.0	4.1	1.4	–
1908	81.1	7.0	3.5	2.8	4.2	1.4	–
1909	82.1	6.5	3.3	2.5	3.9	1.8	–
1910	81.2	6.4	3.5	2.6	4.2	2.1	–
1911	76.8	8.4	4.0	2.7	5.4	2.5	–
1912	75.5	8.3	4.9	2.9	5.2	2.5	0.8
1913	73.7	7.9	5.9	3.1	5.7	2.0	2.8
1914	74.8	7.7	4.7	3.3	5.5	0.6	3.5

Source: LCS balance sheets, NCA.

Although they also benefited from increased consumer spending power in this period, shopkeepers faced many difficulties before 1914. In working-class districts they faced growing competition from multiple shops, but it was the growth of co-operative stores that worried them most.[10] Shopkeepers in working-class districts needed to develop a strong customer base in the provisions trade in order to survive, and one means of doing this was to provide goods 'on tick' to their regular customers, creating both social and economic ties of loyalty. However, the provision of credit was a serious risk for shopkeepers, and in times of trade depression or industrial disputes, demand for credit often exceeded shopkeepers' ability to provide it.[11] Thus, for small shopkeepers co-operatives were a threat because they attracted their best and most reliable customers, leaving behind poorer families who were more likely to seek credit and less likely to repay their debts.

Some urban shopkeepers organized opposition to the spread of co-operative stores. While boycotts and attacks by such private retailing organs as *The Grocer* occurred in the 1860s and 1870s, the 1890s saw much better-organized and sustained opposition. In

[10] Crossick and other analysts suggest that, because shopkeepers identified as businessmen and aspired to similar levels of success as multiple retailers, they were more ambivalent about them than co-operative competition. See Kinloch and Butt (1981), 246, and Crossick (1984), 245.
[11] Johnson (1993), 69.

Scotland traders organized themselves into 'defence associations' and pressured railway companies and other large employers to dismiss employees who were co-operative members. Attacks in the press and coordinated boycotts of local societies occurred throughout the 1890s, culminating in 1896 with a boycott by master fleshers in Glasgow's public market, who refused to sell to co-operative establishments. The SCWS and its member societies fought the boycott in the courts, through the municipal government, and in the press, and moved to purchase their supplies of beef direct from farmers or from North America. Although it continued into the new century, by 1899 several meat sellers had withdrawn from the boycott, allowing co-operators to claim victory.[12] In England, the zenith of the anti-co-operative campaigns came in the early 1900s, although local trade associations engaged in sporadic boycotts in the 1890s.[13] In 1902, the St Helens Society (see Figure 4.5) faced a sustained boycott that became a national cause for the movement as a whole. Established in 1883, by 1900 the society's membership included over half of the town's total population, and plans were afoot for a new central premises. In the summer of 1902 the local Traders' Defence Association inaugurated a boycott on supplies of all manufactured goods to the society and refused to employ co-operative members or their relations in their own shops. Throughout the summer and autumn the campaign received widespread coverage in the national press, and similar associations appeared in towns as far away as Newcastle and Plymouth. Soon a London-based paper, the *Tradesman & Shopkeeper*, appeared and whilst the St Helens boycott died down other anti-co-operative campaigns continued.[14] Throughout the period traders' associations continued to campaign against co-operatives on a variety of fronts, often seeking to get anti-co-operative candidates elected to local councils. Two lines of attack were pursued: first, that dividends were simply rebates for which co-operators paid in advance through higher prices; and secondly, the view that dividends should be taxed as income. In the latter case traders argued that dividends were profits and that co-operative businesses thus had an unfair advantage. In 1905 various traders' associations made their case to a Departmental Committee on Income Tax—which upheld the view that co-operative dividends were not profits, but rather a periodic return to members of the difference between the cost price and the distribution price.[15] Nonetheless, similar arguments would be repeated over the next few decades.[16]

[12] See Kinloch and Butt (1981), 245–63, for a detailed discussion; see also Gurney (1996), 199–200.

[13] For instance in Bolton, a Grocers and Provision Dealers' Association formed in early 1894 and quickly federated to the national organization. Among its stated aims was 'where possible, to fight the Co-operative Stores'. Over the next few years the fifty-plus member association made regular protests against the co-operatives' exemption from paying income tax, encouraged its members to vote against any candidate for town council that expressed views in favour of the movement, and accused the society of selling the products of 'sweated' labour. However in Bolton, where the co-operative accounted for about three-quarters of the total grocery trade, it appears the association was relatively ineffective. See *Bolton Co-operative Record* (hereafter *BCR*) (February 1894), 12; (March 1894), 2; (January 1897), 13.

[14] See Winstanley (1983), 87–8, Crossick (1984), 248–50, and Gurney (1996), 199–202.

[15] *Report of the Departmental Committee on Income Tax*, Cmnd 2575 (1905), xxiii–xxv.

[16] See section 5.5.

FIGURE 4.5. St Helens Co-operative Society, *c.*1910s. One of the St Helens Society's branch stores, location unknown. In 1902 the local Traders' Defence Association led a boycott against the society, leading to the creation of a special co-operative defence fund to support societies facing similar difficulties.

However, co-operators countered private traders' campaigns. Co-operative societies could turn to the CWS for supplies in response to boycotts, and some found business thrived due to the associated publicity. Moreover, the movement's resources were marshalled to support individual societies under attack. In the aftermath of St Helens' experience the Co-operative Union inaugurated a Co-operative Defence Committee and raised funds to support co-operatives facing boycotts. The CWS Board was represented and guaranteed the committee's funds up to £50,000 in autumn 1902.[17] Then in 1906 the Plymouth Co-operative Society won a landmark libel case against the *Tradesman & Shopkeeper*, which had reported that the society was insolvent and that its management was concealing this from members. The publishers had to pay £5,000 in damages, which resulted in the paper's closure.[18] By the end of the decade, the editor of the CWS magazine *Wheatsheaf* felt able to poke fun:

Once upon a time the Traders' Defence Association struck a chill to the heart of the timid Co-operator. Now, 'none so poor to do it reverence.' 'Have you heard,' says the Lowestoft Local Editor to the members, 'that our friends, the traders, are going to make things hum for us? We are to have a free advertisement which, according to their view, will have the desired effect—*of*

[17] CWS balance sheets, 'Committee's Report' (September 1902).
[18] *Wheatsheaf* (May 1906), 162.

what? I know—you know. Increased loyalty to the Society. No Society that has been boycotted but what has, in the end, made progress by it."[19]

Ultimately, such episodes, and growing trade and membership figures, reaffirmed the movement's confidence in the face of external threats.

Meanwhile, CWS and the movement generally recognized the need to strengthen support for co-operation in those parts of the country where progress had been limited. Such 'co-operative deserts' were to be found in pockets across the country, but especially in the south of England. London in particular was a source of concern, notwithstanding the presence there of a major CWS branch. As early as January 1893, the CWS Board were acutely concerned about what they called the 'depression' of co-operation in the capital.[20] In response, the movement launched a propaganda campaign in 1890, with a view to extending the heartland of co-operation, with a grant of £2,000 from the CWS.[21] The idea was that it would establish new co-operative societies funded in part from this grant, and with guidance from the joint propaganda scheme run by the CWS and the Co-operative Union. It proved to be very active indeed in the 1890s. In 1891 representatives were sent to meetings in Mold in Flintshire and Uttoxeter in Staffordshire to take the message to areas where co-operation had yet to establish a footing. Representatives were also sent to Cornwall, to assist those striving to establish societies there.[22] By September 1891 CWS Board members were sitting on the committees of new societies established by the Propaganda Committee in Longton, Bootle, Hull, and Penrith.[23] Significantly, almost from the outset there were those on the CWS Board who argued that such activity should exclusively be controlled by the CWS, or at least that the Wholesale should take the leading role.[24]

Worry about the situation in the capital began to intensify in the early 1890s, when economic difficulties began to take their toll on the London societies. In early 1892, the Hammersmith Society had to go into liquidation, while the West Greenwich society was reported to be in very serious financial difficulty.[25] This was just the tip of an iceberg. Between 1881 and 1892 some seventy-three societies had been launched in the capital, only for them to fail ignominiously.[26] By January 1893 a Joint Committee of the branches of the CWS met in London to discuss the 'depression in London'. So concerned were the assembled representatives that they recommended that the CWS Board provide £3,000 to enable it to establish one or more London societies with several branches, just to keep the movement alive.[27] By April 1893, motions for the CWS to do this were submitted to the next quarterly meeting.[28] The upshot was the establishment in London by CWS and the Co-operative Union of the 'People's Co-operative Society',

[19] *Wheatsheaf* (May 1909), 162.   [20] CWS Board minutes (6 January 1893).
[21] Redfern (1913), 168.   [22] CWS Board minutes (28 August 1891).
[23] CWS Board minutes (23 October 1891).   [24] CWS Board minutes (6 November 1891).
[25] CWS Board minutes (19 February and 4 March 1892).
[26] G. Hawkins, in CU Congress Report (1896), 136.
[27] CWS Board minutes (6 March 1893).   [28] *Co-operative News* (22 April 1893), 397.

which ran a network of branches across the city from the London CWS branch's headquarters in Leman Street. By August 1897 the People's Co-operative Society had 3,387 members, but problems of profitability resulted in falling dividends. Ultimately the society went into voluntary liquidation in August 1899, though it was claimed that the initiative did at least spark a new wave of independent co-operative initiatives in London.[29] Certainly the propaganda initiative continued, and with it the notion that the CWS had a responsibility to take an active role in the spread of co-operative societies, firmly took root. Herein lay the origins of a progressive and proactive role for the CWS, which would lead later in 1934 to the establishment of a special department within the CWS for the purpose of assisting the proliferation of societies—the CWS Retail Society—later the CRS.[30]

4.2 EXPANDING PRODUCTION AT HOME

Before 1914 an increasing proportion of the goods available in co-operative shops were factory-produced, branded commodities. This was a trend which would accelerate in the twentieth century. Whereas previously consumer choice had been restricted to the middle and upper classes, in this period the number of options proliferated for the humble shoppers. Preference for goods, such as the choice between Pears' and Sunlight soap, between Reckitt's or Colman's starch, was now the preserve of the ordinary customer.[31] To meet customer and society demands, the Wholesales now had to supply such branded items. To counteract dependence on external sources, the CWS continued to expand its manufacturing capacity, seeking to produce a greater share of the items sold in co-operative stores. Between 1890 and 1910 it built or acquired more than forty factories, workshops, and mills.[32] It extended its footwear and packaged foods production capacities, and commenced clothing manufacture of various types. In collaboration with the SCWS, the tea department expanded and a chocolate factory was opened in Luton. Taking the SCWS's industrial complex at Shieldhall as a model, in 1903 the CWS opened the multi-factory Pelaw Works on the Newcastle to Sunderland main rail line.[33] Covering four acres, the Pelaw site housed cabinet and clothing factories, a printing works, a grocery packing facility, a drug and drysaltery works, and a dining hall and sports grounds for employees. Such facilities produced an increasing array of co-operative goods, often bearing the name of the place they were made—such as 'Lutona Cocoa' or 'Pelaw Polish' (Figure 4.6).

---

[29] Redfern (1913), 197–8.   [30] See section 5.6.   [31] Kelley (1998), 296–7.
[32] For the dates of commencement of all CWS factories and departments, see the useful appendices in Redfern (1913), 423–30, and Redfern (1938), 597–609.
[33] Redfern (1913), 254 specifically ties the inspiration for Pelaw to the Shieldhall site. On Shieldhall in the period up to 1914, see Kinloch and Butt (1981), 111–16.

FIGURE 4.6. **Pelaw Polish packaging, *c.*1910s.** The CWS often used the place of manufacture to brand its products, including Pelaw Polish, which remained a staple brand in co-operative stores for decades.

But the challenge of private brands in co-operative stores was fierce. Soap illustrates the problem well. Scientific and popular understanding of the relationship between hygiene and the spread of disease had grown, while prevailing social mores connected household cleanliness with respectability. As manufactured soaps and cleaning products were relatively low-cost items, they were now regarded as household necessities rather than luxuries.[34] Total UK soap production rose from 200,000 tons in 1881 to 353,000 in 1906.[35] The industry changed from one dominated by small family firms producing for local markets in 1880, to one of big, wealthy firms selling to the national market by 1900. Thus the CWS faced altogether more formidable competition by the end of the century.

Lever Brothers Limited was in the vanguard of the new soap giants, led by William H. Lever, one of the leading businessmen of the day. Lever began work at his father's Bolton grocery firm, rising to junior partner in 1872 at the age of 21. Two years later, he

---

[34] See Reader (1959), 77–83; Church and Clark (2001), 509; and Cook and Cohen (1958), 217.
[35] Reader (1959), 78; Wilson (1954), 115.

began producing his first line of soaps, which he sold to local retailers. His rise to national prominence was assured by 'Sunlight Self-Washer Soap' in 1884. A new kind of hard soap, 'Sunlight' dissolved more quickly and provided more lather than its rival products—but its component materials required special packaging. Since vegetable oils caused 'sweating' and rancid odours when the soap was exposed to open air, Lever developed soap tablets that were sold in wrapped cartons.[36] In 1885, Lever began producing 'Sunlight' as well as selling it, buying a factory in Warrington that, within a year, produced 450 tons of soap per week.[37] Two years later, he transferred his soap manufacturing business to a new site on the Mersey, where he built the famous Port Sunlight factory village.[38] Meanwhile in 1873, around the same time that Lever was making his first soap, the CWS opened a soap works in a former candle factory in Durham. This was one of the CWS's first manufacturing ventures, and like many of its early efforts it grew slowly from an initial small base through the 1880s. By the early 1890s, however, the marketplace was changing fast—and the Durham factory's small capacity of 35 tons per week was unequal to potential co-operative demand. Lack of capacity for expansion at Durham, and its inland location, away from imported raw materials, forced the CWS to seek a larger and more accessible site.

By the 1890s Lever's innovations in branded soap for the mass market posed a major challenge for the CWS.[39] His grocery experience in the retail marketplace of north-west England made him a feared competitor for the CWS, and in fact his first travelling salesman, H. Whitehead, had been lured away from a co-operative society.[40] In addition to deploying a professional sales force, Lever made extensive use of advertising. By 1888, Sunlight soap was advertised nationally, with larger sales than any other brand in Britain.[41] Advertising costs became a major item of expense for Lever and his rivals. One of Lever's innovations was the gift scheme, in which customers collected soap wrappers in exchange for 'free' items, usually cheaply produced wallets, china, etc. Although co-operative leaders decried these schemes as fraudulent and wasteful,[42] they were clearly popular with many of their own customers. In 1902 Whitehead, now chief salesman for Lever Brothers, reported that sales of Sunlight soap in Lancashire and Yorkshire co-operative societies were down by 25 per cent due to Lever's attempt to discontinue the prize schemes.[43] The problem of bonus coupons and prizes (adopted by manufacturers of tea and cocoa as well as soap) continued to be a subject of debate in co-operative circles throughout the early twentieth century, with the CWS sending out a questionnaire to co-operative managers in 1906 asking for details of their 'bonus trade' and asking whether the Wholesale ought to consider a similar programme for its branded products.[44]

---

[36] Cook and Cohen (1958), 218; Jeremy (1991), 60; Church and Clark (2001), 513, 515.

[37] 'The Assizes', *Times* (16 July 1907), 11.

[38] Cook and Cohen (1958), 217. On Port Sunlight, see Wilson (1954), 142–58; Jeremy (1991), 58–9; and Rowan (2003).

[39] Cook and Cohen (1958), 219.   [40] Wilson (1954), 32.

[41] Church and Clark (2001), 531.   [42] See for example CU Congress Report (1907), 133.

[43] Wilson (1954), 53–4.   [44] The questionnaire was reprinted in full in *BCR* (September 1906), 13.

By the 1890s, expanding production was clearly the order of the day. In October 1894 the CWS opened its new soap works, depicted in Figure 4.7, designed to accommodate an output of 400 tons per week. It was fitted with the latest machinery for producing its thirty different brands of soap, and was located in Irlam near the terminus of the newly opened Manchester Ship Canal.[45] During the same year, Lever Brothers became a publicly held company in order to fund expansion. The importance of the network of co-operative societies as a potential outlet for Lever products was highlighted in Lever's decision in June that year to offer CWS 50,000 5 per cent cumulative preference shares in the new public company.[46] Clearly Lever hoped that if CWS became a shareholder, they would be keen to promote Lever soaps to their member societies. But CWS let the proposal lie and did not respond. Subsequently Lever introduced the 'Lifebuoy' carbolic soap and 'Lux' machine-milled soap flakes, and bought out other soap producers in both the UK and America. By 1900 Lever Brothers and its subsidiaries accounted for about a sixth of the sales of soap in the UK.[47] Sold only in co-operative stores, and usually in competition with private makers' brands, CWS soap sales enjoyed a smaller share of the market. Thus, between 1895 and 1905 the Irlam

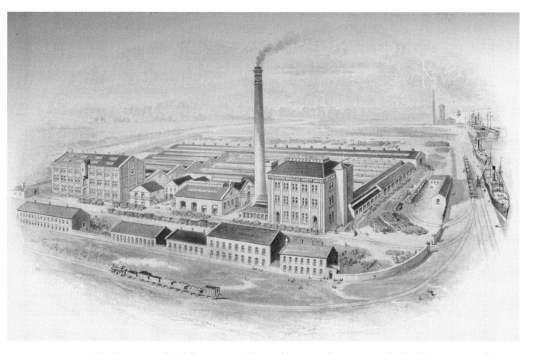

FIGURE 4.7. CWS soap works, Irlam, 1909. Opened in 1894, the purpose-built Irlam soap works was located on the northern bank of the Manchester Ship Canal, eight miles from Manchester. During the First World War, the CWS opened a margarine factory in nearby Higher Irlam.

[45] Redfern (1913), 240–1.   [46] CWS Board minutes (22 June 1892).
[47] Church and Clark (2001), 515, 532–3.

works never produced to full capacity, with output growing from 72 tons per week to 265 tons between 1895 and 1905, while Lever Brothers' total output was around 3,000 tons per week.[48]

By 1905 circumstances had changed. Improvements in refining processes meant that many types of oils and fats once used in soap manufacture were now in demand from food manufacturers for use in margarine and lard, including tallow and coconut oil. Soap makers therefore faced shortages and high prices for these essential raw materials, especially in early 1906. At that time stagnating wages led many consumers to reduce their soap consumption, resulting in falling sales. That July, Lever tried to reduce costs by reducing the size of his soap tablets by one ounce per packet, placing a notice on the wrappers. He also raised the wholesale price to retailers from 20s. to 25s. a ton.[49] Then, in August, Lever caused a major public controversy. At a meeting of northern glycerine producers, Lever proposed that the leading manufacturers should collaborate to economize on manufacturing and selling costs, cementing the deal with an exchange of shares. Arguing that there was a precedent for such arrangements in pricing agreements made by the Soap Manufacturers' Association, Lever argued that economies could be made through centralized manufacturing, combined buying, and reduced expenditure on sales staff and advertising, Annual advertising cost Lever Brothers £500,000 a year by 1906.[50] Lever's major competitors Gossage's and Crossfield's joined the combine together with some smaller firms. Together they accounted for around half of national soap output.[51]

By September 1906, these collective reductions allowed Lever to suspend a £6,000 advertising contract with the *Daily Mail*. This proved to be a costly decision, because the *Daily Mail* and other newspapers owned by Alfred Harmsworth (Lord Northcliffe) launched a crusade against the new 'soap trust' and Lever Brothers. The *Mail* played on fear of 'American-style' monopolists, and gained the support of many small retailers. It highlighted the reduced weight of Lever's soap tablets as a sign of things to come. Throughout October and November 1906 Northcliffe newspapers ran daily headlines such as 'Soap Trust Victims' and 'The 15-ounce Pound', and advised consumers about which soaps they should and should not purchase. By the end of November the negative publicity had reduced sales for the associated companies, and the 'soap trust' was abandoned.[52] Incensed by the damage to his reputation, Lever sued the Northcliffe papers, eventually receiving £91,000 in compensation. But Lever estimated that the affair had cost him about £500,000.[53]

While the *Daily Mail* campaign was costly for Lever Brothers and for the Northcliffe press, for the CWS it was beneficial. No fan of the Northcliffe press and its 'crocodile indignation', the Wholesale nonetheless benefited from the consequent increase in sales of its own-brand soaps.[54] Even after the opening of the Irlam complex, CWS had struggled

[48] Redfern (1913), 241; 'The Assizes', *The Times* (16 July 1907), 11.
[49] Wilson (1954), 72–4; Macrosty (1907, 2001), 169–70.
[50] Wilson (1954), 76–80; Macrosty (1907, 2001), 167.
[51] Macrosty (1907, 2001), 226–7.   [52] Wilson (1954), 80–2; Redfern (1913), 242.
[53] Wilson (1954), 87–8.   [54] *Wheatsheaf* (December 1906), 88.

to sell its own soap to societies. In 1900 it lamented that just over half of the soaps sold through the Newcastle branch were of Irlam make, while in Manchester and London the figures were around 27 per cent.[55] At the June 1900 quarterly meetings CWS leaders acknowledged that co-operatives in the north-east faced less competition, and condemned the lack of loyalty in the other regions. CWS Director Thomas Bland noted that at least the Manchester district's performance was an improvement over 1894, when only 18 per cent of its goods had come from Irlam. Members of the CWS Grocery Committee were sent to visit societies particularly reluctant to buy Irlam soaps.[56] According to another Board member, Thomas Hind, another director, argued that the problem was not quality:

The evidence of those who used this soap...was that it was as good as any other make; but the difficulty was to get the members to take it. (Hear, hear)....He was sorry to say they had greater difficulties with the large societies than with the small ones. The committee were willing to adopt any reasonable steps that would be likely to effect an improvement...but they could not spend £30,000 or £40,000 a year on advertising, because those who bought the soap would have to pay for that outlay.[57]

The *Daily Mail* campaign boosted CWS soap sales, keeping the Irlam works running around the clock during autumn 1906. Output grew from 250 tons per week to over 650 tons.[58] A number of societies passed resolutions to stock only co-operatively produced soaps. This rising demand persuaded the CWS to expand productive capacity. By 1908 it opened an additional soap factory in Silvertown, London, followed in early 1909 by a new works at Dunston upon Tyne, near Newcastle (see Figure 4.8). While sales were higher than before the soap trust agitation, with the Manchester district increasing its percentage of Irlam soaps to 50 per cent in 1909, by the end of that year the CWS was again urging societies to buy more of its soaps, noting that the supplies for the half year had averaged 460 tons when the works were capable of producing more than 900.[59]

Then, in 1910–11, Lever Brothers launched an assault on the co-operative movement. Lever sought legal redress against the growing number of co-operative societies (about 400) which refused to stock his products. In summer 1910 he arranged a series of 'trap orders' to various co-operative societies and then took legal action against them, claiming the societies had fraudulently passed off their own goods as the Lever brands they refused to stock. Writs were served on thirty-eight societies, but the CWS came to their aid.[60] At the first trial in October 1911, the judge criticized Lever for wasting the court's time, suggesting that 'the real ground of offence the plaintiffs entertained against the defendants was that the Co-operative Societies made and sold their own soap and other

---

[55] CWS balance sheets, 'Committee's Report' (March 1900).
[56] *Co-operative News* (16 June 1900), 664.
[57] *Co-operative News* (16 June 1900), 667.
[58] Redfern (1913), 243.
[59] CWS balance sheets, 'Committee's report' (March and December 1909).
[60] Redfern (1913), 245–6; Wilson (1954), 124.

FIGURE 4.8. Workers at CWS soap works, Dunston, c.1910. The Dunston upon Tyne works opened in 1909, as part of the CWS's effort to expand its soap trade. Photographs like this one were taken to demonstrate good working conditions and the use of modern technology in CWS factories, often accompanying articles in the co-operative press.

goods without dealing with the plaintiffs or private makers'. When Lever appealed, the appellate court concurred with the prior opinion, commenting that Lever's action was 'a somewhat audacious claim to a monopoly without warrant in law'.[61] The Lever cases again promoted increased sales of CWS soaps. Although still below CWS production capacity, by 1912 600 societies stocked only CWS soap.[62] Thus, in 1913 the CWS took the further step of refusing to stock private makers' soaps, although societies could of course purchase them from other suppliers. Meanwhile, Lever Brothers focused its efforts on acquiring its competitors, essentially recreating the soap trust of earlier years through corporate acquisitions. By 1914 Lever Brothers owned its major rival, Pear's, and produced almost half of all the soap used in the UK.[63] Nonetheless, legal victories and growing sales maintained co-operative confidence that they could match this competition.

By the early twentieth century many private manufacturers' goods were also heavily advertised, and co-operative society members expected to be able to buy them in

[61] *The Times* (14 December 1911), 3; (4 March 1912), 3.
[62] CWS balance sheets, 'Committee's Report' (December 1912).
[63] Wilson (1954), 120; Church and Clark (2001), 509.

co-operative stores. In response, the CWS tried a variety of methods to persuade societies and their members to choose co-operative productions instead. While historians have criticized co-operatives for their hostility towards advertising, revisionists have recently argued that the movement 'needs to be ranked among the main initiators of the marketing of branded goods and the use of the brand as a communicative device to add value to products which were difficult to differentiate in the minds of consumers'.[64] Whilst many co-operators regarded advertising as frequently dishonest, unethical, and an expensive waste of resources, the CWS realized that to compete it had to raise consumer awareness of its produce. CWS advertisements in co-operative papers, like that in Figure 4.9, sought an ethical approach to selling, highlighting the purity and quality of its goods. The Wholesale also argued that since co-operators owned the factories that

FIGURE 4.9. **CWS advertisement, 1900.** This advertisement, in the 1900 Co-operative Congress report, encouraged co-operative societies and their members to feel pride of ownership in CWS factories and the products they produced. Such messages were common features of CWS branding for much of the twentieth century.

[64] Schwarzkopf (2009), 199. See also Gurney (1996), 65–6 and 128–30, and Kelley (1998).

produced these goods they were therefore responsible for employing workers on good wages and working conditions. By 1900 the CWS magazine *Wheatsheaf* featured articles about its various works, including pictures of the factories, their machinery, and their facilities for workers.[65] In the words of one co-operative: 'buyers of Co-operative soap know that the persons who made it are well treated, having good light, good air, and good wages.'[66]

The CWS also funded exhibitions of co-operative productions, at Congress and in various localities. Groups of employees and members were encouraged to visit nearby CWS factories to see for themselves how 'their' goods were made, excursions that became a common feature of co-operative events. The CWS also supported window-dressing competitions among co-operative employees and created posters and materials to support the display of CWS goods. By 1900 the CWS had begun to employ its own travelling speakers for co-operative events. They delivered lectures illustrated by lantern slides showing every step of a product's journey to their store. It was also possibly the first major commercial organization to use film in the UK.[67] By 1913, the CWS even ran 'Ladies' Concerts' with societies, which featured musical acts alongside the speakers, who distributed free samples of CWS goods. There were also 'Smoking Concerts' for men, these offering CWS tobacco samples.[68] Recognizing that most products were purchased by female consumers, the Wholesale also utilized the Women's Co-operative Guild (WCG).[69] From 1903 the CWS contributed toward the WCG's yearly Congress, and from 1908 made an annual donation to its executive. At the local level it promoted recipe and cooking competitions using CWS goods and encouraged 'Push the Sales' campaigns.[70] But CWS promotional activities faced a serious limitation: they focused inward on the movement and its most active members, and rarely reached external audiences. Indeed, one reason for the neglect of co-operatives' contribution to marketing history is because its advertisements appeared almost exclusively in the co-operative press, rather than national papers and magazines. They were aimed at the converted co-operator, rather than the mass audience of consumers targeted by private advertisers. It was 1916 before the CWS geared its publicity department towards a more outward-facing marketing strategy.[71]

In the meantime, range and volume of CWS goods increased. This did cause some concern about the CWS's relationship with independent producer co-operative societies. The CWS's productive expansion brought them into competition with these

---

[65] For example, in 1906 the *Wheatsheaf* featured long articles on the CWS brush works in Huddersfield and Leeds, the Bristol Depot, and the Middleton Jam and Preserves Works.

[66] *BCR* [leader] (October 1895), 16.

[67] Burton (1994), 18–39; see also Redfern (1938), 430–1.

[68] *BCR* (November 1913), 13; (January 1914), 3; (April 1914), 3.

[69] See Vorberg-Rugh (forthcoming), chapter 4.

[70] CWS balance sheets, 'Agenda' and 'Minutes' (March 1903, March 1908). It is worth noting that, during the controversy between the CU and the WCG in 1914–18, the CWS did not withdraw its annual grant. See Scott (1998), 129–50.

[71] Schwarzkopf (2009), 206–7.

societies, and in some cases involved the absorption of producer societies into the CWS. As shown, the CWS's entry into production had caused controversy within the movement about the relationship between consumer and worker co-operatives. Despite the efforts of the Co-operative Productive Federation (CPF) and the new wave of worker co-operatives established in the 1890s, the consumer movement was dominant.[72] The changing commercial environment of this period favoured large-scale production, and, unlike the smaller worker co-operatives, the CWS had plenty of capital to fund modern factories which could meet the increasing demand of growing consumer societies. Although some societies had strong relationships with nearby producer co-operatives, as was the case in Leicester,[73] by the 1890s it was clear that if the movement wanted more co-operative goods in its shops, it would be the Wholesales that made them.

Even so, when the CWS manufactured items where producer co-operatives were already active, controversy ensued within the movement. In 1892, the CWS Board agreed to a resolution from the Gateshead Society which asked the CWS to establish a printing and stationary business. This caused tension at quarterly meetings, as the CWS had up until then given its printing orders to the Co-operative Printing Society (CPS), providing at least a quarter of the latter's business.[74] This was a further blow to the CPS, which had lost significant business in 1887 when the Co-operative Newspaper Society set up in-house operations to print the *Co-operative News*. With the new printing proposal, the CWS threatened to become a formidable competitor for the CPS. Although the CWS stressed that its initiative was principally aimed at in-house printing for its own operations rather than intended to compete with the CPS for co-operative societies' business, within five years it was already moving into this field, printing co-operative society balance sheets, society histories, and other materials.[75] By 1908 it had three printing works (Longsight, Pelaw, and Leicester), reflecting not only the resources the CWS Board could invest in new enterprises but also its attention to strategic location, so that it could service societies across the country.[76]

The growing prosperity of the movement increased the appetite of societies for CWS produce, and many societies perceived major benefits accruing to them from the location of new productive outlets in their vicinity. Flour milling, in which producer

---

[72] See Cole (1944), 204–8.

[73] In Leicester, the consumer co-operative society's management committee included many who were also involved in the local co-operative productive works, including Amos Mann, one of the founders of the Anchor Boot Works and the treasurer of the Co-operative Productive Federation; he became LCS president in 1908. Meanwhile, John Butcher, the long-time manager of the CWS Wheatsheaf boot factory, was also on the LCS management committee and helped create the Midland Federal Corn Mill in 1875. See Thomson (1911), 102–3, 121–2.

[74] Redfern (1913), 189–91.

[75] CWS Director Thomas Moorhouse, in responding to the questions of Gateshead delegate Mr Thornton at a June 1900 quarterly meeting, noted that the printing department 'hadn't made special point of canvassing their members for trade'—but in the same breath pointed out that they could now offer colour printing. *Co-operative News* (16 June 1900), 665.

[76] Cole (1944), 211.

co-operatives had long been active, especially interested retail societies. By the 1890s new roller technologies made major increases in productivity possible, a development further assisted by new sources of cheap, imported wheat from North America and Eastern Europe. Small, inland mills with little capital for investment were extremely vulnerable. Demand from retail societies grew rapidly, as flour and bread were major items of the working-class diet and formed a significant portion of societies' trade. By 1900 nearly two-thirds of all societies had flour departments, and the largest retail societies had begun to build sizeable bakeries.[77] Moreover, large private mills were being constructed in port cities, which might draw societies' trade. The CWS's large plant at Dunston, constructed between 1889 and 1891, was typical of a whole series of projects to modernize the organization's productive capacity; these involved a brand new boot and shoe works at Enderby in 1888, and the Irlam soap works in 1894. The construction at Dunston accelerated in response to rumours that a consortium of flour millers were planning to set up a joint milling enterprise which would supply half a million consumers from 'the Humber to the Tweed', including many co-operative societies.[78]

Inevitably, tensions between the CWS and producer co-operatives involved in milling continued throughout the 1890s. Following a series of conferences between the CWS and co-operative mills in Lancashire and Yorkshire in the spring of 1901, the Wholesale began to act as agent for several of the 'federal' mills, but this compromise proved to be only a temporary respite, as the small federals were unable to meet all co-operative requirements. In the summer of 1901, CWS Board member William Lander claimed that the weekly demand for flour exceeded the federal mills' output by 10,000 sacks per week.[79] In 1903 both the Hull and Liverpool societies put forward motions asking that the CWS establish corn mills in their areas which gathered some support, though they were rejected by the CWS Board. But after deliberating, it relented, and recommended to the March 1904 meetings that they erect a mill in the Manchester district. In response, the Heckmondwike society moved that, before building a new mill, the CWS should negotiate with the federal mills in the area, to see if they were willing to sell their enterprises.[80] Heckmondwike's resolution passed, and by 1906 two Lancashire mills agreed to sell. The recently refitted Star Mill in Oldham, pictured in Figure 4.10, continued milling under CWS ownership, while the outdated Rochdale mill site later became the Wholesale's paint and varnish works. Also in 1906 the CWS bought the privately built Sun flour and provender mills, located along the Manchester Ship Canal on the new Trafford Wharf site.[81] Although a group of Yorkshire mills decided not to sell, they were eventually bought out by the CWS in 1915.[82] By 1914 there were new CWS mills at

<hr>

[77] The Bolton Society, for instance, had established a bakery by 1885. See Peaples (1909), 139, 143.

[78] Redfern (1913), 229.

[79] Redfern (1913), 235–7.

[80] CWS balance sheets, 'Agenda' and 'Minutes' (March and June 1903); 'Committee's Report' (December 1903); 'Agenda' and 'Minutes' (March 1904).

[81] Redfern (1913), 235–8.

[82] Two of the three Yorkshire 'federals' voted to sell in 1905, but a third decided against it and the negotiations broke down. See CWS balance sheets, 'Committee's Report' (December 1905).

FIGURE 4.10. CWS 'Star' flour mill, Oldham, 1909. Begun as a federal mill by the Oldham Industrial and Oldham Equitable societies in 1870, the original 'Star' mill was destroyed by fire in 1890 and replaced with the latest technology of the time. It was purchased by the CWS in 1906.

Avonmouth, near Bristol, and in Silvertown, along London's Victoria and Albert Docks, and the CWS could claim to be the largest flour millers in the UK.[83] By 1920, whilst some producer co-operatives survived and even thrived, the consumer co-operative model had cemented its dominance. CWS takeovers of worker co-operatives became more frequent, particularly in times of economic crisis. Over time, such buyouts became relatively commonplace and controversy subsided.[84]

The CWS also sought to vertically integrate its operations. As part of its overarching production strategy, the CWS acquired not only productive sites and plants, but also sources of supplies needed to produce the goods they manufactured. A key area in this approach was the CWS's move into farming. In the early 1890s the Board decided to build a jam and preserves works at Middleton Junction (between Manchester and Rochdale), which began operations in the summer of 1896. Whilst the factory was under construction the CWS negotiated the purchase of the Roden Estate in Shropshire, con-

---

[83] Redfern (1913), 238.

[84] For instance, when in June 1908 the CWS purchased worker co-operatives in Birtley, Dudley, and Keighley and expanded into production for its sizeable hardware trade, it passed with little comment from delegates. See CWS balance sheets, 'Committee's Report' (March 1908).

sisting of 740 acres of land including five farms and a residential hall, for £30,000.[85] The aim was for the state to produce fruit and run a creamery. By August experiments were earmarked for 10 to 12 acres.[86] By 1901, the fruit farms and greenhouses covered more than 120 acres, providing strawberries, apples, damsons, plums, pears, and cherries for the Middleton jam works, as well as tomatoes, cucumbers, and other vegetables for pickling. Meanwhile, the CWS opened the estate hall as a convalescent home for co-operators in the summer of 1900.[87] Then in 1903 the CWS purchased the 120-acre Marden fruit farm in Hereford, which had supplied the Middleton works in previous years.[88] By 1908 the CWS had opened a purchasing depot for fruit, vegetables, and cereals in Wisbech, Cambridgeshire, and in 1912 acquired another 820 acres of farmland on the nearby Coldham estate, still being farmed by The Co-operative Group today. Altogether, by 1914 the CWS owned nearly 1,500 acres of farmland in four counties, producing supplies to the value of £23,000.[89]

4.3 CWS GROWTH OVERSEAS

As shown, the CWS's purchasing from foreign markets was a key part of its business strategy in attracting societies' trade. In the 1890s and 1900s the CWS continued to expand its presence in Scandinavia, opening new buying depots in Denmark (Aarhus, 1891; Odense, 1895; and Esbjerg, 1905) and Sweden (Gothenburg, 1895) for the purchase of butter, eggs, and bacon. In addition to purchasing from Scandinavian farmers, many of which were organized in agricultural co-operatives, the CWS also exported some items, including quantities of bran from its Dunston corn mill, used for livestock feed.[90] The CWS also extended its North American operations, opening an office in Montreal in 1894, and increasing its supplies of fruit and other produce from Spain through the opening of the Denia depot in 1896. Altogether, the CWS's expanding purchasing network kept its small fleet of steamships laden with imported foodstuffs, though in the long term, CWS began to move out of shipping in the 1890s as private shipping lines seemed to offer greater flexibility.[91] The importance of foreign supplies to CWS business is perhaps best illustrated by its strong support for the Manchester Ship Canal. J. T. W. Mitchell was among those who gave evidence to Parliament in support of the project and the CWS eventually became the Ship Canal Company's largest shareholder, investing £20,000. When the Canal (see

---

[85] Redfern (1913), 207–9.   [86] CWS Board minutes (24 July and 29 August 1896).
[87] CWS balance sheets, 'Committee's Report' (December 1901).
[88] CWS Board minutes (28 August and 9 October 1903). The CWS kept the foreman on as farm manager, and decided to raise the farm labourers' pay from 15 to 16 shillings a week, replacing the summertime cider allowance with an additional 2s. in pay between April and September; labourers also no longer had to purchase their own pitchforks. CWS Board minutes (30 October and 6 November 1903).
[89] CWS balance sheets, 'Committee's Report' (December 1914).
[90] Redfern (1913), 192–3.   [91] Redfern (1913), 135.

FIGURE 4.11. CWS Board members on opening day, Manchester Ship Canal, 1894. Co-operative leaders gathered aboard the *SS Pioneer* on New Year's Day 1894, and travelled the length of the new canal. In the front row, left to right: Thomas Brodrick (standing); Thomas Tweddell; Captain Rockett, ship's captain; J. T. W. Mitchell; John Shillito; and John Lord.

Figure 4.11), which transformed Manchester into an inland port city, opened on New Year's Day 1894, the first merchant vessel to travel its length was the CWS's *SS Pioneer*, with Mitchell and several other Board members aboard, as well as a cargo of cube sugar from Rouen.[92]

From the 1890s, vertical integration was evident in the CWS's foreign operations. As shown, the CWS had always pursued close relationships with international producers, seeking cost savings and quality control by cutting out the middlemen. From the late 1890s, CWS increasingly focused on owning key sources of supply. The first such experiment in this regard was in Ireland, and began in the mid-1890s. Building on its existing network of buying depots, the CWS moved to acquire creameries to *produce* butter supplies. In the mid-1880s, efforts had been made to bring Irish butter up to the quality of the better-selling Danish variety. In 1889 Horace Plunkett began working with co-operative leaders to establish the Irish Co-operative Aid Association, which subsequently

---

[92] Redfern (1913), 132–4.

became the Irish section of the Co-operative Union. Plunkett led a co-operative propaganda campaign in Ireland, recruiting R. A. Anderson to the cause.[93] The CWS buyer at
its Limerick depot, W. L. Stokes, worked with a local butter merchant to help establish
the country's first co-operative creamery in nearby Drumcollogher, with the CWS
investing some of the initial capital, and the Co-operative Union providing its model
rules and constitution.[94]

Although relations between the CWS and the nascent Irish movement began cor-
dially, matters soon deteriorated. At the 1891 Congress in Lincoln, Mitchell called for
Irish co-operation to be developed in the field of distribution as well as production, indicating the CWS's interest in developing creameries in Ireland (see Figure 4.12). This
antagonized Plunkett and his compatriots.[95] Plunkett believed that producer-owned
dairy co-operatives were better suited to the country's agrarian economy, and CWS
dairy production in Ireland would be a threatening competitor for Irish producer
co-operatives. Plunkett and his supporters went on to form the Irish Co-operative
Agency Society as a joint marketing effort for the productive creameries in 1893,

FIGURE 4.12. CWS creamery, Bunkay, Ireland, 1909. The CWS began opening creameries in
1895, and operated more than forty creameries and extensive auxiliary operations by 1902.
However, heavy losses and ongoing conflict with local producer co-operatives led to the CWS's
gradual withdrawal from the Irish dairying business from 1908.

[93] Robert Andrew Anderson, hired by Plunkett in 1889 to promote co-operatives in Ireland, was to
devote the rest of his long life to the cause. He was appointed the first secretary of the Irish Agricultural
Organization Society (IAOS) in 1894, and took over its presidency in 1932 after Plunkett's death;
Anderson died ten years later. See Anderson (1983) for his autobiographical account of his work.
[94] Bolger (1977), 61–6.   [95] CU, Congress Report (1891), 99.

and the umbrella organization the Irish Agricultural Organisation Society (IAOS) in 1894.[96] Meanwhile, the CWS went forward with its plan, opening its first creamery at Castlemahon (near Limerick), an asset taken over from a failing producer co-operative in 1895. Other CWS creameries and auxiliary operations followed, fuelling a conflict between the CWS and IAOS that would last for years. While the CWS argued that consumer co-operation should take precedence, and that the producer operations favoured landlords and property owners, IAOS increasingly viewed the struggle in nationalist terms, arguing against the 'imperialism' of English consumers over Irish tenant farmers.[97] Over the next decade, the ultimate benefactors of the internecine conflict were the two co-operative movements' private competitors.[98]

For the CWS, Irish dairying turned out to be a costly experiment. By 1902 it operated more than 40 creameries and 50 auxiliaries in Ireland, predominantly in Kerry and Limerick. In addition to operational difficulties and rivalry with IAOS, the CWS blamed its creamery losses on the lack of winter dairying by Irish farmers. In contrast, Danish farmers supplied dairies throughout the year, resulting in a consistent supply of butter.[99] However, the CWS and IAOS made limited progress in winter dairying and CWS dairying losses were considerable. In 1903 the creameries lost more than £12,000, and while losses were not as high in subsequent years the operations were never profitable.[100] Eventually, following a Co-operative Union-brokered conference with the IAOS in 1908, the CWS agreed to exit the Irish creamery business. The process was gradual, as the IAOS did not have the resources to immediately take over all of the CWS operations. Of the 34 creameries and 51 auxiliaries that had gone out of CWS hands by 1912, about two-thirds were purchased by private proprietors.[101]

Despite these difficulties the CWS developed productive facilities and sources of raw materials elsewhere. This was partly a response to competitive pressures. Just as small shopkeepers urged local wholesalers not to sell to co-operatives, multiple firms applied similar pressure on their suppliers. Thus, in the winter of 1899–1900 the CWS faced a boycott by several bacon providers in London. However, the CWS's resources and connections in Ireland and Scandinavia meant that the London 'bacon ring' faced an uphill battle. In 1899–1900 the CWS leased, and then purchased, an abattoir and bacon factory in Herning, Denmark. In January 1900 the Board authorized the construction of a bacon

---

[96] Bolger (1977), 72–5.

[97] For the CWS point of view, see Redfern (1913), 295–305; for that of the IAOS, see Anderson (1983), 76–85; see also Bolger (1977), 195–9, and Cole (1944), 242–52.

[98] See Doyle (2012).

[99] The contrast in CWS relations with Irish dairy co-operatives and the more established dairy co-operatives in Denmark is striking. In its reports the CWS Board reported on Irish 'backwardness' in language that can only have inflamed the IAOS and its supporters. For example, see CWS balance sheets, 'Committee's Report' (December 1903).

[100] The CWS Board published separate accounts for the creameries annually in its December reports, 1903–14.

[101] Redfern (1913), 304–5. Nor was the process over in 1912—in 1916, the CWS Board reported it had 2 main creameries and 6 auxiliaries remaining. CWS balance sheets, 'Committee's Report' (December 1916).

factory in Tralee, Ireland. In addition, the central Grocery Committee in Manchester worked closely with the London branch, drawing on information from its buying staff in both countries to bring in Irish and Danish bacon supplies via firms unconnected with the London ring. By December 1900 the boycott was broken and the move into bacon production was declared a success.[102] Further vertical integration was assisted by the development of additional processing operations at various CWS branches, including a purpose-built factory at Trafford Wharf from 1906, for washing, cutting, and smoking Irish bacon.[103]

Perhaps the most ambitious example of vertical integration during this period involved the CWS's decision to move into tea production. In 1892, Charles Fielding, the head of the tea department, had opposed the idea of the Wholesales acquiring tea plantations or gardens in India or Ceylon, on the grounds that the teas acquired for CWS customers were extremely varied, and could not be supplied from just a few tea estates.[104] But during the course of the 1890s, this view changed radically in response to increasingly ferocious competition from private tea suppliers, who proved adept at winning societies' custom. Branded teas were increasingly in demand, with Hornimans in particular winning over many co-operative customers. By 1899, a number of societies even allowed Hornimans to use their names in advertisements at major railway stations and in the national press, a practice to which the CWS objected vociferously.[105] As early as 1893, the CWS had launched a campaign to push its tea among societies, focusing especially on some fifty-six societies which had not previously purchased tea from the Wholesale.[106] Many private tea companies also began to offer incentives for individual consumers to buy their wares, such as free gifts or 'bonuses'. 'Bonus tea' became a major source of contention within the co-operative movement in the 1890s, with many arguing that the practice was un-co-operative. However, the popularity of 'bonus tea' with the ordinary co-operative consumer meant that even co-operative societies had to offer their own bonus schemes on CWS tea.[107] An additional consideration was the fact that the CWS, in concert with the SCWS, invested a substantial sum in its tea blending and warehousing capacity in the 1890s, opening new premises in London in 1897 (see Figure 4.13).[108] This redoubled the need for the CWS to hold its own in the tea market against this tide of fierce competition.

During the course of the 1890s, the view emerged that, after all, CWS plantations in India or Ceylon might strengthen the ability of the CWS to win custom based on arguments of quality and distinctiveness of product. In November 1897, the question of acquiring estates was placed on the agenda of the Joint Tea Committee of the CWS.[109] The following March, the decision was taken to send a deputation to India and Ceylon

---

[102] CWS Board minutes (11 November 1899; 12 January, 16 March, and 15 December 1900).
[103] Redfern (1913), 307.
[104] *CWS Annual* (1892), 467–8.   [105] CWS Board minutes (14 February 1899).
[106] CWS Board minutes (2 December 1892, 17 March 1893).   [107] Redfern (1913), 216–17.
[108] Redfern (1913), 214.   [109] CWS Tea Committee minutes (8 November 1897), NCA.

with a view to buying tea gardens.[110] Fielding accompanied the deputation in late 1898, and he reported back to the Committee in May 1899.[111] While at this stage no further action was taken, on the basis that the right estates had not yet been found, it was made plain that this was now a CWS priority. Thereafter, in 1902, a purchase of an estate was made in Ceylon in 1902, the first of a series of major acquisitions in India and Ceylon in the years before 1914.[112] (See Plates 5 and 8).

Another major CWS overseas venture stemmed from the soap trade. By 1900 the CWS was acquiring raw materials for soap through its purchasing depot in Sydney, established in 1897. In 1901, it laid plans for a works to boil tallow and extract oil near its Australian depot.[113] However, as shown, soap production was changing with the use of oil extracted from coconut kernel (copra). In 1902 and 1903, Lever Brothers were searching for new supplies of copra in the South Pacific and West Africa, with a view to producing their own coconut oil.[114] In 1910 Lever asked shareholders for £14 million to support these plans, explaining that: 'Soap makers not only in this country but also in America and elsewhere were having to become, in addition to soap makers, their own crushers and producers of many of the raw materials for their use.'[115] By 1911, Lever had

FIGURE 4.13. Tea department, London, 1909. Begun in 1882 in Hooper Square, off Leman Street, the tea department was a joint operation of the CWS and SCWS, formalized as the English & Scottish Joint Co-operative Wholesale Society (E&SCWS) in 1923. This building, on Leman and Great Prescott streets, stood opposite the London branch premises and was opened in 1897.

[110] CWS Board minutes (8 March 1898).   [111] CWS Tea Committee minutes (8 November 1897).
[112] Redfern (1913), 218–19.   [113] CWS balance sheets, 'Committee's Report' (June 1901).
[114] Jolly (1976), 109.   [115] The Times (1 October 1910), 16.

negotiated a treaty with the Belgian government securing commercial control over a vast territory in the Congo, one of the world's largest sources of palm oil.[116] In addition, Lever Brothers also worked with the Colonial Office to secure access to the palm oil trade in British West Africa. Unlike Belgian and French colonies, in British West Africa firms had to purchase their copra directly from the native Africans. But by 1910 companies had negotiated concessions granting them exclusive rights to develop palm oil production in specific areas, using copra supplied by the indigenous tribes. Lever's first concessions were in present-day Nigeria; and in 1912 he secured one in Sierra Leone.[117]

But the CWS were not far behind. In 1913, the CWS won a concession of 314 square miles in Sierra Leone and that October a deputation, consisting of Board members Lander, Joseph English, and George Thorpe, along with soap works manager J. E. Green (all pictured in Figure 4.14), left for Freetown with T. J. Alldridge, the CWS's agent in Sierra Leone, and A. R. Richards, who was to become the CWS's representative in West Africa. Members were reassured that, while the deputation hoped to secure benefits for British co-operators, 'it is not our intention to exploit the poor natives'.[118] In Freetown,

FIGURE 4.14. **Members of the CWS deputation to West Africa, 1913.** Sitting left to right, are Board members George Thorpe, William Lander, Joseph English, and Irlam soap works manager J. E. Green.

[116] For more on this topic, see Wilson (1954), 167–79.   [117] Wilson (1954), 180–3.
[118] *Co-operative News* (18 October 1913), 1376.

the deputation met colonial officials before travelling inland for a meeting with tribal chiefs in Masungbo (see Figure 4.15). Lander explained to a gathering of a thousand the CWS's plans to purchase copra and run an oil-producing factory, together with trading establishments under Richards's direction.[119] Following the CWS visit, representatives from the SCWS travelled to Gold Coast (now Ghana) in the summer of 1914, to investigate palm oil production and cocoa buying.[120] Although the First World War interrupted developments in West Africa to some extent, once hostilities ceased the Wholesales continued to work in the region.

4.4 SERVING CO-OPERATIVE SOCIETIES

The CWS strategy for maximizing societies' commercial loyalty also led it to widen the services it offered to them. As co-operatives grew into larger and more sophisticated operations, so new opportunities arose for the CWS to strengthen links with them

FIGURE 4.15. **West African tribes meeting CWS deputation, 1913.** The CWS deputation met with representatives from ten tribes in Masungbo, about 100 miles inland from Freetown, near the site of the proposed palm oil factory. More than 1,000 people gathered to hear Lander's address and to finalize the concession agreement.

[119] *Co-operative News* (14 February 1914), 212–13; (21 February 1914), 230.
[120] *Co-operative News* (4 July 1914), 860–1; (11 July 1914), 894–5. See also Redfern (1938), 88–91.

through the provision of new services. New CWS departments sprang up to meet these fresh demands. One was the precursor of the modern travel business. Rising incomes and falling transport fares brought travel for pleasure within the scope of working people, who could now afford day trips and even more extended holidays. By the 1880s some larger co-operative societies planned and sold excursions to members during holiday periods, a practice that grew rapidly. In 1905, the CWS Excursion Department commenced. Its first activities were trips to the Isle of Man, arranged with the Midland Railway Company. In addition the department was an agent for the North Wales Steamship Company for journeys to Llandudno with the Lancashire and Yorkshire Railway in 1906.[121] By 1913 the department had a turnover of £80,000. By 1920 the CWS published an annual holiday guide and offered its first overseas excursions, to the battlefield sites of France and Belgium.[122] Other new departments developed as offshoots of 'in-house' CWS services. The Engineering Department at Pelaw offered societies services in 'electric, hydraulic, gas and steam engineering'.[123] Similarly, CWS auditors provided services to co-operative societies after an amendment to the Industrial and Provident Societies Acts in 1913 made annual auditing compulsory. From 1916 the CWS's in-house legal department also took on legal work for societies.[124]

But perhaps the greatest expansion of CWS services to co-operative societies came in 1913 when, together with the SCWS, it took over the Co-operative Insurance Society (CIS). Garnett explains these developments in detail.[125] The CIS had originally begun as a limited company in 1867. In 1899, a few years after changes to the Industrial and Provident Societies Acts made it legally possible, it converted to co-operative status. By 1900 the CIS's primary business was insuring co-operative societies against fire or other accidents, and a small individual life insurance scheme. By 1905 it had begun construction of its new headquarters in Manchester (see Figure 4.16), just across Balloon Street from the CWS, and had branches in Glasgow, Edinburgh, Bradford, Newcastle, and London.[126] In 1906 about 650 societies were members, and the CIS had funds of about £165,000.[127] But the CWS had started its own insurance fund in 1873 following heavy losses through shipwreck.[128] It continued to build its insurance reserve, which reached £500,000 in 1898 following the passage of the Workman's Compensation Act. This prompted some in the movement to advocate the consolidation of the movement's insurance business.

In the summer of 1898, Newcastle branch chairman Thomas Tweddell raised the insurance issue with the CWS Board.[129] He argued that the CWS was not using its insurance funds to maximum capacity, and that the CWS should effectively subsume the CIS, organizing 'an insurance department on similar lines to the banking arrangements'.[130]

[121] CWS Board minutes (17 February 1905, 16 March 1906).   [122] Redfern (1938), 332–3, 429.
[123] CWS balance sheets, 'Committee's Report' (September 1903).   [124] Redfern (1938), 196, 431.
[125] See Garnett (1968), 117–48; for a rather more partisan account, see also Redfern (1913), 331–46.
[126] Garnett (1968), 125–7.   [127] Redfern (1913), 333–4.   [128] Redfern (1913), 97–8, 334.
[129] CWS Board minutes (27 July 1898).   [130] Redfern (1913), 334–5.

FIGURE 4.16. CIS headquarters, Manchester, c.1908. Designed by CWS architects, the CIS opened its headquarters in Manchester, extending the 'co-operative quarter' further along Corporation Street. Five years later, the CWS and SCWS jointly purchased the CIS.

A subcommittee was instructed to explore the possibility of the CWS providing insurance services for the movement generally. In the interim the CIS asked to undertake Workman's Compensation coverage for the CWS, seemingly unaware of CWS moves to swallow up its business.[131] The CWS decided against developing its own insurance department at this time, although it did increase its insurance funds and recommended rule alterations to allow it to expand into other areas of insurance except life assurance. It stressed however that, while it was seeking a full range of insurance powers, initially it only intended to insure its own and members' employees, under the Employers' Liability Act and Workman's Compensation Act. It stressed that it would seek members' approval before moving into other types of insurance.[132] But the opportunities in insurance remained tempting. In 1907 the Finance Committees of the two Wholesales held two special meetings to discuss insurance. In November they formed a joint committee with

[131] CWS Board minutes (27 July, 2 and 27 September, and 28 October 1898).
[132] CWS Board minutes (10 and 23 December 1898).

the CIS to explore joint initiatives in fire and other types of insurance.[133] Then at the
December 1907 quarterly meetings, the Sunderland society moved that the CWS begin
its own Insurance Department, a move supported by other north-eastern societies.[134] By
spring 1908 the CWS had decided that the absorption of the CIS by the CWS and SCWS
was the best course of action. It announced its intended action in June 1908. [135] However,
the June delegate meetings could not agree on the course of action to take, and called on
the Co-operative Union to arbitrate between the Wholesales and the CIS.[136] SCWS
members voted against participating, and by March 1909 the CWS Board retreated from
its support of the Sunderland resolution, leaving it free to consider its strategy.[137] It then
went forward alone and established its own fully-fledged Insurance Department.

Although the CIS's financial reserves nearly doubled between 1906 and 1911, its
resources were massively outstripped by those of the CWS, and it was only a matter of
time before the CWS brought this to bear. Having exercised its 'lender's privilege' in July
1909 to require that all properties built under the CWS Bank's house-building scheme be
covered by the CWS insurance fund, in 1910 it informed societies seeking overdrafts to
build their own premises that they would need to insure them with the CWS.[138] This
re-ignited the debate, which raged at Congress and at conferences throughout 1910. This
time the CWS resisted all calls for arbitration.[139] The debate continued throughout 1911,
while the passage of the National Insurance Act complicated matters further. That
autumn the CWS set up a special Health Insurance section to act as an 'approved society'
under the law, inviting its member societies to act as its local agents, and by summer 1912
the new section had more than 100,000 members.[140] Having had no such success, and
under pressure from its members, the CIS met with the Wholesales in the spring of 1912
to discuss terms for the transfer of engagements, and the Co-operative Union declared
itself in favour of the Wholesales.[141] In the end, once terms were agreed more than 80 per
cent of CIS member societies voted to approve the amalgamation.[142] As an editorial in
the *Co-operative News* put it, the CIS amalgamation had occurred 'Because the
Movement prefers to lodge their faith in the power of the two Co-operative Wholesale
Societies.'[143] By June 1913, the agreement was signed, and the CIS became jointly owned
by the CWS and SCWS.

[133]   CWS Board minutes (19 April, 4 and 18 October, and 1 November 1907).
[134]   CWS balance sheets, 'Agenda' and 'Minutes' (December 1907).
[135]   CWS balance sheets, 'Committee's Report' (March 1908); CWS Board minutes (14 and 28
February, 10 April, 22 May, and 12 June 1908).
[136]   CWS Board minutes (22 May and 12 June 1908); CWS balance sheets, 'Agenda' and 'Minutes',
(June 1908).
[137]   CWS balance sheets, 'Committee's Report' (December 1908); presented to March 1909 quarterly
meeting.
[138]   Redfern (1913), 340–1; CWS Board minutes (24 March and 10 June 1910).
[139]   For the CU's reconstruction of the situation up to this point, see Congress Report (1911), 89–98.
[140]   CWS balance sheets, 'Committee's Report' (September 1911 and June 1912).
[141]   CU Congress Report (1912), 104.
[142]   Garnett (1968), 146. The terms of the agreement were quite favourable to CIS management,
including a guarantee of full employment for three years for all CIS staff.
[143]   *Co-operative News* [leader] (14 December 1912), 1558–9.

4.5 THE STRUCTURAL CHALLENGES OF GROWTH

Co-operative membership grew from an average number of about 800 per society in 1890 to over 2,200 in 1914, creating some very large co-operative societies. While only one society (Leeds) had more than 20,000 members in 1891, by 1911 there were thirteen: Barnsley; Bolton; Bradford; Brightside & Carbrook (Sheffield); Derby; Leeds, Newcastle; Pendleton; Plymouth; Preston; Royal Arsenal (Woolwich); St Cuthbert's (Edinburgh); and Stratford (East London).[144] Larger societies faced new issues, as co-operatives moved from being small community organizations to large, mass membership organizations. Throughout this period, big societies experimented with the development of district voting, local subcommittees, and other means of adapting co-operative democracy on a larger scale.[145] However, these 'mega-societies' were far from the norm. Before 1914 the vast majority of co-operatives remained quite small (see Table 4.8), with 90 per cent of UK co-operative societies in 1891 having fewer than 2,000 members, and a full two-thirds with less than 500. Nonetheless, the trend was towards larger societies. By 1914, 75 per cent of societies had less than 2,000 members, with around 40 per cent at 500 or below.

Another trend, welcomed by co-operative leaders, was a gradual decline in the number of co-operative societies. The 1880s saw the number of distributive societies grow by more than 250 to reach around 1,200, and the figure continued to rise in the 1890s. Around the turn of the century, however, the number of societies stabilized, peaking at 1,453 in 1903 and gradually declining to 1,385 in 1914.[146] Given the difficulties inherent in coordinating more than a thousand independently governed societies, it is unsurprising that national leaders looked to reduce overall numbers. For instance, in 1887 the Co-operative Union and CWS had established a joint effort to help form co-operatives where none existed, lending financial assistance through the CWS Bank where capital couldn't be raised locally and sending staff to assist in canvassing the area. However, in 1900 the CWS Board adapted the 'Propaganda Scheme' to offer existing societies the same kinds of assistance to form branches in the neighbouring towns and villages which had no stores.[147] For co-operative leaders, new branches were preferable, as existing societies had greater experience than new start-up groups, could benefit from economies of scale, and (crucially for the CWS) consolidated orders into larger units rather than adding smaller, less economic ones.

Co-operative leaders also called for voluntary mergers of neighbouring societies. In areas of the country where co-operation was well established, there were sometimes two or more societies operating in close proximity, sometimes competing against one another for members. In 1900, for example, Blackburn hosted seven different co-operative societies (Bank Top, Blakey Moor, Daisyfield, Exelsior, Grimshaw Park,

---

[144] CU Congress Report (1912).   [145] See Webb and Webb (1921), 52–65.
[146] Cole (1944), 371–2.   [147] CWS Board minutes (15 December 1900).

Table 4.8. Size of British retail societies, 1891–1914

Membership	1891		1901		1911		1914	
	# societies	% of total	# societies	% of total	# societies	% of total	# societies	% of total
Over 20,000	1	0.1	4	0.3	13	0.9	21	1.5
15,001–20,000	1	0.1	8	0.6	14	1.0	16	1.2
10,001–15,000	11	0.8	18	1.3	26	1.9	32	2.3
5,001–10,000	22	1.6	49	3.3	76	5.4	70	5.1
2,001–5,000	85	6.2	116	8.1	158	11.3	189	13.8
1,001–2,000	125	9.1	174	12.1	225	16.1	222	16.2
501–1,000	214	15.5	248	17.2	257	18.3	248	18.1
Under 501	916	66.6	822	57.1	631	45.1	573	41.8
Total societies	1,375		1,439		1,400		1,371	

Source: CU Congress Report (1916), 245.

Industrious Bees, and Livesey), while Rochdale itself was home to three (Pioneers, Provident, and Conservative).[148] This reflected the intensely local nature of much co-operative development, and also a tendency for minority groups to split and begin their own society, as was the case in Rochdale.[149] Thus in many localities, overall co-operative membership could be quite large, but divided amongst several societies.

As co-operatives grew neighbouring societies sometimes found themselves in conflict with one another. Successful co-operatives usually sought to expand their businesses by opening branches in new neighbourhoods, thereby reaching additional members. As Scola noted in Manchester in the 1870s, co-operatives followed a somewhat different strategy of expansion from the emerging multiple retailers, whose branches tended to be opened in close proximity to each other. In contrast, co-operative societies scattered their branches in different working-class areas.[150] Problems could arise, however, when two or more societies claimed the same district as part of their trading area, a practice known as 'overlapping'. Although many societies worked out boundary agreements themselves with relative ease, as the Bolton and Farnworth societies did in 1896,[151] protracted battles ensued elsewhere. At the 1899 Congress, James Johnston (Manchester & Salford Equitable) moved for a Special Committee on the subject, commenting on difficulties in Rochdale, where the Provident society was planning to build new central premises within 200 yards of the Pioneers' headquarters at Toad Lane.[152] The Special Committee was formed, and reported to Congress the following year.[153] It pointed out that competition between co-operatives led to pressure to offer higher dividends than were warranted, failure to allocate proper reserves, or, in areas where there was little private competition, higher prices. It also led to societies competing for members by offering credit.[154] Moreover, overlapping led to unnecessary expense through duplication of shops and delivery services. The committee argued that the problem was the tendency for societies to focus on their own progress, rather than that of the movement as a whole.[155]

[148] CU Congress Report (1901).
[149] Cole suggests that the split in Rochdale was political, as despite its non-political policy the Pioneers society's leadership was considered Liberal in respect to local affairs. The catalyst came in 1869 when a recently dismissed manager started the rival Rochdale Provident Society, taking a considerable number of members with him; the two societies remained separate until 1933. See Cole (1944), 73, 94.
[150] Scola (1992), 234–5. For a discussion of private retail expansion from a local and regional perspective, see Stobart (2003), 155–78.
[151] Peaples (1909), 200.
[152] CU Congress Report (1899), 145. The original resolution called for an inquiry into overlapping in both consumer and producer co-operatives; however, an amendment passed which forwarded the producer co-operative question to the CU Productive Committee.
[153] The Special Committee was appointed by the United Board: J. Baldwin (North Western Section); James Deans (Scottish), F. Hardern (North Western); James Johnston (North Western); and Duncan McInnes (Midland; also CWS Director). CU Congress Report (1900), 32–4.
[154] On co-operatives and credit, see Johnson (1985), 144–92; and Vorberg-Rugh (forthcoming), chapter 4.
[155] CU Congress Report (1900), 33–4.

The special committee suggested various measures. It encouraged sectional and district conferences to educate activists and members about the dangers of overlapping. Societies whose operations were 'very closely mixed up' were urged to amalgamate or establish joint committees to agree common prices and dividend rates. Of particular importance was the committee's suggestion of a permanent arbitration board, to be elected annually by the Central Board (the Co-operative Union's executive). The board would be empowered to impose decisions on participating societies, who were expected to agree legally binding contracts on arbitration decisions, including penalties if they did not abide by the rulings. Moreover, the new body was to act wherever it was deemed necessary by the United Board (consisting of all the members of the eight sectional boards), and the Co-operative Union was to be empowered to expel member societies who did not comply.[156] This reflected a conviction among some leaders that the Co-operative Union required more authority over local societies. As noted in earlier chapters, Congress resolutions were not binding, and the Co-operative Union could only persuade in its efforts to shape co-operative policy.

The 1900 Congress received the report with little comment, but recommended it for consideration by societies at conferences during the following year. Notwithstanding progress on the issue in Scotland, little practical action ensued in England and Wales, as one observer noted at the 1906 Congress.[157] A paper to the 1906 Congress largely repeated the points made by the earlier committee, and, noting that 'the whole trend of modern business is in the direction of syndicates, trusts and combines, with large capital, and reduced cost in working expenses', he warned that 'the co-operative movement must work on similar lines'.[158] However, his calls were unsuccessful in shifting opinion at this point.

But at least one senior figure was prepared to try to make progress on the issue. J. S. Gray's presidential address to the 1906 Congress was a milestone. As the Co-operative Union's General Secretary, Gray (pictured in Figure 4.17) was a well-known figure. Assistant secretary to E. V. Neale from 1883 before succeeding him in 1891, Gray was a formidable administrator. Sensationally, he called for the creation of a single, national co-operative society. Gray distinguished between active members, or 'the real co-operators', and those who joined solely for their economic benefit.[159] In effect, Gray presaged what Fairbairn would later identify as a problem in the development of the Rochdale model: the conflict between the short-term individual interest of members and their long-term collective interest in a strong community enterprise.[160] Gray also tackled the issue of relations between the societies themselves, acknowledging the dysfunctionality of the federation. Commenting on the conception of co-operation as a 'state within a state', popular in the movement since its coining by Lord Rosebery in an 1890 Congress speech, Gray challenged its veracity:

We cannot say that the co-operative movement as a whole is a 'State', because each separate society is independent of any of its fellows, and there is no cohesion, except where advantage and

---

[156] CU Congress Report (1900), 34.
[157] CU Congress Report (1906), 365–77.   [158] CU Congress Report (1906), 370–1.
[159] CU Congress Report (1906), 50.   [160] Fairbairn (1994), 16.

FIGURE 4.17. J. C. Gray (1854–1912). Formerly secretary of the Hebden Bridge Fustian Co-operative Society, Gray became the Co-operative Union's assistant general secretary in 1883 and succeeded E. V. Neale as General Secretary in 1891. He retired due to ill-health in 1911 and died the following year.

profit can be shown. Neither can it be said that the local town or village society is a State in itself, because its hold upon its members is so slight and illusory. Even the well-being of the Co-operative Union 'State' and the Co-operative Wholesale Society 'State' is subject to the caprice and fancies of every other society - they may work with or against these institutions, just as they think fit; there is no obligation to remain true to each other.[161]

He stressed the need for greater unity of structure within the movement, in order for it to meet contemporary and future challenges.[162]

Gray's plan for a 'National Co-operative Society' placed the Wholesales at the centre, noting that their national resources and extensive capital made them the 'natural nucleus' of his project of unification.[163] Basing his model on the CWS, Gray proposed the transfer of all local society members and assets to the central body, while modifying its constitution to allow for retail trading and individual membership. Instead of a central Board, the national society would be governed by an elected General Council of 150, which would then appoint committees to oversee the movement's business, educational, and administrative operations. Existing retail societies would become branches of the new organization, and while locally elected committees would remain responsible for their management, they would be subject to the authority of the General Council. Critically,

[161] CU Congress Report (1906), 53.   [162] CU Congress Report (1906), 53.
[163] CU Congress Report (1906), 55.

Gray envisioned a system of centralized buying, to consolidate the movement's purchasing power and favour co-operative productions. Members would continue to be allocated dividends based on their purchases in the national society, but only half of the amount would be available for them to draw out; the rest would be allotted in the form of fixed transferrable shares, receiving a standard rate of interest. Thus, every year half of the movement's total profits would be available 'for the extension and development of co-operative ideas and aims'.[164] In summarizing the advantages of his proposals, Gray included the prevention of overlapping and the creation of uniform dividends, as well as the unification of societies' myriad rules and administrative systems as practical benefits. In a national society, he argued, individuals would have greater security, the movement would be more competitive commercially, and it would have more resources to devote to creating the 'co-operative state' envisioned by their predecessors. Most of all, Gray hoped that co-operators would sacrifice 'a small portion of individual liberty for the common good' and unite around one policy and one system.[165]

At the conclusion of Gray's speech, the audience seemed unsure how to proceed. From the platform, SCWS chairman William Maxwell suggested that those present suspend their judgement for the moment and consider Gray's proposals in more detail at district conferences. In seconding a vote of thanks, the Co-operative Union's W. R. Rae, of the Northern Section, offered some tempered criticism: 'It might be that they would not agree with Mr Gray in all the details of the drill he wanted them to follow; they might desire more Home Rule in some cases; they might not be quite so sure about the glorious results that would follow from the leading of the two Wholesale Societies, but they did feel with Mr Gray that, in the common danger, union was necessary.'[166] In the weeks and months that followed, Gray's speech was the subject of numerous articles and letters in the *Co-operative News*, and many co-operative leaders, local and national, expressed views ranging from overall support to deeply felt outrage. For all the discussion, however, there were no practical efforts to bring Gray's plans to fruition—a reflection perhaps of just how ambitious and divisive they were. Nonetheless, Gray's proposals continued to inspire co-operative reformers in subsequent decades, including the General Co-operative Survey Committee and the co-operative commissions that came in the second half of the twentieth century.[167]

4.6 MANAGING A GROWING ENTERPRISE

Amongst the greatest challenges facing the CWS in the years before 1914 was how to manage its growing operations as it expanded in both scale and scope. In some respects, the CWS experience mirrored that of retail societies as they grew. At their formation, most co-operatives were staffed by their elected management committees in their spare

---

[164] Congress Report (1906), 53.   [165] Congress Report (1906), 60–1.
[166] Congress Report (1906), 65–6.   [167] See sections 5.3, 6.4, and 9.1.

hours, but once business developed, committees began to hire managers to oversee day-to-day operations. Committee members were paid for their time and expenses, but were not formally employed by their societies. As co-operatives expanded, they developed subcommittees to offer more specialized oversight, usually taking charge of a particular department such as grocery or drapery—although few committee members had retail experience themselves. The number of employees grew as business expanded, and societies increasingly developed hierarchical structures under branch and department managers. Over time it became common for larger societies to appoint a secretary, responsible for financial administration, and/or a general manager focused on operations. By the twentieth century, full-time officials had become the norm in many societies.[168]

Managerial staff were appointed by, and reported directly to, the management committees. However, as management became more professionalized, tensions could arise between elected committees and paid officials. Although the Co-operative Union's first *Handbook for Co-operative Committee Members* was published in the early 1920s, its commentary on the differing roles is an accurate depiction of concerns emerging before 1914:

> Committees, too frequently, try to manage the society. This is not their function. Their function is to guide and direct policy.... The more a committee-man knows of the technical side of the society's business the better; but he should not let his knowledge tempt him to interfere with the management of departments, for he will, by so doing, weaken the sense of responsibility in the managers of those departments and probably create friction.[169]

Management committees were often loath to cede much authority to paid staff, and even societies' most senior officials had little voice. While staff were encouraged to be members of their societies, before 1914 most co-operatives prohibited employees from standing for, or voting in, management elections, to ensure that consumer-members retained control.

Despite these constraints, as co-operative societies grew in many parts of the country a new cadre of professional co-operative managers came into being. Managerial functions in co-operatives became increasingly specialized, and by the 1890s societies seeking additional staff could draw upon a pool of experienced co-operative candidates. Whilst societies could, and did, hire managers with a background in private trade, in many cases co-operatives sought to hire candidates with co-operative experience, or to promote from within their existing staff. For instance, the Bolton society's Joseph Pomfret began his employment as a 'check lad' in 1875 and moved up through the society's management, becoming head clerk in 1880, secretary in 1894, and then general manager in 1905. Others moved between co-operative societies, such as tailoring manager Walter Mercer, who had previously worked for societies in Crewe, Colne, and Bury before being hired in Bolton in 1898.[170] By the turn of the twentieth century, co-operative management was gaining increased attention from co-operative leaders, and the

---

[168] For an overview of co-operative store organization in this period, see Webb and Webb (1921), 28–46; Hall (1923) is an excellent source for more detail.

[169] Hall (1923), 104.   [170] Peaples (1909), 484–8, 499–500.

Co-operative Union's Central Education Committee began to develop training courses for employees on topics such as bookkeeping and salesmanship. By 1905, such courses had enrolled more than 1,800 students; soon after a textbook for managers, edited by Sunderland drapery manager R. J. Wilson, appeared.[171] In the years before 1914 two new professional organizations developed, the National Association of Co-operative Secretaries (1909) and the National Association of Co-operative Managers (1912), creating new avenues for officials who sought a broader role for co-operative management.[172] Although in their infancy before the First World War, in subsequent years these organizations worked with the Co-operative Union and other bodies to provide greater attention to employee training, encourage interaction between managers from various societies, and raise the status of officials inside the movement.

Unsurprisingly, CWS management structures shared many of the features of retail societies, from whom its directors were elected. By the 1890s most Board members came to the CWS with long experience as committee members and/or officials of prominent retail societies.[173] Less is known about the recruitment of CWS senior managers in this period, although records suggest that many personnel were able to move up through the administrative ranks. For instance, Edward Jackson, who began his career with the CWS's London branch at the age of 16 in 1886, was later appointed traveller for the Bristol depot in 1899, and eventually became the first manager of the CWS Agricultural Department in 1914. Others came from co-operative societies, like New York Depot manager John Gledhill, or were hired from private employment.[174] As in retail societies, by the turn of the century the CWS had developed a significant administrative hierarchy, and the appointment in 1899 of Thomas Brodrick (pictured in Figure 4.18) as the CWS's first permanent, full-time secretary suggests the Board recognized the increasing importance of professional managers. Brodrick, who began his CWS career at 16 in 1872, had trained as an accountant and played a significant role in CWS development throughout his impressive 51-year career; he received a knighthood in 1922.[175]

Although professional managers were playing a greater role, authority remained vested in the CWS Board, the structure of which had changed little since the establishment of the Newcastle and London branches in the 1870s. The CWS was overseen by a General Committee of twenty, sixteen of whom were elected from the Manchester district. The branch committees in Newcastle and London, each with eight members elected by their districts, appointed two of their ranks to represent them on the General

---

[171] Brown (1937), 29–30.

[172] The two organizations eventually merged with the National Union of Co-operative Officials, established in 1917, to form the National Association of Co-operative Officials (NACO) in 1970. See NCA (GB 1499 NACO).

[173] Redfern (1913), 375–92, provides a biographical index of important figures in CWS history in its first fifty years, which offers insight into the background of early leaders but is often vague as to whether particular CWS directors came from the elected or paid management of their societies.

[174] Jackson (1936); Redfern (1938), 568, 577. The 1938 volume's biographical supplement (565–89) is an additional resource for information on CWS directors and officials, but is far from comprehensive.

[175] Redfern (1938), 573.

FIGURE 4.18. Sir Thomas Brodrick (1856–1925). Having joined CWS in 1872, Brodrick rose to become the CWS's chief accountant in 1884 and its first permanent secretary in 1899. He was knighted in 1922 and retired the following year, after fifty-one years' service.

Committee, and branch decisions were subject to the Board's approval. Like the retail societies, the CWS Board created permanent subcommittees covering different aspects of the business, including finance, grocery, drapery, and productive operations. These subcommittees were replicated at branch level, and the general and branch committees held regular joint meetings. Also like societies' management committees, Board members were paid fees for their time and their travel. Despite the phenomenal expansion of its business, however, their work was considered part-time, which hardly reflected the time required to manage the CWS's numerous concerns.

Matters first came to a head over the fraught relationship between the General Committee and that of the Newcastle branch. In spring 1900, the former decided to exercise its authority over the branches to a greater degree, recommending that the General Committee appoint two representatives to the branch committees, just as the branches appointed two of their number to the main Board. The proposal was attacked by co-operators in the north-east as a ploy to assert excessive control from Manchester. Unsurprisingly, the proposal was rejected by the quarterly meeting in Newcastle.[176] However, at quarterly meetings elsewhere, including in London, the proposal drew very little comment, and the rule change was approved with more than a two-thirds majority.[177]

---

[176] *Co-operative News* (24 February 1900), 192; (17 March 1900), 254–5.
[177] CWS balance sheets, 'Business Paper, special general meeting' (March 1900).

This relatively small constitutional change was to be the beginning of further discussions. District conferences in Newcastle, Macclesfield, and Birmingham debated reorganization of the CWS leadership structure. Other issues were also raised, such as the advancing age of committee members and the proper level of payment for their services. There were recommendations that the CWS establish a superannuation fund to support CWS Board members in retirement, and the subject of pensions continued to be raised over the next few years.[178] Others questioned the ability of a part-time Board, whose appointments to subcommittees were arranged according to an annual rota, to oversee an enormous national and international operation.

By 1904, structural reforms had become a key issue at quarterly meetings. In December, motions from the Newcastle branch and the Reading society called for special inquiries.[179] Although postponed, the Reading proposal resurfaced in the June 1905 meetings, and was passed.[180] The Special Committee of Inquiry consisted of four members elected from the Manchester district, two each from London and Newcastle, and four representatives appointed by the General Committee of whom one each had to be from the branch committees.[181] Its remit covered seven key points: the constitution and method of election of the Board and the branch committees; the age candidates should be eligible for election; whether Board members should be paid a fixed salary; whether there should be a compulsory retirement age for Board members; whether Board members should receive a retirement allowance; whether branch committees were properly represented on the Board; and whether the Board and its committees should be enlarged. Over the next year, the committee visited CWS works and depots, touring factories and interviewing managers in Manchester, Newcastle, London, Bristol, and Leicester, as well as the Roden Estate in Shropshire and the various operations in Tralee, Ireland.[182] In 1906, the committee's report recommended enlargement of the General Committee from twenty to thirty-two members, sixteen from the more populous Manchester district, and eight each from London and Newcastle, dispensing with the branch committees in favour of a truly national board. It also recommended the establishment of four main subcommittees, each with four members from the Manchester district and two each from Newcastle and London: Finance & General Purposes; Grocery & Buying Depots; Drapery, Boot & Shoe, & Furnishing; and Productive. It rejected a proposal for a separate committee to manage the CWS's extensive productive operations, on grounds of complexity.

[178] Redfern (1913), 319.   [179] Redfern (1913), 318–20.   [180] Redfern (1913), 319.
[181] The Board representatives were John Shillito, Thomas Killon, Thomas Tweddell (Newcastle branch), and Henry Pumphrey (London branch). The elected representatives were Thomas Redfearn (Heckmondwike), James Johnston (Manchester); Frank Hardern (Oldham Industrial); William A. Hilton (Bolton); E. J. Graham (Newcastle); William Crooks (Blaydon); T. George Arnold (Royal Arsenal); and Robert Rowsell (Reading). Johnston chaired the committee, and Brodrick served as secretary. CWS, Report of the Special Committee of Inquiry (hereafter SCI Report), July 1906, NCA. The report, dated 12 May, was included with the CWS balance sheets for June 1906. It was subsequently reprinted, with the addition of the amendments proposed by member societies, for the Special General Meetings held 14 and 21 July 1906.
[182] SCI report (July 1906).

On salaries and fees, the report wanted tighter control over General Committee members' activities and expenditure. It wanted a salaried, full-time board, and its proposed amount of £350 per annum was accepted. General Committee members were to be restricted from holding other paid offices, but could retain their positions on their societies' management committees. Although they were empowered to serve on public administrative bodies, such as councils or Boards of Guardians, the report decreed that such offices should not interfere with their CWS duties. In addition, the report argued for specific arrangements for holidays, sick leave, and travel expenses, including the provision of contract tickets for first-class rail fares. It also contended that, as far as possible, meetings should be held weekly—twice monthly in Manchester and once each month at the branches.

The committee decided against setting a maximum age for General Committee candidates, but did require that they state their age on their nomination and voting papers. A set age for retirement was rejected as well. Instead, the report put in place a procedure in which Board members could vote, by three-quarters majority, to request the retirement of a committee member due to age, infirmity, or misconduct. Along with this 'stick', the committee included a 'carrot' to encourage older members to retire, providing allowances of between £2 and £3 a week depending on their years of service. Even here, however, member societies showed their interest in keeping expenses down. In future the newly salaried directors would fund their own retirement through a superannuation scheme. Concern over the age and fitness of CWS Board members would continue to be a source of concern. In the end, the original report was accepted, and the reforms of June 1906 became constitutional. Moreover, the inquiry became the model for future reform efforts. During the First World War, a similar committee would investigate the role and responsibilities of CWS auditors, and during the inter-war years new special committees would instigate additional constitutional reforms.[183]

4.7 CONCLUSIONS

The period 1890 to 1914 could easily be described simply as a period of consolidation and maturation for the CWS, with the strengthening of the organization's productive infrastructure and its domestic and international supply chains. It is certainly true that it saw continuing expansion and could boast ongoing success. Despite all its internecine struggles it was flourishing, and at the time of its Jubilee in 1913 more than three million co-operative members benefited from its profits. Co-operators had built one of the country's largest and most successful businesses, and CWS leaders were keen to share the story—through Percy Redfern's substantial history of the CWS and through a wide array of Jubilee festivities. The formal celebrations began after the quarterly meetings of 13 September, when delegates attended special evening events in Manchester, London,

[183] See section 5.7.

Newcastle, Carlisle, Leeds, Birmingham, Bristol, and Cardiff. After the final meeting in Manchester the following week, 950 dignitaries sat down to dinner in the CWS dining hall at Balloon Street, where they were entertained by two employees' musical groups—an orchestra and a male voice choir. *The Co-operative News* reported that the CWS head-quarters (see Figure 4.19) were lavishly decorated for the Jubilee events, and special bronze medallions cast for the occasion were to be found on every lapel. Throughout the autumn celebrations continued, including a gathering for 'kindred institutions', attended by representatives from the Co-operative Union and SCWS alongside international co-operators representing the ICA and the Austrian, Belgian, French, and German co-operative wholesales. Nor were the festivities simply for the movement's leadership; in October more than 2,500 CWS employees filled the Free Trade Hall for a special Jubilee evening, and sizeable gatherings were also held at CWS branches and premises elsewhere. All employees received Jubilee gifts of 10 shillings and a special 'casket' of CWS goods.[184] In 1913 the movement looked back with pride in its accomplishments, and forward with increasing confidence in co-operation's ability to build a co-operative state within a state.

FIGURE 4.19. **CWS headquarters, Manchester, 1913.** Now known as the Hanover Building, the structure to the left was completed in 1907, and held the CWS's boardroom and Mitchell Memorial Hall. The buildings to the right were later replaced by the current Co-operative Bank headquarters and, behind it, the Printworks complex.

[184] *Co-operative News* (20 September 1913), 1228–35; (27 September 1913), 150–2, 1270–3; (11 October 1913), 1340–1, 1345.

Yet there were already, by the eve of the First World War, growing causes for concern. By 1914 the great retailing multiples had arrived as serious contenders, and had shown themselves willing to escalate the political and ideological attacks on co-operation previously led by small traders and their associations. Moreover, there was a growing realization that faced with such sophisticated, modern retail organizations able to organize on a national basis, the structures of the CWS and the movement at large might be found wanting. This was the true significance of the Propaganda Committee, the acquisition of international sources of supplies, and the efforts to reform the movement through amalgamations or even a national society. Likewise, the 1906 initiative to reform the structure and function of the CWS General Committee betrayed a growing anxiety that co-operation might not enjoy the dominance in the twentieth century which it had established in the latter half of the nineteenth. This would of course, prove to be the case. What is important, however, is that neither the CWS nor the movement at large merely sleepwalked into trouble. Future problems were being anticipated as early as 1900, and plans being drawn up to address them. Yet the difficulty of implementing such strategies for reforming the 'dysfunctional federation' in a diffuse, combative, and democratic movement was already becoming apparent. Much of the twentieth century would merely repeat and reinforce the lesson.

CHAPTER 5

....

WAR AND PEACE, 1914–38

....

LIKE every major institution in British society, the co-operative movement faced major upheaval as a result of the Great War of 1914–18. The first modern 'total war' had seismic consequences. Six million Britons served in the armed forces, and by November 1918 around 1.6 million had been wounded or taken prisoner. Around 745,000 were killed in action, representing 9 per cent of the country's men under 45.[1] Initial efforts to allow business and the economy to operate as they did in peacetime ('business as usual') had to be abandoned by late 1915, and the state extended its authority over every aspect of military and civilian life. This unprecedented growth of state power over the economy inevitably impinged upon the co-operative movement, given its prominent position in national economic life by 1914.

A crucial area, and one which went right to the heart of the co-operative movement's business, was the nation's food supply. In 1914, two-thirds of Britain's food was imported. Provisioning the home front and the military was an enormous challenge. Given that co-operatives had the country's most extensive distribution network and were important manufacturers of staple goods, co-operators expected to play a prominent role in government strategies for the food supply. But until 1917 these expectations were frustrated. Most of the business experts recruited by the state as advisers on food were multiple retailers and other private traders. The co-operative movement was ignored, and even actively discriminated against. Government advisers drawn from the ranks of private traders who had been hostile to co-operation used their influence with politicians and civil servants to keep the co-operative movement at arm's length from policy formation. The movement struggled to adapt to the turbulent conditions of war. Early in the conflict, co-operative leaders joined with other working-class organizations to call for government price controls and national rationing of basic supplies. The effectiveness of German naval warfare created food shortages and soaring prices, fuelling popular discontent. By 1917 the revolution in Russia prompted concerns that food shortage and prices might cause serious unrest in Britain. By then, frustration at three years of being treated as outsiders persuaded the co-operative movement to reverse its policy of political neutrality and establish the Co-operative Party. In the final year of the war the CWS

---

[1] Marwick (1965), 290.

and other co-operative leaders were brought into the Ministry of Food, but by then the movement had concluded that political action was necessary to defend its interests.

The cessation of the war did not end the turbulence, even given high hopes about post-war reconstruction. Demobilization was haphazard and strong trade union power, coupled with post-war inflation, led to much industrial conflict. At the end of the war there were major questions about the nature of post-war society and the political system. The war had seen a dramatic strengthening of organized labour, with trade union membership doubling from four to eight million.[2] Organized labour's active collaboration with government had raised expectations that after the war, unions would be accorded a place in the formation of economic and social policy, and that promises of 'homes fit for heroes' would translate into substantial social reform. At the heart of this was a challenge to the Victorian 'night-watchman' conception of the state, and the notion that the war had shown that the state could, and should, be an active manager of national economic affairs. Reformers' hopes were bolstered by the Representation of the People Act of 1918, which enfranchised all adult men and, for the first time, a substantial proportion of women. The success of the Labour Party at the General Election of 1918, and the election of A. E. Waterson as the first Co-operative Party MP, also raised expectations. Thus the co-operative movement faced a context which was challenging, yet in some respects promising, given the apparent empowerment of working-class people. This radically turbulent political environment confirmed the importance of a more active political role for the co-operative movement through the Co-operative Party, a conviction strengthened by government efforts to tax co-operative surpluses as income. The relationship of the movement, and especially the Co-operative Party, with the organized labour movement in general, and the Labour Party in particular, became matters of crucial importance.

But these expectations of a 'new orthodoxy' of state intervention and social reform were not fulfilled. The post-war boom, fuelled by the relaxation of state controls and the retooling of the industrial infrastructure for peacetime, abruptly ended in late 1920, with a collapse in prices and a sharp rise in unemployment to over two million. Problems were compounded by the coalition government's decision in 1920 to return to pre-war notions of political economy as a means of reviving the fortunes of the financial sector, a course which involved balancing the budget by swingeing public expenditure cuts, as exemplified by the infamous 'Geddes Axe' of 1922.[3] Inevitably this impacted the retailing sector, including the co-operative movement. For the first time since 1894, CWS sales declined in 1921 and 1922. From the mid-1920s there was some recovery, but this was geographically uneven. Areas of heavy manufacturing industry and mining in northern England and South Wales were the hardest hit, and the slowest to recover. Growing American competition and the British decision to return to the gold standard in 1925 reduced the competitiveness of British exports and exacerbated the difficulties of the 'old' staple industries of textiles, iron and steel, shipbuilding, and heavy engineering. In contrast the South and the Midlands saw accelerating growth as a result of the rise of

[2] Cole and Postgate (1961), 552.   [3] See Daunton (2002), 78–94.

new consumer-oriented industries such as motor vehicles and electrical household products such as electric irons, radios, and vacuum cleaners. Consumption in these areas was buoyed by job growth in the new industries, and these regions led the way in the rise of multiple shops and department stores. Such geographical disparities became even more apparent in the 1930s.

After the downturn of 1921–2 the trade of the CWS and the co-operative movement resumed expansion. During the inter-war period co-operative growth was especially prominent in the South and Midlands, while in depressed areas co-operative societies faced tough times. For the CWS, the challenge was to meet the needs and interests of societies in different regions. Some societies in the depressed areas faced liquidation, and in the 1930s the CWS responded by establishing the CWS Retail Society to help support societies in trouble. It also launched initiatives to help growing societies, including new service departments to help meet the challenge from antagonistic private traders. In addition, the CWS developed fixed maximum prices and national advertising programmes for selected goods, and expanded its own product lines in response to producer associations' efforts to prevent co-operatives paying dividends on their goods through resale price maintenance (RPM). Notwithstanding this expansion into new products and services, the CWS's greatest strengths remained in the grocery and provisions markets. After the resumption of free trade in the 1920s, British overseas trade policy changed dramatically in the 1930s as the Great Depression prompted worldwide adoption of protectionism. In 1932–3 the British government abandoned free trade in favour of preferential tariffs for empire goods. The CWS responded to these developments in various ways, including new strategies for working with international co-operative organizations in Australia, New Zealand, and the Soviet Union.

Throughout the inter-war period CWS and the movement struggled to adapt the co-operative model to cope with the turbulent times. At the end of the war, the movement had conducted a major survey into the state of, and prospects for, the movement, and in 1919–20 debated the Survey Committee Report. Although the Survey, rather like J. C. Gray's speech at the start of the century, achieved little in the way of immediate reform, its observations were prescient and foreshadowed the conclusions of later investigations into the movement. The period was, therefore, one of great change in co-operation and its position in British society. This chapter will examine how the CWS and co-operatives adapted to the fast-changing demands of war and an unsettled peace.

5.1 CO-OPERATIVES AND THE FIRST WORLD WAR

In August 1914 the consensus was that the European war would be brief, and that economic and social disruption would be minimal. It was believed that British naval strength would protect food imports, and there would be no need for the state to interfere with the normal operations of international trade and retailing. There were initial problems due to panic hoarding, and disruption of commerce due to cancelled shipping contracts, but these were seen as only temporary difficulties which could be managed. At the start of the war, the CWS moved quickly to try and ensure normality. In early August it reassured societies that it would execute all its contracts for flour, sugar, and butter at the usual prices, although they reserved the right to limit the quantity sold to any one society.[4] In the first week, the CWS Bank reassured societies concerned that members might draw out capital, and quickly arranged an additional £500,000 in credit to guard against a run. The Board instructed its Silvertown flour mill's manager that societies were not to be asked to pay anything toward charges for 'war risks' from its suppliers.[5] In September the CWS reassured societies through the *Co-operative News* that, unless the naval situation changed, it would not raise its flour prices.[6]

Inevitably, the domestic food supply was a concern for Herbert Asquith's Liberal government. Business experts were recruited to a series of advisory committees established to deal with a range of economic problems. First came the Prices Advisory Committee, tasked with dealing with inflation. On 6 August CWS secretary Thomas Brodrick, Board member George Thorpe, and London branch manager William Openshaw attended a meeting at the Home Office, alongside representatives from other large grocery firms, to discuss fixing retail prices. However, when invited to appoint two representatives to the new Committee, the Board decided not to do so, because of the CWS's rigid policies on Board members using their time for CWS work.[7] Given the difficulties they faced in getting representation on government committees during the next three years, this was a decision the Board was to regret. The Prices Advisory Committee therefore represented only private trade, and it shaped government food policy in the early years of the war. Soon after its formation, the committee was required to publish lists of recommended maximum prices for a range of basic goods. The recommendations reflected private traders' estimates of a reasonable margin of profit, which were, unsurprisingly, quite generous. In any case, these were not enforceable by law and many traders took the opportunity to increase prices and margins.[8] Although the initial panic subsided within a few weeks and prices declined, they never returned to pre-war levels.

Expectations of a short war ensured that state intervention was initially kept to a minimum. Two commodities attracted early attention, sugar and wheat. High British sugar consumption made it essential that supplies and prices met demand.[9] But the main supplies from central Europe were now cut off. A Royal Commission on Sugar Supplies was set up in August 1914, and in October recommended a state monopoly of sugar imports. Within weeks the Commission controlled both wholesale and retail prices.[10] As a staple

---

[4] Redfern (1938), 102–3.   [5] CWS Board minutes (7 and 14 August 1914).
[6] *Co-operative News* (19 September 1914), 1188.   [7] CWS Board minutes (7 and 14 August 1914).
[8] Barnett (1985), 37–8.
[9] Sugar was important to working-class consumers, who used it to preserve food and to add flavour to bland diets. Contemporary medical experts argued that sugar's high caloric value made it an important source of nutrition. See Stark (1984), 41–2.
[10] See Stark (1984), 41–2, and Barnett (1985), 31.

of the national diet, bread and therefore imported wheat (about 80 per cent of total supplies) was another source of concern. In autumn 1914 a Grain Supplies Committee was
appointed with orders to build a reserve of two million quarters of wheat by summer
1915. Ironically, its purchases actually helped to drive up world grain prices.[11] The CWS, a
major provider of sugar and one of the country's largest flour millers, was not invited to
participate in either committee, an omission which may have stemmed from its earlier
refusal to sit on the Prices Advisory Committee.

In any case, the CWS was otherwise occupied. By mid-August, 350 of its employees
had joined the armed services. By 1918 about 6,000 had enlisted, causing serious
labour shortages. As in the Boer War, the CWS promised enlisted employees their
former positions on demobilization, and also paid the difference between military
pay and employees' regular wages to the workers' dependants (see Figure 5.1).[12] In
September 1914 the CWS won War Office orders for 200,000 tunics, trousers, and
caps, along with 63,000 blankets, for which the Wholesale charged cost price. The
CWS was also called upon to help victual military encampments. It provided catering for the East Lancashire Territorials and later used the Newcastle branch dining
room to feed locally stationed troops. There were also uncertainties about foreign
branches and overseas shipping. In early September twenty-one staff, family members, and local residents were evacuated from CWS Rouen Depot, using the CWS's
New Pioneer.[13]

During 1915 it became clear that the war would be lengthy and expensive in lives
and resources, and was essentially a test of the industrial might and endurance of the
warring powers. Industry and the military competed for manpower, and the government was compelled to make significant concessions to organized labour in order to
ensure adequate industrial production. In March 1915 an agreement was struck
between the government, the Labour Party, and trade unions. Trade unionists agreed
to settle disputes by arbitration rather than strikes, and to allow the 'dilution' of skilled
labour during the war. In exchange, the government agreed to the resumption of 'normal' industrial relations and trade practices when the war ended.[14] These conditions
applied in those CWS factories that moved to war work, and employees in distribution sought similar agreements as male retail workers left for military service or
better-paid war industries, and were replaced by women. By summer 1915 the Amalgamated Union of Co-operative Employees (AUCE) negotiated a policy with the
CWS and other co-operative societies, in which 'substituted' female workers would

---

[11] Barnett (1985), 27–30.

[12] During the Boer War, CWS paid more than £1,500 to reservists' dependants; CWS balance sheets,
'Committee's Report' (December 1902). In 1914 it continued the policy, and, until the government
legislated provision for the soldiers' dependants, paid three months' wages to employees' widows; see
CWS Board minutes (14 August, 10 September, and 6 November 1914). The total cost was estimated at
over £650,000; Redfern (1938), 118.

[13] CWS Board minutes (7 and 14 August, 18 September, and 2 October 1914). See also Redfern (1938),
101–13.

[14] Cole and Postgate (1961), 512.

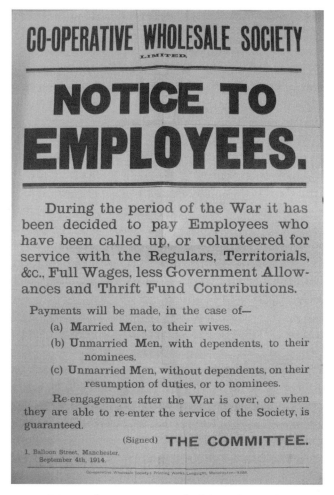

FIGURE 5.1. **Notice to CWS employees, 1914.** As it had done during the Boer War (1899–1902), the CWS paid the difference between wages and military pay to its employees' dependants, and guaranteed their employment on return from service. The total cost of these payments was estimated at £650,000 in 1918.

receive pay equal to that of the men they replaced (after initial training). Under such arrangements substituted workers were to be dismissed at the end of the war, but were required to join a trade union in the interim. However, despite such agreements, high inflation and shortages contributed to tense industrial relations in the CWS and the co-operative movement generally, as it did elsewhere. In 1916 the Co-operative Union (CU) established a mechanism to negotiate hours and wages at district, regional, and national levels, but between 1914 and 1918 the AUCE led seventy strikes for higher wages in retail societies.[15] In summer 1918 an AUCE strike at the Pelaw

[15] See Vorberg-Rugh (2009), 130–4.

works threatened to spread to other CWS operations, prompting the government to intervene.[16]

But just as labour relations inside the movement were becoming more fraught, relations between co-operative leaders and the labour movement were growing closer. Historians have noted that during the war Labour increasingly spoke 'in the name of the consumer', in response to wartime shortages and inflation.[17] However, the role of co-operation in developing this 'labour consumerism' has not been explored. An umbrella organization, the War Emergency Workers' National Committee (WNC), was established in 1914 and responded to government policy on a range of issues, including the civilian food supply. There were representatives on the London-based committee from the CU, the Women's Co-operative Guild (WCG), the Labour Party, and the trade unions. Although the CWS did not participate, it promised help where appropriate.[18] During the initial war panic, and after, co-operative representatives on the WNC's new Food Prices Subcommittee drew information from a range of societies to get information about the prices of staple goods.[19]

As conditions worsened the security of food supplies and the rising cost of living became critical issues. For wholesalers and retailers, war had made supply procurement more difficult, with rising shipping rates and prioritization of military over civilian shipments. But the co-operative movement enjoyed certain advantages. As the CWS only supplied co-operatives, societies did not have to compete with private retailers for this trade. Moreover, as producers, CWS had greater control over the costs of certain items. Its international expertise and networks of depots were also advantages. Before state control of sugar imports CWS sought new supplies through its New York Depot, and it supplemented diminishing butter supplies from Europe with New Zealand butter.[20] Where retail societies were strong, lower prices in their stores compelled other retailers to limit prices. Co-operative societies, mindful of keeping costs down for members, were under less pressure than their competitors to raise prices. Co-operative prices rose, but less quickly than those of private traders. Consequently the movement's membership rose by nearly 500,000 between 1914 and 1916.[21] Nonetheless, as the war went on the CWS's shipping operations were hampered by labour shortages and government restrictions, reducing imported supplies.[22] The German U-boat campaign from February 1915

[16] The strike began over a requirement that employees join a TUC-recognized union, which at that time did not include AUCE due to its disputes with craft unions. See Ministry of Labour, Wages & Arbitration Department file LAB2/164/IC6546/8/1918, National Archives, London.

[17] Barnett (1985), 128; see also Hunt (2000).

[18] See J. S. Middleton to T. Brodrick (6 August 1914) and Brodrick to Middleton (21 August 1914), WNC collection, Labour History Archive & Study Centre (hereafter LHASC), Manchester. The WNC members directly affiliated to the co-operative movement were: Margaret Bondfield (WCG); Mary Gasson (WCG); Henry May (CU and ICA); and B. Williams (CU).

[19] Societies provided their prices for a list of standard goods, as well as those of local private traders and multiple shops. See Box 11, WNC collections, LHASC.

[20] CWS Board minutes (13 November 1914); Redfern (1938), 103.

[21] CU Congress Reports, 1915–17.

[22] The CWS quarterly report for December 1914 reported shipping volumes were down 36 per cent over the same period in 1913, and 24 per cent down in June 1915 from June 1914, with decreased traffic continuing into 1916. See CWS balance sheets, 1914–16.

worsened the situation as it targeted both Allied and neutral supply shipments. In one instance, the CWS lost an £8,000 shipment of butter from its Swedish depot when German forces seized it in the Baltic. Eventually the CWS had to close its Gothenburg operation.[23] The U-boat sinkings and military demands reduced British shipping available by a third by December 1915.[24] Wheat and sugar reserves were swiftly depleted, exacerbating price inflation and shortages, and by early 1916 these were felt acutely by working-class consumers.

As working-class consumers spent a higher proportion of their income (two-thirds) on food than those higher in the social hierarchy, they felt the hardship most severely.[25] As the war dragged on and more items became scarce, working-class dependence on bread grew. In February 1915 Labour MPs demanded the imposition of maximum price limits for essential foods and state control of shortage commodities.[26] The co-operative WNC members also called for state control of wheat and coal at the 1915 Congress.[27] The WNC was preparing a memorandum on the cost of living, and asked the CWS for advice on wholesale price rises. The CWS provided information on changes in the wholesale prices of twenty-two staple items between May 1914 and May 1915. The highest rises were in common-grade flour, which had gone up over 90 per cent, while granulated sugar prices were up nearly 80 per cent and frozen beef was up by over 60 per cent.[28] In July the WNC published the first edition of the memorandum, which it updated and reissued at regular intervals in 1916 and 1918. The CWS and retail societies continued to provide much of the data.[29] This co-operative contribution to the WNC was invaluable in demonstrating the impact of price rises on everyday consumers, both to the general public and to government.

Inflation heightened public anger about inequalities. There was outrage at businesses which plainly profited from higher prices, who were labelled 'profiteers'. There were also concerns about how the government would pay for the war. In 1915, the government tried to address these problems through a new Excess Profits Duty (EPD), which taxed all profits in excess of a pre-war standard, initially at a rate of 50 per cent but later rising up to 80 per cent in 1918. Initially, the co-operative movement welcomed the EPD as an anti-profiteering measure. But the inclusion of co-operative dividends under EPD prompted outrage, as co-operative surpluses had never been treated as profits in law. Most co-operators shared the view that the tax on dividends was 'irregular, unfair, unjust, unprincipled, and most illogical'.[30] Protests, even when coordinated with the support of Labour MPs, were unsuccessful. During 1916 and 1917 CWS paid nearly £1 million in EPD to the government.[31] Societies responded by cutting dividends and

---

[23] Redfern (1938), 118.   [24] Barnett (1985), 70.   [25] Stark (1984), 49.
[26] See Stark (1984), 51; Barnett (1985), 39–42.   [27] CU Congress Report (1915), 150.
[28] WNC 11/248, LHASC.
[29] WNC, *Memorandum on the Increased Cost of Living During the War* (1915); see also WNC Box 7, LHASC.
[30] *Kettering Co-operative Magazine* (November 1916), quoted in Robertson (2010), 156.
[31] Redfern (1938), 148.

selling goods at or near cost price.[32] The CWS lowered prices so much in 1918 that it posted a trading loss, and eventually recovered around £700,000 in rebated wartime EPD.[33] The state's refusal to differentiate between co-operative surplus and private profit continued to be an issue in the inter-war years.

The pressure on working-class living standards continued in 1916. In its second report to Congress, the WNC's co-operative members estimated that the food budget for a working-class family of six was almost 50 per cent higher in February than it had been in August 1914.[34] Although wages for many workers rose during the war, the report noted that the poorer sections of society, including old age pensioners, had suffered acutely.[35] Rising public pressure compelled the Asquith government to impose stronger controls over food supplies. Once again sugar caused concern, as government stocks were depleting rapidly (see Figure 5.2). In July 1916 the government restricted sugar consumption on the basis of the 'datum period', limiting supplies to distributors on the basis of 65 per cent of pre-war sales. Unfortunately, the datum period system caused significant inequalities in distribution. Affluent areas which had purchased more sugar in 1915 received greater supplies, and the system took no account of wartime population movements.[36] For co-operative societies, the datum period had a further inequity: it took no account of their rising membership. These concerns prompted some societies to implement their own rationing systems for members from mid-1916.[37] Such schemes were publicized in the Co-operative News and CWS Price List, and promoted the view that rationing was a fairer solution to supply problems. The datum period system was roundly condemned by a unanimous resolution protesting its use at the CWS's quarterly meeting in December 1916.[38]

In autumn 1916 the Board of Trade established a Food Department, as poor wheat harvests added to mounting food supply problems. The Royal Commission on Wheat Supplies took direct control of purchasing wheat imports that October. By the end of 1916, the state controlled imports which amounted to 75 per cent of the food supply by calories, and two-thirds by weight.[39] However, although the CWS now actively sought representation, the co-operative movement continued to be excluded from government advisory bodies. Despite the CWS's important role in milling and distribution, and the presence of the Millers' Association on the Wheat Commission, co-operators were refused

---

[32] For example, the Ten Acres & Stirchley (hereafter TASCOS) society in Birmingham noted in 1916 that 'The policy of adjusting selling prices in order to provide for a dividend of 1/8 in the £, which was agreed upon at the last quarterly meeting of members, has been carried out. The adjustment has been effected by selling certain commodities in the Grocery Department at practically cost price, thus reducing the general profit.' See TASCOS, *164th Quarterly Report* (3 October 1916), NCA.

[33] CWS Board minutes (11 February 1920).

[34] The Board of Trade food budget from 1904 estimated the total price for such a family at 22s. 6d. According to WNC the same bundle of goods cost 25s. in July 1914, 34s. in August 1915, and 37s. 3d. in February 1916. See CU Congress Report (1916), 165–6.

[35] CU Congress Report (1916), 165–6.

[36] Barnett (1985), 71, 83–4.

[37] On early 'sugar card' systems, see *Co-operative News* (26 August 1916), 875; (10 February 1917), 143.

[38] CWS balance sheets (December 1916).   [39] Barnett (1985), 83–5.

FIGURE 5.2. **Sugar rationing cartoon, 1917.** The original caption read: 'CAPITALIST PROFITEER: "Now, I can get you sugar if I get your sugar card." CO-OPERATOR: "Yes, and so can my stores. They will look after **my interests** and sugar. You are out for **your own interests**, not really to get my sugar."' Courtesy of *Co-operative News* (<www.thenews.coop>).

representation on the grounds that the body was not intended to be representative but instead an expert body.[40] At the December 1916 quarterly meeting, the CWS's William Lander told angry delegates that the government had refused the Wholesales' deputation to the Wheat Commission that autumn, commenting: 'They [CWS] had bombarded the offices in London.... They would proceed to knock at the door of Government again, and let them know that they intended to be heard.'[41]

In December 1916 David Lloyd George replaced Asquith as Prime Minister and reorganized the government. The Food Department was transformed into the Ministry of Food and Lord Devonport was appointed as Food Controller. Devonport (formerly Sir Hudson Kearley) had made his fortune in the grocery wholesaling firm of Kearley & Tonge. Lloyd George, who attributed his success at the Ministry of Munitions to the

---

[40] *Co-operative News* (16 December 1916), 1295, 1309.
[41] *Co-operative News* (23 December 1916), 1327.

appointment of businessmen in executive posts, hoped Devonport would achieve similar results. But Devonport has been seen by historians as woefully incompetent.[42] He became an unpopular figure amongst co-operators and the labour movement. In early January, Devonport met a joint deputation from the WNC and the co-operative movement, which suggested a national rationing system similar to the sugar schemes implemented by many societies. In spite of Devonport's promises to investigate the datum period system and address the inequities in sugar distribution, he failed to act.[43] In January 1917 the CU organized public meetings and conferences in Bristol, Leeds, London, and Edinburgh, to press for co-operative representation on government advisory committees and for stronger state control of prices and supplies.[44] Devonport's advocacy in February 1917 of 'voluntary rationing' by consumers to limit their weekly intake of bread, sugar, and meat was received with scorn by the public and the press.[45] The WCG criticized Devonport's apparent ignorance of the prices of staple foods. It condemned in particular the fact that the middle and upper classes could afford meat prices, whilst working-class families did not have this option.[46] Devonport's new system of Food Committees, appointed by local authorities to deal with problems of distribution and supply, was widely condemned by the co-operative and labour movements for their lack of representation of ordinary consumers, and their domination by farmers and anti-co-operative private traders. In response, the WNC called for Food Vigilance Committees to be formed by trade unionists, co-operators, and working-class women.[47] Supplies and prices caused industrial unrest throughout Devonport's term at the Ministry of Food, as a renewed German U-boat campaign in the spring of 1917 further reduced imports. The retail price of food rose 87 per cent above pre-war levels in January and topped 100 per cent by July.[48] Mounting unrest and strikes reduced munitions production and undermined home front morale. In June 1917 Lloyd George established a Commission of Enquiry into Industrial Unrest, and appointed commissioners to investigate the problems. The Commissioners were unanimous that the rising real price of food was the root of the problem.[49] When the unpopular Devonport resigned he was replaced by Lord Rhondda (formerly D. A. Thomas), and J. R. Clynes, Labour MP, was named as Rhondda's Parliamentary Private Secretary.[50] The aim was to address public concerns about food supplies. Rhondda moved quickly to seek the advice of the labour movement. Within days of taking office, Rhondda met WNC representatives and agreed to some of its proposals, including a reduction in the price of bread which was achieved through government subsidy from September 1917.

---

[42] Barnett (1985), 98.   [43] CU Congress Report (1917), 240, and (1918), 307.
[44] CU Congress Report (1917), 241.   [45] Barnett (1985), 108.
[46] *Co-operative News* (24 February 1917), 194.
[47] *Labour Woman* (May 1917), 150–1. On Food Vigilance Committees, see Hunt (2010).
[48] Barnett (1985), 118.
[49] Commission of Enquiry into Industrial Unrest, No. 2 Division (1917), 13–14.
[50] Barnett (1985), 132 comments that 'Harry May' of CWS was approached to become Food Controller, but declined, saying it would be 'the cemetery of the CWS'. This refers to Henry May, then secretary of the CU Parliamentary Committee. May sat on WNC throughout war, and was the first Co-operative Party candidate for Parliament in 1918.

Bread remained at a fixed maximum price for the duration of the war.[51] Rhondda also recruited trade unionists and co-operators as advisers. T. W. Allen, a CWS director and member of the Joint Parliamentary Committee, was made honorary private secretary to Clynes, and from the autumn of 1917 other CWS representatives joined government committees.[52] Crucially, John Gledhill, long-time head of the CWS's New York buying depot, advised the Food Ministry from August 1917.[53] His unique understanding of the food trade with North America proved invaluable. But the CWS and co-operative leaders remained a minority amongst the private commercial advisers, and were viewed by some with suspicion. Mary Cottrell, who represented the movement on the Milk Control Board in 1918, grumbled that the while the Food Ministry valued the intelligence co-operators could provide, they wanted to limit their influence.[54] However, Rhondda did reconstitute the local Food Committees, insisting that among their twelve members there must be at least one labour representative and one woman, some preferably drawn from local co-operative leaders.[55] These 1,900 committees took over regulating supply and distribution of food in villages, towns, and cities across Britain. Co-operators welcomed this, and the Mitchell Memorial Hall at the CWS headquarters accommodated Manchester's Food Committee (see Figure 5.3). However, while working-class consumer representation increased under Rhondda's leadership, co-operative officials remained a minority on local committees. By November 1917 roughly 15 per cent of Food Committee members were farmers, 12 per cent private traders, and only 2.5 per cent were from the co-operative movement. By the end of food control the co-operative representation rose to 5.5 per cent, but remained a small minority.[56]

Rationing and other food controls took time to implement and shortages worsened throughout the autumn and winter of 1917. Government fears of public unrest were exacerbated by the Russian Revolution, and labour movement groups, including co-operatives, were placed under surveillance.[57] The shifting political context of 1917 began to change traditional co-operative aversion to party political activity. In March 1917 the CWS Board had opposed a resolution for direct representation in Parliament, forwarding an amendment to ascertain whether societies would support political activity with their own funds.[58] But by May its position had changed. At the Swansea Congress more than 100 societies called for the movement's direct representation in Parliament. The CWS's Allen introduced the resolution on behalf of the Joint Parliamentary

---

[51] The WNC suggested this measure in 1915; see typescript of R. Williams's evidence to the Committee on Food Prices, WNC/31/5/55, LHASC. See also Barnett (1985), 111–12.

[52] CWS representatives in the Ministry of Food were: Thomas Killon (Orders), replaced in 1918 by Henry Elsey; Phillip Coley (Wheat); H. J. Youngs (Milk); A. E. Threadgill (Oil and Fats). J. E. Johns (Tea) represented E&SCWS. Some CWS managers, including A. W. Lobb, butter buyer, also served on committees dealing with butter, cheese, and dried fruit, and in the War Department's Cloth Office. William Lander was appointed to the Advisory Committee of Ministry of Reconstruction. See CU Congress Report (1918), 150–1; Redfern (1938), 156–9.

[53] Gledhill died in 1918 and was replaced by W. J. Murphy, who continued to assist the Ministry until decontrol. Redfern (1938), 115–16.

[54] Quoted in Redfern (1938), 164.   [55] Barnett (1985), 127.   [56] Hilton (2003), 65.

[57] Gurney (1996), 214–15.   [58] CWS Board minutes (21 March 1917).

FIGURE 5.3. **CWS Mitchell Memorial Hall, Manchester, 1918.** During the final years of the First World War, the CWS loaned its central meeting hall to the Manchester Food Committee for the duration. Mitchell Hall was destroyed during the Manchester blitz of 1940; this is a rare photograph of its interior.

Committee, and addressed Congress on the difficulties and political exclusion of the movement during the war. He attacked the latter as 'a great national blunder' and criticized the excessive, self-interested, and conservative influence of private traders and vested interests. The resolution passed, 1,979 to 201.[59] This paved the way for the formation of the Central Parliamentary Representation Committee, later renamed the Cooperative Party. An Emergency Conference in London in October 1917, with Allen again in the chair, effectively launched the new party (see Figure 5.4). Anger was heightened by the recent refusal by Lloyd George to meet a co-operative deputation and Rhondda's unwillingness to mandate (rather than recommend) the presence of co-operators on local Food Committees. Writing in November 1917, Bolton Co-operative Society president William Bradley summed up the wartime politicization of many co-operators:

This war had made Co-operators see their weakness with respect to the Government, and he had been led to believe that, like other organisations, they would have to take political action and have direct representation of Co-operation in Parliament.... He had not advocated parliamentary representation until recently, but he felt something must be done. Co-operation was one of the greatest, if not the greatest, retail trade organisation in the country. They had over three million

[59] CU Congress Report (1917), 525–7, 559–60.

À LONDRES.

FIGURE 5.4. Co-operative politics cartoon, 1917. This cartoon appeared on 13 October 1917, the week before the emergency conference in London that formed the Co-operative Political Representation Committee, later the Co-operative Party. Courtesy of *Co-operative News* (<www.thenews.coop>).

members, and yet they had not been able to get representation on many bodies affecting them, and had not a share in arranging prices of food. He did not think that was right.[60]

This defensive approach continued to characterize co-operative politics in the inter-war period, particularly among the CWS leadership. Although the CWS supported the resolutions of the Emergency Conference, it remained concerned about the impact of political activities on its business concerns.[61]

In January 1918, the Ministry of Food created a new advisory body, the Consumers' Council, which became a central pillar of the Lloyd George government's strategy

[60] *BCR* (November 1917), 15.
[61] See CWS Board minutes (11 October 1917), in which the Board decided to support the main resolutions but opposed specific elements of party policy.

FIGURE 5.5. **Mary Cottrell (1868–1969).** From Birmingham's Ten Acres & Stirchley Co-operative Society (TASCOS), Mrs Cottrell was the first woman elected to the society's management committee in 1909 and the first to represent the Midlands on the Co-operative Union's Central Board, from 1917. Following the armistice, she became the first woman elected to the CWS Board, serving from 1922 until her retirement in 1936. She remained an active co-operator into her 90, and lived to be 101.

'to contain increasingly assertive and rebellious consumers by co-opting them'.[62] Although aware of the government's motives and of the Council's limited authority, the co-operative movement and other WNC-affiliated organizations agreed to join.[63] Co-operative representatives on the twenty-member council included Allen as deputy Chair, along with Philip Coley and William Dudley from the CWS Board, William Gallacher and Robert Stewart from the SCWS, and W. H. Watkins and G. Wilson from the Co-operative Union. In addition Cottrell (see Figure 5.5), who would become the first woman on the CWS Board in 1922, served on the Council as a WCG representative. Although the Consumers' Council had only advisory powers, it was nonetheless active, pressing with some success for greater state controls to benefit consumers.[64]

As Lloyd George had intended, the involvement of labour and co-operative organiza-tions in the work of the Ministry of Food gave the state much-needed public legitimacy.

---

[62] Trentmann (2008), 198.

[63] Middleton to J. R. Clynes (28 January 1918), WNC collections, Box 5, LHASC.

[64] For instance, co-operative WNC members reported to the 1918 Congress that they influenced provision of additional milk rations for infants, children, and nursing/expectant mothers in February 1918, through Mary Cottrell's presence on the Milk Advisory Board. CU Congress Report (1918), 307. On the Consumers' Council, see Hilton (2003), 53–78; and Trentmann (2008), 191–241.

Nonetheless, the Consumers' Council gave the movement greater influence than it had enjoyed earlier in the war. In other areas of government a similar process occurred. Following the introduction of conscription in 1916 a system of local military service tribunals, appointed by local authorities, oversaw the granting of exemptions. Heavy front-line losses drove the government to reduce the range of employments considered exempt. Moreover, in some communities, private traders on local tribunals sent co-operative employees to the front whilst exempting their own workers. One society had 102 of its 104 male employees called up, while in another a branch manager was called up on the grounds that it would improve the business of a rival village grocer![65] However, by 1918 co-operators were included in new Regional Advisory Committees set up to address the many grievances caused by conscription. After more men were called up in April 1918, the Joint Parliamentary Committee took up the case of nearly 5,300 co-operative employees in pivotal positions, who had been ordered to serve. Of these they gained exemptions for over 4,000.[66]

Progress was also made on rationing. Local rationing began in several areas in late 1917, and the first national programme (for sugar) was launched in January 1918, soon followed by other scarce commodities including margarine, fats, bacon, and butchers' meats.[67] Under the new system each individual consumer had to be registered with a single retailer for rationed products. By the end of 1917 nearly 8 million people had registered for sugar with co-operatives in England and Wales, and another 1.5 million in Scotland.[68] Although the system was far from perfect, prices came down, and food queues disappeared. Co-operators continued to lobby, as they were still being allocated supplies on the datum period in July 1918.[69] Rationing proved relatively popular, as shortages were now experienced by all classes and allocating supplies to registered customers was considerably more equitable.[70] By July 1918, rationing schemes were operating for sugar, butter, margarine, lard, meat, bacon, and ham. Clynes took over as Food Controller that July, and rationing continued to expand, covering 40 million British civilians by November 1918.[71] By the end of the war, the movement's Parliamentary Committee concluded: 'Not only has the Government realised its tactical mistake in ignoring the co-operative movement in the early days of the war, but the use and effectiveness of its organisation and principles have been recognised as a factor to be counted upon.'[72]

5.2 PEACETIME CONFLICTS, LEFT AND RIGHT

The high cost of the war had been felt by all, including the movement. A memorial in The Co-operative Group's Old Bank Building in Manchester shows the names of 810 CWS employees killed in the First World War. But of course problems continued after

---

[65] Bonner (1961), 141.   [66] CU Congress Report (1919), 166–8.
[67] For details on rationed items and dates of rationing, see Beveridge (1928), 224–5.
[68] Redfern (1938), 134.   [69] CU Congress Report (1919), 163.
[70] Barnett (1985), 151–2.   [71] Stark (1984), 38.   [72] CU Congress Report (1919), 170.

the end of the conflict. Adjusting the economy from a total war footing to peace took time, and was a source of widespread debate and disagreement. In 1917, when a negotiated peace rather than outright victory appeared to be the most likely conclusion to hostilities, a strong consensus emerged that much of the wartime apparatus of state intervention should be kept in place, in order that the country might be prepared for any future resumption of hostilities. This encouraged the view, held by many in the labour movement, that their active involvement in, and support for, the British state would become part of a new post-war orthodoxy for governing the country. This, it was hoped, would pave the way for major industrial and social reforms which would improve the position of the working classes. But the unexpected total victory of November 1918 removed, in the minds of Conservative and Liberal politicians and many business leaders, any notion that such a radical transformation of state economic and social policies would be necessary. Between 1918 and 1921, the conviction took hold in these circles that there should be a resumption of the pre-war principles of balanced budgets, the gold standard, international free trade, and a minimalist state—in other words, business as usual.[73] The scene was therefore set for conflict between those who expected to see permanent change in the role of the state in the economic and social spheres, and those set on a return to the old orthodoxy.

National food supplies remained a pressing issue. Late in 1918 some restrictions on the food supply were lifted, and early in 1919 the government announced plans to close the Ministry of Food within a year. But as rations increased and controls were loosened, food prices began to rise again. This prompted labour unrest, compounded by the effects of demobilization of men from military service and women from wartime employment. There were strikes and renewed outcries of profiteering, increasingly identified with the growth of international combines. One estimate suggested that 60 per cent of British beef imports were controlled by an American meat trust.[74] But the impetus towards dismantling wartime controls gathered momentum. These were said to be hindering private trade and too expensive in light of Britain's huge war debts. By summer 1919 the Ministry of Food's staff had been halved. As unrest continued the Consumers' Council called for the reintroduction of food controls. In August its delegation urged the Prime Minister to make the Ministry of Food a permanent department. Controls were reintroduced on several items, and the Ministry given a stay of execution.[75]

There had been tensions between labour and co-operative bodies during the war over the movement's entry into politics and increasing trade union militancy in co-operative stores and factories, but generally the two movements maintained a united front.[76] However in 1919 divisions resurfaced. Although the 1919 Co-operative Congress supported the continued operation of price controls and the Ministry of Food, in the autumn CWS leaders began to make it clear that they saw this as only a temporary measure. In September

---

[73] Cain and Hopkins (2001), 442–9.   [74] Trentmann (2008), 207.   [75] Barnett (1985), 212.
[76] Tensions has arisen earlier when the CU withdrew its representatives to the WNC in October 1917, expressing concern over its close connections with Labour as the movement was then setting up its own political party; however the row was smoothed over and co-operative representatives returned to the WNC in January 1918. See WNC collections, Box 8, File 1, LHASC.

CWS support for fixing of maximum prices was made conditional upon the proviso that as soon as possible controls would be removed.[77] This brought the CWS into conflict with members of the Consumers' Council, and many within the co-operative movement. All parties agreed that consumers needed protection from high prices, but not on whether state control was the best means of achieving this aim.

Debate about food control continued through the autumn. Labour, socialist, and trade union representatives formed a majority on the Consumers' Council. They wanted a state monopoly of the import of staple foods and a permanent Ministry of Food to oversee supplies and fix prices. They believed the war had proved the necessity of state protection of the consumer, and that the experience of partial decontrol had demonstrated the danger to the working classes from profiteers and international trusts. They argued that the Council's achievements demonstrated the potential for improvements through democratic state control. But while some co-operators agreed with this view, CWS and SCWS representatives did not. The Wholesales found the controls imposed during the war to be very frustrating, not least because of the key advisory roles enjoyed by their private competitors. At best, food control had inserted government intermediaries into co-operative operations; at worst it had restricted their trade and resulted in active discrimination against the movement. Although concerned about growing competition and the impact of cartels, many co-operators felt confident in their ability to hold their own in the marketplace. They believed the best protection for consumers would be further co-operative growth. There was also a strong traditional preference for voluntary action in civil society over state compulsion. The 'Co-operative Commonwealth' was to supplant the existing state, not be imposed by government. Matters came to a head in early 1920. By then, the public was growing impatient with scarcity and rationing. Manufacturers and retailers clamoured for the removal of controls, and the government was keen to reduce the number and scale of wartime ministries in its quest to reduce war debt. Despite protests over milk prices in the winter of 1919–20, in January 1920 milk was decontrolled.[78] In February, the latest Food Controller, Labour MP George Roberts, resigned in order to take up a position in industry.[79] As the position was to be abolished in August 1920, this raised the question of whether he would be replaced. On 19 February the Consumers' Council held a conference in London, hoping to resolve its differences and present a united front to the government. In addition to the Council itself, delegates were invited from across the labour and co-operative movements—including CWS and SCWS, the CU, the National Association of Co-operative Managers, and the WCG. After speeches from the Council's Chair, the former Marxist Henry Hyndman, and others who supported a permanent Ministry of Food, the SCWS's Gallacher spoke in opposition. The Wholesales had had enough of state control, not least through ministries principally advised by the movement's rivals.[80]

---

[77] CWS Board minutes (19 September 1919).

[78] In November 1919 more than 50 WCG branches organized demonstrations against high milk prices. See Trentmann (2008), 204.

[79] *The Times* (6 February 1920), 12.

[80] 'Consumers' Council Conference' (19 February 1920), WNC/ADD/1/25, LHASC.

Responses to Gallacher's speech reflected the depth of the split that had emerged in the Council. Fred Bramley, representing the TUC, condemned Gallacher's position as representing a business rather than a consumers' perspective. Lander, from the CWS, defended the Wholesales, pointing out that they had scrupulously avoided profiteering during the war. Lander praised the Ministry of Food's role in wartime, but rejected entirely the notion that state control should be made a permanent arrangement. Lander's comments were explosively significant, as he had been a member of the Advisory Committee on the Ministry of Reconstruction. He made clear that he viewed the permanent extension of state control in the supply of food as inimical to the aims of co-operation. William Bradshaw (see Figure 5.6), a former co-operative society manager who was now a CWS employee and member of the government's Retail Grocers Advisory Committee, supported the view that the CWS could do a far better job if free of state control. It was an opinion, however, which was not supported by all co-operators. Plymouth's W. H. Watkins, a CU representative on the Council, argued that the rise of international trusts during the war necessitated concerted state intervention.[81]

The conference decided in favour of a permanent Ministry of Food, but it split the co-operative movement down the middle. The Co-operative Union supported a permanent

FIGURE 5.6. Sir William Bradshaw (1877–1955). Having begun his co-operative career as a 'check boy' in Ripley, Bradshaw moved to Grantham in 1903 to become that society's general manager. He was active in the National Co-operative Managers' Association, served in the Ministry of Food during the First World War, and was elected to the CWS Board in 1921. He served as CWS President between 1936 and 1945, and was knighted in 1937.

[81] 'Consumers' Council Conference'.

ministry, while the CWS, SCWS, and the Parliamentary Committee opposed it; the WCG representatives abstained. After a period of division, the Parliamentary Committee brokered a compromise whereby the Wholesales agreed to support a permanent Ministry of Food, provided its role was purely regulatory rather than directive.[82] The 1920 Congress backed this measure, but by then wider opinion was turning decisively against intervention. *The Times*, which had supported the continuation of food control in February, condemned the wastefulness of the Ministry of Food in May. It savagely dismissed the Consumers' Council as 'a pretentious excrescence' representative only of left-wing activists.[83] The Council's influence was on the wane. In October 1920 bread was decontrolled, and in November the last major foodstuff, sugar, was de-rationed. In early January 1921 the Consumers' Council met at the CWS London branch in Leman Street, where they disbanded, declaring the continued need of a government ministry that would defend consumer rights. They noted with some bitterness that government continued to support big business at the expense of consumers.[84]

Although co-operators and organized labour disagreed over state controls, they jointly lamented the entrenchment of capitalist business in the government machine. In addition to the large manufacturers and multiple retailers who had occupied significant positions in various Ministries, after the war small business owners and shopkeepers became a vocal constituency. From the early twentieth century the 'shopocracy' had begun to drift from the Liberal to the Conservative Party, and their influence grew.[85] Although Lloyd George remained Prime Minister after the election of December 1918, the split in the Liberal Party made the Conservatives the majority party in the coalition. Both parties wanted the support of private retailers. Thus, when Chancellor Austen Chamberlain appointed a Royal Commission on Income Tax in October 1919, taxation of co-operative societies was firmly on its agenda. The Commission included one co-operative representative, Henry May, and heard evidence from CWS, SCWS, and CU leaders who argued that co-operative surpluses were savings through mutual trade rather than profits. Private traders contended that all co-operative transactions should be subject to tax. But the Commission's 1920 report satisfied neither side. While dividends paid to co-operative members did not constitute taxable profits, the report argued, surpluses retained by societies as 'corporate entities' were liable in the same manner as private businesses. Practically, this meant that co-operative societies could be taxed on reserve funds. Although May and eight other Commission members objected to this conclusion, the 1920 Finance Act applied the Corporation Profits Tax of 5 per cent to co-operative reserves.[86] The co-operative movement protested, holding emergency conferences in London and Preston in the autumn of 1920. The public pressure had some result, as co-operatives received an exemption from the tax the following year after a close parliamentary vote.[87] Although

---

[82] CU Congress Report (1920), 118.   [83] *The Times* (24 February 1920), 17; (8 May 1920), 17.

[84] 'Statement by the Consumers' Council' (4 January 1921), WNC/ADD/1/87, LHASC.

[85] See Winstanley (1983), 94–104.

[86] The CU created a special committee on income tax, with CWS and SCWS representatives; this reported to the 1920 Congress. See CU Congress Report (1920), 164–78.

[87] Redfern (1938), 241.

the short-term impact of the Corporation Profits Tax was minor, it was a sign of things to come. In the 1930s the movement would face renewed attempts to tax their surpluses in an even less favourable political environment.

5.3 THE GENERAL CO-OPERATIVE SURVEY COMMITTEE

Just before the outbreak of war, co-operators launched the first movement-wide strategic review. Announced at the 1914 Co-operative Congress, the General Co-operative Survey was the first of three attempts in the twentieth century to evaluate co-operative policy and practice, and devise strategies for the movement's future development. The impetus for the Survey came in 1913–14, and was partly inspired by the work of Sydney and Beatrice Webb, who were preparing a report on the movement for the Fabian Society's Research Department.[88] At the 1914 Congress, the CU Central Board cited the need for greater 'solidarity and flexibility' as a reason for the Survey, which was to review the movement's work in education, distribution, and production. Representing the CU Northern Section, W. Clayton cited the growing challenge posed by private traders, especially the emerging multiples.[89] In the Congress discussion it was clear that the Webbs would be asked to participate, but after war was declared they had other priorities, and in the end no external authorities were included. The Survey Committee worked throughout the war, producing four reports between 1916 and 1919.[90] In the process, the Survey presented the movement with a wealth of information about itself, albeit in a format that sometimes made it difficult for larger issues to be clearly identified.[91]

In September 1914 the Central Board met and decided that the Survey Committee would consist of eighteen members: ten elected by the CU United Board; two each from the Wholesales; two from the Co-operative Productive Federation (CPF); and one each from the Scottish and English Women's Guilds. But in October the CWS refused to participate in the committee, and the SCWS quickly followed suit. Further requests for the CWS to contribute were declined.[92] The reason for the CWS's refusal has never been clearly established, but it is likely, as Cole suggests, that both Whole-

---

[88] The report was published in special supplements for the *New Statesman*. The first, on producer co-operatives, appeared 14 February 1914; another on consumer co-operatives appeared 30 May 1914 and included a full-page CWS advert. The latter supplement served as the foundation for the Webbs's subsequent book *The Consumers' Co-operative Movement* (1921).

[89] CU Congress Report (1914), 557–8.

[90] The first three Survey Reports were published in the Congress Reports for 1916–18, whilst the final report was printed separately (along with the 3rd report) for use by district conferences in 1919.

[91] Cole (1944), 293; see also Webb and Webb (1921), 151.

[92] CWS Board minutes (2 October and 27 November 1914; 29 January, 5 February, 5 and 11 March 1915).

sales felt they were woefully under-represented on the committee.[93] Notwithstanding a certain loss of credibility because of the Wholesales' absence, the Survey Committee proceeded in spite of difficulties posed by war and internecine conflicts.[94] The first Survey Committee report to the 1916 Congress analysed the movement's administrative machinery, while the second, in 1917, focused on co-operative education; both were approved. In 1918 Congress delegates voted to accept, rather than approve, the third interim report, ordering its consideration by district conferences.[95] The interim report presented proposals for CU constitutional changes, but deferred several sections (including one on wholesaling and another on production) on the grounds of wartime difficulties in getting information. The final report was prepared in time for the 1919 Congress, but as negotiations were then under way between the CU and the Wholesales on various proposals this too was deferred, and a Special Congress was set up for February 1920.[96]

All of the Survey Committee reports stressed the need for greater coordination and unity across the co-operative movement. Given the dominance of CU personnel in its membership, it is unsurprising the Survey Committee saw the Co-operative Union as the appropriate body to achieve this aim, and sought to strengthen CU authority. Formed in the late 1860s and early 1870s, the CU was intended to serve as the representative central body for the entire movement, by organizing the annual Congress to legislate co-operative policy and providing the machinery to implement it.[97] The CU's elected regional and district boards provided a means of connecting disparate societies, and over time the CU developed departments for educational, legal, and other advisory services, centred at its Manchester headquarters. Like other co-operative organizations, CU membership was voluntary; but unlike co-operative businesses the CU was dependent on societies' payment of membership dues for much of its revenue. In addition, CU leadership had little authority over member societies, as while Congress dictated co-operative policy the CU could not impose sanctions on societies that chose not to enact them. Thus, in comparison with the CWS, the CU (see Figure 5.7) had a broad remit but significantly fewer resources, and had to rely even more heavily on the powers of persuasion to achieve its aims.

---

[93] This would not be the committee's only personnel difficulty. In 1916 A. W. Golightly resigned following his election to the CWS Board, and the WCG's Margaret Llewelyn Davies left due to disagreements over the committee's position regarding auxiliary bodies. The WCG had its own difficulties with the CU during 1914–18, related to the Guild's stance on divorce reform and the CU's concern that the WCG was too autonomous; see Scott (1998), 129–53; Blaszak (2000), 167–84; and Vorberg-Rugh (forthcoming).

[94] The Survey Committee members from the CU were: George Bisset (Scottish Section; died 1918); W. H. Bryant (Western); W. T. Charter (Southern); Robert Fleming (Irish; resigned 1919); A. W. Golightly (Southern; resigned 1916); William Gregory (North-Western); William Millerchip (Midlands); James Pollitt (North-Western); W. R. Rae (Northern); and W. H. Watkins (South-Western). The CPF representatives were Robert Halstead and Amos Mann, while Margaret Llewelyn Davies (WCG; resigned 1916) and Mrs M. Hunter (SCWG) represented the Guilds. Tom Horrocks, Charles Wood, and Professor Fred Hall from the CU staff served as secretaries.

[95] CU Congress Report (1918), 614–29.

[96] CU Congress Report (1919), 50–9.   [97] Cole (1944), 197–201.

FIGURE 5.7. Holyoake House, c.1930s. Completed in 1911 and extended in the 1930s, Holyoake House was erected in the growing 'co-operative quarter' of Manchester, as headquarters for the Co-operative Union. Today the building remains the home of Co-operatives UK, the Co-operative College and other co-operative organizations.

The 1918 report called for the CU to have greater authority over member societies on such questions as overlapping and amalgamation, including the power to expel those who did not conform with Congress-approved policies. The same report called for the CU to be headed by a full-time paid executive, sought an overhaul of the educational executive and its mission, and argued for a leading role for the CU in the Co-operative Party by reconstituting the Parliamentary Committee as a subcommittee under the Central Board.[98] The CU was also to have supervisory powers over all aspects of co-operative organization, including business activities as well as its traditional fields of education, politics, and promotion of the movement.[99] Significantly, while the Survey saw greater centralization as essential, it eschewed proposals for a national society. This reflected the strength of retail society opinion. Although CU appointees to the Survey Committee were generally in favour of a more powerful Co-operative Union, most had come to prominence in the movement as leaders of retail societies, and retained their

[98] General Co-operative Survey (hereafter GCS) (1919), 14–20.   [99] GCS (1919), 13.

suspicion of measures that would limit societies' local, independent identities.[100] Rather than a national society, the Survey Committee's proposed solution was greater coordination of, and more clearly defined roles for, the movement's constituent bodies.[101] The report was especially concerned by loss of trade by retail societies to private traders and multiple shops. Although societies' turnover was expanding, since the turn of the century their average annual sales per member had stagnated, which, given wartime inflation, actually indicated falling volumes of goods sold.[102] Amalgamation was seen as the key to improvements, and larger societies were cited as better equipped to meet the new challenges. Although many societies continued to prioritize high dividends over price competition, the report noted a trend toward reduced prices and moderate dividends, accelerating under the influence of wartime EPD, which they saw as likely to attract more members and customers. Societies were encouraged to widen the range of services and goods they offered to members, particularly co-operative laundries, cafés and restaurants, optical and pharmacy services, funeral services, and milk deliveries. Societies in close geographic proximity were encouraged to pool resources for such developments through the creation of federal organizations, a recommendation which was followed by many societies in the inter-war period. The report noted with approval that co-operative societies were selling a greater proportion of co-operative productions in their stores, rising from around 3 per cent in the early 1880s to around 34 per cent in 1917.[103] However, it criticized production of goods by local federations of societies where this competed with producer societies or the Wholesales, and cited an instance where a group of societies had established a jam factory in competition with the CWS.[104]

The report also commented upon societies which invested capital outside the movement. Data from 1909 showed that about half of societies' total capital was invested in their own undertakings, one-fifth in house property, another fifth in other co-operative businesses, while the rest (about £4 million) went outside the movement, in railway shares, municipal loans, and, controversially, sometimes into private competitors with co-operative businesses.[105] Many societies had limits on share capital that were below the £200 legal maximum. The Committee regarded these as too low. Such restrictions, designed to combat the problem of 'surplus capital' in the nineteenth century, had to be removed because the movement needed all the capital it could gather to finance expansion. There was great scope for capital accumulation by societies, as many members had only very small investments in co-operative share capital, whilst other members used their societies as secure investments but spent little in the stores. According to the report, around two-thirds of retail society members held less than £3 in their society, while about half of societies' total capital was held by one-tenth of the members.[106] The Committee offered a number of suggestions on raising capital, including increasing allocations to reserves and encouraging minimum shareholding requirements linked to

[100] GCS (1919), 48.   [101] GCS (1919), 152.
[102] CU Congress Report (1916), 269–70.   [103] GCS (1919), 143.
[104] GCS (1919), 152. This was the Teeside Co-operative Federation; see Webb and Webb (1921), 94–5.
[105] CU Congress Report (1916), 261.   [106] CU Congress Report (1916), 257.

dividend and share interest rates.[107] Wherever possible societies were to invest capital in the Wholesales and other co-operative organizations, as 'capital which is not directly used in co-operative trade is directly, or indirectly, used against the movement'.[108]

There were numerous proposals for the Wholesales, most demonstrating the committee's suspicion of centralization. At the heart of the recommendations was an effort to strictly limit the Wholesales' role to supplying the movement, rather than exercising any wider powers of leadership.[109] Indeed, the Survey Committee, arguing that the Wholesales were already overstretched, wanted a new federal society to take charge of co-operative banking. The existing CWS Bank was to provide the nucleus of the operation, in which the Wholesales would clearly have a role, but ultimately power would be invested in the new federal society. Alluding to friction between CWS and the CPF, who in some areas were competing, the report argued that a new society would give influence to a wider range of societies within the movement, as well as opening the possibility of trade unions, friendly societies, and other organizations who had opened CWS Bank accounts since the 1910s being able to participate in its management. The report also wanted new federal societies for co-operative investment and to pioneer a mail order business. It criticized the slow growth of the CIS since its takeover by the two Wholesales. Although it hinted that the CIS should once again be a separate society, the Committee decided that the time was not right for such a step.[110] Other areas of CWS business, it argued, were more suited to CU control. In particular, auditing was a service thought best provided by an expanded CU department. A similar argument was made for the transfer of the work of the CWS's Legal Department.[111] It was also recommended that the CU take over the Joint Propaganda Committee, training co-operative organizers and initiating a national co-operative advertising scheme aimed at educating members in co-operative principles.[112]

The CWS management structure was also criticized for its alleged rigidity, which, it was argued, hindered 'lateral expansion' into new areas of enterprise.[113] The report argued for greater democratic scrutiny of balance sheets and expert advisers to help CWS subcommittees with handling the CWS's increasingly complex range of businesses. It wanted CWS employees to be drawn from wider sources within the movement, arguing that employment in the Wholesales was akin to public service. It even suggested the use of civil service-style examinations to recruit staff.[114] The weakness of the CWS's educational provision for its staff, especially in co-operative principles, was roundly condemned, and a role was mooted for the CU Education Department in establishing technical and co-operative classes for employees, as well as the CWS's making better use of local authority trade schools. This was needed to ensure competitiveness with private business and to strengthen the commitment to co-operation as an alternative economic and social system.[115] The Survey Committee ultimately took a very critical stance in its assessment of the future of the Wholesales:

[107] GCS (1919), 70–2.   [108] GCS (1919), 71–2.   [109] GCS (1919), 47.
[110] GCS (1919), 178–83.   [111] GCS (1919), 29–30, 183–4.   [112] GCS (1919), 81–2.
[113] GCS (1919), 50.   [114] GCS (1919), 50–3.   [115] GCS (1919), 18–21.

Every true co-operator desires to see them grown and their usefulness increase. That usefulness, however, is not to be secured by blind growth, but by development which accords with the true function and place of the Wholesale Societies in the movement. Efficiency is essential to success, and, in our opinion, the greatest efficiency cannot be secured by the Wholesale Societies spreading themselves over too many activities or maintaining a constant form of organisation and administration that may be suitable at one stage of development and unsuitable as the societies grow bigger.... We earnestly wish to see a big co-operative movement, but this does not necessarily imply big organisations within the movement.... Moreover, the bigger the Wholesale Societies become, and the more complex their activities become, the greater is the difficulty of the members of the societies exercising effective control, and thus the greater is the tendency for the Wholesales Societies to become bureaucratic and further removed from the rank-and-file members of the movement, a position which contains the germs of disaster from a co-operative point of view. In our opinion the true sphere of the Wholesale Societies is wholesale distribution and production, with concentration upon attempts to secure access to raw materials from sources co-operatively owned.[116]

Needless to say, the Survey Report met with significant resistance from the CWS and its Scottish counterpart. Although some of the report's criticisms were subsequently acted upon in the 1920s, attempts to limit the scope of the Wholesales' business were opposed. The situation was complicated by the Survey Committee's relations with the Central Board. In April 1918, following the publication of the third report, some Central Board members felt the Survey had gone too far in its criticisms of the Wholesales, and defended the CWS's record in such areas as propaganda.[117] The Central Board was aware of grumbles about the longevity and expense of the Survey Committee.[118] In 1919, the Central Board and the Survey Committee argued over who had final ownership of the report and the timing of its submission to Congress. Also, by 1919–20 it was clear that the report itself needed to be amended in light of rapidly changing political and economic conditions. All agreed that better communication with the Wholesales was essential, and the CWS recognized the need for renewed dialogue with the wider movement.[119]

Throughout 1919 efforts were made at compromise between the CU and the Wholesales on the Survey Report. In March 1919 the Survey Committee and Wholesales discussed a new proposal. Rather than a full-time CU executive, the Survey Committee now proposed the expansion of the part-time Central Board, to include representatives from the Wholesales and the CPF. The Wholesales' involvement in the CU would also extend to the Central Board's main committees, including political and propaganda work. These proposals were eventually included as an addendum in the final survey report.[120] While these ideas were under consideration, the Wholesales discussed the Joint Parliamentary Committee with the Central Board, which the Survey Report sought to bring under the sole CU control. In 1918 the Wholesales had declared their intention to deal directly with government on commercial questions rather than through the Parliamentary Committee.[121] During

[116] GCS (1919), 153.   [117] CU Congress Report (1918), 29.
[118] CU Congress Report (1918), 616 and 626.   [119] CU Congress Report (1919), 34–5, 51.
[120] W. H. Watkins continued to support a full-time CU executive; his statement was included in the final report. CWS Board minutes (13 March 1919); GCS (1919), 125–8.
[121] CWS Board minutes (17 June and 4 December 1919).

summer 1919 a committee of the two Wholesales examined the Survey Report and in December the CWS Board accepted its recommendations, including opposition to representation on the Central Board, rejection of a separate banking society, and opposition to any restrictions on the CWS's legal or auditing operations. However, after further negotiations in January 1920, the CWS did accept the CU's offer of representation on a reconstituted Joint Parliamentary Committee.[122]

By the time of the Special Congress in Blackpool in February 1920, the Central Board opposed the most contentious Survey Report proposals for the Wholesales. Although there was some internal dissent, the CU's executive argued against a special banking society and the mail order proposition.[123] The Central Board also voted against a full-time executive, on the basis of cost.[124] The CWS delegates expressed their dislike of many of the proposals, highlighting what they saw as 'an attack on the Wholesale', but adopted a pragmatic approach, defending CWS activities in auditing and legal services on the basis of its superior resources.[125] Ultimately, all points at issue for the CWS were 'remitted and shelved'.[126]

For those who had supported major reforms, the outcome of the five-year General Co-operative Survey Committee was disappointing.[127] Although the Special Congress accepted the report with revisions, there was no strategy or momentum to put it into action. The recommendation to give the Co-operative Union more power over its member societies was granted in theory, but not practically applied. In fact, the CU's leadership was divided over how much authority it should claim, and did not have the resources to effect major changes. Ultimately the CU, like the CWS, was subject to control by its member societies. A delegate to the Special Congress, Mrs Palmer from Southampton, summarized the problems:

I should like to know where is the authority that is going to enforce any resolution passed this morning? There is none. There are many pious resolutions. We have too many forces inclined to conflict.... The Co-operative Wholesale Society will have too much power, and will be regarded as the voice of the movement even if we pass this amendment. The Survey Committee's Report is a good report, and they have done uncommonly well, but how are we going to make their efforts effective? To do that we shall have to refer the whole matter to the whole of societies and ask them whether they are willing to submit to rules and regulations that shall apply throughout the whole country.[128]

Clearly, many retail societies opposed the assertion of central authority by either the CU or the Wholesales.

[122] CWS Board minutes (4 December 1919; 8 and 10 January 1920).
[123] CU Special Congress Report (1920), 27.
[124] CU Special Congress Report (1920), 20, 41. The Special Congress passed an amendment in favour of the full-time executive, but this was not implemented until the CU reorganization of the early 1930s.
[125] CU Special Congress Report (1920), 61–2.
[126] Redfern dismissed the Survey Report in one paragraph, noting of the banking proposals that 'to drag them now from the dust would be unkind'. Redfern (1938), 243.
[127] Webb and Webb (1921), 150.   [128] CU Special Congress Report (1920), 41.

If the Survey Committee failed, it was nonetheless significant. It demonstrated the difficulties faced by the 'dysfunctional federation' and the wider movement in reforming itself despite the seriousness of the competition it faced. Local societies and national societies had different priorities. In particular, retail societies were fundamentally hostile to any initiative to centralize power into national organizations. There were some immediate benefits. Relations between the CU and the Wholesales were improved by the negotiations prompted by the Survey Report, and by increasing awareness of the difficulties posed by the post-war environment. The information gathered in the report was useful in the longer term, and further data was collected that would help strategic planning in the 1930s. Many of the issues highlighted by the Survey remained concerns in the inter-war period, and some of its proposed solutions were eventually implemented by future Co-operative Congresses (see Figure 5.8). At least one historian in the 1960s judged the Survey to be highly prescient, pre-empting much of the analysis and many of the solutions offered by the Co-operative Independent Commission Report of 1958.[129]

FIGURE 5.8. **Co-operative Congress delegates, 1931.** Among the many topics of debate at the Bournemouth Congress of 1931 were changes to the Co-operative Union's constitution, deferred until 1932, and a resolution in favour of cuts to defence spending, which passed easily. The annual Congress has occurred every year since 1869, with the exception of 1944 when it was cancelled due to war conditions.

[129] Bonner (1961), 157. See also section 6.4.

5.4 Troubled times

Of course economic circumstances worsened after 1920. This followed the sharp post-war boom of 1918 to 1920, when inflation had been a serious problem. The British index of wholesale prices (1913 = 100) stood at 229 in 1918 and peaked at 330 in mid-1920. Wage rates climbed in response and by the end of 1920 were nearly twice their pre-war levels.[130] Britain experienced a post-war reconstruction boom in which the co-operative movement participated, alongside other businesses. Together with land for the expansion of their existing works, the CWS purchased new factories and farms. Between 1918 and 1920 the number of CWS productive works grew from 54 to 76. Altogether the CWS outlaid £3.7 million in capital expenditure in 1919 and 1920.[131] This reflected the growing confidence of both the CWS and its member societies, having exited the war with nearly one million additional co-operative members.

Private firms funded their post-war expansion through bank loans or share issues. The CWS also needed capital for its own plans. In 1916 the CWS increased the share capital requirements for new member societies, and encouraged existing ones to follow suit.[132] In 1919 the Wholesale changed its rules to pay 6 per cent on shares, reflecting the rising interest rates of the time and the CWS's need to attract societies' investment.[133] The same year, the CWS issued £2.5 million in development bonds, followed by a second issue in 1920 of more than £4.5 million. The bonds were popular with co-operative societies, and were promoted widely in the movement and to trade unions.[134] In 1920 the share capital holding requirements were further increased, to one £5 share for every two members.[135] Throughout this period the CWS sent 'financial propagandists' around the country to promote greater investment in societies and the Wholesales. The 'Campaign for Co-operative Capital' tapped into the political radicalism of the time, with lecturers speaking to mass meetings in front of banners stating, 'Unless the workers control capital, capital will control the workers' (Figure 5.9).[136]

Then, early in 1921, the post-war bubble burst. Prices fell together with production and trade. That year unemployment reached 2.1 million, and remained above 1.5 million

---

[130] Cole (1944), 273.

[131] Special Committee of Inquiry (hereafter SCI) (1929), NCA, 53; Redfern (1938), 225.

[132] Share capital requirements had been raised previously. In 1871, societies held one £5 share per twenty members. This became one share per ten members in 1873, three shares per twenty members in 1890, one share per five members in 1904, and three shares per ten members in 1916. Over the same period the SCWS share capital requirement remained at one £1 share per member. In 1917, the CWS reported 300 existing members had come up to the new limit, adding £500,000 in share capital. See GCS (1919), 131–2; CWS balance sheets, 'Committee's Report' (June 1917).

[133] CWS balance sheets, 'Committee's Report' (September 1919).

[134] A report on the second issue suggests that co-operative societies were the biggest market. In the first month, sales totalled over £335,000—£308,000 came from societies, nearly £27,000 from individuals, and only £100 from trade unions. CWS Board minutes (5 and 26 February 1920).

[135] CWS balance sheets, 'Committee's Report' (June 1920).

[136] South Wales was one of the areas targeted; see *Wheatsheaf* (January 1921), 10–11.

FIGURE 5.9. **CWS campaign for capital, 1920.** During a public meeting in South Wales, CWS lecturer F. C. Crowther (pointing, at right) made the case for increased co-operative investment in the Wholesale. Later in the 1920s Crowther helped design CWS training programmes and was founder and producer of the Balloon Street Players, a theatre group for the CWS's Manchester employees.

until 1924.[137] The combination of low consumer spending and rapid deflation led to drastic losses in the manufacturing and distributive trades. When the CWS reported a £3.4 million loss on its half-year trade to its September 1921 quarterly meeting, it made national headlines. Efforts were made to soothe panic in certain parts of the movement.[138] In 1922 annual profits after allocations for depreciation were just over £110,000 on sales of nearly £81 million.[139] The problem for the CWS was that societies had been hard hit by the slump and were reducing their purchases, as many had large stocks of goods that had to be sold at a loss. Societies had to cut dividends, hampering their efforts to attract and retain members' trade. In 1921 more than a third of co-operative members received dividends under 1s. in the pound, while some received none at all.[140] The global nature of the crisis meant that the CWS also suffered losses abroad. There were debts owed by

[137] Garside (1990), 5.   [138] TASCOS, 184th quarterly report (ending 27 September 1921), 4.
[139] CWS balance sheets, 'Committee's Report' (June and December 1922).
[140] Purvis (2012), 10–11. For instance, TASCOS saw its dividends drop from 1s. at the start of 1921 to 6d. in May 1921; it fell to its lowest level of 2d. in the £ in November 1922 and didn't begin to recover until August 1923. It did not return to a 1s. dividend until February 1926. See Vickrage (1950), 93–4 and 108–9.

struggling co-operative organizations in newly independent parts of Eastern Europe which threatened to turn bad.[141] However, the CWS consoled itself with its foresight in having built large reserves, and sought to reassure societies even as they appealed for greater loyalty. By mid-1922 efforts to raise capital for the movement had been replaced by calls for greater loyalty by societies to co-operative producers. The CWS did not fully recover until the second half of 1923, when it was able to pay its first dividend to member societies since the end of 1920.[142] Thereafter the CWS's fortunes improved, although economic instability remained the salient feature of the 1920s.

The slump hit hardest those regions which had been most prosperous before the war: the industrial heartlands which produced and exported textiles, coal, and steel. War-time economic mobilization in Europe had enabled rivals, such as Japan, to begin to challenge Britain's global dominance in textiles. Between the wars, the British economy went through a painful process of readjustment, as new consumer industries, selling principally to the domestic market, rose and the traditional export staple industries experienced decline.[143] Industrial regions in Scotland, the North of England, and South Wales struggled throughout the inter-war years, particularly following the overpric-ing of exports by the return to the gold standard in 1925. These were of course precisely the heartland of co-operative growth in the nineteenth century, further exacerbating the movement's difficulties. Other areas of the country, especially the Midlands and the South, recovered more quickly, as a result of the rise of new industries. These therefore offered the best prospects for co-operative growth in the inter-war period. Economic conditions in the heavy industrial areas were worsened in the 1930s by the Great Depression of 1929–33, and the collapse of international trade and global retreat into protectionism which followed. Unemployment rose from 2.3 million in 1930 to 3.4 million in 1932, and only fell below 2 million in 1937.[144] In this context, the CWS admit-ted that the last half of 1931 saw the most difficult period in its history. Nonetheless its investments were sound and its sales healthy enough to continue to pay dividends of 3d. per share.[145]

Unlike the slump of the early 1920s the CWS was better able to weather the difficulties of the 1930s. This was because the movement had experienced strong growth in the South and parts of the Midlands where the new industries (motor vehicles, aircraft, chemicals, domestic electrical goods) were located. London societies saw the real value of their sales increase by 410 per cent between 1920 and 1938, while those around Bir-mingham saw 278 per cent growth. In contrast, in the depressed region of east Durham, sales were more than 37 per cent lower in value over the same period, while those in Lancashire and Yorkshire were at or below their 1920 levels in 1938.[146] These 'new'

---

[141] For example, the CWS's Arthur Varley travelled to Bucharest in 1921 to negotiate over a £440,000 debt. In spring 1922 CWS auditors expressed concern over the possible consequences of foreign debts. See CWS Board minutes (19 August 1921; 16 March 1922).

[142] CWS balance sheets, 'Committee's Report' (December 1920–December 1923); CWS Board minutes (7 July 1922).

[143] Jefferys (1954), 40.   [144] Garside (1990), 5.

[145] CWS balance sheets, 'Board's Report' (January 1932).   [146] Purvis (2012), 18–21.

co-operative areas ensured that the CWS's overall growth in the inter-war period was strong despite the broader economic difficulties. This mirrored Britain's wider economy, which experienced an overall rise in living standards and consumer spending which disguised the gap between regions. But geography did pose challenges to the CWS's business model. It had to meet the divergent needs of its various member societies, small and large, urban and rural, depressed and prosperous. Societies in declining areas needed financial assistance whilst those in the 'new' co-operative areas sought an ever-wider range of consumer goods, as new methods of production and new types of products appeared on the market. The changing economic conditions also led to challenges for CWS leadership, as societies to the south sought greater representation and those in the declining regions struggled to defend their positions despite weakening trade (see Table 5.1). At the same time, constitutional changes passed in 1921 linking voting rights to the amount of a society's purchases, rather than the number of its members, altered the CWS's internal politics.[147] This gave more advantage to smaller but more loyal societies as against the larger societies whose purchases were more likely to bypass the Wholesale.

Changing conditions of global trade also posed challenges to the CWS. The business had flourished in the era of free trade, and many of its leaders were devoted to it.[148] But with the collapse of world trade and rise of protectionism in the 1930s, the movement had to adapt to very different conditions. By the early 1930s Britain had introduced tariffs on imports and preference for imports from within the British empire. But the CWS was not entirely unprepared. Throughout the 1920s it increasingly imported goods from the Dominions (see Figure 5.10), developing close relationships with agricultural co-operatives in New Zealand (see Plate 10) and Australia. In conjunction with a New Zealand agricultural co-operative, in 1921 the CWS formed a joint enterprise, the New Zealand Produce Association Limited (NZPA), to source dairy goods and, later, frozen meat.[149] By the 1930s the CWS Bank was heavily involved in financing the export of Australian wheat to the UK, through Westralian Farmers Ltd, to which the CWS advanced £200,000 in 1931 to help finance its warehousing and other operations. The CWS also opened a depot in New Zealand in 1932, though in the difficult circumstances of the period, it struggled throughout that decade.[150] In addition, throughout the inter-war period the CWS increased sales to co-operatives overseas, particularly to Soviet Russia (see Table 5.2). It acted as a buying

---

[147] The April 1921 quarterly meeting passed the following changes: one vote per society based on CWS membership, one for the first £10,000 in CWS purchases, and one additional vote for each complete £20,000 following, based on the prior year's trade. In 1938 the qualifying amounts became £12,500 and £25,000 respectively; see SCI (1937), 24 and Redfern (1938), 244.

[148] In response to a Manchester Chamber of Commerce survey asking whether it favoured full free trade policies or a variety of levels of protection, the CWS responded in favour of unlimited free trade; see CWS Board minutes (27 May 1930). See also reports on the CWS's J. T. Davis, *Manchester Guardian* (30 May 1930), 15.

[149] See SCI (1929), 38–9.

[150] CWS Board minutes (10 November 1931, 14 March 1933).

Table 5.1. CWS domestic sales, England and Wales, 1920–35

	Manchester (£)	% of total	Newcastle branch (£)	% of total	London branch (£)	% of total	Total (£)
1920	55,819,208	54.2	18,757,093	18.2	28,442,540	27.6	103,018,841
1925	40,746,636	55.6	11,313,089	15.4	21,236,709	29.0	73,296,434
1930	42,800,143	52.1	10,029,735	12.2	29,278,767	35.7	82,108,645
1935	47,134,900	49.2	10,649,512	11.1	38,101,729	39.7	95,886,141

Source: CWS balance sheets, 1920–35.

Table 5.2. CWS sales to foreign and dominion countries, 1920–35

	1920 (£)	1925	1930	1935
Russia	–32,207	363,975	794,569	453,904
Total foreign and dominion	360,166	684,865	1,132,770	758,791

Source: CWS balance sheets, 1920–35.

agent for overseas societies in Argentina, Australia, Bermuda, Newfoundland, and South Africa.[151] Whilst the CWS had adapted to imperial preference, and was even represented on the Empire Marketing Board from the mid-1920s, in the early 1930s political and economic shifts presented new challenges.[152] The rise of commodity marketing boards protecting domestic agricultural producers, as well as the imposition of quotas on foreign imports, further tested the adaptability of CWS business operations.

But CWS proved adept at turning to advantage its well-established international network, and its unique blend of banking and wholesaling activities (see Figure 5.11). This was exemplified by a remarkable deal struck with the New England Fish Company in 1933 by the CWS's New York depot. Under this, the CWS lent that company $500,000 at 5 per cent per annum. The deal was struck at a time when the US banking system was still on its knees following the Wall Street Crash of 1929 and the subsequent banking crisis. Many American businesses were desperate for alternative sources of capital. But the deal involved an additional level of sophistication which operated to the CWS's benefit. The New England Fish Company owned all the shares in the Canadian Fishing Company, a firm which caught and canned sockeye salmon on the Pacific Coast, at their Carlisle Cannery on the Skeena River. Under the deal, the CWS had the right to purchase all of the output from this cannery. If the New England firm defaulted on the loan, its shares in the Canadian Company would be forfeit to the CWS. The deal thus secured a regular supply of tinned salmon for the tables of British co-operators, from a source relatively unhindered by protectionist measures, since Canadian imports were subject to the British policy of imperial preference. It is likely that the interest on the loan substantially covered the costs of CWS purchases from the Canadian Fishing Company, as a result of this sophisticated convergence of banking and transnational expertise. It is a deal reminiscent of some of the operations of post-Second World War multinational corporations. Furthermore, the deal allowed for a chance to renegotiate the supply deal with the Canadian Fishing Company when the loan was due to be fully repaid in 1944.[153]

During these intensely difficult years, CWS also proved willing to assist overseas co-operative movements. In October 1931 it advanced £100,000, secured on supplies

[151] CWS Board minutes (15 October 1929).
[152] CWS Board minutes (31 December 1926).   [153] CWS Board minutes (24 February 1942).

FIGURE 5.10. **Window display of CWS provisions, c.1930s.** Labelled 'CWS Provisions—The Sunshine of Life', this window display highlighted the availability of foreign goods, including Australian lemons, imported by the CWS. The unknown society was participating in the movement's national window dressing competition, which became an annual event in the 1920s.

of grain, to the Romanian Central Co-operative Society to enable it to continue to buy produce from peasants in that country. [154] The CWS New York Depot also began to supply the German CWS with lard in 1931.[155] Perhaps most controversial was the CWS's business with the Soviet Union. In 1923, the CWS formed a joint enterprise, the Russo-British Grain Export Company, established with Arcos, Centrosojus, the Soviet grain exporting organization, and three other British firms.[156] The company specialized in the export of Russian grain to Britain, and from the mid-1920s the CWS advanced considerable sums to it, totalling around £1 million by the early 1930s.[157] In July 1932 the CWS agreed to a new loan of £800,000 to the Russo-British company, at a time when starvation was beginning to ravage the Russian population as a direct consequence of Stalin's agricultural collectivization policy.[158] Of course, the CWS were not alone in being misled about the true nature of Stalin's regime and the consequences of his policies. In 1934 Soviet wheat exports fell, and by 1935 the CWS agreed with the other parties that the Russo-British Grain Export Company

[154] CWS Board minutes (20 October 1931).
[155] CWS Board minutes (29 December 1931).   [156] See SCI (1929), 38–9.
[157] CWS Board minutes (24 November 1931).   [158] CWS Board minutes (26 July 1932).

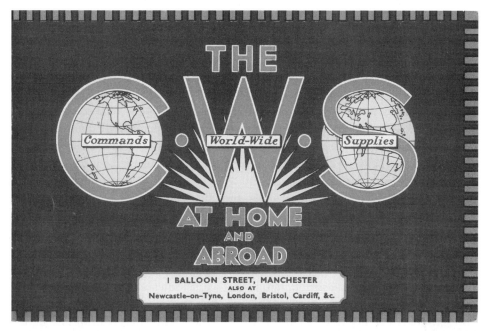

FIGURE 5.11. *CWS at Home and Abroad* **pamphlet, *c.*1930s.** Pamphlets like this one highlighted the national and international scope of CWS enterprise. By the end of the 1930s, there were over 150 CWS in factories in England and Wales, and operations in Europe, the Americas, Africa, and Australasia.

should be dissolved.[159] Other CWS dealings with the USSR were equally extensive and complex. For instance, the CWS Bank made advances to the Soviet butter organization Soyusprodexport and the Moscow Narodny Bank to ensure supplies of butter, not only to the CWS, but also to NZPA, which the CWS Bank supported through loans.[160] In 1931, 30,000 casks each were supplied to the CWS and to NZPA. Between 1926 and 1933, the CWS and NZPA were supplied with 690,000 casks of Siberian butter, facilitated by CWS advances which totalled over £3.5 million.[161] Between 1924, when the CWS Bank first started to deal with the Soviet Union, and 1933, it earned £975,364 in interest on its dealings.[162]

In other areas, the CWS Bank proved to be an important agent of CWS overseas strategy. In 1932 it extended credit of £90,000 to the NZPA to enable it to supply the CWS with butter and cheese.[163] It also supplied credit to its Argentinian suppliers of wheat and butter.[164] In this way the CWS Bank came to play an important role in ensuring a supply of produce to the CWS and its overseas clients, demonstrating that the CWS was sufficiently sophisticated to cope with many aspects of the difficult global conditions of the 1930s.

---

[159] Redfern (1938), 295.   [160] CWS Board minutes (11 April and 2 May 1933).
[161] CWS Board minutes (12 February 1934).   [162] CWS Board minutes (17 October 1933).
[163] CWS Board minutes (23 February 1932).   [164] CWS Board minutes (10 and 11 May 1932).

5.5 THE CWS AND INTER-WAR POLITICS

The state and political parties had a major impact on the CWS and co-operative business in the 1920s and 1930s. The early 1920s were particularly turbulent, with three governments in as many years in 1922–4. Amidst the rise of the Labour Party as a significant force, the decline of the hopelessly split Liberals, and the increasingly dominant Conservatives, the fledgling Co-operative Party tried to find its feet. However, in the 1920s the relationship between the Co-operative Party and the movement had not been defined. The CWS remained sceptical, and feared that a separate Co-operative Party might make more enemies than friends, broadly favouring a position of political neutrality. But the movement was divided on this question. Some CWS member societies and Board members had strong ties to Labour, while others in the movement were opposed to co-operatives' becoming tied to one party, or being involved in party politics at all. At a meeting with Co-operative Party representatives after the 1922 election, the CWS sought to clarify its position, noting that while individual Board members were free to act as they wished, the CWS was 'essentially a trading concern, and, as such, it is not advisable to be involved in Party Political Strife'. [165] Nonetheless from 1919 on the CWS made an annual £1,000 contribution to the party, justifying it on the basis of the party's work for co-operative business affairs. Similarly, while the CWS was happy to self-identify as part of a workers' movement (see Figure 5.12), its relations with trade unions were a further complication. On the one hand, CWS links with trade unions were strengthening through the growing number of unions using the CWS Bank. Trade union branch CWS bank accounts grew from 900 in 1918 to over 8,000 in 1922. In addition, CWS member societies resolved in 1919 that all CWS employees be members of a union recognized by the Trades Union Congress (TUC). This was reaffirmed in 1928. [166] The CWS Bank extended credit to trade unions during the three-month miners' strike of 1921, and the CWS gave financial support to societies in the north-east and other mining areas. However, the strike led to friction on the co-operative side, as many trade union debts were slow to be repaid and local societies faced difficulties as a consequence. [167] Meanwhile relations between co-operatives and their employees were tense throughout the early 1920s, as the CWS and societies sought to lower labour costs through wage reductions and staff cuts. [168]

---

[165] CWS Board minutes (14 December 1922).

[166] This was the subject of some controversy. In 1921, 375 employees at the CWS tobacco factory protested the compulsory measure and throughout the 1920s there were various efforts to rescind or reframe the resolution. In April 1922, the Board asked that the condition not apply to managers, buyers, and heads of departments; this was rejected. See CWS Board minutes (19 August 1921); CWS balance sheets, 'Agenda' and 'Minutes' (January 1919, April 1922); Redfern (1938), 272–3.

[167] CWS Board minutes (9 June 1921); see also Gurney (1996), 226.

[168] Discussions of wage revisions featured regularly in Board minutes between July 1921 and early 1923, whilst efforts to reduce staff at productive factories from December 1922 led to the most serious stoppages. See CWS Board minutes (6 December 1922) on the dispute's origins.

FIGURE 5.12. 'A Colossus of Commerce' drawing, 1929. This image, taken from a CWS pamphlet, used the familiar façades of CWS commercial buildings and factories to highlight the collective ownership of its business by working-class consumers.

The complicated relationship between co-operatives and trade unionists came to a head during the General Strike of 1926. The CWS faced a dilemma as a business and as a social movement. The TUC called out co-operative employees on the same terms as those of private companies and many CWS operations were suspended or curtailed. In addition, although the TUC initially promised to facilitate CWS efforts to deliver essential food supplies, after the first week its position hardened and it offered no exceptions for co-operative deliveries. Meanwhile CWS member societies desperate for supplies turned to private traders. Despite a deputation to the TUC on 8 May, including members of the CWS's Board and the Co-operative Party's A. V. Alexander, the movement won no concessions. The CWS then turned to the government, who pledged their assistance. The move was justified on the grounds that the CWS had no alternative.[169] These problems hampered efforts to build relations between the Co-operative and Labour Parties, and it was not until after the strike had ended that progress could be made. In early 1927 the TUC General Council and a delegation from the CU and CWS set up a joint committee to discuss relations between the two movements. The CWS wanted co-operative immunity from strikes if trade union wages and conditions were in place, as well as protection from demands for higher wages and better conditions than were asked of private employers. By 1928 progress was made and the TUC agreed

[169] On the CWS experience of the General Strike, see *Wheatsheaf* (June 1926), 81; and Redfern (1938), 265–71.

in principle that co-operatives were 'entitled to special consideration'.[170] Although this did not entirely settle the question, relations improved.[171]

Still, CWS remained uncertain about closer relations with the Labour Party. It continued its donations to Co-operative Party funds, but also projected an image of neutrality. When in 1927 some member societies pressed for the cessation of the CWS's donation, the CWS defended the donation because Co-operative MPs could defend co-operative interests in Parliament. In the aftermath of the 1927 Congress in Cheltenham, which created a formal alliance between the Labour and Co-operative parties, the CWS placed a statement on the front page of its monthly *Wheatsheaf* magazine, to reinforce its party political neutrality: 'The CWS will not be affected by the Cheltenham resolution. No funds which the CWS holds on behalf of Societies or others can be touched by any outside Party or Movement. CWS funds are the property of its Society-Members, and are subscribed and used for trading and allied purposes.'[172]

Labour's emphasis on the leading role of the state in economic and social affairs was a concern for the CWS, and clashed with the voluntarist tradition of many co-operators.[173] Labour's advocacy of municipal trading in areas of business where co-operatives were active, such as the coal and milk trades, was a particular source of criticism, although the CWS did agree to consider a 1931 proposal for municipal savings banks.[174] Co-operators also expressed concern over Labour interest in state purchasing of commodities, favouring instead co-operative marketing through wheat pools rather than government intervention.[175] Even under the Labour government of 1929–31, the CWS and the movement gained little ground on key issues such as legislation on restrictive trade practices. Perhaps their greatest concern, however, was the Agricultural Marketing Act of 1931, which allowed agricultural producers to elect boards to control the marketing and sale of different commodity groups. In November 1930 the CWS expressed grave concerns over the Bill, criticizing the excessive interference with tried and tested existing methods. It argued that the Bill placed the interests of producers before consumers.[176] Labour promises that consumer protections would follow were dashed by the split and fall of the government in August 1931.

Co-operatives faced hostility from the Conservatives, who were in government for most of the inter-war period. Private retailers had become a significant constituency in the Tory Party, and their views were supported by much of the popular press. As a result, the movement won no concessions on the question of restrictive trade practices from the National or Conservative governments of the 1930s. Between 1931 and 1935 the

---

[170] CWS Board minutes (14 January, 11 February, and 17 March 1927; 3 February 1928).

[171] In 1926 a National Conciliation Board was set up to adjudicate issues between trade unions and retail co-operative societies, but CWS did not participate. After protracted negotiations it agreed a separate conciliation framework in 1937. See Jones (1939), 10.

[172] *Wheatsheaf* (July 1927), 97.   [173] See Manton (2008).

[174] CWS Board minutes (5 January 1931). The CWS joined the Co-operative Party's Committee on Municipal Trading at its formation in 1927; see CWS Board minutes (17 and 23 February 1927).

[175] Cole (1944), 277; see also CWS Board minutes (11 March and 1 April 1930).

[176] CWS Board minutes (4 November 1930).

sole Co-operative MP (William Leonard, Glasgow) was a marginal figure. Despite the CWS's long experience in international trade with the Dominions and elsewhere, its offer of advisers for the government's delegation to the Ottawa conference, which set up the system of imperial preference tariffs, was rebuffed in the summer of 1932.[177] Later that year, Chancellor Neville Chamberlain set up a committee to investigate income tax. In December 1932 the committee called for the taxation of co-operative reserves, and the government duly acted on its advice. The Wholesales and the CU campaigned against the measure, including a petition to Parliament with 2.3 million signatures, but the tax remained in place.[178] The movement interpreted the tax as evidence of the political strength of the private retail lobby.[179] It also railed against further tax burdens imposed by the National Defence Contribution of 1937, in the midst of extensive co-operative debate over rearmament and Britain's political response to the expansion of Nazi Germany.[180] Thus the prevailing mood of the CWS and the movement on the political front in the 1930s was one of grievance and frustration at the prevailing hostile political climate (see Figure 5.13).[181]

5.6 DOING BUSINESS IN TROUBLED TIMES

The inter-war period was a difficult one for all businesses, and throughout the 1920s and 1930s societies in depressed areas looked to the CWS for assistance. In the past the CWS had helped societies in difficulties, providing financial and staff support. In the 1920s many societies in depressed areas struggled to keep their businesses afloat, and some were deeply in debt to the CWS. The Sunderland society was a case in point. In June 1927, it was reported that the Sunderland society, despite making a net profit of only £130 and owing more than £30,000 to the CWS (of which nearly £25,000 was overdue), had decided to pay its members a 1s. dividend. In response, the CWS threatened to withdraw its credit unless Sunderland agreed that future dividends be subject to CWS approval, and CWS advice was followed. Despite agreeing to this in September, three months later Sunderland reneged and decided to pay an 8d. dividend. The CWS responded by threatening to end their help and to report Sunderland to the Registrar of Friendly Societies.[182] But in mid-1929 the CWS relented and agreed to write off much of the interest on its overdue accounts, on the grounds that the society had reorganized, reduced its expenses, was now purchasing 96 per cent of its supplies from the CWS.

---

[177] CU Congress Report (1933), 103.   [178] CU Congress Report (1933), 47–55; Cole (1944), 327.

[179] *Wheatsheaf* (December 1933), 178.

[180] On co-operatives and the peace movement in this period, see Burton (1994), 52–61; and Flynn (2009).

[181] See, for example, J. J. Worley's presidential speech to Congress in 1938, in CU Congress Report (1938), 477.

[182] CWS Board minutes (7 June, 1 September, 8 and 29 December 1927).

FIGURE 5.13. Co-operatives and private traders cartoon, 1934. The original caption read: 'Trader (to referee): "Send him off! I can't keep him from scoring!"' Courtesy of *Co-operative News* (<www.thenews.coop>).

This was agreed, notwithstanding Sunderland's overdue accounts and unpaid overdrafts totalling over £62,000 (against its share capital of £83,000).[183]

   Problems like this prompted the 1928 Congress to resolve that the CWS should enter the retail trade in areas where there were few co-operatives.[184] In part, this was an extension of the CWS's involvement in the Joint Propaganda Committee, which had assisted in the formation of new societies and branches in 'co-operative deserts' for decades. It also implicitly acknowledged that only the Wholesales had the resources to promote co-operatives in new areas and support those in difficulties. In Scotland the SCWS had established retail branches since 1908 in regions without co-operatives and had also taken over failing societies.[185] In England and Wales this was to be the model for the CWS Retail Society (later the CRS). After economic conditions worsened in the 1930s, the need to assist societies in trouble became more pressing. In early 1930 the CWS Board set up a subcommittee to develop a structure for the new organization. Under the scheme, the CWS Retail Society's management was controlled by the CWS Board, who guaranteed all capital and interest. Local meetings of branch members would elect advisory committees, who would maintain local engagement in the society. While committees

[183] CWS Board minutes (29 May 1929).   [184] CU Congress Report (1928), 420–4.
[185] Kinloch and Butt (1981), 221, 290–1.

were to have limited oversight over business operations, branches could become auton-omous societies by vote of 75 per cent of the membership.[186] The CWS Retail Society was officially launched at the January 1934 quarterly meeting.[187] It was not until 1936 that the long-troubled Cardiff society became the first CWS Retail branch, whilst more than forty societies remained under CWS supervision. Many of these would become CWS Retail branches in later years.

The experience of societies in Britain's growing regions was significantly different. Growth of large-scale manufacturing of consumer goods increased the range and vari-ety of items available to those who could afford it. New types of products reached the market (see Figure 5.14), while other goods, such as men's clothing, became increasingly differentiated according to rapid changes in fashion. Transport improvements made it easier to travel long distances to shop. Variety was wider, but also more national, as demand for particular types of goods by region declined. As Jefferys noted, the increase

FIGURE 5.14. Window display of CWS electrical goods, c.1930s. Originally a producer co-operative, the CWS acquired the Dudley bucket and fender works in 1908 and continued to produce hardware at the site. In 1935, the CWS expanded its works to make 'Dudley' brand elec-trical goods, including vacuum cleaners, electric washers, toasters, and hairdryers.

---

[186] CWS Board minutes (30 September 1930).
[187] CWS balance sheets, 'Board's Report' (January 1934). The vote led to another wave of dissatisfaction in the press; see *Wheatsheaf* (March 1934), 33.

in variety was partly the outcome of improved production processes, but was also the result of intense competition in both manufacturing and retailing.[188] These were the conditions under which the CWS had to compete in London, Birmingham, and other growing areas in the South and Midlands.

In early 1924, as the movement began to recover from the post-war slump, the Board published a report entitled 'Trade Passing the CWS', on the old problem of weak society loyalty in purchasing from the Wholesale. This was the result of a CWS survey of 66 per cent of societies, representing more than 83 per cent of individual members. Four main reasons were identified for trade bypassing the Wholesale: prices; lack of variety in styles; the demand for proprietary goods; and the use of local sources of supply. On the first point, the Board noted that many societies had been forced to sell items at or below cost during the downturn, and had sometimes turned to cut-rate suppliers or lower-quality goods to meet the pressure.[189] However throughout the inter-war period CWS prices became a significant issue, driving the CWS to cut costs in an effort to attract trade in the South and Midlands where price competition proved more important than high dividends in attracting trade. On the second point, the CWS noted that this concern most often referred to the drapery and allied trades. Here the Board seemed to deny their own findings, suggesting that the choice of goods it offered was in fact adequate.[190] This obduracy in questions of fashion stemmed partly from a co-operative ideological commitment to 'production for use' rather than to meet changeable fashions.[191] The demand for proprietary articles, whose sale was often the subject of strict trade conditions in the inter-war period, was a further difficulty, and the CWS noted the particular issue of brand loyalty in the case of tobacco and cigarettes, conceding the need for greater attention to image, display, and advertising in order to win custom for co-operative brands. Finally, the continued convenience and price benefits of some local sources of supply was also recognized, particularly in relation to fresh food items, though the CWS argued it had a proven track record in supplying large societies with milk, greengrocery, meat, and other items.[192] Indeed, as Table 5.3 demonstrates, grocery items continued to make up the bulk of CWS sales.

As for the previous period, records from the Leicester Co-operative Society (LCS) offer a window into the procurement strategies of retail societies in the inter-war period.[193] Whilst Leicester's experience cannot be taken as typical, it nonetheless offers some insight into the changing nature of co-operative trade. In 1914, the society was over fifty years old, with a membership of over 21,700, share capital of nearly £275,000, and annual sales of more than £500,000.[194] By 1920 membership rose to 34,000, growing to nearly 57,000 in 1930 and to more than 73,000 in 1938, when its share capital had grown to £1.2 million and its sales to £2.4 million.[195] After the difficulties of the early 1920s LCS prospered, and by the early 1930s had added a range of new departments, including

[188] Jefferys (1954), 41–3.
[189] 'Trade Passing the CWS', in CWS balance sheets (March 1924), 1–2, NCA.
[190] 'Trade Passing the CWS', 2.   [191] Gurney (1996), 233–7.   [192] 'Trade Passing the CWS', 3–4.
[193] See section 4.1.   [194] CU Congress Report (1915), 604;
[195] CU Congress Report (1921), 568; (1931), 590; (1939).

Table 5.3. Per cent of CWS domestic sales in grocery category, 1920–35

	Manchester	Newcastle branch	London branch	Total[a]
1920	81.2	84.3	84.1	78.8
1925	71.0	75.5	75.8	82.7
1930	79.2	83.4	80.7	81.9
1935	81.2	84.3	84.1	82.0

[a] Domestic trade does not include trade with SCWS or the E&SCWS.

Source: CWS balance sheets, 1920–35.

optical, chemists, funeral services, wireless sales, and even hairdressing.[196] As Table 5.4 demonstrates, CWS purchases represented roughly a third of LCS purchases during the 1920s, and, following a slump during the Great Depression, were on the rise in the latter half of the 1930s. Whilst grocery items made up the majority of LCS orders from the CWS throughout the period, shown in Table 5.5, by the mid-1920s the proportion of grocery orders was diminishing and the LCS was purchasing a wider variety of the Wholesales' goods. The growth in the 'bakery' category after 1930 is partly explained by the closure of the LCS's own corn mill, but what is particularly interesting is the growth in purchases from an increasingly wide array of CWS departments. For instance, in 1935, 2.2 per cent of Leicester's total purchases from the CWS were for its coal department, 1.3 per cent for its growing travel operations, and 1.8 per cent for support functions such as delivery and a building department.[197] Although these were small percentages in themselves, such figures demonstrate both the increasing range of societies' business and the CWS's interest in developing new products and services to maintain societies' trade.

One of the key issues for the CWS in developing its inter-war trade was the development of fixed price lines. Many multiple chains had sold their goods at nationally advertised prices for decades, but the varied dividend and price policies of the hundreds of co-operative societies made national advertising and pricing difficult. In the early 1920s, however, the CWS experimented with fixed price lines in a small way, focusing on the boot, drapery, and soap trades. These goods were advertised in co-operative media, but increasingly the CWS also advertised elsewhere, including post offices and even private newspapers.[198] In 1929 the CWS created a special subcommittee on fixed prices, ordered the preparation of press articles for CWS magazines on the subject, and planned a series of conferences with retail societies to consult on the items best suited to the policy.[199] One *Wheatsheaf* article stressed the competitive pressures behind the move: 'While co-operators have been busy changing the *principles* of trade, the private firms and combines that advertise and sell in all parts at one price in each case, have changed the *scope*

[196] LCS balance sheets (1914–38), NCA.   [197] LCS balance sheets (1935), NCA.
[198] CWS Board minutes (29 September and 13 October 1922).
[199] CWS Board minutes (15 October and 19 December 1929).

Table 5.4. Leicester Co-operative Society purchases by source, 1914–38

	CWS (%)	Other co-ops	LCS Corn Mill[a]	Other sources[b]
1914	32.7	2.4	11.0	53.9
1915	34.8	2.1	13.2	49.9
1916	34.9	2.1	14.7	48.3
1917	32.8	1.8	12.5	52.8
1918	34.2	2.1	9.5	54.2
1919	37.7	2.2	7.8	52.4
1920	36.1	2.1	7.4	54.3
1921	31.6	1.7	9.0	57.8
1924	32.5	2.1	7.1	58.3
1925	31.8	2.2	7.3	58.6
1926	30.5	1.7	7.2	60.5
1927	33.1	2.0	7.5	57.3
1928	33.6	2.5	5.8	58.1
1929	32.6	2.4	5.2	59.8
1930	29.5	2.1	4.5	63.9
1931	30.4	1.9	–	67.8
1932	29.2	2.3	–	72.7
1933	30.7	2.4	–	66.9
1934	32.0	2.2	–	65.7
1935	35.0	2.2	–	62.8
1936	36.0	2.1	–	61.8
1937	37.2	1.9	–	60.9
1938	41.7	1.8	–	56.5

[a] LCS closed its corn mill in 1930.
[b] Other sources were predominantly private suppliers, but the overall total includes a small number of internal transfers from LCS departments (not tallied separately).

Source: LCS balance sheets, NCA; no data recorded for 1922–3.

of trading.'[200] A subsequent piece highlighted CWS consultation with societies as part of the price-setting strategy, in contrast to the arbitrary fixing of prices by private firms without such consultation.[201]

Indeed, many private manufacturers, through their trade associations, were beginning to impose a system of resale price maintenance (RPM), whereby retailers had to sell the product at a price set by the producer. Like the Proprietary Trade Articles Association (PATA), which had battled with the movement since 1906, several trade associations imposed restrictions on co-operatives' offering dividend on their products. These

[200] *Wheatsheaf* (June 1930), 87–8.
[201] *Wheatsheaf* (October 1930), 146. By mid-1930 CWS referred to 'fixed maximum prices' in all its literature; see CWS Board minutes (29 July 1930).

Table 5.5. Leicester Co-operative Society purchases from CWS, 1914–38

	Grocery (%)	Drapery	Clothing	Boot/shoe	Furnishing	Butchery	Bakery	Other[a]
1914	74.8	7.7	4.7	3.3	5.5	0.6	3.5	–
1915	72.8	7.1	4.1	2.8	4.7	0.6	7.8	–
1916	76.1	6.2	2.7	2.0	4.7	2.1	6.2	–
1917	76.0	5.3	1.9	2.0	4.6	2.4	7.9	–
1918	77.8	7.7	2.6	2.2	5.9	0.1	3.1	–
1919	76.7	6.2	3.0	2.2	7.1	1.3	2.9	–
1920	79.5	5.2	3.4	1.9	6.4	1.1	2.3	–
1921	80.7	4.2	0.6	1.4	6.0	0.2	5.4	–
1924	80.3	3.7	0.5	0.7	5.3	0.7	5.5	3.3
1925	79.4	4.1	0.6	0.8	5.6	1.1	4.2	4.2
1926	80.3	4.2	0.5	0.8	5.5	1.5	3.1	4.1
1927	77.8	4.1	0.7	1.1	5.6	2.1	4.1	4.5
1928	77.4	5.1	1.8	1.6	5.3	1.7	2.8	4.3
1929	75.9	5.4	3.1	1.8	5.0	1.7	3.5	3.6
1930	73.8	6.5	2.1	2.1	5.5	1.2	3.6	5.2
1931	71.1	6.7	2.2	2.3	5.1	2.2	4.3	6.1
1932	68.7	6.4	2.1	1.8	5.1	1.9	4.5	9.5
1933	65.4	5.4	2.2	2.0	4.9	3.7	6.2	10.2
1934	65.9	5.7	2.3	1.9	4.9	3.7	7.2	8.4
1935	64.4	5.2	2.2	2.8	5.1	4.2	7.7	8.4
1936	64.4	4.7	2.8	2.0	4.7	2.7	9.4	9.3
1937	66.0	4.2	1.9	1.9	4.1	2.6	10.6	8.7
1938	68.6	3.3	1.9	1.7	3.3	2.3	7.3	11.6

[a] 'Other' category includes purchases for 'miscellaneous departments' as well as dairy (from 1924), coal (1928), chemists (1931), travel (1931), support departments (1932), and funerals (1935).

Source: LCS balance sheets, NCA; no data recorded for 1922–3.

included the Association of Photographic Manufacturers, who sought to restrict co-operative dividends on their products in 1930.[202] During the inter-war period, the CWS tried to fight such restrictions, even closing accounts with suppliers who agreed to sell goods on PATA's extensive lists.[203] The most famous incident, however, was the case of radio manufacturers who suddenly informed the CWS in the final months of 1933 that they would no longer allow dividend payments on wireless sets. In response the CWS quickly brought out its own brand radio, named 'Defiant', with two models available in the shops by December and a further thirteen available by the following year (see Plate 15). In a *Wheatsheaf* article the CWS proudly noted that 1,000 societies representing 5.5

[202] See CWS Board minutes (24 June 1930). Although CWS buyers advocated signing the agreement and noted that SCWS had already done so, the Board refused.
[203] CWS Board minutes (5 May 1921 and 24 August 1922).

million members had refused to sign the wireless agreement in 1933, although six societies with 60,000 members had.[204] Although the Defiant was a famous case, many societies quietly signed agreements with various manufacturers in the inter-war period,
under pressure from members to sell branded items and in order to maintain trade in
unsettled times.

Although there were many instances of the 'dysfunctional federation' in action in
the inter-war period, in the midst of heightened competition and a negative political
and economic climate, the component parts of the co-operative movement did find
new ways to work more closely together. For the CWS, developing fixed price policies
in consultation with other parts of the movement was part of a broader attempt to
achieve greater commercial cohesion within the movement. Working with the
National Association of Co-operative Managers, they developed district and national
consultative committees to make decisions on developing fixed prices and advertising
campaigns.[205] A key area of CWS innovation was in its use of film. Having already
made extensive use of film in its 'co-operative capital' campaigns of the early 1920s, in
1928 the CWS produced its first 'story' films for screening in local cinemas, provided
to societies at a subsidized price. Such films combined advertisements for specific
CWS products with messages about co-operative ideals, framed through the experience of 'typical' consumers at co-operative stores. By the early 1930s societies could
draw on the CWS's Film Library Service, and 'cinema lectures' proved popular tools
for member engagement. During the 1937–8 season the CWS estimated that 237,000
people had attended nearly 1,200 screenings of its films.[206] By the end of the 1930s these
productions were becoming more elaborate. The 1937 colour production *Co-operette*
starred well-known comedian Stanley Holloway and featured musical numbers with
dancers dressed as CWS products![207]

There were signs of greater coordination across the movement as well, culminating in
the creation of the National Co-operative Authority in 1932, which brought together
leaders from the CU, Wholesales, Co-operative Party, and auxiliaries. Although the
Authority had no power to impose policy, it did provide a more unified national voice
and greater coordination on matters of policy and trade.[208] The CWS proved willing to
work with the CU on joint committees related to trade, advertising, and technical education, while the joint Trade and Business Conference, inaugurated in 1921, brought
together retail society managers and CWS officials to discuss wider trade policy and led
to several key initiatives in the inter-war period.[209] Perhaps the greatest of these was the
Ten Year Plan, inaugurated in 1934 and timed for completion during the centenary of the

---

[204] *Wheatsheaf* (January 1934), 7.   [205] CWS Board minutes (20 December 1929).

[206] Burton (1994), 27.

[207] Many co-operative films, including *Co-operette*, are contained in the National Co-operative Film
Archive, NCA. Original films are deposited with dedicated film archives; NCA has viewing copies.

[208] See Whitecross (forthcoming).

[209] William Bradshaw, future CWS president, was instrumental in gaining support for the Trade and
Business Conference. A CWS employee in 1917, he was elected to the Board in 1921, and was knighted
in 1937. See Redfern (1938), 196 and 198.

Rochdale Pioneers. Organized by a joint committee of the CU and CWS, the plan used the CU's regional and district committees to set annual trade and membership targets for societies, and developed national advertising campaigns to push co-operative productions and encourage members to use the entire range of societies' services (see Plates 7 and 11). A separate plan, inaugurated in 1936, aimed at improving and modernizing cooperative educational provision.[210] Throughout the 1930s the Ten Year Plan focused the movement's attention on the strategic problems it faced, and encouraged closer collaboration between retail societies, the CU, and the Wholesales in finding solutions. However, it is difficult to assess its long-term impact, as the plan was abandoned after the start of the Second World War.

5.7 REORGANIZING THE CWS, 1929 AND 1937

In 1928, after extensive discussions, the CWS Board proposed major revisions in representation on the Board to reflect geographic changes in membership and trade. The Board wanted a reduction in the number of Newcastle district representatives, to be redistributed in favour of the growing London district, with the Manchester representation remaining unchanged. But so controversial did this prove that the membership voted instead for a Special Committee of Inquiry (SCI), to investigate a broad array of management and constitutional issues, as had been done in 1906. Like its predecessor, the 1929 SCI report reflected the changing views of member societies and CWS leaders on how best to approach the changing business climate. Intriguingly, two of the eleven members of the 1929 SCI, Professor Hall and W. T. Charter, had served on the Survey Committee. The SCI interviewed a cross-section of the movement, but also took on board research into modern management methods used by foreign co-operative businesses as well as British private industrial firms.[211] In 1937, there came a second SCI, again prompted by arguments over regional representation. Although this report was more limited in scope, it reported on the outcomes of the 1929 recommendations and put forward new plans of its own. R. F. Lancaster (see Figure 5.15), CWS's secretary and most senior administrator, served as secretary to both inquiries.

At the heart of both the 1929 and 1937 reports was the issue of the geographical shift in membership and trade, and how it should be reflected in representation on the CWS Board. The 1929 inquiry proposed a reduction in the number of Board members from 32 to 28, which was generally popular, but more controversially proposed a national system of voting as more appropriate to a business that was increasingly national in scope. However, neither the CWS nor its member societies were ready in 1929 to abandon regional representation. Instead, delegates voted to redistribute Board representation,

---

[210] See Topham (1935), Woods (1935), and National Educational Council (1936).
[211] SCI (1929), 6.

so that 14 members were from the Manchester district, 8 from London, and 6 from Newcastle. The reduction in numbers was to be achieved through retirements, as several members were approaching the mandatory retirement age.[212] However, when the 1937 inquiry published its findings, advocacy of national voting was strong once more. Modern CWS operations were planned nationally, its goods were nationally advertised, and its competition was increasingly national in nature. It noted that current directors reported that their duties increasingly prompted them to take a national perspective on the business.[213] The report outlined a new two-round voting procedure, beginning with a regional candidate selection round, based on the CU regions rather than the former CWS districts. The number of candidates each region would select was determined on the basis of CWS purchases, whilst the balance between large and small societies was achieved by candidate selection being based both on the highest number of individual votes and the highest number of societies' voting. The selected candidates would then go forward to national election.[214] Although the proposals clearly allowed for some continued regional identity within the CWS, their successful passage in 1937 reflected the increasingly national perspective of both the CWS Board and its member societies.

Another key SCI concern in 1929 was with the Board's organization and oversight of its gargantuan operations. The report listed the responsibilities of each of the Board's main committees and questioned the efficacy of a system where 200 managers were directly responsible to the Board, and Directors conducted weekly visits to factories and departments.[215] Thus the 1929 SCI argued for the creation of permanent subcommittees of the three main committees (Finance, Grocery, and Drapery), organized around single industry or commodity groups. Departments and works would be coordinated along similar lines and managed accordingly. All boot works, for example, would be under one senior manager who would then report to the Board subcommittee. The report also approved of the CWS's practice of forming national trade advisory committees, in which managers in similar operations shared their expertise. Although there was a specific list of powers that were not to be delegated to subcommittees, such as property transactions, major investments, new ventures, appointments of staff, and any working relations with competitors, the report was nonetheless an important step in moving the Board to be more involved in strategic decision-making and less in operational management.[216] The 1937 SCI reported with approval on the outcome, recognizing that it gave Directors more time to focus on policy. The report also noted with pleasure that the move away from routine visits, and the new policies of group management and joint buying across similar operations, were demonstrating benefits.[217]

The 1929 inquiry also proposed new Sales Investigation Departments at the three main branches. These departments were to monitor retail societies' purchases, and to investigate where the CWS was failing to win sufficient trade. Societies were also to be

---

[212] CWS Board minutes (20 June 1929).   [213] SCI (1937), 8.   [214] SCI (1937), 10–12.
[215] SCI (1929), 7–10.   [216] SCI (1929), 11–14.   [217] SCI (1937), 29.

FIGURE 5.15. Sir Robert F. Lancaster (1883–1945). In 1916, Lancaster moved from Newcastle to become CWS solicitor, heading up the new Legal Department in Manchester. In 1923, he was appointed secretary, and served in the CWS's top administrative post until his death in 1945. In the 1930s he was honoured by the Danish and Canadian governments for his contributions to international trade, and was knighted in 1944.

invited to approach the department to initiate discussions and settle complaints. The SCI clearly hoped these departments would lead both to a more systematic approach by CWS to meeting societies' trading needs and to strengthening relations with societies' buyers.[218] However, the 1937 report alluded to an initial lack of confidence from officials and managers on both sides when the departments were initiated, and indicated that they had not achieved the expected results. Accordingly, the inquiry suggested that the departments be developed into Consumer Research operations.[219] The departments were now to undertake extensive market research analysis, investigate new industrial trends and inventions, and advise the CWS on its packaging, presentation, and public appeal (one novel example of contemporary advertising can be seen in Figure 5.16). Although the 1937 report did not make a formal recommendation on the subject, consumer research became a subject of much discussion in co-operative media in the following year, with several officials (including Percy Redfern) supporting more work in this area.[220]

[218] SCI (1929), 16.   [219] SCI (1937), 30.
[220] SCI (1937), 30; *Co-operative Review* (December 1938), 358–9.

The SCI of 1929 recommended that co-operative funds should be invested in private companies to ensure a measure of co-operative control over them.[221] This was a radical proposal given that the CWS had been keen to keep co-operative capital inside the movement. It reflected a growing awareness of just how formidable private competition was becoming. Moreover, the CWS was willing to act, using its financial resources in this way to defend its competitive position. In 1929, the CWS purchased shares in the Southern Oil Company, a firm supplying refined oils for margarine production which was independent of the Lever combine.[222] However, Southern Oil wanted to ensure that any alliance between the two companies did not attract public attention, owing to the hostility it might cause within the industry. Thus, CWS purchased shares in Southern Oil, but through an intermediary, the Westminster Bank.[223] The CWS also had the financial power to invest in its private suppliers, and was willing to do so if it could secure a trade advantage. For example, in September 1929 representatives of the sugar refiners Tate & Lyle offered to sell 88,000 shares to the CWS at the price of 30s. per share. In its discussions the CWS noted that in the prior half-year more than 73 per cent of its sugar purchases were from the company, and it was suggested that a liaison officer could be appointed between the two directorates, with a view to securing the best ongoing trading arrangements. Although the CWS decided against the proposal in October, however, in the following month the Board narrowly voted to authorize reopening the discussions. By January 1930 the deal was made.[224] In the 1937 SCI report a suggestion aimed at limiting competitors' access to information about the CWS freed the Board from having to announce to general meetings when they planned to begin a new enterprise. The provision passed.[225]

Although the 1937 report was more limited than its predecessor, it did make one interesting new recommendation of its own. This related to CWS and retail trading, and would develop into a key area of the Wholesale's development in the years after the Second World War. Following on from the creation of the CWS Retail Society three years before, the inquiry recommended a further expansion into retailing. Although it stressed that the CWS would agree not to engage in any activity without the consent of nearby societies, 'the inadequacy or complete absence of retail effort in some areas…and, furthermore, restrictive legislation, clearly point to the fact that CWS is the best medium for undertaking classes of trade such as, for example, funeral furnishing and chemist shops'. The rule change, passed by delegates, would be a spur to CWS activities in these areas in subsequent years. The suggestion, and its passage by delegate societies, suggested a greater willingness to accept CWS central control during a period of heightened competition.

---

[221] SCI (1929), 40. However the report argued for some transparency, advocating annual reporting of the amount invested, the dividend accruing, and the amount of CWS trade with firms in which it invested.

[222] On Lever Brothers, see sections 4.2 and 4.3.

[223] CWS Board minutes (28 June and 16 July 1929).

[224] CWS Board minutes (1 October and 5 November 1929; 7 January and 21 May 1930).

[225] SCI (1937), 38–9.

FIGURE 5.16. CWS milk bottle top adverts, *c.*1930s. Printed on cardboard and used to cap milk bottles, societies purchased advertisements like these to communicate with their members and customers. In addition to promoting the quality, purity, and affordability of co-operative goods, some messages highlighted the differences between co-operatives and their competitors.

5.8 CONCLUSIONS

The First World War and the inter-war period had been a severe test for the CWS and the movement at large. For most of the period it faced tough commercial competition from a retail sector increasingly dominated by large-scale producer combines and multiple chains. It also had to contend with governments which were deeply unsympathetic to co-operation in practice and principle, and which directly attacked co-operative profits through the tax system. In addition, once the wartime problems of inflation and shortages receded, they were replaced by major problems of economic downturn, protectionist obstacles to international operations, and contracting markets. How did the CWS and the movement fare?

Superficially, it can be argued that both the CWS and the movement identified the threats they faced and were able to contain them, at least for a time. This was evident in the willingness to use the CWS's sophisticated overseas networks to adapt to the difficulties presented by protectionism, and to utilize the range of CWS operations to open new opportunities in uncongenial circumstances. In the end, the CWS and the wider movement showed a willingness to reform structures and practices to adapt to the tougher environment, in diverse arenas from political activities to consumer research and marketing. This was not a movement impervious to the need for change. It demonstrated that it had leaders who were prepared to argue for internal reforms to meet changing circumstances, and engage in the difficult work of building a sufficient consensus to achieve their aims.

But the period also demonstrated that longstanding divisions within the 'dysfunctional federation' placed limits on how far, and how fast, the movement could adapt. The bitter arguments over the Survey Committee Report revealed deep-seated rivalries between the CU and the Wholesales, and a visceral opposition among retail societies to anything which might challenge their independence. As a result, the Survey Report was watered down in subsequent discussions between the component bodies within the movement in the early 1920s, and proved an ineffective blueprint for creating a more united and cohesive national, social, and commercial entity. On the whole, the reforms achieved in the inter-war decades came when the movement was able to unify in its own defence, rather than from proactive initiatives. It proved difficult for the disparate movement to develop the long-term strategic coherence that was needed to enable co-operation to anticipate and pre-empt what would prove an even faster changing social and commercial environment after the Second World War. As a result, many of the issues and problems which were not adequately addressed in the 1920s and 1930s would re-emerge in far more difficult circumstances, and the question of fundamental reform had to be revisited once more.

PART II

RETREAT AND RENAISSANCE

....

CHAPTER 6

CO-OPERATION IN RETREAT

War and Decline, 1939–73

....

6.1 HISTORIANS AND CO-OPERATIVE RETREAT

FEW periods have attracted so much historical interest in the British co-operative move-ment as the Second World War and the quarter of a century after the cessation of hostili-ties. The reasons for this are not hard to identify. The famous 'long boom' of the 1945–73 period saw striking changes in living standards, consumer behaviour, and social struc-ture, all of which had revolutionary implications for patterns of consumption and the retail trade. At a basic level, Leigh Sparks shows that consumer expenditure, as calcu-lated at 1985 prices, quadrupled between 1950 and the mid-1970s.[1] More presciently, he describes the emergence of radically different consumers, affluent individuals and their households, less engaged in their local communities or collective activities generally, less loyal to traditional social or economic institutions (including co-operatives), and much more choosy and fickle in their tastes. By the 1960s, the trappings of affluence increasingly included technological mass innovations such as the motor car and the household refrigerator, which revolutionized shopping patterns by making possible the weekly shop at large supermarkets (increasingly, the latter were relocated to suburban sites where relatively cheap land enabled the provision of mass car parking) instead of the daily trip to the local store. Such trends were also reinforced by changes in employ-ment patterns. Full employment and the financial demands on households of the new consumerism led to the entry of larger numbers of women into the ranks of paid employ-ment. This in turn increased the attraction of the 'one-stop' weekly shopping expedition to the supermarket in place of daily visits to smaller specialist stores. Meanwhile the TV ratcheted up consumer awareness of an ever expanding range of commodity brands and

---

[1] Sparks (1994), 5.

promoted consumption as a definer of status and self-image rather than just an activity to meet need.[2] Easier credit and the emergence of hire purchase fuelled the resulting consumer boom.

This was a rapidly changing world in which the British co-operative movement struggled to hold its own. The fortunes of co-operatives in Britain seemed to be in stark contrast to those of private sector rivals in the retail trade, especially the multiple firms which had been gathering strength throughout the twentieth century. The period saw the share of the retail market enjoyed by British consumer co-operatives almost halve, from 12 per cent in 1951, to 7.5 per cent by 1971.[3] The share in its particular area strength, food, fell from 17.1 per cent in 1951 to 11 per cent by 1971; but this was eclipsed by co-operatives' plummeting share of non-food from 6.5 per cent to just 3.3 per cent in the same period. While the full scale of the decline only became fully apparent from the mid-1950s, many co-operative leaders were already concerned during the Second World War about the growing competition the movement faced. Loss of market share was not the only problem. During the twenty years after the war, it became apparent that the membership base of the movement was weakening. This was not manifested initially as falling membership, though as John Walton has pointed out, the membership records of many societies are notoriously suspect for this period, with the possibility of dead members remaining on the books.[4] Rather, contemporaries began to note a growing apathy among members, with lower attendance and participation in co-operative activities, and fewer coming forward to stand for office or committees. In the mid-1950s, J. A. Banks of the University of Liverpool and E. N. Ostergaard of the University of Birmingham were commissioned by The Co-operative College to prepare a major study of the internal democracy of retail societies. This was followed by a similar study by Ostergaard and A. H. Halsey in the early 1960s. Both cited member apathy as a major cause of concern for the movement, and offered various strategies for reviving a solid core of activists.[5] In 1963, one commentator sourly remarked (revealing the sexist attitudes of the time) that only co-operative employees and housewives seemed to find the time to stand for office, and stated bluntly that 'direct democracy has ceased to function effectively'.[6] As Walton shows, by the 1970s society membership records, for all their shortcomings, tell an unequivocal story of declining numbers.[7]

Of course historians have been especially concerned about the reasons for the apparent inability or reluctance of the movement to address its mounting difficulties. Why was it that the decline seemed to prove irreversible, in spite of numerous investigations

[2] Sparks (1994), 6–12.   [3] Byrom (1982), 47.

[4] J. K. Walton in Black and Robertson (2009), 23.

[5] Sir Jack Bailey, 'A Declining Democracy', in *Co-operative Review* (March 1965), 86. The Ostergaard and Banks study was published as part of the 'Co-operative College Papers' series.

[6] 'The Challenge Before Us' (a synthesis of two letters published in the Co-operative Party's 'Monthly Letter'), *Co-operative Review* (March 1963), 67.

[7] Walton in Black and Robertson (2009), 23.

and attempts at reform? What were the obstacles which stymied most, if not all, initiatives to modernize the movement without sacrificing its essential co-operative values? As shown, the necessity for changing the structures and practices of the movement was identified by successive generations of co-operative leaders, and these did from time to time result in efforts to implement reform and change. These initiatives aimed to change both the operations of retail societies and those of central bodies such as the Co-operative Union and the two Wholesales. Perhaps the most notable of these in the immediate post-war period was the Co-operative Independent Commission which was established in 1955 and reported in 1958. But this was by no means unique, and further efforts at reform followed in the 1960s, with another internal report by CWS Head of Market Research in 1963 ('The Role of the CWS'), and a major report by a Joint Reorganization Committee in 1965. As will be seen, while these initiatives did stimulate attempts to reorganize the movement, or at least parts of it, none was really successful and all encountered resistance from one source or another. For historians, the key question is why the movement proved so difficult to reform, notwithstanding the fact that the formidable challenges which faced it were clearly recognized.

On this point, a number of views have emerged. In the late 1980s, Müller argued that the decline of British co-operative business resulted from several factors, including the rise of powerful competitors in the private sector and, especially by the 1970s, the emergence of consumer society, in which many of the previously loyal working-class members and customers of co-operative retail societies began to 'shop around'. Of these, Müller identifies the dissipation of traditional co-operative loyalties and attitudes among the more affluent working class as most important. 'It was as if', says Müller, 'the driving force which had called these organisations into existence, and the self-confidence and the willpower of the working people to bring about economic and social changes were exhausted.' Thus for him, decline was as much social and ideological in origin, as commercial and economic.[8] It was a wider transformation of British society and economic behaviour which proved so challenging for the movement, because it undermined the very spirit of co-operative engagement and activism which had historically been the source of its dynamism. More recently Gurney has offered an explanation which takes this analysis slightly further. He contends that the post-war period witnessed the emergence of a new culture of individual consumption and consumer 'rational choice', in place of older notions of working-class loyalty to 'the co-op', the co-operative ideal of fostering production and consumption to meet 'real' needs rather than the fabricated desires of mass advertising, and suspicion of 'exploitative' capitalist retailers. Crucially, Gurney argues that this might not have been inevitable, had the supposed allies of the co-operative movement in the Labour Party constructed a post-war settlement based upon co-operative principles of social ownership and the development of institutions to protect and shape consumer interests, rather than displacing co-operative ideas of socialist reconstruction by a more prominent role for the state in economic and social

---

[8] F. Muller, in Brazda and Schediwy (1989), 124–5.

affairs. The error was subsequently compounded by Labour's slavish acceptance of mass individual consumerism, as both a reality of, and indeed a desirable feature of modern life, a view epitomized in the work of the party's most influential thinker of the 1950s, Anthony Crosland. This absence of strong political support for co-operative ideas at the very time when the movement needed it most was exacerbated by the even more zealous embrace of mass individual consumerism by the Conservatives, and a continuance of their thinly disguised hostility to co-operation as an idea. Co-operative decline was thus political, as well as social and cultural in origin.[9] Gurney's damning assessment of the Labour Party's indifference and even hostility to the interests of the co-operative movement is supported by Manton, whose work on Labour's attitudes to consumerism and the retail industry underlines just how marginal the co-operative movement and co-operative principles were in Labour thinking after 1945.[10]

While acknowledging the significance of such socio-cultural and political factors, Johnston Birchall, one of the most influential historians of the British and international movements, stresses the formidable challenges posed by the new consumer society and especially by competition from the multiple retail chains. Many of the multiples had become capital rich as a result of flotation as public companies, and were therefore advantageously placed to relocate and re-equip their shops. But Birchall contends that the most serious obstacles hindering efforts to modernize and reform the co-operative movement to meet the challenge lay within the movement itself. For him, it was the dogged independence of the retail societies, and their suspicion of what they saw as centralizing tendencies of the Wholesale societies, the Co-operative Union, and among those advocating reform such as the Independent Commission Report authors in 1958, which stymied the coherence of reform initiatives for much of the post-war period. Birchall contends that by the 1960s there were three discrete factions within the movement, each perceiving its future very differently. First, there was a 'localist' faction, especially strong among many local retail societies, which jealously defended the principle of the local autonomy of societies, and which was buoyed up by examples of successful small societies in certain parts of the country. The second faction took the opposite tack and argued for the absorption of all the retail societies and national bodies into one, single national society, which would then be powerful enough to rationalize the business of the movement in ways analogous to the methods employed by the large multiples as they progressed from being regional to becoming national entities. Between these emerged a 'regionalist' faction, convinced that the creation of large regional societies through the amalgamation of smaller ones could provide a structure which would make rationalization easier to achieve, but whilst maintaining a high degree of local autonomy.[11] Thus the root of the movement's inability to reform and adapt quickly enough lay in its structural fragmentation and the enduring belief in retail society autonomy. Lawrence Black, in his assessment of the response of the movement to the report of the Co-operative

---

[9] Gurney (2005), 983–7.   [10] Manton (2009), (2008), (2007).
[11] Birchall (1994), 159–60.

Independent Commission, also notes the inability of the movement to cohere around virtually any of its recommendations as internal divisions produced inertia.[12] In his comparative study between the British and Norwegian movements, Ekberg also stresses the problems of division and adherence to local autonomy as factors which frustrated efforts to reform the British movement. This contrasted with the relative success of their Norwegian counterparts who maintained a largely consistent, if gradual, strategy of coordinated modernization in which local societies were prepared to follow the lead of the central leadership of the movement. But Ekberg offers the caveat that in part the differing outcomes also reflected differences in the quality of competition each respective movement faced from private retail chains. In Britain, the movement faced a range of formidable competitors who left it little time to adapt, while the Norwegian co-operators, faced with less effective opponents, could afford to take time to maintain coherence through a slower strategy of persuasion. Thus in Britain problems of movement fragmentation were greatly exacerbated by the rapid emergence of formidable private sector operators who were, notwithstanding a limited degree of autonomy allowed to store managers, able to adapt to the new consumer environment comparatively quickly. Crucially, they were unencumbered by the time-consuming democratic processes which national co-operative leaders faced, particularly the need for careful persuasion of recalcitrant retail societies.[13]

Perhaps inevitably, some historians have focused upon the quality of the movement's leadership and its determination to implement effective change. Among these, Leigh Sparks is perhaps the most critical of several generations of its leaders during the three decades after the war.[14] Like others, Sparks concedes the difficulties of speedy adaptation in the face of fierce and rapidly emerging competition, and he also recognizes the difficulty of implementing centralizing reform in a vast federal democracy of societies, each jealous of its own independence. But ultimately for Sparks it was the lack of a clear vision of reform which was the principal culprit for co-operative failure, especially in the crucial period of the war and just after, and the absence of clear-headed, strong, and determined leadership at a time when this was beginning to play a crucial role in the business world.[15] Most recently, Martin Cohen has offered perhaps the most damning indictment of the leadership of the movement, arguing that in the immediate post-war period it was 'complacent and overconfident', and wilfully ignorant of the changing consumption and savings habits of its members and customers.[16] Cohen paints a picture of an ideologically hidebound movement, so locked into its leftist views that it missed almost entirely the radical shifts in consumer behaviour occurring in the post-war decades. Those parts of the movement which grasped these changes, such as the Co-operative Permanent Building Society, which eventually renamed itself as the Nationwide Building Society,

---

[12] L. Black, in Black and Robertson (2009), 38–41.
[13] Ekberg (2008), 295–8; Ekberg, in Black and Robertson (2009).
[14] Sparks (1994).   [15] Sparks (1994), 52–4.
[16] Cohen (2012), 154 and 159.

gradually distanced themselves from the movement and the idea of co-operation generally.[17] However, the CPBS's withdrawal from the movement probably reflected generally bad publicity about the consumer movement arising from financial difficulties faced by a number of societies at the time, rather than any ideological rejection of co-operation per se.

The argument presented here includes many of these elements in its explanation of the difficulties both for the movement and the CWS during this period. But it will offer a number of important and distinctive contentions. First, it will argue that the longstanding tensions within the movement generally—between autonomous local retail societies and the CWS, between the CWS, CRS, and Co-operative Union, and between the CIS and the CWS Bank (soon to become The Co-operative Bank)—were the principal obstacles to effective reform; thwarting, delaying, or distorting numerous initiatives to restructure the movement under united leadership and a clear plan to take on the radically changed consumer environment of post-war Britain. Secondly, it will challenge the view offered by contemporaries in the 1950s (especially Crosland and others on the Co-operative Independent Commission) and some historians, that the CWS and the movement generally were complacent and lacked the creative will and leadership to address the problems the movement faced. In fact, it will be shown that as early as the 1940s, key figures within the CWS and the movement more generally recognized the need for adaptation to meet the different commercial environment likely to emerge after the end of the war. Moreover, it will be shown that not all of the initiatives from these sources were unsuccessful; but the embedded problems of division within the 'dysfunctional federation' prevented the emergence of a truly coherent plan for change capable of implementation. Thirdly, it will become clear that for reasons beyond the control of the CWS or other bodies within the movement, some of the changes that did occur, in the short run at least, made the co-operative federation even more dysfunctional, rendering effective reform more difficult. The result was a period of stuttering and incoherent change within the CWS and the movement, in many instances well thought out and argued for, but in the end implemented too slowly and partially to meet the challenge of modern consumer society and formidable multiple chain competitors. How these developments unfolded will be the subject of this chapter, and to a large extent the pattern was set in the Second World War.

6.2 WAR—AGAIN

When war broke out again in September 1939 it was clear that the co-operative movement, and especially the CWS, was much better prepared than it had been in 1914 (see Figure 6.1). In part this reflected a wider appreciation of what modern war would mean.

[17] *Co-operative Gazette* (23 April 1970).

FIGURE 6.1. **Sandbagging the entrance to Mitchell Memorial Hall, Manchester, 1939.** Despite the best efforts of workers from the CWS traffic department to protect the headquarters building, bomb damage destroyed the upper storey in December 1940, including Mitchell Memorial Hall (see Figure 5.3). In London's East End, cellars at the CWS's London branch were used as shelters for employees made homeless in the blitz, and were also used to house air raid personnel and local police; the society's own fire brigade was kept busy throughout, protecting CWS and neighbouring property.

No longer did politicians and business leaders expect that 'business as usual' would prevail in a context of global conflict, and as is clear, plans had been laid long in advance of 1939 to cope with the demands of a major war between advanced industrial societies. The deterioration in international relations prompted the British governments of the 1930s to commence rearmament, and to begin to plan a wartime economy, including organization of food supplies and the management of consumption through rationing. The co-operative movement was better placed to have an influence over this process than in the First World War. By 1939 there were nine Labour MPs who were sponsored by the movement, and hundreds of local councillors. Most were unafraid to make their voices heard. The continued growth of the membership of the movement during the inter-war period, and its successful commercial inroads into southern England, had established it as a truly national organization which could not be ignored in an era of total war. As Birchall shows, by the end of the 1930s the CWS was a formidable organization, employing a quarter of a million people in a wide range of production, distribution, and financial activities, from farms to factories.[18] It also ran a global operation in procuring commodities, with major depots and branches across the world. These were frequently involved in complex financial as well as trading transactions, the importance of which was not missed by a wartime coalition government under extreme pressure to preserve international supplies of food and raw materials in the face of German naval power.

As a result, the CWS came to play a pivotal role in the government's strategy for procuring overseas food supplies. Together with Spillers and Rank, in 1938 the CWS took responsibility for buying and sustaining the national wheat reserve.[19] Throughout the war, the CWS's links in Canada were particularly important. In January 1940 it was given responsibility for purchasing wheat there up to a value of £500,000, a government decision which elicited an offer from the CWS to take over all of the British government's purchasing at Canadian ports.[20] The government availed itself of the robust CWS network in Canada, ordering 4 million bushels of wheat through it in May 1940.[21] By 1943, the CWS was also handling a substantial share of the trade from Canada in tinned and frozen fish, at the express request of the British Food Mission in Ottawa.[22] In light of the CWS's successful activities in Canada in the 1930s, this is perhaps unsurprising. Its overseas fishing commercial operations in Canada in the 1930s, a decade of protectionism, stagnant trade, and difficulty, were remarkable for their sophisticated coordination of local knowledge acquired through its New York and Canadian branches, and deployment of its financial resources and banking expertise. This was evident in the dealings shown in the last chapter between the CWS and the New England and Canadian Fishing Companies in the early 1930s.[23] The CWS also supplied commodities to the Allied powers, particularly to Polish troops and civilians in Russia through Poland Supply Co., agents for the Polish Ministry of Labour in exile.[24] Indeed, so important did this relationship become, that shortly after the end of the war, Labour's new Foreign Secretary, Ernest Bevin, asked that a CWS representative join a British co-operative delegation visiting Warsaw to develop links with the Polish movement, in an effort to strengthen British links with that country generally.[25]

More generally, both the CWS and the retail societies played a crucial role in the war effort, particularly in the implementation of rationing and in wartime production. In fact, the co-operative movement, through its parliamentary representatives, were among the most vociferous proponents of implementing a rationing system which would ensure that all could access necessities fairly and with as little disruption as possible.[26] The presence of A. V. Alexander in the government as First Lord of the Admiralty also

[18] Birchall (1994), 136–7.   [19] Richardson (1977), 83.
[20] CWS Board minutes (30 January 1940)   [21] CWS Board minutes (21 May 1940).
[22] CWS Board minutes (8 June 1943).   [23] See section 5.4.
[24] CWS Board minutes (14 October 1941).   [25] CWS Board minutes (25 September 1945).
[26] Richardson (1977), 93–9.

helped ensure that the movement would be represented at the highest levels.[27] CWS factories were also drawn into the government's centrally planned industrial economy, particularly its efforts to rationalize production of war matériel and other essential commodities through a policy of concentration of production into the larger and most efficient factories. The CWS took a proactive line in advising the Board of Trade which factories would be best equipped for certain lines of production.[28] In May 1941 its advice on where to concentrate boot and shoe production in its core 'nucleus' factories in the East Midlands was accepted by officials at the Board of Trade.[29] In addition, leading CWS officials were seconded onto a wide range of economic and production advisory committees.[30] The upshot was that the CWS came to play a crucially important role in the war effort, producing large quantities of military uniforms, rifle parts, assault boats, and military equipment, as well as aircraft parts. This was in addition to its role in international trade and as the largest single supplier of food and other household essentials. All of this amounted to the movement enjoying an esteemed and valued position in national economic life which it had previously never achieved. It was a position bolstered by an expansion of its activities into new fields. During the war, the CWS Bank increased its loans to local authorities struggling desperately to cope with bomb damage and the disruption of war. Thus in March 1941, the CWS Board agreed to make £500,000 in loans to local authorities.[31] The CWS did this whilst also playing a leading role in helping retail societies severely affected by war damage (see Figure 6.2), especially though generous loans from the CWS Bank. In February 1941 the Portsea Island society was awarded an interest-free loan of £30,000 so that it could secure premises to replace its flattened bakery.[32]

As a result, the Second World War is seen as the zenith of the fortunes of the CWS and the movement generally. But it was also of course a highly unusual period in terms of economic management. The British state was compelled to operate a command economy, in which the 'normal' strictures of a market economy did not apply. This has contributed to the criticism, voiced by Cohen, Sparks, and others, that the co-operative movement became complacent, conservative, and paid little or no attention to the task of planning for a changed post-war world.[33] The only widely acknowledged attempted reform was the abortive attempt in 1944 to merge the CWS and SCWS.[34] But this ignores the evidence. In fact, both the CWS and the movement more widely were engaged throughout the war in trying to foresee what the post-war social and economic climate would be like, and in trying to plan for a range of eventualities. Such efforts began early in the war. In an analysis which anticipated one of the key conclusions of the Co-operative Independent Commission

---

[27] Bonner (1961), 219.   [28] CWS Board minutes (25 March 1941).
[29] CWS Board minutes (27 May 1941).   [30] Richardson (1977), 87–90.
[31] CWS Board minutes (8 April 1941).   [32] CWS Board minutes (4 February 1941).
[33] Cohen (2012), 154; Sparks (1994), 27. Sparks in particular takes the CWS to task for 'not grasping the opportunities from the changes under way'.
[34] Sparks (1994), 27.

FIGURE 6.2. Bomb damage, Holyoake House, 1940. The Manchester blitz in December 1940 destroyed the upper storey of the Co-operative Union's headquarters. Many societies faced far worse damage. For example, in one night Portsmouth's Portsea Island society lost its central premises, grocery warehouse, several workshops, the dispatch department, offices, a meeting hall, two grocery branches, and its bakery.

over a decade later, R. H. Palmer identified in 1941 that a key problem for the movement and the CWS was the huge number of societies, which limited the capital available for investing in new stores and outlets, and made it difficult for retail societies to meet the demands of an increasingly competitive consumer market. But Palmer recognized that amalgamations between societies could not be enforced from above. The democratic nature of the movement and the strong tradition of retail society autonomy meant that amalgamations would have to be achieved by persuasion and incentives. Palmer argued for the creation of District Societies, which ten or fifteen societies in a locality could join as members. Palmer anticipated that these district societies could form the basis of future voluntary amalgamations by member societies, when the advantages of scale became fully apparent. Ultimately Palmer envisaged the movement would evolve beyond recognition:

In time, the position might be reached that instead of ten or twenty retail societies in each District, as well as a District Society, there would be only the District Society, the whole of the retail societies having eventually agreed to amalgamate with the District Society. When that situation has been reached in every District the Movement would comprise sixty ordinary societies, all big scale co-operative organisations, covering a wide area and providing a co-operative service for all or most of the needs of the consumer.[35]

Where amalgamations could not be achieved, alternative forms of retail society collaboration needed to be promoted, such as Federal Societies, where resources could be pooled to provide the means for opening joint retail society bakeries, dry goods stores, and for other commodities.

The CWS was also keen to address the need for reconstruction of the movement after the war was over. As early as March 1942, it signalled its broad agreement with calls from Palmer and 184 retail societies for a major reorganization of the movement, and agreed that it should be represented on any body established for planning such changes.[36] The CWS was especially attracted by the district/federal society initiative. In August 1943 it signalled that it was prepared to invest substantially in new district or federal societies, up to 50 per cent of the required capital if necessary.[37] Moreover the CWS was prepared to act on this pledge. In September 1942, the CWS became involved in a local initiative in North Wales to set up a Federal Society which would establish a federal dry goods store and bakery. It agreed to subscribe capital as a member and to nominate some of its directors to sit on the board of the new society.[38] Similar initiatives attracted CWS support or interest in Manchester, Durham, and Kent.[39] The CWS also opened an internal debate on post-war reform. In March 1942, it responded positively to a call from representatives of co-operative bodies on the National Co-operative Authority (a body established to facilitate more effective collaboration between sections of the movement), and from Palmer, for some kind of national forum on the reorganization of the movement post-war.[40] In June 1943, it accepted a request for its own views on reorganization and began its own deliberations, with a view to producing a memorandum.[41] It submitted the memorandum, and a subsidiary document calling for the amalgamation of the CWS with the independent co-operative productive societies.[42] But these were merely first musings, and soon after the Grocery Committee was instructed to undertake its own investigation into preparations for the peace.[43] Its remit was wide. It was instructed to review the whole of the CWS's system for producing, procuring, and distributing goods

[35] 'The District Society: Plan for a Complete Co-operative Consumer Service', 260–1. Based on an address given by Palmer to Co-operative Managers in Manchester *Co-operative Review*, 9 September 1941, Vol. 15. See also Pickup (1942).
[36] CWS Board minutes (10 March 1942).
[37] CWS Board minutes (17 August 1943).
[38] CWS Board minutes (22 June 1943).
[39] Manchester initiative: Durham: CWS Board minutes (23 June 1943); CWS Board minutes (11 January 1944); Kent: CWS Board minutes (17 October 1944).
[40] CWS Board minutes (10 March 1942).
[41] CWS Board minutes (20 July 1943).
[42] CWS Board minutes (17 August and 21 September 1943).
[43] CWS Board minutes (2 November 1943).

to the retail societies. Radical options were to be considered, including, if necessary, the rationalization of CWS production, and the standardization of management practices in all CWS centres around the country. Just two weeks later, in mid-November 1943, the body set up by the Authority to consider post-war changes, the Advisory Committee on Post-War Problems, submitted its interim report to the CWS Board for its views.[44]

The report was thorough and quite radical. It called for exploration of more centralized buying arrangements for the whole movement, rather than individual society buyers venturing into the market and being unable to secure the best deal. There was some debate about whether this could be achieved by national centralization, or by retail societies combining locally to buy jointly, but the principle of collective bulk buying being likely to secure better terms from manufacturers was clearly identified. Moreover, it was approved by the CWS Board. What makes this particularly fascinating is that similar ideas were to be suggested by later initiatives to reform the movement, yet it first appears to have been mooted during the supposedly sterile years of the Second World War. Other radical changes were considered by the report and approved by the CWS. It fully endorsed Palmer's policy of promoting the creation of District or Federal Societies, which would in time reduce through amalgamations the numbers of societies the CWS had to deal with. It even promoted the idea of the CWS adopting a leading role in the initiatives to reform buying for the movement. In the area of marketing it especially wanted major changes. Modernization of production was certainly identified as an area for change by the report, advocating a fund of £100,000 be set aside for investment in new experiments in manufacture. It also called for a larger and more modern marketing department, which would apply the latest knowledge and techniques in market research and branding. Perhaps most significantly of all, it required a report from the CWS on how it might reorient itself to the post-war environment.

Significantly, the CWS had helped formulate this call for a plan from itself to meet post-war conditions. In July 1943 it had asked the Head of its Market Research Bureau, Fred Lambert (see Figure 6.3), to begin preparing his own report for CWS consumption, provisionally entitled 'The Reorientation of the CWS', and the idea was promoted by CWS representatives in the Advisory Committee on Post War Problems.[45] Lambert's report was submitted to the Advisory Committee for its views in December 1943.[46] While no copy of Lambert's memorandum appears to have survived, it seems that he strongly endorsed many of the Advisory Committee's findings. Lambert is an important but neglected figure in the history of the CWS. He was a major influence within the CWS, a professional employee who imbibed the ethos of the movement, and who developed a keen sense of the challenges which confronted it in the dramatically changing environment of post-war Britain. Lambert first joined the CIS in the late 1920s, leaving a year or so later to take a Commerce degree at the University of Manchester. He joined the CWS in 1932, and quickly emerged as a serious analyst of the organization, working

[44] CWS Board minutes (16 November 1943).
[45] CWS Board minutes (21 December 1943).
[46] CWS Board minutes (21 December 1943).

FIGURE 6.3. **Fred Lambert.** A pivotal figure in the CWS's development, Lambert began his career with the CIS in 1927. He went on to head the CWS's market research operations, and played a key role in the reorganization of the 1960s. At his retirement in 1970, then chief executive Sir Arthur Sugden said of him: 'Few men have exercised such a basic and continuous influence on CWS development.'

closely with its most prominent historian, Percy Redfern. He was involved with one of the major analytical reviews of British co-operation, the famous Carr-Saunders survey of the late 1930s. Appointed to lead the Market Research Bureau during the Second World War, Lambert quickly emerged as an important thinker about the future development and reorganization of the movement and the CWS. Certainly he seems to have been instrumental in the drafting of the CWS's 'Policy and Programme for Post War Development', published and considered at a series of delegate conferences on 27 April 1944.[47] It would not be the last contribution which Lambert would make to debates about the future of the CWS.

In the preamble, the report was clear that the CWS and the co-operative movement would face unprecedented changes to the commercial environment in which it would operate post-war:

We have become increasingly conscious that developments are taking place in the commercial world and in trading practice which can only be met only by the adaptation of the co-operative trading organisation to meet changed social and economic conditions, and without losing the essentially democratic spirit of the Movement. In many industries the scale and nature of

[47] Report by the Co-operative Wholesale Society Ltd on its Policy and Programme for Post-War Development, 1944.

operations have been changing and widening rapidly for many years. Improved transport arrangements have greatly increased the area which can be served from a particular point and have considerably modified the shopping habits of consumers. Rising incomes on the one hand, and declining costs of production on the other have widened the range and variety of goods and services purchased by working people, who form the mainstay of the co-operative movement. The combined effects of increased demand, improved facilities for transport and distribution, and the application of science and machinery in the technique of production, have resulted in considerable changes in the system of supply of consumers' goods and particularly the production and distribution of manufactured articles.[48]

The changes mooted in the report were far reaching, and in many ways pre-empted plans for reform championed by the Co-operative Independent Commission and later bodies. In food and other consumables such as tobacco, the report envisaged a post-war expansion of demand, and therefore advocated rebuilding CWS productive capacity, which had been severely damaged by wartime bombing of cities such as Manchester and London, and expanding it beyond pre-war levels. This would involve new sugar, butter, and tobacco factories, and ones producing yeast and breakfast cereals for the first time, and even a new factory in Irlam for refining cooking oil. But it paid particular attention to the likely growth of more substantial household investments. It foresaw that in due course, a larger number of working-class families would be able to afford what had formerly been regarded as luxury items—especially 'dry goods' such as furniture, radios, and what would now be referred to as 'white goods' (refrigerators etc.). To meet this demand, the report called for major changes in the way the movement was organized generally, and specifically in the relationship between the CWS and retail societies. Predictably, it reasserted its support for the promotion of District Societies or Federal Societies which could create larger, more efficient and attractively located dry goods outlets than the traditional small stores that made up the bulk of co-operative provision (see Figure 6.4).[49] It called upon the CWS to provide financial or other support for such initiatives.[50] It called for changes in the traditional methods of operation in the dry goods field by which the CWS and the retail societies could collaborate more closely. The report anticipated that retail societies might see this as a veiled attack on their autonomy. To ease such fears, the report stressed that it 'did not envisage any fundamental change in the local organisation and character of the bulk of the Movement's trading activities'.[51] Nonetheless, it proposed the establishment of CWS-controlled bazaars, and mail order selling.[52] The report also urged a major overhaul of the buying activities of the CWS, with major reviews of the workings of a number of departments.[53] It also called for movement by the CWS into a number of new lines of activity, in response to what it saw

[48] Report by the Co-operative Wholesale Society Ltd, 3.
[49] Report by the Co-operative Wholesale Society Ltd, 9.
[50] Report by the Co-operative Wholesale Society Ltd, 10.
[51] Report by the Co-operative Wholesale Society Ltd, 4.
[52] Report by the Co-operative Wholesale Society Ltd, 10.
[53] Report by the Co-operative Wholesale Society Ltd, 5.

FIGURE 6.4. **CWS goods at the counter, c.1940s.** Prior to the introduction of self-service in the late 1940s, customers brought their orders to the counter to be filled by shop assistants. This publicity photo includes a variety of CWS products on display, from soap flakes and custard powder to table salt.

as likely new consumer demands. These included domestic and industrial refrigerators, toys, household tools, and a range of other goods.[54] It also wanted the CWS to branch out into pharmacy (see Figure 6.5) through the establishment of a National Co-operative Chemists society.[55] Plans were also offered for the establishment of a national motor trades service run by the CWS for retail societies.[56] Perhaps most ambitious were plans to increase the number of CWS Bank branches around the country, and the extension of its services to a large number of local authorities.[57]

All in all, it was quite a comprehensive plan to overhaul the movement, and the CWS's role within it. Yet historians have largely focused on just one of its recommendations, the

[54] Report by the Co-operative Wholesale Society Ltd, 9.
[55] Report by the Co-operative Wholesale Society Ltd, 10.
[56] Report by the Co-operative Wholesale Society Ltd, 8.
[57] Report by the Co-operative Wholesale Society Ltd, 4.

FIGURE 6.5. Pharmacy branch, Chatham, c.1940s. By the 1940s many co-operatives, like this society in Kent, operated pharmacy branches. In 1945, the CWS and some retail societies joined forces to create the National Co-operative Chemists.

planned merger between the CWS and SCWS. In fact the report was far sighted in its anticipation of a radically different retail environment post-war, and showed little indication of complacency or an unwillingness to consider that the world was changing. Quite the reverse was the case. Yet, as with so many previous and later blueprints for reform, the report was implemented only partially. Resistance to the merger meant that the CWS and SCWS would continue as separate entities until the 1970s, while there remained a great deal of resistance within retail societies, who viewed efforts at reform from above as an unwelcome challenge to their independence.

6.3 POST-WAR CHALLENGES AND INERTIA, 1945–55

In spite of the CWS's intentions to reform itself and the movement, the first decade after the war proved frustrating and disappointing for these ambitions. In March 1948, J. M. Peddie, one of the Board's directors, expressed his frustration at the slow progress made in developing new specialist shops. He was especially dismayed at how little had been done to establish specialist stores selling fruit and vegetables and radios.[58] Later that year J. S. Paterson of the SCWS was also deeply critical, contending that the movement had lost its way and lacked a coherent plan. He blamed the 'parochial outlook' of many local retail society leaders, and their unwillingness to follow any kind of central leadership.[59] In essence the difficulty was twofold. First, many retail societies remained unconvinced of the need for the radical change in the fundamental structure of the movement along the lines signalled in the CWS 1944 report. If one considers the performance of co-operatives in the immediate post-war period, it is not hard to see why they held this view. Superficially at least, co-operation continued to do well in the first ten years after the war, and in terms of market share it seemed to be holding up reasonably well, partly because the rise of the multiples as a major competitive force really only gathered momentum after the abolition of rationing and as the post-war boom began to significantly increase consumer purchasing power. Thus in terms of overall market share the movement fell only from 12 per cent in 1951 to 10.8 per cent in 1961, with falls in food and non-food being from 17.1 to 15 per cent and from 6.5 to 5.6 per cent respectively.[60] Moreover, in some areas the movement seemed to lead the field (see Figure 6.6). Thus as late as 1957, it led the way in the provision of self-service shops, with co-operative societies running 2,003 self-service shops against just 881 by the large multiples, amounting to just over 60 per cent of the self-service stores in Britain.[61] What seemed less significant at the time, but became crucially important later, was the small size of these co-operative self-service stores. It would be the multiples which would prove best placed to exploit the potentialities of self-service in terms of scale. Secondly, central to the problem of reform was that ultimately no body within the movement, not even the CWS or the Co-operative Union, held the power to force change through. This was, after all, the essence of co-operative democracy as understood by retail societies for over a hundred years. It meant the autonomy of the local society, and its right to determine its own future, without any checks from centralized bodies, whose role was to support and serve the retail societies, not dictate to them. Moreover, retail societies themselves were diverse entities, with different practices, views, and aspirations. Some were well run, some were not; some stuck to time-honoured practices such as the central importance of maximizing the dividend to members, others by the early 1950s were alive to the greater attractiveness to many consumers (including co-operative members) of lower prices. Some societies, including many of those in London, embraced self-service, while others were fiercely resistant. In practice this meant that securing a consensus for change across the movement in the early 1950s was nigh impossible, even though there were instances of local societies collaborating on a practical level.

---

[58] *Co-operative News* (27 March 1948).   [59] *Co-operative News* (10 April 1948).
[60] Byrom (1982), 47.   [61] Shaw and Alexander (2008), 68.

FIGURE 6.6. **Self-service shop, Blackley, 1949.** This Blackley Society branch in north Manchester was one of around 400 co-operative shops operated on partial or full self-service lines in 1949. Co-operatives led the introduction of self-service in Britain in the 1940s and 1950s.

This is a crucial point in the debate about the quality of the leadership of the movement and the CWS in this period. Leadership is an ambiguous concept, the meaning of which changes according to the context. Unlike the multiples, which increasingly from the 1950s developed shareholder value-driven 'command and control' management structures investing the power to make change happen into the hands of senior executives, the CWS and Co-operative Union had to try to build a consensus for reform. They had to persuade and cajole rather than direct. Inevitably this meant that co-operative leadership involved protracted efforts to persuade and educate, and frequently a willingness to compromise to achieve objectives incrementally or even only partially. Inevitably, although this was the only form of leadership possible in such a diverse and democratic movement composed of fiercely independent retail societies, it looked to many observers, who were unschooled in the co-operative movement's culture and democratic structures, like prevarication, weakness, and a lack of vision. Ultimately, the ability of the movement's leaders to effect reform depended upon the amenability of retail societies *en masse* to accept the need for change, and this was just not possible given the diverse and conflicted state the movement was in by the 1950s and 1960s. The point made by contemporaries such as Ostergaard and Halsey, and historians such as

Walton, about declining member participation in retail society decision-making, made the problem even worse. Many societies were left with ageing and conservative leaders who were frequently out of touch and sympathy with the fast-changing milieu of British society. Such local leaders all too frequently failed to grasp the urgency for change on a grand scale. There is much truth in the notion that by the mid-1950s, the central problem for the movement was not that its national leaders were weak, but that the movement itself had become effectively un-leadable as a national entity.

Certainly historians have been quick to point out the formidable problems which were emerging for the movement by the 1950s. It was not only that the multiples reacted more swiftly and decisively in response to the 'consumer society'. There were also major strategic and financial issues which were to prove increasingly problematic for retail co-operation. First, there was the question of the dividend. The rise of the multiples sharpened competition on price in the grocery and other trades. Traditionally, co-operatives had built loyalty through payment of the dividend; but as competition in price became tougher, securing sufficiently high returns to finance the dividend put pressure on the ability of co-operatives to both keep prices competitive and pay the 'divi'. As Cohen correctly points out, the war had entrenched support of the dividend in some societies, when price controls imposed during the conflict removed the tension between price competition and sustaining high dividends. This meant that key interest groups in many societies were obdurate in support of high dividends, even though it sometimes contributed to the high prices which drove customers and members elsewhere.[62] Ekberg shows that even the Co-operative Union supported the continuation of a flat-rate dividend on purchases in its report to Congress in 1954, in response to experiments by some societies under which dividend was only paid on more profitable lines of business. In due course, by the 1960s many societies gave up paying dividends altogether as they lost market share and encountered deepening financial difficulties, and some followed the example of private retailers in offering trading stamps as an incentive to shoppers. Initial opposition to this from the CWS and the Co-operative Union soon gave way to official endorsement by the end of the 1960s. But this did not in the end produce the reversal of falling market shares hoped for.[63] Furthermore, dividends also drained much-needed funds from initiatives to modernize shops and the supply chains and networks needed to feed them effectively. Thus, as Alexander shows, while the London Co-operative Society tried to compete with the multiples in the mid-1960s by developing self-service and its own supermarkets, it simply lacked the resources to support them adequately with supply infrastructure.[64] Both Sparks and Ekberg assert that this was a problem for the movement nationally, and a factor in the delay in addressing the issue.[65] Secondly, Black also makes the point that declining membership loyalty led to many of them simply withdrawing their capital from societies. He estimates that by the end of the 1950s average capital holding per member had fallen by as much as two-thirds compared to twenty

---

[62] Cohen (2012), 150.   [63] Ekberg (2008), 263–9.
[64] Alexander (2008), 489–508, 495 and 504.   [65] Sparks (1994), 42; Ekberg (2008), 141–2.

years earlier.[66] Thus capital shortages, compared to the formidable access to capital enjoyed by the multiples, was undoubtedly a problem for the movement, and it stemmed from an unwillingness to change existing structures and practices sufficiently quickly and in a concerted and organized way.

But added to this were also formidable problems outside the control of the movement, and this did not only include the competitive advantages of the multiples. Manton and Gurney's contention that the movement enjoyed few political friends, and that this was reflected in government policy, has already been mentioned. Gurney's argument that the post-war Labour government missed an opportunity to shape the retail environment in ways which might have helped co-operation is a fair one, though of course such changes might not have survived the succeeding period of Conservative dominance in the 1950s and early 1960s. In one area, however, shifts in government policy certainly did not favour the movement, though ironically it supported the changes. Ever since the 1930s, many manufacturers had operated policies of Resale Price Maintenance (RPM). Under this, either individual or groups of manufacturers set a minimum retail price at which their goods could be sold. The policy was especially aimed at the retail co-operatives, who were felt by many manufacturers to be cutting the prices of manufactures by stealth through the dividend.[67] In the 1930s, many manufacturers simply refused to sell goods to the retail co-operatives if they paid dividend on them. Much to the chagrin of the movement, RPM was given legal status by the Retail Price Maintenance Act of 1940. From this point on, the movement devoted a great deal of effort to the complete repeal of the legislation and the effective outlawing of RPM in practice. It became, as Stewart shows, a symbol of the movement's aspiration to be the effective mouthpiece for and defender of consumer rights. Ultimately, of course, RPM was abolished, first collective RPM in 1956 and then individual firm RPM in 1964, much to the pleasure of the co-operative movement. But Stewart captures the irony of this: the real winners of RPM abolition were not co-operatives, but the multiple chains who, freed from the constraints of price controls, were sufficiently efficient to push down prices of manufactures to levels the less efficient co-operative societies simply could not match. Thus the abolition of RPM proved yet another factor in the retreat and diminishing market shares of the co-operatives.

In light of this, it is easy to dismiss the CWS's good intentions of the 1944 Report as so much hot air. But this would not be fair. CWS leadership had, in fact, produced some changes for the better, though not on anything like the scale or with the speed anticipated and needed. The spread of self-service had been actively and effectively promoted by the CWS and the Co-operative Union. Thus in 1951, Lambert of the CWS and J. A. Hough of the Co-operative Union produced a joint report on the progress of self-service shops, which became almost a guide on how to operate self-service effectively.[68] Moreover by the time of the launch of the Co-operative Independent Commission in 1955, a

---

[66] Black, in Black and Robertson (2009), 43.
[67] Stewart (2012).   [68] Lambert and Hough (1951).

number of the Federal Societies encouraged by CWS since the war years had been established. The problem was that change and reform rested upon the willingness of retail societies to engage in planning for change, and this they were not prepared to do with anything like the urgency the realities of the situation demanded.

6.4 THE CO-OPERATIVE INDEPENDENT COMMISSION, 1955–8

By the early 1950s even the most obdurate retail society committee could not help but notice the changes which were taking place in the high street, as the multiple chains began to compete energetically for trade. As a result, by 1954 there was a groundswell of opinion for a new inquiry into the state of the movement and how it needed to change to meet the demands of the new commercial environment. In 1955, the Co-operative Congress called for an 'Inquiry Commission of suitable persons not engaged in co-operative management or administration, who shall be charged with the responsibility of surveying the whole field of co-operative production and marketing, both wholesale and retail'.[69] The CWS Board was certainly supportive of this move. As early as 1954 it recognized that it needed to be much more aware of the activities of its rivals. In November of that year, the Policy and General Purposes Committee strongly recommended that the CWS take up full membership of the British Institute of Management (founded in 1947), in order to access the latest thinking on managerial practice. Tellingly, it noted the tendency for the CWS to be rather too insular in its outlook, and that it now needed to 'cross fertilize' its ideas with those of private enterprise:

It would bring the Society, through its managers and officials, into contact with other managers and executives facing common management problems, and, in so doing, would broaden and widen their attitude. We tend to be very insular in the Co-operative movement, and sometimes are not as alive as we should be to the remarkable trends and developments which are taking place in management practices outside.[70]

This was hardly the attitude of a body resistant to change, and as will be seen, when the Co-operative Independent Commission (CIC) was constituted, the CWS took a keen interest and participated very enthusiastically.

As Ekberg shows, the general mood within the movement when the Commission was launched was not at all pessimistic, perceiving the motive to be one of adjustment to modern trends rather than any massive overhaul of business practice. This was evident

---

[69] *Co-operative Independent Commission Report*, vii.

[70] Report to the CWS Board by the policy and general purposes committee re: Resolutions of the shareholders passed on the recommendations of the recent inquiry committee and matters arising therefrom, CWS Board minutes (30 November 1954).

from the view of the Co-operative Union Chairman, John Corina (no opponent of modernization himself), as expressed at the 1955 Co-operative Congress.[71] An independent commission was deemed the best option, principally because of the need for a cold external eye on the commercial activities of the movement, free from the complex internal tensions which existed within the movement. But the choice of the personnel of the Commission (pictured in Figure 6.7) was, as Black rightly says, controversial.[72] The two main driving forces on the Commission were its Chair, Hugh Gaitskell (shortly to succeed to the Leadership of the Labour Party), and Tony Crosland, who took over as secretary to the Commission in early 1956. As Manton shows, the Labour Party's attitude to the co-operative movement had been problematic for some time, and the arrival on the

FIGURE 6.7. Members, Co-operative Independent Commission, 1955. Co-operative dignitaries joined CIC members for this photograph in 1955. Top row (left to right): Anthony Crosland; Robert Southern (CU General Secretary); Donald Dow (SCWS Board); John Corina (CU Chairman), Leonard Cooke (CWS Board); A. E. Jupp (CPF); E. J. Ravenhill (Birmingham Co-operative Society); and J. T. Murray. Bottom row: Dr James Jefferys; Margaret Digby; Prof. D. T. Jack; Hugh Gaitskell MP; Col. F. J. L. Hardie; and F. C. Pette. Lady Margaret Hall joined the CIC later that year.

[71] Ekberg (2008), 172.   [72] Black, in Black and Robertson (2009), 35.

Commission of these two particular individuals did not presage a sympathetic perspective. Both Gaitskell and Crosland were part of an emerging new generation of Labour leaders who largely rejected Labour's traditional antipathy to capitalism, and who took the view that the future lay in a modern egalitarian welfare state, underpinned by a mixed economy in which private enterprise would be the principal driving force creating the wealth necessary to fund social reform. Crosland was the principal architect of this strategy, which was articulated in his 1956 work *The Future of Socialism*. Implicit in this perspective was an acceptance of the superiority of private capitalism in many fields, but especially in the new fast-growing consumer industries. This inclined Crosland and Gaitskell to a quite critical view of the co-operative movement, which they associated with the more outmoded traditions of the Labour movement. Other members of the Commission were controversial for different reasons. A key figure was the academic J. B. Jefferys, who had published in 1954 the leading text on the history of the retail trade, *Retail Trading in Great Britain, 1850–1950*, which had charted the rise of the multiple challenge to the co-operative movement. He had since been made secretary of the International Association of Department Stores, a position which gave him a unique insight into the problems of large retail movements like co-operation, but which also made him appear to be a somewhat suspect advocate of the movement's rivals.[73] Alan Sainsbury, of the rising multiple chain, was viewed in a similar light. Less controversial were the industrial consultant J. T. Murray, Margaret Digby of the Agricultural Producers' Federation and the Horace Plunkett Foundation, Alderman Pette of the Middlesbrough Society, and the economists Professor D. T. Jack and Lady Margaret Hall who joined the Commission after its establishment. Colonel Hardie, the final member, was to gain a certain notoriety through his minority report, which called for the creation of single national co-operative societies in Scotland and England, to replace the thousand or so autonomous retail societies in those countries.

Most accounts of the CIC focus upon its reports and recommendations, and these will be considered here also. But what have received far less attention are the process of investigation which the Commission undertook, and the role of the CWS in it. Yet this was crucially important, not only in determining the nature of the report which the CIC produced, but also for its chances of implementation. The CWS, and especially its leading planner, Frederick Lambert, took a very keen and critical interest in the Commission and the people on it. He was especially critical of the appointment of Jefferys, for whose work he had very little respect. Lambert also saw Jefferys's role on the International Association of Department Stores as problematic, as it would restrict the information which the CWS could afford to share with him.[74] One member of the Board, Leonard Cooke, made clear that the CWS needed to take a leading role not only in advising the Commission, but also in implementing any resulting programme of reform. Cooke, pictured in Figure 6.8, cited the modest success in implementing some of the reforms advocated in its 1944 report, and argued that with some important reforms in

[73] Black, in Black and Robertson (2009), 35.
[74] Lambert to Buckley, 16 June 1955, Correspondence of Frederick Lambert, NCA.

FIGURE 6.8. **Sir Leonard Cooke (1901–76).** A leading advocate of reform within the co-operative movement, Cooke was elected president of the CWS Board in 1960 and was knighted in 1965. He chaired the Joint Reorganization Committee in 1965 and retired shortly after its programme was implemented, in 1966.

the structure of the movement, the CWS could be the vehicle for more successful reform. Cooke did not beat about the bush, acknowledging that this would mean a substantial surrender of their autonomy by retail; societies:

None of these efforts can become truly national, however, whilst retail societies enjoy complete local autonomy. Nor can any future national development be planned on this basis. The democratic nature of the movement precludes the imposition of authority but should not prevent on the part of Retail Societies the delegation of many of their trading activities to a Central Organisation. Unanimous acceptance of these ideas would enable co-operative trade to be conducted by a truly nationally coordinated society. It is submitted that the CWS is the only national co-operative organisation that can undertake this co-ordination by the extension of its present producing and wholesaling activities into the field of retailing.[75]

Cooke argued that by bolstering CWS authority over the movement, this would provide the means for rationalizing the supply of produce to societies, the creation of streamlined business management and practices across societies, a better strategy for developing a store portfolio better suited to the needs of the market, and generally a much more rational use of the movement's resources. '*Britain* would have' argued Cooke, 'a *unified—*

[75] Memo by L. Cooke, presented to the CWS Policy Committee on 19 March 1956. Lambert Correspondence.

and not a divided—Co-operative Movement'. This was a very radical call for a major restructuring of the movement in which there would be a major concentration of power in the hands of the CWS, which was, in Cooke's view, the 'natural' vehicle for commercial reform. It is important, however, to stress that while most of the Board would certainly subscribe to the need for reforms which would dilute retail society autonomy in certain key areas, not all were prepared to go as far as Cooke. Many, after all, were key figures in retail societies, and some regarded an important aspect of their role on the Board as to represent those societies and defend their autonomy. Even those who supported Cooke baulked at the likely response of retail societies to Cooke's almost bald assertion that they should surrender autonomy to the CWS. This meant that Cooke did not in the end secure unanimous support for his radical plan, though strenuous efforts were made to reach a compromise position which could be presented to the CIC. As will be seen, internal division within the CWS Board would prove the undoing of its aspirations to become the leadership of reform.

CWS drafted a 60-page-plus statement of its analysis of the state of the movement, which it presented to the CIC in the spring of 1956. The statement provided the most lucid account of the development of British co-operation to date, and identified a number of key obstacles which had to be addressed. These included the age-old problem of the dysfunctional federation—a movement of retail societies which varied in size and activities, ran stores which were no longer truly appropriate for the geographical areas they served due to geographical and demographic change, and remained doggedly autonomous and resistant to central direction.[76] The report also cited a lack of integrated planning between the wholesale societies on the one hand and the myriad of retail societies which made the efficient supply of the latter with produce of the right quality and in the right quantities almost impossible to achieve.[77] It identified the lack of sufficient numbers of specialist stores across the country in such fields as greengrocery and specifically dry goods, where the movement remained alarmingly weak.[78] This could only be addressed by creating more centralized structures; a chain of shops across the country which would be subject to much greater control by a central body such as one of the wholesale societies.[79] The report also criticized retail societies for their lack of loyalty to the CWS in key areas such as dry goods, and provided evidence which suggested that support for the CWS from the societies had actually declined since before the war. While retail societies continued to source between 75 and 80 per cent of their groceries from the CWS, the figures for other produce had fallen alarmingly; down from 61 per cent in 1938 to 47 per cent in 1954 for drapery, from 49 to 45 per cent in menswear, from 59 to 46 per cent in footwear, and from 66 to 41 per cent in furniture and hardware.[80] Other problems cited included the frequently negative attitude towards the CWS among the staff of many retail societies, and their lack of professionalism generally. Since CWS produce

[76] CWS statement to CIC, 33, NCA.   [77] CWS statement to CIC, 34.
[78] CWS statement to CIC, 35–6.   [79] CWS statement to CIC, 38.
[80] CWS statement to CIC, 40–1.

could only be sold through retail societies, and retail societies were not obliged to sell CWS goods, this made advertising CWS goods (see Figure 6.9) prohibitively expensive and ineffective, compared to manufacturers able to get their goods to market across the full spectrum of outlets. This particular problem would be exacerbated when TV advertising became the norm after the mid-1950s. On pricing, the CWS noted with irritation that retail societies often did not follow its advice on the pricing of CWS produce, frequently over-pricing it and discouraging customers. Crucially, the CWS was extremely critical of the absence of coordinated buying by retail societies. This, it said, made it impossible for the CWS to plan its own production or its own purchasing arrangements with external suppliers. It outlined efforts made by the CWS to improve this by voluntary

FIGURE 6.9. CWS advertisement, c.1950s. Advertisements like this one were produced by the CWS for co-operative societies, who replaced 'Anytown Co-operative Society' with their own trading name. The 'particular men' series advertised CWS 'made to measure' tailoring services as leisure wear for miners, bus drivers, milk roundsmen, and salesmen during their off hours.

agreement, but was quite adamant that major reform in this area was essential.[81] In reviewing progress towards reform since the 1944 report, the 1956 statement highlighted some areas of success, but stressed that progress had been disappointing in such key areas as mail order and the development of bazaar trading, precisely because of a lack of co-operation from retail societies.[82] In reviewing these failures, the report clearly signalled the need for reform which would deliver greater central control to CWS:

These ventures, in fact, do not demonstrate the inability of the national organisation to tackle a problem, but the powerlessness of the central organisation, in existing circumstances, to implement a national and rational solution to difficulties.[83]

In many ways, the logic of report was for centralization of power into the hands of the CWS at the expense of the retail societies, to make it an instrument of modernization and national direction. But given the strong traditions of local autonomy within the movement, and the absence of constitutional authority for any co-operative body to compel retail societies to accept change, this was always going to be a hard idea to sell to the wider movement. In its final section, the statement drew back somewhat from the thrust of its own argument. It argued that since the democratic nature of the movement prevented the CWS imposing its ideas, then retail societies needed to collectively delegate some of their trading activities to a central body—namely the CWS. This plea, in the sixth section of the report, was deliberately vague and intended to minimize the antagonism of the retail societies, and to gloss over disagreements within the CWS leadership over what exactly was required—but in so doing it did rather weaken the report's impact.[84]

In fact, the CWS Board and senior employees such as Lambert agonized over this part of the report. Lambert's position in the CWS initiative became very important, when he and Hough of the Co-operative Union were seconded as advisers to the CIC in December 1955.[85] Lambert's role was to advise the CIC on aspects of co-operative production, wholesaling, personnel management, recruitment, training, and salaries; but he also reported back to the CWS Board in an effort to guide their dealings with the CIC. The initial reception of the report by the CIC, while not hostile, did signal some important differences of emphasis between it and the CWS. The CWS report had mentioned the difficulties of dealing with over a thousand different societies, and the need to encourage federal approaches to overcoming some of the problems concerned with coordinating buying and the development of new stores in areas of rapid change and development. But the idea of encouraging societies to amalgamate in order to reduce the number of societies and more effectively pool their resources was implicit rather than stated. Greater centralized control by the CWS of the movement was the driving logic behind

[81] CWS statement to CIC, 41–4.   [82] CWS statement to CIC, 48–9.
[83] CWS statement to CIC, 49.   [84] CWS statement to CIC, 61.
[85] Minutes of 2nd meeting of CIC, 22 December 1955, CIC/1/2/2, NCA.

the CWS's position, though as will be seen there was a lack of clarity and agreement over how this might be achieved. Yet the notion of society amalgamations and federal responses to some of the movement's problems quickly became a major focus of the CIC's mooted solutions. Indeed, as early as late August 1956, on Lambert's advice the CWS found itself trying to play catch-up in this field, approaching retail societies with a view to promoting the idea of federal joint ventures in respect of department stores. This was at least partly motivated by a desire on the part of the CWS to be seen to be aligning itself with some of the CIC's key emerging arguments, a strategy clearly intended to maximize CWS influence in the Commission's deliberations.[86]

But Lambert began to see problems in the all-important concluding section 6 of the CWS Statement to the CIC and its recommendations for changes in the relationship between the CWS and the retail societies. CIC stress on retail society amalgamation as a crucial element in reform of the movement might, he felt, be seen as contradictory to the CWS's plea for the establishment of some kind of national body to which the societies would delegate authority. Larger, amalgamated societies might be seen as more than capable of implementing the necessary changes in commercial practice without any controversial surrender of the enlarged retail societies' autonomy.[87] Moreover, the vagueness of the wording of the crucial section 6 of the CWS Statement, itself a fudged compromise to mask divisions within the Board and to avert a negative response from the retail societies, left hostages to fortune. Lambert correctly anticipated that when the CIC interviewed the CWS representatives, this aspect of the report would be subject to detailed scrutiny, and that a clear response was essential, if CWS influence over the CIC was to be established. The problem was that it was open to a number of different interpretations. Did it mean, mused Lambert, the complete control of all co-operative activity under a single board of directors? Or did it mean the creation of a series of specialized organizations, largely controlled by CWS, but focused upon specific trades such as dry goods? If the latter, would they be linked by some kind of overarching structure of control? Of course, the question of how much control over such bodies the retail societies should enjoy would also be a major question which would have to be answered if the CWS's proposals were to be taken seriously. Lambert noted that there was already evidence that a more strident line for rapid centralization under the authority of the CWS would meet with widespread resistance from the movement. A consultation exercise with some fifty or so retail societies had indicated that they would vociferously reject any attempt by the CWS to assert central control. Lambert's preference therefore was for a rather subtle line to be adopted. Under this, CWS representatives to the CIC would speak of centralization of power in the hands of the CWS as a long-term and gradual aspiration, rather than an immediate objective. The CIC would be asked to support the idea that the CWS should be the vehicle for any major new initiatives of reform on a national basis, rather than propose the creation of new separate independent national bodies which would not be subject to CWS

[86] Report by Buckley, Secretary to the Policy and Resources Committee of the CWS, to that Committee on 28 August 1956, Lambert Correspondence.

[87] Lambert to Buckley, 28 August 1956, Lambert Correspondence.

control.[88] Even then, CWS representatives would need to have well-rehearsed answers to numerous questions, such as the extent to which retail societies would be prepared to co-operate with the CWS approach, how the changes would impact upon the relationships between the CWS and other major components of the movement such as the Co-operative Union, and how such issues as co-operative democracy would be addressed. Lambert was prescient in his belief that if the CWS was to shape the deliberations of the CIC, it would need to be able to offer convincing answers to a host of detailed questions. His private fears that this would not be achieved were also realized.

In the event, the CWS failed abysmally to persuade the CIC that it could become the vehicle for reform, and that greater authority and power should be vested in it. There were several reasons for this failure. First, the CWS was of course just one interest group lobbying the CIC for change. As part of its deliberations, members of the CIC embarked upon fact-finding visits to retail societies across the country. The impressions they gleaned were frequently unflattering to not only the retail societies concerned, but also the CWS. When Jefferys and Crosland visited the Birmingham society, for example, questions about the CWS's pledge 'we match your terms or resign' when supplying societies were met with 'ribald laughter':

The departmental managers said the actual CWS reply, when presented with a private commodity at a lower price, was 'we just don't know how they can do it', followed by total inactivity. They all thought the CWS wholesale role was outmoded in the case of the large society, which could almost always buy cheaper.[89]

Similarly, the Crawley society (with which Crosland was deeply impressed as a model for future societies to follow) criticized the CWS for too much red tape, slowness of delivery, and a lack of coordination between its various departments.[90] A senior buyer for the Royal Arsenal Co-operative Society told Crosland and Jefferys that the quality of CWS women's clothing and electrical goods did not match that of private manufacturers.[91] Margaret Digby and Crosland were treated to a tirade against the CWS by the Berkhamsted and Hemel Hempstead society, because of the former's insistence, during abortive loan negotiations, that any loan to construct a new store would be contingent upon the society promising 75 per cent purchasing loyalty to CWS.[92] These negative perceptions, especially on the part of Crosland, were only reinforced by his visit to meet a small group of CWS directors (all from the Dry Goods Committee) in Manchester on 27 April 1956. The Oxford-educated Crosland's patrician outlook perhaps influenced his dismissive impressions of the capabilities of the men before him:

[88] Undated note by Lambert on the CIC, Lambert Correspondence.
[89] Jeffreys and Crosland's visit to the Birmingham society, 18 June 1956, Papers of Hugh Gaitskell, C309.2 CIC Reports on Visits, Vis/CARC/6, 2, University College, London.
[90] Crosland's visit to the Crawley society, 5 March 1957, Gaitskell Papers, C309.2 CIC, Vis/CARC/19, 2–3.
[91] Crosland and Jeffrey's visit to the Royal Arsenal Co-operative Society, London, 9 April 1956, Gaitskell Papers, C309.2, Vis/CARC/2, 6.
[92] Crosland and Digby's visit to the Berkhamsted and Hemel Hempstead society, 4 June 1956, Gaitskell Papers, C309.2, Vis/CARC/5, 1.

Their average calibre was not outstanding. I would say that two (Noble and Kemp) were distinctly able, one (Gosling, the Chairman) had been but was now wholly given over to clowning, three (Dodd, Pickup and Robinson) were decent chaps struggling very conscientiously with a job that was too big for them and one (F. Cooke, not to be confused with Len Cooke) a total passenger who never once opened his mouth. (Depressingly, Cooke was both the youngest and the most recently elected).[93]

The CWS directors were politely heard out, though it was plain that Crosland was less than impressed by CWS claims of retail society disloyalty, and was clearly aware that the latter offered a very different analysis of the problems of the movement. A second problem was that during the course of formal discussions with the CIC in March 1957, the CWS delegation of Lord Williams, L. Cooke, B. T. Eccles, H. Kemp, and J. M. Peddie were utterly unable, in the eyes of the Commission, to offer an 'agreed or consistent outlook', resulting in inconclusive and 'ragged' discussions.[94] The situation deteriorated even further at the subsequent meeting between the CIC and the CWS representatives on 19 July 1957, when blatant disagreements surfaced on the CWS side. Leonard Cooke, always a 'hawk' on the question of asserting CWS control over the movement, argued for the complete surrender of buying power and financial control by the retail societies to the CWS, confining the autonomy of the former to such issues as membership, education and propaganda, and the appointment of managers at a junior level. Lord Williams (pictured, Figure 6.10) openly contradicted Cooke, arguing that such a view not only lacked support in the Board, but that it had never even been properly debated by it. Neither did he believe that retail societies would accept such a policy. The meeting eventually broke up, and whatever hopes the CWS, Lambert, and others had entertained that they would be the leaders of reform had been utterly lost.[95] So dimly were the CWS regarded by members of the CIC by this stage that one of the Commissioners even argued that the CWS was the central problem, and that it needed to be dismantled, with its functions being transferred to a technical department answerable to the Co-operative Union.[96]

The CIC did of course go on to publish a report with important recommendations. The report was published as a book, and its recommendations widely distributed and discussed in the financial press. It was quite damning about the condition of many retail society shops, which had become a byword for drabness.[97] Recommendations were aimed at both the retail societies and central bodies such as the CWS. In respect of the retail societies, unsurprisingly amalgamation was very high on the agenda, with the aim of replacing the 1,000 or so societies with 200–300. This would avoid waste, duplication

---

[93] Crosland on meeting CWS directors in Manchester, 27 April 1956, Gaitskell Papers, C309.2 CIC, Vis/CARC/4.

[94] Minutes of 17th meeting of CIC, 5 April 1957, CIC1/2/18; referring to meeting with CWS on 15 March 1957, NCA.

[95] Minutes of 22nd meeting of CIC, 19 July 1957, CIC1/1/24.

[96] Paper: 'The Co-operative Problem' by John Murray, Gaitskell Papers, C.309.6.

[97] Co-operative Independent Commission Report, 44–9.

FIGURE 6.10. **Lord (T. E.) Williams (1892–1966).** Born in Wales, Williams began his employment with the Ynyshir co-operative society at the age of 14, and later moved to the Royal Arsenal society in Woolwich. After serving in the First World War, Williams returned to Woolwich and became active in politics, standing unsuccessfully for Parliament in 1931 and later serving on the Labour Party executive from 1931 to 1936. He became Lord Williams of Ynyshir in 1948, and served as CWS Board president from 1951 to 1957.

of services, and make it much easier to rationalize and reorganize the provision of stores.[98] It argued that the retail societies should aim to match or better the multiple chains in price, and that ultimately price competitiveness should take precedence over maximizing dividends.[99] It wanted retail societies to be much more vigilant in building up reserves for investment in new stores and outlets.[100] It also demanded much better salaries and training for society managers, to attract the best products of the grammar schools and the universities.[101] The report wanted the Co-operative Union to strengthen the quality of support services it gave to societies, especially in such areas as staff training.[102] But central to the aim of modernizing the movement was the creation by the

[98] *Co-operative Independent Commission Report*, 242.
[99] *Co-operative Independent Commission Report*, 238.
[100] *Co-operative Independent Commission Report*, 239.
[101] *Co-operative Independent Commission Report*, 240–1.
[102] *Co-operative Independent Commission Report*, 243.

Co-operative Union and the Wholesale Societies of a new federal society, the Co-operative Retail Development Society (CRDS). The remit of this body was to provide common services for retail societies designed to help them modernize their stores and operations, and to bring the movement in line with developments among the multiples.[103] As part of this more general rationalization of retail society activities, the CRDS should, where appropriate, help organize national specialist chains of shops in such fields as footwear and other dry goods lines.[104] To the Wholesale societies, the report made additional recommendations, specifically concerned with the governance of the organization. It argued for a revamped model under which the elected lay board would confine its role to general supervision of the running of the organization by a full-time managerial board chosen to run the organization on a day-to-day basis.[105] In essence, the Commission looked to instil in the movement some of the latest managerial techniques and principles which guided the multiples, and modern capitalist organizations generally. The authors of the report (especially Crosland) expressed scepticism about what they regarded as some of the more idealistic aspirations of co-operation, especially the notion of an active democracy in which the bulk of the membership would actively participate in the running of the co-operatives. 'But we deceive ourselves' said the report, 'if we suppose such persons will ever be more than a small minority of the community. Most people wish to attend to their families and cultivate their gardens.'[106] It might have been the mantra of the new consumer age.

There was a minority report, penned by Colonel Hardie, which came close to the views of Leonard Cooke, calling for the establishment of two single, integrated national societies for Scotland and England and Wales. But its ideas found little favour with the rest of the Commission, who regarded this idea as both wide of the mark in terms of what was required, and extremely unlikely to win the support of the movement necessary for its recommendations to become reality.[107] In fact, it should perhaps have saved such condescension for its own recommendations, since very quickly it became clear that there was widespread resistance to many of the proposals, notwithstanding some vaguely positive initial noises. Both Black and Ekberg provide examples of the rapidly gathering resistance to the report and its recommendations. By 1960, most of the key proposals had been rejected by Co-operative Union Congresses and by the membership of the CWS.[108] The idea of an independent CRDS proved to be as unpalatable to retail societies as it did to the wholesale societies: both saw it as a potential threat to their autonomy. Not all was lost; at least one of the recommendations for the creation of national specialist stores bore fruit, in the form of Society Footwear (from 1964 Shoefayre), the national co-operative footwear chain, established

---

[103] *Co-operative Independent Commission Report*, 251–3.
[104] *Co-operative Independent Commission Report*, 252.
[105] *Co-operative Independent Commission Report*, 220.
[106] *Co-operative Independent Commission Report*, 17.
[107] S. J. L. Hardie, *Minority Report on the Organisation of the Co-operative Movement to derive the greatest possible advantage for the movement*; CIC Report, 270–84.
[108] Black, in Black and Robertson (2009), 174–6.

in 1959 jointly by the CWS and SCWS.[109] But the notion of a coherent strategy for modernizing both the movement's organization and its material assets was utterly lost. The main reasons for this new failure have already been alluded to: principally the stubborn reluctance of retail societies to surrender their autonomy, and an enduring complacency about the movement's overall trading position. It is likely that the rather dismissive attitude of the Commission's leaders towards co-operative principles, an outlook which, as Manton's work suggests, was endemic in the Labour Party of the 1950s, also alienated many co-operators. But perhaps crucially, the Commission failed to embrace key allies, who might have significantly enhanced the chances of success. Of these, the CWS was potentially the most important. The CWS statement to the Commission and the efforts of key figures such as Lambert and Cooke, indicate that there was a genuine willingness to embrace reform, even if there was not a clear consensus about what exactly was required. Yet their willingness to take the lead in any modernization initiative was not welcomed by the CIC, which seemed to regard the CWS as a major part of the problem rather than a possible solution. As a result, CWS leaders became as alienated and resistant as other sections of the movement. For a body led by politicians, the CIC proved to be curiously inept at navigating its way through the internal political landscape of the co-operative movement, and at identifying and winning over key allies.

6.5 The 1960s and early 1970s: Deepening difficulties and the CWS response

But of course the problems of intensifying competition and loss of market share did not abate (see Table 6.1). By the mid-1960s, some of the competitors of the CWS were becoming aware of the increasing fragility of the loyalty of some retail societies to the CWS, and were aggressively courting them. Thus in 1964, independent producers of preserves and marmalade sought to buy their way into the retail society trade by undercutting

Table 6.1. Co-operative share of UK retail trade, 1951–81

Year	Food (%)	Non-food (%)	All (%)
1951	17.1	6.5	12.0
1961	15.0	5.6	10.8
1971	11.0	3.3	7.5
1981	9.2	2.5	6.4

Source: Byrom (1982), 47.

[109] Muller, in Brazda and Schediwy (1989), 97.

CWS produce.[110] Similarly, in 1965, the large margarine producer Van Den Berghs (VDB) launched an aggressive campaign to persuade societies to buy their margarine from VDB instead of the CWS. They circulated to societies 'alleged market research intelligence' which suggested that societies which sold VDB products did much better than those selling CWS margarine. Reluctantly the Market Research Department conceded that while the sales of margarine by societies who remained loyal to CWS margarine fell on average by 5.5 per cent, those who sourced it from VDB did much better. There was even strong evidence of the latter 'loss-leading' with VDB products, because they felt it enhanced their attractiveness to consumers so much.[111] VDB were not the only margarine producer avidly targeting retail societies. In 1964, the Birkenhead society (see Figure 6.11) had negotiated a unique deal to purchase 'Echo' margarine from Unilever at rock bottom prices, while Kraft even offered retail society branch managers free hospitality in local hotels![112] In addition, the near 'fratricidal' competition among lard producers had led to a number of non-co-operative producers tempting retail societies with price offers which must have incurred losses for the producers in some cases.[113] Competition by non-co-operative suppliers of bacon was also described as 'fierce'.[114] The pattern was, if anything, bleaker in dry goods. In the half-year to 10 July 1965, every line of CWS drapery and clothing reported a decrease in sales on the previous year, with the ferocity of competition from the private trade being cited as a principal reason.[115] Competition from other private trade multiples with retail societies was equally cut-throat, with many of the former selling such commodities as sugar as loss leaders.[116] In tea, for so long one of the great staples of the retail society, the situation was becoming increasingly worrying by the early 1960s. The Market Research department noted in early 1964 that the virtual abandonment of RPM in tea had led to many private retailers using tea as a loss leader, with many retail societies simply unable to match them.[117] The ferocity of direct competition from the supermarket multiples was also increasingly taking its toll on retail societies.[118]

[110] Distributive Undertakings under the Control of the Grocery Committee: Notes on the Trading Activities and Results for the 26 weeks ended 11 July 1964 (for use by Directors at Ordinary General Meeting of CWS) 8 October 1964, 33.

[111] Distributive Undertakings under the Control of the Grocery Committee: Notes on the Trading Activities and Results for the 52 weeks ended 9 January 1965 (for use by Directors at Ordinary General Meeting of CWS) 24 April 1965, 41–2.

[112] Productive Undertakings under the Control of the Grocery Committee: Notes on the Trading Activities and Results for the 26 weeks ended 11 July 1964 (for use by Directors at Ordinary General Meeting of CWS) 30 September 1964, 21–2.

[113] Productive Undertakings under the Control of the Grocery Committee, 38–9.

[114] Productive Undertakings under the Control of the Grocery Committee, 14–15.

[115] Dry Goods Committee, Statistics and Reports for 26 Weeks ended 10 July 1965, 5–9.

[116] Dry Goods Committee, Statistics and Reports, 55.

[117] Distributive Undertakings under the Control of the Grocery Committee: Notes on the Trading Activities and Results for the 26 weeks ended 11 January 1964 (for use by Directors at Ordinary General Meeting of CWS) 14 April 1964, 57.

[118] Distributive Undertakings under the Control of the Grocery Committee: Notes on the Trading Activities and Results for the 26 weeks ended 11 July 1964 (for use by Directors at Ordinary General Meeting of CWS) 8 October 1964, 33.

FIGURE 6.11. **Birkenhead Co-operative Society supermarket, c.1950s.** By the 1950s and 1960s, more co-operative members were purchasing their groceries from purpose-built supermarkets like this one, on Woodchurch Road in Birkenhead. New store formats, changing consumer tastes, and increasing price competition were part of the rapidly changing retail environment of the period.

In these circumstances change in the movement was unavoidable, as market forces drove many societies into deep financial trouble. As a result, the process of amalgamation, so stridently promoted by the CIC, developed a momentum of its own, as societies merged to pool resources and membership in the face of dwindling profits and numbers. The Co-operative Union had tried to take heed of the CIC recommendations, ordering its own *National Amalgamation Survey* in 1960.[119] By the time it was published, the number of societies had already been reduced from around 1,000 in 1950 to 875.[120] In line with the CIC, it also called for a reduction in the number of societies to around 300. In practice, of course, the survey and indeed the Co-operative Union itself carried no more weight than did the CIC, and inevitably, this ambitious target was not achieved as quickly as hoped. There were still about 539 societies in 1967—a marked reduction by mergers since the 1960 report, but not as rapid as either CIC or the Co-operative Union had called for.

[119] Co-operative Union, *National Amalgamation Survey* (1960).
[120] Ekberg (2008), 184.

Nonetheless, the trend was clear. Of particular significance was the role of the CRS (Co-operative Retail Services, see Figure 6.12), the subsidiary of the CWS set up in 1934 to promote co-operation in those parts of the country where there were few co-operative societies.[121] In practice, the CRS became a kind of 'ambulance service' for societies in trouble, in some cases stepping in to take control of the failing society. It represented an incursion by the CWS indirectly into retail, and in its statement to the CIC, the CWS had presented its work in a positive light, as evidence of the ability of the CWS to take a lead in the reform of retailing generally.[122] Certainly the CRS became even busier during this period in taking over failing societies. In 1950, the CRS had a turnover of £6,462,426 and had inherited a membership of 128,573.[123] By the mid-1970s it had taken over 162 societies, and the turnover of the organization had grown to £287 million per annum.[124] By 1975 it had a membership of 136,424.[125] In the process, the CRS began to take on an identity of its own, increasingly seeing itself as an autonomous body operating within the co-operative movement, rather than being a mere appendage of the CWS. By the mid-1990s, CRS retail outlets predominated over their CWS rivals (following CWS's late entry into retailing in the 1970s) in large swathes of England and Wales, including Wales, the south-west (Devon, Somerset, and Cornwall), Cambridgeshire, and a large swathe of Yorkshire, stretching into north-east Lancashire. In contrast, the CWS was strong in retailing by then in Newcastle and the far north-east, parts of the East Midlands, and in the south-east. In this way, the rivalry took a distinct geographical manifestation. How did this come to pass, given CRS origins as a CWS vehicle? In part this stemmed from the very process of absorbing societies into the CRS. Under the constitutional arrangements for the CRS, members of societies absorbed into it were given rights of democratic representation in the running of the CRS. Branches of the CRS were constituted around the societies inducted into the organization, and on a regional basis these could elect representatives to the Management Committee of the CRS (in time this became a fully-fledged Board of Directors, and became known as the Board of the CRS). Theoretically, the CWS retained control of the Management Committee of the CRS, constitutionally controlling six of the eleven positions on that committee. But increasingly the non-CWS members of the committee came to see the CRS as possessing an identity of its own, effectively representing the substantial cohort of individual co-operative societies the CRS had inherited. Over time, this sense of separate identity even seems to have filtered into the outlook of some of the management committee representatives from the CWS.[126] The upshot was that the CRS gradually evolved into a rival centre of power to the CWS and the Co-operative Union; with a strong sense of its claim to democratic legitimacy and its unique presence in the retail world. It represented a trend of even greater fragmentation, arguably just when the movement really needed greater unity.

---

[121] See section 5.6.   [122] CWS statement to CIC, 61.
[123] Taken from CWS annual balance sheets, NCA.
[124] Richardson (1977), 234–44 and 362–3.   [125] CWS balance sheets.
[126] CWS statement to CIC, 83–7.

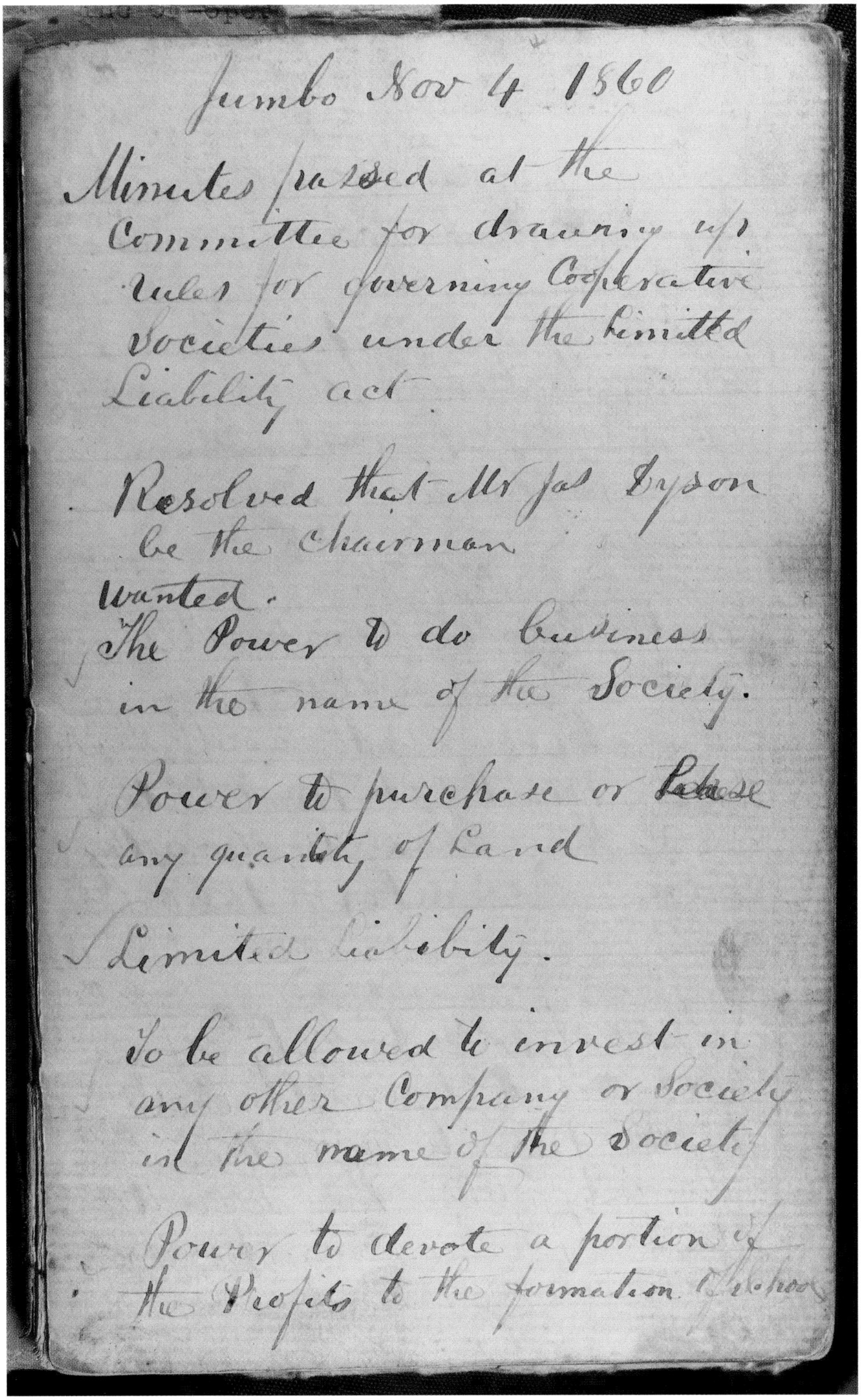

Jumbo Nov 4 1860

Minutes passed at the
Committee for drawing up
rules for governing Cooperative
Societies under the limitted
Liability act.

Resolved that Mr Jas Dyson
be the chairman

Wanted.
The Power to do business
in the name of the Society.

Power to purchase or lease
any quantity of Land

Limited liability.

To be allowed to invest in
any other Company or Society
in the name of the Society

Power to devote a portion of
the Profits to the formation of schools

PLATE 1 'Jumbo Farm' minute book, 1860. The first page of minutes taken by William
Cooper, one of the Rochdale Pioneers, which record a series of meetings in 1860–3 that led
to the North of England Co-operative Wholesale Society.

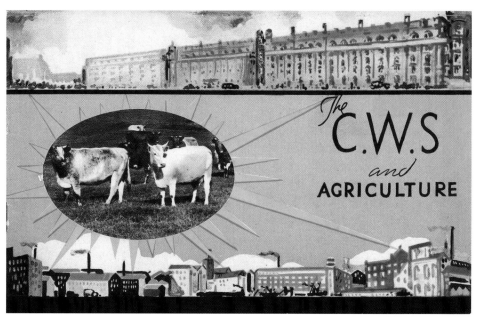

PLATE 2 **CWS and agriculture, c.1900s and 1936.** The Roden estate in Shropshire (above) was the first farm purchased by CWS, in 1896. The hall, dating from 1860, was converted into a convalescent home for co-operators, and opened in 1900. By 1936, when this pamphlet (below) was published, the CWS owned nearly 18,000 acres of farm and pasture land.

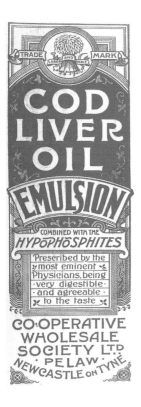

PLATE 3 CWS packaging, *c.*1910s–30s. After the Proprietary Articles Traders' Association, formed in 1906, refused to sell chemists' goods to co-operatives if they paid dividend on these items, CWS developed its own products (left) at its Pelaw Drug and Dysaltery Works. By the 1930s, CWS produced an extremely wide variety of branded goods, including basic commodities as well as more exotic items (below).

PLATE 4 CWS armistice programme, 1918. One week after the Armistice, on November 19, CWS members, employees, and officials gathered in Mitchell Memorial Hall in 'Greetings to Peace'. The final total of CWS employees killed was 810; 94 were decorated for their service.

PLATE 5 **Co-operative tea labels, *c.*1930s and 1940s.** By the 1930s, E&SCWS sold an enormous variety of blends and packages of tea to co-operative societies, at home and abroad. Its products included a special blend for Argentina's 'El Hogar Obrero' co-operative society and for the British Red Cross during the Second World War.

CO-OPERATIVE
PICTURE LECTURE

Moving and Still Pictures by Kinema and Lantern

"PRODUCTION ᶠᴼᴿ USE"

(The aim of the C.W.S.)

Illustrated by Kinema Films, and from 60 to 80 beautifully coloured Lantern Pictures. Duration, 1 hour.

From the
Sources
of
Supply

WEST AFRICAN DEPOT.

Direct
to
the
Consumer

A Special Propaganda Lecture prepared for the

CAMPAIGN FOR CAPITAL

Also for Trade and Membership.

For Synopsis see page 3

PLATE 6 'Campaign for Capital' pamphlet, c.1920s. This promotional pamphlet was used by CWS lecturers touring the country in the early 1920s as part of a campaign to increase members' investment in co-operative societies and the Wholesales. The illustrated lectures included moving images as well as lantern slides of CWS products and premises, including CWS' West African depot.

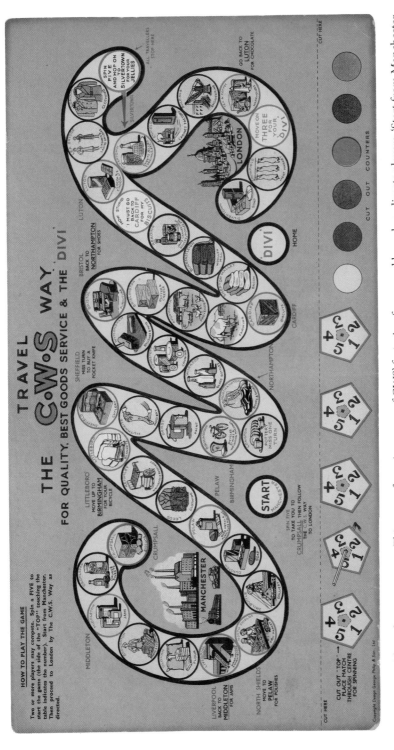

PLATE 7 CWS board game, c.1930s. This game, featuring many of CWS' factories, farms, and branches, directs players: 'Start from Manchester. Then proceed to London by the C.W.S. Way.'

Tea Picking for
ENGLISH & SCOTTISH JOINT C.W.S

Shipping
ENGLISH & SCOTTISH JOINT
C.W.S Tea

ENGLISH & SCOTTISH JOINT C.W.S
Tea Blending

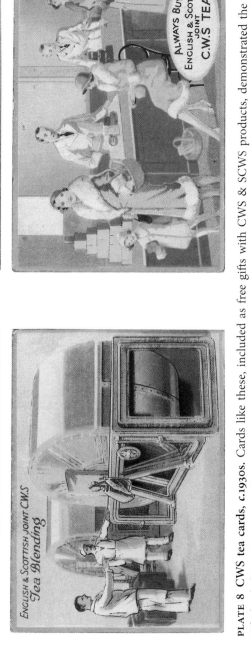

ALWAYS BUY
ENGLISH & SCOTTISH
JOINT
C.W.S TEA

PLATE 8 **CWS tea cards, c.1930s.** Cards like these, included as free gifts with CWS & SCWS products, demonstrated the Wholesales' involvement at all stages of the supply chain, from its tea estates in India and Ceylon to co-operative store counters.

PLATE 9 **CWS Bank and SCWS headquarters buildings, *c*.1930 and 1977.** By 1930, the CWS Bank had grown large enough to require a separate building (above), to accommodate account holders. The SCWS' Morrison Street headquarters in Glasgow (below), built in 1893, became home in 1977 to a CWS hypermarket. In the late 1990s the building was redeveloped and converted into flats. Nearby, a SCWS warehouse built in 1876 was destroyed by fire in 2011.

C·W·S: FIFTY YEARS 1881-1931
IN DENMARK

PLATE 10 CWS in Denmark and New Zealand, *c.*1930s. In 1931, CWS printed a pamphlet (above) commemorating the jubilee of its first Danish operation, a buying depot in Copenhagen. In 1921, CWS formed a joint venture with agricultural co-operatives in New Zealand, importing butter, cheese and meat and exporting tea, clothing, and household goods.

PLATE 11 **CWS advertising, *c.*1930s and 1940s.** Advertisements often featured the 'woman with the basket' (above), a common symbol used by the Women's Co-operative Guild and the movement to demonstrate the power of female consumers in the movement. Waveney products (below) continued the co-operative practice of branding goods based on location. The CWS Lowestoft factory, opened in 1929, stood on the River Waveney in Suffolk.

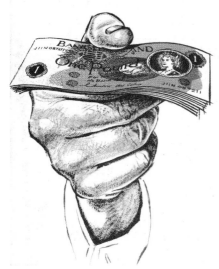

DIVIDEND

IS BETTER THAN GIFT STAMPS

- keep hammering this message home by reproducing the specimen advertisement in your local press, in your Society's magazine and balance sheet, and as leaflets for distribution in your branches and by roundsmen, and by displaying the window bills on *all* your branches.

From the Co-operative Union Ltd., Holyoake House, Hanover Street, Manchester 4.

Produced for the Co-operative Union Ltd., by the C.W.S. Public Relations Division, and printed by the C.W.S., Warrington

PLATE 12 Dividend vs. dividend stamps, *c.*1950s and 1960s. In the 1950s, the Co-operative Union and CWS tried to counteract the growing use of gift stamps by private retailers (above). In the late 1960s, however, many societies replaced the traditional dividend with 'dividend stamps', produced by CWS from 1968 (right).

Perspective View of Section for
Chocolates, Sweets & Delicacies.

MANAGER.

C. W. S. LTD.
SHOPFITTING DEPT
MANCHESTER & LONDON.

MOBILE
GROCERY

Come Co-operative Shopping

SOCIETY'S NAME
AND ADDRESS

PLATE 13 **Types of shop, *c.*1930s and 1960s.** Above, a drawing for a confectionary counter in a large co-operative emporium, produced by the CWS shop fitting department in the 1930s. Below, a mobile grocery shop branded with the 'Come Co-operative Shopping' strapline of the early 1960s. For decades, many societies used mobile shops to expand their trade to adjacent villages and rural areas.

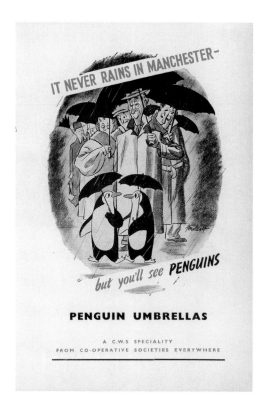

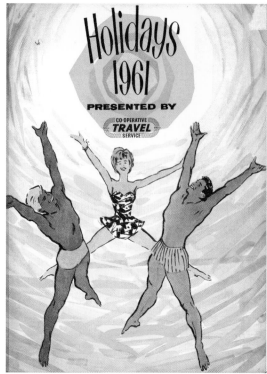

PLATE 14 CWS advertising, rain and shine, 1949 and 1961. Co-operative leaders often commented on CWS' ability to provide products and services to members 'from cradle to grave'. By the mid-twentieth century these included umbrellas to protect from Britain's wet weather, and package holidays to escape from it.

PLATE 15 Defiant advertising, *c.*1930s and 1960s. When wireless manufacturers refused to sell radios to co-operative stores if they paid dividends on their products, CWS began to produce its own 'Defiant' brand radios (right). The name became an iconic brand for CWS audio equipment and, in the 1950s and 1960s, televisions.

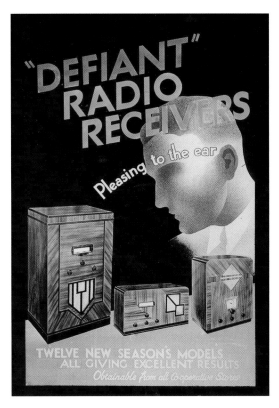

PLATE 16 CWS advertising, *c.*1960s and 1970s. Longstanding CWS brands such as 'Waveney' (left) were phased out with the introduction of the 'Co-op' brand in the late 1960s. The new branding was also used for CWS' non-food trade (below).

PLATE 17 'Your caring sharing Co-op' poster, *c.*1980s. Advertising campaigns in the late 1970s and early 1980s used the strapline 'Your caring sharing Co-op'. This poster emphasized CWS' British manufacturing operations as well as the variety and quality of its own-brand products.

PLATE 18 CIS, c.1920s and 2000s. The CIS'
motor insurance business expanded rapidly
in the 1920s as automobiles became more
common (left). In 2005, The Co-operative
Group transformed the landmark CIS tower
(above) by replacing deteriorating concrete
tiles with more than 7,000 photovoltaic solar
panels, which now generate 180 megawatt
hours of renewable energy each year. Photo
above, courtesy of The Co-operative Group.

PLATE 19 '99 tea' packaging, *c.*1920s, 1960s, and 2000s. Marketed in the 1920s as 'prescription tea' and the 'No. 99' blend (above left), '99 Tea' went on to become an enduring CWS brand. In the 2000s, The Co-operative Group converted the brand to the Fairtrade standard, building on the earlier conversion of its own-brand chocolate and coffee. Photo at lower left, courtesy of The Co-operative Group.

PLATE 20 **Rochdale Pioneers Museum and 1 Angel Square, Manchester, 2012.** Visitors from around the globe continue to visit the Rochdale Pioneers Museum (right), in the original building where the Pioneers' Society opened in 1844. Below, architectural drawings show the new headquarters of The Co-operative Group in Manchester, opened in 2013. Image below, courtesy of The Co-operative Group.

FIGURE 6.12. CRS store, Wales, *c.*1960s. In 1936 the first CWS Retail Society branch opened in Cardiff, and by the 1960s the CRS was developing into a sizeable retail operation, with regional strengths in Wales, south-west England, Yorkshire, and north-east Lancashire.

Such fragmentation was evident in other parts of the movement. Key components of the movement increasingly saw themselves as separate entities, some even distancing themselves from it, as did the Co-operative Permanent Building Society, which became the Nationwide in 1970.[127] Two other major institutions of the movement, the Co-operative Insurance Society (CIS) and The Co-operative Bank (as CWS Bank became known in 1968), certainly did well in this period. The bank, which had been steadily building its portfolio of local authority, trade union, and other accounts during the post-war period, was one of the few components of the co-operative movement that could point to material success. Its profits more than doubled between 1945 and 1965, from £167,565 to £373,034; with a significant jump in profits from £178,871 in 1963 to £329,202 in 1964. Its numbers of current and deposit accounts rose from 54,857 to

---

[127] Cohen (2012), 163.

143,225 and from 39,415 to 54,823 respectively between 1945 and 1963.[128] The CIS also grew impressively. Its premium income rose from £32 million in 1952 to £76 million in 1962.[129] By 1968 it was the second largest industrial and ordinary life insurer in Britain and in life insurance was competing directly with Prudential, the market leader.[130] But as Garnett, the CIS historian, noted in 1968, the CIS had achieved this success by pursuing limited objectives and focusing exclusively on its own business.[131] There was little attempt to link with The co-operative bank in developing new financial products or identifying new markets, and the CWS seems to have taken the view of both the CIS and the bank, that they should largely be left to their own devices. As a result, the movement increasingly operated in silos, with little coordinated attempt to develop a planned approach to the development and growth of the business. In addition, the trend towards amalgamation produced results which had not been anticipated by the CIC when it recommended an amalgamation strategy. It anticipated that fewer, larger societies would make for easier coordination of activities, and in which leadership from the CWS and the Co-operative Union would be more easily executed. Fred Lambert rightly anticipated the flaw with this argument in 1963, and his words proved to be remarkably prophetic:

> The bulk of CWS trade is now done with large retail societies. In their food operations these societies are bigger than most wholesalers; they can run their own warehouses and buy on relatively favourable terms. They probably think they can do better than they really can and as a society grows in size it usually tends to become more independent of the CWS...Regardless of any other considerations, there is therefore an inherent tendency for retail societies, as they grow in size, to grow away from the CWS, and to seek to perform for themselves functions at one time undertaken by the CWS. This is reflected in a steady decline in loyalty.[132]

Thus as societies became larger they would be less inclined to follow the lead of the CWS or any other central body, viewing themselves as viable and vibrant commercial organizations in their own right. Thus the development of strong central leadership for the movement would become more difficult, not less.

But the early 1960s did see some efforts to improve the position of CWS. The 100th anniversary of the foundation of the organization in 1963 was certainly an occasion for reflection on its progress, amid the national celebrations during the course of that year. The decade saw more tangible evidence of efforts at reform both within CWS and the movement more widely. The completion of the CIS tower (see Figure 6.13) in the decade, and the CWS New Century House (Figure 6.14)—both which still figure prominently in the Manchester skyline—signalled that some measure of modernization was being attempted. The CWS could even point to some products in the previous decade which had captured the public imagination, notably its coup in securing the collaboration of

---

[128] Co-operative Bank statistics from CWS balance sheets, NCA.
[129] Garnett (1968), 294.   [130] Garnett (1968), 297–9.   [131] Garnett (1968), 300.
[132] F. Lambert, 'CWS in the 20th Century: Notes on the Basic Problem', 1–2, in a bundle of documents entitled 'The Role of the CWS', NCA.

FIGURE 6.13. **CIS tower, Manchester, c.1960s.** Completed in October 1962, the CIS tower was a national sensation as one of Britain's first skyscrapers, and at nearly 400 feet high was for many years the tallest building in Manchester.

the famous footballer, Stanley Matthews (see Figure 6.15), in the design of the CWS-produced football boots which bore his name. Moreover, contrary to notions that CWS was slow to see its problems, real (though unsuccessful) efforts were resumed to reform the organization in the early 1960s. At the centre of the new ideas was, once again, the Head of the Market Research Bureau, Fred Lambert. As will be seen, while Philip Thomas, CWS's CEO in the late 1960s, has been heralded by some as the 'great lost hope' of co-operative reform during this period, in fact many of the most important ideas were being developed within the CWS, several years before Thomas joined the organization. On this point, the response of the CWS leadership to the CIC report should be considered. There was undoubtedly disappointment and frustration at the CIC's refusal to accept the CWS's bid to lead reform. This jaundiced the attitude of some on the Board to the CIC report, but key figures such as Lambert, and elected members such as Lord

Peddie, were spurred into revisiting some of their earlier ideas about the leadership role of the CWS, and how to revive the fortunes of the movement more generally. Certainly leading figures in CWS refused to ignore the wider changes which were occurring in the retail world. In 1962, Lord Peddie, H. J. Cadogan, and H. N. Whitehead of the CWS Board visited the USA to witness the latest methods of organization of the retail trade there. They came back with their belief in the need for urgent reform greatly strengthened. On their return, they asked Fred Lambert to prepare a detailed report reviewing the current position of the CWS in light of the American visit, and to present it to the Policy Committee of the CWS. At its meeting on 1 April 1963, the Policy Committee set up a subcommittee of three directors (one each from the Finance, Grocery, and Dry Goods Committees) to review the whole position of the CWS within the co-operative movement. Their deliberations were to be informed by Lambert's document.[133] The remit of the subcommittee was far reaching: to focus on the question of the CWS's leadership role, and to consider solutions to problems, some of which would prove decades ahead of their time. The subcommittee was to explore ways in which the CWS could become 'the unifying element in the structure of the movement'. It was recognized that this would involve substantially altering the relationship between the CWS and retail societies, possibly with the CWS becoming a provider of services for retail societies rather than a supplier of goods to them on the basis of a commercial relationship. The idea was mooted, some thirty years before it became a reality, that the CWS should aspire to become a buying agency for societies, rather than a traditional wholesaler which sold to them. It was also asked to consider how the CWS could take the lead in the rationalization of co-operative warehousing facilities across the country, to ensure a better and more rational use of resources. As Alexander's work on the implementation of self-service in London suggests, such an exercise was long overdue.[134] The aim was for the subcommittee to report to a major trade conference of the movement scheduled for October 1963, but its findings were also intended to inform a major review of 'Top Management' processes being undertaken by the policy committee for the CWS Board.[135]

Lambert's initial advisory document to the subcommittee is an eloquent rebuttal to those, like Sparks and Cohen, who dismiss the capacity within the CWS for leadership during this period. From the outset, Lambert stressed that there needed to be a complete overhaul of the relationships which existed between the various parts of the movement to ensure that it compete effectively with the multiples. Unequivocally, only the CWS could provide the leadership needed to implement reforms, argued Lambert. Referring to the 1962 US deputation's findings, Lambert suggested that there were three possible avenues for the CWS to pursue improvements. First, it could merely confine its efforts to improving its own efficiency as a producer and wholesaler of goods, without troubling itself about the wider relationships within the movement. Secondly, it could try to go beyond this, to establish the CWS as the 'unifying element' in the movement, without undermining the

---

[133] Minute of the Policy Committee of CWS 1 April 1963, 'The Role of the CWS'.
[134] Alexander (2008).
[135] Minute of the Policy Committee of CWS 1 April 1963.

FIGURE 6.14. New Century House, Manchester, 1963. The companion building to the CIS tower, the formal opening of New Century House coincided with the CWS's centenary. Like its taller counterpart, it was designed by CWS architect G. S. Hay, in association with Sir John Burnett, Tait, and Partners.

traditions of local organization within it. Lambert envisaged a radical change in the relationship between the CWS and the societies, under which the CWS would gradually become the buyer for retail societies and provider of other services to it. Thirdly it could adopt an ultra ambitious strategy of trying to turn the CWS into the nucleus of a single national co-operative society as mooted by Hardie and Cooke at the time of the CIC.[136] Lambert was clear that the third option would incite such hostility within the movement that it could not be openly pursued in the short term, though in the more distant future it might become feasible. Neither did Lambert believe the first option to be adequate on its

[136] F. Lambert, 'The CWS in the Twentieth Century: Observations', 2–4, 'The Role of the CWS'.

FIGURE 6.15. **Stanley Matthews's in-store signing, c.1960s.** One of the most famous English footballers of the twentieth century, Matthews played for Stoke City (1932–47, 1961–5) and Blackpool (1947–61) during his long career. He signed a sponsorship deal with CWS in 1949, helping design the football boots which bore his name; these remained a popular item in co-operative stores through the 1960s.

own. He argued that it needed to be combined with the second strategy, which would involve the CWS substantially altering its operations, moving into buying for, rather than selling to, the retail societies. Lambert recognized that developing the kind of relationships he envisaged would inevitably have to be the result of negotiation, experiment, and trial and error—in this respect he envisaged a programme of change that would be flexible, both in terms of objectives and time scale, for achievement.[137] Lambert also pointed out that unless steps were taken towards the CWS developing this relationship, it was more than likely that the retail societies would drift even further away from the CWS. Thus the development of an integrated supply structure for the movement, with the CWS at its centre, was essential for the preservation of the CWS as a major body within it.[138] So impressed were the subcommittee with Lambert's arguments that in May 1963 they adopted his basic approach and invited him to sit on the committee.[139]

[137] Lambert, 'CWS in the Twentieth Century: Memorandum', May 1963, 3–6, 'The Role of the CWS'.
[138] Lambert, 'CWS in the 20th Century: Notes on the Basic Problem', 3–5.
[139] Minutes of subcommittee on the role of the CWS, 16 May 1963, 2, 'The Role of the CWS'.

In his later memoranda for the subcommittee, Lambert tried to flesh out what his general proposals might mean in practice. For the CWS it meant a reorientation of activities away from selling to societies towards buying for them as part of an integrated operation, developed on a voluntary basis. It meant developing a much more collaboratively based approach to marketing and advertising, and change in the basis upon which CWS was remunerated by societies for supplying them—probably 'cost plus' rather than sale to the societies at a market price.[140] It also meant a complete overhaul of CWS's warehousing policy, so that CWS warehouses across the country would stock goods required by the societies.[141] Lambert was clear that he anticipated some resistance to his strategy, and that as such there would have to be a special central body established which would, in a flexible way, manage relations with the retail societies and other bodies, and gradually press the policy of integration forward over time.[142] What is interesting here is that Lambert's prescription for change, unlike the CIC, fully grasped the political obstacles and realities of trying to reform a movement in which power was dispersed and no one body had the requisite authority to impose its will. Change could not be swift and programmatic, but through gradual persuasion and a central authority in place which could respond to opportunities for change as they arose. Lambert offered not only a plan for reform, but a strategy for implementation: a notion of leadership adapted to the needs of a democratic movement. Significantly, again the subcommittee accepted Lambert's advice.[143] Ultimately, in its report to the Policy Committee in November 1963, the subcommittee endorsed Lambert's arguments, arguing that the Policy Committee now needed to secure the approval of the CWS Board to reconstitute the Policy Committee as a Planning and Development Committee with the power to work out a truly detailed strategy based on the subcommittee's findings.[144]

Of course the CWS Board responded to these recommendations very positively. In November 1964 it authorized the establishment of the Joint Reorganization Committee (JRC), consisting of Board members and elected members of the shareholding retail society shareholders, under the chairmanship of that arch reformer Leonard Cooke.[145] The committee met thirteen times and its report was published and circulated to societies in August 1965.[146] Its recommendations were wide ranging. It advocated major changes in the operating structures of the CWS, calling for the appointment of full-time professional executive officers who would be answerable to a newly constituted part-time Board of thirty elected members, whose job would be to supervise the work of the new executive officers, rather than engage in direct day-to-day management themselves.[147]

---

[140] Role of the CWS, document 3, Consequential Policy Decisions, 12 June 1963, 'The Role of the CWS'.
[141] Role of the CWS, document 3; Role of the CWS Document 5: A First Approach to Action, 11 July 1963, 'The Role of the CWS'.
[142] Role of the CWS Document 4, 21 June 1963, 3–6, 'The Role of the CWS'.
[143] Minutes of meeting of subcommittee on the Role of the CWS, 26 June 1963, 'The Role of the CWS'.
[144] Interim Report of the Subcommittee on the Role of the CWS, 20 November 1963; 'The Role of the CWS'.
[145] Report of the Joint Reorganization Committee (Manchester CWS 1965); terms of reference.
[146] Richardson (1977), 276.
[147] Report of the Joint Reorganization Committee, 41–7.

But the main thrust of the report, very much following the work of Lambert, was on reform of the problematic relationship between the CWS and the retail socie-ties. It set out the objective of producing a more integrated movement, in which the CWS would move towards a relationship with the retail societies under which it would increasingly buy for them and coordinate its activities much more closely with them.[148] A special Trade Audit department was to be set up (Lambert's central authority for implementing the plan) to supervise what was intended, and indeed had to be, given the dispersal of power throughout the movement, a gradual redrawing of the relation-ship between CWS and the retail societies. While the report made concrete constitu-tional changes to CWS, its plans for reforming relations with the wider movement rested upon gradual persuasion and consensus building. This would prove just as difficult as in the past.

Nonetheless, the report was approved and adopted by the CWS in October 1965.[149] It paved the way for the election of the new part-time Board, and the appointment of the new executive officers to run the restructured CWS. In March 1966, nominations were invited for the part-time Board, which was elected ready for its first meeting on 4/5 May 1966.[150] It was chaired by Sir Leonard Cooke, whose commitment to radical change seemed to promise that this 'new beginning' would continue in earnest. The Board pro-ceeded to appoint its executive officers, and in January 1967, Philip M. Thomas, then 42 years old, was appointed (see Figure 6.16). The appointment of Thomas was in itself indicative of a new radicalism. Thomas was the first ever outsider to the movement to be appointed CEO (and until the appointment of Euan Sutherland as CEO of The Co-oper-ative Group in 2012, the only such external appointment), and this signalled a recogni-tion that new ideas were needed at the top. He was appointed because of his experience in the fast-changing food retail industry. He had been secretary and executive director at Associated British Foods, and brought a formidable reputation for a commitment to ruthless efficiency. He appointed several key members of his team—Arthur Sugden, a CWS insider who had been Controller of CWS Edible Fats and Oils Division, was made Deputy Chief Executive Officer (Food). G. K. Medlock, a co-operator since 1938 and a director of the CWS for over six years, was made Deputy Chief Executive (Non-Food). D. S. Smith, formerly of Boots Pure Drug Company, was appointed as Deputy Chief Executive Officer (Administration).[151] Thomas was in fact only in office from February 1967 till his tragic death in a plane crash on 20 April 1968, but during that time he made major strides towards modernizing and restructuring the CWS and in trying to alter its relations with the wider movement. The creation of three divisions—food, non-food, and administration—represented a major restructuring and streamlining of the CWS's internal operations, and in the essential task of beginning to redefine relations with the retail societies. There was also a major rationalization of CWS warehousing and produc-tive capacity which involved some controversial closures such as the historic Leman

---

[148] Report of the Joint Reorganization Committee, 15–25.   [149] Richardson (1977), 289.
[150] Richardson (1977), 293.   [151] Richardson (1977), 297–8.

FIGURE 6.16. **Phillip Thomas (1925–68).** Recruited from outside the co-operative movement, Thomas was appointed chief executive of the CWS in 1967. The following year, the 43-year-old Thomas and his wife, Elsie, were killed in a plane crash while on holiday in South Africa.

Street premises in London.[152] Under Thomas the CWS began to take a much tougher line with societies who came to it for financial help—in future the CWS would have to be convinced that these societies were running their affairs efficiently before even considering assistance. Of crucial importance in piloting the desired new relationship with the retail societies was the launch in 1968 of 'Operation Facelift', a CWS-led scheme for the refurbishment of retail society stores and the provision for them of the new 'CO-OP' national symbol, a logo designed to project a fresh and common identity across the country (see Figure 6.17). Within six months, some 1,300 shops had been so modernized.[153] Thus by the time of Thomas's death, the new strategy appeared to be bearing fruit.

This modernization and professionalization of CWS was complemented by the Co-operative Union's *Regional Plan for Co-operative Societies* published in January 1968. This was the result of the Amalgamation Survey carried out by the Co-operative Union in the wake of the CIC report. The plan called for the amalgamation of societies into fifty large regional societies, which would have the resources and coordinating capacity to make the desired collaboration between the CWS and the retail societies easier to achieve.[154]

[152] Richardson (1977), 306–7.   [153] Birchall (1994), 154.
[154] *Regional Plan for Co-operative Societies* (1968).

FIGURE 6.17. Ellesmere Port Co-operative Society store, 1970. The introduction of the new 'CO-OP' symbol in 1968 was coupled with a CWS-led programme of store modernization, known as 'Operation Facelift'. Despite such efforts many co-operative societies continued to struggle with the rapid changes in the commercial environment, as price competition increased and many retailers moved to larger shops outside city centres.

It received vocal support from parts of the co-operative media, which saw it as an essential first step in the movement's fight-back against the growing dominance of the multiples.[155] Coupled with the JRC and Thomas's ruthless reform of CWS practices, there now seemed to be a real prospect of success—but it was to prove as illusory as earlier initiatives.

6.6 Conclusions

Writing ten years after the death of Thomas, R. Byrom, who as a CWS director had been involved with the subcommittee working on reform in 1963, reflected on the progress made on the bold initiatives of 1967–8. He noted first of all that the co-operative

---

[155] J. Jacques (CU Chairman), (1968).

movement's share of national retail trade had continued to slide, from 9 to 7 per cent.[156] Whilst Byrom was at pains to list the improvements made in the relationship between the CWS and the retail societies, he readily conceded that they were far from being transformed in the way anticipated at the time of the reforms of the late 1960s.[157] Similarly, while Byrom celebrated what he saw as the success of Operation Facelift, he lamented that the movement was still a divided one, in which some of the larger societies entertained 'misconceived ideas of self sufficiency and independence'.[158] Bluntly he had to concede that:

Despite the success of the last decade, few would deny there has been insufficient progress in the rationalisation and coordination of retail inventories, especially in non-food. Within retail societies, pre-JRC purchasing methods and purchasing organisations have been retained, virtually intact.[159]

In the end, Byrom called for a redoubling of efforts to make the initiatives outlined under the JRC a reality, but there can be no mistaking the undercurrent of disappointment and quiet acknowledgement of failure in his article.

In light of this it would be easy to concur with Sparks and Cohen that this represented a failure of leadership, not least by the CWS. But this would be unfair. Leadership in the context of the co-operative movement meant the persuasion of disparate and fiercely independent interests across the movement to accept a common strategy for reform. 'Command and Control' style central leadership, so beloved by management strategists since the 1980s, was simply not an option. A more subtle, painstaking, protracted, and messier approach to leadership was required, which was about winning the hearts and minds of frequently difficult and independent-minded local leaders. This required sensitive and politically astute setting of objectives which were achievable rather than attempts to impose over-ambitious 'master plans' to revolutionize the movement. In men such as Fred Lambert, Leonard Cooke, and of course Philip Thomas, the CWS and the movement more generally really did have leaders of the requisite calibre. The problem was that as the processes of market decline and amalgamation into larger and more independent retail societies gathered momentum, the movement simply became more difficult to lead. This was compounded by the emergence of the CRS as an effective rival centre of power to the CWS, and the tendency for other major organizations such as the CIS and the bank to be regarded as quasi-separate and independent, and whose functioning should be left to their own devices. In short, it was not a failure of leadership that scuppered the reforms of this period—it was the fact that the movement was becoming almost un-leadable.

---

[156] R. Byrom (Controller Retail and Services Division CWS) (1978), 49.
[157] Byrom (1978), 53.
[158] Byrom (1978), 56.
[159] Byrom (1978), 57.

CHAPTER 7

ADAPTING THE BUSINESS MODEL, 1973–90

HAVING analysed the failings of the immediate post-war years and outlined how fundamental features of co-operation such as the 'divi' were fading into obscurity, it is now important to assess how senior CWS management responded in the 1970s and 1980s to what was increasingly regarded as terminal decline. Although regionally based and independently minded co-operative societies were emerging from the late 1960s, this was more a response to acute financial difficulties, rather than a direct result of the 1968 Regional Plan. Moreover, competitive pressures from multiple retailers were intensifying at a time when macro-economic pressures precipitated the end of over two decades of full employment, a trend exacerbated by a highly damaging process of deindustrialization which created serious unemployment in regions which had been heavily populated by co-operative retailers. In addition, inflationary tendencies were sparking intense industrial relations difficulties, while global issues such as precipitous increases in oil and other commodity prices limited growth prospects. Another worrying feature of the early 1970s was a secondary banking crisis which contributed significantly to the uncertainty that in 1973 prompted Bank of England officials to persuade the SCWS to merge with the CWS when its bank hit problems. This move also highlights the importance of what in 1971 had become The Co-operative Bank, because in stark contrast to the SCWS's financial arm this venture was rapidly developing into a major business in its own right. Indeed, this chapter will demonstrate how from the 1970s The Co-operative Bank contributed an increasing proportion of the CWS's annual surplus. While to a certain extent this reflected the performance challenges experienced by some of the CWS's core activities, the bank's growing status and market penetration would by the 1990s become a key dimension of the organization's commercial viability.

While the rise of The Co-operative Bank will form an important part of this chapter, the key issue to be addressed is how the CWS's business model was undergoing radical change. In the first place, as the SCWS had opened many retail branches in what had been co-operative 'deserts', its absorption into the CWS precipitated the latter's conversion into a retailer. Moreover, with even larger retail societies merging into the CWS from the 1970s, the nature of the organization was changing dramatically. This radical twist to the CWS's business model would inevitably have major repercussions for the movement as a whole, because not only did it complicate the ownership structure, it also aroused the suspicions of both English and Welsh retail societies, as well as the CWS's longstanding retail arm, the CRS. Returning to a common theme running throughout this history, one can consequently emphasize how the dysfunctional nature of the co-operative movement persisted right up to the 1990s. Of course, just as we have noted in preceding chapters, efforts were made by CWS senior executives to cope with these internal challenges, especially during the 1980s when Dennis Landau became CEO. It is also fair to point out that more effective marketing, production, and distribution techniques were either developed or imported as a means of improving performance in the face of intensifying competition. On the other hand, as Sparks has emphasized,[1] the CWS proved incapable of creating 'change agents' who could overcome local resistance. Crucially, it was simply not credible for senior management to argue that because co-operative retailing was structured along lines that were different from those of other multiple retailers, it was just too challenging to adapt. As a consequence, and in spite of exhortations to change, by the 1990s the movement was in crisis mode and predators were circling, indicating how it was being undermined by institutional sclerosis and limited leadership perspectives.

7.1 MACRO-ECONOMIC TRENDS AND CONSUMER BEHAVIOUR

Before delving into the fascinating way in which this debate unravelled, it is first of all necessary to understand the prevailing socio-economic and political contexts that provide the essential backdrop to the CWS's late twentieth-century evolution. In particular, it is vital to note that by the early 1970s macro-economic conditions had changed markedly, bringing to an abrupt end what had been a post-war era of low unemployment and steady economic growth. Although a 'stop-go' economic cycle had been apparent in the 1950s and 1960s, 1973 witnessed the onset of a period characterized by deep cyclical depressions. The key event of 1973, of course, was the enormous increase in oil prices instigated by OPEC and war in the Middle East, precipitating a global recession that severely affected international trade. In addition, commodity (especially food) prices rose significantly from the late 1960s, a trend that would have serious implications for all retailers. This also coincided in the UK with a process of deindustrialization, whereby manufacturing employment fell in both absolute and relative terms, with the loss of significant numbers of jobs in regions such as east Lancashire, central Scotland, north-east England and South Wales, namely, areas where co-operative retailing had traditionally been extensively represented. As Table 7.1 reveals, not only did unemployment rise

---

[1] Sparks (1994), 52.

Table 7.1. Macro-economic indicators, 1950–90

Years	Unemployment (% of workforce)	Years	GDP growth (average % p.a.)	Years	GDP per head (£ at 1980 prices)	Years	Inflation (average % p.a.)
1950–64	2.5	1951–73	2.8	1951	2,226	1950–67	3.8
1965–73	3.1			1966	3,138	1968–73	7.5
1974–81	6.8	1973–79	1.3	1976	3,918	1974–80	15.9
1982–87	11.3	1979–87	1.8	1985	4,465	1980–87	6.9

Source: Derived from Crafts and Woodward (1991), 1–25.

dramatically after 1973, GDP growth struggled to exceed 2 per cent up to the late 1980s and inflation became a major issue. This prompted the creation of the term 'stagflation' to describe the 1970s, while sluggish growth rates, rampant deindustrialization, and inflation meant that the 1980s were no better for many working-class communities.

Exacerbating these trends, and linked directly with the rapid growth in prices during the 1970s especially, was an acutely difficult industrial relations scene, with the number of days lost through strikes reaching record levels for the post-war era. This problem was especially acute in 1971 and 1973, when the coal industry was severely affected by wage disputes, culminating in a three-day working week and energy rationing in the latter year. The engineering industry and public sector were also badly disrupted by the same problem, resulting in major disputes in 1978–9 that have gone down in history as the 'Winter of Discontent'.[2] In spite of legal changes to the status of trade unions introduced by Conservative governments of 1979–83 and 1983–7, these problems persisted into the 1980s, culminating in another major coal industry strike in 1984–5. These disputes once again impacted especially on working-class communities, not least in coal-mining regions, significantly affecting the fortunes of those retail societies located in or around those areas. Although Table 7.1 indicates that living standards (measured by GDP per head) were rising impressively in the 1970s and 1980s, there were enormous regional disparities between those areas suffering from deindustrialization and the buoyant south-east of England. Indeed, while by the 1980s British citizens were much more affluent, the 1980s were especially marked by an increase in pay inequality,[3] providing a challenge to those retail societies which relied entirely on working-class consumers. Crucially, however, while other multiple retailers responded to these trends by attempting to attract different types of consumer, as we shall see shortly co-operatives would appear to have failed to cope with the polarization that affected their customer base.

Another feature of the 1970s and 1980s, largely arising from the deep British macroeconomic difficulties, was the high interest rates that prevailed consistently throughout this period. Linked inherently to the replacement of Keynesian with monetarist policies, interest rate policy was used by successive governments as a blunt weapon either to curb inflation and demand or help resolve balance of payments crises. This resulted in long periods—mid-1970s; 1979–84; and early 1990s—when double-digit interest rates featured prominently, exacerbating the general sense of crisis that prevailed at those times. The most immediate impact of high interest rates was felt especially on consumption, given their effect on mortgage payments and credit card bills. On the other hand, because high interest rates were used to boost the value of sterling, conversely they reduced the price of imports on which the UK relied heavily. However, while this could well be regarded as useful if it controlled food and commodity prices, adversely it also served to cheapen the price of imported manufactured goods. In particular, British textile manufacturers were devastated by a flood of cheap imports that

---

[2] For a detailed survey of these issues, see Morgan (1990).
[3] Chapman and Temple (1994).

by the early 1980s resulted in 5,000 redundancies per month in the clothes sector.[4] This created major problems for the CWS's clothing factories, mostly located in the East Midlands, precipitating the loss of 1,100 jobs between 1975 and 1980 and large-scale rationalization in the 1980s.

It is consequently apparent that in many respects the general socio-economic environment was not particularly conducive to the movement. In addition, the early 1970s was marked by a range of technical changes that would impact decisively on major wholesalers and retailers, not least decimalization (1971), the replacement of purchase tax by VAT, the introduction of metric measures, and the UK's entry into the European Economic Community (all in 1973). Consumer pressure groups such as *Which?* and the Consumers' Council were also much more vocal in highlighting any trading abuses, indicating how the legal environment was much more demanding. Of course, all of these factors, alongside rampant inflation, deindustrialization, and deteriorating industrial relations were entirely beyond the control of any trader. On the other hand, while the 'stagflation' of the 1970s and heavy unemployment of the 1980s affected all retailers, this not only exacerbated the competitive tensions that had been building since the 1950s, but it is also worth noting that the spatial focus of co-operative trading outlets meant that the movement was disproportionately affected. The key issue was whether the movement was prepared to respond effectively to these tensions, by adopting an appropriate structure and strategy—in effect, altering a business model that was widely regarded as anachronistic. For example, while rampant inflation can cause acute uncertainty amongst consumers, well-organized retailers can use this as an opportunity to manage stocks and develop effective purchasing strategies that would boost profitability.[5] A related issue is the extent to which consumers understood the purpose of co-operative trading by the 1970s, given the much greater levels of affluence and rampant consumerism that had emerged in the full employment society of post-war Britain. When combined with the rapidly changing urban landscape, which either dismantled many working-class neighbourhoods or changed them radically, it is no surprise that co-operative traders were struggling to adapt to conditions which were fundamentally different to those prevailing earlier in the century.

While these regional disparities were to become a major feature of late twentieth-century Britain, the significant increase in living standards recorded in Table 7.1 provided the consumption power that retailers proved all too willing to exploit. Indeed (using an index based on 1985 = 100), Sparks has noted that personal disposable income increased from 65 in 1965 to 122 by 1990, fuelling a rise in consumers' expenditure on food from £8.2 billion to £27.5 billion (at current prices), respectively.[6] Linked closely with this trend was a significant decline in the number of retail outlets, from approximately 550,000 in 1950 to 350,000 by 1990.[7] In particular, this period was characterized by the demise of the local grocery store, to be replaced by much larger retail outlets such as the superstore (25,000 square feet or

---

[4] CWS Board Minutes (CWSBM), 14 June 1980.   [5] Sparks (1994), 46–7.
[6] Sparks (1994), 6–7.   [7] Sparks (1994), 15–17.

more), hypermarkets (over 50,000 square feet), and regional shopping centres (such as Brent Cross, opened in 1976 as a harbinger of things to come). This was also linked to the advances in mobility afforded by increasing car ownership, because while in 1950 83 per cent of households did not own a car, by 1990 this had fallen to just 22 per cent, allowing more people to drive to shops located away from traditional centres.[8] This encouraged British retailers to invest in new types of outlet: while in 1962 there was not a single superstore or hypermarket in the UK, by 1986 there were 470, mainly operated by Sainsbury's (63), Tesco (109), and ASDA (93), while Marks & Spencer was venturing into the 'all things to all people' approach to retailing. Although by that time co-operative societies operated seventy-four of these units (for example, see Figure 7.1), they were not integrated into a national distribution system until much later, minimizing their impact on retail effectiveness.[9]

Clearly, by the 1970s consumers were both better informed and much more mobile and affluent than previous generations, offering those retailers with the resources and strategy enormous opportunities to build sales. Another key factor in this changing scenario was the dramatic change to working-class communities, in that a dedicated slum clearance programme initiated in the early 1950s and accelerated during the following two decades resulted in the relocation of a significant proportion of the urban population.[10] As almost all co-operative outlets had been built to service traditional working-class communities characterized by multiple rows of terraced houses, many were left isolated by the construction of either high-rise tower blocks or new towns built well away from older centres. This helps to explain why between 1967 and 1982 co-operative retail societies closed 18,000 shops, as these premises were no longer needed.[11] Although 8,000 outlets were still trading under the CO-OP label, it is apparent from Table 7.2 that their share of the grocery trade was falling drastically. Above all, Table 7.2 highlights how even though the grocery trade grew significantly from £1.5 billion in 1973 to £13.1 billion by 1992,[12] both co-operatives and local independent shops lost out significantly to the increasingly powerful multiple traders such as Sainsbury's, Tesco, and ASDA, which proved to be much more adept in responding to these socio-economic trends.

Of course, it is easy to exaggerate the efficiency of these multiples, especially in view of the knowledge that until the power struggle of the 1970s and Operation Checkout was initiated Tesco rarely achieved the desired levels of performance.[13] Similarly, although Sainsbury's was innovative up to the 1980s, it had lost its market dominance to Tesco by the 1990s, while by the 1990s ASDA had overextended itself and was close to bankruptcy before the Walmart takeover. Of much greater importance to local retail societies up to the 1980s was the competition offered by regional and other multiples, as well as a new breed of discount stores—Kwik Save and Fine Fare—which penetrated UK retail markets, as Table 7.2 reveals. The key issue was the ability of CWS and retail society executives to cope with these trends, adapting both the business model and co-operative

---

[8] <http://www.20thcenturylondon.org.uk/car-ownership>.   [9] Davies and Sparks (1989).
[10] Morgan (1990), 117–18, 312–15.   [11] Byrom (1982), 46.
[12] Sparks (1994), 15.   [13] For a definitive study of this firm, see Sparks (2008).

FIGURE 7.1. **Walsall Co-operative Society shopping centre, Cannock, c.1970s.** When it opened in Cannock, Staffordshire in 1975, this 28,500 square foot shopping centre was the town's largest retail store. Designed and engineered by the CWS, the project cost over £425,000 and included a dry goods section, a travel bureau, and a banking service as well as the society's 'Krazy Kuts' supermarket.

brand to the increasingly demanding requirements of late twentieth-century retailing. As we shall see, these challenges merely served to highlight what Sparks described as the 'institutional paralysis' that appeared to characterize the whole movement's attitude to the need for change,[14] issues which we shall now go on to analyse in much greater detail.

7.2 MERGING WITH SCWS

If the British co-operative movement needed a stark reminder that the general environment was no longer as accommodating as it had been, then the collapse of the SCWS offered a prompt that could not be ignored. Of course, as we shall see, the reasons behind the SCWS's problems were unconnected to macro-economic conditions. Moreover, after implementing its 1965 *Review of Organisation*, it is also vital to stress that performance was improving significantly during the 1970s, with turnover of what would become

---

[14] Sparks (1994), 47.

CWS (Scotland) Retail rising from £30 million in 1973 to £80 million (at current prices) by 1977.[15] Nevertheless, as a direct result of mismanagement at the SCWS Bank, in the spring of 1973 the CWS was persuaded to use its much larger financial reserves to absorb the Scottish organization and effect a merger that others had envisioned several times in the twentieth century. The reluctance to agree to a merger, indeed, highlights once again the strength of views on local and regional independence, because in 1944 and following the debates stimulated by both the 1958 Commission and 1968 Regional Plan it was always clear that SCWS management and staff loathed the idea of linking up with their English counterpart.[16] Even though there had been extensive collaboration on such matters as tea production and packaging, Scottish co-operators firmly resisted the economic logic of combining with the CWS to cope with the mounting socio-economic challenges of the late twentieth century. The Scottish National Party was also generating widespread support in the late 1960s and early 1970s, providing an ironic political background to the story as it unfolded.[17]

When analysing the SCWS's evolution, it is first of all essential to remember that the Scottish movement operated on the basis of a different business model from the CWS, having become an extensive retailer in its own right by the 1940s. The first retail branch had been established in 1908, in what was described as the 'co-operative desert' of Elgin,[18]

Table 7.2. Share of grocery trade, by leading retailers and type of outlet, 1973–92

	1973	1976	1980	1984	1988	1992
Sales through grocers £bn.	1.5	2.4	5.1	7.1	8.6	13.1
	%	%	%	%	%	%
Sainsbury's	8.2	8.9	12.5	16.7	19.0	20.5
Tesco	7.4	7.9	13.4	14.0	15.3	17.4
ASDA	3.3	5.7	8.4	9.8	9.4	10.7
Kwik Save	1.1	2.2	4.1	4.6	4.7	8.7
Safeway[a] (ind. until 1987)	–	1.3	1.3	2.7	5.1	8.2
Lo-cost	–	–	–	2.1	0.9	1.2
Gateway	–	–	–	6.3	10.8	6.3
Waitrose	–	1.3	1.2	1.3	1.6	1.4
Other grocery multiples	15.8	16.7	9.2	8.9	6.8	5.4
Co-ops	20.5	21.5	18.1	14.6	12.5	10.1
Total independent grocers	29.9	23.1	16.6	12.9	11.3	9.3

[a] I am indebted to Dr Jim Quinn for providing this data.
Source: Taylor Nelson AGB/TCA and Superpanel, recorded in The Grocer.

[15] This section has benefited from Kinloch and Butt (1981).   [16] Kinlock and Butt (1981), 315–17.
[17] Morgan (1990), 182–3.   [18] Kinlock and Butt (1981), 222.

while over the following sixty-one years another ninety-nine retail branches were opened across Scotland. By 1960, the SCWS was also linked to 179 separate retail societies which had purchased shares in the secondary co-operative.[19] In assessing the impact of this issue, it is important to remember that while over 70 per cent of the Scottish population lived in the central belt between Glasgow and Edinburgh, the remaining 30 per cent was spread across difficult terrain, including the many islands that contained small populations. Moreover, while the independent retail societies were located in either the central belt or other cities, most of the SCWS's retail branches were in the more dispersed regions, creating major logistical challenges for an organization that was struggling to compete with the multiple traders. Kinloch and Butt also explain that while up to the 1950s the vast majority of the movement's customers were concentrated in central Scotland's inner-city tenements, thereafter many were moved into either expansive housing schemes or new towns located outside traditional centres.[20] It was estimated that the Glasgow societies lost approximately 200,000 members as a result of these changes, breaking forever the community bonds that had underpinned the earlier growth of co-operative trading. Furthermore, as labour-intensive industries such as coal-mining, shipbuilding, textiles, and heavy engineering experienced severe difficulties from the 1960s, Scottish unemployment started to rise alarmingly, significantly affecting the SCWS's core consumers.

Another feature of these dramatic migrations was the deep irony that some of the capital raised by local authorities to fund their housing programmes was provided by the SCWS's shareholders, namely, Scottish co-operative retail societies. This highlights another major challenge facing the SCWS, namely, the rapid decline in loan capital available to the movement: having peaked in 1946 at £22.1 million, by 1968 loan capital had fallen to just £6.9 million. Even though the SCWS raised its loan rates to match the significant increases in bank rate between 1951 and 1973, not only did societies withdraw large sums to invest in local authority debt, but also individual members preferred to spend their savings on the expanding range of consumer goods, depriving the movement of capital for either modernization or rationalization. This problem was also accentuated by the significant increase in retail society indebtedness to the SCWS, from £3 million in 1948 to £11 million by 1965, largely to fund the accelerating popularity of hire purchase schemes, highlighting how the organization was beginning to feel the impact of a liquidity crisis that would seriously damage its ability to respond to mounting external challenges.[21]

Although this combination of population movements and internal illiquidity would have tested the mettle of senior management at the SCWS, by far the most serious challenge facing co-operative retailing was what appeared to be the inexorable rise of regional multiple traders such as Laws, Wm. Low, Hintons, and Hillards. (At that time, Sainsbury's and Tesco did not have a significant presence in Scotland.[22]) These trends

[19] Kinlock and Butt (1981), 89–102.   [20] Kinlock and Butt (1981), 38–9.
[21] Kinlock and Butt (1981), 318–19 and 393.   [22] Sparks (1996).

were also exacerbated by what we have already noted with regard to Scottish housing developments, leaving co-operative stores isolated from their former customers. While the co-operative movement had pioneered self-service from the early 1940s, and still led the field in this respect by the 1960s, the paucity of capital to spend on superstores meant that the regional multiples were rapidly surpassing the SCWS. Furthermore, most retail societies refused to extend opening hours to accommodate the changing patterns of employment, especially for women, an increasing proportion of whom were moving into full-time employment. The abolition of the cash dividend in 1968 across almost all Scottish retail societies further reduced any loyalties that working-class consumers might have retained. Even though a stamp reward scheme—confusingly called the 'Dividend Stamp'—was extensively adopted in Scotland, this failed to stimulate demand for co-operative goods at a time when the population movements earlier described were also breaking up traditional working-class communities that had shopped extensively at local co-operative stores.

The most obvious manifestation of all of these problems was the trend in Scottish co-operative retail sales: although over the 1948-68 period average annual sales per member rose from £88 to £159, by the 1960s it was increasingly apparent that a severe slowdown was being experienced across all societies. Indeed, an absolute fall in Scottish societies' sales occurred between 1966 (£168 million) and 1969 (£162 million), while over the 1960s as a whole in real terms (at 1960 prices) a fall of almost 30 per cent had been recorded (from £160 million in 1960 to £113 million in 1969).[23] As a direct consequence of this decline, the net surpluses recorded by Scottish societies fell from £13 million to just under £6 million, respectively, further accentuating the liquidity issues highlighted earlier. Another key trend in the SCWS was concentration into a smaller number of retail societies, with just 106 remaining by 1972, compared to 220 thirty years earlier. Indeed, the number of retail societies had fallen by over 50 per cent between 1942 and 1972, largely because of mergers between failing operations that sought the sanctuary of either a neighbour or the SCWS, as well as a handful of liquidations. As we saw in the last chapter, however, absorbing societies that were in financial difficulties would only serve to exacerbate the organization's liquidity challenges, in that accumulated debts merely became additional burdens to the SCWS. While the CWS's solution had been the formation of the CRS to rescue failing societies, it was 1966 before the Scottish Co-operative Retail Society (SCRS) was formed. Within six years, twenty-nine societies had joined the SCRS, with sales totalling £16.5 million, reflecting what Kinloch and Butt describe as 'the culmination of years of decay amongst a significant group of Scottish societies'.[24] In 1970, the SCRS's operations were also integrated with the SCWS's retail outlets, by dividing Scotland into five regions, with CASCO (Central and South) at the core covering Glasgow and much of the central Scotland belt. This was part of a broader reorganization instituted in 1968 which (as we shall see later) proved successful in creating a platform for growth in the 1970s.

---

[23] Kinloch and Butt (1981), 394.   [24] Kinloch and Butt (1981), 345.

Creating the SCRS, of course, was only one dimension of the response SCWS made to the external challenges undermining the movement after the 1950s. Another function which received a lot of managerial attention was in-house production, given the acute problems these businesses experienced from the early 1950s. SCWS production actually peaked in 1953, while at current prices over the period 1960–72 output fell from £23.45 million to just £12.4 million.[25] The Shieldhall complex of co-operative factories was especially badly affected by this trend, while elsewhere flour mills, soap works, footwear factories, and laundries were closed in response to mounting losses. A key factor in these decisions was the need for fresh investment in modern production facilities if the SCWS was going to compete with specialist manufacturers, a challenge that the cash-strapped organization simply could not meet. Crucially, Scottish retail societies increasingly preferred to purchase goods from private suppliers, rather than take relatively expensive SCWS products. Only in the 1980s did Shieldhall receive the kind of investment required,[26] by which time manufacturing in Scotland was a shadow of its former prominence.

FIGURE 7.2. SCWS Centenary House, Glasgow, c.1968. Built to celebrate the SCWS's 100th anniversary, Centenary House was designed by Kenneth Masson, the SCWS's chief architect from 1936 to 1968. The building, adjacent to the former SCWS headquarters erected on Morrison Street in 1893 (see Plate 9), now houses Glasgow Council offices.

[25] Kinloch and Butt (1981), 348.   [26] CWSBM, 23 January 1982.

While rationalizing its productive capacity was an essential response to the changing post-1945 environment, it was imperative by the mid-1960s that the SCWS should undergo root-and-branch reform if it was to survive. This prompted SCWS to commission a firm of consultants, John Tyzack & Co., to investigate the possibilities and recommend a plan of action, resulting in the *Review of Organisation* published in November 1965.[27] The key dimension of the changes instigated after 1965 was the appointment of a central professional team run by a chief executive and financial controller, while the Board was reduced in size from twelve to nine. The business was divided into five divisions, the managers of which reported directly to the chief executive, while central services such as marketing, purchasing, and training were revamped and invigorated. A new headquarters had also been built by 1968, Centenary House in Glasgow (see Figure 7.2), opened by Her Majesty the Queen. This also coincided with the CWS's 'Operation Facelift', a campaign to refurbish the co-operative image and boost marketing and sales activities.[28] Although the first SCWS chief executive (William Dorking) resigned within a few months of his appointment, mainly because a general meeting gave the Board authority to curb his powers, once J. S. Marshall was elevated from his post of food division controller in 1967 the reforms started to take effect.

While this restructuring was an essential first step in recovering the fortunes of a movement that in Scotland was experiencing a drastic fall in sales, mounting illiquidity, and growing indebtedness, above all it was vital to persuade the retail societies to work more closely with the SCWS. This prompted discussion of what was termed 'contractual obligations', by which societies would give 100 per cent of their trade to the SCWS. By 1968, however, only 66 of the remaining 145 retail societies had signed up to this deal, representing just 31 per cent of Scotland's co-operative sales. This indicates how in the year of its centenary the SCWS was still struggling with the traditional problems of a dysfunctional federation that rarely seemed to accept the need for collaboration. Although over the following four years the number of societies fell by 27 per cent, to 106, and further rationalization of the productive activities was implemented, stimulating a partial recovery in sales and profitability, most societies insisted on retaining their independence. There had also been some discussion of the SCWS merging into the CWS, an Integration Committee having been established in 1968. This was at least the fourth time that merger talks had been conducted, executives of the two organizations having met in 1916, 1944, and as recently as 1962 to discuss this possibility. After much local debate, however, in 1970 the SCWS rejected the merger proposal, expressing the Board's wish to remain independent of English control.[29] Given the broader context of a resurgent Scottish National Party and discovery of substantial gas and oil deposits in the North Sea, this decision did not surprise many people. Moreover, in stark contrast to what we shall record in both this and the next chapter about relations between the CWS and CRS, in January 1973 the SCWS and SCRS merged, bringing over 400 shops into an integrated operation. A month earlier, the SCWS had also changed its name to Scottish Co-operative Society (SCS), as part of its attempts to improve image and pursue further integration

---

[27] Kinloch and Butt (1981), 356–71.   [28] See section 6.5.
[29] Kinloch and Butt (1981), 209–10 and 342.

across the movement. All these initiatives, however, were brought to a dramatic end by a banking crisis that precipitated a dramatic change in ownership and structure.

In stark contrast to the CWS's early move into banking, the SCWS's banking department had only opened in 1946, as a means of asserting some independence from the expensive charging policies of the large Scottish commercial banks.[30] The SCWS Bank, however, struggled from the outset, because it inherited an investment portfolio dominated by low-yielding assets that, after interest rates started to rise after 1951, had to be sold off at a loss. This illiquidity was compounded by the mistaken policy of relying on loans made against the security of its own investments, because as interest rates continued to rise into the 1970s it became a net borrower. After rejecting suggestions in 1964–5 of either closing the bank or merging it with the CWS Bank, further borrowing from both Scottish banks and the CIS was used to counteract the pressures imposed by the mounting debts of retail societies. It was also in this context that the SCWS Bank management started to invest in Sterling Certificates of Deposit (SCD), a device first used from 1968 by British banks to certify that a sterling deposit had been made, but paying only fixed interest rates set when the certificate was issued. SCD trade by British banks expanded rapidly over the following five years, reaching £5.3 billion by March 1973, largely because bankers realised that they could be readily traded and speedily liquidated.[31] Where the SCWS Bank fell foul was in borrowing at high interest rates to purchase long-dated SCD, breaking the banker's axiom that one never borrowed short to lend long. It was clearly a mistaken strategy, based in large part on the SCWS Bank's desire to gain credibility within Scotland's intimate banking community. By February 1973, the SCWS Bank held £90 million in SCD, almost all of which yielded less than the cost of how they had been financed. Even more worryingly, and unbeknown to SCWS management, the SCWS Bank had committed to buying £365 million in SCD at such a rate that a loss of £25 million was being projected by the Bank of England.

While no records have survived to explain the rationale behind the SCWS Bank's investment strategy, it is clear that the Glasgow operation was trying to persuade the Scottish banking community based in Edinburgh that its management was capable of building a substantial business. However, such losses would not only disrupt the fluid market in SCD, but also precipitate a crisis at the SCWS. Responding especially to the first implication, and having been informed of this impending disaster by Lord Diamond (a former Labour government cabinet minister) on 23 February, the Bank of England moved swiftly to effect a rescue strategy, creating a syndicate from amongst the clearing banks that had lent the SCWS Bank funds to purchase SCD at rates which would have bankrupted the client. This proved to be decisive in staving off a crisis in the SCS, but clearly it was only a short-term stop-gap that was dependent on Bank of England support; a longer-term solution was required. Above all, it was clear that the SCS Bank would never be capable of raising funds from other banks, forcing SCS senior management to approach the CWS for a rescue package that involved a full merger. Reflecting

---

[30] Kinloch and Butt (1981), 241 and 366–70.
[31] This section is based on Capie (2010), 529–31.

the urgency of the situation, after being informed on 7 March of the SCS's difficulties, by 19 March the CWS Board had accepted the proposal, following which on 21 March a meeting of the two boards ratified the agreement. The general manager of The Co-operative Bank, Lewis Lee, played a key role in these discussions, given the acute urgency created by the SCS Bank's dangerous investment strategy, substantially enhancing his reputation both within the movement and across British banking. As we shall see in the next section, this assisted The Co-operative Bank's drive for wider recognition at that time, while in absorbing the SCS Bank's enormous debt Lee was able to avert a major crisis that could have had disastrous consequences for the movement in Scotland.

Over 100 years of independent trading had consequently been brought to an end within a few weeks, largely because of the actions of a department that would appear to have been out of control. Although it was another three weeks before SCS shareholders were informed of the deal, it was ratified at a special meeting on 12 May and the transfer of all Scottish assets to the CWS was confirmed on 9 June at a general meeting.[32] Inevitably, a publicity gloss was put on the CWS–SCS merger, stressing how it ought to allow both organizations to exploit extensive economies of scale and scope in the highly competitive markets in which both operated, reduce replication in areas such as marketing and advertising, and consequently generate better returns for members on both sides of the border. In reality, however, this was a humiliating turn of events for the SCS, in that its Bank management had been allowed to pursue a disastrous investment strategy unchecked by any notions of financial probity. To reflect the scale of the financial crisis, bearing in mind that the total amount of SCS share and loan capital was just £18.1 million in 1972, the bank syndicate had by June 1977 been obliged to provide £29 million to cover the losses on SDC trading. The CWS alone by February 1974 had paid out £5.5 million to meet SCS commitments. On the other hand, following the late 1960s rationalization and reorganization programmes, the SCS brought a reserve of £20 million to the CWS, while sales volumes were improving in the early 1970s, generating in 1972 a surplus in excess of £2 million. Moreover, what would become CWS (Scotland) Retail increased its turnover by 266 per cent between 1973 and 1977, reaching £80 million, substantiating the more optimistic statements made at the time of the merger. Whether in the long term this would help the CWS adapt its business model and cope with its internal and external challenges we shall analyse later in this chapter; in the mid-1970s, however, it would appear to have been a step in the right direction towards greater integration and closer coordination of a highly dispersed set of businesses.

While this positive interpretation of an enforced merger resonated across the movement, after CWS auditors conducted a detailed investigation of the £90 million in assets that they had inherited from the SCS, some serious irregularities were also discovered in a subsidiary, Centenary Finance Co Ltd, that had been responsible for handling car leases.[33] Having been formed in 1970 as part of the SCS Bank, by 1973 it was responsible for £3 million worth of business, but auditors discovered that fraud valued at approximately £1 million had been perpetrated, resulting in the Scottish Fraud Office being informed of the

---

[32] Kinloch and Butt (1981), 364–74.   [33] CWSBM, July 1973.

problems. As we shall see in Chapter 8, while fraud was not exactly rampant across the Co-operative movement, there were serious problems in certain sections that reflected badly on the corporate governance structures prevailing up to the 1990s.

7.3 EXPANDING THE BANK

Whatever the short- or long-term implications of the CWS–SCS merger, for The Co-operative Bank, of course, this was a challenge that management would certainly not have anticipated when in 1972 it was converted from its original function as the CWS banking department. As we saw in Chapter 3, after creating a loan and deposit department in 1872, then converting it into the CWS Bank in 1876, this institution had enjoyed respectable progress up to the 1960s. Apart from serving the financial needs of both the CWS and a significant proportion of the English and Welsh retail societies, by the 1930s over 10,000 trade unions had opened accounts with the bank, as well as over 11,000 mutual organizations and clubs.[34] This growth prompted the CWS to move the bank from its original Manchester premises in Balloon St into a dedicated building close by on the corner of Corporation St and Hanover St. At that time, only five branches had been opened, three of which were in London to serve the trade unions and CWS depot. Instead of branches, the bank relied on retail societies to act as agents, 2,500 of which had been appointed by 1934. Although personal accounts were only initiated in 1910, by 1935 there were over 46,000, accounting for 67.5 per cent of all accounts, but just 17.4 per cent of credit balances. Crucially, however, as it was not a member of the London Clearing Houses Association, it was dependent on one of the major joint stock banks (National Provincial) to clear its cheques. This highlights the bank's limited status in a banking industry that until the 1990s was dominated by a small number of London-based joint stock banks.[35]

Although the CWS Bank's assets had increased steadily in the inter-war era, from £20 million in 1920 to £114 million by 1939, it was the Second World War that prompted rapid growth, largely because of tight governmental controls on both consumption and capital expenditure. As a consequence, by 1946 CWS Bank assets had risen to £259 million, with an investment portfolio of £237 million, mostly made up of government securities. In the late 1940s, its customer base was also extended by the decision of many Labour-controlled local authorities to switch their accounts to the CWS Bank. By the mid-1960s, 281 local authorities had made this move, bringing £3.3 billion in turnover to the bank, while the number of accounts increased to 135,000, compared to 68,204 in 1935.[36] While this prompted the Bank of England in 1947 to grant the CWS Bank the status of being an 'Authorized Bank', allowing participation in foreign exchange business, in effect this made little difference to its dependence on National Provincial as its clearing agent.

[34] Further detail on the CWS Bank's history can be found in Carr-Saunders et al. (1938), 165–7.
[35] Wilson (1995), 192–3.   [36] CWS, 'Story of the CWS Bank', 1963.

Moreover, given the scale of the competition from much larger clearing banks, it was difficult in the post-war era to break into new markets and evolve into a fully-fledged component of the industry.

When one considers the post-1945 development of the CWS Bank, it is essential to understand two key characteristics of the English banking industry. First, as we have just noted, it was dominated by a small group of London-based joint stock banks that ran the London Clearing Houses Association. There were just eleven London clearing banks in 1959, the last one of which to join the Association was the District Bank (in 1936). Directly as a result of several mergers, however, by 1970 the 'Big Four' (Barclays, Lloyds, Midland, National Westminster) accounted for over 70 per cent of clearing bank liabilities, with two smaller banks (Williams & Glyn's and Coutts) taking another 5 per cent. These banks by 1976 were responsible for 81 per cent of all non-cash payments in Great Britain.[37] Secondly, the Bank of England dictated interest rate policy to all banks,

FIGURE 7.3. **Bus advertising, The Co-operative Bank, c.1970s.** Advertisements like these reflect the rising public profile of The Co-operative Bank in the 1970s. Advertising campaigns high-lighted the bank's ties with retail co-operative societies, building on the strapline 'Your Caring, Sharing Co-op', introduced in 1977.

[37] Wilson (1979), 35.

limiting competition amongst the clearing banks to the extent of their branch networks. A 1968 Monopolies Commission report on banking even described them as 'soporific', given the limited competition that had prevailed since the 1940s.[38] Although after over three decades of tight controls and effective cartelization in 1971 the government attempted to introduce greater competition, by enacting a new policy entitled *Competition, Credit and Control*, the nature of British banking militated against innovation, senior management having settled for a cosy cartel that put up substantial barriers to new entrants.[39]

These features of British banking clearly provided formidable challenges to the further development of the CWS Bank. Even though twelve new bank branches and nine sub-offices were opened in the 1950s, and by 1965 approximately 5,000 agency outlets had been established within retail society outlets, it was incapable of exploiting the enormous surge in popular banking from the 1960s. Bank executives were also anxious to bring to the CWS's attention that over the period 1946–68 the proportion of the bank's business attributable to co-operative activities had fallen from 79 per cent of net funds to just 13 per cent,[40] while in the following twelve months this fell to 9 per cent. Crucially, though, not being a fully-fledged clearing bank was constraining further growth of the CWS Bank, persuading the bank's general manager, B. D. Jacob, and Alfred Wilson, CWS chief executive, that efforts ought to be made to change its status. In the first place, the name was changed to The Co-operative Bank in September 1968, while over the following year detailed research was undertaken into the possibility of floating the business as a joint stock company. Although Wilson was willing to support this move, at a September 1969 board meeting his co-directors refused to sanction the proposal.[41] After a month's further work, however, which involved consultations with both the Bank of England and specialist legal advice, the Board proved more amenable. This put in train a series of steps that resulted in The Co-operative Bank being converted into a company,[42] wholly owned by the CWS. Finally, in 1971 an Act of Parliament was secured, allowing the bank to throw off the shackles of the 1876 legislation and become a limited company in 1972.

Another crucial figure in these developments was Lewis Lee (see Figure 7.4), because he became general manager in 1971 just as the changes were taking place, J. D. Jacob having had to retire due to ill-health. Having joined the bank in 1936, after completing an economics degree at the University of London, Lee's rise up the hierarchy was only interrupted by the Second World War, when he served with distinction as a pilot with Bomber Command.[43] By 1964, he had become assistant general manager, working closely with Jacob to effect the decisive changes to The Co-operative Bank's status. While he recognized that the bank's key role up to the 1960s was its ability to influence retail societies, by controlling the supply of overdrafts and loan capital, Lee was especially keen to break into the clearing bank cartel, the first step towards which was to make

[38] Wilkinson and Balmer (1996), 25.   [39] Wilson (1995), 190–3.

[40] CWSBM, March 1969.   [41] CWSBM, 17 September 1969.

[42] CWSBM, September 1969.   [43] Obituary in *Independent on Sunday*, 13 April 2004.

The Co-operative Bank a member of the British Bankers' Association, following which an application to join the Clearing Houses Association was made. The basic elements of this strategy were developed at a meeting of Bank directors on 13 August 1973. The four major clearers, however, proved less than welcoming, given The Co-operative Bank's recent growth, forcing Lee to endure some hard bargaining with the cartel. The election of a Labour government in 1974 finally helped to persuade the Bank of England that The Co-operative Bank could be a viable member of the clearing committee, resulting in its election to this highly influential body in 1975. No doubt the CWS's rescue of the SCS would also have convinced other banks that The Co-operative Bank was capable of dealing with severe challenges, while its expanding business was also regarded as another clear sign of financial credibility.

These decisive changes to The Co-operative Bank's legal and operational status would clearly provide Lee with the platform on which to develop a highly ambitious strategy. Apart from retail banking, the bank had also been expanding its range of activities. For example, in 1969 Co-operative Commercial Bank Ltd was formed, to provide the bank's larger customers with opportunities to trade in inter-bank and currency markets.[44] A year earlier, a controlling interest in FC Finance Ltd was acquired at a cost of £1.75 million,[45] creating a vehicle to extend the bank's funding of the hire purchase and leasing activities of retail societies. At the same time, The Co-operative Bank was especially keen to build a stronger presence in the rapidly expanding retail banking market, selling itself as the alternative to the major clearing banks by competing

FIGURE 7.4. Lewis Lee (1920–2004). At the helm of The Co-operative Bank from 1971 to 1988, Lee was instrumental in the organization's development into a significant player in the British banking industry. During his tenure the bank introduced free current accounts, became the first new clearing bank in forty years, and worked with trade unions to form Unity Trust Bank.

[44] CWSBM, December 1969.   [45] CWSBM, February 1969.

aggressively for new accounts (see Figure 7.3). The Co-operative Bank's relatively small size would always be its most significant advantage in competing with its much larger rivals, because it was not burdened by substantial overheads. Crucially, given the introduction of new computerized technologies by the American banks that encroached on the British market at that time,[46] Lee was willing to pioneer both strategies and structures that other clearing banks proved slow to adopt. Computer technology had been employed extensively by the CWS Bank since the early 1960s, but amongst a series of radical moves was the 1977 decision to spend £7 million developing a new site in Skelmersdale for the construction of Delf House, a centralized operating centre to which by 1979 all technical functions had been transferred. This represented a radical innovation for British banking, which until the 1990s mainly operated through a series of regional offices. Having provided The Co-operative Bank with a highly efficient organization that was relatively easy to coordinate, in the late 1970s Lee secured £4 million from CWS to construct a new headquarters on what had been its first base, 1 Balloon St. This seven-storey building symbolized how The Co-operative Bank was intent on developing a modern, innovative business that would compete effectively with its British rivals.

While these organizational and infrastructure improvements were being implemented, Lee was also planning a series of innovations, not least in marketing. A significant move in this respect was the appointment in 1973 of what was the British banking world's first marketing director, Terry Thomas (see Figure 7.5), who helped Lee achieve his vision of converting The Co-operative Bank's customer base from its traditional concern with co-operatives and trade unions into a personal banking service. Having worked at the antecedents of what in 1968 became National Westminster Bank, Thomas had not only been responsible for introducing new marketing techniques into the major clearing banks, but also popularizing credit cards as a new banking service. Described 'as an avuncular, jolly, caring Welshman',[47] Thomas was able to work closely with Lee in developing a marketing strategy that would set The Co-operative Bank apart from its larger rivals, especially in building a stronger presence in personal banking. The first bold step was to announce in December 1973 the introduction of free banking, abolishing all charges on personal accounts that remained in credit, as well as paying interest on current accounts. Of course, this coincided with the Bank of England's attempts to increase competition in British banking, the sector having been carefully controlled since the Second World War. Although this largely resulted in a major surge in credit, adding significantly to the inflationary forces at play in the early 1970s (see Table 7.1), the relaxation enacted by the Bank of England provided a conducive environment for The Co-operative Bank's ambitions.

In announcing free personal banking and paying interest on current accounts, and in the process sending shock waves around the industry, The Co-operative Bank heralded its intention to challenge the major clearing banks in the market that they had dominated for almost a century. Significantly, it was 1984–5 before the larger rivals introduced free banking, providing The Co-operative Bank with a significant period in

---

[46] Ferguson (2009) 2.   [47] Interview in *Observer*, 9 April 1995.

FIGURE 7.5. Terry Thomas, later Lord Thomas. Thomas joined The Co-operative Bank in 1973, as marketing manager; he became chief executive following Lewis Lee's retirement in 1988. Two years after Thomas's own retirement in 1995, he became Lord Thomas of Macclesfield.

which to build up market share. To make a major impact in this market, however, The Co-operative Bank required much more extensive access to customers. This prompted a significant augmentation of its branch network, which by 1980 had exceeded sixty towns, with plans to reach 100 by the 1990s. Building on its established agency network in retail societies, in October 1975 the 'Handybank' concept was announced, offering customers an opportunity either to open a bank account or deposit/withdraw money in purpose-designed facilities that employed the kind of strong promotional techniques widely used in retailing.[48] Trials were first conducted in Bolton and Wigan, but by May 1976 it was being rolled out across the UK to 700 co-operative stores. In addition, 3,500 stores were identified as 'Cash-a-Cheque' points, providing a more limited service, yet reflecting the commitment to personal banking. By 1979, customers could also avail themselves of new services such as a retail credit card, Handycard, and personal credit service, Handyloan. Co-operative Bank customers had been offered a Barclaycard since 1972, but the Handy innovations demonstrated how the movement had decisively overcome its traditional aversion to providing credit. While initially these services were initially managed by Barclaycare, by 1982 the Skelmersdale processing centre had taken

[48] CWSM, October 1975.

over, by which time over 100,000 Handycards and £33 million worth of Handyloans had been sold. This also proved to be good for retail societies, in that the bulk of the credit secured at either Handybank or Cash-a-Cheque points was used to purchase goods in their stores, demonstrating the mutually beneficial nature of these strategies. By the time a Co-operative Visa card was launched in 1980, this had become a major part of the bank's business, confirming to potential customers that it was capable of offering comparable products to those of its major rivals.

Apart from focusing a considerable amount of attention on personal customers, Co-operative Bank made some ambitious forays into other markets. For example, when in 1979 the newly elected Conservative government announced a loan-guarantee scheme to support small firms, Lee was the first chief executive to express support. Indeed, it was another year before the major banks agreed to adopt the scheme, at a time when record numbers of firms were going bankrupt as a result of the global recession that struck at the heart of business confidence. As a keen advocate of co-operative principles, Lee was also anxious that The Co-operative Bank should not forget its earliest supporters in the trade union movement, leading in 1984 to the creation of Unity Trust Bank. Although in West Germany and Israel similar trade union banks had been flourishing for several decades, when launched auspiciously on May Day Unity Trust offered a range of services to trade unions and operations such as social enterprises, with the initial capital of £2.5 million provided in equal measure by The Co-operative Bank and a small group of leading trade unions. Terry Thomas was seconded from the bank to run Unity Trust, providing him with extensive senior management experience that would serve him well in the 1990s. By 1987, Unity Trust had gained full banking status, while as a direct result of a share issue in 1986 most of the leading unions and the TUC had provided funds, ensuring its success at a time when the movement was under severe pressure.

While these activities proved successful, however, it was the personal banking market that occupied Lee and his senior management team. Having established a reputation for innovation, during the 1980s they worked hard to extend coverage through both additional branches and retail societies as a means of attracting more customers. The product range was also extended in the early 1980s, when mortgages, travellers' cheques, and various savings schemes were launched. This coincided with the 1982 announcement that the total number of customers had exceeded one million, compared to 192,000 in 1970, while by 1988 there were 1.5 million accounts in ninety-two branches, 586 Handybanks (see Figure 7.6), and 2,700 Cash-a-Cheque points. This certainly confirmed the efficacy of Lee's strategy, fully justifying the drive to join the clearing committee in 1975 and creating a highly profitable component of the CWS. At the same time, as illustrated, until the 1990s The Co-operative Bank was unable to generate significant surpluses. In 1981, along with its rivals The Co-operative Bank was also hit by the Special Tax on Deposits, a measure devised by government to shore up its ailing finances. Although The Co-operative Bank was only obliged to pay £3.2 million to the Exchequer, as this represented 88.9 per cent of its pre-tax profits for that year, this was regarded as grossly unfair, because the comparable figure for the four largest clearing banks was just 19.85

per cent, even if it was an average of £78.7 million.[49] The substantial investments in both central services and new branches also imposed significant charges on profits throughout the 1980s, limiting the availability of funds for other parts of the CWS. This forced the bank in 1988 to take the exceptional move of issuing £40 million in preference shares on the open market, in order to fund both the continued expansion of its branch network and additional financial services. For the first time, and again reflecting the lack of co-operation across even complementary activities, the bank also agreed to work with the CIS, in order to sell each other's products, emphasizing its recognition that further expansion was not going to be possible by relying on the CWS alone. It was in these circumstances that the bank was rocked by a major economic crisis that affected all British institutions, the repercussions from which were to have a significant influence on its strategy.

During the mid-1980s, the City of London endured a series of radical changes that culminated in what was widely known as the 'Big Bang' of December 1986.[50] At the core of these changes was deregulation of the financial services industry, reflecting the free market doctrines of the incumbent Conservative government that since its election victory in 1979 had been responsible for stimulating rapid growth in this sector. While these policies certainly worked, especially in attracting international finance houses into the City, they also sparked a ferment of speculative investment activity which culminated in a resounding crisis that started on 19 October 1987, or 'Black Monday', when stock markets around the world fell alarmingly. Although the markets recovered within a year, the most damaging impact of this crash was a period of relatively high interest rates, precipitating a severe recession that lasted until 1991. Moreover, the 1986 Building Societies Act precipitated further radical change in British banking, in that these institutions were then allowed to become fully-fledged banks that competed extensively in the personal market. It was an inauspicious time to take over as chief executive, but having worked closely with Lewis Lee in developing the bank's expansion strategy, and especially in devising a highly successful series of marketing campaigns, Terry Thomas was keen to succeed when his boss retired in 1988.

Appointing Terry Thomas as chief executive of The Co-operative Bank proved to be a highly successful move, because not only had he been responsible for key innovations during the previous sixteen years, but he also oversaw a period of rapid expansion that ensured a steady supply of funds at a time when the CWS was struggling to generate surpluses. Initially, though, and directly as a result of the late 1980s financial crisis, The Co-operative Bank struggled badly in what up to the early 1990s was an extremely difficult time for British financial institutions. Apart from the increase in competition arising from the 1986 Building Societies Act and the introduction in 1984–5 of free banking by all of the major clearing banks, The Co-operative Bank was by then carrying a much larger overhead in the form of Delf House, a bullion centre (in London) and expanding branch network. As Figure 7.7 records, after seventeen years of surpluses, in

[49] CWS, 'It must never happen again', press release issued in April 1982 decrying the Special Tax.
[50] Wilson (1995), 235–6.

1988–9 The Co-operative Bank revealed a substantial loss (£10.4 million) that shocked many in the CWS.[51] When in the following year yet another loss (£7.21 million) was recorded, serious questions were being asked about the viability of sustaining this activity, not least because as we shall see in section 7.4 the CWS's performance was deteriorating even further than it had done in the 1970s. We will analyse how The Co-operative Bank under Terry Thomas effected a remarkable recovery from its late 1980s crisis in Chapter 8, but major concerns were being expressed at that time about the wisdom of

FIGURE 7.6. In-store banking, Blackburn Co-operative Society, c.1970s. The Co-operative Bank's in-store facilities for cheque cashing and other services, launched under the name Handybank in 1975, were unique to the banking industry. However, such services had long roots in the co-operative movement, as many co-operative societies had acted as agents for the CWS Bank for decades.

[51] Interview with Simon Williams.

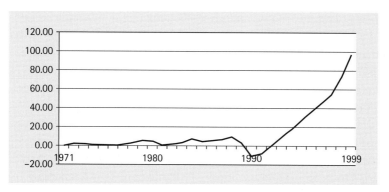

FIGURE 7.7. Net profits of The Co-operative Bank, 1971–99 (£ million).

investing so extensively in this activity at a time when other parts of the CWS were leaking cash and competition was squeezing margins.

7.4 RATIONALIZATION AND INVESTMENT

Although these debates about the bank would only emerge in the 1990s, as we saw in Chapter 6 the movement had throughout the 1950s and 1960s been extensively engaged in discussions relating to its deteriorating (absolute and relative) performance.[52] Again repeating themes already elaborated, the focus of this discussion was placed mostly on food retailing, ignoring the continued success of non-core areas such as insurance, banking, funeral services, and travel. Of course, given that in 1970 food retailing (including dairy) accounted for almost 75 per cent of all co-operative trade, it was clearly vital that considerable attention should be paid to this component of the business, especially as its rivals in this sector were investing massively in new facilities and systems. As Bamfield had noted, using 1963 as 100, by 1976 the volume of sales stood at 90.7, while the number of co-operative shops had fallen from 28,300 to 11,700, respectively.[53] Tesco also experienced a similar reduction in retail outlets over this period, but with the obvious caveat that its management was also investing in new locations and enhanced store layouts.[54] Tesco and other multiples also took advantage in the 1980s of the Conservative government's move to establish Enterprise Zones in depressed regions, using the subsidies offered to build expansive stores that rapidly came to be seen as the way forward for British retailing. Surprisingly, not a single co-operative store featured in these Zones, reflecting a failure of vision on the part of the CWS, CRS, and regional co-operatives. The movement was not assisted by the liquidity crisis that had beset both the CWS and local societies from the late 1960s—retail societies had withdrawn almost £100 million

[52] See sections 6.3–6.5.   [53] Bamfield (1978a), 18.
[54] Sparks (2008), 21–5.

from CWS reserves between 1950 and 1970[55]—a trend that significantly limited the extent and nature of its response. Of course, some effort was put into developing The 'CO-OP' brand and initiating national marketing campaigns, while significant efforts were made both to revamp internal management structures of the larger societies forged through merger, as well as adapting the trading and distribution systems. Nevertheless, although absorbing the SCS's retail operations brought new challenges to the CWS, it is apparent that senior management was struggling to reorient a business model that was beginning to wilt in the face of stiffening competition.

This was the scenario that Alfred Wilson (see Figure 7.8) inherited when first he was asked to stand in as Acting CEO, following Philip Thomas's untimely death in 1968, and then ultimately offered the permanent CEO post in February 1969.[56] Having worked for the CWS since 1946, rising to the position of membership secretary in 1962, Wilson was well aware of the challenges facing the movement as it moved into the 1970s. It would be his responsibility to provide the kind of leadership required in coping with these challenges, allowing Thomas's radical structural changes time to bed in and adapt the organization to internal and external challenges. Although Thomas's three deputies were reduced to a single post, when in 1972 Arthur Sugden was appointed to that role after D. S. Greensmith resigned, it is apparent from even a cursory glance at the Board minutes for this period that senior management adopted a highly proactive approach to tackling the CWS's challenges. Sugden also sustained this momentum when he became the next CEO in June 1974,[57] agreeing to fresh terms and conditions for this key role fashioned by a sub-committee of the Board. Another important appointment at that stage was the elevation of Dennis Landau from his post of Food Controller to Deputy CEO,[58] because he would play a leading role in the rationalization of CWS activities during the 1970s. The CWS was especially concerned with modernizing facilities in both the production and distribution sectors of the CWS, raising the levels of productivity in order better to compete with rivals at a time when, as we saw at the beginning of this chapter, the British economy was undergoing some traumatic times. As we shall see, however, it is debatable whether senior management would ever achieve the kind of performance levels to which other multiples aspired. This highlights the fundamental issue of the extent to which vision was subjugated to institutional lethargy; whether internecine conflict was used as an excuse to avoid innovation. For example, the eight regional centres controlling the CWS's distribution system were never managed as effectively as the way in which Tesco developed at exactly the same time, indicating how a lack of organizational depth hindered progress across the co-operative movement.

By the time Arthur Sugden had taken over as CEO, co-operative trading was under intense pressure to adapt to the difficult economic environment of the mid-1970s. This prompted the introduction of a new marketing strapline, 'Your Caring, Sharing Co-op', alongside the first major national advertising initiative. As we shall see later, a stronger ethical flavour to CWS activities was also emerging from the 1970s, for example the deci-

[55] CWSBM, January 1970.   [56] CWSBM, 5 February 1969.
[57] CWSBM, August 1973.   [58] CWSBM, July 1973.

FIGURE 7.8. **CWS executives greet Co-operative Bank of Nigeria manager, 1973.** Left to right: Co-operative Bank deputy general manager Neville Wilson; Chief Ayodele Onagoruwa; CWS chief executive Alfred Wilson; and Co-operative Bank general manager Lewis Lee. The Co-operative Bank of Nigeria was established in 1954 with assistance from the CWS Bank.

sion to cease sourcing certain commodities from South Africa, and banning fox-hunting on its property. On the other hand, it is also fair to note that the CWS failed to publicize this extensively, indicating the lack of marketing competencies across the organization at a time when other retailers were building substantial teams aimed at differentiating their offering. One should also stress that the 'Caring, Sharing Co-op' initiative was later rebranded as 'The Co-operative Difference' (see Plate 17), largely because few local and regional societies were willing to follow the Manchester lead. Although some societies did emphasize their ethical commitment to their local communities (see Figure 7.9), The 'Caring Sharing' initiative ultimately failed because of what Landau claimed was an 'unwillingness of the retail societies to live up to its promise, rarely paying much more than lip service to ideas emanating from Manchester'.[59] This ignores the acute difficulties experienced by many societies at that time, prompting the abandonment of the 'divi', making it extremely difficult for them to use the 'sharing' aspect of the advertising initiative, given that this rang hollow to all but the very committed. This highlights how the intrinsic meaning of co-operative membership was being significantly diluted, leaving societies vulnerable to competition from which they could barely be distinguished, a trend that the CWS did very little to halt at that time. This contrasts sharply with the success Tesco achieved with its 'Operation Checkout',[60] indicating the

[59] Interview with Dennis Landau.   [60] Sparks (2008), 21–5.

enormous organizational differences between co-operatives and their multiple rivals. Just as in the late nineteenth century, many private manufacturers also used their small armies of travellers and representatives to negotiate tempting deals with retail societies, a factor which encouraged independence and defiance amongst even the smallest operations. The CWS failed to counter this dynamic, frequently using it as an excuse for failing to improve performance, rather than tackling reform at this most fundamental of levels. Above all, it was the membership and their representatives who decided the destiny of co-operative trading, rather than executives residing in their spacious Manchester offices, revealing the full extent of the conundrum that faced both sides when considering integration and synergy.

Of course, the acid test of the CWS's drive both to modernize co-operative commercial activities and integrate the movement more extensively must ultimately rest on commercial performance. Writing in the mid-1970s, Richardson felt confident

FIGURE 7.9. **Donating dividend stamps, Birmingham Co-operative Society, 1972.** Outside the Birmingham society's high street store, members donated dividend stamps to support the charity Action for the Crippled Child. The campaign was part of a national promotion featuring comedians Eric Morecambe and Ernie Wise.

enough to conclude his study by claiming that: 'Far from sinking into decrepitude the Co-ops have taken on a new lease of life. There is a new buoyancy and energy.'[61] This view was supported by Bamfield, who detected a 'revival' that had been based on: a restructuring of internal management structures across both local societies and the CWS; the creation of regional societies; and the benefits of 'Operation Facelift'.[62] Delving deeper into these issues, however, it is unclear whether the evidence totally supports these claims. On the one hand, as revealed, both turnover and surplus increased impressively in the mid-1970s (see Figures 7.10 and 7.11), providing observers with some grounds for optimism, especially when in 1977 the CWS recorded respective figures of £1.44 billion and £18.8 million. On the other hand, while by 1980 turnover had grown to almost £1.9 billion, the surplus had plummeted to £6.3 million, giving rise to widespread concern about the CWS's ability to generate enough capital for the much-needed investment in enhanced facilities. In this respect, and as we shall note later, while Bamfield emphasizes how rationalization of both productive and retailing capacity helped to reduce the cost structure of an extremely cumbersome organization, the loss of 42 per cent of all co-operative jobs between 1966 (232,000) and 1976 (135,000), allied with the closure of 56 per cent of all co-operative stores, was much more closely linked to competitive failure.[63] It was also in 1977 that Tesco launched the 'Operation Checkout' programme,[64] prompting an enormous surge in investment which was matched by its main rival, Sainsbury's. These campaigns made such a conclusive impact on British retailing that all thoughts of a CWS recovery were

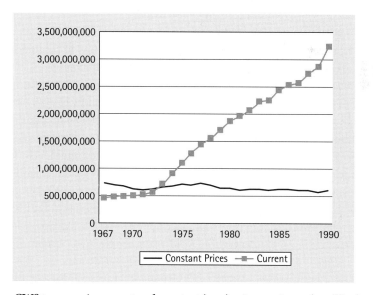

FIGURE 7.10. CWS turnover in current and constant (1974) prices, 1967–90 (£ million).

[61] Richardson (1977), 335.   [62] Bamfield (1978a).
[63] Bamfield (1978a), 22.   [64] Sparks (2008), 30–5.

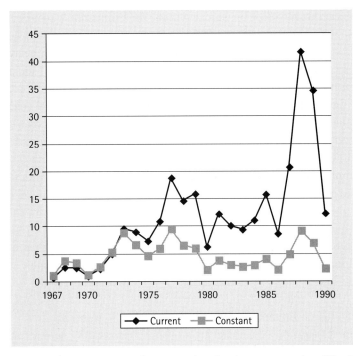

FIGURE 7.11. CWS surplus in current and constant (1974) prices, 1967–90 (£ million).

brought to a decisive end, placing even more pressure on management to reverse the decline in market share experienced since the 1950s.

Another crucial issue was the failure of the first Regional Plan to reduce the number of societies from 650 to the intended fifty regional operations in England and Wales, because by 1976 there were still 217, operating at different levels of efficiency. While Figure 7.12 reveals how the period 1966–72 was characterized by an intense merger movement, the surge in liquidations also reveals that much of this activity was a response to increasingly acute commercial difficulties, rather than a desire to link up together. Although by 1976 the twenty largest societies accounted for 62 per cent of total co-operative turnover,[65] one should also add that as they had developed distribution, marketing, and retailing strategies that reinforced regional loyalties, this discouraged closer collaboration. Moreover, CRS was by 1976 a major business in its own right, having acquired over fifty societies since the mid-1960s and building turnover to £330m. In 1974, a second Regional Plan was launched by the Co-operative Union, in the hope that continued concentration would achieve the 1968 target of twenty-five societies. As Figure 7.12 reveals, however, after the peak years of 1968–71, merger activity waned significantly, even though more societies were being absorbed into either the CRS or CWS. Crucially, in spite of these changes the movement's share of

[65] Bamfield (1978a), 19.

retail trade continued to fall, undermining Bamfield's claims of a mid-1970s revival (see Table 6.1).

Before elaborating further on these organizational and commercial issues, it is important to gain a sense of the debate across the movement about how it should respond to its challenges. As we have seen throughout this history, it is possible to identify a range of views in this debate, most of which were dictated by either vested interests or ideological positions. Above all, in spite of successive appeals to create a 'National Society', conflict between the CWS and local societies, not to mention the deepening rift between the CWS and CRS, ensured that the lack of central coordination continued to hamper overall performance. This highlights once again the fundamental importance of democratic principles as the abiding influence on co-operative structures, leading Sparks to note that:

The society structure and the democratic Co-operative principles devolve power to the hands of more people than in corporate retailers, but at the same time do not impose strategic and operational control mechanisms on these people, as corporate retailers would.[66]

Moreover, apart from accentuating the isolation of local societies, this also stifled the recruitment of fresh managerial talent capable of injecting new ideas into a sclerotic organization characterized by sluggish decision-making and outmoded processes. While one could argue that this academic analysis fails to accommodate adequately the core principles of a movement that had flourished for well over a century, an obvious riposte would be to reflect on the possibility that the movement had not only lost its

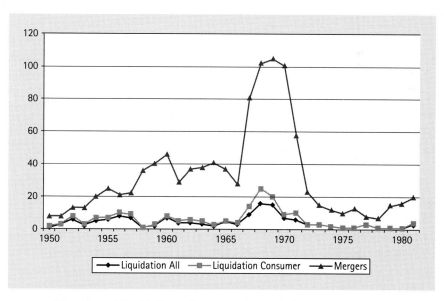

FIGURE 7.12. Mergers and liquidations of co-operative societies, 1950–82.

[66] Sparks (1994), 50.

formerly dominant retailing position, it was not stretching the bounds of possibility to say that its very survival was being questioned.

In emphasizing the key role played by democracy in underpinning the ideology of a movement that had survived for well over a century, it is also important to remember some of the factors highlighted in section 7.1, namely, the dissolution of working-class neighbourhoods and the post-war emergence of a much more fluid and affluent society. Of course, while these factors were beyond the control of the CWS and local societies, they were having a significant impact on the nature and extent of the British shopping experience, especially in former working-class neighbourhoods that were enormously affected by slum clearance and rehousing programmes. It is also vital to combine this trend with the rise of a much more individualistic society that prized consumption and status over community spirit. As a consequence, it is perhaps not surprising that by the 1990s co-operative membership was almost one-third lower than it had been in the mid-1960s (see Appendix). Of course, intensifying competition from multiple retailers provided another key element in this increasingly difficult external environment, but this merely accentuated what had been a decisive socio-cultural shift that decisively affected the viability of local co-operatives. When combined with the power vested in boards that rarely engaged with their membership, it is apparent that by the 1980s any claims that the movement as a whole was based on democratic traditions could easily be challenged by looking at the extent to which members were consulted on key matters. Indeed, as we shall see over the following two chapters, many societies had become little more than fiefdoms dominated by a small clique, undermining both the democratic principle and any efforts to integrate the movement more effectively. While democracy was constantly used as a defence against the 'National Society' advocates, in reality this was used as a means of defending vested interests at a time when traditional loyalties were dissolving and consumerism replaced community as a key social driver. Moreover, it is also worth repeating the earlier point that an organizational lethargy restricted the influx of fresh talent into a movement that was in desperate need of new ideas and dynamic management.

It is in this context that we must judge the efforts of successive CWS management teams to encourage greater synergy and coordination across the movement. While from the vantage point of the twenty-first century it is easy to accuse them of neglect and apathy, on the other hand there were successive failures to drive through much-needed change, allowing institutional barriers to continue to resist reform. Above all, one must question whether sufficient work was done to set a new path for the movement as a whole, encouraging vested interests to adapt to the challenging environment. While throughout the 1970s Alfred Wilson and his successor as CEO, Arthur Sugden (Figure 7.13), worked industriously at finding solutions to the challenges faced by both the CWS and the movement as a whole, it is clear that little of substance was changed. Indeed, given the continuing decline in market share, not to mention the static performance of turnover and surplus, the CWS failed to provide the kind of leadership required to lever co-operative trading out of this vicious downward spiral. By the time

Dennis Landau was elevated from his deputy role to CEO, it was clear that unless decisive action was taken, then the slump would continue.[67]

While Landau's overall aim as CEO was to improve CWS's commercial performance, there would appear to have been three essential features to the strategy he outlined as the means of implementing that vision: increased integration across the CWS's limited retailing activities; developing closer links with retail societies; and vigorous rationalization of production and distribution activities, along with improved marketing and sales strategies.[68] Before going on to assess the degree of success achieved in implementing these strategies, it is also important to stress that Landau realized the importance of building an appropriate organizational structure capable of delivering results. In this context, Landau tightened up the managerial controls introduced in the late 1960s, especially in terms of monitoring cash flow across the organization. Another refinement was the reorganization in 1984 of the CWS into seven groups—Food Manufacturing; Milk; Fresh Foods; Retail Planning; Retail Management Services; Fuel and Motor Trades; and Non-Food Manufacturing. This provided much greater focus for the executive team, while with two groups linked to retailing it was clear that the CWS was beginning to

FIGURE 7.13. Sir Arthur Sugden (1918–2003). Born in Manchester, Sugden joined the CWS at the age of 14 but left to serve in the armed forces, becoming a major. After his return, he qualified as an accountant and moved up through CWS management, becoming deputy chief executive in 1971. He served as CWS chief executive from 1974 to 1980.

[67] CWSBM, 30 April 1980.

[68] These issues were extensively discussed at successive board meetings in the early 1980s. CWSBM, October 1980–July 1984.

switch its emphasis. The Retail Management Group had started life in 1968 as the Development Group, formed specifically to coordinate areas such as store improvements, product packaging, and quality.[69] This involved bringing together the formerly separate functions of estate management, architecture, engineering supplies, packaging, stationery, and the central laboratories, providing an opportunity to bring much greater coordination to the way that the CWS projected its image to consumers in its expanding retail operations.

Having effected these organizational refinements, and at the same time attempting to present a more cohesive image to customers and broader stakeholders, the new groups were also subjected to intense analysis in the 1980s, with CWS directors receiving detailed reports that highlighted both the challenges faced in various marketplaces and how well equipped the group was to cope with them.[70] By 1986, a Co-operative Trade Committee had also been formed, to replace the Wholesale/Retail Trade Committee, composed of representatives from the CWS, CU, and the nine largest retail societies. The aim behind this move was clearly to focus CWS resources on implementing strategies, bearing in mind the classic maxim that organizations need to ensure that structure and strategy are closely intertwined if they are going to improve performance. This highlights the efforts made by the CWS's Board in debating strategy and adapting the organization to these changed priorities. The question remains, however, whether all of these strategies were undermined by either the inherent institutional sclerosis and internecine difficulties that had been building over recent decades, or alternatively a lack of drive and leadership that would radically alter these dynamics.

One of the key factors in this scenario was the drive to achieve greater integration of co-operative retailing, CWS and other commentators recognizing that this would provide opportunities to capture economies of scale and scope for a movement that was struggling to compete. As we have already noted, both Regional Plans (1968 and 1974) had dismally failed to deliver concrete results: even though almost 500 independent societies disappeared between 1963 and 1976 (see Figure 7.12), there were still 217 trading at the end of that period.[71] This prompted extensive debate throughout the 1970s and early 1980s concerning the ability of local retail societies to withstand the mounting competition from multiple retailers such as Tesco, Sainsbury's, and ASDA which were able to coordinate their activities much more effectively from a strong central organization. By 1980, there were still 210 independent retail societies, and while as we noted earlier the leading twenty accounted for two-thirds of all co-operative sales, there was mounting evidence that both large and small societies lacked the resources to invest in either facilities or programmes that would make up for the continuing loss of market share. Moreover, those mergers that did occur in this period were from a position of weakness, in that the CWS and CRS were obliged to absorb societies because they could no longer survive as independent entities. For example, the CWS took over the Belfast

---

[69] CWSBM 5, 18 December 1982.   [70] CWSBM, June 1982–August 1983.
[71] Bamfield (1978a), 18.

Co-operative Society in 1982, as well as the even larger Royal Arsenal in 1985, while in 1981 the CRS acquired London Co-operative Society.

While on the one hand bringing these substantial societies into the CWS and CRS was an essential element in the drive to coordinate retailing, on the other hand these three societies brought with them cumulative losses exceeding £30 million. For example, in 1981–2 London Co-operative Society had lost £10.7 million, in addition to which further adjustments totalling £11.2 million had to be made to its accounts, adding significantly to the financial burden the CRS was inheriting.[72] By that time, The Co-operative Bank was threatening to withdraw overdraft facilities, forcing the London Board to seek CRS support or face bankruptcy. Indeed, such was the level of indebtedness being carried by the CRS in the early 1980s that it was essential for the CWS to step in when Royal Arsenal was obliged to accept the need for a merger, having recorded in the early 1980s losses of £10 million per annum on an annual turnover of £165 million. The CWS consequently borrowed £30 million to cover these losses and absorb this substantial business into a creaking organization. Inevitably, though, with interest charges rising inexorably on the increased borrowings, this ate decisively into CRS and CWS surpluses at a time when funds were required to improve competitiveness across the co-operative retailing sector. Given the earlier significant reduction in CWS reserves, arising from the propensity of retail societies to withdraw their funds, by the 1980s the CWS was clearly severely hampered in its drive to compete with better-endowed multiple retailers. Interest charges especially remained a major problem throughout the 1980s, with UK interest rates remaining high between 1979 and the mid-1990s, exacerbating the challenges associated with intensifying competition (see Table 7.2) that were forcing even more retail societies to seek refuge in either the CWS or CRS. The lack of funds, however, should not be regarded as the only problem, in that after the mergers the CWS failed to change either store formats or organizational dynamics; in effect, the opportunities associated with merger were not seized at that time, further diminishing competitive advantage at a time of intensifying competition. The CWS's impact was consequently much more rhetorical than actual, with market share continuing to fall throughout the 1980s in spite of continued concentration of co-operative trading.

Another dimension of this missed opportunity was the implications associated with the CRS's continued expansion. As Figure 7.12 indicates, while the number of mergers declined significantly after 1970, the scale of the losses absorbed by the CWS and CRS increased substantially. Crucially, for the CRS it was becoming impossible to withstand this kind of pressure, given its complete dependence on the CWS and internally generated funds, forcing the CWS to accept the need to absorb more failing societies. When combined with the competitive pressures emanating from multiple traders, this was bringing into question the viability of operating two organizations at a time when it was essential to bring as much of the movement together as possible. Landau (see Figure 7.14) was especially keen to deal with this recurring issue, specifically by initiating extensive

---

[72] CWSBM, September 1982.

discussions about a merger between the CWS and CRS. On his appointment as CEO, Landau had insisted that he should also sit on the CRS Board, in order to engineer closer collaboration between the two largest co-operative trading bodies. Such had been the apparent success of this manoeuvre, indeed, that by December 1982 a Tripartite Committee had been created, involving representatives of CWS and CRS boards and chaired by a CU representative. Over the following six months, in a succession of meetings that took up a considerable amount of senior management time, the Committee worked on a set of recommendations that was presented to the respective boards in February 1983. This plan involved the creation of a holding company, frequently referred to across the movement as 'The New Society', which would coordinate the merged activities of the CRS and CWS, ultimately bringing the CIS and The Co-operative Bank into this body, as well as providing greater momentum behind the absorption of larger retail societies into a Co-operative 'Group'.[73] As we shall see in Chapter 9, this pre-empted by almost twenty years the creation of The Co-operative Group, providing the leadership and cohesion that would underpin a commercial recovery.

It is apparent from both CWS Board minutes and interviewing key figures that considerable effort was put into these negotiations, senior CWS managers especially devoting extensive resources to drawing up proposals and lobbying for broad support. After the initial proposals were discussed at board level in February 1983, however, it was apparent

FIGURE 7.14. **Sir Dennis Landau.** After a successful career at Cadbury Schweppes, Landau joined the CWS as food controller in 1971 and became deputy chief executive in 1974. He served as CWS chief executive from 1980 to 1992.

[73] CWSBM, February 1983.

that significant problems would be encountered in implementing a scheme that effectively allowed the CWS to absorb the CRS. The first problem that Landau and his team had to contend with was the ill-health of the CRS CEO, R. A. (Alfred) Lee, who absented himself from the meetings early in 1983. Eventually, in September 1983, Lee retired on health grounds, to be replaced by W. H. Farrow (Figure 7.15). Although Beaumont claims that an ideologically committed group of left-wing activists from the London Co-operative Society had infiltrated the CRS Board after the 1981 merger, their role at that time can easily be exaggerated. The core issue was leadership, in that no consensus could be reached on whether Landau or Farrow should run the combined operations. As a direct result, when it became apparent that the CWS's corporate members were more inclined to support Landau, by the end of 1983 Farrow decided to withdraw from the discussions and reassert CRS independence. This issue was also compounded by the differences in membership structures, in that while the CWS had by the 1980s a substantial number of individual members as a result of its recent acquisition of many retail societies (see Table 7.3), decision-making was dominated by the corporate membership. In contrast, individual members had a strong voice in the CRS, a feature that its Board wanted to sustain.

FIGURE 7.15. E. W. Farrow. Following the retirement of Alfred Lee, Farrow became chief executive of the CRS, serving from 1983 to 1987. Farrow's long co-operative career began in Oldham at the age of 14, and by the early 1980s he was a well-known co-operative leader, having recently led the North Midlands Society into a merger with Greater Lancastria that formed the nucleus of United Co-operatives.

Table 7.3. Number of retail societies joining the CRS and CWS, 1956–95

Year	CRS	CWS
1956–60	26	–
1961–5	37	–
1966–70	47	–
1971–5	17	1
1976–80	4	14
1981–5	12	22
1986–90	4	4
1991–5	11	11

Sources: CRS balance sheets and *Co-operative Statistics* (1956–95).

The collapse of this round of talks, after consuming months of valuable management time when it could be least afforded, was symptomatic of the tone of CWS–CRS relations over the following seventeen years, because the desire of CRS leadership to dominate 'The New Society' certainly soured relations and ensured that integration would be resisted. Even though as Table 7.3 reveals both continued to absorb struggling societies, CRS leadership entrenched their independence in a movement that continued to be characterized by a lack of co-operation. The CRS's independence was also further reinforced by various rule changes, starting in 1977 when it was agreed that the CWS no longer had the right to nominate the CRS's chairman, while the post of CRS secretary was also moved from the CWS to the CRS CEO. Although in 1987 the CWS was able to secure the election of Harry Moore as Farrow's successor as CEO, leading to further discussions of a CWS–CRS merger, in effect this became an attempt by the latter to acquire its larger counterpart. The origins of these discussions was a report commissioned by the CWS from Peat Marwick McLintock, the prominent accountancy firm (now part of KPMG), which outlined the financial shortcomings of running two separate bodies.[74] It was unfortunate, though, that elements within the CRS were merely exploiting Landau's imminent retirement as an opportunity to acquire the CWS. This not surprisingly provoked a strong response from the CWS, resulting in yet another missed opportunity to forge a much stronger central core. By the time Landau had retired in June 1992, the two secondary co-operatives were as far apart as at any time in their history, preventing rationalization at a crucial time in the movement's history.

In spite of the failure to bring the CRS into the CWS fold, it is apparent from Table 7.3 that the latter succeeded in absorbing more societies. While developing closer relations with retail societies was especially close to Landau's heart, having committed himself from the outset of his tenure as CEO to travel around the country to talk to senior managers in both small and large operations, most of the mergers were a consequence of competitive failure. Similarly, the emergence of larger regional groupings during the

[74] CWSBM, October 1987.

1970s resulted in an even greater unwillingness to work with either the CWS or CRS. While Landau later vividly claimed that 'We encouraged the mergers then the mergers spat in our face!',[75] it is apparent that CWS leadership was outmanoeuvred by the regional groupings that emerged from the 1970s because they developed an even stronger sense of their importance and independence as a result of consolidation. An excellent example of this trend was the creation in May 1983 of United Co-operatives Ltd, a merger of the Lancastria and North Midland groups that had already resisted CWS entreaties to collaborate more closely, not least because of their geographical proximity in the north-west of England. As we shall see more explicitly over the next two chapters, however, United Co-operatives resisted these approaches, developing a highly independent (and successful) approach to its commercial strategies. Indeed, United demonstrated what was achievable, while the CWS continued to struggle against both internecine conflict and overwhelming competition from the multiples.

This resistance to efforts at leadership by the CWS became even more intense in the 1980s, notwithstanding the movement's continued loss of market share (see Table 7.2). As we noted earlier, Landau was especially keen to create greater cohesion across the movement, specifically encouraging the part-time CWS directors who voted through his policy changes to support these initiatives on returning to their local societies. In his 1982 New Year message to the movement, after reporting that he had visited many retail societies to discuss greater harmonization, Landau stated that the CWS ought to 'get closer to our retail society colleagues—the people we exist to serve'.[76] In spite of the clear economic case for greater integration, however, such pleas frequently fell on deaf ears at regional and local levels, undermining attempts at capturing the economies of scope and scale available across the movement. In effect, retail societies looked on the CWS as a lumbering bureaucracy that was incapable of offering either the leadership or managerial resources required to improve performance. An excellent example of this fractious relationship was the complaint tabled by Portsea Co-operative Society at the 1980 AGM, accusing the CWS of encroaching excessively into retailing.[77] Although this ignored the absorption of many retail societies in order to avoid the disappearance of co-operative trading, the complaint reinforces the point that most societies refused to accept rhetorical pleas to bring about much-needed rationalization and integration.

While the first two aspects of Landau's plan were dependent on the collaboration of other parts of the movement, the third—to develop and enhance the CWS's distribution and production activities—was an activity that the organization could pursue itself. Improving the efficiency of CWS factories was an especially important aim, given the imperative need to keep its products and services competitive with the significantly larger alternative suppliers that dominated various industries by the 1980s.[78] Given the macro-economic challenges and socio-economic changes described in section 7.1, consumers were much more selective when choosing either where to shop or on which brands they would rely. These trends obliged the CWS to place an even greater emphasis

---

[75] Interview with Sir Dennis Landau.   [76] CWSBM, January 1982.
[77] CWSBM, June 1980.   [78] See Hannah and Kay (1977).

on the use of modern technology and premises if the factories were going to compete. It was also notable that the CWS was the only major multiple retailer which was still involved in production, all of the others having retreated from this form of vertical integration and used their buying power to negotiate with suppliers. This phenomenon also needs to be combined with the rise of the retailer brand, with multiples developing close relationships with specialist manufacturers and suppliers which were capable of then developing products in response to requests for volume orders.

As we saw in the last chapter, CWS production activities had dwindled significantly from the 1930s peak, when as a vertically integrated operation it ran over 200 factories and workshops manufacturing an extremely diverse range of products.[79] In the 1960s especially capacity had been severely reduced, either by selling operations (for example, the Derby paint works and Birmingham cycle factory), concentrating production into a single large plant (for example, preserves in Stockport, see Figure 7.16), or entering into joint ventures with rivals (for example, J. Lyons & Co in baking, and Fatstock Marketing in bacon). The CWS had since the 1960s struggled to generate much of a surplus from its manufacturing activities, recording returns on sales of less than 1 per cent throughout the 1980s, even though sales rose from £1.81 million in 1980 to just under £3 million by 1990. This reveals yet another weakness in the CWS's portfolio, reflecting a failure to ensure that activities remained competitive at a time when other manufacturers were investing heavily in new technologies. By 1987, the CWS was operating just thirty-five units (excluding dairies), ten of which were food-related. At the same time, it is also worth noting that in the period 1984–93 the CWS invested £75.2 million in upgrading these operations,[80] indicating how a modernization programme was initiated. One of the most effective investments was the £3.1 million spent between 1973 and 1976 rebuilding the Crewe tea factory, providing the CWS with a highly efficient source of its most successful single product.

Another example of the way in which the CWS pursued this programme was at Shieldhall, Glasgow. Having inherited this complex from SCS when it merged into CWS in 1973, it became apparent that while Shieldhall (shown in Figure 7.17) represented a valuable cluster of businesses, covering everything from furniture and clothing production, printing and stationery, and food and drinks packing, it was vital to update much of the plant and machinery. The Shieldhall complex had actually been opened in 1887, and even though some of the facilities had been improved during the 1950s and 1960s there remained problems with the plant and factories. The CWS consequently decided in 1978 to instigate radical changes to what was branded a 'co-operative industrial estate', resulting in a three-year programme of improvements that would create a highly efficient cluster of businesses capable of providing retail societies with relatively cheap, but good-quality, goods.[81] The surviving factories in the CWS's manufacturing network were similarly revamped—the glass containers business at Wigan and Worksop benefited from £10 million worth of investment between 1978 and 1981[82]—creating a much more

---

[79] See section 6.5.   [80] CWSBM, January 1994.
[81] CWSBM, April 1978.   [82] CWSBM, November 1981.

FIGURE 7.16. **CWS confectionary works, Reddish, *c.*1960s.** This factory, in Stockport, was built in the late 1930s. It was modernized in the 1960s when the CWS consolidated its preserves and confectionery production. It was sold to Rank Hovis McDougal in 1989.

efficient and profitable group that up to the early 1990s contributed effectively to the CWS's performance as a conglomerate.

The rationalization and modernization of the CWS's productive capacity was clearly a much-needed aspect of the way this Leviathan was being brought under stronger central direction. When combined with the other dimensions of the CWS's strategies, at the very least it represented the realism which was beginning to feature prominently in New Century House, as opposed to the doggedly traditionalist approach that had dominated previously. At the same time, in focusing production primarily on food it is also vital to stress that this represented the slowest-growing sector of retailing in which competition was at its most intense. Of course, especially in sectors such as clothing, footwear, and houseware, as we noted in section 7.1 the CWS just could not compete with the much cheaper imported goods that since the early 1970s had been flooding into the domestic market. Indeed, the UK clothing industry was struggling badly, especially in the 1979–82 recession, when 5,000 jobs were disappearing every month.[83] This trend made it even more imperative that loss-making factories should

[83] CWSBM, June 1980.

FIGURE 7.17. SCWS Shieldhall complex, Glasgow, 1969. The factory complex at Shieldhall began with boot, shoe, and tailoring works in 1887 and included sixteen factories by 1914. As with the CWS Pelaw Works, many SCWS goods were branded 'Shieldhall'. Following the merger, in the late 1970s CWS initiated a modernization programme at Shieldhall, including a new drinks works.

be either closed or sold, but at the same time it forced the CWS to depend even more heavily on the slow-growing food sector, limiting the prospects for real growth in turnover and surpluses for investment.

Another important dimension of the CWS's productive activities, of course, was the dairy business, given that in 1976 it still supplied 30 per cent of all bottled milk to UK consumers (see Figure 7.18).[84] This market position was strenuously defended throughout the late twentieth century, through both significant investment programmes in modern plant and restructuring the business. For example, in 1984 the CWS committed £1.85 million to enhancing the Belfast dairy plant,[85] while during the 1980s each of the regions were requested to initiate a process of merging plants and distribution networks, in order to achieve economies of scale and scope.[86] At the same time, co-operative retailers failed to adapt to the new packaging techniques that would decisively

[84] CWSBM, October 1976.   [85] CWSBM, July 1984.
[86] CWSBM, July 1984.

switch consumption away from the traditional bottle that was delivered at the doorstep every day to more flexible coated cardboard containers that could be purchased at the weekly shop in superstores. This was yet further evidence that co-operative trading was tied to traditional techniques that were rapidly being overhauled by the more flexible multiple retailers, undermining commercial performance across the broad gamut of CWS activities.

Linked to these changes in productive capacity was an attempt to improve the distribution and marketing of co-operative goods. As we saw in Chapter 6, although in 1963 the CWS had initiated a plan to build regional distribution centres, as a first step in reducing the enormous number of warehouses that had been built since the late nineteenth century, due to resistance from regional retail societies by the mid-1970s only 35 per cent of total co-operative grocery sales were supplied through this system.[87] While from the mid-1970s much greater effort was put into persuading societies to sign up to what became a network of eight warehouses, all coordinated through the Co-operative Retail Liaison Committee, as we shall see in section 9.1 even the most substantial retail societies such as United Norwest were reluctant to honour the aspiration and promises of this body, preferring instead to utilize their own systems. This again highlights the limitations imposed by the movement's federal structure, because

FIGURE 7.18. Co-operative milk float, Sharston, c.1980s. In 1985, doorstep deliveries accounted for more than 80% of milk sales, and the CWS's Milk Group accounted for about 28% of the liquid milk market. This milk float, delivering in south Manchester, probably belonged to the Norwest society, which had a processing dairy in the vicinity.

[87] Richardson (1977), 326–7.

even though the benefits of securing significant savings from bulk buying and distribution were evident to all, few societies were willing to accede to CWS control of their buying policies.

Given this reluctance to think collectively on such fundamental aspects of retailing, it is also no surprise that imposing a common CO-OP label across the movement proved to be problematic. We noted earlier that the CWS had been obliged to adapt its slogan 'Your Caring Sharing Co-op' to 'The Co-operative Difference', as a means of persuading more retail societies to participate in this attempt at presenting consumers with a cohesive image. Similarly, space was frequently taken in *Co-operative News* to project a common brand,[88] while consumer surveys were conducted to assess the efficacy of this activity. We shall return to a study of CWS marketing in the next chapter, but it is nevertheless clear, given the definitive evidence in Table 7.2 on declining market share, that such marketing drives were failing to make the kind of impact CWS had anticipated. Above all, whether one considers retailing, manufacturing, or distribution, the movement lacked decisive leadership in coping with the late twentieth-century challenges, allowing the dysfunctional federation to continue to dominate.

Having made this critical point, it is vital to stress some of the positive aspects of the CWS's investment strategy during the 1980s. In particular, and responding to the way in which multiple traders were investing enormously in superstores and hypermarkets, in 1982 the CWS established a Superstores Group, the first act of which was to tour the USA in order to learn valuable lessons from the originators of this organizational form.[89] This resulted in the purchase of twenty-two superstores from Mainstop, at a cost of £25 million,[90] reflecting its intention to try to match its competitors and move away from its traditional dependence on the local convenience store format. This strategy was even more advanced in Scotland, where in both Paisley and Inverness superstores were constructed in the late 1970s, replacing a string of local stores. By the mid-1980s, even though over 60 per cent of co-operative grocery trade took place in small stores (under 4,000 sq. feet), the CWS was operating sixty superstores (see Figure 7.19), as well as another 120 that occupied between 15,000 and 20,000 square feet,[91] indicating the extent to which the business was trying to compete with its main rivals. While in Chapter 8 we shall assess whether this was a sensible strategy, given the heavy presence of rivals in this retailing sector, it is difficult to be critical of the CWS, given the contemporary preoccupation with large store formats and the desire to pursue a unidirectional strategy at Tesco, ASDA, and Sainsbury's. On the other hand, one must stress that the co-operative commitment to superstores proved to be a temporary phenomenon, diverting attention away from the convenience store strategy that had always been a prominent feature of co-operative retailing.

---

[88] CWSBM, April 1982. [89] CWSBM, June 1982.
[90] CWSBM, October 1982. [91] CWSBM, November 1982.

FIGURE 7.19. Royal Arsenal Co-operative Society superstore, Southwark, 1970s. In the 1970s and 1980s, many co-operative societies developed superstores and hypermarkets and by 1982 the CWS had established a Superstores Group. By the mid-1980s, the CWS operated around 60 superstores, although small format stores accounted for nearly two-thirds of its total trade.

7.5 CONCLUSIONS

This discussion of how the CWS was investing in a superstore format that was becoming increasingly popular for British consumers reflects how by 1990 the organization's business model was already being transformed. In part, of course, adaptation and transformation was forced upon CWS executives, in that the acquisition of the SCS and accession of an increasing number of struggling retail societies extended the business directly into retailing. While the CWS was also clearly committed to revamping production and distribution facilities from the 1960s, either modernizing these functions as a means of improving their competitiveness or closing down a substantial part of its capacity, it was apparent that the traditional business model was no longer viable as retailing took up more of its resources. Crucially, executives realized that the expanding retail network not only provided more direct access to consumers, but also an expanded market for the output of its manufacturing and distribution operations. This changed emphasis became especially apparent in the early 1980s. As Landau stated in a 1984 address to CWS managers:

... We should shift our procurement and distribution role away from 'profit' towards a basis of 'cost and service', that we must remove the speculative, stockholding and selling elements from our wholesaling and become instead a distributor, buying on behalf of retail societies.[92]

[92] CWSBM, January 1984.

This closely echoed the sentiments expressed by Lambert in the early 1960s, indicating that over this twenty-year period very little had changed: while there was plenty of rhetorical exhortation from the centre, this failed to persuade retail societies to collaborate more effectively with the CWS, other than those in the deepest financial trouble. In his AGM speech of May 1987, Landau went on to add that the CWS needed 'to focus proper attention and resource on the development of the extensive retail operations in which [we have] become involved'.[93] Although he recognized that this was a long-term process, largely contingent on an improvement in profitability, the new focus on retailing indicated how the business model was beginning to adapt. Crucially, as the data in Table 7.2 reveals, this process was taking far too long to influence market share, indicating that rhetorical exhortation was simply not working.

In evaluating this process, it is important to stress that the CWS was severely handicapped by two fundamental internal challenges. In the first place, and certainly in contrast to the major multiple retailers that were capable of mobilizing substantial financial resources, the CWS could never generate the scale of funds required to revamp all of its activities. While to a certain extent this failing can be attributed to the severe late 1960s decline in financial reserves, the key factor was a sluggish growth in profitability and the acquisition of a host of loss-making retail societies, eating substantially into accumulated reserves. Even though The Co-operative Bank developed impressively during the 1970s and 1980s, by the end of the period profits were difficult to come by in that sector, accentuating the CWS's liquidity challenges. Even though the CWS acquired forty-one retail societies between 1973 and 1990, Figure 7.10 illustrates that in real terms turnover growth was virtually non-existent, highlighting the commercial failings of a business that was just not responding effectively to the market challenges. Moreover, as Figure 7.11 reveals, while there were periods (late 1970s and again in the late 1980s) when the surplus increased significantly at both current and constant prices, the CWS was never able to generate the kind of returns that a competitor such as Tesco or Sainsbury's could produce. This is apparent from comparative data, because while in the period 1969–78 the CWS invested an annual average of £42 million on all parts of its expansive business, Tesco spent an average of £22.5 million on retailing alone, while the equivalent figure for Sainsbury's was £19.5 million.[94] Similarly, and introducing the second internal challenge, it is not clear whether the movement was ready to accept the kind of leadership role to which the CWS was aspiring. Indeed, as we have stressed many times in this and previous chapters, the dysfunctional nature of the co-operative federation ensured that New Century House was always kept at arm's length by even its corporate membership. In simple terms, even if the CWS had been well endowed with financial resources, it is not clear that executives would have been able to pursue their strategies as effectively as necessary in an increasingly competitive market environment. In addition, the CRS's resistance to all entreaties to integrate with its parent organization compounded the difficulties associated with achieving the synergies required if the CWS was going to improve its performance.

[93] D. Laudau (1987), 7.   [94] CWSBM, April 1980.

Overall, it is difficult to exonerate CWS executives from any blame for the continued decline in market share, poor financial performance, and retrenchment in traditional markets; effective leadership places as much emphasis on accepting responsibility for both success and failure. Returning to the accusations made by Sparks concerning the alleged inability of CWS executives to act as 'change agents' capable of overcoming resistance,[95] it is clear from what we have seen in this chapter that while institutional sclerosis and internecine conflict severely afflicted the movement up to the 1990s, limiting the effectiveness of strategic or structural changes, it is difficult to detect the kind of drive required to effect real change. Another issue which ought to be emphasized was the obstacles this sclerotic organization put in place when considering an infusion of fresh talent; as Melmoth noted when entering the CWS in the mid-1970s, the organization was more like 'a monastery' than a modern business with effective human resource strategies.[96] These organizational issues were also further compounded by the commercial position in which the CWS found itself, because in competing against much better-resourced multiple retailers which from the 1970s operated highly integrated organizations that adopted most of the latest improvements in logistics and automated warehousing, strategic decision-making lacked dynamism. In view of declining market share, limited financial resources, and weak marketing efforts, it was apparent to almost all external observers that it was time to adapt the business model to these challenges. At the same time, as a direct result of its acquisition of an increasing number of failing retail societies, the CWS was evolving from its original function as a secondary into a primary co-operative, while the role of independent societies (CWS's shareholder members) was also diminishing. We shall now move on to assess how in the 1990s a new style of leadership addressed this challenge, reinvigorating the CWS and reaffirming co-operative values and principles while opportunistically seizing a chance created by external intervention to leverage the entire movement into a new era.

[95] Sparks (1994), 52.   [96] Interview with Sir Graham Melmoth.

CHAPTER 8

....

THE WATERSHED DECADE

....

HAVING highlighted how between the 1940s and 1980s co-operative trading experienced significant deterioration in commercial performance, with market share especially in steep decline and the movement as a whole proving notoriously slow to respond effectively, it is fascinating to assess how from the 1990s a recovery would appear to have been initiated, belying contemporary predictions of a painfully slow demise. One ought to stress that this was an iterative process, with each step building on the foundations laid by earlier initiatives. Nevertheless, this overcame what had been the major problems—ineffectual leadership and an ossified management structure, a lack of fresh managerial talent, tensions between the member-elected Board and senior managers, and conflicts between the CWS and other bodies such as the CRS—that lay at the heart of the problem. As one external commentator noted, while CWS executives attempted to ape their corporate counterparts in other parts of British business, they were unable to replicate the organizational changes that were taking place.[1] Of course, the key issue facing the CWS was coordinating the disparate, sprawling Leviathan-like business empire, and in particular creating an organization capable of exploiting the potentially enormous economies of scale and scope across the entire co-operative 'family'. At the same time, CWS managers also needed to come to terms with the dynamics associated with a changing membership structure, given the incursion of individual consumers into a structure that had been originally built around corporate members. As the voice of individual consumers had always been absent from CWS deliberations, this heightened the tensions between the secondary co-operative and its primary shareholders, and especially with the CRS, limiting the prospects of greater collaboration.

In dealing with these challenges, we shall see how the late 1990s offered an opportunity that was seized with alacrity by the CWS. Indeed, a watershed was forged by a new style of leadership that was much more determined both to alter radically the CWS's business model, yet at the same time reinforce the co-operative mission and philosophy. The initial personification of this leadership style was manifested in Graham Melmoth, who in the early 1990s was prominent in pushing through a reaffirmation of co-operative principles, working closely with the International Co-operative Alliance (ICA). At the same time, prompted by a series of scandals involving managers at both the CWS and

---

[1] Interview with John Sandford. See J. F. Wilson (1995), chapter 6, for insights into British corporate developments.

retail societies that struck at the very heart of a movement built on the claim to be an ethical trader, radical changes to the corporate governance system were also introduced. These changes coincided with the emergence of a much more ethical approach to trading, starting with The Co-operative Bank, but spreading to many other parts of the CWS, stridently differentiating the business from its main rivals. Having been appointed to the CEO post in 1996, Melmoth was then confronted in 1997 by a City financier's attempt to buy the CWS, providing the opportunity for co-operative opinion to coalesce around the need for change. Crucially, in exposing the fundamental differences between the movement's core values and principles and those of an unscrupulous world of finance, Melmoth vigorously highlighted its value to society, using the takeover bid to engineer a chain of events that would prove crucial in altering the CWS's commercial trajectory.

While focusing on these decisive changes, and providing the essential background to what will be analysed in Chapter 9, it is also important to correct a bias in the extant literature,[2] namely, an excessive focus on the CWS's retail and distribution activities. As we have stressed many times in previous chapters, the CWS was a Leviathan operating across a wide range of commercial activities, including banking, insurance, manufacturing, farming, property, and specialist retail businesses such as funeral services, travel, opticians, and motor services. A central plank of Melmoth's vision for the CWS was to create 'a family of co-operative businesses' that was not only capable of improving performance, but also achieving commercial synergies.[3] At the same time, by looking more closely at The Co-operative Bank and the funeral services business, it is possible to detect how their customer-facing approach provided a template on which later strategies would be based. Again, it is vital to stress that this was an evolutionary process, but the lessons learned from building highly successful banking and funeral services businesses would prove invaluable to how the CWS evolved. Above all, it was in the late 1990s that the CWS and the broader movement started to respond to the challenges that over the previous three decades had undermined its whole *raison d'être*, providing a sound base for what would happen in the early twenty-first century.

8.1 EARLY 1990S RATIONALIZATION AND CORPORATE GOVERNANCE REFORM

Even though up to the early 1990s there had been some progress in starting to move the CWS away from its outdated business model to one based much more on a realistic assessment of its changed orientation—namely, building the retail operation and switching from 'selling to' to 'buying for' co-operative societies—progress was stinted by the dysfunctional nature of a movement that had for many decades proved resistant

---

[2] See for example the work of Ekberg (2008).
[3] See Co-operative Commission (2001); and Yeo (2002).

to radical measures. Another severe economic slump had also struck the UK economy in the late 1980s, reducing demand and intensifying competition amongst retailers. A damaging side-effect of this recession was the return of high interest rates, reaching 15 per cent in 1992 when the pound sterling was rudely ejected from the European Exchange Rate Mechanism, forcing successive governments to protect the currency for the rest of the decade. This compounded the problems that had limited the CWS's ability to invest extensively in its ageing stock of shops, factories, and distribution facilities, because with borrowings having exceeded £300 million by 1991[4] and The Co-operative Bank struggling to generate the kind of results it had recorded in the expansionary 1980s, liquidity remained a major challenge. The internecine hostilities between the CWS and CRS, alongside a reluctance on the part of retail societies to work more closely with other parts of the movement, also limited the prospects of achieving many of the economies of scale and scope available in an organization covering such a wide range of activities.

In view of these internal and external challenges, it is perhaps no surprise that multiple retailers such as ASDA, Tesco, Sainsbury's, and Safeway continued to extend their share of British consumption (see Table 7.2). The big success story of the 1990s, of course, was the rise to prominence of Tesco, under the vigorous management of Terry Leahy, knocking Sainsbury's from its top spot (in market share) and obliging Morrison's to merge with Safeway in order to compete.[5] With out-of-town retail parks having replaced the corner-shop at the end of every street as the preferred place to buy not only food, but also most consumer durable goods,[6] their market share increased decisively: while in 1950 multiple retailers accounted for just 20 per cent of British grocery sales, by 1971 this had more than doubled to 41 per cent, rising to 81 per cent by 1998. By capturing the economies of scale and scope available in highly integrated distribution systems that served ever-larger retail outlets, these firms attracted an increasing proportion of British food and other types of consumption. Tesco also developed a multi-directional retail strategy, investing in both convenience stores and larger units as a means of catering for different types of consumer.[7] As Table 8.1 reveals, co-operative stores' share of total UK retail trade fell inexorably from its 1950 peak, reaching just 4.4 per cent by 2000. While the CWS and retail societies had attempted to match the strategies of their better-resourced private rivals, most notably by building superstores and hypermarkets (like that in Figure 8.1), the late twentieth century was clearly characterized by sluggish competitive performance that proved difficult to transform.

Returning to the themes already outlined in previous chapters, and referring specifically to the arguments presented by Ekberg, internal political obstacles to coordinated reform within the movement became even more intractable in the post-war period. While the number of retail societies fell from over 500 during the Second World War to just 42 by 2002, the emergence of large and relatively well-resourced regional co-operatives inspired an even stronger sense of independence from the CWS.[8] Indeed, some of

---

[4] CWSBM, 31 January 1991.   [5] Sparks (1994).   [6] Sparks (1994), 3–19.
[7] Sparks (1994).   [8] Ekberg (2008), 59 and 300.

Table 8.1. Co-operative societies' share of total
UK retail trade, 1900–2000

Year	Share of total UK retail trade (%)
1900	15
1950	23
1960	21
1970	15
1980	12
1990	5.5
2000	4.4

Sources: Data for UK supplied by Dr Jim Quinn from research
conducted in *The Grocer*.

the larger retail societies developed their own wholesale activities to rival those of the
CWS, just as the CWS had branched out into retailing, replicating functions and curtail-
ing their ability to take advantage of mass, national-scale buying in bulk. The ingrained
spirit of regional and local independence, and a lukewarm, occasionally hostile, attitude

FIGURE 8.1. **CWS superstore, Nottingham, 1994.** Superstores like this one, renovated by the
CWS following the Greater Nottingham society merger in 1992, were seen as critical to
co-operative retail strategy in the early 1990s.

towards the CWS which had characterized relations within the movement since the formation of the CWS in 1863, lived on into the 1990s. Apart from the failure to secure economies of scale and scope, there was also conclusive evidence of a failure to match the multiples on productivity. While there were big variations across the multiples, with Tesco outpacing its rivals significantly in the 1990s, sales per square foot in co-operative outlets stagnated at just one-half of those achieved in the multiple retailers.[9] In simple terms, increasingly affluent and well-informed consumers were turning elsewhere for their purchases, indicating that the CO-OP brand was undoubtedly suffering from a negative image that resonated more of a former age, especially compared to the shiny retail 'palaces' of multiple retailers and their well-developed brands. As Seth and Randall summarized the movement's early 1990s predicament, there was 'no capital, no strategy, no store profile, in essence no co-operation.'[10]

This dismal analysis of the movement's competitive prospects is well borne out in Figures 8.2 and 8.3, which respectively reveal how in terms of turnover and surplus the 1990s proved in real terms (at 1974 prices) to be just as challenging as the three previous decades. The turnover data was especially unconvincing, with a brief surge in 1993 that tapered off badly over the next five years, while at constant prices it remained flat

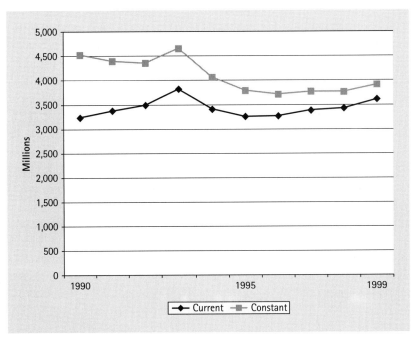

FIGURE 8.2. CWS turnover in current and constant (1974) prices, 1990–9 (£ million).

[9] Seth and Randall (1999), 140–3.   [10] Seth and Randall (1999), 142.

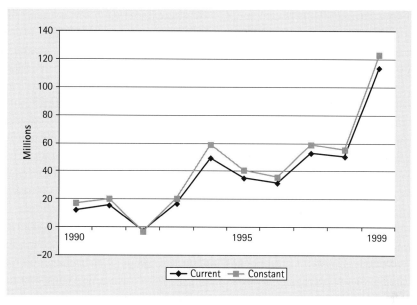

FIGURE 8.3. CWS surplus in current and constant (1974) prices, 1990–2000 (£ million).

throughout the decade. More worryingly, the CWS recorded a trading deficit in 1992 (of £2.85 million). The trading surplus was, indeed, under intense pressure throughout the early 1990s, a point substantiated by the revelation that in 1990 the CWS made more profit (£13.6 million) on selling redundant property than on all other businesses (£6.1 million). In this context, the CWS failed to imitate other multiples which sold their property on leaseback terms, thereby raising substantial quantities of capital by leveraging their assets.[11] Even though there was a recovery in profits up to 1995, the mid-1990s slump in CWS surplus came at a most unfortunate point in its history, as we shall see later. One should also stress that the late 1990s surge was mainly a result of booming profits from The Co-operative Bank, a story we shall relate in section 8.2, while the food retailing business that accounted for over 70 per cent of CWS turnover continued to struggle in response to the aggressive strategies pursued by its rivals.

Given this distinctly unimpressive performance, as well as the widely publicized data in Table 8.1, it was consequently clear that the CWS needed to pursue radical solutions that might either inject fresh capital into the business or help to reverse what many felt was a process of institutional decline. With the CWS's debts having risen to over £300 million by 1991, largely as a result of accepting the accession of so many failing retail societies, it was especially important to reduce interest payments, thereby freeing up resources for investment in more expansive strategies. The CWS had even resorted to borrowing £14 million from its pension scheme, all of which was repaid through the issue by S. G. Warburg of £50 million in debenture capital.[12] At the same time, as much

[11] Sparks (1994).   [12] CWSBM, 12 January 1994.

greater emphasis was being placed on the switch from 'buying for', rather than 'selling to' retail societies, senior management was beginning to question whether the CWS needed to retain its remaining manufacturing activities. As we noted in the last chapter, a key feature of Landau's period as CEO had been both the closure of many non-food factories and modernization in key areas such as dairy, flour processing, and tobacco. Landau's successor, David Skinner (shown in Figure 8.4), sustained this programme, resulting in a total of £75.2 million being invested in these facilities between 1984 and 1993, significantly improving the competitiveness of own-brand goods. This can be substantiated by noting that by 1993 24 per cent of output was being sold to non-co-operative retailers, the CWS having set up a marketing arm, F. E. Barber, specifically to sell to this type of customer. By 1994, however, compared to 200 manufacturing operations in 1945, CWS had just two creameries, ten food, and two textiles factories, with sales of £304 million and 3,250 employees.[13] While this strategy proved extremely successful—in 1990 the return on capital employed in food manufacturing was 20.1 per cent, a record that was only exceeded by funerals (20.5 per cent) and farms (24.1 per cent), while food retailing languished at just 5.8 per cent—there was considerable concern that competitors offering single runs of products at marginal cost would undermine performance.[14] Indeed, Skinner prompted extensive debate amongst CWS directors over the issue of selling the manufacturing operations,[15] as he recognized both the value of capitalizing on what was

FIGURE 8.4. **David Skinner.** After six years as the deputy in charge of retail and services, Skinner took over as the CWS's chief executive from 1992 to 1996. During his tenure he pursued additional amalgamations that increased the CWS's retail operations, including mergers with societies in Brighton, Cumbria, Kent, and Nottingham.

---

[13] CWSBM, 12 January 1994.   [14] CWSBM, 15 September 1993.
[15] CWSBM, 9 December 1992; 20 January, 14 June, and 12 January 1993.

still a commercially viable business and further adapting the business model to trading conditions.

Before analysing this adaptation process further, a vital feature of this move was the person who led the purchase, Andrew Regan, an entrepreneur with impeccable contacts amongst blue-chip City institutions and prominent household and food products firms.[16] Regan's first venture into business had been in 1985, when at the age of just 18 he had established Cadismark Household Products. Using his close contacts with David Thompson, the chief executive of the leading food processor Hillsdown Holdings, he acquired one of that firm's subsidiaries, Hobson, merged it with Cadismark and proceeded to recruit a management team capable of building a flourishing business.[17] It was as chief executive of Hobson that in 1994 Regan came to prominence, when he borrowed £30 million from Lloyds Bank and floated £80 million worth of shares, underwritten by the Swiss Banking Corporation, to purchase for £111 million the CWS's food manufacturing operations, including F. E. Barber.[18] Crucially, this deal included a three-year agreement to continue to supply CWS customers, worth £220 million per year, providing Hobson with a sound business model. The sale was finally completed in May 1994,[19] but from the outset Regan demonstrated a ruthless streak that set him apart from his co-operative counterparts: even though he had assured CWS executives that existing employees would not be affected by the acquisition,[20] he immediately closed two factories and sold off a further two operations, reflecting a desire to improve productivity across his new business. In 1995 he also paid £2.85 million for a two-year extension to the original deal to supply the CWS, significantly enhancing the value of his streamlined operation.

While as we shall see later this contract negotiation became the subject of legal investigations, having such a secure source of custom proved extremely lucrative. One should also stress that this extension had been negotiated with Allan Green, Deputy Head of Food at CWS, but without the involvement of CWS Board members, who were only informed of the deal in 1997, by which time it was apparent that this executive had been supplying Regan with considerable quantities of confidential CWS data. It was also discovered that Hobson had paid £2.4 million into a private Swiss bank account to Ronald Zimet of Trellis International, a company registered in British Virgin Islands, in return for allegedly acting as an intermediary in the contract extension negotiations. The failure to provide an adequate explanation for this payment later persuaded Swiss Banking Corporation to withdraw its services to Regan's business, resulting in the latter starting an ill-fated relationship with Hambros Bank.[21] Crucially, though, Hobson was such a

---

[16] Regan's father, Roger Regan, had been chairman of Fine Art Wallcoverings up to 1993, at which point, and largely as a result of a shareholder revolt against incumbent management, he was appointed chairman of Spring Ram, the building materials group that had recently experienced severe difficulties. *Independent*, 12 July 1993.

[17] *Sunday Telegraph*, 13 February 1994.   [18] CWSBM, 2 February 1994.

[19] CWSBM, 27 May 1994.   [20] CWSBM, 30 March 1994.   [21] *Independent*, 24 April 1997.

highly attractive proposition that in December 1995 Hillsdown Holdings paid £121 million for the business, reportedly making Andrew Regan a £3 million profit on his original investment, after paying off his financial supporters.[22]

Regan will return to prominence in section 8.3, when we will analyse his attempt to buy the CWS. His 1994 intervention, though, was an essential part of the CWS's response to the multi-faceted challenges it faced by the early 1990s. Specifically, apart from providing the opportunity to reduce its borrowings by one-third, the sale of all remaining manufacturing operations reflected the decisive move into 'buying for' both its own retail outlets and those of the remaining societies. While retaining exclusive use of the CO-OP brand, the CWS was from 1994 free to source products anywhere that offered the best price. At a time when the surplus had only just recovered from its 1992 losses, and turnover was struggling to increase in real terms, it was clearly essential for the CWS to pursue this strategy as ruthlessly as possible, even if it meant transferring jobs to the private sector. Of even greater importance than the sale of food factories, however, was the creation in 1993 of the Co-operative Retail Trading Group (CRTG), principally as a result of the work of CWS's head of retail, John Owen, and leading retail society CEOs such as Bob Burlton. Although CRTG initially involved just the CWS and three other societies (Anglia; Oxford, Swindon and Gloucester; and Central Midlands), by the late 1990s the top sixteen retail co-operatives had joined. Indeed, of all the innovations introduced at that time the CRTG would have the most effective long-term impact on co-operative trading, because by coordinating all of the buying activities of these operations it was able to use their considerable buying power to secure much cheaper supplies of all commodities. Such was its success that by 1999 even the CRS had joined the CRTG, creating an organization which by then possessed buying power of £4.5 billion and giving considerable credence to the 'buying for' strategy.[23] At the same time, one might wonder why the CRTG needed to be created, given that the CWS had been formed as long ago as 1863 to perform the 'wholesaling' function for its member societies. The CIC had in the 1950s also identified the deficiencies that CRTG was intended to resolve, highlighting how the dysfunctional nature of CWS prompted the creation of a new organization that attempted to match the multiples' supply mechanics.

Another positive sign of what was increasingly regarded as an emerging consensus on the need for change was the transfer in April 1990 of North Eastern Co-operative Society to the CWS. Of course (see Table 7.2), societies had been acceding to either the CRS or (after 1973) the CWS for many decades, mostly because inherent trading difficulties had virtually bankrupted them. Bringing North Eastern into the CWS, however, marked a decisive switch in emphasis, because it was trading profitably and appeared to have a good future. This regional society had been created in 1968, directly as a result of the aggressive drive initiated by Philip Thomas in his brief period as CEO. As Hughes remembers in his revealing memoirs,[24] Thomas ruthlessly used the mounting debts

---

[22] *Sunday Times*, 9 February 1997.   [23] *Sunday Business*, 11 July 1999.
[24] Hughes (2000), 141–9.

owed by fifteen retail societies in the north-east to The Co-operative Bank as a blunt weapon to merge them into a more viable unit that could withstand contemporary competitive conditions, and especially the mounting competition from Fine Fare. Having recently brought Sunderland Co-operative Society back from the brink of bankruptcy, Hughes and a small team managed to secure the agreement of executives at most of the region's societies, including the more robust operations in Newcastle, Darlington, and Blyth. Even though Thomas had tragically died by the time the North Eastern Co-operative Society (NECS) came into existence in April 1969, within a year over thirty societies had been merged into the regional society, creating a business with 1,300 shops and an annual turnover of £70 million. Eighteen months later, 400 shops had been closed, a new out-of-town superstore was being constructed at Castletown, and the NECS had embarked on a modernization programme that made it a model for counterparts across the country. Apart from importing American retailing and marketing ideas to improve productivity and image,[25] the NECS was also responsible for a progressive range of innovations over the following two decades that ensured continued profitability.

By 1990, the NECS was generating sales of £350 million. While its surplus of £6 million was relatively low, especially compared to the multiples, a substantial £30 million investment programme had been initiated, including the construction of a 38,000 square feet hypermarket at Stockton and opening 127 convenience stores under its '8-till-8' facia. Another key part of its activities was Associated Co-operative Creameries Ltd (ACC), a £50 million federal dairy business owned jointly with the CWS that supplied a wide range of products across the country using advanced chilled distribution systems imported from the USA.[26] It was this interaction with ACC that prompted the NECS to consider complete integration into the CWS, given the enormous potential in creating a retailing group with annual sales of almost £1 billion. For example, merging the 127 '8-till-8' convenience stores with the 208 'Late shop' stores run by the CWS afforded considerable buying and distribution opportunities.[27] Negotiations consequently intensified in 1989 between the NECS's head, Neil Arnold, and the CWS's secretary, Graham Melmoth, resulting in an announcement in April 1990 that trumpeted how: 'It is the first time that a large, successful society has been willing to join us of their own volition.'[28]

This 'merger from strength' provided a clear signal to the rest of the movement that concentration was a positive move which could benefit all parties. On the other hand, while up to 2000 CWS North Eastern was able to retain a regional identity that the CWS had promised throughout the negotiations, thereafter it was carefully integrated into the national business alongside the failing societies that had merged into the CWS. Crucially, other viable regional societies refused to follow the NECS's example, fearing total

[25] Hughes (2000), 185–92.   [26] Hughes (2000), 28.
[27] *Grocer*, 28 April 1990.   [28] *Guardian*, 25 April 1990.

assimilation into an organization that was still regarded as antiquated. A total of twenty-two societies merged into the CWS and CRS over the following five years (see Table 7.3), but all of these were a result of acute commercial difficulties. This process was pursued with particular vigour by the CEO, David Skinner, who regarded the acquisition of other co-operative societies as key to the development of the CWS as a retailer. Just as we noticed in the last chapter, the CWS was regarded with great suspicion by the regional societies that had emerged since the 1970s, not least its closest neighbour, United Co-operatives Ltd, created in May 1983 through the merger of the Lancastria and North Midlands societies. As we shall see in section 9.1, United replicated a considerable proportion of the CWS's activities, from distribution through to retailing, highlighting the widespread reluctance of these regional societies to accede to entreaties to engage in the movement towards 'One Society'. In conjunction with the CRS, United even went as far as creating a rival to the CRTG, the Consortium of Independent Co-operatives, undermining further any attempt to synchronize buying across the movement.

By far the most virulent opposition to the idea of 'One Society', however, emanated from the largest retail co-operative society, the CRS; or more specifically 'One Society' under CWS leadership. The principal commercial reason behind this rivalry was the CWS's increased focus on retailing, the function for which the CRS (see Figure 8.5) had originally been established. Although CRS activists such as Bert Beaumont (Barnsley)

FIGURE 8.5. CRS 'Pioneer' store, Wales, c.1990s. During the 1990s the CRS operated different types of store under various names, including 'Pioneer' for discount retail outlets, 'Leo's' supermarkets, 'Stop and Shop' convenience stores, and the non-food chains 'Living' and 'Home World'.

proposed that the CWS ought to hive off its retailing operations into a separate business and focus on its original role as a secondary co-operative,[29] it is clear from what we have seen of the 1980s and 1990s that the latter was committed to expanding further into retail. As we also noted in Chapter 7, since 1977 various rule changes had significantly reduced the CWS's control over the CRS, a process that intensified after the London Co-operative Society transferred into the CRS, bringing with it a highly politicized left-wing group dominated by members of the National Federation of Progressive Co-operators (NFPC). Apart from undermining all talks of a CWS–CRS merger, this group also encouraged the CRS's CEO, Harry Moore, in 1990 to seek a ruling from the Chief Registrar of Friendly Societies over whether the CWS should be able to dominate its board.[30] As the Chief Registrar ruled in the CRS's favour, in March 1991 the CWS was obliged to agree that it could only nominate three directors (as opposed to eight of the sixteen), while at general meetings its vote was reduced to 10 per cent (as opposed to 50 per cent). Following further discussions in 1993, the CWS finally agreed to withdraw completely from appointing people onto the CRS's board, on condition that all of its share capital should be refunded, marking the end of a relationship that had been in existence since 1934.

Immediately after these legal changes, in 1994 the BBC's *Money Programme* ran an article advocating the benefits of merging the CWS and CRS, featuring an interview with Harry Moore on the advantages of 'One Society'. This publicity persuaded the CWS and CRS to publish a pamphlet entitled 'The Time is Right', with a board composed of regional representatives (but not other retail societies). However, it soon became clear that CRS saw this as an opportunity for a reverse takeover, with the new Society to be run by Harry Moore (pictured in Figure 8.6). As direct result, CWS withdrew from the discussions, leading to a deep rift between the two organizations that proved calamitous for the CRS. Having realized that a merger was not going to happen, the CRS not only developed its own logo, but also a new management team was recruited in from outside the co-operative movement, creating major difficulties that as we shall see later resulted in heavy and consistent losses and declining sales.

In analysing the reasons why the CRS and CWS would appear to have been at logger-heads throughout this period, Beaumont is highly critical of the role played by the NFPC, arguing that this group 'constructively weakened' the former,[31] not least in filling the lay board with politically motivated candidates who lacked a broad understanding of the commercial realities in which the society operated. On the other hand, while as we shall see in the next chapter the CRS's commercial performance deteriorated significantly during the 1990s primarily as a result of its Board's failure to engender the necessary debate about strategy and its link with trading reality,[32] the impact of the political influences on the CRS can be overstated. Above all, at the root of the CWS–CRS tensions was the influence individual members could have on the business, because as a secondary

[29] *Co-operative News*, 25 October 1991.   [30] Beaumont (1997), 17.
[31] Beaumont (1997), 19–20.   [32] Beaumont (1997), 22.

FIGURE 8.6. **Harry Moore.** Having begun his career as a petroleum chemist with Shell, Moore moved into retailing with Littlewoods before joining the CRS in 1977. As chief executive from 1988 to 1998, Moore led the CRS during the height of its rivalry with the CWS.

co-operative the CWS was more concerned with its corporate members to which a dividend was still paid. This is key to understanding why the CRS refused to merge into the CWS, even if in commercial terms there were strong reasons why the two should have combined forces much earlier (see Figure 8.7).

This discussion of the way in which CRS was being run also highlights another major debate of the 1990s, because as a direct result of a series of scandals in various societies that occurred in the 1980s and early 1990s, an enormous question mark was placed over the movement's corporate governance structure. In particular, these scandals struck right at the heart of the institutional constraints facing those who were advocating the creation of 'One Society', because they revealed in the starkest form how some societies were run purely in the interests of a small clique. We have in previous chapters discussed what can be described as a 'democracy deficit' within the movement as a whole, a situation in which accountability was so weak that few safeguards existed to protect the vast majority of members. Of course, it is difficult to envisage a system that would have accommodated the millions of people who in the 1990s were still co-operative members, but at the same time it is clear that the 'democratic deficit' was not only open to abuse, but it also restricted the flow of talent into senior echelons of management at a time when fresh ideas were very much needed. At the core of this

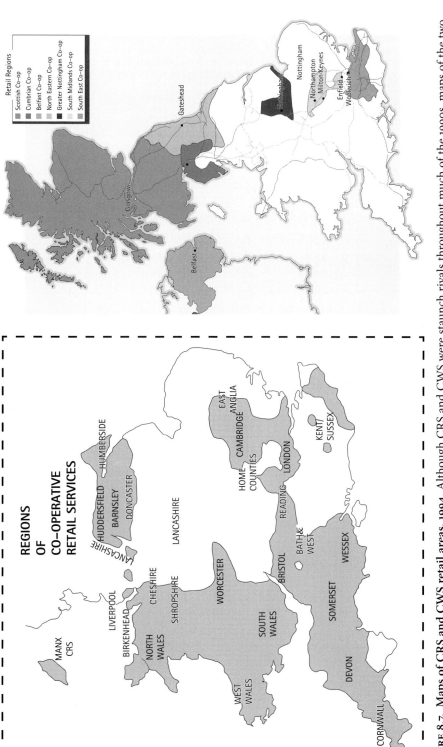

**REGIONS
OF
CO–OPERATIVE
RETAIL SERVICES**

MANX
CRS

LIVERPOOL
BIRKENHEAD
NORTH
WALES
CHESHIRE
SHROPSHIRE
LANCASHIRE
LANCASHIRE
HUDDERSFIELD
BARNSLEY
DONCASTER
HUMBERSIDE
WORCESTER
WEST
WALES
SOUTH
WALES
BRISTOL
BATH &
WEST
READING
HOME
COUNTIES
CAMBRIDGE
EAST
ANGLIA
LONDON
KENT
SUSSEX
SOMERSET
WESSEX
DEVON
CORNWALL

Retail Regions
Scottish Co-op
Cumbrian Co-op
Belfast Co-op
North Eastern Co-op
Greater Nottingham Co-op
South Midlands Co-op
South East Co-op

Glasgow
Gateshead
Belfast
Birmingham
Nottingham
Northampton
Milton Keynes
Enfield
Woolwich

FIGURE 8.7. **Maps of CRS and CWS retail areas, 1994.** Although CRS and CWS were staunch rivals throughout much of the 1990s, maps of the two organizations' trading areas demonstrated the logic behind efforts to merge their retail operations. However, as they had been in the 1980s, merger discussions in 1994–5 were unsuccessful.

issue, of course, was the extent to which membership had lost most of its meaning once the 'divi' had been abandoned by most societies in the late 1960s. While active involvement in society activities had been declining significantly since the 1940s, it had been the 'divi' which secured customer loyalty. It was also clear that the membership lists kept by societies were grossly out of date, probably containing hundreds of thousands of names of people that were no longer alive. Crucially, society meetings were attended by small cliques of activists who dominated key elections to influential posts, thereby controlling how the society allocated resources, secured supplies, and the extent to which it would collaborate with either other societies or the CWS.

Although it is invidious to focus on specific cases, by providing some examples it helps to indicate the extent to which the 'democratic deficit' resulted in such low levels of accountability that certain individuals exploited the gaps almost at will. An especially high-profile case was linked with CWS Engineering, highlighting the inadequate nature of auditing processes across the organization, given the millions of pounds lost to fraudsters operating a false invoicing scam.[33] Another of these cases involved executives at Central Midlands Co-operative Society, based in Lichfield, who were bribed by the managing director of a Leamington Spa fruit and vegetable wholesaler, Griffin and Steel, to the tune of £5.7 million over the course of a thirteen-year orgy involving £700-a-night prostitutes, lavish holidays, and trips to Wimbledon. The bribes only came to light as a result of a tax inspector asking Faulkner how he could afford to fund the ten homes he owned, prompting a detailed investigation that coincided with the bankruptcy of Griffin and Steel in 1992, revealing the depth of the fraud. Apart from obliging customers to pay higher prices for their vegetables, the scandal did untold harm to the movement's image at a time when as we shall see later ethical trading was being developed as its marketing strapline. This image was also tarnished further when fraud revelations at societies as far apart as Perth, Airedale, Gloucester, Milton Keynes, and Long Eaton gave the impression that far from being ethical, co-operatives seemed to be corrupt havens that allowed ruthless executives to exploit opportunities at will.

While it is important to stress that business corruption was by no means unique to co-operatives—high-profile cases such as Maxwell, BCCI, Guinness, Polly Peck, and Ferranti International revealed extensive corruption in the private sector—the key issue was the extent to which this influenced consumers at a time when ethical trading was becoming the CWS's hallmark. However, what happened during the 1991 merger between two major societies, United and Norwest, was to have much wider implications for the movement as a whole. In negotiating this merger, the respective chief executives, Harry Lovatt and Rod Aspray, not only linked their salaries and retirement packages to turnover (which would obviously rise considerably after the merger), but also failed to inform their boards of directors, composed of lay members who remained totally ignorant of the deals. As a consequence, when Lovatt and Aspray took early retirement, their joint pay-off amounted to £5.4 million, as opposed to an anticipated £1.4 million.[34] As if to compound the

---

[33] Interview with Paul Smedley.   [34] *Manchester Evening News*, 13 May 1993.

situation, after the first sole chief executive (John Thomson) was obliged to resign just nine months in post, following allegations of financial irregularities,[35] widespread concern was expressed at the £370,000 severance payment he received. The scandals certainly provided a challenging introduction to United Norwest for the next chief executive, Martin Beaumont, a person who will feature prominently in Chapter 9.

In view of this flurry of financial and managerial scandals, it was incumbent on the movement to respond effectively and eradicate the growing impression of an organization that was riddled with corruption and unethical behaviour. The private sector had already moved to deal with its corporate governance challenges, by establishing in 1991 the Cadbury Committee and introducing fresh guidelines that were intended to instil greater confidence in reporting mechanisms and executives' accountability to their shareholders.[36] Although later scandals would demonstrate that the Cadbury review never went far enough, it highlighted the need to address corporate governance issues as a first step in clarifying management responsibilities, especially in large-scale organizations that were affected by an extensive divorce between control and ownership. Pictured in Figure 8.8, Lloyd Wilkinson, Co-operative Union (CU) General Secretary, was especially keen to respond to what the United Norwest scandal had revealed about the apparent lack of transparency in the actions of executives, leaving lay board members ignorant of important financial transactions. This resulted in the formation of a Corporate Governance Working Group (CGWP), chaired by Brian Harvey, Co-operative Bank professor of corporate social responsibility at Manchester Business School.

Aimed at improving the way in which co-operative societies are managed and controlled, the terms of reference provided by the CU for the CGWP focused on directors' responsibilities, board organization, the relationship between members and management, drafting an ethical code, recommending legislation to support any changes, and any other relevant matters that the CGWP came across in the course of their deliberations. As the CGWP consisted of enthusiastic and committed individuals such as the chief executive of Oxford, Swindon and Gloucester Co-operative Society, Bob Burlton (pictured in Figure 8.9), a constant critic of the existing corporate governance systems, it was going to penetrate to the heart of the issues. The other members of the CGWP were Brian Jones (former executive director of The Co-operative Bank), Tom Philbin (Leicestershire Society president), Finney Swift (CWS pensions manager), George Cunningham (Musselburgh and Fisherrow president), William MacLaughlin (KPMG partner), and Ian Snaith (law lecturer at the University of Leicester), providing a mixture of experience and expertise. Given that they only started meeting in October 1993, producing a comprehensive report within six months that offered a wide range of reforms was an impressive performance. In total, forty-two recommendations were presented to the CU Congress in May 1994, covering a wide range of issues, from the conduct of meetings through to remuneration packages and contracts, and including accountability to both lay directors and members. Referring indirectly to the recent spate of scandals, part V was devoted to directors' responsibilities,

---

[35] *Guardian*, 15 January 1993.   [36] Charkham (1995), 248–9.

FIGURE 8.8. **Lloyd Wilkinson.** The Co-operative Union's general secretary from 1974 to 1999, Wilkinson pushed for co-operative governance reforms following a series of scandals in the early 1990s.

stating that they should '... exercise the highest standards of honesty, integrity and good faith, and at all times to act in the best interests of the society rather than in their own interests or in the interests of any other person or body'.

Of course, having to write this as a basic expectation reveals the awful level to which behaviour had deteriorated, forcing the movement as a whole to accept responsibility for an abrogation of responsibility. After having been approved by the CU Congress, curiously it took until July 1995 before a booklet entitled 'Corporate Governance: Code of Best Practice' was published and distributed widely, offering all societies an opportunity to reform a key dimension of their activities. It is also important to note that the ICA (Europe) conducted investigations and workshops on corporate governance from May 1994, taking the lead from British developments that proved to be highly influential in fashioning a code for all European co-operatives.

If CWS executives had been unable to persuade the remaining retail societies to merge into 'One Society', there was a wide consensus over the new code. At the same time, there was a parallel modernization and reaffirmation of what were widely regarded as 'The 1844 Rochdale Principles' by the ICA. The 'Rochdale Pioneers' had not formulated their 'Principles' until the 1860s, indicating how a mythical element had become the norm across the co-operative movement. The reform process was started in 1992, when

FIGURE 8.9. **Bob Burlton**. A prominent co-operative leader and long time head of Midcounties Co-operative (formerly Oxford, Swindon & Gloucester) from 1987 to 2006, Burlton helped found the Co-operative Retail Trading Group (CRTG) in 1993 and served on the Corporate Governance Working Group (CGWG) in 1994. He is past Chair of The Co-operative Group (2004–7) and of The Co-operative Bank (2007–10).

Sven Åke Böök, a leading figure in the Swedish co-operative movement who worked with Professor Ian MacPherson of the University of Victoria, Canada, produced a revised set of Principles at that year's ICA Congress. Böök had originally raised the issue of the revision of the Principles at the Congress of 1988, culminating in *Co-operative Values in a Changing World* which was published for the 1992 ICA Congress. There followed several years of discussion, redrafting, and further debate, with final acceptance of what are listed in Table 8.2 at the October 1995 ICA Congress held in Manchester. Apart from replacing 'Promotion of education' with a more comprehensive commitment to 'Education, Training and Information', the revised Principles are notable for the failure to mention financial issues such as surplus distribution and interest payments, focusing instead on internal dynamics and community issues. These changes reflected the dramatic changes that had occurred since the 1960s to co-operatives across the world, especially in terms of their ability to provide financial benefits to their members.

Another key point to make about the 1995 Principles is the role played by Graham Melmoth (CWS secretary) in ensuring that they were accepted at the 1995 ICA Congress. While Böök and MacPherson were the key architects behind the changes, as Chair of the 1995 Congress held in Manchester Melmoth played a leading role in the adoption process. This provided an excellent opportunity to highlight how CWS executives were helping to modernize a movement that many felt was losing its way. One can see from Table 8.2 that

Table 8.2. A comparison of the 1844 Rochdale Principles and ICA 1995 Principles

1844 Rochdale Principles	ICA 1995 Principles
Open membership	Voluntary and open membership
Democratic control	Democratic control
Distribution of surplus in proportion to trade	Member participation
Payment of limited interest on capital	Autonomy and independence
Political and religious neutrality	Education, training, and information
Cash trading	Co-operation among co-operatives
Promotion of education	Concern for community

while the 'Pioneers' had focused on democratic trading, the key emphasis of the 1995 Principles was democracy, member involvement, and encouraging greater co-operation across the movement. This reflected Melmoth's desire to strengthen what he regarded as a distinctive feature of the movement. As he often noted, 'We are nothing if not a membership-driven organisation.'[37] Above all, alongside the corporate governance reforms, the movement was recognizing the imperative need to differentiate itself from private sector rivals that operated on much more commercially oriented principles. As we shall also see later, it was primarily as a result of playing this influential role that in November 1996 Melmoth (pictured, Figure 8.10) became CWS chief executive, defeating his principal rival, John Owen, the head of retail. This provided him with the opportunity to progress his idea of building a 'family of co-operative businesses', integrating the Leviathan in a way that had never occurred in the CWS's history. Crucially, having made these decisive changes to both the corporate governance structure and the principles upon which the movement was based, by the mid-1990s the CWS and retail societies were able to support the 'ethical trading' programme more convincingly, while much more focused consideration was being given to the need to address what is involved in co-operative membership, issues that were very close to Melmoth's personal philosophy.

8.2 The 'family', The Co-operative Bank, and ethical trading

As we noted in the introduction to this chapter, one of the principal failings of some highly authoritative analyses of the CWS's performance has been the tendency to focus only on food retailing, to the neglect of other parts of the Leviathan that demonstrated a degree of dynamism. The CWS's business portfolio, of course, was highly diverse, highlighting how,

---

[37] Interview with Sir Graham Melmoth.

FIGURE 8.10. **Sir Graham Melmoth.** As secretary from 1975, Melmoth oversaw numerous societies' amalgamation into the CWS, and was Chair of the International Co-operative Alliance (ICA) when it adopted the 1995 statement of co-operative identity, values, and principles. He became CWS chief executive in 1996, successfully repelled an attempted takeover bid the following year, and led the organization through its merger with CRS, retiring as CEO of The Co-operative Group in 2002.

even though food retailing dominated the business (accounting for 70 per cent of turnover), and the CWS was the largest farmer in the UK (with 80,000 acres), it also possessed a huge property portfolio worth £104 million (at 1997 values), the travel agency ran 256 shops, and the funeral services businesses operated out of 359 outlets, generating sound returns that justified the continued investment in these sectors.[38] Of course, this also ignores other activities such as the creameries and dairy businesses trading as ACC had developed into a major business by the late 1990s with a turnover of £300 million and accounting for one-third of all milk doorstep deliveries. Similarly, the Shoefayre chain of 260 shoe shops was not integrated into the CWS, having been formed in 1964 as an independent secondary co-operative when the CWS, CRS, and six retail societies combined their operations. This created a major business headquartered in Leicester, the centre of Britain's shoe-making industry. The same format was adopted with regard to the pharmacy activities, in that National Co-operative Chemists had since 1945 been operating as a secondary co-operative coordinating a nationwide network.

While it is essential to remember that the CWS was a highly diversified conglomerate—indeed, *the* most diversified conglomerate in British business—another dimension of this

---

[38] Data taken from a report published in *Manchester Evening News* (Business Section), 21 April 1999.

point is the way in which some of the businesses developed and expanded. In particular, one might argue that had the CWS been able to imitate their strategies, the conglomerate would never have suffered so badly after the 1960s. By far the most spectacular of these stories is The Co-operative Bank, but before assessing how this operation provided a template on which the CWS built its branding profile it would also be useful to examine the funerals business and how it developed a powerful market position. Although it was 1890 when the first known co-operative funeral was conducted, by Manchester and Salford Society,[39] and by 1936 at least 250 societies operated what were known as funeral furnishing departments, it was 1930 before the CWS opened a monumental masons works in New-castle, followed by its own funerals business in 1934. By the mid-1950s, co-operative funeral furnishings was worth over £3 million, but as this was dispersed across 379 societies, considerable thought was put into coordinating this expanding business, as well as securing an even larger share of the market. The momentum behind these moves came mainly from what had been the SCWS, which accounted for 45 per cent of all burials in Scotland, resulting by 1981 in the creation of CWS Funeral Furnishings, with headquarters in Glasgow and a turnover of £14.6 million.

Over the course of the following twenty years, this business expanded considerably, recording a turnover of £172 million by 2003 and accounting for one-quarter of the British market. Crucially, though, while bringing the formerly dispersed activities together under a single headquarters had improved performance, crucial to this success was a combination of several strategies: the business was very much customer-facing, having been embedded extensively into local communities; and extensive acquisitions of both co-operative and private funeral businesses, eliminating competition and expanding market share. This policy of what was described in 1981 as 'controlled expansion and acquisition,'[40] alongside the effective integration of a customer-facing business, underpinned the continued growth of a highly successful business that by the 2000s was recording profits averaging almost 10 per cent of sales. In short, had CWS imitated this approach to developing its business portfolio much earlier than the 2000s, the Leviathan would have been much more successful than it was in the late twentieth century.

Another template that the CWS might well have imitated was The Co-operative Bank, not least because since the 1970s it had significantly expanded in terms of both numbers of customers and market share. In the early 1990s, it had also made the first decisive moves towards projecting an ethical image, the chief executive (Terry Thomas) and his marketing manager (Simon Williams) having developed this policy in response to a serious slump in profitability in the late 1980s and early 1990s. As we saw at the end of section 7.2, profits had slumped alarmingly and losses appeared for the first time after the major recession precipitated by 'Black Monday' in October 1987 (see Figure 7.11). Of course, the recession of the late 1980s and early 1990s undermined bank profitability

---

[39] Information supplied by The Co-operative Funeralcare to Lauren Thomas, Simone Bilton, and Robyn Lyness (University of Liverpool undergraduates working on a strategy report).

[40] CWSBM, 2 December 1981.

across the sector, exacerbating these competitive pressures at a time when the rate of increase in account-holders was tapering off. As all of the larger clearing banks had by 1985 adopted free banking and many building societies were also encroaching on the traditional banking market, The Co-operative Bank was no longer able to differentiate itself clearly from its much larger rivals. Such were the challenges, indeed, that in the early 1990s Thomas was prompted to pursue a strategy that might have been regarded as highly speculative, but which in fact would underpin a significant growth in both customers and profits. The key influence behind this strategy was Simon Williams, a marketing specialist who had previously worked for Bass plc on major brands such as Carling Black Label.[41] Having joined The Co-operative Bank in 1988 when it was beginning to struggle financially, he was clearly faced with the major challenge of helping to turn round what was a struggling organization.

The specific challenge which Williams and his team set themselves at an internal management conference in 1988 was to develop a positioning strategy that would help to boost market share. Codenamed 'Project Genesis', this involved five market research projects, evidence from which was used to determine how the bank could link more closely with customer sentiment. Some of the early innovations developed by Williams and his team involved changing the logo and improved marketing materials, in order to differentiate Co-operative Bank from its parent organization. This reflected a growing dissatisfaction with how CWS was responding to market pressures, an attitude that had also been prevalent in funeral services. Williams also worked closely with the Butterfield Day Devito Hockney agency, bringing fresh ideas into the team. While some of this work was nothing more than a series of superficial modifications to advertising literature, it was increasingly recognized from the market research that not only were customers concerned about where banks invested their funds, but also The Co-operative Bank already had a reputation as an ethical operation with high levels of customer satisfaction rating. Building on these findings, the team realized that this empathy between Bank and customers could also be further strengthened if its strategies resonated more closely with beliefs and aspirations. Researching the idea more thoroughly, this persuaded Williams to advocate a much stronger ethical stance as The Co-operative Bank's distinctive characteristic, especially as none of its much larger rivals had ever shown any interest in pursuing this approach.[42] When Terry Thomas announced the strategy at a CWS Board meeting, however, deep concerns were expressed at such a move, even though ironically the CWS had been advocating an ethical trading stance since its very foundation. Indeed, during the 1980s the CWS's stance against South Africa and such issues as fox-hunting demonstrated a commitment to ethical issues, even if little of this was used in a coordinated fashion to differentiate the organization from its rivals. There were even calls for Thomas's resignation from some directors,[43] reflecting the highly

---

[41] Williams had been responsible for such popular advertising slogans as 'I'll bet he drinks Carling Black Label'. Interview with Simon Williams.
[42] Interview with Simon Williams.   [43] Williams; Macclesfield (2008).

conservative nature of this key feature of the hierarchy. Thomas nevertheless persevered, arguing convincingly that the strategy could well reverse the bank's recent poor performance.

After further internal debate, the campaign was finally launched in 1991, announcing a core positioning statement that left nobody in any doubt:

The Co-operative Bank is a different kind of bank, committed to an alternative, socially responsible approach to the provision of banking services. We aim to achieve this by ensuring that we are both responsible and conscientious in regard to where our money comes from and what we do with it.[44]

This revealed to all actual and potential customers and other stakeholders that The Co-operative Bank would never do business with particular types of client, namely, heavy polluters, arms manufacturers, tobacco and pharmaceutical firms that tested products on animals, blood sports enthusiasts, and 'oppressive Third World regimes'. Of course, one ought to note that the bank was not currently dealing with any of these types of customers—as the *Observer* commented, firms such as GEC (the UK's leading defence manufacturer) 'probably ha[d] more lazy money than the Co-op Bank could raise on even its sunniest days'[45]—but by pushing this image it was hoped that informed individuals would switch their accounts to an operation which trumpeted ethical values.

Launched at the same time as the announcement of its second consecutive loss, The Co-operative Bank's ethical strategy was a bold move aimed at reversing what had become a disastrous commercial record. The biggest risk was not losing customers—only seven commercial firms moved their accounts—but converting a niche operation into what in the early 1990s was an even smaller niche. This raises a key issue, because while in the 1990s carefully designed marketing campaigns (like that in Figure 8.11) disseminated the ethical message widely, at a time when movements such as 'Stakeholder Capitalism' and corporate social responsibility started to gather momentum, it is clear that other factors played a major role in the 1990s recovery. Indeed, The Co-operative Bank admitted in 2003 that only 19 per cent of its profits were attributable to customers who had signed up for ethical reasons, indicating that this was only one of its strengths. Of much greater importance was doing basic banking functions effectively, producing impressive customer satisfaction ratings: a MORI FS survey noted in 2002 that 97 per cent of Co-operative Bank customers reported themselves as at least 'satisfied' with the service, compared to 91 per cent for the sector as a whole.[46] This contrasted sharply with what the CWS had been doing, not least in terms of its relationships with retail societies. Although market share only moved from 2 per cent in 1990 to 3.5 per cent by 2003, by which time over 3 million customers had opened accounts with The Co-operative Bank, compared to just over one

---

[44] Co-operative Bank publicity flyer.   [45] *Observer*, 9 April 1995.
[46] *Observer* (9 April 1995), 11–12.

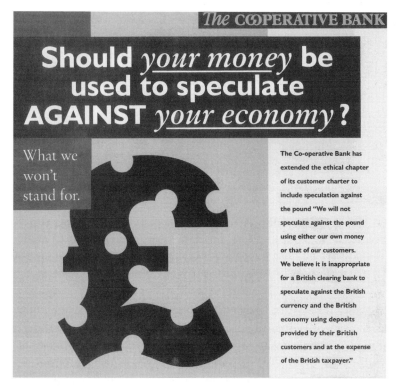

FIGURE 8.11. The Co-operative Bank advertisement, c.1990s. This advertisement from the 1990s highlights The Co-operative Bank's customer charter, stating: 'We believe it is inappropriate for a British clearing bank to speculate against the British currency and the British economy using deposits provided by their British customers and at the expense of the British taxpayer.'

million in 1990, as one can see from Figure 7.11 profitability had improved impressively over that period, providing CWS with a reliable source of capital for investment in its core business.

The ethical banking strategy was consequently only one dimension of the bank's recovery from the early 1990s problems; even though a resonance with broader movements proved to be extremely useful, of much greater importance was a combination of improved internal processes and technological innovation. On taking over as chief executive in 1988, Thomas had actively recruited a senior management team capable of significantly enhancing all aspects of the business, from human resource management to marketing, significantly improving internal organization. The key issue in maintaining the high levels of customer satisfaction, however, was the continued commitment to technological innovation, sustaining what had been since the 1970s a major dimension of its operations. For example, the bank not only joined the LINK network (with 50,000 ATMs), but also placed 1,500 of their own ATMs in locations where either rivals had closed branches or next to a co-operative convenience store. Launched in 1999, smile (see Figure 8.12) was also one of the UK's first internet banks, signing up 650,000 new

smile the internet bank

FIGURE 8.12. smile logo. Launched in 1999, smile grew quickly, attracting 650,000 customers in its first three years. Like its parent, The Co-operative Bank, smile drew on its relationship with co-operative societies, including a 2002 promotion that placed stickers with the smile logo on the bananas sold in co-operative stores. Courtesy of The Co-operative Group.

customers within three years. This indicated how the bank was able to move business away from the expensive branch network to telephone or internet banking, offering a quality service that was clearly appreciated by the increasing number of account-holders.

Crucially, one ought to conclude that the impressive increase in profitability after the early 1990s crisis, from losses averaging £8.5 million in 1990–1 to a surplus of almost £100 million by 1999 (see Figure 7.11), was based mostly on sound organizational princi-ples and continued technological innovation that ensured customers were satisfied with the quality of service offered. While ethical banking continued to feature prominently in marketing drives in the 1990s and 2000s, this was but one of the characteristics of a niche operation that proved to be the CWS's major success story. Ironically, though, in 1994 Thomas discovered that The Co-operative Bank was going to be sold, the CWS hav-ing commissioned its merchant bank, Warburg's, to secure a sale.[47] This move was prompted by the growing liquidity crisis across co-operative trading, with debts having risen above £300 million at a time of high interest rates, combined with poor levels of profitability in the core food business. Although Thomas and his board were very much against this move, they responded by attempting to interest a European co-operative bank, DG Bank of Germany being one of the principal contenders. Much to Thomas's surprise, however, by 1996 the CWS had decided to abandon its plan to sell The Co-operative Bank, having realized that its profits were vital to the conglomerate's recov-ery. It was a curious incident in CWS history which indicated how major decisions could be hidden from even those most directly affected; in spite of the corporate governance changes outlined in the last section, decision-making still continued to be shrouded in

[47] Macclesfield (2008).

secrecy, reflecting the opacity of an organization that struggled to come to terms with the demands of modern business ethics.

The Co-operative Bank was clearly the CWS's success story of the 1990s. While organizational improvements were undoubtedly more important to its recovery than the adoption of an ethical strategy, the combination of these innovations underpinned the improvement in performance recorded in Figure 7.11. At the same time, one can nevertheless claim that the bank's adoption of an ethical strategy was more important in converting CWS marketing to this approach. While, as we have just seen, Terry Thomas had been extremely nervous about announcing the introduction of the bank's ethical strategy at a CWS Board meeting in 1991, it rapidly became clear to senior management that the highly positive response to what the bank was doing could very well assist the recovery of the distribution and retail operations. Of course, one might argue that co-operative trading had always been ethical, in that one of the primary reasons behind the creation of retail societies had been to cope with the widespread adulteration of food. Similarly, from the 1970s some CWS managers headed by Bill Shannon and John Bowes were beginning to realize that this was one way of differentiating their goods from those of the other multiple retailers.[48] By the late 1980s, there was also considerable debate within the CWS about the blue logo that had by then been in use for twenty years, prompting the marketing team to conduct detailed research into rebranding Co-op goods and shop fronts. Although the Food Controller, David Skinner, resented this interference in what he felt was his managerial territory, the head of marketing, Campbell Weir, encouraged his team to reposition its brand and offer consumers a more progressive image.

As with many initiatives, the introduction of ethical trading into the CWS was piecemeal and iterative, the marketing team having already introduced aspects of this programme by adapting the movement's historical interest in ethical retailing to address the concerns of a new generation of consumers who were increasingly well informed on environmental issues.[49] Under Campbell Weir, who had been given responsibility for developing the 'Co-operative Brand', a team headed by Bill Shannon had been developing slogans such as 'Eat right, eat well' and working with the major retail societies to introduce campaigns such as 'Freedom Foods' and the 'Green Range'. Indeed, by the 1990s CWS had pioneered the use of clear labelling that educated consumers about the nutritional value of own-brand food products (see Figure 8.13). Apart from making a strong link with the movement's mid-nineteenth-century concerns with food adulteration, this work also provided an excellent example of what the co-operative commitment to education and training meant in practice. In 1985, the CWS and CRS had also severed all supply links with the South African apartheid regime, while in 1989 an 'Environmental Care' campaign was started, establishing them as the first retailers to offer 'green' products. Crucially, in 1992 the CWS made its first move into retailing fair trade products, which led ultimately by 1996 to

---

[48] Interview with Bill Shannon.   [49] Docherty (2008), 205.

FIGURE 8.13. *The Lie of the Label II* pamphlet, *c.*1990s. The success of The Co-operative Bank's ethical strategy fuelled new attention to socially responsible initiatives in other areas of CWS business. During the 1990s the CWS moved to provide clear nutrition information on its own-brand foods and developed a series of consumer education materials on topics including product labelling (shown here), environmental concerns, animal testing, and healthy eating.

Fairtrade certification of the movement's entire own-brand lines of coffee and chocolate.[50] While it was 2001 before all co-operative coffee and chocolate was genuinely Fairtrade, building on how The Co-operative Bank had rolled out its ethical policy, this marked a decisive turn to the movement's activities. Of course, some efforts had been made by the CWS to develop such initiatives since the 1970s, but little coordination had ever been attempted, indicating how marketing was subjugated to the distribution and (later) retailing activities. By the mid-1990s, however, the CWS and the remaining retail societies were capitalizing on the growing public interest in Fairtrade products, contributing extensively to their increased popularity. The CWS was also a founder member of the Ethical Trading Initiative, an organization created in 1997 to improving working conditions in developing economies, while in the following year Co-op '99 Tea' became the first mainstream food product to be marketed using ethical criteria (see Plate 19).

The iterative nature of this progressive adoption of ethical trading during the 1990s, culminating in the CWS's introduction of Fairtrade bananas in 2000 (sourced from the

[50] See Bowes (2010), 125–39.

Volta River Estates, Ghana), marked a radical transformation in the way that goods were being marketed and retailed.[51] Of course, these initiatives might appear to be just another marketing strategy designed to obviate the depressing decline in market share, but they were in fact highly significant for a movement whose status and reputation had been eclipsed by the multiple retailers which had come to dominate UK consumption patterns. Ever since the CIC report, much of what the CWS had attempted had been imitative and reactive, aping the likes of Tesco, Sainsbury's, and ASDA in the forlorn attempt to stem what to many seemed an inevitable decline; the turn to ethical trading represented a genuine attempt to differentiate the Co-op from its competitors, and effectively returning to the movement's core values. Even the aping strategies had been shallow imitations of what the multiples had achieved, the CWS having failed to adopt the rigorous distribution and marketing techniques that Tesco especially had introduced since the 1970s. Crucially, the success of its ethical trading initiatives demonstrated to people inside and outside the CWS that the movement could connect with the concerns of modern consumers; it was not simply a nostalgic enterprise based on outmoded values and principles. This encouraged the CWS, Co-operative Bank, and CRTG in 1998 to create a 'Brand Group' that would forge a highly effective marketing campaign based on the Fairtrade marque. This campaign was based on the emergence of the 'responsible retailer' concept, effectively linking the CWS into the most significant socio-economic trend of the last generation, as ethical trading moved out of a tiny niche sector into the mainstream of British retailing and consumption patterns.[52]

While there are many factors which have underpinned a revival in the CWS's commercial fortunes over the last twenty years, there is no doubt that adopting the 'responsible retailer' concept was fundamental to this trend. As we shall see later, this also ran in parallel with Graham Melmoth's campaign to reaffirm the values and principles inherent to the co-operative movement, having played a leading role in drafting the ICA's 1995 revisions. Just at the time that Melmoth was beginning this campaign, however, the CWS was rocked to the core by an event that challenged its very existence. The repercussions arising from this event would prove crucial to how Melmoth was able to move the CWS into a different era, reflecting both the widespread recognition that change was essential and the vision that he brought to the movement.

8.3 REGAN'S TAKEOVER BID

One of the most traumatic events in recent British co-operative history was the attempted takeover in 1997 of the CWS by Lanica Trust Ltd. Coming at a time when the CWS was struggling with substantial challenges, this represented a full-scale assault on

---

[51] Bowes (2010), 126.   [52] Docherty (2008), 34.

its independence, just when some of the equally old mutual building societies were being converted into public limited companies by a wave of 'carpetbaggers'. Described by the *Sunday Times* as 'one of the boldest takeover attempts the City has ever seen,'[53] the two factions could not have been more different: the predator was a 31-year-old entrepreneur, Andrew Regan, backed by 'blue-chip' City names such as Hambros, Schroder, and Nomura; while in contrast a 134-year-old CWS was showing weaknesses that critics claimed were fatal. Much to the surprise of these critics, however, under the imaginative leadership of its chief executive, Graham Melmoth, the CWS not only saw off Regan and his backers, but emerged from the experience in much better shape to tackle its challenges. It is consequently possible to refer to a 'Regan Paradox', because while he set out to acquire and asset-strip the CWS, thereby undermining the British co-operative movement, he actually achieved exactly the opposite effect, sparking a revival that accelerated over the following fifteen years. It was a *cause célèbre* of 1997, highlighting how, in spite of its apparent weaknesses, the CWS proved capable of both defending itself and seizing the opportunity to lay the foundations for the achievement of a radical reorganization capable of underpinning a commercial revival of considerable proportions. Indeed, in the late 1990s the CWS managed to overcome the residual organizational resistance to greater integration in a series of moves that resulted in the creation of what came to be known as the 'co-operative family'.

Before analysing the takeover bid and its consequences, it is important to understand the context in which this occurred. The Conservative governments of 1979–97 had been intent on deregulating the British financial system, introducing a range of liberalizing measures that undoubtedly fuelled the rapid expansion of what is euphemistically called 'the City'.[54] These measures included deregulating international financial transactions (1979–81), eradicating restrictive practices, and computerizing London Stock Exchange activities (the 'Big Bang' in 1986), while the privatization of many public sector utilities added considerably to the City's prosperity. Another innovation was the 1986 Building Society Act, which permitted these financial institutions to demutualize, as long as 75 per cent of the membership voted in favour.[55] While a clause was inserted into this Act which prescribed a qualifying period of two years before members could benefit from the process, in 1989 the courts overruled this safeguard, resulting in a group of what have passed into the vocabulary as 'carpetbaggers' who activated in favour of demutualization. As a result, starting with the Abbey National Building Society in 1989, by 2000 ten major building societies had demutualized, accounting for two-thirds of this sector's assets.[56] This highlighted what to many was the spirit behind Conservative reforms, in that mutuality was exchanged for a promise of financial remuneration, sparking a tidal wave of demutualizations that would affect the CWS adversely in 1997.

---

[53] *Sunday Times*, 27 April 1997.
[54] For more detail, see Kynaston (2002). See also Wilson (1995), 233–41.
[55] These issues are also covered in Myers et al. (2011).   [56] See Pollock (2008).

At the same time, British business was also indulging in one of its frequent bursts of intensive merger and acquisition activity, creating an environment in which few commercial operations could afford to reveal any weaknesses. Certainly, the intensity of this activity enhanced the growing impression that British business was driven more by the struggle for corporate control, rather than improving performance and competitiveness; that retaining shareholder loyalty was more important to senior management than innovation and productivity, placing the prime emphasis on money-making, as opposed to organizational culture and loyalty to employees. Several high-profile scandals also revealed some of the murkier aspects of City activities. While these incidents represented only a small fraction of the booming range of City transactions, when the public read about the illegal operations of people such as Robert Maxwell, Ernest Saunders, and James Guerin,[57] this significantly tarnished the City's reputation at a time when successive governments proved unwilling to introduce stronger corporate governance regulations.

It was in this milieu that Andrew Regan operated, using impeccable contacts with blue-chip City institutions and entrepreneurs linked to household and food products to build a flourishing business empire. As we noted earlier, in 1994 he had used these contacts to provide the resources for his firm, Hobson, to purchase the CWS's food manufacturing operations, including the subsidiary trading as F. E. Barber, for £111 million. Part of this deal was a three-year agreement to continue to supply CWS customers, worth £220 million per year, providing Hobson with a sound business model. Such was the importance of this supply contract that in 1995 Regan paid £2.85 million for a two-year extension to the original deal, significantly enhancing the value of his streamlined operation.

While superficially this deal looked like a good piece of business for both parties, as we shall see later they became the subject of detailed legal investigations. In the first place, one should stress that the contract extension had been negotiated with Allan Green, Deputy Head of Food at CWS (see Figure 8.14), but without the involvement of CWS Board members, who were only informed of the deal in 1997, by which time it was apparent that this executive had been supplying Regan with considerable quantities of confidential CWS data. As we saw earlier, this deal also involved Ronald Zimet of Trellis International, while by December 1995 Hillsdown Holdings had paid £121 million for the business, reportedly making Andrew Regan £3 million on his original investment.[58] Crucially, these deals established Regan's City reputation as somebody capable of raising large sums of money and generating appreciable returns within a short period of time, characteristics that were regarded as highly attractive to a financial community driven by short-term imperatives. As one contemporary noted: 'Regan is one of an elite band of young City dealmakers whose recent adventures have set the world of high finance alight... They all play the business world like a roulette wheel and so far their numbers

---

[57] Guerin was the American businessman who defrauded Ferranti of approximately £210 million by merging his firm into the august British electronics venture. See Wilson (2013).
[58] *Sunday Times*, 9 February 1997.

FIGURE 8.14. Allan Green and David Chambers in *Co-operative News*, 1993. This news item highlighted Green and Chambers's leadership of CWS Retail operations; both men later served prison sentences for providing Andrew Regan with confidential information during his attempted CWS takeover in 1997. Courtesy of *Co-operative News* (<www.thenews.coop>).

have come up.'[59] In order to exploit this reputation further, in October 1996 Regan made a successful £4 million hostile bid to acquire New Guernsey Securities as his vehicle to launch further acquisitions, renaming it Lanica Trust Ltd and spinning off a subsidiary called Galileo to handle acquisitions. Counting amongst his supporters such prestigious City names as Hambros Bank, Schroders, Jupiter Tyndall, and Killik & Co, Regan also recruited a formidable management team, including David Lyons, the Rea Brothers financier who had advised CWS on the sale of its food manufacturing activities. The City clearly responded favourably to these developments, because Lanica's share price rose from 58p to 1950p within four months, in anticipation of more lucrative deals.[60] Not wanting to disappoint his backers and admirers, using the Galileo subsidiary Regan put together a bold £500 million bid for CWS's non-food businesses, including its opticians, funeral parlours, garages, and travel agencies.

As we shall see later, it is now known that a large quantity of CWS data had been illegally acquired to inform Galileo's bid, leading to several court cases that trundled on for a further six years. Nevertheless, after the *Sunday Times* produced a sensational revelation on 9 February 1997 that Regan was about to launch this bid,[61] the business world was aghast at the scale and audacity of his intentions. Regan also put about the story that as a schoolboy in Macclesfield, he had allegedly been puzzled by the sight of a chauffeur-driven Jaguar dropping off a friend every morning, especially as the car was owned by a CWS manager who enjoyed yachting. This anecdote was used as part of his publicity drive aimed at convincing anybody who would listen that the CWS needed to be revamped, implying that its executives were somehow no longer sticking to the socialist principles that underpinned the movement.[62] It was also a point that resonated with informed opinion, most commentators agreeing that the CWS was in need of radical change, its management having lived off a legacy that was rapidly diminishing in value. While the London Stock Exchange was immediately obliged to suspend Lanica's shares, in order to suppress any further speculation, Regan stood astride the City as the epitome of its ethos and attitudes, with support from highly prestigious institutions that were anticipating another financial bonanza.

Prior to the *Sunday Times* exposé on 9 February about Regan's intentions, Graham Melmoth, the newly appointed CWS chief executive, had already been tipped off by his City contacts of Regan's intentions, providing him with invaluable time to initiate a robust riposte. It was not in this person's character to accept such an assault without offering a response that would shake the City establishment to its roots. Melmoth had joined the CWS as co-operative secretary in 1975, after having been trained in several London firms as a company secretary.[63] As he had always sympathized with left-of-centre political views, espousing an ideological commitment to co-operative principles, the Manchester job reflected his own social democratic tendencies. Initially, though, he was sorely disappointed by the culture of an organization that had become what he described as a

[59] *Express on Sunday*, 16 February 1997.   [60] *Express on Sunday*, 16 February 1997.
[61] *Sunday Times*, 9 February 1997.   [62] *Sunday Times*, 27 April 1997.
[63] This section is based on an interview with Sir Graham Melmoth.

'monastery', with intense internal rivalries undermining the co-operative principle and a Board totally dominated by successive CEOs who rarely consulted others on strategy. Indeed, Melmoth almost left the CWS within a year of securing the post, but persevered in the hope that opportunities might arise to change what he felt was a self-defeating culture. Reflecting his intense commitment to co-operative principles, as we noted earlier he had also played a leading role in the ICA's drive to reaffirm and modernize the '1844 Rochdale Principles', culminating in the publication of *Co-operative Values in a Changing World*. More importantly, Melmoth had worked effectively to impose greater coordination across the CWS and local retail societies, successfully placing the co-operative secretary's office at the heart of an organization that had traditionally allowed distribution (and more recently, retail) executives to control strategy and structure. It was primarily as a result of this influential role that in November 1996 Melmoth was appointed CEO, defeating his principal rival, John Owen, the head of retail. CWS managers remember vividly how, when informed of the Board's decision to appoint Melmoth at a managers' meeting, Owen and his retail team were so shocked that the room fell silent.[64] To nobody's surprise, Owen left the CWS shortly after to pursue a career in the private sector.

Although Melmoth's rise to prominence was undoubtedly based on his strong commitment to co-operative values and principles, one should also stress that he had demonstrated considerable organizational talent in starting to pull together a business empire which, as we have noted many times, had traditionally been internally divided and dysfunctional. Crucially, it was the secretary's department that negotiated the assimilation of local co-operative societies into the CWS, providing Melmoth and his team with the opportunity to effect greater coordination over the disparate movement. Crucially, he had assembled a team of committed co-operative managers that shared both his strong belief in the movement's principles and the desire to build an organization capable of converting these principles into commercial success. While two of the team were also involved in the corruption scandal surrounding the 1997 takeover bid, this did not undermine their commitment to pursue the new CEO's vision. Skinner actually kept Melmoth at a distance during the latter months of 1996, mainly because as a retailer he had supported Owen's candidature for CEO, leading many to view the CEO designate's team as a 'government in exile'.[65] Nevertheless, by the beginning of 1997 they were ready to launch a radical campaign to renew the movement's commitment to its core values and principles.

One of Melmoth's first actions as chief executive, reflecting his belief that a strong commitment to the philosophical principles and values of co-operation should come from the top, was to publish a booklet entitled *Managing Change through People*.[66] This outlined his commitment to co-operative values and explained that the organization should 'work for the long-term success of the co-operative sector'. Although he acknowledged that the CWS had been undergoing 'a metamorphosis' in the past decade, not least through the acquisition of substantial retailing operations, he felt that to build on these foundations and cope with the increasingly competitive marketplace it was necessary to place an especial

---

[64] Interview with Dr Bill Shannon.   [65] Interview with Dr Bill Shannon.
[66] CWS BM, 6 November 1996.

emphasis on four key dimensions, *Performance-People-Communication-Planning*. It was a radical manifesto that left nobody in any doubt about how and why Melmoth and his team would drive the CWS forward, not least because it was followed by the introduction of an extensive training programme, initially for the top 200 managers and later for over 1,000, conducted by the Co-operative College, inculcating the message into the very fabric of the organization. He also commissioned Bill Shannon to write a report on the 'co-operative dimension' in retailing, indicating to that part of the organization that he was intent on inculcating the values and principles into the core of a disparate business. Externally, Melmoth also offered the prospect of much closer collaboration between CWS and CRS,[67] given that relations between these two organizations had deteriorated to such an extent that they were almost 'warring factions'.

Melmoth had clearly given himself an ambitious agenda in attempting to overcome toxic historical features of a movement that was at the same time struggling to compete with the major multiple retailers. At the same time, even though Melmoth had been tipped off about the Regan bid, it still came as a massive shock to the movement. Business editors of broadsheet newspapers, notably the *Sunday Times* and *Sunday Telegraph*, devoted many column inches to highlighting CWS weaknesses, implicitly supporting Regan's bid. Melmoth was consequently obliged to counter this adverse publicity by commissioning the CWS's merchant bank, S. G. Warburg, and solicitors, Linklater Paine, to build a defence against Regan. Internally, Alan Prescott took the lead in harnessing CWS resources behind the defence, keeping senior managers especially focused on the need to repel Regan. While this team boosted the CWS's chances of repelling Regan, not least because of the creative work of Warburg's Brian Keelan, it is nevertheless vital to stress that the predator was also the victim of his own tactics, in that it rapidly became apparent that Lanica executives were being fed information of a highly confidential nature to support the bid. For example, one Sunday newspaper published the CWS's financial results before they had been officially released,[68] while Green later admitted that he had provided Board minutes, property valuations, and profit forecasts.[69] The feeling that confidential information was being leaked to Regan sparked a forensic internal investigation of executive activities, including expenses claims and telephone records, revealing that Green and Chambers were most likely to be responsible. A firm of corporate investigators, Control Risks Group, was also hired, securing photographic evidence of Regan meeting these CWS executives in the car park of a Buckinghamshire hotel,[70] during which boxes of CWS documents were being ferried from one car to another. Apart from showing a film of this incident to a High Court judge, the CWS was able to use this ammunition in a highly subtle way, by privately alerting Regan's backers about the highly dubious nature of his business practices. Melmoth likened the strategy to isolating a battleship by attacking its supporting flotilla, thereby rendering it vulnerable to counter-attacks and negating its offensive potential.[71]

[67] *Independent*, 5 November 1996.   [68] *Sunday Times*, 13 April 1997.
[69] *Guardian*, 26 April 1997.   [70] *Guardian*, 17 May 1997.
[71] Interview with Sir Graham Melmoth.

FIGURE 8.15. Andrew Regan in *Co-operative News*, 1997. On 18 March 1997, as the Lanica affair unfolded, the front page of the *Co-operative News* taunted Regan's misunderstanding of the CWS's membership structure and compared him unfavourably with nineteenth-century CWS leader J. T. W. Mitchell. By May 1997 Regan had resigned all of his directorships, and moved his family to Monaco, where he went on to run an investment business. Courtesy of *Co-operative News* (<www.thenews.coop>).

Before explaining how all of this was played out in a blaze of publicity (see Figure 8.15), it is vital to explain the three key stages through which the bid passed. As we have already seen, the first stage was Galileo's plan to bid £500 million for the CWS's non-food businesses. Once Lanica's shares had been suspended on 10 February 1997, however, it is clear that over the following six weeks Regan and his advisers started to hatch an even more ambitious bid, estimated at approximately £1.2 billion, for the whole of the CWS, with Nomura Securities (the world's largest financial trader) providing the bulk of the capital. Using confidential information supplied by Green and Chambers, Regan had calculated that if the organization was broken up into palatable portions, an estimated £1.8–2.0 billion could be generated, making him a substantial fortune on a single deal.[72] This once again highlighted how under different management the CWS's considerable resources could be leveraged to generate much better returns, reflecting badly on its lethargic organizational dynamic. To expedite matters, Allied Irish Bank was lined up to buy The Co-operative Bank, while Sainsbury's was going to be offered the retail network, achieving the kind of financial synergy to which City denizens aspired. The rumour machine was also cranked up to inform opinion-makers of the plans, further enhancing Regan's reputation as one of the City's emerging stars.

[72] *Sunday Telegraph*, 27 April 1997.

Having laid solid foundations within the financial community, it is important to stress that in spite of the advice emanating from David Lyons and the illicit material coming from Green and Chambers, the predators were guilty of pursuing a misdirected strategy. This error was based on a fundamental misinterpretation of CWS's membership structure, because Regan thought that if he offered £1,000 to each of what he calculated to be 500,000 active members, this would facilitate the transfer of ownership into Galileo. It was a strategy that had handsomely rewarded the 'carpetbaggers' converting mutual building societies into public limited companies. Indeed, the Alliance & Leicester Building Society was going through exactly this process in April 1997. As various commentators explained, however, this strategy was flawed, in that the CWS's individual members, which were at that time numbered in the millions, elected representatives onto regional committees, which in turn elected CWS Board members.[73] It is also worth noting that the corporate members stood firm against Galileo, refusing the money offered for their votes, decisions which ran counter to what we have noted with regard to the remaining retail societies' aversion to collaborating with the CWS. As Regan required 75 per cent of the membership to vote in favour before ownership could be transferred, this seemed highly unlikely even to the most optimistic of his supporters. In addition, Regan would also need approval from the Registrar of Friendly Societies, something that was never assured. Furthermore, as the Board (dominated by retail societies) rejected Regan's request to engage in talks, this made it impossible for Galileo to succeed with its strategy. Regan had made a fatal error, albeit one that was never tested in practice because of his other failings.

Of course, while the second stage was unfolding Melmoth and his team were by no means inactive, because it was in this period that an internal audit team headed by Paul Smedley was filtering through expenses claims and telephone logs, as well as commissioning Control Risk to follow Green and Chambers to their secret rendezvous with Regan and advisers.[74] As a result of certain early 1990s corporate governance scandals that were described earlier, Smedley's team had developed a series of techniques that uncovered a host of illegal activities, including hotel expenses that indicated clearly how Green and Chambers had been meeting Regan regularly.[75] By the time Regan was ready to launch his bid for the whole of the CWS, Melmoth was consequently well armed to forestall the process with a series of lethal strikes that destroyed the predatorial 'flotilla' with devastating speed and ruthlessness. The first of these strikes was fired before Regan had officially placed his bid, when on 17 April not only were Green and Chambers suspended from their CWS positions, on the grounds of what a CWS press release claimed was a 'suspected recent serious breach of trust',[76] but Melmoth also wrote to Lord Hambro (head of Hambros Bank) enquiring about the £2.4 million payment to Ronald Zimet in 1995. This certainly destabilized Regan's team, especially as it was followed on the day after by the CWS requesting an injunction both blocking the use of the confidential information that Green and Chambers had leaked to the predators and requiring its return to the CWS.

[73] *The Times*, 19 April 1997; *Grocer*, 26 April 1997.
[74] CWS paid £70,000 for Control Risks' services. *Financial Times*, 21 April 1997.
[75] Interview with Paul Smedley.   [76] *Financial Times*, 18 April 1997.

The full extent of the accusations against Green, Chambers, Regan, Lyons, and Hambros Bank was revealed at a second hearing on 25 April, when Mr Justice Lightman concluded that the bid had patently been based on 'iniquitous conduct'.[77] This view was reached after the CWS's QC, Christopher Clarke, explained how almost all of the documents passed by Green and Chambers to Regan had been given to Hambros Bank, which in turn had provided copies to seventeen organizations that wished to benefit from the bid (including HSBC, Lloyds Bank, Goldman Sachs, JP Morgan, and Price Waterhouse). Lightman was consequently in no doubt that the actions of Regan, Lyons, Green, and Chambers had been 'clearly dishonest', extending the ban on using all information to Hambros Bank and Travers Smith Braithwaite. In a forlorn attempt to rescue the situation, on 24 April Lyons wrote to all twenty-eight CWS directors, including a copy of the 72-page Galileo bid, encouraging them to convene a special general meeting of all members to consider a sale. The CWS chairman, Lennox Fyffe, refused to entertain the document, insisting that all directors return it 'unopened and unread', effectively terminating the process on a day that Galileo returned seven boxes of CWS material.[78] Melmoth also continued to write to both Hambros Bank executives and Regan, requesting explanations about the veracity of documentation used in compiling the bid and hinting at criminal prosecutions, further embarrassing the City establishment at a time when its less scrupulous activities were coming under closer scrutiny.[79]

Apart from terminating the Regan bid, Mr Justice Lightman's ruling was clearly a serious indictment of what Melmoth described as 'illegal activity that strikes at the heart of the City'. Even the key executive at the CWS's investment bank, Brian Keelan of Warburg's, was willing to concede that: 'It has not been a good week for the City. It's been ugly.'[80] This sparked the third and longest stage in the bid process, because while Regan had been soundly defeated, the CWS announced that it would not only pursue its predators for appropriate compensation, but also prosecute all parties involved in the bid. Information relating to the mysterious payment to Ronald Zimet of Trellis International had already been passed to the Serious Fraud Office (SFO), given that the CWS was convinced it was a bribe paid to Green and Chambers to extend the Hobson supply contract in 1995, both men having denied that any intermediary had been involved in the negotiations.[81] Green and Chambers were formally dismissed from the CWS on 27 April, while entreaties were made to the relevant authorities to investigate possible insider trading in Lanica's shares, given their rapid increase in value prior to February 1997 from just £2 to almost £20. Although Sir Chips Keswick, chairman of Hambros Bank, was obliged to issue a public apology to the CWS, as well as sharing with Travers Smith Braithwaite a compensation package of approximately £1 million to cover CWS's legal and other costs,[82] in 1998 this company was fined £270,000 (plus £80,000 costs) by the Securities and Futures Authority

[77] *Guardian*, 26 April 1997.   [78] *The Times*, 24 April 1997; *Daily Mail*, 24 April 1997.
[79] *Daily Telegraph*, 24 April 1997.   [80] *Guardian*, 26 April 1997.
[81] *Daily Express*, 22 April 1997.   [82] *Independent*, 29 April 1997.

for using confidential information.[83] The CWS also dropped its private case against Green, Chambers, Regan, and Lyons when on 12 May they paid an estimated £750,000 to cover legal and other costs,[84] leaving all actions in the hands of the SFO.

It was September 1999 before the SFO charged Green and Chambers with corruption, and in the following month issued a warrant for Regan's arrest (as he was by then living in Monaco), having finally decided that the mysterious £2.45 million payment to Trellis International was a bribe to secure an extension of the Hobson–CWS supply agreement.[85] In the interim, the SFO investigated not only this payment and the actions of Regan and Lyons, but also County Produce, a bogus farming co-operative set up by Lanica as a means of convening a special CWS meeting to vote on the bid. Such was Regan's status by May 1997 that he had resigned from all of his other directorships,[86] while Galileo was placed in voluntary liquidation and the Stock Exchange refused to refloat Lanica's shares. At that point, he moved his family to Monaco, from where he ran an investment syndicate that by the end of 1999 had made him an estimated £50 million.[87] Finally, after a trial that lasted almost six months, in April 2002 Green and Chambers were convicted of each receiving a £1 million bribe, crimes for which they were given jail sentences of three-and-a-half years, a £50,000 fine, and forced to refund the bribe (including interest). To the amazement of many, the jury failed to reach a verdict on Regan, who had been accused of stealing £2.45 million from F. E. Barber plc for the purposes of bribing Green and Chambers. At a subsequent retrial in January 2003, the judge ordered yet another trial with a fresh jury, but in August 2003 this resulted in a not-guilty verdict, allowing him to return to his Monaco investment business.

8.4 Impact

There was widespread recognition in April 1997 of the resounding nature of the victory achieved by Graham Melmoth and his team, with prolific newspaper coverage announcing how the 'Knightsbridge whizz-kid'[88] had been humbled by the Manchester-based CWS.[89] Apart from defeating Regan, Melmoth was anxious to stress that: 'We have uncovered much evidence of activity that does strike at the heart of the City.' Speaking immediately after the decisive court hearing, he was also convinced that: 'We are not

---

[83] Three executives (Nigel Pantling, Peter Large, and Andrew Salmon) were also fined for their parts in the bid. *Scotsman*, 17 September 1999. In December 1997, Hambros Bank was bought for £300 million by Société Générale.

[84] *Financial Times*, 13 May 1997.

[85] Paul Thomas, the solicitor advising on the 1995 CWS–Hobson deal, was also charged on the same day. *Independent*, 22 September 1997.

[86] These included the NAAFI and Select Catalogues. *Independent on Sunday*, 25 May 1997.

[87] *Sunday Telegraph*, 21 November 1999.

[88] *Scotsman*, 26 April 1997.

[89] See further coverage in *Independent, Observer, Daily Telegraph*, and *Sunday Telegraph*, all of which on 26–7 April 1997 devoted full-page articles to Regan's demise.

here to celebrate. It's the end of a chapter in the life of the society that is part of the fabric of British society. It's 135 years old, and it's been doing good for all that time and intends to carry on doing so.'[90]

Two weeks earlier, using a football analogy he had described the CWS as 'a third division player', when compared to 'first division' firms such as Tesco, Sainsbury's, and ASDA. In particular, he was keen to stress the need to gain promotion as quickly as possible, highlighting the dangers of sustaining the status quo.[91] Indeed, it is vital to stress that while Melmoth did not have any experience of food retailing, he was well aware of the need to improve performance in what was by then the CWS's core business. He had read and absorbed the detailed report written by Sparks,[92] as well as many other dismal assessments of the CWS's commercial performance, using this as further evidence of the need to change course. The 1997 CWS annual meeting had proved difficult for senior management, because many corporate members used the opportunity to highlight how Regan's bid had emerged because of widely acknowledged weaknesses in both structure and strategy.[93] Melmoth responded by arguing that he wanted to forestall future bids by developing a 'successful co-operative business', with the emphasis placed on all three words.[94] Above all, CWS management wanted to avoid the implications of one headline, 'Funeral postponed',[95] because if Regan had achieved anything, it was revealing the inherent weaknesses in a rambling, uncoordinated organization that possessed some highly valued assets worth approximately £2 billion. Indeed, in April 1999 the US takeover specialist Babcock & Brown tabled a £2 billion offer for the CWS. One must stress, though, that this bid faded as rapidly as it had emerged from the City rumour-mill once the Americans realized that they faced a defence based on strength, rather than perceived weaknesses.

This highlights what we can regard as the 'Regan Paradox', because while he assembled his bid on the premiss that the CWS was in decline, the decisive leadership demonstrated by Melmoth and his team both during the bid and over the following years provided the foundations for a recovery in fortunes. Again, it is essential to stress that one can easily exaggerate the significance of the 1997 bid, given that through mergers and rationalization the CWS had been pursuing a more integrated structure since the 1980s. Indeed, many would stress the essential importance of an active membership, in stark contrast to the situation in building societies which were succumbing to the 'carpetbaggers'.[96] Crucially, the CWS was driving forward on a mission to reassert the importance of membership to co-operative identity, Melmoth arguing consistently that unless consumer members received tangible benefits from being part of the organization, then support would melt away. On the commercial front, the rapid adoption of an 'ethical trader' brand (see Figure 8.16) was also instrumental in fuelling sales growth,

[90] *Daily Telegraph*, 26 April 1997.   [91] *Daily Express*, 9 April 1997.
[92] Sparks (1994).   [93] *Daily Telegraph*, 19 May 1997.
[94] Interview with Sir Graham Melmoth.   [95] *Northwest Business Insider*, May 1997.
[96] Interviews with Russell Gill and Mervyn Wilson.

FIGURE 8.16. **CWS lorry advertising Fairtrade, *c.*2000s.** Even before the creation of the Fairtrade marque in 1994, CWS stocked fairly traded Cafédirect coffee from 1992, and by 2000 had introduced its first own-brand Fairtrade products. Courtesy of The Co-operative Group.

alongside key organizational changes made possible by much closer integration through the CRTG and further mergers.[97] At the same time, it is vital to stress that many executives would have been in favour of further essential changes to the commercial structure of the CWS by the time Melmoth had retired as chief executive in 2002.[98] Nevertheless, Melmoth's status in April 1997 as the 'defender of co-operative values' provided him with the momentum to press forward with even more radical changes. In May 1997, he was also able to appoint his right-hand man during the Lanica bid, Alan Prescott, to the position of deputy chief executive, strengthening the team as key agents of change and prefacing significant organizational and strategic changes over the following five years.[99] Moreover, the general political climate proved highly conducive, in that after almost eighteen years of Conservative government, the electorate moved decisively in favour of 'New Labour', offering the rich promise of a fairer and more balanced society. To many, the key issue facing the CWS was a combination of, first, coordinating the disparate, sprawling business empire, and secondly, reasserting the voice of individual members in a movement that had developed an enormous distance between its management and consumers. The way in which this eventually occurred is one of the initial issues that we

[97] These issues are further developed in Myers et al. (2011).
[98] Interview with Martin Beaumont.   [99] *Financial Times*, 2 May 1997.

shall address in Chapter 9, where the creation and development of The Co-operative Group will be analysed.

Above all, though, it is vital to avoid the perception that these events can be seen in isolation, because there was an evolutionary character to the whole process that reflected the way in which the CWS had adapted to its environment over the course of its fascinating history. Although the robust rejection of Regan's bid had provided the kind of stimulus the CWS needed to prompt radical change, this was merely yet another stage in the organization's evolution. Of course, imaginative organizational and marketing drives, not least the 'responsible retailer' initiative, were vital additional dimensions to the 1990s changes, but these built on earlier programmes that had contributed to the later successes. In this sense, the 'Regan Paradox' was of vital importance in highlighting CWS's commercial weaknesses and reviving some of the dynamism that had been so evident in its first decades. Melmoth's major contribution was to use the takeover bid as a figurative 'stick' to beat his board into agreeing with his aim to build a 'family of co-operative businesses'. Just to reinforce the message, this was used as the subtitle to the second Co-operative Commission's report,[100] leaving nobody in any doubt that change was both essential and achievable. In particular, many felt that the CWS was simply not able to compete effectively in what was an increasingly challenging marketplace. Furthermore, in reaffirming the values and principles of the co-operative movement, this reinforced the commercial vision, resonating closely with the marketing drive based on 'ethical trading' that had underpinned The Co-operative Bank's increasingly impressive performance.

We shall now go on to assess the extent to which this impacted on the CWS's performance from the late 1990s, outlining how even higher levels of concentration and integration were achieved, eschewing the regional solution that many had advocated in the previous decade.[101] While many battles had yet to be fought and won, not least in persuading societies to link up with the CWS, change was coming to be regarded as essential if the movement was going to survive and flourish. Crucially, the post-1997 revival was built solidly on the values and principles first espoused by the Rochdale Pioneers almost 140 years earlier, reaffirming the central role of individual membership and the benefits one can derive from joining the movement. Moreover, this idealism appealed to a generation of managers that had entered the CWS from Britain's expanded higher education sector in the 1960s and 1970s—young people who were interested in a business career, but whose left-of-centre sympathies made co-operatives especially appealing. It was no coincidence that the pace of reform accelerated just as this generation reached positions of real power and influence within the movement; but especially in such key organizations as the CWS, CRS, and Co-operative Bank. In this sense, British co-operation, for all its difficulties, avoided the loss of ideological purpose which has been instrumental in the demise of co-operative movements elsewhere, notably in France, Germany, and Austria.

[100] Co-operative Commission (2001).   [101] Sparks (2002); Cook (1982).

CHAPTER 9

···

'FALLING TOWARDS THE CENTRE'

A Twenty-First-Century 'Renaissance'

···

THE late 1990s had clearly been a pivotal stage in the CWS's evolution, awakening staff at all levels to the possible consequences of continued decline and atrophy. Of course, as we have outlined in the last two chapters, a host of initiatives had been launched since the late 1960s aimed at both compensating for the loss of market share and adapting the business model to much-changed circumstances. Amongst the most notable of these was the increased concentration of retailing into the CWS and CRS, focusing much more on 'buying for', rather than 'supplying to', as the principal role of the CWS, as well as creating the CRTG to improve this function, disposing of the manufacturing operations, and introducing ethical trading as a key differentiator from its multiple rivals. In addition, one should stress how The Co-operative Bank and funeral services became shining beacons of improved performance, based on a highly customer-focused strategy and carefully integrated structure. While these innovations did not halt the CWS's continued loss of market share, largely because they were not pursued as rigorously as necessary in the challenging circumstances, they provided elements of a package that successive CEOs were able to develop from the late 1990s. The three CEOs—Graham Melmoth (1996–2002), Martin Beaumont (2002–8), and Peter Marks (2008–13)—were very different in style and background; they have been described respectively as 'diplomat, modernizer and entrepreneur'[1]—but each contributed enormously to a radical change in orientation and achievement. In many ways, they could also be described as 'lucky generals', moving into the top position when the time was right to make the changes required to effect performance improvements. Indeed, by exploiting the cathartic nature of Regan's 1997 takeover bid, Melmoth initiated a process that his successors have been able to extend, precipitating a 'fall towards the centre' in terms of focusing activity within the CWS and its successor, The Co-operative Group, a process

---

[1] Interview with Russell Gill.

accelerated under Beaumont and Marks, contributing enormously to what some have described as a 'renaissance' in the movement's fortunes.

In analysing these claims, we shall be especially interested in the iterative nature of strategic decision-making, and especially how this built on the many initiatives of the previous three decades. This exercise will highlight the conducive political environment for change that prevailed from the late 1990s, because such were the changes to the movement's internal dynamic that traditional obstacles to reform were either marginalized or removed altogether, while a highly popular Labour government also proved supportive of the change agenda. In simple terms, the attitudes that created what we have consistently described as a dysfunctional federation waned dramatically from the late 1990s, resulting in the replacement of senior managers unsympathetic to change by a generation of modernizers who recognized that the CWS had to adapt or disappear. The major corporate members were also much more prone to accommodate this 'fall towards the centre', because while the large regional societies had been an essential staging point in this process, by the 2000s it was increasingly apparent that combination was the only means of surviving the onslaught from intensifying competition.

Another key feature of this era was the successful reaffirmation of co-operative values and principles, and specifically a resurgence in the voice of individual members as the CWS evolved from being a secondary into a primary co-operative. As we saw at the end of Chapter 8, the 2001 Constitutional Review was responsible for introducing the kind of governance standards that would facilitate much more forceful individual member involvement, creating the three-tier democratic structure which was effectively supported by the revitalized member relations department. These processes significantly diminished the source of much of the conflict between the CWS and retail societies, confirming the efficacy of a growing desire to differentiate 'the co-op' from its competitors and provide an appropriate climate for the 'responsible trader' campaign that had gathered effective momentum in the 1990s. These solid foundations were developed during the 2000s, often in association with an aggressive merger strategy that boosted market share, especially in the convenience store sector of retailing.

At the same time, while The Co-operative Bank experienced some difficulties after 2005, careful attention was also paid to other non-core businesses such as funeral services and healthcare (pharmacies) as a means of building on the concept of a 'family of co-operative businesses'. Nevertheless, it is vital to note that this was not a simple linear process of improving market share and profitability, because enormous challenges still needed to be overcome in effecting this 'renaissance'. Furthermore, although Peter Marks was rightly able to claim by 2009 that 'the co-op...was back in the premiership', improving significantly on Melmoth's 1999 accusation that the CWS was distinctly 'third division', the pressures to sustain that position remain. By 2010, however, claims of a 'renaissance' in co-operative fortunes were widely accepted, even though after the financial crisis of 2008 the British economy experienced severe bouts of recession. This chapter will assess how a 'renaissance' was achieved, culminating in extremely optimistic statements by the incumbent CEO that in spite of recession co-operative trading was once again vibrant and increasingly profitable, with individual members fully represented in a transparent, democratic structure.

9.1 MELMOTH, THE CRS, AND THE 'FAMILY' CONCEPT

It was clear by the summer of 1997 that Melmoth's victory over Regan, combined with an unwavering commitment to co-operative values and principles, would provide him with invaluable ammunition when pressing forward with his reform agenda. Melmoth was especially keen to convert what to many appeared to be an uncoordinated Leviathan-type collection of businesses into what became a core element of his strategy, namely, creating a coherent 'family of successful co-operative businesses'. As he was often heard to say, equal emphasis had to be placed on all of the last three words in this quotation,[2] reflecting his belief that the key to success was coordinating the Leviathan and generating the profits required for an essential modernization process. Indeed, as well as initiating a programme based on reaffirming co-operative values and principles,[3] Melmoth also instigated a radical Strategic Review of CWS operations, with a view to achieving the degree of coordination required to improve commercial performance. This dual emphasis on philosophical and commercial priorities would later be described as the distinct 'co-operative advantage', again reinforcing the movement's desire to differentiate itself from the enormous retail companies that competed aggressively for consumers' attention.

Apart from advocating the complete rationalization and streamlining of the CWS's procurement system, as well as modernizing store interiors and improving product lines, the 1997 Strategic Review was especially noteworthy for the highly controversial decision to abandon the hypermarket and superstore sectors of food retailing in order to place much more focus on the local convenience store (hereafter, c-store).[4] As we shall see later, it was at least another eight years before this decision could be completely implemented, given that since the 1970s the CWS (and other major retail societies) had invested significantly in large store formats made popular in the UK by Sainsbury's, Tesco, and ASDA. Of course, the CWS was not alone in diverting resources into c-stores, because in response to late 1990s planning restrictions on out-of-town stores, Sainsbury's and Tesco were investigating this option.[5] Nevertheless, the CWS's decision stimulated considerable debate across the movement, in that by 1996 77 superstores had been opened, as well as 1,397 supermarkets and 102 department stores, all of which would be either closed or sold off by 2005. An even bigger source of debate was how many of these

---

[2] Interview with Sir Graham Melmoth.   [3] See section 8.3.
[4] Hallsworth and Bell (2003).   [5] Wood et al. (2006).

outlets were exchanged with multiples for c-stores, some challenging the values the CWS placed on their assets.[6] Clearly, though, the Board was convinced that as part of the strategy aimed at differentiating the CWS from its rivals, the c-store format could be developed as the basis for future growth. It was a matter, as Melmoth argued both at the time and in retrospect, of dropping the 'me too' approach to retailing, because the CWS had slavishly imitated its rivals over the previous two decades, but with no palpable impact on competitiveness and market share.[7] Of course, it was essential that the c-stores (see Figure 9.1) should be located in appropriate places, highlighting the issues raised in Chapter 7 about the impact of extensive slum clearance programmes on retail societies.[8] The CWS nevertheless decided in 1997 to focus its retail strategy on c-stores, prompting significant investment in both new facilities and an aggressive acquisition policy that would eventually significantly boost market share.

FIGURE 9.1. **Co-operative 'late shop' in Kirton, Lincolnshire, c.1995.** Although CWS and other co-operative societies had invested in superstores and hypermarkets since the 1970s, following a strategic review in 1997 CWS shifted its focus to developing its convenience and small format stores.

[6] Correspondence with Leigh Sparks.   [7] *Daily Mail*, 13 January 2002.
[8] See section 7.1.

Melmoth had clearly given himself an ambitious agenda in attempting to overcome toxic historical features of a business model that was struggling to compete with the multiple retailers. Again, as we shall discuss later, it is essential to remember that from the 1990s other parts of the CWS—banking, insurance, and funerals—were performing extremely well, generating improved returns that kept the conglomerate afloat. As food retailing continued to represent over 70 per cent of total turnover, however, focusing resources on what was by then regarded as the CWS's core business was vital. Moreover, with market share falling dramatically from its formerly dominant position of the 1950s (see Table 8.1), not only were commentators quick to condemn performance, but also predators circled the Leviathan with a view to asset-stripping its prized possessions, most notably The Co-operative Bank, funeral services, and an extensive property port-folio (including the well-placed premises in the centre of Manchester). Above all, it was essential to improve the degree of co-operation across the movement, given the frequent criticism that as the CWS was not working with the CRS, this represented 'an undeniable death wish'.[9] As Melmoth had promised at the time of his appointment to work more closely with the CRS, this was yet another challenge he needed to tackle.

To many, the key issue facing the CWS, and indeed the movement as a whole from the 1960s, was rationalizing the number of operations and securing the economies of scale and scope available in a geographically dispersed, sprawling business empire. It was also seen by many as essential that the CWS ought to merge with the CRS, a move that by the late 1990s would create a business with turnover approaching £5 billion. The replication of activities across the CWS and CRS is highlighted in Table 9.1, while by adding United Co-operatives as a third comparator one can readily see that considerable opportunities existed to integrate operations and achieve the kind of synergistic benefits that multiples had already secured. As we saw in Chapter 8, United Co-operatives had been formed in April 1991 by merging two major societies, creating an organization that refused stead-fastly to collaborate with the CWS, even though it operated in the geographical region surrounding Manchester. Although that merger was surrounded by scandal,[10] once the new CEO, Martin Beaumont, started to impose more rigorous management systems on the business it started to generate amongst the best returns in the movement. We shall look closer in section 9.2 at United Co-operatives' strategy, but above all it is vital to stress that in allying itself with the CRS through a buying operation, as well as pursuing a highly independent strategy, this reflected the deep divisions across the three major societies.

The development of a separate buying operation by the CRS and United Co-operatives is an excellent illustration of the hostility that had often been expressed towards the CWS. At the heart of this tension was the difference in membership structure, in that the CRS and United Co-operatives were primary co-operatives owned by individual con-sumers, while the CWS was still a secondary co-operative that was primarily controlled by its corporate membership, providing the individual members acquired through

---

[9] Hallsworth and Bell (2003), 141.   [10] See section 8.1.

Table 9.1. Overlapping businesses in CWS, CRS, and United Co-operatives, 2000

	CWS	CRS	United Co-operatives
Locations	Scotland	South-east	North-west
	Northern Ireland	South-west	North Midlands
	North-east	Wales and Borders	North Wales
	Nottingham	Northern	
	South Midlands		
	South-east		
Sectors	Food	Food	Food
	Household goods		Household goods
	Clothing		Clothing
	Travel		Travel
	Funerals	Funerals	Funerals
	Opticians		Opticians
	Automobiles	Automobiles	Automobiles
	Agriculture		Pharmacies
	Dairies		
	Banking		
	Insurance		

mergers with failing societies with very little voice in the organization. Consequently, even though creating and developing the CRTG had been a considerable success for the CWS, indicating to all inside and outside the movement what could be achieved by exploiting its considerable buying power, the CRS and United Co-operatives still refused to participate. By 1997, the CRTG was responsible for sourcing £3 billion worth of retail sales for sixteen retail societies, offering centralized buying, marketing, and pricing that operated out of the CWS's Manchester headquarters. The CRS, however, was so reluctant to collaborate with the CWS that in 1996 it combined with four other major societies (United Co-operatives, Portsea Island, Tamworth, and Yorkshire) to create a rival to the CRTG, named the Consortium of Independent Co-operatives.[11] Along with the construction of its expensive headquarters building in Rochdale, the Consortium was yet further evidence of the CRS's stubborn resistance to all entreaties to synchronize this crucial aspect of modern multiple retailing. Although the Consortium was able to boast by 1997 that it sourced £2 billion-worth of goods, it lacked the centralized functions developed by the CRTG, limiting the latitude with which its five members could source their own goods. This not only undermined the Consortium's buying power, but

[11] *Grocer*, 25 January 1997.

commentators were also aware that the existence of two operations severely constrained the economies of scale that the movement potentially possessed.

Of course, as we noted in Chapters 7 and 8 (see Table 7.3), such had been the intensity of co-operative mergers since the late 1960s that there was inevitably less potential in this rescue strategy. Nevertheless, whether or not the creation of the CRTG and the Consortium can explain the need for societies to merge into larger operations, Melmoth was convinced that it was essential to combine the CWS and CRS. This conviction prevailed in the CEO's mind in spite of the CRS's open hostility to a merger, an attitude based mainly on the membership differences just highlighted and compounded by the aspirations of Harry Moore to run a combined operation.[12] As we noted in Chapter 8, after the decisive 1993 constitutional changes, the CRS had succeeded in marginalizing CWS influence on its Board,[13] eliminating at least in the short term any prospect of a merger. Moreover, the (heavily politicized) lay composition of the CRS's Board failed to hold its executives to account for their increasingly poor commercial judgements. Nevertheless, as Figures 9.2 and 9.3 reveal, the decline in turnover after 1996 and mounting losses over the following three years were placing enormous question marks over the CRS's ability to survive as a trading entity.

By the late 1990s, the CRS's dismal performance was becoming a major issue for the entire movement, not least because its CEO, Harry Moore, and the lay Board continued to resist Melmoth's invitation to merger talks. When it was revealed that Moore had even met Andrew Regan to discuss whether the CRS would support a takeover bid, this

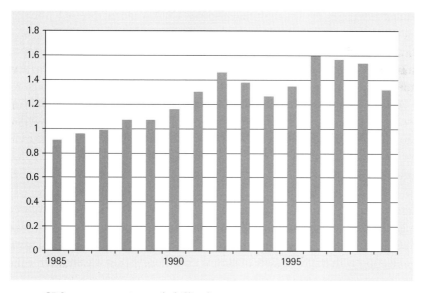

FIGURE 9.2. CRS turnover, 1985–99 (£ billion).

[12] See section 8.1 for an analysis of these issues. [13] See Beaumont (1997), 19–22.

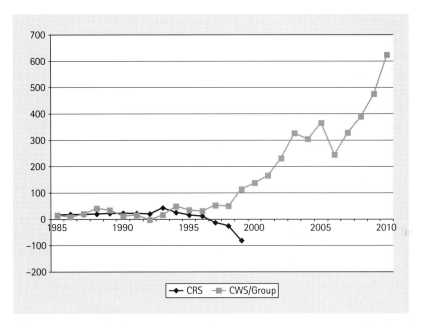

FIGURE 9.3. Surplus/deficit of CRS and CWS/The Co-operative Group, 1985–2010 (£ million).

exacerbated what was already a fraught relationship.[14] Of course, innovations such as the Consortium indicated that the CRS was attempting to turn around a very difficult situation, even if joining the CRTG would have been more effective for an operation that was struggling badly. The CRS also replaced Moore as CEO, when in May 1998 Andy Meehan was recruited from Storehouse, bringing a fresh approach to the challenges. In spite of his lack of experience in co-operative trading, as a trained accountant with a honed business mind, Meehan quickly grasped the nature of the problem facing the CRS.[15] Amongst Meehan's earliest initiatives was a marketing drive to push own-brand foods, while in 1999 CRS closed fifty-two of its non-food stores that traded under the names Living and Homeworld. Although these initiatives lacked the kind of restructuring of retail branding that multiples such as Tesco and ASDA-Walmart had pursued, at least the CRS was attempting to turn around what was an increasingly depressing commercial scenario. Crucially, and much to the astonishment of many within the movement, Meehan also announced that the CRS would withdraw from the Consortium and make all future purchases through the CRTG, bringing the CRS decisively into the CWS's orbit.[16] Although Meehan refused to accept that this was the inevitable prelude to a merger with the CWS,[17] many observers felt that once both parties realized the benefits of working in an organization with buying power of almost £5 billion, then it was inevitable that they

---

[14] *Independent on Sunday*, 27 April 1997.

[15] *Manchester Evening News*, 25 July 2000.

[16] The Consortium continued to operate on behalf of United Co-operatives and two other retail societies until 2007.

[17] *Supermarketing*, 30 April 1999.

would combine.[18] Melmoth also seized this opportunity to initiate yet another round of merger discussions, persuading Meehan to attend a series of meetings between June and October 1999. In view of the commercial difficulties facing the CRS by the late 1990s (see Figures 9.2 and 9.3), Meehan was obliged to accept the need to put aside the traditional aversion to the CWS and accede to a merger, the Board reluctantly acquiescing in this decision after considerable debate.

When in October 1999 the CWS–CRS merger was announced, commentators were unanimous in their views of both Melmoth's negotiating skills and the beneficial impact combination would have on commercial performance. Although the merger was not fully operational until 2001, along with other major structural and strategic innovations across the Manchester-based organization this represented a significant tipping-point for the movement's commercial activities, after several decades of strife and decline. Crucially, the merger changed the nature of the organization, specifically prompting the shift in the balance from corporate to individual membership, because of the influx of the much larger CRS membership base. It also allowed Melmoth and his team to move decisively towards creating the 'family of co-operative businesses' that lay at the root of his organizational aspirations.

Before going on to assess this rationalization programme, however, it is necessary to consider a vital development that would have significant long-term effects on how the CWS and its successor organization would evolve. Perhaps the most significant impediment to a merger between the CWS and CRS had been the CRS Board's reluctance to be subsumed into the existing CWS governance model. At the same time, successive CWS CEOs had also bemoaned the effectiveness of the CWS Board, complaining that it was comprised of representatives from regional co-operatives who showed little loyalty and commitment to the CWS. It was also apparent, even before the CWS–CRS merger, that the CWS was changing, with more and more emphasis being placed upon its retailing activities as a primary co-operative, leading to the conclusion that the voice of the individual member needed to be heard more clearly in the boardroom and in the corridors of New Century House in Manchester. From the most inauspicious of circumstances, a solution to this conundrum emerged which allowed many of these previously insoluble issues to be tacked, enabling a new governance model to be established. This highlights how after the CRS Board had agreed to transfer engagements to the CWS, two separate streams of activity were pursued: first, a relatively swift process of commercial integration, to ensure that the obvious business benefits might be realized quickly but also to prevent a further haemorrhaging of the CRS; and secondly, a much longer period of deliberation over a new democratic structure, based not on what had existed in the CWS or CRS but which addressed the concerns of members from the CWS, CRS, and independent societies.

Whilst the executives from both organizations started to create a single business operating model, the task of designing a new governance model was left to a Constitutional Review Board, comprising equitable representation from all stakeholders. The mandate

---

[18] *Sunday Business*, 11 July 1999.

for this Board was to start with a blank sheet of paper and to design a 'fit for purpose' governance model, both reflecting best practice in corporate governance and ensuring equitable representation for representatives of individual members and independent societies; in effect, a model that might become an asset to the business in making wise decisions, rather than a millstone which compounded the dysfunctionality of the business.[19] This work took some twelve months to complete, including extensive consultations with members from all regions and independent societies, led by the combative and independently minded CWS secretary, Nick Eyre, a lawyer by background who had been recruited by Melmoth from the building society sector, establishing his pugilistic credentials by taking the fight to Regan in the post-Lanica legal wranglings. Supporting Eyre was Stephen Connah, CRS secretary, who was an honourable voice of reason in the chaotic final years of that society. Supported by Moira Lees, Eyre's deputy, the Review Board picked over every conceivable area of governance, working to the mantra that 'nothing is agreed until everything is agreed'. During this intervening period, the majority of the existing CRS Board was bolted onto the CWS Board, creating a hugely unwieldy and dysfunctional, if temporary, Board, which had the effect of reminding all that there was a real need to design more workable governance structures. While CWS and CRS regions also continued to operate in parallel over this time, what started as 'never the twain shall meet' began to evolve into a developing appreciation of one another's strengths, as well as a recognition of the common interests that existed, particularly between the representatives of individual members.

When the Constitutional Review team made its final recommendations in May 2001, it had achieved what for decades had seemed impossible, namely, consensus. The new Group Board would be comprised of representatives from eight newly created regions, some of which were made up wholly of members from the CWS (such as Scotland, Northern Ireland, and North Eastern & Cumbrian), some wholly CRS (such as South West, Wales & Borders, and Northern) and two which were a mixture of co-operative traditions, many of which pre-existed a CWS–CRS divide (South East and Central & Eastern). Independent societies also retained their voice on the Board, though importantly they now formed a minority, indicating that the primary co-operative business model predominated over the federal. Below board level, eight new regional boards were established (shown in Figure 9.4), operating with significant delegated powers from the Group Board, covering matters such as scrutiny of business operations, approval of capital expenditure in their region, and responsibility for approving branch closures. Forty-five area committees were also established, providing a voice for the local member and championing co-operative values and principles in local communities. For the first time, these committees would be elected by postal and internet voting, giving many more members the opportunity to elect their representatives, an innovation that would radically improve the claim to be a democratic organization. Apart from these structural refinements, it is vital to note that a Group Board-level values and principles committee was formed. Crucially, this committee was given equal status with other board subcommittees such as audit, risk and remuneration, and appointments, ensuring that

---

[19] We are indebted to Russell Gill for advice on this section.

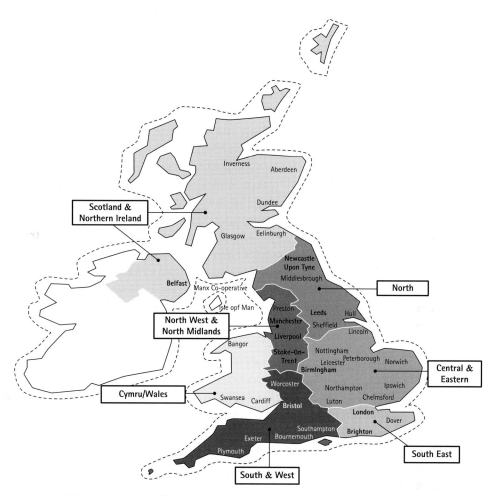

FIGURE 9.4. The Co-operative Group regions, 2001 to present. In The Co-operative Group's current democratic structure, co-operative members elect representatives to forty-eight area committees, which in turn elect representatives to the seven regional boards. The Board of Directors is made up of fifteen representatives elected from regional boards and five elected representatives from independent co-operative societies that are members of The Co-operative Group. This structure evolved from arrangements first agreed following the 2001 Constitutional Review. Courtesy of The Co-operative Group.

the need to champion co-operative values would become a central consideration at a strategic level, involving both members and management in the process. This united the wishes of Melmoth and his acolytes and those members ideologically committed to promoting the values of co-operation. This formalized the priority given to the ethical agenda, and also ensured that traditionally esoteric member relations activities became much more mainstream in the business.

Having decided on this new structure, following elections to the lower-tier representative bodies, there was an influx of new members as some existing directors chose to leave, taking compensation for loss of office. The new Group Board first assembled towards the end of 2001. The first Chair was Keith Darwin, the well-respected CEO of Lincoln Co-operative Society, who replaced Lennox Fyfe in order to build on the consensus achieved by the Constitutional Review. Of course, it was inevitable that tensions would exist between the executive management team and the Board and Regional Boards; indeed, these tensions proved to highly constructive in stimulating debate about the difficult decisions which needed to be taken, such as the disposal of loss-making but well-loved businesses and branches. On the other hand, many of the priorities pursued by the executive management team—improving retailing standards, creating a more confident co-operative brand, and revitalizing membership by reintroducing dividend—were what members had been demanding for years, extending the consensus on co-operative priorities in a way which had been absent during the previous dysfunctional era. Indeed, as might be expected with any board, it was frustration about the stalling commercial performance of the Group which prompted debate across the organization. This was to an extent exacerbated by conflict between the Group's commercial interests and those of the second largest co-operative, United Co-operatives, whose CEOs Martin Beaumont and then Peter Marks were also Group Board members whilst at the same time busily establishing a highly successful challenger to the Group within the movement. As we shall see later, further refinements were added after 2007, but ostensibly this structure has prevailed ever since 2001, providing a more transparent and appropriate governance model for the combined business. Interestingly, though, Melmoth was convinced that in order to confirm the efficacy of these changes, it was necessary to secure support from the incumbent Labour government, in order to give the initiatives even more powerful momentum.

A recurring theme of this history has been the vague nature of British co-operation's relationship with the major political parties. Of course, in the mid-1950s Labour politicians had played a prominent role in attempting to lead efforts at reforming the movement, Hugh Gaitskell in particular fashioning the 1958 Commission Report.[20] On the other hand, what up to the 1990s was a distinctly socialist Labour Party proved to be largely indifferent to the values and traditions of co-operation. Paradoxically, though, many MPs received financial support from co-operative societies, revealing the movement's failure to leverage support as a condition of this funding. At the same time, the movement's traditional allegiance to Labour alienated a Conservative Party that was in government from 1979 to 1997. Moreover, it was Conservative policies that encouraged demutualization of most building societies, providing the legal basis for Regan's takeover bid. While in the late 1990s co-operators could anticipate a more conducive political environment, given that Tony Blair's 'New Labour' government was elected in 1997 on 'A Third Way' manifesto offering a hybrid approach to socio-economic issues, New Labour ideologists proved neutral when approached to support the movement.

In spite of the apparent apathy shown by New Labour, Melmoth was convinced that his modernization programme needed political support if it was going to achieve lasting change. After all, Blair was elected with such an enormous majority that any association with this charismatic leader would benefit the CWS, indeed the whole movement. Melmoth

---

[20] See section 6.4.

consequently lobbied Downing St relentlessly, finally achieving his aim of persuading Blair to sponsor the establishment of a second Co-operative Commission. Chaired by John Monks, General Secretary of the Trades Union Congress, and populated by a balanced mixture of co-operative executives, politicians and trade unionists, and business people, the Commission started work on 29 February 2000. Its terms of reference were agreed by Blair and Melmoth, focusing on both radical improvements in commercial performance and greater social inclusion, with the scope to range across a wide variety of issues that had hindered progress. Although the Commission was based in London, to which a substantial number of submissions were sent, regional hearings were also held in Oxford, Loughborough, Edinburgh, and Manchester, ensuring an extensive dialogue with co-operative societies, trade unions, and many other interested parties. Remarkably, within eleven months the Commission had produced its report, entitled *The Co-operative Advantage. Creating a Successful Family of Co-operative Businesses* (see Figure 9.5), within a week of the creation of a new society forged from the CWS–CRS merger, The Co-operative Group.

As the report's title indicates, while Melmoth did not sit on the Commission, he was clearly influential in helping the team fashion an overall vision for the movement. No less than sixty recommendations were made by the Commission, under the topics identified in Table 9.2. Of central importance, however, was the suggestion of a new Mission Statement that would 'stretch' the movement, namely: 'To challenge conventional UK enterprise by building a commercially successful family of businesses that offers a clear co-operative advantage.' The report went on to define what was meant by a 'co-operative advantage': 'Excellent products or services with distinct competitive benefits derived from our values and principles, our rewards for members or our commitment to the communities we serve.'[21] This was also linked into the introduction of key performance indicators, rigorous auditing and reporting structures, and improved corporate governance regimes that would enhance accountability. Although clearly the retail societies would be the principal delivery vehicles for this Mission, the Commission wanted an enlarged Co-operative Union (CU) to monitor progress, with a view to reporting by 2006 the extent to which the movement was 'stretching' itself.

As Bamfield has noted, by incorporating such concepts as a mission statement, key performance indicators, auditing and corporate governance, the 'approach is more Business School than Fabian Society.'[22] It is also clear from Table 9.2 that there are many similarities with the recommendations made in 1919 and 1958,[23] especially in the first three categories; even though the aims were couched in a different vocabulary, issues such as greater integration, improved branding and distribution, and raising the return on capital employed featured in all three reports. Above all, though, the 2000–1 Commission placed considerable emphasis on achieving the 'co-operative advantage', provoking widespread debate about what this meant and the feasibility of ever achieving what

[21] Co-operative Commission (2001), 84–5.   [22] Bamfield (2002), 50.
[23] See sections 5.3 and 6.4.

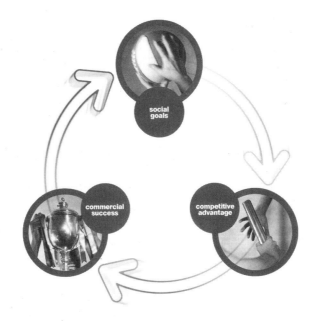

the co-operative advantage

Creating a successful family of Co-operative businesses

The Report of the Co-operative Commission
January 2001

FIGURE 9.5. *The Report of the Co-operative Commission, 2001.* Entitled *The Co-operative Advantage*, the Co-operative Commission's report put forward the 'virtuous circle' concept, in which co-operatives' commercial success is used to fund their social goals, which in turn produce a competitive advantage.

Sparks regards as a vague concept. Moreover, he goes on to add that: 'If there is an identifiable "Co-operative Advantage" as the Report keeps on saying, then why would consumers vote to relinquish this?'[24] In other words, if there is an 'Advantage', why is this extra protection needed to engender consumer loyalty, because the decline in market share demonstrated that consumers were not convinced there was anything differentiating co-operative trading from any other form of retailing. Ideally, of course, the report was correct in offering a vision based on achieving a 'virtuous circle' linking social goals, competitive advantage, and commercial success,[25] harmonizing with what Melmoth was

[24] Sparks (2002), 11–12 and 23.   [25] Co-operative Commission (2001), 18–19.

trying to achieve within the CWS. Nevertheless, as Sparks was quick to argue: 'The co-operative advantage has to be earned not assumed, and much business pain will have to be endured to earn such a standing.'[26] Moreover, the Commission failed to cost out the necessary changes required in achieving the 'co-operative advantage', while in advocating a doubling of the average return on capital employed this ignores the simple arithmetic that would still leave co-operative retailing 40 per cent below its major competitors.

In highlighting these deficiencies in the Commission's report, Sparks was voicing widespread scepticism concerning the ability of a movement that had endured forty years of decline to implement the necessary changes. Following his earlier damning analysis of the CWS's performance,[27] Sparks outlined how in stark contrast to its principal rivals the UK's largest co-operative society was deficient in three crucial respects: store formats; branding; and logistics. Although Melmoth's 1997 Strategic Review had decisively switched the focus of CWS retailing to c-stores, leading to a mass sell-off of its superstores, Sparks emphasized that the most successful multiple retailers such as Tesco and Sainsbury's operated a 'multi-format' range that included hypermarkets, superstores, and c-stores. This was also backed up vigorously by the maintenance of a strong, unified corporate brand that consumers recognized and valued, with a logistics system that ensured steady improvements in service and quality.[28] While the Commission argued that co-operative consumers 'should experience service that is better than that provided by peer competitors',[29] Sparks was again sceptical of the movement's ability to achieve a benchmark that was being set by its rivals. Moreover, given the way that society had changed so radically since the apogee of co-operative trading's influence in the 1940s, the movement would have to work hard in persuading consumers that membership offered a sufficient advantage to persuade them to shop at co-operative outlets.[30] Indeed, as Bamfield argued, the Commission's recommendations concerning social audits and the creation of a Community Task Force not only resembled the failed Co-operative Development Agency, but also diverted both management time and capital funds from the core task of improving commercial performance.[31] One might also note that the Co-operative Commission ran concurrently with a Competition Commission review of food retailing, the report from which almost entirely neglected to mention co-operative trading. This demonstrated in graphic form that the sector had by then been reduced to a marginal position; that, indeed, it was a 'third division player', as Melmoth had noted in April 1997.[32]

While a Special Co-operative Congress convened in November 2001 and the 2002 Co-operative Congress enthusiastically endorsed the Co-operative Commission's report, and even the sceptics acceded that it stood more chance of succeeding than its

---

[26] Sparks (2002), 22.   [27] See section 7.4.   [28] Sparks (2002), 16–18.
[29] Co-operative Commission (2001), para. 10.1.   [30] Sparks (2002), 20.
[31] Bamfield (2002), 48–9.   [32] See Competition Commission (2000); and section 8.4.

Table 9.2. Co-operative Commission Report recommendations

1. Re-establishing the Co-operative Advantage (16 recommendations)
   - Commercial performance improvement
   - Societies' performance
   - Financial auditing
   - Social performance improvement
   - Social auditing
   - CRTG
   - Financial services
2. Successful Co-operative Business in the 21st Century (6)
   - Branding and image
   - The co-operative logo
   - E-commerce and new technologies
   - New sectors
3. Membership Participation and Securing the co-operative movement Legacy (8)
   - Membership
   - Securing co-operative assets
4. Effective Management for Change and Development (10)
   - Boards, management and staffing
5. National, Regional and Local Societies (13)
   - Lifelong learning
   - Co-operative foundation
   - Political structures and affiliations
   - The co-operative press
   - Regional issues
   - National issues for UK government
6. The Social Economy and Co-operation (4)
   - Social economy and community task force
   - Housing
   - UKCC and Co-operative Union
7. Mission Statement and Next Steps (4)
   - Mission Statement
   - Implementation

Source: Sparks (2002), 9.

1919 and 1958 predecessors,[33] there were clearly serious reservations about its ability to produce the results required. In many ways, however, one might argue that having secured prime ministerial support for the Commission, and Tony Blair having written an enthusiastic foreword to the report espousing the hope that it would 'help chart the

---

[33] Bamfield (2002), 50; Sparks (2002), 25.

route towards a successful future for this movement',[34] Melmoth had succeeded in his principal aim of giving his mission and strategy the highest level of political support. The report was even launched from 10 Downing St, feeding off Blair's widespread popularity; prior to the unfortunate military incursions into Iraq and Afghanistan, his backing would prove extremely useful in persuading the rest of the movement to accept the need to create a thriving 'family of co-operative businesses' based on reaffirmed values and principles. Following his resounding success over Regan's takeover bid, this gave Melmoth the political authority to set the agenda for a movement that had in the past resisted CWS entreaties to 'fall towards the centre'. When combined with the CRS's commercial crisis, this authority provided him with the momentum to merge it into the CWS by 2000, relabelling the organization as The Co-operative Group (CWS) Ltd in the following year.

By 2001, the structure and strategy of The Co-operative Group (hereafter, the Group) had clearly changed markedly, especially compared to the dysfunctional, opaque, and uncompetitive organization that had prevailed up to the 1990s. At the same time, one should stress that Melmoth regarded these as merely the first step in achieving his broader aim of building the 'family' into an integrated network that would thrive. Apart from integrating all of the retailing and distribution activities into the Group (see Figure 9.6), in 2002 The Co-operative Bank and CIS merged to form Co-operative Financial Services (CFS), building further on the 'ethical banker' platform devised a decade earlier. Nevertheless, much work still needed to be done, not least in terms of branding, marketing and integrating the disparate parts of the Leviathan. While one can convincingly argue that at the very least solid foundations had been laid, organizationally and politically, this was only the start of a process that over the following decade would accelerate impressively. It is vital to remember that in addition to its banking and insurance activities, the Group was the largest farmer in the UK, it also possessed a substantial property portfolio worth £104 million (at 1997 values), the travel agency ran 256 shops, there were almost 200 pharmacies and opticians, as well as 359 funeral services outlets, each requiring focused management and resources in order to sustain their presence in those markets.[35] At the same time, as we have already noted, since the mid-1990s the Group had been relying enormously on the profits generated by Co-operative Bank (see Figure 8.3), while market share had continued to plummet and sales volumes were at best stagnant (in real terms).

These posed significant challenges to the Group, and other societies, demonstrating that in spite of Melmoth's achievements in bringing the CWS and CRS together, as well as creating Co-operative Financial Services, much still needed to be done. Having admitted in 1997 that the CWS was 'a third division player', when compared to 'first division' firms such as Tesco, Sainsbury's, and ASDA,[36] with market share at an all-time low of 4.4 per cent in 2000 it is unlikely that Melmoth could claim the Group had been

---

[34] Co-operative Commission (2001), p. 1.
[35] Data taken from a report published in *Manchester Evening News (Business Section)*, 21 April 1999.
[36] *Daily Express*, 9 April 1997.

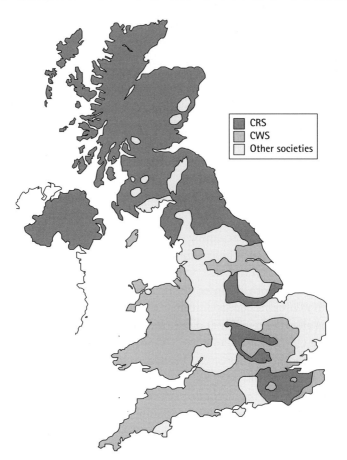

CRS
CWS
Other societies

FIGURE 9.6. Map of CWS, CRS, and independent societies' retail operations, c.2000.

promoted to a higher division. On the positive side, however, terminating the 'me too' strategy that between 1970 and 1996 had resulted in the drive to open a large number of superstores was a decisive move towards the c-store format as the CWS's preferred modus operandi. Similarly, instituting an extensive programme aimed at training all staff in the values and principles for which the movement stood was a key dimension of a campaign that included 'ethical banking' and the emergence in 1995 of the 'Responsible Retailer' initiatives. Following on from this work, and partly arising from the Co-operative Commission's recommendations, Simon Williams, Bill Shannon, and John Bowes had succeeded in developing a 'Brand Group' that would finally standardize this crucial aspect of the retailing activities, an issue we shall pursue in the next section. It is also noticeable that by 2002 the CRTG was operating a central marketing, buying, and pricing system for approximately 60 per cent of co-operative trading, representing turnover of £5 billion. Finally, Melmoth had started the process of binding the 'family of co-operative businesses' together, for example by encouraging the cross-selling of products across the Group's highly diverse range of businesses.

These were all significant achievements, especially when one compares the highly dysfunctional nature of co-operative activities in the early 1990s and its apparent propensity to allow extensive fraudulent criminality to flourish. While one might cogently argue that this was a process which should have been initiated decades earlier, typically, when Melmoth was knighted in January 2002 for his services to the movement, he diverted much of the praise onto the movement as a whole, arguing that the knighthood was a tribute to the efforts of many people who had participated in the recent changes.[37] Of course, this honour was regarded as a fitting reward for a person who had committed his considerable energy and talent to reconfiguring key activities. Nevertheless, while Melmoth had initiated some fundamental changes, there remained significant challenges that commentators had highlighted when critiquing the Co-operative Commission's report. One might argue that in just six years it would have been impossible to reverse what by the late 1990s had been forty years of continuous decline; a Leviathan-type organization such as the CWS would require much longer to deal with such a legacy. On the other hand, Melmoth and his team had laid some solid foundations on which his successors could effectively build. As a consequence, when Sir Graham Melmoth retired in October 2002 there were few critics of an executive who had both saved the CWS from a hostile predator and persuaded the CRS to abandon its independent stance. He also had the satisfaction of reporting in 2002 a 48 per cent increase in operating profit on 2001, indicating that commercial performance was improving,[38] albeit from what most regarded as a very low base. Above all, though, Melmoth had built his strategy around the reaffirmation of the values and principles that were at the heart of British co-operation, as well as reviving the voice of individual members in co-operative affairs, providing a conducive environment for ethical trading to become its differentiating brand and c-stores to take centre stage.

9.2 BEAUMONT, MERGERS, AND MARKET SHARE

While Melmoth was rightly pleased with his five-year tenure as CEO, one of his abiding regrets was a failure to pave the way for his chosen successor, Alan Prescott. Having played a key role in the 1997 takeover struggle, Prescott had been appointed as Deputy CEO, contributing extensively to the Strategic Review and many of the changes that took place thereafter. Much to the CEO's surprise, however, rather than Prescott the CWS Board chose as his successor Martin Beaumont (see Figure 9.7), the CEO of United Co-operatives. Apart from having had a private education, topped off with a Cambridge University economics degree, Martin Beaumont was a very different type of executive from those who had populated senior CWS posts. Having spent the first sixteen years of his career as a chartered accountant with Peat Marwick Mitchell, becoming a partner

---

[37] *Daily Mail*, 13 January 2002.   [38] *Independent*, 1 May 2002.

FIGURE 9.7. **Martin Beaumont.** As part of The Co-operative Group's support for BBC Children in Need, Beaumont was photographed in his office with mascot Pudsey in 2006. Following a long career at KPMG, Beaumont joined the Norwest society shortly before it merged with United Co-operatives, and served as United's chief executive from 1992. In 2002 he became The Co-operative Group's chief executive, serving until 2008. Courtesy of The Co-operative Group.

with general practice and management consultancy responsibilities, in the late 1980s he had moved to Egremont, a publishing company, as head of finance, where he established a wide reputation for astute financial management. In 1990, he was invited to join Norwest Co-operative Society as chief financial officer. He was initially to operate in the same role at United Co-operatives after the April 1991 merger that created the third largest retail society,[39] but following the revelations of financial mismanagement by the incumbent CEO, Beaumont was swiftly moved into this key role.

As Table 9.1 indicates, with headquarters in Stoke-on-Trent United Co-operatives operated in a large territory that included the West Midlands, North Wales and northwest England, creating a business which by 1999 boasted a turnover of £710 million. In explaining why Beaumont was appointed as the Group's CEO, it is vital to note that in certain respects United Co-operatives could be regarded as a pace-setter. For example, it was the first society to dispose of its superstores, using the capital to invest in the c-store format that the CWS would eventually adopt as its preferred option. Beaumont was also not slow to recruit senior executives from the private sector, as a means of injecting fresh ideas into key functions such as branding, marketing, and financial management. In particular, he was keen to emphasize the link between co-operative

---

[39] See section 8.1.

membership and consumers, encouraging cross-selling of services across its extensive retailing activities (see Table 9.1). Even though he had joined the CWS's Board in 1996, United continued to operate separately, even allying with the CRS in the creation of the Consortium of Independent Co-operatives. In this respect, his appointment as the Group's CEO in 2002 came as a great surprise to many in the movement, not least his predecessor. Nevertheless, although Sir Graham was suspicious of his successor, given his work at United Co-operatives, it will become clear that Beaumont proved to be highly effective in sustaining the late-1990s initiatives.

When Beaumont moved from his former Stoke headquarters to the Group's much larger premises in Manchester, he was instantly struck by the stark differences between the two organizations.[40] Even though he was impressed with the branding work being developed by Bill Shannon's team, it was apparent that the Group lacked a vigorous marketing function that would fully harness the advantages of this work. At the same time, as his arrival coincided with the implementation of the 2001 Constitutional Review, he benefited from the introduction of a more transparent, member-oriented structure that would prove more appropriate for the change agenda than its cumbersome, opaque predecessor. Although he was critical of the lack of commercial experience on the Group Board, creating some tensions from the outset, a constructive relationship emerged at that level, facilitating the introduction of radical measures aimed at improving profitability. In effect, Beaumont was keen to adapt what had been achieved at United Co-operatives to the Leviathan controlled from Manchester, overriding the historical legacy of a highly dispersed organization and implementing the best aspects of both the Constitutional Review and Co-operative Commission.

It is clear that Beaumont brought a fresh management philosophy to the Group, improving what he regarded as weak systems such as human resources and information technology, as well as transforming the way in which decisions were implemented across the sprawling organization. As he later explained: 'The only solution is a clear vision for change and the sheer hard work and determination to deliver.'[41] The essential steps taken in achieving this end were: develop a sound business strategy for each of the businesses, challenging older traditions in the process and disposing of non-core activities; enhance the marketing and sales functions; link these to membership; and import managerial talent where necessary. An excellent example of this approach was the recruitment of Guy McCracken, who joined the Group in May 2005, after having spent twenty-five years working in Marks & Spencer's food division. Apart from effectively integrating new acquisitions into the retailing network, McCracken proved crucial in moving the Group closer to its major rivals, adopting a much more customer-facing approach to retailing that was manifested in much-improved store fascias and improved training for workers at all levels.

While integrating and enhancing the co-operative retailing experience was clearly an essential process if the Group was going to increase its market share and boost turnover,

---

[40] Interview with Martin Beaumont.   [41] *Co-operative News*, 1 June 2005.

another crucial aspect of this work was the need to develop a much stronger co-opera-tive brand that consumers both recognized and valued. In this respect, one of the key recommendations from the Co-operative Commission was that a movement-wide Brand Panel should be established, overcoming a historical legacy of inconsistent stand-ards, different names and fascia, and confusing and incoherent marketing activities that had prevented retail societies from maximizing their full potential. Above all, it was also widely felt that the CO-OP logo was tainted by the past era of decline. Even though some effort had been expended by CWS executives on marketing, this had never been truly effective in overcoming these deficiencies, while a movement-wide approach recog-nized that even the newly formed Co-operative Group could not on its own change pub-lic perception about the Co-operative's Brand values.

Aside from the Brand work undertaken within the CWS and Co-operative Bank by people like Bill Shannon, Simon Williams, and John Bowes, the Brand Panel established in 2001 was able to draw upon experiments which had taken place elsewhere, for exam-ple in the Oxford, Swindon & Gloucester society under CEO and Group Board member Bob Burlton. Amongst other innovations, Burlton had championed the MOCA Princi-ples (Marketing Our Co-operative Advantage) developed by Tom Webb, a professor at Saint Mary's University, Nova Scotia. Much of this early work was led by Wendy Wrigley and Terry Hughton, both longstanding CWS employees who had been amongst the gen-eration of managers inspired by the co-operative management culture encouraged dur-ing Melmoth's era. Their work had also been central to the development of 'Responsible Retailing' initiatives such as Fairtrade and honest labelling,[42] giving the Brand Panel a solid foundation on which to innovate. Specifically, the Brand Panel developed a new brand—'The Co-operative'—to replace the tired CO-OP logo, as well as agreeing a set of standards which should be met by those societies wishing to adopt the brand. Aside from the Group, however, while some societies were enthusiastic advocates of the new approach, others lacked commitment, because either they did not believe change was necessary or they thought that a common brand was a distraction. This reinforced the increasingly influential arguments of those who were advocating still greater consolida-tion into 'One Society'.

While the work of the Brand Panel was truly innovative and potentially of tremen-dous import for the movement as a whole, initially its programme of action lacked momentum; it was vital to appoint an experienced marketer who could take the consen-sus which had been achieved and execute this into a customer-facing strategy. This lack of momentum persuaded Martin Beaumont to appointed Zoe Morgan for this task. Having worked for the high street chemist Boots and HBOS Bank, Morgan brought extensive experience in this crucial area, building on the work of the Brand Panel and earlier work by CWS marketing experts such as Simon Williams, Bill Shannon, and John Bowes. Morgan's major contribution was to execute for the first time in co-operative history a brand strategy that united the Group's businesses, including food, travel, funeral, and financial services. Under 'The Co-operative' banner, common fascia were

[42] Docherty (2008), 205–31.

FIGURE 9.8. The Co-operative Group pharmacy and food stores, Poynton, 2012. Initiatives begun in 2005 brought the diverse array of co-operative businesses, including food, banking, travel, pharmacy, and funeral services, together under common branding for the first time. Courtesy of The Co-operative Group.

introduced for each business, as in Figure 9.8, that would resonate with consumers in every one of its 3,400 outlets. In a highly novel demonstration of what was about to be rolled out, at the 2005 Congress the marketing team had what was called 'Co-operation Street' built, providing a mock-up of the new shop colours and branding, following which forty shops in various parts of the country were revamped. This significantly re-invigorated one of the oldest retailing brands in the UK, offering customers a single, fresh brand identity that enhanced its positioning; it was game-changing in a most radical way. A pilot-study operating in sixteen stores over twelve months demonstrated significant sales growth, compared to a similar control group, leading Morgan to claim: 'This will have a major impact on the way consumers perceive our operations on the High [Main] Street. For the first time our family of businesses will be united under one common brand, which will go hand in hand with defined operational standards for each business.'[43] Such was the impact of this innovation that in 2006 a group of US co-operative leaders had visited the Group to assess its impact.

---

[43] *Co-operative News*, 2 September 2006.

While this marketing innovation in itself was widely regarded as instrumental in improving the Group's presence, it should also be linked closely with the relaunch in 2005 of the membership offer. As we have noted several times, the fragmentation of the link between membership and trading with the Society had become a major issue by the 1990s, not least because while corporate members of the Group were still paid a dividend, the millions of individual members received nothing, the 'divi' having been abandoned by most societies in the late 1960s. Although membership records were bloated by possibly millions of dormant accounts, whose owners had long since lost any meaningful contact with the society they purported to own, it was nevertheless regarded as essential that the Group should return to one of the core features of co-operative consumption. A Dividend Card had been introduced by the CWS in 1996, but this was not a member benefit scheme, having been devised to compete with the phenomenally successful Tesco Clubcard, a loyalty scheme which had recruited fourteen million consumers. This again highlights the 'me too' nature of the CWS's strategy, in that like the investment in superstores it was merely responding to what rivals had already pioneered. On the other hand, it demonstrated a possible route towards a new approach to member reward, using the language of loyalty. This was a point that the Co-operative Commission picked up as part of its analysis of declining individual membership, prompting the commissioners to call for the introduction of a single, national card-based scheme to be used across the movement (see Figure 9.9). It also recommended that dormant members be cleared off share registers, as part of the move to involve individual members in the governance of their co-operatives.

The views of the Co-operative Commission clearly chimed effectively with the mood of the time. In particular, following the CWS–CRS merger, representatives of individual

FIGURE 9.9. The Co-operative Group membership card. Although an earlier 'dividend card', introduced by CWS in 1997, was a loyalty scheme that offered bonuses on own-brand products, in 2006 The Co-operative Group returned to the 'true dividend', sharing a portion of its surplus with members in proportion to their purchases of goods and services. Courtesy of The Co-operative Group.

members from both societies believed it was imperative that customer members should be able to receive a share of profits—a dividend. Similarly, the independent societies which had continued to receive a corporate dividend, even in leaner years, supported the move, with Bob Burlton playing a leading role in advocating a relaunch of the 'divi'. This added sense of urgency encouraged Martin Beaumont to prioritize the work that had already been started in the late 1990s, resulting in the design of a new membership proposition that was carefully interwoven into the developing work on 'The Co-operative' Brand, while negotiations with other leading co-operative societies ensured that a common approach to promoting membership would be adopted across the movement. Another key development was to encourage employees to become members, given that historically the CWS (and subsequently the Group) had surprisingly low levels of employee membership. At the same time, there was a clear desire to align the tradition of member relations activity with a developing Social Goals agenda, re-emphasizing the claims to offer a distinct 'co-operative difference'. By 2005, using the same basic functionality which had supported the 1990s loyalty scheme, but repositioning the offer so that it became a mechanism for distributing the surplus to members, a personal 'divi' scheme had been relaunched, with all appropriate publicity. Even if the Co-operative Commission's vision of a single membership scheme operating across the entire movement has not been achieved, the 'divi' relaunch has effectively marginalized the previous dysfunctionality that dogged progress up to the 1990s. Crucially, it was more than a loyalty card; it was a vital component in the common approach towards membership that effectively supported the creation of 'The Co-operative' brand.

By the time the Group was named in 2006 as the UK's most trusted retailer, this demonstrated how the revitalization of the brand and the relaunch of the personal 'divi' was giving real substance to its drive to be seen as the 'responsible retailer'. When in 2007 a NOP survey named the Co-op Brand as the most ethical in the UK, this confirmed the efficacy of the work done for many years by key individuals such as John Bowes, Bill Shannon, and Simon Williams, providing Zoe Morgan with the expertise to highlight how ethical trading can effectively underpin the marketing strategy. Moreover, personal membership also started to rise once again, after many decades of stagnation and even decline, demonstrating that even in the twenty-first century consumers were willing to associate themselves with the co-operative movement. While prior to the relaunch of the 'divi' in 2005, membership stood at 1.1 million, within a year this had risen to 1.6 million, and by 2012 it had rocketed to over 7 million.

Given this creative approach towards both projecting a cohesive image to consumers and garnering customer loyalty, it is also worth repeating what we discussed in Chapter 8 relating to the way in which, first, the CWS and then the Group pursued 'Responsible Retailing'. In particular, as Schwarzkopf has noted: 'The track record of the Co-op brand in pushing fair-trade products, responsible retailing and advertising self-regulation on the agenda of British marketing culture is outstanding.'[44] This claim is based on how Fairtrade products were launched through co-operative outlets during the 1990s,

---

[44] Schwarzkopf (2009), 217.

including bananas, chocolate, Chilean wine, pineapples, and coffee. The strategy was also linked with the introduction of product lines with much-reduced sugar, salt, and fat content, forcing the advertising industry to revise how products were sold to children. Indeed, the Group has fundamentally changed the attitudes of British retailers to these issues, prompting the major chains to reconsider their attitudes towards what in the 1990s were regarded as mere gimmicks. In quoting a 1924 CU document that claimed 'the co-operative store is in reality the outpost of a new civilisation', Schwarzkopf highlights how by the twenty-first century this had taken on a completely different complexion, reflecting the Group's wide reputation for its ethical stance.[45] Moreover, the Group was also willing to exploit these achievements as aggressively as its rivals, demonstrating the value of having a marketing team capable of directly influencing activities across the Leviathan. Other innovations included the introduction of eco-friendly policies in the insurance and retailing operations, including the installation of 7,000 solar panels on the iconic CIS Tower, as well as nineteen wind turbines on other Manchester premises. While some of this activity would only make a tiny difference to the Group's carbon footprint, every opportunity was taken to instil in the workforce a commitment to environmental awareness, as part of a cohesive sustainability strategy which reinforced other dimensions of its ethical stance.

It is consequently clear that the Group was beginning to adapt progressively to the commercial and organizational challenges that had beset the Leviathan since the 1950s. Other innovations included the adoption of a more open organizational structure, replacing the old command-and-control modus operandi that had prevailed for many decades with a much more proactive approach to decision-making. Although the Group had always employed some highly talented individuals, a key feature of the last three chapters has been the inability of senior management to mobilize this resource as effectively as possible, largely because the traditional modus operandi had allowed 'barons' in key roles to resist change. Recruiting dynamic executives such as McCracken and Morgan was an intrinsic feature of this transformational process, but above all this was about changing the mindset of an organization that since the early twentieth century had atrophied. Another aspect of this strategy was the 2005 decision to reduce by 600 the number of staff employed at New Century House, demonstrating that the Board was serious about overhauling the organization, as well as eliminating the excessive replication of functions that had arisen as a result of diversification and vertical integration.

The Leviathan-nature of the Group has been a consistent theme of this history, illustrating how over the decades businesses had been added to the portfolio in response to perceived needs. Of course, as we saw in Chapter 8, manufacturing had been sold off in 1994, but as part of further rationalization major disposals were made in the early 2000s, adjudged against the core criteria of whether activities were either commercially unsound or lacked a link to the core business of retailing. Although mistakenly accused by some of 'selling the family silver', by the spring of 2004 a significant reduction in agricultural production had been enacted, the Goliath footwear business had been sold, and

---

[45] Schwarzkopf (2009), 217.

efforts were being made to sell the ACC milk processing and distribution operation.[46] In addition, sales of superstores continued, as an essential feature of the c-store strategy, bringing funds into the remaining businesses that could be used to support fresh initiatives. Indeed, it is estimated that the Group generated £8 million from these disposals,[47] while rationalizing both headquarters activities and agriculture would diminish what was an enormous cost base. This to a large extent mitigated criticism of the Group's strategy, not least because there was extensive evidence that these funds were being used productively in its marketing and image-building activities as critical dimensions of its rejuvenation.

Another crucial dimension of the Group's evolution at that time was the way in which funds were diverted to the acquisition of an increasing number of retail outlets, mainly in support of its c-store strategy. Even though other multiple retailers were encroaching extensively on the c-store sector—a major threat was the Tesco Express format, while others were acquiring high-street locations as part of the drive to develop a multi-format approach to retailing—the Group sustained its commitment to a strategy that had been rolled out in the late 1990s. As we noted in the last chapter, one of the problems with this strategy had been the major housing programmes pursued across the UK by local authorities, leaving many co-operative stores isolated from its traditional customers. To obviate this challenge, the CWS/the Group pursued an aggressive acquisition strategy, buying significant numbers of c-stores either to boost or create market share. By far the most significant move was the purchase of Alldays for £131 million from the receiver, adding 600 stores instantly to the c-store network. In June 2003, the Group also spent £30 million on seventy-five c-stores and thirty-five newsagents formerly owned by the Balfour chain. As these outlets were located mostly in the south of England, they proved to be valuable additions to a network that was largely focused on more northern territories. Another sixty-four c-stores were also purchased a year later in the south-west of England, when three chains accepted £15 million from the Group.[48] Collectively, these acquisitions added 750 stores to the Group network, providing a significant boost to market share at a time when this was at an all-time low.

While this aggressive acquisition strategy was clearly an essential component in the recovery programme that had started in late 1990s, as many British firms had discovered when pursuing similar expansion plans,[49] it was vital to integrate the new components swiftly and effectively, otherwise synergy would never be achieved. At the same time, the Group was also faced with the equally enormous challenge of integrating CWS and CRS activities, not to mention switching emphasis from superstores to c-stores across both networks. As the Group's results by 2005 indicate, however, there was little evidence that the full benefits of acquiring c-stores were being generated. Indeed, as Figures 9.10 and 9.11

---

[46] *Co-operative News*, 4 May 2004.   [47] CGBM, January 2005.
[48] These chains were Plymouth and Cornwall Convenience Stores Ltd, Devon and Cornwall Convenience Stores, and Somerset and Bristol Convenience Stores.
[49] Wilson (1995).

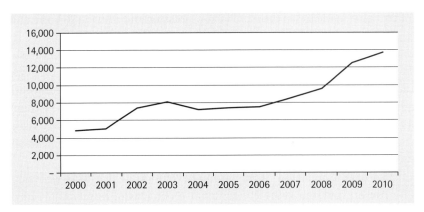

FIGURE 9.10. Gross income of CWS/The Co-operative Group, 2000–10 (£ billion).

reveal, growth in both turnover and profitability was poor, principally because of problems in the food retailing division which still accounted for over 70 per cent of the Group's business. This reveals one of the most disappointing aspects of the early twenty-first century, in that assimilating Alldays especially into the Group network proved to be a major challenge that management only sluggishly overcame. Indeed, only after McCracken was recruited in 2005 did this process improve, indicating that the Group still lacked the dynamic leadership required to ensure its acquisition strategy resulted in effective implementation. The sharp decline in profitability in 2004 also prompted Beaumont to initiate Project Exchequer in 2005, resulting in 600 New Century staff losing their jobs. Crucially, though, it was essential to overhaul the Group's logistics system, given a historic under-investment in this key component of a nationwide distribution network. A major step forward was the construction in 2005–6 of a purpose-built National Distribution Centre in Coventry, which would become the heart of the CRTG's service to what by then were 3,300 Group shops.[50] As by that time the CRTG was serving the entire co-operative retail system, this significantly improved productivity across the movement, offering rich opportunities for the future.

While the way in which the Group was relatively slow to integrate fully all of the new acquisitions into the CWS–CRS retail network, by 2005 a much clearer way forward was being developed in response to the recent disappointing results. Of course, the early 2005 economic difficulties exacerbated the challenges experienced by all retailers, but above all it was essential to overhaul the Group's internal processes if it was going to improve performance. This resulted in the elaboration of a six-point 'revitalization programme'. While Beaumont admitted that it was 'not rocket science or management speak. They are simply what we have to do,' he wanted the Group's modus operandi to change radically. The six priorities were:

1. To turn the food business round; 2. To reduce costs while raising the Group's game; 3. To get the business portfolio right; 4. To rejuvenate the Co-op brand; 5. To win the hearts and minds of employees; and 6. To build a new CIS whilst investing in the bank to ensure growth.[51]

[50] *Co-operative News*, 2 August 2006.   [51] *Co-operative News*, 1 June 2005.

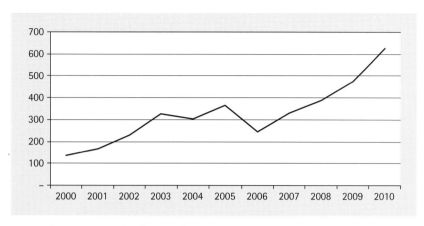

FIGURE 9.11. Operating profit of CWS/The Co-operative Group, 2000–10 (£ million).

Judging from what we have already noted in this section, the first four priorities had evidently been work-in-progress since Beaumont's appointment as CEO in 2002. The fifth, however, arose from a MORI survey of all the Group's 64,000 staff, 12,801 of whom responded in a frank and constructive manner. Not surprisingly, while 64 per cent were happy with job security, 48 per cent expressed dissatisfaction with remuneration systems. More worrying was the consensus that the Group still had some way to go in creating a human resource strategy that engendered a conducive environment in which a majority of employees could flourish, in line with co-operative values and principles. The new HR director, Richard Bide, who had been recruited from Centrica, was also committed to responding effectively to the questionnaire's findings. This again reflects the Group's desire to import appropriate skills in order to achieve the organizational improvements necessary across a business that needed radical reform.

If the first five of Beaumont's priorities were closely linked to aspirational improvement, the sixth was highly specific to a part of the Group's business portfolio, namely, the insurance arm of the CFS. Although we have not devoted much attention to the CIS,[52] given that it is such a specialist business with a long and detailed history, it is clear that even small deviations in the performance of a business with such an enormous financial base could seriously affect the Group. Indeed, in 2003–4 the CIS was adversely affected by both fundamental changes in pension provision and a drastic write-down of £285 million in the value of its investment portfolio. As this was the first time the CIS's balance sheet had been consolidated into the Group's figures, Beaumont noted that: 'It's sod's law that this would happen this year.'[53] While there was never any danger of the CIS experiencing the same kind of difficulties that struck down Equitable Life in 1999, emergency action was required to ensure that it would swiftly turn around a record that was extremely worrying. Profit had actually fallen by 48 per cent in 2003–4, from £61.7

[52] See sections 4.4, 5.3, 6.5, 7.2, and 7.4 for references to CIS, as well as Garnett (1968).
[53] *Independent*, 24 April 2003.

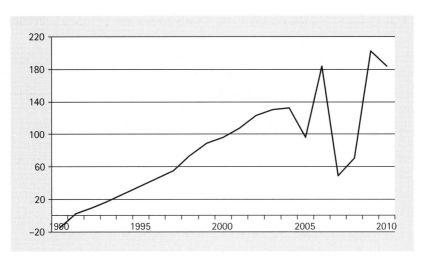

FIGURE 9.12. Operating profit of The Co-operative Bank, 1990–2010 (£ million).

million to £32.2 million, but such was the speed of the recovery that by 2005 the CIS was again returning much-improved profits of £66.5 million. Nevertheless, the CIS was obliged to shed 2,500 jobs in 2004, as part of the business's response to this crisis. Unfortunately, however, it was also in 2005 that Co-operative Bank profits started to slide. Having recorded a growth in profits every year since 1992 (see Figure 9.12), The Co-operative Bank's performance deteriorated badly from 2005, due to a combination of intense competition in retail banking and £31.8m of investment write-downs through the bank's relatively small exposure to structured investment vehicles. A year earlier, Mervyn Pedelty had left as CEO of the CFS. His successor, David Anderson, was charged by the Group board with bringing the bank's operations much more effectively into the wider organization, reflecting the process of integration that was by then under way.

While the CFS was struggling to sustain the role it had played in supporting the CWS/the Group during the 1990s and early 2000s, it is important to stress that one of the key dimensions of this era was how considerable effort was put into improving performance and balancing resource allocation across the 'family of co-operative businesses'. As we noted earlier, from the outset Beaumont had not been averse to disposing of loss-making businesses, a strategy that was further illustrated when in 2004 the ACC was sold for £75 million to Dairy Farmers of Britain (DFB), based in Nantwich. Similarly, after accumulating losses of £15.4 million between 2004 and 2006, and in spite of a shop refurbishment programme initiated in 2005, by the end of 2006 Shoefayre's 317 shops had been transferred to rivals Shoezone. On the other hand, considerable success was achieved in two other retailing operations, Pharmacy and Funeralcare. By the time the Pharmacy business had been converted into Co-operative Healthcare in 2007, becoming the third largest pharmacy chain in the UK, this robust business was generating sales of £541 million and a surplus of £27 million, having more than doubled in size since 2000 as a result of carefully planned acquisitions. Co-operative Funeralcare (see Figure 9.13) had similarly been successful in sustaining its competitive advantage, producing a surplus in 2007 of £28.5 million on sales of £234 million, continuing its highly effective customer-facing strategy built on acquisitions and continued service quality improvements.

Although other non-core businesses such as Travelcare and Farmcare were never able to match these performance levels, Beaumont ensured that their management teams continually strove to adopt more progressive business methods that were being developed in other parts of the 'family'. While Travelcare struggled to cope with the highly cyclical nature of this business, a brief analysis of Farmcare will provide clear evidence

FIGURE 9.13. The Co-operative Funeralcare hot air balloon, Sheffield, c.2010. In recent years, The Co-operative Group has found creative ways to market its Funeralcare business, including the use of its hot air balloon (above) at community events. The Group is the UK's leading funeral provider, responsible for more than 100,000 funerals each year. Courtesy of The Co-operative Group.

of how the non-core activities were responding to the challenges set by the new management style. The CWS had been farming since the acquisition of the Roden estate in June 1896, developing over the course of the following century into Britain's largest farmer, with 80,000 acres either directly owned or leased for the production of a wide range of produce for co-operative societies. While arable crops, fruit, and vegetables accounted for the bulk of output, what by the late-1990s was called CWS Agriculture also made wine, honey, and beer, as well as farming turkeys for the lucrative Christmas trade. However, as part of the specialist retail division it was widely accepted that Agriculture lacked co-ordination and effective integration into food retailing; that, in effect, it was 'a basket case', according to the woman who would run the business from 2000, Christine Tacon, making losses averaging almost £4 million by the early 2000s.[54] This prompted a radical restructuring of what by 2007 was known as Co-operative Farms (see Figure 9.14), involving more careful coordination of output with the needs of the Group outlets, improved training schemes for farm workers and managers, and the sale of 30,000 acres regarded as surplus to requirements. Crucially, by 2010 Co-operative Farms was made a component of the mighty Food Retail division, ensuring that its output would be integrated directly into the Group's food supply chain. These innovations also facilitated an improvement in commercial performance, because in 2010 Farms generated sales of £32.8 million (compared to £21.1 million in 2003) and a surplus of £4.5 million.[55] Moreover, a much more sustainable approach towards farming had been instituted, linking closely with the Group's growing reputation for ethical management.

While some of the older businesses were being revamped, reflecting a new-found entrepreneurial spirit within the Group, some new ventures were launched in 2006, Legal Services and Energy. Based in Bristol, but closely linked with the CIS, Legal Services was created to provide members with conveyancing, will-writing, and probate management services. The Energy business was even smaller, starting with eight wind turbines at Coldham, Cambridgeshire, funded jointly by Scottish Power and the Group, but with plans to invest further in a sustainable business that harmonized well with the Group's ethical stance. Although relatively small-scale operations at the outset, their formation reflected a desire to tap into markets that offered rich promise of future expansion at a time when serious questions were being asked about the balance of activity across the 'family'. The investment in wind farms was also publicized as part of the Group's sustainability strategy, further enhancing its reputation in this increasingly congested aspect of British business activities.

With the CFS no longer generating the kind of returns that had sustained the CWS/ the Group during the 1990s and early 2000s, however, and the new ventures producing a negative cash flow, clearly the focus of management attention would be even more heavily oriented towards the core business of food retailing. Of course, this had been the case throughout the period covered by the last two chapters, given that as this business accounted for over 70 per cent of total turnover it needed to generate appropriate

---

[54] Interview with Christine Tacon.
[55] CGBM, February 2011; and interview with C. Tacon.

FIGURE 9.14. The Co-operative Farms packaging, garden peas, *c.*2010s. As in the past, co-operative own-brand products demonstrate the movement's ethics through their packaging. This bag, made from degradable plastic, includes information about 'Five a day' portions of fruit and vegetables, and states that its peas are 'Conventionally Grown—reducing, banning and controlling pesticide use.' Courtesy of The Co-operative Group.

returns. As Table 9.2 reveals, during the early 2000s Food Retail was struggling to increase both sales and surplus in the face of intense competition from major rivals such as Tesco and Sainsbury's, while Safeway had been merged into Morrisons, Walmart had rejuvenated the ailing ASDA network, and new multiples such as Aldi and Lidl were beginning to make a significant impact at the cheaper end of the retail sector.[56] This indicates that in spite of the enormous investment in both acquisitions and shop refurbishments, not to mention the highly innovative marketing strategies implemented since the mid-1990s, the Group continued to struggle to increase market share. As a direct consequence, by the end of 2006 yet another major co-operative merger was being considered, when negotiations between the Group and United Co-operatives were initiated (see Figure 9.15). While the CWS–CRS merger in 2000 had been momentous, this had been a response to the latter's deteriorating commercial performance, sustaining a tradition of defensive mergers. The Group–United merger, on the other hand, would

[56] Interview with Leigh Sparks.

FIGURE 9.15. *Stronger Together* report, 2007. Mergers with co-operative societies including United Co-operatives (2007) and the Plymouth & South West society (2010) meant that by the end of its first decade as The Co-operative Group, the organization accounted for 85 per cent of UK co-operative trading. Courtesy of The Co-operative Group.

occur from a position of considerable strength, because the latter had consistently recorded healthy surpluses and boasted a proud record of retailing innovation. Above all, the merger offered the prospect of moving towards the 'One Society' ideal that some visionaries had advocated since the early twentieth century. The merger negotiations between the Group and United were clearly going to occupy a substantial proportion of management time in 2006–7, not least because of the extensive overlaps between the two businesses (see Table 9.1) and a history of limited co-operation. Indeed, United had been one of only a handful of societies which had refused to follow the Group's 2006 branding initiative. While ironically United's CEO, Peter Marks, advocated the creation of a National Society at the 2006 Co-operative Congress, he also announced that United would 'do their own thing' on branding and marketing.[57] As the government had just

[57] *Co-operative News*, 25 May 2006.

Table 9.3. Food Retail Division sales and surplus, 2000–10

Year	Sales (£ million)	Surplus (£ million)
2000	2,308	34.5
2001	2,600	69.5
2002	2,859	82.0
2003	3,071	122.0
2004	3,042	75.0
2005	2,983	71.6
2006	3,038	92.5
2007	3,677	93.0
2008	4,500	219.0
2009	7,500	218.0
2010	7,520	383.0

asked the Competition Commission once again to assess whether the dominance of multiple retailers was beneficial to consumers, there was a complacent feeling at the Congress that the intense competition of previous decades was going to diminish. Nevertheless, the two boards worked closely throughout the latter months of 2006 and early part of 2007 to pave the way for a merger that would create the world's largest consumer co-operative. Again, returning to a previous point, these negotiations were conducted from mutual positions of strength, the Group having reported a 17.6 per cent improvement in profitability for 2006 (see Figure 9.11), while United had just boosted trading profits by 16.6 per cent (to £62.2 million) on a turnover of £2.2 billion. Having recently acquired the large co-operative societies in Sheffield (December 2006) and Leeds (January 2007), as well as buying the Williams pharmacy chain, United was building a formidable presence across the north of England that would effectively complement what the Group had developed.

Given the undoubted strength of United, however, and even though it was much smaller than the Group, a vital issue in the merger negotiations would be the question of who would run the combined business. In this context, it is important to stress that in October 2006 Martin Beaumont announced his retirement as CEO, to take effect from October 2007, after five years in the top position, preceded by ten years as CEO of United Co-operatives. As Bob Burlton stated at the Group's 2007 AGM, Beaumont's 'strong leadership' and clear vision had ensured 'incredible progress' over the previous six years.[58] While one can excuse the hyperbole, it is certainly reasonable to note that by 2007 the Group was in a much healthier state. Of course, as we have consistently argued in this chapter, the foundations laid by Sir Graham Melmoth, and especially forging the

[58] *Co-operative News*, 24 May 2007.

merger between the CWS and CRS, were of paramount importance. Beaumont also sustained the earlier work that was developing a stronger link between personal membership and 'The Co-operative' brand, resulting in the rehabilitation of 'the divi' in 2005. In addition, the business model had been effectively modernized, especially in key areas such as distribution and financial control. Closely linked with these innovations was the development of a highly creative marketing campaign masterminded by Zoe Morgan, awakening the potential in the brand and exploiting more effectively the Group's reputation as a 'responsible retailer'. Recruiting dynamic executives such as Zoe Morgan was also symptomatic of Beaumont's desire to revitalize the organizational culture, bringing fresh talent into the Group as a means of ensuring it was utilizing modern techniques. This provided the dominant Food Retail business to develop progressively at a time when rivals were investing massively in new store formats, and especially in developing the c-store strategy on which the Group had gambled since the mid-1990s. The aggressive acquisition strategy also supported this drive to boost Food Retail's performance, as well as assimilating the CRS and the new stores, in order to build market share and sales volumes in the face of intense competition. However, it was felt by some on the Board that the increased professionalism of the Group had come at a price, with a bulging cost base and a lack of entrepreneurial instinct, which led directly to a major exercise to reduce corporate costs as well as an increasingly fractious relationship between the Board and management. Whilst the commercial performance of the Group had undoubtedly improved by the time Beaumont had left the Group, it was widely recognized that there was considerable scope for his successor to take the Group's profitability to another level.

Apart from the improvements effected to Food Retail's results, Beaumont had also been keen to ensure that non-core businesses benefited from these organizational and marketing innovations. One of the most difficult challenges had been dealing with the CIS's investment problems, obviating a major crisis in what was an important component of the 'family of co-operative businesses'. Another vital element in this respect was integrating the CIS more effectively into the CFS, encouraging the insurance team to work more closely with Co-operative Bank executives in securing the kind of synergies that would boost profitability. Other significant non-core areas such as Funeralcare and Pharmacy also benefited from the growing insistence that standards across the 'family' should rise, with continued emphasis being placed on further acquisitions to boost market share and integrating them into the marketing and branding campaigns. This highlights how the drive to develop a governance structure capable of achieving these aims was central to building what Beaumont claimed was 'a strong platform for the next phase of The Co-operative Group's development'.[59] Indeed, as the 'modernizer' of the three CEOs responsible for revitalizing the Group, Beaumont had achieved what many of his predecessors had failed to do, namely, transforming an organizational culture and business model that had proved inappropriate to the requirements of twenty-first-century

[59] *Co-operative News*, 25 October 2006.

retailing. Above all, by (slowly) integrating new acquisitions, invigorating the marketing and communications sides of the business, and recruiting the kind of talent required to implement these aims, Beaumont provided a legacy on which his successor could build. In effect, by 2007 the Group had a viable business model that through the personal dividend was built on a commitment to co-operative values and principles, differentiating it from its major rivals—Tesco, Sainsbury's, ASDA, Morrisons, Aldi, and Lidl—and driving the organization forward in a highly decisive and committed way.

9.3 MARKS AND THE 'RENAISSANCE'

Having emphasized how under Martin Beaumont the Group had improved its fortunes, and returning to the theme of this chapter, the third essential step in the recovery process started in October 2007, when Peter Marks (Figure 9.16) took over as CEO. His appointment certainly seemed appropriate, in that since 2000 he had been CEO of United Co-operatives, the society that in 2007 merged with the Group to create the world's largest consumer co-operative, with combined sales in excess of £8 billion. Another important appointment was the Chair of The Co-operative Group Board, in that previously this had always been a representative of the CWS/the Group's corporate membership, reflecting the power base they had within the structure. In 2007, however, Len Wardle, the south-east's representative of individual members, was elected to the Chair. This was highly symbolic, because it decisively signalled to the co-operative world that the Group was by then a primary co-operative. Len Wardle (Figure 9.17) has also continued to chair the Board in a highly balanced way, providing the CEO and his executive team with the kind of constructive criticism that such a body ought to give in challenging them to justify their commercial strategies.

In assessing Peter Marks's core working philosophy, it is important to stress that while as we noted earlier the relationship between the Group and United had never been especially productive, with the latter having as recently as 2006 refused to follow the former's branding lead, Peter Marks was very much in favour of concentrating co-operative trading into 'One Society'. When commenting on United's absorption of Sheffield Co-operative Society in 2006, Marks noted that: 'In this business, scale is important. There's a recognition that consolidation ultimately is necessary to sustain our future.'[60] More importantly, after listening to a radio interview conducted with Terry Leahy (Tesco CEO) on the morning he was going to address the 2006 National Retail Consumer Network conference, Marks decided to rip up his speech and deliver a decisive message. Leahy had been asked why Tesco was moving into convenience stores, given that the Group had invested significantly in that type of retailing. His response was both startling and extremely disconcerting: 'There's only one winner in convenience stores, and it

---

[60] *Yorkshire Post*, 20 September 2006.

FIGURE 9.16. **Peter Marks.** Having started his co-operative career stacking shelves for the York-shire society in the late 1960s, Marks rose through the ranks to become its chief executive in 2000, a role he continued in after its merger with United Co-operatives in 2002. He became chief executive of The Co-operative Group in 2008, following the United merger, and retired in May 2013. Courtesy of The Co-operative Group.

isn't the co-op.' This enraged Marks, resulting in a fevered day's work with his corporate affairs director, Mark Craig, to write a blunt speech advocating the creation of 'One Soci-ety'.[61] The core message in Marks's revised speech was that 'the movement either had to change or it would go bust'.[62] While many in the audience disliked the explicit nature of this statement, not to mention the implication that the movement had been too slow to respond to competitive pressures, the realists in the audience accepted the logic behind his case for 'One Society' as the major vehicle capable of achieving the levels of integra-tion required to compete with its major rivals.

As Peter Marks and his team were highly focused on driving commercial perform-ance for the newly merged business, he was happy to leave the design of a new constitu-tional settlement to the Group Chair Len Wardle and Group Secretary Moira Lees (Figure 9.18). The latter, of course, was a veteran of the CWS–CRS merger negotiations and consequent governance revisions, bringing a degree of understanding of the com-plications that few could match. Supported by a highly experienced membership team, many of whom had started their career in the rarefied atmosphere of the CRS in the

---

[61] Interview with Peter Marks.   [62] *Co-operative News*, 21 March 2011.

FIGURE 9.17. **Len Wardle.** An elected member from the South East region, Wardle has chaired The Co-operative Group's board since 2007; he joined the CWS Board in 1992. Courtesy of The Co-operative Group.

1990s, and including Russell Gill, this second Constitutional Review of the decade carefully knitted together the priorities for the representatives from the incoming United with the practical needs of the much larger and complex Group democratic structure. It is nevertheless vital to remember that the three-tiered structure agreed in 2001 was retained, while individual members were still regarded as the core of the organization. Over the course of the last five years, the membership department has applied this core philosophy to a dynamic campaign that has seen individual membership rise to about 7 million by 2012. Although an occasional critic of the democratic structure, Peter Marks has said that directors have always backed the key commercial decisions which he has recommended; while they have challenged management to prove the business case for these decisions; ensuring that co-operative values remain at the centre of how the Group does business, Marks has never had a major move rebuffed.

Looking more closely at some of the detailed constitutional changes of the 2007–12 era, it is important to note that at Group Board level it was decided to create two new subsidiary boards covering Food and Specialist Retail, operating alongside the existing Financial Services board. This recognized the reality of the size and complexity of the Group, because it was hardly sensible for the strategic oversight of major businesses like funerals or pharmacy to be a bolt-on at the end of the agenda whilst focus was given to bigger businesses. As part of the creation of subsidiary boards, it was also agreed that Independent Professional Non-Executive Directors (IPNEDS) could be appointed to fill skills gaps—which were an almost inevitable consequence of relying upon the democratic structure to populate boards. IPNEDs had been a reality for some years on the CFS Board, as a result of stipulations laid down by the Financial Services Authority, and

FIGURE 9.18. Moira Lees. Having joined CWS as a management trainee in 1981, Lees became deputy secretary in 1996 and worked closely with then-CWS secretary Nick Eyre on the Governance Review Board during the merger with CRS. In 2007, Lees became the first female secretary in The Co-operative Group's history. Courtesy of The Co-operative Group.

this experience had convinced many in the Group that this independent voice would lead to better governance and decision-making. Interestingly, one of the first IPNEDs to be appointed to the Food Board was a senior executive from Kingfisher plc, Euan Sutherland, who in December 2012 was announced as Peter Marks's successor as Group Chief Executive, an issue we shall assess in the final chapter.

Peter Marks had come from a very different background from his two predecessors: while Melmoth and Beaumont had started their careers in a professional capacity, much to his parents' disdain Marks had left St Bede's Grammar School, Bradford, mid-way through his A-levels, eschewing academic qualifications in favour of stacking shelves for his local co-operative store and concentrating more on his life-long interest in rock music.[63] It was only as a result of his manager's ability to spot potential in the young Marks that he agreed to participate in some training programmes that involved a half-day of in-house education and two nights per week at a local college. This imbued him with a retailing mentality which was based on tough negotiations over prices and quality, committing himself to a commercial dynamic that would dominate a highly successful career. Using these skills, he took a store manager's position in Bradford, but after eight years in retailing he seized the opportunity created by the retirement of Yorkshire Co-operative Society's personnel manager to move into a senior management position. By the 1980s, he had moved back into retailing, as head of Yorkshire's funeral care business, following which he consecutively ran the department stores and food retail divisions. After impressing colleagues with his committed approach to improving Yorkshire's

---

[63] Interview with Peter Marks.

performance, by 2000 he was made CEO of an operation that was almost immediately absorbed by United Co-operative Society. With United's CEO moving on to take over the newly created Co-operative Group, this created a vacuum that Marks was more than willing to fill, becoming CEO on Beaumont's departure in May 2001. By 2007, with United reporting record profits of £62.4 million on a turnover of £2.2 billion, the business had sustained its impressive performance, developing especially a highly robust food retailing business that would complement the Group's recent efforts.

Marks was clearly committed to extensive consolidation of the once disparate co-operative movement, having just absorbed Sheffield Co-operative Society in January 2007, as well as boosting United's pharmacy chain by acquiring nine shops in Leeds and Harrogate from the Sheard Group and Saffer Chemicals. Even though United and the Group had not collaborated closely, for example on such matters as branding, he was keen to persuade his Board to move towards the 'One Society' ideal he had forcefully advocated at the 2006 Co-operative Congress, working closely with Martin Beaumont to ensure that the merger would be effected. This was no easy process, given the hostility of some United board members to being absorbed into the much larger Group. Nevertheless, as the robust development of United under Marks's stewardship was often held up as a shining example of how co-operative societies ought to be managed and developed, he was in a strong position to achieve his aims for both the Group and the movement as a whole. As he would later admit, in pursuing these aims Marks was never frightened of upsetting people if he felt that this was an acceptable price to pay for making progress. 'Sure, I've ruffled some feathers, but you don't change a business like this without doing that' is how he summarized his management style.[64]

It was this no-nonsense approach that would be used to awaken the Group to its full potential, driving the Leviathan forward in a positive frame of mind. It will become apparent that in his six years as CEO, a series of overlapping themes dominated: first, the extensive integration of the Leviathan business empire; secondly, further significant acquisitions that boosted scale in key parts of the Leviathan; thirdly, the aggressive pursuit of standardized branding and shop refits; and fourthly, a 'renaissance' in Group fortunes. With specific regard to the latter, it is possible to see Marks as a 'lucky general', in that he inherited an organization that had been radically overhauled by his predecessors, with a highly effective branding and marketing campaign that set the Group apart from its major rivals, allied with the reintroduction of the 'divi' in 2005. On the other hand, Marks was also very much the architect of his own success, ruthlessly pursuing strategies designed to lift performance and exploit further the inherent advantages of the Leviathan.

Having noted Marks's ruthlessness, it is also fair to highlight how significant figures across the movement were sceptical of Marks's commitment to co-operative values and principles, regarding him as a hard-nosed retailing expert who was more interested

---

[64] Interview with Peter Marks; and *Sunday Times*, 22 August 2010.

in doing deals and boosting sales and profits.[65] Indeed, Sir Graham Melmoth publicly stated in the *Co-operative News* that: 'Peter Marks wouldn't know a co-op principle if it crept up and smacked him in the face.'[66] Of course, this was far from the truth, in that since becoming a store manager in Bradford in his twenties Marks had been as committed as any other employee to what the movement represented. At the same time, he was a realist, arguing that while being an ethical retailer differentiated co-operatives from their rivals: 'In my view, ethics are a tie-breaker—everything else—price; quality—has to be as good as the competition.' Crucially, he was keen to stress that had co-operatives merely focused on ethics, values, and principles: 'We were on our way to becoming the most ethical business in the corporate graveyard.'[67] This highlights how he can be regarded as a critical friend of co-operative values and principles; while he remained committed to this ethos, it was the commercial dynamic which motivated him more than any philosophic notions. Moreover, he would frequently argue that as the vast majority of members rarely did anything but shop at co-operative stores, it was essential to retain their loyalty through good service and provide value-for-money propositions, rather than appeal to their philosophical leanings. Although this approach did not gel with many of the purists in the movement, it ensured that once he took the Group reins the expanded business would be run as a commercial operation that had to compete with much more integrated multiples anxious to boost market share.

One of the first challenges Marks faced was how best to integrate United into the Group, because while the latter was much larger and more diverse than its smaller counterpart, there was considerable overlap across the core and non-core activities (see Table 9.1). His aim was to create 'one business in one year',[68] illustrating how he was never willing to take half-measures. In his keynote address to the Co-operative Congress in 2008, Marks also explained that by the time of his retirement he wanted not only to increase the Group's market share, but also rejuvenate membership activity as a key feature of co-operative shopping.[69] After persuading Martin Beaumont to bring his retirement forward by one month, Marks then proceeded to create an executive management team capable of bringing the two businesses together.[70] This exercise would inevitably cause considerable friction, in that while Marks was evidently looking for the best talent to perform the key functions, his decisions resulted in some departures. Key members of Beaumont's Executive, including his deputy CEO, Paul Hewitt, Nick Eyre (secretary), Zoe Morgan (Marketing), Bryan Portman (Financial Controller), and Guy McCracken (Food Retail), left The Co-operative Group, to be replaced by a new ten-strong executive team. This included six of Marks's team from United, including Martyn Wates (Financial Controller), Tim Hurrell (Food Retail), and Patrick Allen (Marketing). As he stated

---

[65] Interview with Sir Graham Melmoth.   [66] *Co-operative News*, 23 January 2007.
[67] Interview with Peter Marks.   [68] *Co-operative News*, 23 May 2007.
[69] *Co-operative News*, 10 July 2008.
[70] Beaumont went on to become Chair of Kind Consumer, an operation that existed to encourage ethical trading.

when the team was announced: 'By any standard, this is an experienced and talented team, with a proven track record in delivering commercial success aligned to our co-operative values and social goals.'[71] One of Marks's first decisions was to postpone the TV brand launch developed by Zoe Morgan and her team. He calculated that insufficient of the Group's stores had been converted into the new brand facia and the required operating standards were still not embedded. This gave a clear signal to all in the organization that the new CEO was ready to take hard decisions.

One of the key strategies that both Beaumont and Marks had pursued was increasing market share, given its significant decline over the previous four decades (see Table 6.1). In particular, this had prompted an aggressive acquisition strategy throughout the 2000s, resulting in the purchase of significant numbers of c-store outlets. A move that Beaumont resisted, however, was Marks's suggestion, made as early as 2005, that United and the Group should combine to acquire the Somerfield chain (see Figure 9.19).[72] Beaumont had rightly argued that the Group was not ready at that time to make such a major move, given the difficulties it had experienced in absorbing all of its other acquisitions. On the other hand, it was clear to Marks that Somerfield represented such an excellent fit with the Group's food strategy that he was keen to rehabilitate the plan when he took over as CEO. Itself the product of a series of mergers involving the Dee Corporation's purchase of Kwik Save and some smaller operations, Somerfield still had 750 outlets after several divestments and some sales arising from intervention from the Competition Commission. This proved extremely attractive to the Group,

FIGURE 9.19. 'Welcome to the Family' advertisement, 2009. The Co-operative Group's acquisition of Somerfield for £1.57 million in March 2009 doubled the Group's market share in food retailing. Courtesy of The Co-operative Group.

[71] *Co-operative News*, 23 May 2007.   [72] *Co-operative News*, 21 March 2011.

resulting in Somerfield's purchase in March 2009, for £1.57 million. It was a move that instantly doubled the Group's share of the retail food market, from 4.5 per cent to 7.2 per cent, putting it into fifth place behind Tesco, ASDA, Sainsbury's, and Morrisons. As Marks noted when revealing the Group's 2008 results: 'We needed to win back some market share, and Somerfield came on the market...It was rocket fuel for the business, a real transformational deal.'[73] Another key point to make about the Somerfield acquisition was its timing, at the height of the 2008–9 financial crisis. Indeed, it was the biggest corporate takeover of that year, indicating that as capitalist enterprise was taking such a buffeting only co-operatives not affected by Stock Exchange volatility were capable of engineering such moves. This reinforces Marks's claim that by 2008 the Group was an organization which had the appetite and resources to contemplate highly ambitious moves which leveraged a radical improvement in status and impact.

While the Somerfield acquisition was an extremely significant move for the Group, it also coincided with a new sense of self-confidence across the organization, building on the significant benefits arising from the merger with United. Indeed, as early as 2008 Marks was talking about a 'renaissance' in the Group fortunes, evoking a rich picture of the Group's potential in developing what he called 'a superb brand proposition' based on ethical trading (see Figure 9.20), backed by a £1.5 billion investment programme aimed at boosting sales and profitability.[74] As Figures 9.10 and 9.11 indicate, both gross income and operating profits rose appreciably after the static mid-decade years, boosting optimism across both the Group and the movement as a whole that the problems of the past had been banished. This was reflected in Peter Marks's pronouncement in September 2009 that the Group was 'back in the premiership',[75] referring back to Sir Graham Melmoth's 1997 admission that CWS was a 'third division player' behind the likes of Tesco, Sainsbury's, and Morrison's.[76] Sustaining this football analogy, and in the process denigrating his home-town club, in May 2009 he boldly stated that: 'We were Bradford City, League Two...We are now in the Premier League, perhaps Spurs, but aiming to be right at the top as Manchester United.'[77] Such bullish outpourings from the CEO went a long way to convince all stakeholders that the Group was in a much better position than for possibly sixty years, generating improved returns on a much-increased turnover. The CRTG also continued to play a key role in this recovery, in that as by 2002 it was servicing every UK co-operative society, the £4 billion worth of buying power it generated by 2010 provided extensive economies of scale and scope. Another vital indication of the Group's performance was the enormous decrease in the importance of The Co-operative Bank to group profits, in that in 2000 it accounted for 91.3 per cent of the surplus, while by 2010 this had fallen to 33.4 per cent. Over that same period, turnover rose from £4,853 million to £13,691 million, clearly indicating how the mergers, acquisitions, and rationalizations had paved the way for a general

[73] *BBC News*, 11 December 2009: <http://news.bbc.co.uk/1/hi/business/8392663.stm>.
[74] *Co-operative News*, 23 May 2008.   [75] *Daily Post*, 25 September 2008.
[76] See section 8.4.   [77] *Mail on Sunday*, 10 May 2009.

FIGURE 9.20. The Co-operative Fairtrade and 'Truly Irresistible' products, c.2010s. The Co-operative Group established a premium own-brand range, 'Truly Irresistible', in 2003, and has continued to transition its own-brand products to Fairtrade standards. Courtesy of The Co-operative Group.

improvement. One should also remember that the improvements in turnover and profitability had been achieved against the backdrop of what most authorities have described as the worst recession since the 1930s, as many Western industrial economies wrestled with the consequences of how the financial community had indulged in wild speculation of the most irresponsible type.

Underpinning this impressive commercial performance was a series of highly creative marketing and advertising campaigns that built significantly on the innovations developed under Zoe Morgan between 2005 and 2007. Prior to her departure, Morgan had secured a major coup when she persuaded Bob Dylan to allow the use of one of the most enigmatic protest songs of the twentieth century, 'Blowin' in the wind'. It was extremely unusual for Dylan to agree to the use of his music for commercial purposes,[78] a stance that was only modified when he realized that 'Blowin' in the wind' was to be used to reinforce a message of change in a TV campaign extolling the virtues of ethical banking and ethical retailing. Although Marks postponed the launch of that campaign until he was totally confident that the retailing network was capable of providing the essential operational back-up, it was a brave decision by the Group to run with 'Blowin'

---

[78] He had allowed Apple to use a song ('Someday Baby') to appear in a global TV campaign for iPods.

in the wind', especially as it was regarded as a 1960s anthem for those disaffected with the establishment. Nevertheless, it underpinned a multimillion-pound relaunch of The Co-operative Group's image in February 2009. Such was the impact of this creative campaign that many regarded it as game-changing and highly dramatic, demonstrating a new sense of confidence across the Group that it was indeed a major player in British retailing.[79] This was also followed by extensive TV advertising campaigns, using the voice of a leading actor (John Hannah) to publicize the slogan 'Good with food', epitomizing the ethical trader stance for which the Group was rightly famous. Internally, to reinforce these campaigns a 'Four betters' programme was launched in 2007, highlighting the need to improve the Group's shops, products, service, and execution.[80] Plans were also drawn up to redevelop the sprawling and grossly outdated Manchester offices, leading to a highly ambitious relocation programme that would result in the construction of a highly prestigious headquarters.

Having emphasized a renewed sense of self-confidence within the Group, as well as indicating how through the 'Four betters' campaign the Group was invigorating its value proposition, it is important to stress that while the Somerfield acquisition had impressed many commentators, just as with the Alldays purchase the Group struggled with the integration of its stores into the existing network. As we shall see in the final chapter, the Group also experienced a significant slide in food sales after 2010, indicating that the heady confidence of 2009–10 was being dissipated as established rivals such as Tesco, Sainsbury's, and Morrison's continued to compete vigorously in a market that had also been entered by new firms such as Aldi and Lidl. One critic asked:

What does the Co-operative stand for anymore? What do they offer that other chains can't? They are an ethical fairtrade business but that doesn't wash when customers within the UK are finding things tough. They too want value and don't want to be penalised with higher prices because the Co-op is their local store. Customers liked the appeal of Somerfield and its general appeal, the Co-operative has a reputation for high prices with availability being a challenge in the early days which was a far cry from the slick Somerfield operation.[81]

This highlighted the constant need in retailing to re-evaluate one's offering, given the intense competition provided by both new and older rivals that continued to invest substantially in their premises and systems, an issue to which we shall return in the final chapter. Above all, one must question whether in benefiting from its acquisitions by boosting market share, the Group was also persuading consumers that its value proposition was appropriate to the intensely competitive marketplace, a challenge with which all retailers must wrestle.

Regardless of these problems, however, the Group remained supremely confident of its ability to continue to absorb additional businesses. Apart from the Somerfield acquisition, this confidence was also expressed in the October 2008 announcement that the CFS was negotiating to acquire Britannia Building Society. Based in Leek,

---

[79] <Guardian.co.uk>, 28 January 2009.   [80] The Group Annual Report, 2007.
[81] Dresser (2012).

Staffordshire, Britannia was the second largest building society in the UK, with assets exceeding £37 billion and over 250 outlets. Before the merger could go ahead, it was necessary to await the passing of the Building Societies (Funding) and Mutual Societies (Transfers) Act, known as the Butterfill Act after its sponsor, Sir John Butterfill MP. This 2009 Act gave building societies greater freedom to merge with other companies, as well as changing the current restrictions on the way they are allowed to raise money, providing the requisite statutory authority for the two parties to engage in formal negotiations when passed in January 2009.[82] By 1 August 2009, the merger had been completed and Britannia formally became part of the CFS, creating a business with £70 billion worth of assets, nine million customers, and over 12,000 employees. It was also decided that Britannia's former CEO, Neville Richardson, would run the CFS.[83]

At the time, this was presented as an important step towards creating a larger, ethically sensitive alternative to shareholder-owned banks so recently found wanting by events. In 2009, as The Co-operative Bank was seen as being untarnished by the scandals emerging from revelations about bankers' activities in the lead up to the 2008 financial crisis, the Group was able to ride the wave of public popularity. In this context, using Dylan's 'Blowin' in the wind' in TV adverts captured this mood in a most effective way. It is also worth noting that while The Co-operative Bank and Britannia initially retained their independent products and brands, an integration programme was enacted, including the decision to rebrand all Britannia branches and products as Co-operative, ensuring that synergistic benefits arose from such a merger.

Another vital feature of the Britannia acquisition by 2011 was the addition of 245 branches to The Co-operative Bank's network, by converting the building society's operations into fully functioning bank outlets. Apart from advertising how this contrasted sharply with the general attitude of British banks, which since 1990 had closed 7,555 branches as part of their drive to cut costs, it demonstrated how customer service remained a distinguishing characteristic of its operations.[84] Later that year, the CFS also announced that it would bid for over 600 branches that Lloyds Bank was being obliged to sell as a condition of taking taxpayers' funds to bail it out of the deep troubles arising from mismanagement in the years leading up to the 2008 financial crisis. The CFS put into effect a detailed planning exercise that would by September 2012 result in its offer being accepted. The planned acquisition was expected to boost the number of branches past 1,000 and give The Co-operative Bank 10 per cent of the UK banking market, indicating that it had made impressive progress since 1990. The deal was to cost the CFS an initial £350 million, with possible further payments up to 2027 of £400 million. However, in April 2013 the Group announced its withdrawal from the negotia-

---

[82] *Guardian*, 13 October 2008.   [83] *Co-operative News*, 4 August 2009.
[84] *Evening Standard*, 9 June 2011.

tions, citing the economic climate and increasing regulatory requirements in the financial services sector and arguing that the deal would no longer be in the best interests of its members. Nonetheless, financial services remain a key element of the Group's portfolio.

9.4 Conclusions

By the early twenty-first century, and perhaps for the first time in its history, one can speak of a truly coherent, national co-operative trading operation. Moreover, given the impressive improvements in both turnover and operating profits after 2007, few rejected the claims of a 'renaissance', especially as they were underpinned by a significant growth in the Group's share of its core food retail market. While Peter Marks's aspiration of 'One Society' was in 2010 still just that, namely, an aspiration, the Group by then accounted for 85 per cent of all co-operative trading, while the CRTG supplied the needs of every retail society. This had all been made possible by the decisive changes of the late 1990s, giving successive CEOs the authority to press forward with a modernization agenda that member societies had previously resisted. A process of 'falling toward the centre', either through mergers that resulted in the much-expanded Group or strategic alliances through the CRTG, eased the dysfunctional problems that had consistently beset progress in the twentieth century. The post-1997 revival was also built solidly on the values and principles first espoused by the 'Rochdale Pioneers' almost 150 years earlier, restoring the benefits individual members can generate from shopping at co-operative outlets. Moreover, this idealism appealed to a generation of managers that had entered the CWS from Britain's expanded higher education sector in the 1960s and 1970s—young people who were interested in a business career, but whose left-of-centre sympathies made co-operatives especially appealing. It was no coincidence that the pace of reform accelerated just as this generation reached positions of real power and influence within the movement; but especially in such key organizations as the CWS and The Co-operative Bank. It is also apparent that the marketing and branding activities based on ethical trading which had first emerged in the 1970s and developed aggressively after 2001 gave the CWS and later the Group a significant position in the highly sensitive mass-consumption markets for food and banking. These were all decisive contributors to what has already been described as a 'renaissance' in co-operative fortunes since the turn of the millennium, all of which demonstrate that both continuity and radical change were vital factors in this process.

The CWS, then the Group, had consequently adapted itself to a highly challenging environment in what must be regarded as a very short period, especially when compared to its long history. The decisive leadership, imaginative organizational and marketing drives, and the aggressive merger strategies all combined to achieve a 'renaissance' that underpinned the Group's performance. Moreover, the revival of the 'divi' by 2005, combined with radical corporate governance changes that provided individual members with much-enhanced opportunities to influence decisions, meant that democracy had meant something to those who shopped at Group outlets. Whether or not this turnaround was permanent is a difficult question to answer, but it provides us with an opportunity to consider the present and future of co-operative trading in a concluding chapter that will provoke debate on this crucial issue.

CHAPTER 10

....

CONCLUSIONS

....

WHEN in 2010 The Co-operative Group annual report publicized a new vision based on the maxim 'To build a better society by excelling in everything we do', this reflected a new-found confidence across an organization that just thirteen years earlier had been regarded as being in terminal decline and requiring radical surgery if it was ever going to recover. Not only did commentators accept Peter Marks's claim that the Group had experienced a 'renaissance' in its fortunes, but also the incumbent coalition government expressed at least rhetorical interest in mutual and employee ownership, while authoritative observers of the British business scene strongly advocated a mutual type of ownership as the alternative organizational form to the public company with dispersed share ownership.[1] As the CWS had since the late 1990s been reinvigorating the member-led model that had been at the heart of the work of the 'Rochdale Pioneers', this ensured that the opacity which had been central to co-operative society management for many decades had been banished into the mists of time, creating a much more transparent, mutually beneficial business model that proved to be far more successful. With turnover having risen to £13.6 billion in 2010, on which a surplus of £625 million was made, the Group certainly seemed to have overcome the challenges it had faced up to the 1990s, achieving this improvement in the face of the worst recession since the 1930s. While the reasons behind this 'renaissance' have been examined in some detail over the last two chapters, it is now necessary to assess the extent to which this will be sustained, as well as provide both an overview of the business's evolution and some insights into the Group's status at the time of its 150th anniversary. Of course, historians who embark upon exercises in futurology do so at their peril. Predictions of business fortunes are notoriously prone to embarrassing contradiction by events. This is doubly so in the turbulent context since 2008. As such, the authors issue an important caveat emptor in respect of any tentative speculations offered here.

---

[1] Ownership Commission (2012).

10.1 EVOLUTION OF THE BUSINESS MODEL

The most obvious starting point for this analysis is to track the ways in which the business model had evolved in response to strategic decisions that altered the way it operated and how it created value for its stakeholders. Having begun as a secondary co-operative, owned by several hundred primary retail co-operatives, the business model on which the CWS was built relied largely on the provision of goods and services for its shareholders, in return for a corporate dividend that was paid annually on a pro rata basis. As the early chapters outline, the CWS responded to this brief in highly creative ways, establishing not only a wide range of manufacturing and distribution activities, but also international provision networks that ensured its stakeholders were supplied with a wide range of goods at reasonable prices. This culminated in a Leviathan-type business conglomerate that was the most diversified and vertically integrated organization in the UK by the 1940s, while co-operative retail societies accounted for one-quarter of British retail trade.

While it is clear that up to the 1940s the CWS's business model proved to be appropriate to Britain's socio-economic and cultural environment, over the course of the next fifty years this came under intense pressure. Indeed, given the dramatic changes to both retailing and Britain's socio-economic characteristics from the 1950s especially, retail societies experienced such intense financial pressures that a substantial number sought refuge in, first, the CRS, and later, the CWS. Apart from adding considerably to the CWS's liquidity problems, starving key functions of much-needed investment capital, this also fundamentally altered the membership structure, especially after the SCWS merged into the CWS, following its 1973 banking crisis. Having operated as a secondary co-operative owned by corporate members, the acquisition in 1973 of extensive retailing activities owned by individual members presented the CWS with a wholly original challenge. As a consequence, from 1973 the CWS was operating a hybrid business model based on both distribution and retailing, with the latter gathering considerable momentum over the following twenty-five years as more societies merged into the Manchester-based organization. Although it is difficult to be precise about membership numbers, largely because an accurate record was not kept by either the CWS or the retail societies, it was clear by the 1990s that individual members had far less status than their corporate counterparts. As almost all retail societies had abandoned the personal 'divi' by the late 1960s, there was little incentive for customers to become members, and individual members found it extremely difficult to express their voice in a CWS geared toward societies. This 'democratic deficit' was also the source of considerable conflict between the CWS and the retail societies, and especially the CRS, a feature that largely explains why the former failed to persuade the latter to collaborate more extensively in response to intensifying competition and a severe downturn in market share. As we have noted several times in our analysis, the co-operative movement consequently developed a highly dysfunctional character, with leadership of both the CWS and the retail societies failing to navigate opinion towards a mutually agreeable consensus on the best way forward.

Resolving this membership conundrum, and at the same time adapting the hybrid business model, remained a major source of debate across the movement over the course of the late twentieth century, at a time when the co-operative share of retail trade was falling, reaching a nadir of 4.4 per cent by 2000. It was only as a result of severe external provocation, in the form of an attempted takeover of the CWS in 1997, that the movement finally responded effectively to the internal and external challenges. The key to understanding these responses was a reaffirmation of co-operative values and principles, allied with a commitment to ensuring that all members should receive benefits, while at the same time much greater emphasis was placed on leveraging the advantages in scale and mutual benefit to provide a better service to individual consumers. Although the process had already started in 1992, with the creation of CRTG as a reflection of the switch from 'selling to' to 'buying for' co-operative societies, while in 1994 the remaining manufacturing operations were sold, by 2000 the business model had effectively been adapted, with the emphasis placed much more on food retailing. This essential adaptation was also followed by the merger of the CRS into the CWS, resulting in the creation of The Co-operative Group (hereafter, the Group) in 2001, while considerable efforts were made to build a standardized brand image based on 'The Co-operative' that consumers would recognize and value. The re-creation of a membership dividend scheme in 2005 was another vital step along the recovery road, fulfilling the organization's commitment to spreading the benefits of membership wider than the remaining retail societies. Although as we saw in Chapter 9 the movement had been slow to respond to the hugely successful loyalty card schemes developed by Tesco and Boots, at least by 2005 the 'divi' was once again being used as the essential differentiating factor between 'The Co-operative' goods and those of its rivals.

By the time the Group had also acquired United Co-operatives in 2007, creating a business that accounted for 75 per cent of all co-operative trading, the business model was based on the concept of an integrated retailing operation, destroying the image of a dysfunctional federation. Not only were both surplus and turnover rising impressively, but also the acquisition in 2009 of Somerfield reflected a new-found sense of self-confidence, as well as boosting market share to just over 7 per cent, compared to the miserable 4.4 per cent in 2000 recorded for all co-operative societies. Of course, in light of the ruthlessly competitive nature of this sector only time will tell if the acquisition proves to be successful in the long term. Nonetheless, by 2009 the Group could rightly claim to have experienced a 'renaissance' in its fortunes, becoming Britain's fifth largest food retailer, with a recognizable, standardized brand that was heavily advertised. Similarly, a major investment programme in store branding, national advertising campaigns, and technology improvements began to come to fruition. These game-changing campaigns provided categoric evidence that 'The Co-operative' was a force to be reckoned with, significantly reversing the decades of decline experienced up to the 1990s.

A sub-theme running through this story was, of course, the relatively dynamic performance of other businesses such as The Co-operative Bank and Funeralcare. Based on a customer-focused strategy, and extensively supported by aggressive external growth through acquisitions, both of these businesses had developed a viable business model that proved extremely effective. Indeed, had the CWS imitated this business model much earlier, then it would not have experienced such difficulties in the late twentieth century. The Co-operative Financial Services' acquisition of Britannia Building Society in 2009 provided further evidence of the movement's new sense of self-confidence, coming just a year after the Somerfield purchase and coinciding with the TV advertising campaign featuring Bob Dylan's 'Blowin' in the wind'. The Co-operative Group had also been investing in new businesses such as energy and legal services, sustaining its Leviathan-like image of a core (food retailing) that in 2010 still accounted for 60 per cent of turnover, with a wide range of other activities that were increasingly integrated into mainstream activities, where possible.

There is little doubt that by 2010 the Group had made the decisive move away from being a dysfunctional federation into an integrated retailer, reasserting itself in the marketplace and continuing to operate in a wide range of business sectors, from food retailing to banking, funeral care, pharmacies, and travel. Reflecting the Group's new willingness to take hard decisions on failing businesses, the latter was also the subject of a recovery strategy when in response to deep troubles in the travel agency business a joint venture with Thomas Cook was negotiated in 2011. While the Group's Board was heavily criticized by some members for this approach, particularly around the use of the Co-operative brand, this was seen as a way of coping with the impact of a global recession that had seriously affected tourism since 2008. It is also important to add that the Midlands Co-operative Society was a party to this deal, bringing its 100 travel agencies together with the Group's 360 and Thomas Cook's 780 to create the largest business of its type in the UK. The Competition Commission sanctioned the deal in August 2011, and even though some shops were closed as a result of some rationalization of capacity, saving the new group up to £35 million per annum, it was hoped this would provide a basis for commercial recovery.[2]

In view of the continuing deep economic difficulties faced by the UK, as well as many other industrialized economies in Europe and North America, it was apparent that businesses needed to be strategically adaptable and ready to take hard decisions when necessary. Moreover, widespread revulsion at the behaviour of the reckless bankers responsible for the financial crisis of 2007–8 created a space for ethically run businesses, providing an opportunity for the Group to publicize its long-term record in this respect. Indeed, as we have seen especially in the last chapter, at no time had the Group deviated from its commitment to co-operative values and principles, and especially its devotion to member benefits. In 2011, an Ethical Plan was published, laying out a set of radical goals aimed at cementing its reputation as the most socially responsible business in the UK. The core pledges in this Plan were:

- Growing membership from 6 million to 20 million by 2020, with the aim of making every customer a co-owner;
- The most radical Fairtrade conversion programme ever undertaken;

[2] *BBC News*, 16 August 2011. <http://www.bbc.co.uk/news/uk-england-cambridgeshire-14550184>.

- £11 million to support co-operative growth, and the launch of a £20 million international Co-operative Development Loan Fund;
- Doubling financial support for renewable energy and energy efficiency projects, from £400 million to £1 billion by 2013;
- And, the world's first ethically screened general insurance products, which will support over two million policies.

While it is important to stress that the first aim was dropped almost as soon as the Plan was launched, the Group preferring to stress the need to retain good customers and convert them into members, considerable effort was put on publicizing its status as the only major retailer that is owned by consumers, rather than a small group of shareholders. Another dimension of this activity was a campaign to encourage more people to 'Join the Revolution', using the historic link with the 'Rochdale Pioneers' to illustrate the point. An extensive TV, press, and social media campaign was also pursued, providing guidance on how people could either set up their own co-operative businesses (using the Group's Enterprise Hub), fund community projects, or campaign for change or simply purchase ethical products and services, such as Fairtrade and ethical investments. At a time when the coalition government's rhetorical commitment to a 'Big Society' focused greater public attention on community involvement, the Group's campaigns sought to demonstrate their ethical credentials, indicating that while few taxpayers' resources were devoted to the government's programme, there was a broadly accepted need to supplement state action.

These efforts were clearly vital in maintaining public appreciation of what co-operative trading was all about, capitalizing on governmental messages about community and social responsibility. At the same time, returning to the question raised earlier, it is important to ask whether or not the 'renaissance' can be sustained. Indeed, given the Group's recent relatively poor commercial performance, it is not clear whether consumers accepted claims of a 'Co-operative Difference'. Looking at the last set of data generated by the Group, addressing the first half-year trading in 2012 and comparing them with the same period in 2011, not only had Group gross sales risen by just £13 million (£6,559 million, compared to £6,546 million), but underlying Group operating profit had also fallen from £264 million to £174 million.[3] While in July 2012 the Group announced a three-year, £2 billion investment programme, adding considerably to net borrowings that stood at £1.52 billion (compared to £1.4 billion in June 2011), there is mounting evidence that the renaissance has stalled, with consumers preferring the c-store chains of other multiples such as Tesco and Sainsbury's, while the recently established multiples such as Aldi and Lidl have eaten into every multiple's share of the market. The Group was consequently obliged to halve its interim dividend to 0.5p per loyalty point, Peter Marks explaining this by arguing that 2010–12 was the toughest trading environment he had seen for forty years.[4]

³ <http://www.co-operative.coop/corporate/Press/Press-releases/Headline-news/Interim-results-for-The-Co-operative-Group-for-the-26-weeks-ended-30-June-2012/>.
⁴ *Manchester Evening News*, 19 December 2012.

Although one can accept that the economic environment continued to prove difficult, this could hardly be used as a reasonable explanation for the Group's deteriorating commercial performance. After all, the growth in turnover and surplus of 2008–10 was achieved in the face of the most severe recessionary years, conditions which rival multiples had also been obliged to endure. Of course, as consumers outside the much more affluent south-east of England have continued to be affected by bouts of recession and sluggish economic growth, compounded by the retreat of the public sector in unemployment 'hotspots', this could well explain the rise of Aldi and Lidl. These trends consequently raise a question relating to whether in benefiting from its acquisitions by boosting market share, the Group had achieved its purpose of persuading consumers that its value proposition was appropriate to the intensely competitive marketplace. Given the poor figures returned for the first half of 2012, this suggests that the Group achieved quick gains from its acquisitions, but that real change has not been achieved in persuading consumers that there was a 'Co-operative Difference'. Furthermore, the Group has been extremely slow to react to the online revolution which has transformed retailing in a highly radical way, while other multiples have seized this opportunity and used it to boost sales.

Another issue that has arisen recently is both the performance and reputation of The Co-operative Bank. In the first place, while by 2011 revenue had hit the £1.0 billion mark for the first time, underlying operating profit fell 67.9 per cent to £36.9 million. The key reasons behind this poor performance were, first, acute difficulties with the non-core corporate loan book, and secondly, ongoing uncertainty in the Eurozone. Moreover, when in January 2013 the Financial Services Authority (FSA) imposed a fine of £113,300 on The Co-operative Bank for 'failing to handle payment protection insurance complaints fairly', this struck at the heart of its claim to be Britain's leading ethical financial institution. Although it is fair to note that other banks have been hit much harder by the High Court judgement that payment protection insurance had been extensively mis-sold since the 1990s, The Co-operative Bank had set aside $130 million to compensate its customers, meaning that no customers were adversely affected by the delay.[5] This reflected the bank's continued commitment to customer responsiveness. Moreover, while its bid to purchase 632 Lloyds' branches proved unsuccessful the bank's management remain keen to develop its customer relationship banking offer.

Of course, it is hardly credible to claim that in the course of a few years all of the dynamism apparent in achieving the 'renaissance' that was so widely publicized in 2010 had dissipated. Indeed, one would argue that in 2013 there is even more dynamism and entrepreneurial flair across the Group's core and non-core businesses, reflecting well on the organizational culture change that had occurred since the 1990s. It is especially noticeable that Food Retail has recently benefited from the introduction of a new management team, headed by Steve Murrells, the former CEO of Tesco's One Stop c-store chain and more recently CEO of Tulip UK (Britain's leading food producer). One of Murrells's major initial tasks was to sustain both the expansion programme, adding

[5] *Daily Mail*, 5 January 2013.

eighty new stores to the network in 2012, as well as completing the implementation of the award-winning SMART stock management system that had already increased product availability in stores to over 97.5 per cent. In addition to SMART, the supply chain network was also overhauled through the introduction of a purpose-built network with one national distribution centre and nine regional centres, creating the capacity to handle 32,000 deliveries a week.[6]

In spite of these radical innovations, as well as continuing to spend considerably on advertising and marketing, the static turnover data and falling profits demonstrate that the Group was struggling to persuade consumers of the co-operative value proposition. While 'Good with food' had been an appropriate strapline for the resurgence recorded since 2006, it became increasingly necessary to think about a more generic statement that reflected the changing balance across the Group's business portfolio. After all, the acquisition of Britannia Building Society in 2009, the continued strong performance of the pharmacy and funerals businesses, and the establishment of a legal services business indicated clearly that the Group was not simply a food retailer. Indeed, the recent expansion of legal services can be regarded as a sign that the Group has become much more innovative in finding new business areas in which it can address the needs of contemporary consumers. This was why in July 2012 the Group trademarked a new strapline, 'Here for you for life', in an attempt to move on from 'Good for everyone' as the corporate brand. This will mean that 'Good with food' and 'Good with money' will be dropped in favour of 'Here for you for life', denoting both trust in co-operative ethics and the extent of the Group's business portfolio.[7] Moreover, this is reminiscent of co-operative societies' earlier efforts to provide 'cradle to grave' services to their serving customer-members. At the same time, it recalls Peter Marks's phrase, that by the 1990s: 'We were on our way to becoming the most ethical business in the corporate graveyard.' As he went on to add: 'In my view, ethics are a tie-breaker—everything else, price, quality, has to be as good as the competition.' This highlights the eternal challenge facing co-operative businesses, in that while one might operate ethically and extol the virtues of co-operative values and principles, consumers rarely buy on the basis of philosophical posturing. Moreover, the 2012 decision to sell and lease back its new headquarters demonstrates another ongoing challenge for the Group: the need to adopt different strategies to its PLC competitors in raising capital. In the 2010s, as it has done throughout its history, the Group continues to seek a balance between its need to be competitive in the marketplace to attract and retain consumer-members, and its efforts to reform market practice to its members' benefit.

Whether or not the 'Here for you for life' campaign will succeed in persuading more people to use co-operative services is of course a matter for future research. Nevertheless, it indicates how the business model was continuing to adapt to both internal and

---

[6] The Co-operative Group interim results, <http://www.co-operative.coop/corporate/Press/Press-releases/Headline-news/Interim-results-for-The-Co-operative-Group-for-the-26-weeks-ended-30-June-2012/>.
[7] *Grocer*, 4 August 2012. <http://www.thegrocer.co.uk/companies/supermarkets/the-co-operative-group/good-with-food-had-a-good-run-now-the-co-op-must-move-on/231491.article>.

external challenges, while in the 2010s the Group was clearly much better placed to respond rapidly to dynamic and challenging situations. Having sustained the original business model until the dramatic changes of the period 1973–2000, it was clear that in the early twenty-first century attitudes had become much more responsive, providing a conducive environment for change. Indeed, while there has been a recent slump in profitability and turnover growth has been non-existent, the Group continues to look to reposition itself as a provider of multiple services, rather than merely a food retailer. The challenge for the future will be to assess whether such a wide range of businesses should be sustained, challenging traditional loyalties to some core and non-core activities that might well not be sustainable.

In this context, it was perhaps no surprise that the Group's board chose as Peter Marks's successor a CEO who had extensive experience of working outside the movement. With the proposed Lloyds' deal still in progress, the conventional wisdom suggested that someone from the financial services sector would be appointed. Therefore, although some expressed astonishment,[8] when it was announced that Euan Sutherland was going to take over from Peter Marks in May 2013, it reflected the Group's ability to be creative about such crucial appointments. Sutherland had for several years been a non-executive director of Co-operative Food's board, but his principal role was COO of home improvements group Kingfisher, the owner of leading brands such as B&Q and Screwfix. This extensive experience of a highly competitive retail sector will stand him in good stead in the years ahead as he copes with the challenges facing the Group, and especially the need to persuade consumers that its value proposition is appropriate and dependable. Whether the Group will be able to increase its customer (and member) base is the greatest challenge, because this will provide the fuel to achieve further growth across its businesses.

The Co-operative Group faces all of these challenges confident that it now has the organizational dynamism and (human and financial) resources to cope with whatever is thrown in its way. As if to epitomize this new-found sense of self-confidence, one need only look at the magnificent headquarters building, 1 Angel Square, Manchester, that the Group will occupy in 2013 (see Plate 20). Just as the CIS Tower and New Century House were built in the 1960s to mark the 100th anniversary of these businesses, Angel Square denotes an appropriate iconic image, as well as maintaining the Group's links with sustainability through the adoption of an architectural design that is environmentally friendly. At the same time, the old buildings will be located directly opposite what will become part of a redevelopment of the 'co-operative quarter' known as NOMA adjacent to Manchester's 'Cultural Quarter' which since the 1990s has generated considerable momentum. This will sustain the Group's contribution to Manchester, not only as a major employer in its own right, but also in highlighting the co-operative movement's broader contributions to society.

One hundred and fifty years on from its founding, The Co-operative Group retains its place at the centre of British co-operative enterprise, as well a unique status in British

---

[8] *Manchester Evening News*, 19 December 2012.

business. Born of the Industrial Revolution, co-operatives in the twenty-first century operate in a very different world from the one in which they were created, resulting in extensive adaptation of its business model to meet the changing needs of members and customers. Over a century and a half, the Group and its members have made innumerable contributions to British life, arguing through their enterprises that 'business' and 'society', 'profit' and 'principles', need not be antithetical constructs. The survival, and revival, of the Group, as well as the continued development of co-operative models in various contexts, suggests that many Britons agree. For the future, two issues remain central for the future development of The Co-operative Group and the movement more generally. First, one must question how to create a dynamic, active, and participating membership which can reinvigorate the movement's democratic ethos, but without this preventing the Group responding nimbly and effectively to fast-changing global markets. Secondly, as the traditional local loyalties which tied members to their local societies fade, how can a new generation of co-operators be inspired to become active in the movement?

Clearly, the ethical dimensions of co-operative business strategies are being built upon to attract new blood to the movement. But it is also clear that the global retreat of the state as a major social provider, in response to endemic problems of debt, coupled with deeply jaundiced views of the moral suitability or competence of traditional shareholder-led organizations to step into the breach, offers new opportunities to build a substantial bedrock of active co-operators across the UK. The European Commission's prioritization of 'Social Innovation' in its research plans for the late 2010s and 2020s, to encourage new social enterprises and initiatives to fill the void left by a retreating state, suggest that the UK coalition government's pronouncements about the need to promote a 'Big Society' of mutuals, co-operatives, and similar enterprises is neither isolated to the British Isles nor likely to be a passing fad. The flowering of co-operative schools since 2008, many under the auspices of the Co-operative College, shows just how quickly new co-operatives, run by newly inducted and energetic co-operators, can emerge. In this sense, should a larger sector of mutuals and local co-operatives emerge, its relationship with the Group will become a fascinating question. For the Group, already extending its role in financial and legal services, and already operating an Enterprise Hub to assist the formation of new co-operatives, such a new and dynamic sector could prove to be not only an important new market, but also an important new constituency of political allies in securing co-operation legally. Certainly in recent years the Group has worked closely with other mutuals in lobbying politicians of all hues through the joint pressure group Mutuo. An expansion of the co-operative and mutual sector could only lend this more weight.

There is little doubt that, as the twenty-first century progresses, the Group will experience new threats to its business from old and new competitors, in an environment of rapid globalization and seemingly constant change. Yet the fundamental challenge for the Group remains the same as it has always been: finding the means to adapt its democratic structures and translate its ethical principles to address the needs of new generations of consumers, using the proceeds of success in the contemporary marketplace to fund a vision for a more equitable and sustainable future. The experience of The Co-operative Group to date suggests that both profits and principles are necessary to sustain co-operative business. How, or if, this is achieved in the decades to come, is a tale for future historians.

Table showing annual figures for membership, turnover and surplus/deficit, 1864–1999.[1]

Year	Membership in societies affiliated to CWS	Sales/distributive trade (£)	Net surplus/deficit (£)
1864	18,337	51,875	306
1865	24,005	120,754	1,850
1866	31,030	175,489	2,235
1868[2]	59,349	331,744	4,411
1869	74,737	412,240	4,862
1870	79,245	507,217	4,248
1871	89,880	677,734	7,626
1872	114,588	758,764	7,867
1873	134,276	1,153,132	11,116
1874	168,985	1,636,950	14,233
1875	198,608	1,964,829	20,684
1876	249,516	2,247,395	26,750
1877	276,522	2,697,366	36,979
1878	274,649	2,827,052	29,189
1879	305,161	2,705,625	34,859
1879[3]	331,625	2,645,331	42,746
1880	361,523	3,339,681	42,090
1881	367,973	3,574,095	46,850
1882	404,006	4,038,238	49,658
1883	433,151	4,546,889	47,885
1884	459,734	4,675,371	54,491
1885	507,772	4,793,151	77,630
1886	558,104	5,223,179	83,328
1887	604,800	5,713,235	65,141
1888	634,196	6,20,0074	82,490
1889	679,336	7,028,944	101,984
1890	721,316	7,429,073	126,979
1891	751,269	8,766,430	135,008
1892	824,149	9,300,904	98,532
1893	873,968	9,526,167	84,156
1894	910,104	9,443,938	126,192
1895	930,985	10,141,917	192,766
1896	993,564	11,115,056	177,419
1897	1,053,564	11,920,143	135,561
1898	1,118,158	12,574,748	231,256

Year	Membership in societies affiliated to CWS	Sales/distributive trade (£)	Net surplus/deficit (£)
1899	1,179,609	14,212,375	286,250
1900	1,249,091	16,043,889	289,101
1901	1,315,235	17,642,082	288,321
1902	1,392,399	18,397,559	336,369
1903	1,445,099	19,333,142	297,304
1904	1,594,145	19,809,196	332,374
1905	1,635,527	20,785,469	304,568
1906	1,703,564	22,510,035	410,680
1907	1,768,935	24,786,568	488,571
1908	1,845,415	24,902,842	371,497
1909	1,925,517	25,675,938	549,080
1910	1,991,576	26,567,833	462,469
1911	2,067,776	27,892,990	579,913
1912	2,160,191	29,732,154	613,007
1913	2,272,496	31,371,976	636,119
1914	2,336,460	34,910,813	840,069
1915	2,535,972	43,101,747	1,086,962
1916	2,653,227	52,230,074	1,519,005
1917	2,748,277	57,710,132	1,150,732
1918	2,854,584	65,167,960	-16,488
1919	3,088,136	89,349,318	31,183
1920	3,341,411	105,439,628	-64,210
1921	3,457,556	80,884,661	-4,851,235
1922	3,494,335	65,904,812	111,268
1923	3,567,410	66,205,566	510,798
1924	3,662,765	72,888,064	865,773
1925	3,778,659	76,585,764	1,053,504
1926	3,876,695	75,292,233	1,094,288
1928[4]	4,020,332	86,894,379	1,530,969
1929	4,454,793	87,294,025	1,379,672
1930	4,565,372	89,288,125	1,396,974
1931	4,884,090	85,313,018	1,344,218
1932	5,138,124	81,498,234	1,692,157
1933	5,352,310	82,769,119	1,729,223
1934	5,488,364	82,120,864	1,473,838
1935	5,983,810	90,177,672	2,052,498
1936	6,155,964	98,283,975	2,095,481
1937	6,379,274	107,691,527	2,569,412
1938	6,581,337	119,851,542	2,799,095
1939	6,765,194	125,015,316	2,891,485
1940	7,020,544	131,357,439	2,974,722
1941	7,078,362	142,889,444	3,890,388
1942	7,309,579	144,307,408	3,823,533
1943	7,439,813	157,395,338	5,185,683
1944	7,544,315	166,834,649	4,845,869
1945	7,699,409	183,514,745	4,843,505

(*continued*)

Table (*continued*)

Year	Membership in societies affiliated to CWS	Sales/distributive trade (£)	Net surplus/deficit (£)
1946	7,852,875	182,776,340	4,982,357
1947	7,976,177	205,957,079	6,281,055
1948	8,240,867	223,231,506	6,854,037
1949	8,380,463	252,469,693	7,012,214
1950	9,299,664	321,641,923	6,890,123
1951	9,557,602	359,141,772	5,777,852
1952	9,800,011	398,344,136	4,531,886
1953	9,951,666	420,887,591	6,452,828
1954	10,079,167	401,522,832	6,782,538
1955	10,295,616	418,073,209	7,239,001
1956	10,554,983	444,285,406	7,336,486
1957	10,824,453	453,960,174	7,427,928
1958	11,064,735	463,274,603	9,514,857
1959	11,307,260	467,867,807	8,133,148
1960	11,496,284	475,565,896	8,078,099
1961	11,647,032	465,170,491	7,531,034
1962	11,728,481	479,388,939	7,485,504
1963	11,822,706	480,184,395	5,802,825
1964	11,909,932	488,496,661	4,903,232
1965	11,946,568	487,859,688	5,224,654
1966	11,737,879	490,943,840	3,766444
1967[5]		472,948,456	740547
1968		483,364,478	2,603578
1969		493,076,000	2,511000
1970		506,145,000	1,004000
1971		526,021,000	2,322000
1972		581,361,000	4,994000
1973		720,785,000	9,582000
1974		912,610,000	8,986000
1975		1,114,503,000	7,334000
1976		1,278,496,000	10,906000
1977		1,442,871,000	18,791000
1978		1,560,555,000	14,635000
1979		1,707,885,000	15,885000
1980		1,881,658,000	6,290000
1981		1,965,368,000	12,258000
1982		2,069,795,000	10,123000
1983		2,231,519,000	9,401000
1984		2,251,032,000	11,024,000
1985		2,437,352,000	15,834,000
1986		2,537,015,000	8,638,000
1987		2,572,900,000	20,729,000[6]
1988		2,743,233,000	41,666,000
1989		2,870,000,000	34,639,000
1990		3,239,900,000	12,329,000
1991		3,380,900,000	15,553,000

Year	Membership in societies affiliated to CWS	Sales/distributive trade (£)	Net surplus/deficit (£)
1992		3,494,500,000	-2,582,000
1993		3,825,500,000	16,768,000
1994		3,409,500,000	49,391,000
1995		3,261,850,000	35,102,000
1996		3,271,750,000	31,529,000
1997		3,385,200,000	52,910,000
1998		3,431,170,000	50,473,000
1999		3,616,120,000	113,894,000

[1] The statistics for the period 1864–1949 were taken from the *The People's Yearbook* (CWS, 1950), 131–2.

The statistics for the period 1950–67 were taken from annual *CWS Balance Sheets, Board Report & Grand Summary*.

The statistics for the period 1968–99 were taken from annual *Co-operative Union Statistics*.

[2] The financial year ran October to October up to 1868, when it changed to January, therefore there are no statistics for 1867. The 1868 statistics therefore reflect a 65-week period, October 1866–January 1868.

[3] The start/end of the financial year changed to December in 1879, therefore there are two entries in this table for 1879, the latter reflecting a 51-week period starting January 1879 and ending in December 1879.

[4] Financial year changed to January from December in 1928, therefore the statistics for 1928 reflect the period December 1926–January 1928.

[5] From 1967 the membership/shareholder information was no longer available in the sources consulted.

[6] 1986 figures restated to reflect changes in accounting policies on Investment and Goodwill.

BIBLIOGRAPHY

1. ARCHIVAL SOURCES

National Co-operative Archive (NCA)

The Co-operative Group collections
The Co-operative Group annual reports, 2001–12.
Co-operative Wholesale Society (CWS) and The Co-operative Group board minutes and
    subcommittee minutes (where extant), 1863–2012.
CWS balance sheets, 1864–2000.
Correspondence of Frederick Lambert.
Report by the Co-operative Wholesale Society Ltd on its Policy and Programme for Post-
    War Development, 1944.
'The Role of the CWS' documents, 1962–3.

Other NCA collections
Co-operative Retail Services, Northern Region Collection (NCRS).
Co-operative Union (CU) Congress Reports.
Co-operative Independent Commission (CIC) records.
Leicester Co-operative Society (LCS) balance sheets.
Midland Co-operative Society Collection (MID).

Other collections
House of Commons Parliamentary Papers, Proquest
    Commission of Enquiry into Industrial Unrest. No. 2 Division (1917). *Report of the*
    Commissioners for the North-Western Area, Including a Supplemental Report on the
    Barrow-in-Furness District. House of Commons Command Papers, Cd. 8663.
    Report of the Departmental Committee on Income Tax, Cmnd 2575, 1905.
Labour History Archive and Study Centre (LHASC), Manchester
    War Emergency Workers National Committee (WNC) collections.
National Archives, London
    Ministry of Labour, Wages & Arbitration Department files LAB2/164/IC6546/8/1918.
University College, London
    Papers of Hugh Gaitskell, C309.2 CIC.

2. INTERVIEWS AND CORRESPONDENCE

Beaumont, Martin (The Co-operative Group chief executive, 2002–7), interviewed 31 January 2011.
Gill, Russell (Employed in co-operatives since 1992; current head of membership,
    The Co-operative Group), interviewed 15 July 2012.

Hulme, Martin (Employed in co-operatives since 1990, current managing director for estates, The Co-operative Group), interviewed 13 December, 2010.

Jones, Roger (CWS deputy secretary, 1983–96; secretary, 1996–8), interviewed 8 September 2010.

Landau, Sir Dennis (CWS food controller, 1971–4; deputy chief executive, 1974–80; chief executive, 1980–92), interviewed 9 July 2011.

Lees, Moira (CWS management trainee, 1981; CWS/The Co-operative Group deputy secretary, 1996–2007; current secretary), interviewed August 2010.

Marks, Peter (The Co-operative Group chief executive, 2007–13), interviewed 25 June, 2012.

Melmoth, Sir Graham (CWS secretary, 1975–96; chief executive, 1996–2002), interviewed 7 September 2010.

Sandford, John (KPMG, 1977–2010; audited CWS/The Co-operative Group accounts), interviewed 9 August 2011.

Shannon, Bill (CWS manager 1965–81, 1985–2002), interviewed 10 November, 2010.

Smedley, Paul (CWS security manager, 1986–99), interviewed 19 April, 2011.

Sparks, Leigh (professor of retail studies, University of Stirling), correspondence December 2012.

Tacon, Christine (head of farms, The Co-operative Group 2000–11) interviewed 13 April 2012.

Williams, Simon (manager, The Co-operative Bank 1988–2008), interviewed 16 July 2011.

Wilson, Mervyn (employed in co-operatives since 1973; current principal, the Co-operative College), interviewed 20 January, 2011.

3. Newspapers and periodicals

Bolton Co-operative Record [BCR]
Co-operative Directory
Co-operative Gazetie
Co-operative News
Co-operative Review
Co-operative Wholesale Society Ltd Annual
Daily Express
Daily Post
Daily Telegraph
Euroweek
Evening Standard
Express on Sunday
Financial Times
Grocer
Guardian
Independent
Labour Woman
Manchester Evening News
Manchester Guardian
Northwest Business Insider
Observer

People's Year Book
Plunkett Foundation Yearbook
Scotsman
Sunday Business
Sunday Telegraph
Sunday Times
Supermarketing
The Co-operative Gazette
The Co-operative Review
The Co-operator
The Times
Wheatsheaf

4. PUBLISHED WORKS, THESES, PAPERS ETC.

Alexander, A. (2008). 'Format Development and Retail Change: Supermarket Retailing and the London Co-operative Society', *Business History*, 50/4: 489–508.

Anderson, R. A. (1983). *With Plunkett in Ireland: The Co-op Organiser's Story*. Reprint edition. Dublin: Irish Academic Press.

Bamfield, J. (1978a). 'The Revival. Part 1', *International Journal of Retail Studies*, 6/2: 18–23.

Bamfield, J. (1978b). 'The Revival. Part 2', *International Journal of Retail Studies*, 6/3: 14–18.

Bamfield, J. (1998). 'Consumer-Owned Flour and Bread Societies in the Eighteenth and Early Nineteenth Centuries', *Business History*, 40/4: 16–36.

Bamfield, J. (2002). 'Can the Co-operative Commission Do the Trick?', *Journal of Co-operative Studies*, 35/1: 44–51.

Banks, J. A., and Ostergaard, G. (1955). *Co-operative Democracy: A Study of Aspects of the Democratic Process in Certain Retail Co-operative Societies*. Manchester: Co-operative Union.

Barnett, L. M. (1985). *British Food Policy During the First World War*. London: Allen and Unwin.

Battilani, P., and Schröter, H. (eds.) (2012). *Cooperative Business Movement, 1950 to the Present*. Cambridge: Cambridge University Press.

Beaumont, H. (1997). 'The Co-operative Board of Directors—Democratic Developments in CWS and CRS', Institute of Co-operative Directors Fellowship Programme.

Benson, J., and Ugolini, L. (eds.) (2003). *A Nation of Shopkeepers*. London: I. B. Tauris.

Beveridge, W. H. (1928). *British Food Control*. Oxford: Oxford University Press.

Birchall, J. (1994). *Co-op: The People's Business*. Manchester: Manchester University Press.

Birchall. J. (1997). *The International Co-operative Movement*. Manchester: Manchester University Press.

Birchall, J. (2011). *People-Centred Businesses: Co-operatives, Mutuals and the Idea of Membership*. Basingstoke: Palgrave Macmillan.

Birchall, J., and Kettison, L. H. (2009). *Resilience of the Cooperative Business Model in Times of Crisis*. Geneva: International Labour Office.

Black, L. (2009). '"Trying to Sell a Parcel of Politics with a Parcel of Groceries": The Co-operative Independent Commission (CIC) and Consumerism in Post-War Britain', in L. Black and N. Robertson (eds.), *Consumerism and the Co-operative Movement in Modern British History*. Manchester: Manchester University Press, 33–50.

Black, L., and Robertson, N. (eds.) (2009). *Consumerism and the Co-operative Movement in Modern British History*. Manchester: Manchester University Press.

Blackman, J. (1963). 'The Food Supply of an Industrial Town: A Study of Sheffield's Public Markets 1780–1900', *Business History*, 5/2: 83–97.

Blackman, J. (1967). 'The Development of the Retail Grocery Trade in the Nineteenth Century', *Business History*, 9/2: 110–17.

Blaszak, B. J. (2000). *The Matriarchs of England's Cooperative Movement: A Study in Gender Politics and Female Leadership, 1883–1921*. Westport, Conn.: Greenwood Press.

Bolger, P. (1977). *The Irish Co-operative Movement: Its History and Development*. Dublin: Institute of Public Administration.

Bonner, A. (1961). *British Co-operation*. Manchester: Co-operative Union. Revised edition 1970.

Bowes, John. (2010). *Fair Trade Revolution*. London: Pluto Press.

Brazda, J., and Schediwy, R. (eds.) (1989). *Consumer Co-operatives in a Changing World*. Geneva: International Co-operative Alliance.

Briggs, A., and Saville, J. (eds.) (1960). *Essays in Labour History*. London: Macmillan.

Brown, W. H. (1937). *The Co-operative Manager*. York: National Co-operative Managers' Association.

Bryer, R. A. (1997). 'The Mercantile Laws Commission of 1854 and the Political Economy of Limited Liability', *Economic History Review*, 50/1: 37–56.

Burton, A. (1994). *The People's Cinema: Film and the Co-operative Movement*. London: National Film Theatre.

Byrom, R. (1978). 'The Consumer Movement', *Society for Co-operative Studies Bulletin*, 48–63.

Byrom, R. (1982). 'A Future for Consumer Co-operatives in Britain?', *Society for Co-operative Studies Bulletin*, 45: 46–51.

Cain, P. J., and Hopkins, A. G. (2001). *British Imperialism 1688–1900*. Edinburgh: Pearson.

Capie, F. (2010). *The Bank of England: 1950s to 1979*. Cambridge: Cambridge University Press.

Carbery, T. F. (1969). *Consumers in Politics: A History and General Review of the Co-operative Party*. Manchester: Manchester University Press.

Carnevali, F. (2004). '"Crooks, thieves and receivers": Transaction Costs in Nineteenth Century Industrial Birmingham', *Economic History Review*, 57/3: 533–50.

'Car Ownership' (2012). <http://www.20thcenturylondon.org.uk/car-ownership>.

Carr-Saunders, A. M., Florence, P. S., and Peers, R. (1938). *Consumers' Co-operation in Great Britain: An Examination of the British Co-operative Movement*. London: George Allen and Unwin.

Chandler, A. (1990). *Scale and Scope: The Dynamics of Industrial Capitalism*. Cambridge, Mass.: Harvard University Press.

Chapman, P., and Temple, P. (1994). 'The Question of Pay', in T. Buxton, P. Chapman, and P. Temple (eds.), *Britain's Economic Performance*. London: Routledge, 299–301.

Charkham, C. (1995). *Keeping Good Company: A Study of Corporate Governance in Five Countries*. Oxford: Oxford University Press.

Church, R., and Clark, C. (2001). 'Product Development of Branded, Packaged Household Goods: Coleman's, Reckitt's and Lever's', *Enterprise and Society*, 2/3: 503–42.

Claeys, G. (2002). *Citizens and Saints: Politics and Anti-Politics in Early British Socialism*. Cambridge: Cambridge University Press.

Clayton, J. (1908). *Robert Owen: Pioneer of Social Reforms*. London: Fifield.

Cohen, M. (2012*). The Eclipse of 'Elegant Economy': The Impact of the Second World War on Attitudes to Personal Finance in Britain*. Farnham: Ashgate.

Cole, G. D. H. (1944). *A Century of Co-operation*. Manchester: Co-operative Union.

Cole, G. D. H., and Postgate, R. (1961). *The British Common People, 1746–1946*. University Paperbacks, London: Methuen.

Competition Commission (2000). *Supermarkets: A Report on the Supply of Groceries from Multiple Stores in the UK*. London: HMSO.

Cook, A. L. (1982). 'A Future for Consumer Co-operation in Britain? Regionalisation: The Last Opportunity', *Society for Co-operative Studies Bulletin*, 46: 29–36.

Cook, P. L., and Cohen, R. (1958). *Effects of Mergers: Six Studies*. London: George Allen and Unwin.

Co-operative Commission (2001). *The Co-operative Advantage: Creating a Successful Family of Co-operative Businesses*. Manchester: Co-operative Union.

Co-operative Party (1933). *Failure of the National Government*. Manchester: Co-operative Union.

Co-operative Union (CU) (1968). *Regional Plan for Co-operative Societies*. Manchester: Co-operative Union.

Co-operative Wholesale Society (CWS) (1965). *Report of the Joint Reorganisation Committee*. Manchester: CWS.

Cornforth, C., Thomas, A., Spear, R., and Lewis, J. (1988). *Developing Successful Worker Co-operatives*. London: Sage Publications.

Crafts, N., and Woodward, N. (1991). *The British Economy since 1945*. Oxford: Clarendon Press.

Creighton, S. (1996). 'Battersea: The "Municipal Mecca"', in B. Lancaster and P. Maguire (eds.), *Towards the Co-operative Commonwealth: Essays in the History of Co-operation*. Manchester: Co-operative College and History Workshop Trust, 35–8.

Crossick, G. (1984). 'Shopkeepers and the State in Britain, 1870–1914', in H. Crossick and H. G. Haupt (eds.), *Shopkeepers and Master Artisans in Nineteenth-Century Europe*. London: Methuen and Co, 239–69.

Crouzet, F. (1982). *The Victorian Economy*. London: Methuen.

Daunton, M. (2002). *Just Taxes: The Politics of Taxation in Britain, 1914–79*. Cambridge: Cambridge University Press.

Davies, S., and Sparks, L. (1989). 'Spatial Distribution of Retailing', *Transactions of the Institute of British Geographers*, 14: 74–89.

Davis, P., and Worthington, S. (1993). 'Cooperative Values: Change and Continuity in Capital Accumulation, The Case of the British Cooperative Bank', *Journal of Business Ethics* 12: 849–59.

Digby, M. (1951). *Agricultural Co-operation in the Commonwealth*. Oxford: Basil Blackwell.

Docherty, B. (2008). 'A Truly Co-operative Venture: The Case Study of Co-operative Food, a Retailer Response to Fair Trade', *Journal of Strategic Marketing*, 16/3: 205–31.

Doyle, P. (2012). 'Resistance, Conflict and Nationalism: The Development of the Irish Co-operative Movement in County Kerry before World War One', paper delivered to European Social Science History Association. Glasgow, 11–14 April.

Dresser, S. (July 2012). 'The Co-operative—That Good with Food?', <http://www. groceryinsight. com/blog/2012/07/the-co-operative-that-good-with-food/>.

Ekberg, E. (2008). *Consumer Co-operatives and the Transformation of Modern Food Retailing: A Comparative Study of the Norwegian and British Consumer Co-operatives, 1950–2002*. Oslo: University of Oslo.

Ekberg, E. (2009). 'Consumer Co-operation and the Transformation of Modern Food Retailing: The British and Norwegian Consumer Co-operative Movement in Comparison, 1950–2002', in L. Black and N. Robertson (eds.), *Consumerism and the Co-operative Movement in Modern British History*. Manchester: Manchester University Press, 51–68.

Ekberg, E. (2012a). 'Confronting Three Revolutions: Western European Consumer Co-operatives and their Divergent Development, 1950–2008', *Business History*, 54/6: 1004–21.

Ekberg, E. (2012b). 'Organization: Top Down or Bottom Up? The Organizational Development of Consumer Co-operatives 1950–2000', in P. Battilani and H. Shröter (eds.), *The Cooperative Business Movement, 1950 to the Present*. Cambridge: Cambridge University Press, 222–42.

Fairbairn, B. (1994). 'The Meaning of Rochdale: The Rochdale Pioneers and the Co-operative Principles'. Occasional Papers Series. Saskatoon: Centre for Co-operative Studies, University of Saskatchewan.

Ferguson, N. (2009). 'Siegmund Warburg, the City of London and the Financial Roots of European Integration', *Business History*, 51/3: 364–82.

Flanagan, D. (1969). *A Centenary Story of the Co-operative Union of Great Britain and Ireland, 1869–1969*. Manchester: Co-operative Union.

Flynn, A. (2009). '"Mothers for peace": Co-operation, Feminism and Peace. The Women's Co-operative Guild and the Anti-War Movement between the Wars', in L. Black and N. Robertson (eds.), *Consumerism and the Co-operative Movement in Modern British History*. Manchester: Manchester University Press, 138–54.

Foster, J. O. (1974). *Class Struggle and the Industrial Revolution*. London: Weidenfeld and Nicolson.

Friberg, K. (2005). *Workings of Co-operation: A Comparative Study of Consumer Co-operative Organisation in Britain and Sweden 1860 to 1970*. Växjö: Växjö University Press.

Garnett, R. G. (1968). *A Century of Co-operative Insurance*. London: Allen and Unwin.

Garnett, R. G. (1972). *Co-operation and the Owenite Socialist Communities in Britain 1825–45*. Manchester: Manchester University Press.

Garside, W. R. (1990). *British Unemployment 1919–1939*. Cambridge: Cambridge University Press.

Gorsky, M. (1998). 'The Growth and Distribution of English Friendly Societies in the Early Nineteenth Century', *Economic History Review*, 51/3: 489–511.

Gurney, P. (1996). *Co-operative Culture and the Politics of Consumption in England, 1870–1930*. Manchester: Manchester University Press.

Gurney, P. (2005). 'The Battle of the Consumer in Post-War Britain', *Journal of Modern History*, 77/4: 956–87.

Gurney, P. (2012). 'Co-operation and the "New Consumerism" in Inter-War England', *Business History*, 54/6: 905–24.

Hall, F. (1923). *Handbook for Members of Co-operative Committees*. Manchester: Co-operative Union.

Hallsworth, A., and Bell, J. (2003). 'Retail Change and the United Kingdom Co-operative Movement—New Opportunity Beckoning?', *International Review of Retail, Distribution and Consumer Research*, 13/3: 301–15.

Hannah. L., and Kay, J. (1977). *Concentration in Modern Industry*. London: Macmillan.

Henriksen, I., and O'Rourke, K. H. (2005). 'Incentives, Technology and the Shift to Year Long Dairying in Nineteenth Century Denmark', *Economic History Review*, 58/3: 520–54.

Hibberd, P. (1968). 'The Rochdale Tradition in Co-operative History: Is it Justified?', *Annals of Public and Co-operative Economics*, 39: 531–7.

Higgins, M., and Mordhorst, M. (2008). 'Reputation and Export Performance: Danish Butter Exports and the British Market, *c.*1880–*c*1914', *Business History*, 50/2: 185–204.

Hilton, M. (2003). *Consumerism in Twentieth-Century Britain: The Search for a Historical Movement*. Cambridge: Cambridge University Press.

Hingley, M. (2010). 'Networks in Socially Embedded Local Food Supply: The Case of Retailer Co-operatives', *Journal of Business Marketing Management*, 4: 111–28.

Hodson, D. (1998). '"The Municipal Store": Adaptation and Development in the Retail Markets of Nineteenth Century Urban Lancashire', *Business History*, 40/4: 94–114.

Holyoake, G. J. (1893a). *Self-Help by the People: The History of the Rochdale Pioneers*. London: Swan Sonnenschein.

Holyoake, G. J. (1893b). *The History of the Rochdale Pioneers 1844–1892*. London: George Allen and Unwin.

Hughes, D. (2000). *A Journey to Remember*: Beamish: County Durham Books.

Hunt, K. (2000). 'Negotiating the Boundaries of the Domestic: British Socialist Women and the Politics of Consumption', *Women's History Review*, 9/2: 389–410.

Hunt, K. (2010). 'The Politics of Food and Women's Neighborhood Activism in First World War Britain', *International Labor and Working-Class History*, 77: 8–26.

International Co-operative Alliance (ICA) (1995). 'Statement of Co-operative Identity, Values and Principles', <http://2012.coop/en/what-co-op/co-operative-identity-values-principles> [accessed 1 December 2012].

ICA et al. (2012). *World Co-operative Monitor: Exploring the Co-operative Economy*. Brussels: ICA.

Jackson, E. (1936). *Service for Democracy, or Fifty Years with the CWS*. Manchester: Co-operative Press.

Jaques, J. (1968). 'The Regional Plan: A Comment for the New Year', *The Co-operative Review*, 42/1: 1.

Jefferys, J. B. (1954). *Retail Trading in Britain 1850–1950*. Cambridge: Cambridge University Press.

Jeremy, D. J. (1991). 'The Enlightened Paternalist in Action: William Hesketh Lever at Port Sunlight Before 1914', *Business History*, 33/1: 58–81.

Johnson, P. (1985). *Saving and Spending: The Working-Class Economy in Britain 1870–1939*. Oxford: Clarendon.

Johnson, P. (1993). 'Small Debts and Economic Distress in England and Wales, 1857–1913', *Economic History Review*, 46/1: 65–87.

Jolly, W. P. (1976). *Lord Leverhulme*. London: Constable.

Jones, B. (1894). *Co-operative Production*. Oxford: Clarendon Press.

Jones, Frank (1939). *Story of the National Conciliation Board*. Manchester: Co-operative Union.

Kalmi, P. (2007). 'The Disappearance of Co-operatives from Economics Textbooks', *Cambridge Journal of Economics*, 31: 625–47.

Kelley, V. (1998). 'The Equitable Consumer: Shopping at the Co-op in Manchester', *Journal of Design History*, 11/4: 296–7.

Kinloch, J., and Butt, J. (1981). *History of the SCWS*. Glasgow: CWS.

Kirk, N. (1985). *The Growth of Working Class Reformism in Mid Victorian England*. London: Croom Helm.

Kirk, N. (1998). *Change, Continuity and Class: Labour in British Society 1850–1920*. Manchester: Manchester University Press.

Kynaston, D. (2002). *City of London*, iv: *Club No More, 1945–2000*. London: Pimlico.

Lambert, F., and Hough, J. A. (1951). *Self Service Shops: A Joint Report*. Manchester: Co-operative Union.

Lancaster, B., and Maguire, P. (eds.) (1996). *Towards the Co-operative Commonwealth: Essays in the History of Co-operation*. Manchester: Co-operative College and History Workshop Trust.

Landau, Sir D. (1987). 'The Role of the CWS', *Journal of Co-operative Studies*, 60 (August): 6–13.

Macclesfield, Baron Thomas (2008). *An Inclusive Community with Integrity*. Durham: The Memoir Club.

Macrosty, H. W. (1907). *The Trust Movement in British Industry: A Study of Business Organisation*, Reprint edition 2001, Kitchener, Ontario: Batoche Books.

Manton, K. (2007). 'Playing Both Sides against the Middle: The Labour Party and the Wholesaling Industry 1919–1951', *Twentieth Century British History*, 18/3: 306–33.

Manton, K. (2008). 'The Labour Party and Retail Distribution, 1919–1951', *Labour History Review*, 73/3: 269–86.

Manton, K. (2009). 'The Labour Party and the Co-op, 1918–58', *Historical Research*, 82/218: 756–78.

Marwick, A. (1965). *The Deluge: British Society and the First World War*. London: Bodley Head.

Mathias, P. (1983). *The First Industrial Nation: An Economic History of Britain 1700–1914*. 2nd edition, London: Routledge.

Mills, C., and Davies, W. (2012). *Blueprint for a Co-operative Decade*. Brussels: International Co-operative Alliance.

Morgan, K. (1990). *The People's Peace*. Oxford: Oxford University Press.

Muller, F. (1989). 'The Consumer Co-operatives in Great Britain', in J. Brazda and R. Schediwy (eds.), *Consumer Co-operatives in a Changing World*. Geneva: International Co-operative Alliance, 45–138.

Mutch, A. (2006). 'Public Houses as Multiple Retailing: Peter Walker and Son, 1846–1914', *Business History*, 48/1: 1–19.

Myers, J., Maddocks, J., and Beecher, J. (2011), 'Resting on Laurels? Examining the Resilience of Co-operative Values in Time of Calm and Crisis', in A. Webster, L. Shaw, J. K. Walton, A. Brown, and D. Stewart (eds.), *The Hidden Alternative: Co-operative Values, Past, Present and Future*. Manchester: Manchester University Press and United Nations Press, 306–26.

National Educational Council (1936). *Ten Year Plan for Co-operative Education*. Manchester: Co-operative Union.

Navickas, K. (2011). 'Nudism, Incendiaries and the Defence of Rural "Task Scopes" in 1812', *Northern History*, 48/1: 59–73.

The Ownership Commission (2012), *Plurality, Stewardship and Engagement*. Borehamwood: Mutuo.

Peaples, F. W. (1909). *History of the Great and Little Bolton Co-operative Society*. Bolton: Bolton Co-operative Society.

Pérotin, V. (2012), 'The Performance of Workers' Co-operatives', in P. Battilani and H. Shröter (eds.), *The Cooperative Business Movement, 1950 to the Present*. Cambridge: Cambridge University Press, 195–221.

Pickup, F. (1942), 'District Plan: Prospects', *Co-operative Review*, 16/2 (January).

Pollard, S. (1960). 'From Community Building to Shopkeeping', in A. Briggs and J. Saville (eds.), *Essays in Labour History*. London: Macmillan, 74–112.

Pollock, I. (September 2008). 'Not Such a Good Idea after All?', <http://news.bbc.co.uk/1/hi/business/7641925.stm>.

Porter, J. H. (1971). 'The Development of a Provincial Department Store 1870–1939', *Business History*, 13/1: 64–71.

Purvis, M. (1986). 'Co-operative Retailing in England, 1835–1850: Developments beyond Rochdale', *Northern History*, 22:198–215.

Purvis, M. (1990). 'The Development of Co-operative Retailing in England and Wales, 1851–1901: A Geographical Study', *Journal of Historical Geography*, 16/3: 314–31.

Purvis, M. (1998). 'Stocking the Store: Co-operative Retailers in North-East England and Systems of Wholesale Supply, circa 1860–77', *Business History*, 40/4: 55–78.

Purvis, M. (1999). 'Crossing Urban Deserts: Consumers, Competitors and the Protracted Birth of Metropolitan Co-operative Retailing', *International Review of Retail Distribution and Consumer Research*, 9/3: 225–43.

Purvis, M. (2012). 'Revisiting Hard Times: Consumers' Co-operation in Interwar Britain', paper delivered to European Social Science History Association. Glasgow, 11–14 April.

Randall, A. (1991). *Before the Luddites: Custom, Community and Machinery in the English Woollen Industry, 1776–1809*. Cambridge: Cambridge University Press.

Randall, A. (2006). *Riotous Assemblies: Popular Protest in Hanoverian England*. Oxford: Oxford University Press.

Reader, W. J. (1959). 'The United Kingdom Soapmakers' Association and the English Soap Trade, 1867–1896', *Business History*, 1/2: 77–83.

Redfern, P. (1913). *The Story of the CWS*. Manchester: CWS.

Redfern, P. (1938). *The New History of the CWS*. London: J. M. Dent and Sons and CWS.

Richardson, W. (1977). *The CWS in War and Peace 1938–1976*. Manchester: CWS.

Ritchie, T. (1887). *The Relation of Co-operative to Competitive Trading, with Special Reference to High and Low Dividends*. Manchester: Co-operative Union.

Robertson, N. (2010). *The Co-operative Movement and Communities in Britain: Minding their own Business*. Farnham: Ashgate.

Robertson, N. (2012). 'Collective Strength and Mutual Aid: Financial Provisions for Members of Co-operative Societies in Britain', *Business History*, 54/6: 925–44.

Rose, M. E. (1977). '"Rochdale Man" and the Staleybridge Riot', in A. P. Donajgrodzki (ed.), *Social Control in Nineteenth-Century Britain*. London: Croom Helm, 185–206.

Rowan, J. D. (2003). 'Imagining Corporate Culture: The Industrial Paternalism of William Hesketh Lever at Port Sunlight, 1888–1925', Ph.D. thesis (Louisiana State University).

Rubin, G. R. (1986). 'From Packmen, Tallymen and "Perambulating Scotchmen" to Credit Drapers' Associations, c1840–1914', *Business History*, 28/2: 206–25.

Samy, L. (2012). 'Extending Home Ownership before the First World War: The Case of the Co-operative Permanent Building Society, 1884–1913', *Economic History Review*, 65/1: 168–93.

Sanchez Bajo, C., and Roelants, B. (2011). *Capital and the Debt Trap: Learning from Co-operatives in the Global Crisis*. Basingstoke: Palgrave Macmillan.

Schwarzkopf, S. (2009). 'Innovation, Modernisation, Consumerism: The Co-operative Movement and the Making of British Advertising and Marketing Culture, 1890s–1960s', in L. Black and N. Robertson (eds.), *Consumerism and the Co-operative Movement in Modern British History: Taking Stock*. Manchester: Manchester University Press, 197–221.

Scola, R. (1975). 'Food Markets and Shops in Manchester 1770–1870', *Journal of Historical Geography*, 1/2: 153–67.

Scola, R. (1992). *Feeding the City: The Food Supply of Manchester 1770–1870*. Manchester: Manchester University Press.

Scott, G. (1998). *Feminism and the Politics of Working Women: The Women's Co-operative Guild, 1880s to the Second World War*. London: Routledge.

Seth, A., and Randall, G. (1999). *The Grocers: The Rise and Rise of the Supermarket Chains*. London: Kogan.

Shaw, G., and Alexander, A. (2008). 'British Co-operative Societies as Retail Innovators: Interpreting the Early Stages of the Self-Service Revolution', *Business History*, 50/1: 62–78.

Shaw, G., Alexander, A., Benson, J., and Jones, J. (1998). 'Structural and Spatial Trends in British Retailing: The Importance of Firm Level Studies', *Business History*, 40/4: 79.

Smale, W. (11 December 2009). 'Co-op Supermarket Chain Enjoys Somerfield Boost', <http://news.bbc.co.uk/1/hi/business/8392663.stm>.

Snell, K. D. M. (2012). 'Belonging and Community: Understandings of "Home" and "Friends" among the English Poor, 1750–1850', *Economic History Review*, 65/1: 1–25.

Sparks, L. (1994). 'Consumer Co-operation in the UK 1945–93', *Journal of Co-operative Studies*, 79: 1–64.

Sparks, L. (1996). 'Retail Trading in Scotland', *Environment and Planning A*, 1465–84.

Sparks, L. (2002). 'Being the Best? Co-operative Retailing and Corporate Competitors', *Journal of Co-operative Studies*, 35/1: 7–26.

Sparks, L. (2008). 'Tesco: Every Little Helps', Institute of Retail Studies, University of Stirling.

Stark, J. G. (1984). 'British Food Policy and Diet in the First World War'. Ph.D. thesis (London School of Economics).

Stedman-Jones, G. (1984). *Languages of Class: Studies in English Working Class History 1832–1982*. Cambridge: Cambridge University Press.

Stewart, D. (2011). '"A party within a party"? The Co-operative Party–Labour Party Alliance and the Formation of the Social Democratic Party, 1974–81', in A. Webster, L. Shaw, J. K. Walton, A. Brown, and D. Stewart (eds.), *The Hidden Alternative: Co-operative Values, Past, Present and Future*. Manchester: Manchester University Press and United Nations Press, 137–56.

Stewart, D. (2012). 'The British Co-operative Movement and the Politics of Resale Price Maintenance 1949–64', delivered at 'Mainstreaming Co-operation: An Alternative for the 21st Century' conference, Manchester, 3–5 July.

Stobart, J. (2003). 'City Centre Retailing in Late Nineteenth- and Early Twentieth-Century Stoke-On-Trent: Structures and Processes', in J. Benson and L. Ugolini (eds.), *A Nation of Shopkeepers*. London: I. B. Tauris, 155–78.

Stobart, J., and Hann, A. (2004). 'Retailing Revolution in the Eighteenth Century? Evidence from North West England', *Business History*, 46/2: 171–94.

Thompson, E. P. (1971). 'The Moral Economy of the English Crowd in the Eighteenth Century', *Past and Present*, 50/1: 76–136.

Thomson, S. J. (1911). *Social Redemption: Or, the Fifty Years' Story of the Leicester Co-operative Society Ltd, 1860–1910*. Leicester: Leicester Co-operative Society.

Toms, S. (2012). 'Producer Co-operatives and Economic Efficiency: Evidence from the Nineteenth-Century Cotton Textile Industry', *Business History*, 54/6: 855–82.

Topham, E. (1935). *Ten Year Plan: Notes for Speakers*. Manchester: Co-operative Union.

Trentmann, F. (2008). *Free Trade Nation: Commerce, Consumption, and Civil Society in Modern Britain*. Oxford: Oxford University Press.

Vickrage, H. M. (1950). *Seventy-Five Years of Co-operative Endeavour: A History of the Ten Acres and Stirchley Co-operative Society Limited*. Stockport: CWS.

Vorberg-Rugh, R. (2009). 'Employers and Workers: Conflicting Identities over Women's Wages in the Co-operative Movement, 1906–18', in L. Black and N. Robertson (eds.), *Consumerism and the Co-operative Movement in Modern British History*. Manchester: Manchester University Press, 121–37.

Vorberg-Rugh, R. (forthcoming). 'Co-operative Contradictions: Business, Labour and Gender in the British Co-operative Movement, 1880–1920'. D. Phil thesis (University of Oxford).

Walton, J. K. (1996). 'The Making of a Mass Movement: The Growth of Co-operative Membership in Lancashire 1870–1914', in B. Lancaster and P. Maguire (eds.), *Towards the Co-operative Commonwealth: Essays in the History of Co-operation*. Manchester: Co-operative College and History Workshop Trust, 17–28.

Walton, J. K. (2009). 'The Post-War Decline of the British Retail Co-operative Movement: Nature, Causes and Consequence', in L. Black and N. Robertson (eds.), *Consumerism and the Co-operative Movement in Modern British History*. Manchester: Manchester University Press, 13–33.

Walton, J. K. (2012). 'Revisiting the Rochdale Pioneers'. Unpublished paper.

Webb, B. P., and Webb, S. (1921). *Consumers' Co-operative Movement*. London: Longmans, Green.

Webster, A., Shaw, L., Walton, J. K., Brown, A., and Stewart, D. (eds.) (2011). *The Hidden Alternative: Co-operative Values, Past, Present and Future*. Manchester: Manchester University Press and United Nations Press.

Webster, A. and Walton, J. K. (eds.) (2012). 'The Business of Co-operation: National and International Dimensions since the Nineteenth Century', special issue, *Business History* 54:6.

Whitecross, A. (forthcoming). 'Co-operative Commonwealth or New Jerusalem? The Co-operative Party and the Labour Party, 1931–1951'. Ph.D. thesis (University of Central Lancashire).

Whyman, P. B. (2012). 'Co-operative Principles and the Evolution of the "Dismal Science": The Historical Interaction between Co-operative and Mainstream Economics', *Business History*, 54/6: 833–54.

Wilkinson, A. and Balmer, J. M. T. (1996). 'Corporate and Generic Identities: Lessons from the Co-operative Bank', *International Journal of Bank Marketing*, 14/4: 22–35.

Wilson, H. (1979). Royal Commission into the Functioning of Britain's Financial Institutions. London: Her Majesty's Stationery Office (HMSO), 35.

Wilson, C. (1954). *The History of Unilever: A Study in Economic Growth and Social Change*. Vol. i. London: Cassell and Company.

Wilson, J. F. (1995). *British Business History, 1720–1994*. Manchester: Manchester University Press.

Wilson, J. F. (2013). *Ferranti, A History*, iii: *Management, Mergers and Fraud, 1987–1993*. Manchester: Manchester University Press.

Wilson, J. F., and Popp, A. (eds.) (2003). *Industrial Clusters and Regional Business Networks in England, c.1750–1970*. Aldershot: Ashgate.

Winstanley, M. J. (1983). *The Shopkeeper's World 1880–1914*. Manchester: Manchester University Press.

Wood, S., Lowe, M., and Wrigley, N. (2006). 'Life after PPG6—Recent UK Food Retailer Responses to Planning Regulation Tightening', *International Review of Retail, Distribution and Consumer Research*, 16/1: 23–41.

Woods, G. S. (1935). *The Ten Year Plan: The Part to be Played by Managers, Officials, and Departmental Managers*. Manchester: Co-operative Union.

Wrigley, C. (2009). 'The Commemorative Urge: The Co-operative Movement's Collective Memory', in L. Black and N. Robertson (eds.), *Consumerism and the Co-operative Movement in Modern British History*. Manchester: Manchester University Press, 157–73.

Yeo, S. (ed.) (1988). *New Views of Co-operation*. London: Routledge.

Yeo, S. (1995). *Who Was J. T. W. Mitchell?* Manchester: Co-operative Press.

Yeo, S. (2002). *A Chapter in the Making of a Successful Co-operative Business: The Co-operative Wholesale Society 1973–2001*. Manchester: Zeebra Publishing.

INDEX

....